INTERMEDIATE MICROECONOMICS
WITH MICROSOFT EXCEL

This unique text uses *Microsoft Excel®* workbooks to instruct students. In addition to explaining fundamental concepts in microeconomic theory, readers acquire a great deal of sophisticated Excel skills and gain the practical mathematics needed to succeed in advanced courses. In addition to the innovative pedagogical approach, the book features explicitly repeated use of a single central methodology, the economic approach. Students learn how economists think and how to think like an economist. With concrete, numerical examples and novel, engaging applications, interest for readers remains high as live graphs and data respond to manipulation by the user. Finally, clear writing and active learning are features sure to appeal to modern practitioners and their students. The Web site accompanying the text is found at www.depauw.edu/learn/microexcel.

Humberto Barreto is the Elizabeth P. Allen Distinguished University Professor at DePauw University. He earned his Ph.D. from the University of North Carolina at Chapel Hill. Professor Barreto has lectured around the world on teaching economics with computer-based methods, including Spain, Brazil, Poland, India, Burma, Japan, and Taiwan, and spent one year as a Fulbright Scholar in the Dominican Republic. He has taught National Science Foundation (NSF) Chautauqua short courses using simulation. He has received two teaching awards, the Indiana Sears Roebuck Teaching Award and the Wabash College McLain-McTurnan Arnold Award for Teaching Excellence. Professor Barreto's research focuses on the history of economic thought and improving the teaching of economics. His book, *The Entrepreneur in Microeconomic Theory*, was translated into Arabic in 1999. He is co-author, with Frank Howland, of an innovative text, *Introductory Econometrics: Using Monte Carlo Simulation with Microsoft Excel®*, published in 2006 by Cambridge University Press.

INTERMEDIATE MICROECONOMICS WITH MICROSOFT EXCEL

HUMBERTO BARRETO

DePauw University

CAMBRIDGE
UNIVERSITY PRESS

CAMBRIDGE
UNIVERSITY PRESS

University Printing House, Cambridge CB2 8BS, United Kingdom

One Liberty Plaza, 20th Floor, New York, NY 10006, USA

477 Williamstown Road, Port Melbourne, VIC 3207, Australia

314-321, 3rd Floor, Plot 3, Splendor Forum, Jasola District Centre, New Delhi - 110025, India

79 Anson Road, #06-04/06, Singapore 079906

Cambridge University Press is part of the University of Cambridge.

It furthers the University's mission by disseminating knowledge in the pursuit of education, learning and research at the highest international levels of excellence.

www.cambridge.org
Information on this title: www.cambridge.org/9780521899024

First published 2009

A catalogue record for this publication is available from the British Library

Library of Congress Cataloging in Publication data
Barreto, Humberto, 1960–
Intermediate microeconomics with Microsoft Excel / Humberto Barreto.
p. cm.
Includes bibliographical references and index.
ISBN 978-0-521-89902-4 (hardback)
1. Microeconomics. 2. Microsoft Excel (Computer file) I. Title.
HB172.B32 2009
338.5078´5554 – dc22 2009000652

ISBN 978-0-521-89902-4 Hardback

Thanks to my friends and colleagues, Frank Howland and Kay Widdows.

Gracias a mi familia, Tami, Tyler, Nicolas, y Jonah.

Contents

Contents

Preface

In the competitive world of textbooks, different is definitely bad. Authors and publishers, like politicians, stay in the safe middle. Straying too far from the herd is almost a sure way to fail. Fear is strong, but it apparently can be overcome – after all, you are reading a spectacularly unconventional textbook.

The most obvious difference between this book and the usual fare is the use of Microsoft Excel to teach economic theory. This enables students to acquire a great deal of sophisticated, advanced Excel skills while learning economics. No other book does this.

The use of Excel drives other differences. Excel requires concrete, numerical problems instead of the abstract functions and graphs used by other books. Excel's Solver makes possible presentation of numerical methods for solving optimization problems and equilibrium models. No other book does this.

Because numerical solutions are readily available, this book is able to present and explain analytical methods that have been pushed to appendixes or completely ignored in mainstream texts. Problems are solved twice – once with Excel and once with equations, algebra, and, when needed, calculus. No other book does this.

Finally, this book is organized differently. It explicitly repeats a single central methodology, the economic approach, so students learn how economists think and how to think like an economist. Other books try to do this, but none brings the economic way of thinking explicitly to the surface, repeating the message in every application.

I wrote this book because I learned Visual Basic and quickly realized that enhancing a spreadsheet with macros made possible a whole new way of teaching economics. When my students loved this approach, I wanted to share it with others.

Because this book is so different, it probably will not challenge the top sellers. It will be the unusual professor who is willing to try something this new. It requires that the professor care enough about students and teaching to invest time and energy in mastering the material. Of course, I think the rate of return is quite high. My hope is that, though few in number, a committed, enthusiastic core of adopters will enable this book to survive.

Thank you for trying this unique entry into the competitive market for micro theory textbooks. I hope you find that the reward was worth the risk.

Thanks to Scott Parris and Cambridge University Press for supporting and promoting this work. Thanks also to Peggy Rote and Linda Smith for their excellent production and editorial assistance – you really improved the final product.

User Guide

This book is essentially a manual for how to actively work with and manipulate the material in Excel. This section explains how to properly configure Excel, provides instructions for downloading all of the materials and software, offers a few tips before you begin, and describes the organization of the files.

Minimum Requirements

This book presumes that you have access to and a working knowledge of Excel. In other words, you can open workbooks, write formulas that add cells together, create charts, and save files. As you will see, however, Excel is much more than a simple adding machine. It can be used to solve optimization problems and perform comparative statics analysis.

There are many versions of Excel. You will need Excel 1997 or better. In Excel 2007, be sure to save the workbooks in the special "Excel macro-enabled workbook" format, which carries the .xlsm extension. If you save the workbook as an Excel workbook with the .xlsx extension, the macros will not be saved and functionality will be lost.

These materials were created and are optimized for use with Windows Excel, but they can be accessed with a Macintosh computer running older versions of Excel. Starting with Mac Excel 2008, Visual Basic is not supported. Modern Macs can run Windows programs with software such as *Parallels* or *Boot Camp*.

To make sure that Excel is able to run the *Visual Basic* macros in the workbooks and add-ins, security must be properly set. Please carefully follow the instructions that appear next before attempting to open the Excel files or add-ins that accompany this book.

Properly Configuring Excel

The procedure is different in Excel 2007 than in earlier versions of Excel. Instructions for Excel 2007 and earlier versions are provided below.

Excel 2007

Step Click the Office button at the top left corner of the screen, and then click the Excel Options button at the bottom of the dialog box.

Step In the *Excel Options* window, select the *Trust Center* heading, then click the Trust Center Settings . . . button as shown in Figure 1.

Step In the Trust Center, select the *Macro Settings* heading, choose the "Disable all macros with notification" option (this is often the default), and check the "Trust access to the VBA project object model" as shown in Figure 2.

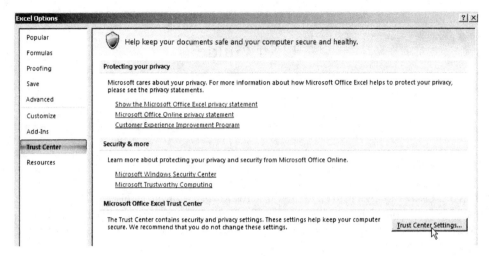

Figure 1. Excel Options.

Disabling macros with notification means that you will be given the opportunity to run the macros embedded in an Excel workbook. Trusting access to the VBA project object model enables the add-ins to function properly and is a critical setting. Many problems with Excel add-ins are rooted in the failure to trust access. Please confirm that this crucial setting is correct before continuing.

Step Finish configuring Excel by clicking OK at the Trust Center and Excel Options dialog boxes.

Opening a Workbook

Figure 3 shows that, when opening a workbook with macros, Excel 2007 will alert you to their presence with a security warning under the ribbon (and right above the formula bar).

Click the Options button, then click "Enable this content" to allow the buttons and other controls in the workbook to function properly.

For workbooks not included with this book, do *not* enable macro functionality unless you are completely confident that the workbook is safe.

You may also receive the warning displayed in Figure 4 when opening a workbook with macros.

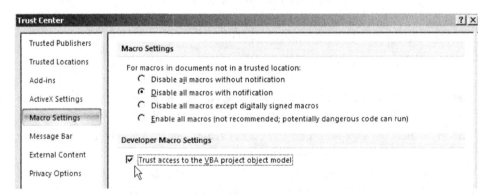

Figure 2. Trust Center.

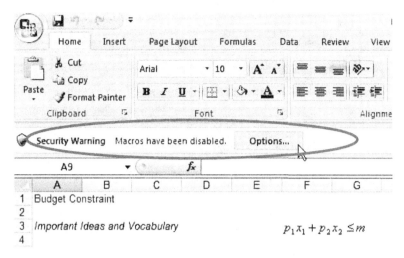

Figure 3. Opening a workbook with macros.

Click the Enable Macros button to have access to the features in the workbook, but do not enable macros if you are unsure of the source.

Properly Configuring Older Versions of Excel (from 1997 to 2003)

Step From Excel, execute Tools: Macro: Security as shown in Figure 5.

Step At the Security Level tab, make sure that High is NOT selected. Medium will always give you a warning that the file you are about to open has macros, and then you can decide whether or not to run the macros (or open the file). Low is (quite reasonably) not recommended since Excel will automatically run all macros with no warning or prompt. Choose the Medium security level as shown in Figure 6.

Step Click the Trusted Sources tab and make sure both boxes are checked so that installed add-ins have access to your Visual Basic projects (that is, your workbooks). See Figure 7.

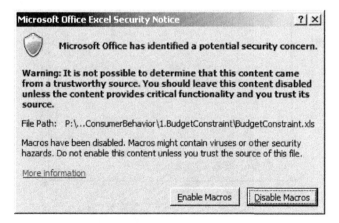

Figure 4. Macros warning.

User Guide

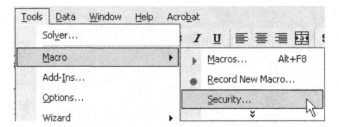

Figure 5. Accessing the Security dialog box.

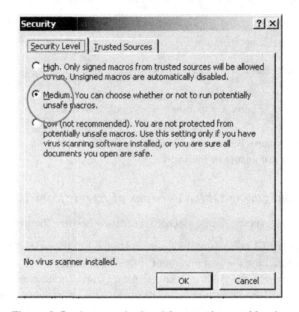

Figure 6. Setting security level for opening workbooks.

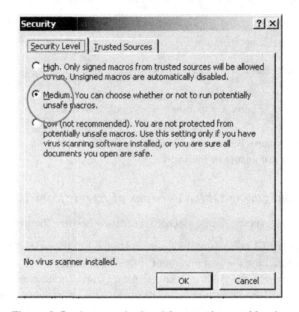

Figure 7. Setting security for add-ins.

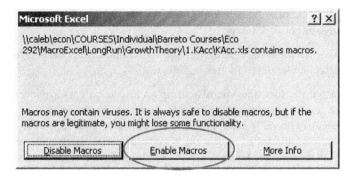

Figure 8. Click Enable Macros when opening a trusted workbook.

With Excel's security correctly configured, you are ready to open macro-enabled Excel workbooks and use the add-ins.

Step When opening an Intermediate Microeconomics with Microsoft Excel workbook, always click the Enable Macros option, as shown in Figure 8.

Aside: Using Excel with a Macintosh

Mac users with versions of Excel that support Visual Basic also need to set security. Both steps, trusting access to Visual Basic projects and enabling macros to run, are required. Excel's Help explains how to do this.

Mac users know that there can be problems working with Windows files and Microsoft Excel does have some cross-platform compatibility issues. Fortunately, when opening the Windows-created workbooks that accompany this book, the content remains true. The display in Mac Excel, however, may not be optimal. Mac users may notice imperfections (such as cutting off text in buttons). You can adjust the Zoom in Mac Excel to improve the display.

In addition, Solver in Mac Excel can be a bit temperamental. Make sure you run Excel's Solver before attempting to open a workbook that uses Solver. If you have trouble opening a workbook (e.g., you get an error message that says, "Can't find project or library"), always try the following simple fix: quit Excel, open Excel, execute Tools: Solver and click Close, then open the workbook.

If you have a modern Mac, a better approach to utilizing these files relies on software such as Parallels or Boot Camp to run Windows on the Macintosh computer. This will improve speed, display, and Solver performance.

Accessing and Using the Excel Files: <www.depauw.edu/learn/microexcel>

With Excel properly configured, you are ready to download the files that accompany this book. You may download all of the files (about 5 MB in a compressed, zip archive that expands to 15 MB) to your hard drive, but do not distribute these files without permission.

Step Launch your favorite browser and go to <www.depauw.edu/learn/microexcel>.

Step Click Excel Workbooks from the menu (on the top, right corner of the page).

Step Click the MicroExcel.zip link and save the file on your desktop (or other location on your hard drive or network server).

Step Double-click the saved MicroExcel.zip archive and extract the files by simply dragging the MicroExcel folder out of its archive folder.

Having extracted the files, the MicroExcel.zip archive is no longer needed and may be deleted. You are free to move the MicroExcel folder to another location.

With Excel security properly configured and the files downloaded, you are almost ready to begin. Take a few minutes to review the remainder of this user guide, which includes troubleshooting, tips (including how to draw in Word), using Solver, and the organization of files.

Troubleshooting

At some point, something will go wrong while you are working with an Excel file. Your computer may freeze or you will not be able to perform a particular task. The first step to overcoming difficulties is to simply start over. Often closing a workbook and reopening it is sufficient, but you may have to quit Excel or restart your computer.

You should revisit the instructions and read carefully to make sure you are following each step closely. For example, in newer versions of Excel, you need to run Solver before accessing macros that use Solver. The instructions point this out, but it is easy to overlook this step.

You may get an error message like that shown in Figure 9. If you click the End button, the message will disappear and you will return to where you were working in Excel. Clicking the Debug button takes you to Visual Basic and highlights the offending line of code, as displayed in Figure 10.

In some cases, you may be able to figure out how to fix the error. In Figure 10, an attempt to take the log of a negative number has triggered an error in the subroutine named test.

You are not expected to be proficient in the Visual Basic programming language, but you may be able to quickly diagnose and correct problems. An updated set of the latest versions of these workbooks and add-ins will be maintained at <www.depauw.edu/learn/microexcel>. If you have persistent problems with a workbook or add-in, please check the web site for an updated, corrected version. You will also find contact information for technical support on the web site.

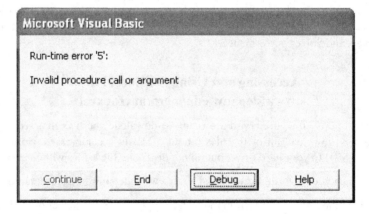

Figure 9. Example error message.

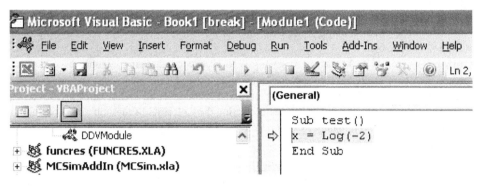

Figure 10. Debugging in Visual Basic.

Common Problems

If buttons or other controls do not work, check to make sure that you have enabled macros (as shown in Figure 3 for Excel 2007). If the Comparative Statics Wizard add-in does not work, check to make sure that you have trusted access to Visual Basic projects (as shown in Figure 2 for Excel 2007).

Visit the web site at <www.depauw.edu/learn/microexcel> to see a list of other problems and solutions.

Tips and Conventions

In this book, a *figure* refers to a variety of graphics, including charts and pictures of portions of a sheet (also known as a screenshot). A chart or range of cells is often displayed in this printed book as a figure, but you should look at the live version on your computer screen. Thus, in addition to a caption, many figures have a source line indicating their location in the Excel workbook.

The book follows Excel's naming convention for workbooks and sheets, [workbook-name]sheetname. If the caption of a figure says, "[FoodStamp.xls]BudgetConstraint," then you know the figure can be found in the FoodStamp.xls workbook in the *BudgetConstraint* sheet. Sheet names in the printed text are italicized to help you locate the proper sheet in a workbook.

Cells are referenced as [workbookname]sheetname!celladdress. So, for example, [RiskReturn.xls]OptimalChoice!B6 refers to cell B6 in the *OptimalChoice* sheet of the RiskReturn.xls workbook.

You may need to adjust your display or the objects in Excel. Use the Zoom button to magnify the display. You can also right-click objects such as buttons (Why Bias?) or scroll bars (◀ ▶) to select and move them. Once you open a workbook, you can save it to another location or name (by executing File: Save As . . .) and make whatever changes you wish. This is the same as underlining or writing in a conventional, printed book.

Drawing in Word

Q&A and Exercise questions often ask you to draw diagrams in Word. Here are a few tips and tricks to make this easier.

- Word 2007 has a completely new drawing interface. Click Insert on the ribbon, then Shapes (in the Illustrations group) to access line and arc tools. The Text Box tool is in the Text group.

After placing a text box on your graph (for labels or explanation), double-click its outline and use the Shape Fill and Shape Outline options on the ribbon to make the object transparent and remove the box.

- In earlier versions of Word, the first step is to access the Drawing Toolbar by executing View: Toolbars: Drawing. You should also execute Tools: Options: General and uncheck the "Automatically create a drawing canvas" option. Text box fill and outline can be removed by double-clicking the text box outline, then selecting the Colors and Lines tab and choosing no fill under Fills and no line under Colors. You should also remove the grid snap.

Installing Solver

Excel's Solver is a numerical optimization add-in (an additional file that extends the capabilities of Excel). It is imperative that you successfully load and install the Solver add-in because without it, neither Solver nor the Comparative Statics Wizard will be available. The procedure is different in Excel 2007 than in earlier versions of Excel. Instructions for Excel 2007 and earlier versions are provided subsequently.

Excel 2007

Here are the instructions from Excel's Help:

1. Click the Microsoft Office Button 🔲 , and then click Excel Options.
2. Click Add-Ins. Then in the Manage box, select Excel Add-ins.
3. Click Go.
4. In the Add-Ins available box, select the Solver Add-in check box, and then click OK.
   Tip: If Solver Add-in is not listed in the Add-Ins available box, click Browse to locate the add-in.
   If you get prompted that the Solver add-in is not currently installed on your computer, click Yes to install it.
5. After you load the Solver add-in, the Solver command is available in the Analysis group on the Data tab.

Installing Solver in Older Versions (from 1997 to 2003)

Click on the Tools heading on the menu bar and select the *Solver...* item.

If Solver is not listed in the Tools menu, select *Add-Ins...* from the Tools menu bar. In the Add-Ins dialog box, scroll down and check the Solver add-in.

After selecting the Solver add-in and clicking on the OK button, Excel takes a moment to call in the Solver file and adds it to the Tools menu.

If the Solver add-in is not listed in the Add-Ins dialog box, click on the Select or Browse button and navigate to the Solver add-in (called solver.xla in Windows and Solver on the MacOS) and open it. It should be in the Library directory in the folders where Microsoft Office is installed.

If you cannot find the Solver add-in, try using the Mac's Find File or Find in Windows to locate the file. Search for "solver." Note the location of the file, return to the Add-Ins dialog box (by executing Tools: Add-Ins . . .), click on Select or Browse, and open the Solver Add-In file.

Still can't find it? Then it is likely that your installation of Excel failed to include the Solver add-in. Run your Excel or Office Setup again from the original CD-ROM and install the

Solver add-in. You should now be able to use Solver by clicking on the Tools heading on the menu bar and selecting the Solver item.

Although Solver is proprietary, you can download a trial version from Frontline Systems, the makers of Solver, at <www.solver.com>. In addition to the basic Solver add-in, this web site provides information on other numerical optimization algorithms.

Organization of Files

Figure 11 shows the contents of all of the materials included with *Intermediate Microeconomics with Microsoft Excel*. These files may be downloaded from <www.depauw.edu/learn/microexcel> (as explained earlier in this user guide).

The Answers folder contains answers to questions posed in Q&A sheets in each Excel workbook. Think of the Q&A material in the Excel workbooks as self-study questions.

There are also questions at the end of each chapter called Exercises. Readers do not have easy access to the answers to the exercise questions. To see these answers, you must be an instructor and register online at <www.depauw.edu/learn/microexcel>.

The SolverCompStaticsWizard folder contains files that use the Comparative Statics Wizard Excel add-in. When used in conjunction with Excel's own Solver add-in, these files enable numerical comparative statics analysis of optimization problems and equilibrium models.

Active Learning

There are many books devoted to microeconomics. This one is different because it is not meant to be simply read. A great deal of the value of this book lies in the Excel workbooks and additional materials. By reading the book and following instructions carefully, you will become a sophisticated user of Excel and learn a great deal of mathematics and, most importantly, economics.

Having properly configured Excel (especially trusting access to Visual Basic projects and enabling macros when opening a workbook) and downloaded the files from <www.depauw.edu/learn/microexcel>, you are ready to begin. Enjoy!

⊞ 🗀 0.Introduction
⊞ 🗀 1.ConsumerBehavior
⊞ 🗀 2.TheoryoftheFirm
⊞ 🗀 3.MarketSystem
⊞ 🗀 Answers
⊞ 🗀 SolverCompStaticsWizard   Figure 11. Organization of the supplementary materials.

Introduction

Economics is the science which studies human behavior as a relationship between given ends and scarce means which have alternative uses.

Lionel Robbins

Economists use a particular framework to interpret observed reality. This framework has been called the economic way of thinking, the economic approach, and the method of economics.

This book is different from the many other books that attempt to teach microeconomics in three ways:

- It explicitly applies the recipe of the economic approach in every example.
- It uses concrete examples via Microsoft Excel in every application, which enables the reader to manipulate live graphs and learn numerical methods of optimization.
- It is written in a terse, word-minimizing fashion. The majority of the content is in the Excel workbooks that accompany the book.

You learn by doing, so let's begin.

The Tech Support Example

Suppose that you manage a tech support service for a major software company.

You have two types of callers:

- Regular customers
- Preferred customers

Preferred customers have paid extra money for faster access, which means they expect to spend less time waiting on hold. There are equal numbers of the two types of customers and they call with equal frequency.

Management has given you a fixed number of worker hours per day to answer calls from users needing help.

1

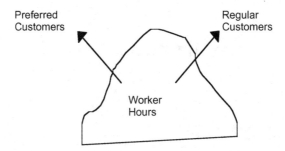

Figure 1. Allocating a scarce resource to two competing ends.

Daily, you have 10 workers, each working 8-hour shifts, and 5 part-time workers (4-hour shifts). Thus, you have 100 hours per day to support customers calling for help. These hours comprise your Total Resources.

When customers call, an automatic message is played asking the caller to input an ID number and the caller is put on hold. The ID number is used to identify the caller as a regular or preferred customer.

Keeping callers on hold creates frustrated, unhappy customers. The callers are already angry since something has gone wrong with the software and they need help. The faster you get support to the caller the better.

The time waiting (the amount of time, in seconds, that the caller is on hold) depends on the number of worker hours available to answer the calls.

To keep things simple, suppose time waiting = 6000/worker hours.

So, say there are 100 worker hours available to answer calls in a day. Dividing 6000 by 100 yields 60, which means the hold time is 60 seconds.

If, on the other hand, only 10 worker hours are available, then the hold time is 600 seconds (since $6000/10 = 600$). Ten minutes is a long time to wait on the phone!

Given that you have two types of callers, you must decide how to allocate your worker hours.

The more you allocate to one type of caller, the lower that type of caller's wait time. That's the good news.

The bad news is that the fixed amount of support resources means that more time devoted to one type of caller results, by definition, in fewer hours to the other type and, therefore, higher waiting times for the other type.

So the general structure of the problem is clear: You must decide how to allocate scarce support resources (worker hours) to two competing ends. Figure 1 shows a simplified picture of the problem.

A Complication

It is unclear exactly what preferred customers expect.

Do they expect to get help twice as fast or 10 times as fast as regular customers?

To incorporate the fact that the preferred customer merits greater attention, management gives you a value weight parameter. The value weight tells you how much more valuable the preferred caller is compared to the regular caller.

The objective function is 6000/RegHours + ValueWeight*6000/Pref-Hours.

In the objective function, the time spent waiting by the preferred caller is Value Weight*6000/PrefHours. PrefHours is the number of worker hours allocated to preferred callers. If value weight = 1, then preferred and regular callers are equally valuable.

Management has decreed that value weight = 2; you (the call center manager) cannot change this parameter.

So, if you decide to allocate 50 hours each to the regular and preferred customers, then both types of customers will wait 6000/50 = 120 seconds and your objective function will be 120 + 2*120 = 360 seconds. Is there a better allocation, one that yields a smaller total time waiting (adjusted with the value weight), than 50/50?

This concrete problem, how to allocate 100 worker hours to answering calls from regular and preferred customers in order to minimize value weighted total time waiting, has a concrete solution.

Setting Up the Problem

We will solve this problem by first setting it up. Optimization problems can always be set up the same way. The three parts to the setup are the goal, the endogenous variables, and the exogenous variables.

The goal is synonymous with the objective function. Endogenous variables are those variables that can be controlled by the decision maker. They are also known as choice variables. Exogenous variables are given, fixed constants that cannot be changed by the decision maker. The exogenous variables (sometimes called parameters or independent variables) form the environment under which the decision maker acts.

In the tech support problem, we can organize the information like this:

1. Goal: minimize total time waiting (value weighted)
2. Endogenous variables: worker hours allocated to preferred and regular customers
3. Exogenous variables: total worker hours and value weight.

Step Open the Excel workbook Introduction.xls and read the *Intro* sheet, then go to the *SetUp* sheet to see how this problem is laid out.

This workbook (along with all of the files that accompany this book) is available for download at <www.depauw.edu/learn/microexcel>. The user guide has detailed instructions on how to properly configure Excel before downloading and opening these files.

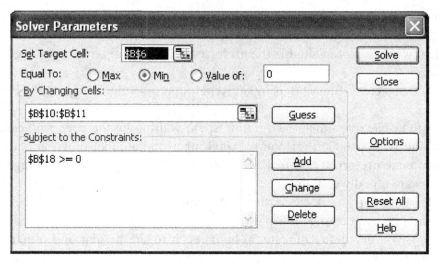

Figure 2. The Solver dialog box.

Step Try the three questions in column A (below the goal, endogenous, and exogenous variables). Check yourself by clicking the See Answer buttons.

Finding the Initial Solution

There are two ways to solve optimization problems:

- Analytical (algebra and calculus) methods
- Numerical (computer) methods.

We will ignore the analytical approach in this example and concentrate on numerical methods.

Step In Excel 2007, click Data in the Ribbon, then Solver (in the Analysis group) to bring up the Solver dialog box (as in Figure 2). (In earlier versions of Excel, execute Tools: Solver.) If Solver is not available, then use the Add-in Manager (as explained in the user guide) to install it.

Note that the important information is already entered. The target cell is the (value weighted) total time waiting, the changing cells (the endogenous variables) are the worker hours devoted to the regular and preferred customers, and the constraint is that the sum of the worker hours not exceed the 100 hours you have been given.

The SolverInstructions.doc file in the SolverCompStaticsWizard folder has documentation on each of the Solver options in the dialog box.

Step Click the Solve button to find the solution to the problem.

You, the call center manager, have optimally allocated your scarce resources. It makes sense that preferred callers have more hours allocated to them because they are more valuable.

Comparative Statics

We have found the initial solution, but we are usually much more interested in a follow up question: How will the optimal solution change if the environment changes?

Comparative statics is a shorthand way of describing the following procedure: Change an exogenous variable, holding the other parameters constant, and track how the optimal solution changes in response to the shock.

Like finding the initial solution, comparative statics can be done via analytical (algebra and calculus) and numerical (computer) methods.

The Comparative Statics Wizard (CSWiz) add-in was used to explore how the optimal allocation of total worker hours would change if worker hours were increased by 10 hours.

Step See the results of the comparative statics analysis by going to the *CS1* sheet.

The results (produced by the CSWiz add-in) show that increased total worker hours are allocated to regular and preferred customers in a stable pattern.

The Comparative Statics Wizard add-in will be introduced later and you will learn how to do your own comparative statics analyses.

Introducing Optimization

This chapter used an example of an optimization problem to show how Excel's Solver can find the optimal solution. It introduced the basics of optimization, including the three parts of every optimization problem:

• Goal (or objective function),
• Endogenous variables, and
• Exogenous variables.

In the chapters that follow, you will learn how to use analytical methods to solve optimization problems. You will also learn how to do comparative statics analysis via analytical and numerical methods.

Exercises

Open Word and answer the following questions. Save the document and print it when you are done.

1. Suppose Management decides that preferred customers are three times as important as regular customers, so that the value weight = 3. With 100 workers hours, what is the optimal solution? Describe your procedure and report the optimal values of PrefHours and RegHours.
2. Compared to the initial solution, when value weight = 2, what is the change in the number of hours allocated to the preferred customers?

3. The percentage change in value weight is 50% (from 2 to 3). What is the percent-
    age change in the number of hours allocated to the preferred customer?

References

Each chapter in this book ends with references. A citation for the epigraph (lead
quotation) of the chapter is provided. Chapter references may also contain
citations documenting sources used, additional information on the history of a
concept or person, and suggestions for further reading.

The epigraph to this chapter is found on page 16 of the second edition of *An Essay
on the Nature and Significance of Economic Science* by Lionel Robbins. This book
was originally published in 1932 and the second edition is available online at
<www.mises.org/books/robbinsessay2.pdf>. Robbins clearly lays out a definition
of economics based on optimization and comparative statics. Robbins made the
definition of economics (in the epigraph to this chapter) famous, but he includes a
footnote that cites various precursors who used a similar description of economics.

For more on Robbins, visit <www.econlib.org/library/Enc/bios/Robbins.html>.
This site says that Robbins' *Essay* is "one of the best-written prose pieces in
economics."

Nobel laureate Gary Becker's *The Economic Approach to Human Behavior* (first
published in 1976) has a classic introductory chapter on the meaning of the
economic approach and applies economic analysis to such non-standard topics as
discrimination, crime, and marriage. Becker's statement, "what most distinguishes
economics as a discipline from other disciplines in the social sciences is not its
subject matter but its approach" (p. 5), greatly extends the scope of economics.

An introductory economics text called *The Economic Way of Thinking* (first
published in 1973) by Paul Heyne focuses on the tools of analysis used by
economists. It is full of interesting applications and ideas. The current version is the
11th edition, authored by Heyne, Boettke, and Prychitko.

Part I

The Theory of Consumer Behavior

Perhaps science does not develop by the accumulation of individual discoveries and inventions.

Thomas S. Kuhn

The Theory of Consumer Behavior posits that buyers choose the bundle of goods that maximize satisfaction, subject to a budget constraint. There are many applications from this basic idea. The material is organized as shown in Figure I.1.

By changing the price of a good, holding everything else constant, we can derive a demand curve. This is the most important concept in the Theory of Consumer Behavior.

Although deriving demand is undoubtedly our prime objective, Figure I.1 also shows the flexibility of the Theory of Consumer Behavior. It can be applied to such wide-ranging topics as charitable giving, driving a car, and asset allocation.

This part concludes with search theory and behavioral economics – special topics built from relaxing assumptions in the basic theory.

After finishing the Theory of Consumer Behavior (from which we get demand), we tackle the Theory of the Firm (and derive the supply curve). The third and final part is the Market System, which studies supply and demand as a resource allocation mechanism.

References

The epigraph is from the second page of the introductory chapter to Thomas S. Kuhn's classic, *The Structure of Scientific Revolutions* (originally published in 1962). Kuhn argued that progress in science is not generated by bit-by-bit puzzle solving (what he called normal science), but that periods of calm are followed by crises that lead to paradigm shifts. The book was as revolutionary as the material it covered, causing debate and controversy in philosophical and scientific circles.

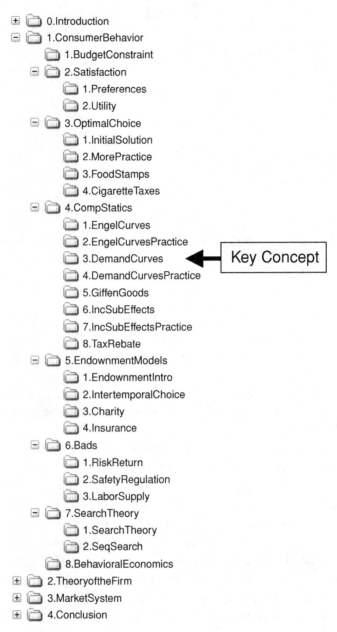

- ⊞ 📁 0.Introduction
- ⊟ 📁 1.ConsumerBehavior
  - 📁 1.BudgetConstraint
  - ⊟ 📁 2.Satisfaction
    - 📁 1.Preferences
    - 📁 2.Utility
  - ⊟ 📁 3.OptimalChoice
    - 📁 1.InitialSolution
    - 📁 2.MorePractice
    - 📁 3.FoodStamps
    - 📁 4.CigaretteTaxes
  - ⊟ 📁 4.CompStatics
    - 📁 1.EngelCurves
    - 📁 2.EngelCurvesPractice
    - 📁 3.DemandCurves ⬅ Key Concept
    - 📁 4.DemandCurvesPractice
    - 📁 5.GiffenGoods
    - 📁 6.IncSubEffects
    - 📁 7.IncSubEffectsPractice
    - 📁 8.TaxRebate
  - ⊟ 📁 5.EndownmentModels
    - 📁 1.EndownmentIntro
    - 📁 2.IntertemporalChoice
    - 📁 3.Charity
    - 📁 4.Insurance
  - ⊟ 📁 6.Bads
    - 📁 1.RiskReturn
    - 📁 2.SafetyRegulation
    - 📁 3.LaborSupply
  - ⊟ 📁 7.SearchTheory
    - 📁 1.SearchTheory
    - 📁 2.SeqSearch
  - 📁 8.BehavioralEconomics
- ⊞ 📁 2.TheoryoftheFirm
- ⊞ 📁 3.MarketSystem
- ⊞ 📁 4.Conclusion

Figure I.1. Content map with focus on consumer behavior.

Modern economics pays little attention to its own history and how it changes. The epigraphs in this book highlight important contributions and individuals in the development of modern microeconomic theory.

1.1

Budget Constraint

1.1.1

Budget Constraint

If we hold money income constant and allow the price of X to change, the price ratio line will rotate about a pivot on the Y axis.

Milton Friedman

The basic idea of the Theory of Consumer Behavior is simple: Given a budget constraint, the consumer buys a combination of goods and services that maximizes satisfaction (utility). By changing a price, *ceteris paribus* (everything else held constant), we derive a demand curve.

This chapter focuses on the budget constraint and how it changes when prices or income change. We cannot answer the question of how much the consumer wants to buy with the budget constraint alone, but the buyer's budget is obviously a key factor in predicting buying behavior.

The Budget Constraint in the Abstract

$$p_1 x_1 + p_2 x_2 \leq m$$

This equation says that the sum of the amount of money spent on good x_1, which is the price of x_1 times the number of units purchased, or $p_1 x_1$, and the amount spent on good x_2, which is $p_2 x_2$, must be less than or equal to the amount of income, m, the consumer has available. You can spend less, but not more, than what you have.

Obviously, the model would be more realistic if we had many products that the consumer could buy, but the gain in realism is not worth the additional cost in computational complexity. We can easily let x_2 stand for "all other goods."

Another simplification allows us to transform the inequality in the equation to a strict equality. We assume that no time elapses so there is no saving (not spending all of the income available) or borrowing. In other words, the consumer lives for a nanosecond – buying, consuming, and dying the same instant. Once again, this assumption is not as severe as it first looks. We can incorporate saving and borrowing in this model by defining one good as present consumption and the other as future consumption. We will use this modeling technique in a future application.

Assuming away time, the budget line is defined as

$$p_1 x_1 + p_2 x_2 = m$$

It can be rewritten in the form of the equation of a line via a little algebraic manipulation:

$$p_1 x_1 + p_2 x_2 = m$$
$$p_2 x_2 = m - p_1 x_1$$
$$x_2 = \frac{m}{p_2} - \frac{p_1}{p_2} x_1$$

The intercept, m/p_2, is interpreted as the maximum amount of x_2 that the consumer can afford. By buying no x_1 and spending all income on x_2, the most the consumer can buy is m/p_2.

The slope, $-p_1/p_2$, also has a convenient interpretation: It states the rate at which the market requires the consumer to give up x_2 in order to acquire x_1. This is easy to see if you remember that the slope of a line is simply the rise (Δx_2) over the run (Δx_1). Then,

$$\frac{\Delta x_2}{\Delta x_1} = -\frac{p_1}{p_2}$$

A Numerical Example of the Budget Constraint

Step Open the Excel workbook BudgetConstraint.xls and read the *Intro* sheet, then go to the *Properties* sheet to see an example of a budget constraint.

Figure 1.1.1.1 shows the organization of the sheet. As you can see, the consumer chooses the amounts of goods 1 and 2 to purchase, given prices and income.

With $p_1 = \$2/$unit, $p_2 = \$3/$unit, and $m = \$100$, the equation of the budget line can be computed.

Step Click on the scroll bars to see the red dot, the consumption bundle, move around in the chart. Notice that clicking on the horizontal scroll bar increases the buyer's purchases of good 1 while holding good 2 purchases constant. The red dot is an ordered pair that represents an amount of x_1 and x_2.

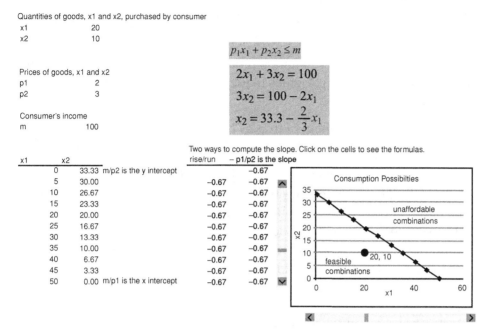

Quantities of goods, x1 and x2, purchased by consumer

x1	20
x2	10

$$p_1 x_1 + p_2 x_2 \le m$$

Prices of goods, x1 and x2

p1	2
p2	3

$$2x_1 + 3x_2 = 100$$

$$3x_2 = 100 - 2x_1$$

Consumer's income

m	100

$$x_2 = 33.3 - \frac{2}{3}x_1$$

Two ways to compute the slope. Click on the cells to see the formulas.

x1	x2		rise/run	– p1/p2 is the slope
0	33.33	m/p2 is the y intercept		–0.67
5	30.00		–0.67	–0.67
10	26.67		–0.67	–0.67
15	23.33		–0.67	–0.67
20	20.00		–0.67	–0.67
25	16.67		–0.67	–0.67
30	13.33		–0.67	–0.67
35	10.00		–0.67	–0.67
40	6.67		–0.67	–0.67
45	3.33		–0.67	–0.67
50	0.00	m/p1 is the x intercept	–0.67	–0.67

Figure 1.1.1.1. The budget line.
Source: BudgetConstraint.xls!Properties

By rewriting the budget constraint equation as a line and then graphing it, we have a geometric representation of the consumer's consumption possibilities. All points inside or on the budget line are feasible. Points northeast of the budget line are unaffordable.

By clicking the scroll bars you can easily see that the consumer has many feasible points. The big question is, Which one of these many affordable combinations will be chosen? We cannot answer that question with the budget constraint alone. We need to know how much the consumer likes the two goods. That is the subject of the next chapter.

Changes in the Budget Line – Pivots (or Rotations) and Shifts

Step Proceed to the *Changes* sheet.

The idea here is that changes in prices cause the budget line to *pivot* or *rotate*, altering the slope, but keeping one of the intercepts the same, while changes in income *shift* the budget line in or out, leaving the slope unchanged.

Step To see how the budget line pivots, experiment with cell K9 (the price of good 1). Change it from 2 to 5. The chart changes to reveal a new budget line. The budget line has rotated around the *y* intercept because if the consumer decided to spend all income on x_2, the amount that could be purchased would remain the same.

If you lower the price of good 1, the budget line rotates out. Confirm that this is true.

Step Changing cell K10 alters the budget line by changing the price of good 2. Once again, change values in the cell to see the effect such changes have on the budget line.

Step Next, click the Reset button to return the sheet to its initial values and work with cell K13. Cut income in half.

The effect is dramatically different. Instead of rotating, the budget line has shifted in. The slope remains the same because prices have not changed.
Increasing income shifts the budget line out.
This concludes the basics of budget lines. It is worth spending a little time playing with cells K9, K10, and K13 to reinforce the way budget lines move when there is a change in a price or income. These shocks will be used again when we examine how a consumer's optimal decision changes when prices or income change.
Remember the key lesson: Change in price rotates the budget line, but change in income shifts it.

Funky Budget Lines

In addition to the standard, linear budget constraint, there are many more complicated scenarios facing consumers. To give you a flavor of the possibilities, let us review two examples.

Step Proceed to the *Rationing* sheet

In this example, in addition to the usual income constraint, the consumer is allowed a maximum amount of one of the goods. Thus, a second constraint (a vertical line) has been added. When the maximum is above the x_1 intercept (50 units), this second constraint is said to be nonbinding.
As you can see from the sheet, this lops off a portion of the budget line.

Step Change cell E13 to see how changing the rationed amount affects the budget constraint.

Step Proceed to the *Subsidy* sheet.

In this example, in addition to the usual income constraint, the consumer is given a subsidy in the form of a fixed amount of the good.
Food stamps are classic example of subsidies. Suppose the consumer has $100 of income, but is given $20 in food stamps (which can only be spent on food), and food (x_1) is priced at $2/unit. Then the budget constraint has a horizontal segment from 0 to 10 units of food because the most x_2 (other goods) that can be purchased remains at m/p_2 from 0 to 10 units of food (since food stamps cannot be used to buy other goods).

Step Change cell E13 to see how changing the given amount of food (which is the dollar amount of food stamps divided by the price of food) affects the budget constraint.

We will return to the food stamp example in a future application.

The Budget Constraint as Consumption Possibilities

The budget constraint is a key part of the optimization problem facing the consumer. By graphing the constraint, we can immediately see the consumer's options.

Changing prices has a different effect on the constraint than changing income. If prices change, the budget line rotates around the intercept (of the unchanged price). A change in income, however, shifts the entire constraint and leaves the slope unaffected.

The basic budget constraint is a line, but there are many other scenarios faced by consumers in which the constraint can be kinked. The flexibility of the constraint is one of the powerful features of the Theory of Consumer Behavior.

The constraint is just one part of the consumer's optimization problem. The desirability of goods and services, also known as tastes and preferences, is another important part. The next chapter explains how we model satisfaction from consuming goods and services.

Exercises

Open Word and answer the following questions. Save the document and print it when you are done.

1. Use Excel to create a chart of a budget constraint that is based on the following information: $m = \$100$ and $p_2 = \$3$/unit, but $p_1 = \$2$/unit for the first 20 units and \$1/unit thereafter. Copy your chart and paste it in your Word document.
2. If the good on the y axis is free, what does the budget constraint look like?
3. What combination of shocks could make the new budget line be completely inside and steeper than the initial budget line?
4. What happens to the budget line if all prices and income doubles?

References

The epigraph of this chapter can be found on page 48 of Milton Friedman's revised edition of his *Price Theory* text. The book is essentially his lecture notes from the famous two-quarter price theory course that Friedman delivered for many years at the University of Chicago. It is interesting to see how Micro was taught back then, especially how little emphasis was placed on mathematics. The problems in appendix B are truly thought provoking.

1.2
Satisfaction

1.2.1

Preferences

[Indifference] curves are negatively sloped, pass through every point in commodity space, never intersect, and are concave from above. The last-mentioned property implies that the marginal rate of substitution of X for Y diminishes as X is substituted for Y so as to maintain the same level of satisfaction.

C. E. Ferguson

The key idea is that every consumer has a set of likes and dislikes, desires, and tastes, called *preferences* over all goods and services.

Preferences allow the consumer to compare any two combinations or bundles of goods and services in terms of better, worse, or the same. The result of such a comparison can be described as follows:

Strictly preferred – the consumer likes bundle A better than bundle B
Indifferent – the consumer is equally satisfied having bundle A or bundle B
Weakly preferred – the consumer likes bundle A better than bundle B or is indifferent between them

In terms of algebra, you can think of strictly preferred as greater than ($>$), indifferent as equal ($=$), and weakly preferred as greater than or equal ($\geq$).

If the consumer can rank any two bundles, then by repeated comparison of different bundles the consumer can rank all possible combinations from best to worst.

The consumer's preferences can be *revealed* and *mapped* by having her choose between bundles.

Three Axioms

Three fundamental assumptions are made about preferences to ensure internal consistency:

1. Completeness – the consumer can compare any bundles and render a preferred or indifferent judgment.

2. Reflexivity – this identity condition says that the consumer is indifferent when comparing a bundle to itself.

3. Transitivity – this condition defines an orderly relation among bundles so that if bundle A is preferred to bundle B and bundle B is preferred to bundle C then bundle A *must be* preferred to bundle C.

Completeness and reflexivity are easily accepted. Transitivity, on the other hand, is controversial. As a matter of pure logic, we would expect that a consumer would make consistent comparisons. In practice, however, consumers may make intransitive, or inconsistent, choices.

An example of intransitivity: You claim to like Coke better than Pepsi, Pepsi better than RC, and RC better than Coke. The last claim is inconsistent with the first two.

In mathematics, numbers are transitive with respect to the comparison operators greater than, less than, or equal to. Because 12 is greater than 8 and 8 is greater than 3, clearly 12 is greater than 3.

In sports, outcomes of games can easily yield intransitive results. Michigan might beat Indiana and in its next game Indiana could defeat Iowa, but few people would claim that the two outcomes would guarantee that Michigan will win when it plays Iowa.

When we assume that preferences are transitive, it means that the consumer can rank bundles without any contradictions. It also means that we may be able to determine the consumer's choice between two bundles based on answers to previous comparisons.

Displaying Preferences via Indifference Curves

We can describe a consumer's preferences with an *indifference map*, which is made up of *indifference curves*.

A single indifference curve is the set of combinations that give equal satisfaction. If two points lie on the same indifference curve, this means that the consumer sees these two bundles as tied – neither one is better or worse than the other.

A single indifference curve and an entire indifference map can be generated by having the consumer choose between alternative bundles of goods. We can demonstrate how this works with a concrete example.

Step Open the Excel workbook Preferences.xls and read the *Intro* sheet, then go to the *Reveal* sheet to see how preferences can be mapped and the indifference curve revealed.

Step Begin by clicking the `ask ?` button. For bundle B, enter 4,3, then click OK.

We are using the coordinate pair notation so 4,3 identifies a combination that has 4 units of the good on the x axis and 3 units of the good on the y axis.

The sheet records the bundles that are being compared in columns A and B and the result of the comparison in column C. The choices are being made by a virtual consumer whose unknown preferences are in the computer. By asking the virtual consumer to make a series of comparisons, we can reveal the hidden preferences in the form of an indifference curve and indifference map.

Notice that Excel plots the point 4,3 on the chart. The green square means the consumer chose bundle B. This means that 3,3 and 4,3 are not on the same indifference curve.

Step Click the ask ? button again. This time offer the consumer a choice between 3,3 and 2,3.

This time the consumer chose bundle A and a red triangle was placed on the chart, meaning that the point 3,3 is strictly preferred to the point 2,3.

These two choices illustrate the concept of *insatiability*. This means that the consumer cannot be sated (or filled up) and more is always preferred to less. 4,3 is preferred to 3,3, which is preferred to 2,3 because good x_2 is held constant at 3 and this consumer is insatiable, preferring more to less.

To reveal the indifference curve of this consumer, we must offer tougher choices, where we give more of one good and less of the other.

Step Click the ask ? button again. This time offer the consumer a choice between 3,3 and 4,2.

The consumer decided that 3,3 is better. This reveals important information about the consumer's preferences. At 3,3, the consumer likes one more unit of x_1 less than the loss of one unit of x_2.

Step Click the ask ? button several times more to figure out where the consumer's break-even point is in terms of how much x_2 is needed to balance the gain from the additional unit of x_1. Offer 4,2.5 and then try taking away less of good 2, such as 2.7 or 2.9. Once you find this point, you have located two points on a single indifference curve. If it is difficult to see the points on the chart, use the Zoom control to magnify the screen (say to 200%).

You should find that this consumer is indifferent between the bundles 3,3 and 4,2.9.

Step Now click the 100 Random ? button. One hundred pairwise comparisons are made between 3,3 and a random set of alternatives. It is easy to see that the consumer can compare each and every point on the chart to the benchmark bundle of 3,3 and judge each and every point as better, worse, or

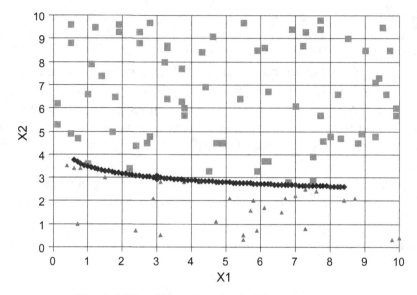

Figure 1.2.1.1. Revealing the indifference curve.
Source: Preferences!Reveal

the same. The bundles that are the same to this consumer compared to 3,3 all lie on the same indifference curve.

If we connect the bundles that are equivalent to 3,3, as in Figure 1.2.1.1, we reveal the indifference curve through the benchmark point for this consumer.

Step To recreate Figure 1.2.1.1, click the indifference button.

The Indifference Map

Every combination of goods has an indifference curve through it. We often display a few representative indifference curves on a chart and this is called an *indifference map*, as in Figure 1.2.1.2.

Any point on the curve farthest from the origin, in Figure 1.2.1.2, is preferred to any point on the indifference curve below it. The arrow indicates that satisfaction increases as you move northeast to higher indifference curves.

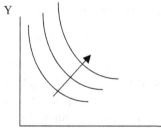

X   Figure 1.2.1.2. An indifference map.

There are many (in fact, an infinity) of indifference curves and they are not all drawn in when we draw an indifference map. We draw just a few curves. We say that the indifference map is *dense*, which means there is a curve through every point.

Marginal Rate of Substitution

Now that we have elicited a single indifference curve from the virtual consumer in the Excel workbook, we can define and work with a crucial concept in the Theory of Consumer Behavior – the marginal rate of substitution, or MRS.

The MRS is a single number that tells us the willingness of a consumer to exchange one good for another from a given bundle.

Step Click the Copy Picture button, then click the New Preferences button, and then display the indifference curve for this new consumer (by clicking the Indifference button).

Notice that the indifference curve is different than the original one. It is a different consumer. You can use the buttons to offer this consumer bundles that can be compared with the 3,3 benchmark bundle, just like before.

The key idea here is that at 3,3, we can measure each consumer's willingness to trade x_2 in exchange for x_1.

Initially (as shown in Figure 1.2.1.1 and in the picture you took), we saw that the consumer was indifferent between 3,3 and 4,2.9. For one more unit of x_1, the consumer is willing to trade 0.1 units of x_2. Then the MRS of x_1 for x_2 at 3,3 is measured by $-0.1/1$, or -0.1.

With our new virtual consumer, the MRS at 3,3 is a different number.

Step Proceed to the *MRS* sheet. Click on the Indifference button. Not only is the indifference curve through 3,3 displayed for this consumer, it also shows some of the bundles that lie on this indifference curve.

You can compute the MRS at 3,3 by looking at the bundle below 3,3. How much x_2 is the consumer willing to give up in order to get 0.1 more of x_1? This ratio, $\Delta x_2 / \Delta x_1$, is the slope of the indifference curve, or the MRS.

The MRS also can be computed as the slope of the indifference curve at a point by using derivatives. Instead of computing $\Delta x_2 / \Delta x_1$ along an indifference curve from one point to another, one can find the instantaneous rate of change at 3,3. We will do this later.

The crucial concept right now is that the MRS is a number that measures the willingness of a consumer to trade one good for another. The MRS is negative because the consumer gives up some of one good to get more of another. The bigger in absolute value, the more the consumer is willing to trade the good on the y axis for the good on the x axis.

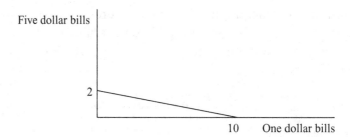

Figure 1.2.1.3. Perfect substitutes.

Funky Preferences and Their Indifference Curves

We can depict a wide variety of preferences with indifference maps. Here are some examples.

Example 1: Perfect Substitutes – Constant Slope

Say a consumer has one $5 bill and five $1 bills (as long as we are not talking about several hundred dollars' worth of bills).

The indifference curve would look like Figure 1.2.1.3.

This consumer is indifferent between having 10 $1s and 2 $5s because it is $10 either way. There is another point, 5,1, which also lies on the indifference line.

You could argue that there is an indivisibility here and there are actually just three points that should not be connected by a line.

Example 2: Perfect Complements – L Shaped Indifference Curves

Suppose the goods in questions have to be used in a particular way, like cars and tires. Ignoring the spare, you need four tires for a car. Having more tires does not help you if you still have just one car.

Figure 1.2.1.4 illustrates the indifference map for this situation. Eight tires with one car gives the same satisfaction as four tires with one car. This indifference map tells us that eight tires and two cars is preferred to four tires and

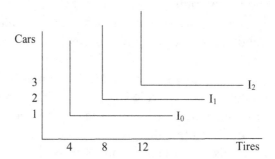

Figure 1.2.1.4. Perfect complements.

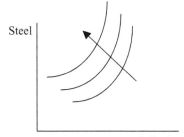

Figure 1.2.1.5. A bad.   Pollution

one car (or eight tires and one car) because the middle L-shaped indifference curve (I_1) is farther from the origin than the lowest indifference curve (I_0).

Example 3: Bads

What if one of the goods is actually a bad, like pollution? Figure 1.2.1.5 shows the indifference map in this case.

Along any one of the indifference curves, more steel and more pollution are equally satisfying because pollution is a bad that cancels out the additional good from steel.

The arrow indicates that satisfaction increases by moving northwest, to higher indifference curves.

Example 4: Neutral Goods

What if something is neither good nor bad? Then it is neutral and the indifference map looks like Figure 1.2.1.6.

The horizontal indifference curves for the neutral good on the x axis in Figure 1.2.1.6 tell you that the consumer is indifferent if offered more x. The arrow indicates that satisfaction rises as you move north (because y is a good and having more of it increases satisfaction).

These are just a few examples of the situations that can be depicted with indifference curves. When we want to describe the basic, general case, as in Figure 1.2.1.2, economists use the phrase "well-behaved preferences."

Another technical term that is often used in economics is *convexity*, as in convex preferences. This means that midpoints are preferred to extremes. In

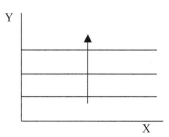

Figure 1.2.1.6. Here x is a neutral good.   X

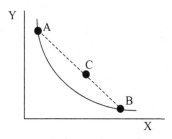

Figure 1.2.1.7. Convex preferences.

Figure 1.2.1.7, there are two extreme points, A and B, which are connected by a dashed line. Any point on the dashed line, like C, can be described by the equation $zA + (1 - z)B$, for $0 < z < 1$. This equation is called a convex combination.

If preferences are convex, then midpoints like C are strictly preferred to extreme points like A and B. Sometimes, convexity is used as another way of saying that preferences are well behaved.

An important property that arises out of well-behaved, convex preferences is that of *diminishing MRS*. The MRS will start large (in absolute value) at the top left corner, like point A in Figure 1.2.1.7, and get smaller and smaller as we travel down the indifference curve to point B. This makes common sense. The consumer is readily willing to trade a lot of *y* for *x* when he has a lot of *y* and little *x*. When the amounts are reversed, such as point B, a small MRS means he is willing to give up very little *y* for more *x*.

Indifference Curves Reflect Preferences

Preferences, a consumer's likes and dislikes, can be elicited or revealed by asking the consumer to pick between pairs of bundles. The indifference curve is that set of bundles that the consumer finds equally satisfying.

The MRS is a single number that measures the willingness of the consumer to exchange one good for another at a particular point. If the MRS is high (in absolute value), the indifference curve is steep at that point and the consumer is willing trade a lot of *y* for a little more *x*.

Standard, well-behaved preferences yield a set of smooth arcs (like Figure 1.2.1.2), but there are many other shapes that depict different kinds of goods and the relationship between goods.

Exercises

Open Word and answer the following questions. Save the document and print it when you are done.

1. What is the MRS at any point if *x* is a neutral good? Explain why.
2. If the good on the *y* axis was a neutral good and the other good was a regular good, then what would the indifference map look like? Use Word's Drawing Tools to draw a graph of this situation.

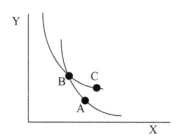

Figure 1.2.1.8. An indifference map.

3. Indifference curves cannot cross. Use Figure 1.2.1.8 to help you construct an explanation for this claim. Note that point C has more x and y than point A; thus, by insatiability, it must be preferred. The key lies in the assumption of transitivity.

4. Suppose we measure consumer A's and B's MRS at the same point and find that $MRS_A = -6$ and $MRS_B = -2$. What can we say about the preferences of A and B?

References

The epigraph is from page 26 of C. E. Ferguson's *Microeconomic Theory* (revised edition, 1969), a popular micro text in the 1960s and 1970s. In the preface Ferguson wrote, "This is a textbook; its content is taken from the public domain of economic literature. Conventional topics are treated in conventional ways; and there is no real innovation." Perhaps, but Ferguson adopted a much more mathematical presentation and added content, including general equilibrium theory, that made his book different.

1.2.2

Utility Functions

[A] cardinal measure of utility is in any case unnecessary; only an *ordinal* preference, involving "more" or "less" but not "how much," is required for the analysis of consumer's behavior.

Paul A. Samuelson

Previously, we showed that a consumer has preferences, which can be revealed and mapped.

The next step is to identify a particular functional form, called a *utility function*, which faithfully represents the person's preferences. Once you understand how the utility function works, we can combine it with the budget constraint to solve the consumer's optimization problem.

Cardinal and Ordinal Scales

Jeremy Bentham (1748–1832) was a utilitarian philosopher who believed that, in theory, the amount of utility from consuming a particular amount of a good could be measured. So, for example, if you ate an apple, we could hook you up to some device that would report the number of "utils" of satisfaction received.

Bentham also believed that utils were a sort of common currency that enabled them to be compared across individuals. He thought society should maximize aggregate or total utility, and utilitarianism has come to be associated with the phrase "the greatest happiness for the greatest number." To continue the example, if I get 12 utils from consuming the apple and you get 6, then I should get the apple.

This view of utility treats satisfaction as if we could place it on a *cardinal* scale. This is the usual number line where 8 is twice as much as 4 and the difference between 33 and 30 is the same as that between 210 and 207.

Near the turn of the 20th century, Vilfredo Pareto (1848–1923, usually pronounced pa-ray-toe) created the modern way of thinking about utility. He held that satisfaction could not be placed on a cardinal scale and that you could never compare the utilities of two people. Instead, he argued that utility could be measured only up to an *ordinal* scale, in which there is higher and lower, but no way to measure the magnitude between two items.

Notice how Pareto's approach matches exactly the way we assumed that a consumer could choose between bundles of goods as preferring one bundle or being indifferent. We never claimed to be able to measure a certain amount of satisfaction from a particular bundle.

For Pareto, and modern economics, the numerical value from a particular utility function for a given combination of goods has no meaning. These values are like the star ranking system for restaurants.

Critic A uses a 10-point scale to judge 14 restaurants.

Critic B uses a 1000-point scale to judge the same 14 restaurants.

We would never say that B's worst restaurant, which scored 114, is better than A's best.

Instead, we compare their *rankings*. If A and B give the same restaurant the highest ranking (regardless of the score), it is the best restaurant.

Now suppose we are reading a magazine that uses a 5-star rating system. Restaurant X is a 4 star and Restaurant Y is a 2 star.

X is better, but can we conclude that X is twice as good as Y? Absolutely not.

An ordinal scale is ordered, but the differences between values are not important.

Monotonic Transformation

Once we reveal the consumer's indifference curve and map, all we need to do is get a function that faithfully represents the indifference curves.

There are many (in fact, an infinity of) functions that could work. All the function has to do is preserve the consumer's preference ranking.

A *monotonic transformation* is a rule applied to a function that changes (transforms) it, but maintains the original order of the outputs of the function for given inputs.

For example, star ratings can be squared and the rankings remain the same.

Suppose that X is a 4- and Y a 2-star restaurant.

Square the star rankings.

X now has 16 stars and Y has 4 stars. X is still higher ranked than Y.

In this case, squaring is a monotonic transformation.

Can we conclude that X is now four times better? Of course not. Remember that the star ranking is an ordinal scale so the distance between items is irrelevant.

It is a fact that the MRS (at any point) remains constant under any monotonic transformation. This is an important property of monotonic transformations that we will illustrate with a concrete example.

Cobb-Douglas: A Ubiquitous Functional Form

Step Open the Excel workbook Utility.xls and read the *Intro* sheet, then go to the *CobbDouglas* sheet to see a concrete example of this utility function.

$$u(x_1, x_2) = x_1^c x_2^d$$

In economics, a function created by multiplying variables that are raised to powers is called a Cobb-Douglas functional form.

Step Follow the directions on the sheet (in column K) to rotate the chart and to see that an indifference curve is a top-down view of the function. The utility function itself, in 3D, is a hill or mountain (that keeps growing without ever reaching a top – illustrating the idea of insatiability).

With a utility function, the indifference curves are contour lines or level curves. The curves in 2D space are created by taking horizontal slices of the 3D surface. Every point on the indifference curve has the exact same height, which is utility.

Step The exponents (c and d) in the function express "likes and dislikes." Try $c = 4$ then $c = 0.2$.

The higher the c exponent, the more the consumer likes x_1 because each unit of x_1 is raised to a higher power as c increases. Notice that when $c = 4$, the fact that the consumer likes x_1 much more than when $c = 0.2$ is reflected in the shape of the indifference curve. The steeper the indifference curve, which means the higher the MRS (in absolute value), the more the consumer likes x_1.

Step Proceed to the *CobbDouglasLN* sheet, which takes a monotonic transformation of the Cobb-Douglas function. It applies the natural log function to the utility function.

Recall that the natural logarithm of a number x is the exponent on e (the irrational number 2.7128 . . .) that makes the result equal x. You should also remember that there are special rules for working with logs. Two especially common rules are $\ln(xy) = y \ln x$ and $\ln(xy) = \ln x + \ln y$. We apply these rules to the Cobb-Douglas utility function when we take the natural log of the utility function.

$$u(x_1, x_2) = x_1^c x_2^d$$
$$\ln u = \ln \left[x_1^c x_2^d \right]$$
$$\ln u = c \ln x_1 + d \ln x_2$$

The *CobbDouglasLN* sheet applies the natural log transformation by using Excel's LN() function.

Step Make sure the exponents are the same in both the *CobbDouglas* and *CobbDouglasLN* sheets.

Step Compare the yellow-backgrounded cells in the two sheets to see that the two combinations continue to lie on the same indifference curve, even though the utility values of the two functions are different.

The fact that the yellow-backgrounded cells remain on the same indifference curve after undergoing the natural log transformation demonstrates the meaning of a monotonic transformation. The utility values are different, but the ranking has been preserved.

Economists often use the Cobb-Douglas functional form for utility (and production) functions because it has very nice algebraic properties where lots of terms cancel out.

The Cobb-Douglas function is especially easy to work with if you remember the following rules:

$$\text{Algebra Rule: } \frac{x^a}{x^b} = x^{a-b} \text{ and } (x^a)^m = x^{am}$$

$$\text{Calculus Rule: } \frac{d(cx^a)}{dx} = acx^{a-1}dx$$

Practice: Say you work on a problem and you arrive at

$$x^4 = 16$$

How can you solve for x?

Apply the Algebra Rule:

$$(x^4)^{1/4} = (16)^{1/4}$$
$$x = 2$$

We will use these rules frequently.

Expressing Other Preferences with Utility Functions

Step Proceed to the *PerfSub* sheet, then the *PerfComp* sheet, and finally the *Quasilinear* sheet.

Note that we can represent many different kinds of preferences with utility functions.

An important point is that there are many (to be more exact, an infinity) of possible utility functions available to us. We would want one that faithfully reflects the consumer's preferences. We can always apply a monotonic transformation and it will not alter the consumer's preferences.

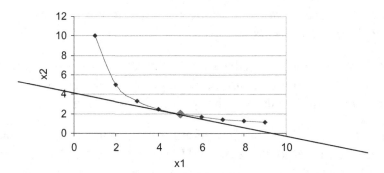

Figure 1.2.2.1. Computing the MRS.
Source: Utility.xls!MRS

Computing the MRS for a Utility Function

Step Proceed to the *MRS* sheet to see how the MRS can be computed. There are two options:

1. A Discrete-Size Change

$$MRS = \frac{\Delta x_2}{\Delta x_1}$$

2. An Infinitesimally Small Change

$$MRS = \frac{dx_2}{dx_1} = -\frac{\frac{\partial U}{\partial x_1}}{\frac{\partial U}{\partial x_2}}$$

We will use a concrete example to illustrate how these two different ways to compute the MRS are applied. Consider the utility function, $x_1 x_2$. It is Cobb-Douglas because the exponents (implicitly) are 1.

1. The discrete-size change computes the MRS *from* one point to another.

Suppose we are interested in the indifference curve that gives all combinations with a utility of 10. Certainly 5,2 works (since 5 times 2 is 10). It is the red dot in the graph on the *MRS* sheet (and in Figure 1.2.2.1).

From the bundle 5,2 (a coordinate pair), if we gave this consumer 1 more unit of x_1, by how much would we have to decrease x_2? A little algebra tells us.

We know that $U = x_1 x_2$ and the initial bundle 5,2 yields $U = 10$. We want to maintain U constant and $x_1 = 6$ because we added a unit to x_1, so

$$U = x_1 x_2 \rightarrow 10 = 6 x_2 \rightarrow x_2 = 10/6.$$

We have two bundles that yield $U = 10$, 5,2, and 6, 10/6. Then, we can compute the MRS as the change in x_2 divided by the change in x_1. The change in x_2 is $-1/3$ (because 10/6 is 1/3 less than 2) and the change in x_1 is 1, so starting from the point 5,2, the MRS from $x_1 = 5$ to $x_1 = 6$ is $-1/3$.

This is the calculation done in Excel in cell MRS!C18.

2. The infinitesimally small change computes the MRS *at* a particular point.

Another way to compute the MRS uses the calculus approach. Instead of a "large" change in x_1, we take an infinitesimally small change, computing the slope of the indifference curve not from one point to another, but as the slope of the tangent line (as shown in Figure 1.2.2.1).

For this simple utility function, we could simply notice that, holding utility constant at 10, we can rewrite the function as x_2 in terms of x_1, then take the derivative.

$$x_2 = \frac{10}{x_1}$$

$$\frac{dx_2}{dx_1} = -\frac{10}{x_1^2}$$

At $x_1 = 5$, the MRS at that point is $-10/25$ or -0.4. If you need help with derivatives, the next chapter has an appendix that reviews basic calculus.

This relies on the ability to write x_2 in terms of x_1. If we have a utility function that cannot be easily rearranged in this way, we will not be able to compute the MRS. There is, however, a more general approach. The procedure involves taking the partial derivative of the utility function with respect to x_1 (called the marginal utility of x_1) and dividing by the partial derivative of the utility function with respect to x_2 (called the marginal utility of x_2). Here is how it works.

With $U = x_1 x_2$, the derivative is pretty simple: $dU/dx_1 = x_2$ and $dU/dx_2 = x_1$. Thus,

$$MRS = -\frac{\dfrac{dU}{dx_1}}{\dfrac{dU}{dx_2}} = -\frac{x_2}{x_1}$$

Because we are considering the point 5,2, we evaluate the MRS at that point (which means we plug in those values), like this:

$$MRS = -\frac{x_2}{x_1}\bigg|_{\substack{x_1=5 \\ x_2=2}} = -\frac{2}{5} = -0.4$$

The ratio of the marginal utilities gives the same answer as the dx_2/dx_1 method. Both are using infinitesimally small changes to compute the instantaneous rate of change of the indifference curve at a particular point.

Note that the ratio of the marginal utilities approach requires that you divide the marginal utility of x_1 (the good on the x axis) by the marginal utility of x_2 (the good on the y axis). Since we used $\Delta y/\Delta x$ in the discrete change approach, it is easy to confuse the numerator and denominator when computing the MRS via the derivative. Remember that dU/dx_1 goes in the numerator.

Step The *MRS* sheet implements the calculus procedure in column C. Click on a cell, such as C18, to see the formula.

Comparing the Discrete Size (Δ) and Infinitesimally Small (d) Methods

Notice that the two procedures yield different answers. The discrete change approach tells you the MRS as measured *from $x_1 = 5$ to $x_1 = 6$* is $-1/3$, whereas the derivative method says that the MRS *at $x_1 = 5$* is -0.4.

The difference is due to the fact that the two approaches are applying a different size change in x_1 to a curve. As the discrete-size change gets smaller, it approaches the derivative measure of the MRS. In Figure 1.2.2.1, the discrete change approach is computing the rise over the run using two separate points on the curve, while the calculus approach is computing the slope of the tangent line.

Step The *MRS* sheet also makes clear that monotonic transformations preserve the MRS at every point. Look at the values of the cells in the yellow highlighted row. The MRS for a given approach are exactly the same. In other words, columns C, H, and M are the same and columns D, I, and N are the same. The MRS remains unaffected when the utility function is monotonically transformed.

Step Finally, alter the step size on the *MRS* sheet (in cell B7) from 1 to 0.5. The indifference curve displays changes because the points being plotted are now closer together. Notice that columns C, H, and M are closer to the MRS = -0.4 value at $x_1 = 5$ in columns D, I, and N. Set cell B7 to 0.1. Now the values for the MRS computed from one point on the indifference curve to another point on the curve are almost the same as the value of the MRS computed as the slope of the tangent line. The reason why is obvious: The change in x_1, the step size, is much smaller so the point-to-point approach is converging to the slope of the tangent line approach.

Utility Functions Represent Preferences

Utility functions are equations that represent a consumer's preferences. The idea is that we reveal preferences by having the consumer compare bundles, and then we select a functional form that faithfully reflects the indifference curves of the consumer.

In selecting the functional form, there are many possibilities and economists often use the Cobb-Douglas form. The value of the utility function itself is meaningless and any monotonic transformation (that preserves the preference ordering) will work as a utility function. Monotonic transformations do not affect the MRS.

Exercises

Open Word and answer the following questions. Save the document and print it when you are done. See the appendix to the next chapter for help with derivatives.

The utility function, $U = x - 0.03x^2 + y$, has a quasilinear functional form. You can see what it looks like by choosing the Polynomial option in the *Quasilinear* sheet.

1. Compute the value of the utility function at bundle A, where $x = 10$ and $y = 1$. Show your work.
2. Working with bundle A, find the MRS as x rises from $x = 10$ to $x = 20$. Show your work.
3. Find the MRS at the point 10,1 (using derivatives). Show your work.
4. Why do the two methods of determining the MRS yield different answers?
5. Which method is better?

References

The epigraph can be found on page 91 of the revised edition of *The Foundations of Economic Analysis*, by Paul Samuelson. This remarkable book, written by one of the greatest economists of the 20th century, took economics to a new level of mathematical sophistication. Samuelson could not have picked a better opening quote, "Mathematics is a Language," by J. Willard Gibbs.

1.3
Optimal Choice

1.3.1

Initial Solution for the Consumer Choice Problem

Joseph Louis Lagrange, the greatest mathematician of the eighteenth century, was born at Turin on January 25, 1736, and died at Paris on April 10, 1813.... In appearance he was of medium height, and slightly formed, with pale blue eyes and a colourless complexion. In character he was nervous and timid, he detested controversy, and to avoid it willingly allowed others to take credit for what he had himself done.

W. W. Rouse Ball

The *budget constraint* shows the consumer's possible consumption bundles.

The standard, linear constraint is $p_1x_1 + p_2x_2 = m$.
There are many other situations, such as subsidies and rationing, which give more complicated constraints with kinks and horizontal/vertical segments.

The *indifference map* shows the consumer's preferences.

The standard situation is a set of convex, downward sloping indifference curves.
There are many alternative preferences, such as perfect substitutes and perfect complements.
Preferences are captured by utility functions, which accurately reflect the shape of the indifference curves.

Our job is to find the combination (or bundle) that maximizes satisfaction (as described by the indifference map or utility function) given the budget constraint. The answer will be in terms of how much the consumer will buy in units of each good.

The optimal solution is depicted by the canonical graph in Figure 1.3.1.1. This canon is not a cannon as in a weapon that fires projectiles. The word *canonical* is used here to mean standard, conventional, or orthodox. In economics, a canonical graph is a core, essential graph that is understood by all economists, such as a supply and demand graph.

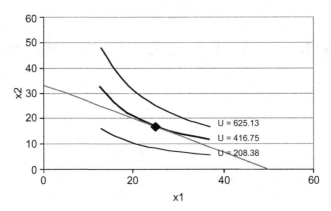

Figure 1.3.1.1. Displaying the optimal solution.

It is no exaggeration to say that Figure 1.3.1.1 is one of the most fundamental and important graphs in economics. It is the foundation of the Theory of Consumer Behavior and with it we will derive a demand curve.

Finding the Initial Solution

There are two ways to find the optimal solution:

- Analytical methods using algebra and calculus – conventional, paper and pencil
- Numerical methods using a computer (Excel's Solver)

Analytical Approach

Unfortunately, constrained optimization problems are harder to solve than unconstrained problems. The appendix to this chapter offers a short calculus review along with a list of common derivative and algebra rules. If the subsequent material makes little sense, see the appendix and then return here.

Because this is a constrained optimization problem, the analytical approach uses the method developed by Joseph Louis Lagrange.

Lagrange's brilliant idea is based on transforming a constrained optimization problem into an unconstrained problem and then solving by using standard calculus techniques. In the process, a new endogenous variable is created. It can have an interesting economic interpretation.

There is a recipe:

1. Rewrite the constraint so that it is equal to zero.
2. Form the Lagrangean function.
3. Take partial derivatives with respect to x_1, x_2, and λ.
4. Set the derivatives equal to zero and solve the system of equations for x_1, x_2, and λ.

A Concrete Example

Suppose the consumer has a Cobb-Douglas utility function with exponents equal to 1 and a budget constraint, $2x_1 + 3x_2 = 100$ (which means the price of good 1 is \$2/unit, the price of good 2 is \$3/unit, and income is \$100).

The problem is to maximize utility subject to the budget constraint. This problem is not solved directly. It is first transformed into an unconstrained problem, and then the unconstrained problem is solved.

We apply the recipe developed by Lagrange.

1. Rewrite the constraint so that it is equal to zero:

$$0 = 100 - 2x_1 - 3x_2$$

2. Form the Lagrangean:

$$\max_{x_1, x_2, \lambda} L = x_1 x_2 + \lambda(100 - 2x_1 - 3x_2)$$

Note that the Lagrangean function, L, is composed of the original objective function (in this case, the utility function) plus a new variable, λ (the Greek letter lambda) times the rewritten constraint. λ is called the Lagrangean (or Lagrange) multiplier.

3. Take partial derivatives with respect to x_1, x_2, and λ:

$$\frac{\partial L}{\partial x_1} = x_2 - 2\lambda$$

$$\frac{\partial L}{\partial x_2} = x_1 - 3\lambda$$

$$\frac{\partial L}{\partial \lambda} = 100 - 2x_1 - 3x_2$$

The derivative used here is a partial derivative, denoted by ∂, which is a lowercase Greek letter d (which is why sometimes δ is used as a symbol for the partial derivative). The partial derivative symbol is often read as the letter d, so the first equation is read as "d L d x-one equals x-two minus two times lambda." It is also common to read the derivative in the first equation as "partial L partial x one."

The partial derivative is a natural extension of the regular derivative. Consider the function $y = 4x^2$. The derivative of y with respect to x is $dy/dx = 8x$. Suppose, however, that we had a more complicated function, like this: $y = 4zx^2$. This function says that y depends on two variables, z and x. We can explore the rate of change of this function along a single dimension by treating it as a partial function, meaning that we hold all other variables constant. Then the partial derivative of y with respect to x is $\partial y/\partial x = 8zx$ and the partial derivative of y with respect to z is $\partial y/\partial z = 4x^2$.

The partial derivative enables us to use the derivative on multivariate functions. Remember to treat other variables as constants when taking a partial derivative.

4. Set the partial derivatives equal to zero and solve the system of equations for x_1, x_2, and λ:

$$\frac{\partial L}{\partial x_1} = x_2 - 2\lambda = 0$$

$$\frac{\partial L}{\partial x_2} = x_1 - 3\lambda = 0$$

$$\frac{\partial L}{\partial \lambda} = 100 - 2x_1 - 3x_2 = 0$$

There are many ways to solve this system of equations, which are known as the first-order conditions. A common strategy involves moving the λ terms to the right-hand side and then dividing the first equation by the second one, like this.

$$x_2 = 2\lambda$$

$$x_1 = 3\lambda$$

$$\frac{x_2}{x_1} = \frac{2\lambda}{3\lambda}$$

The λ terms then cancel out, leaving us with two equations (the one above and the third equation from the original three first-order conditions) and two unknowns (x_1 and x_2).

$$\frac{x_2}{x_1} = \frac{2}{3}$$

$$100 - 2x_1 - 3x_2 = 0$$

The top equation has a nice economic interpretation. It says that, at the optimal solution, the MRS (slope of the indifference curve) must equal the price ratio (slope of the budget constraint).

From the top equation, we can solve for x_2.

$$x_2 = \frac{2}{3}x_1$$

We can then substitute this value into the second equation to get the optimal value of x_1.

$$100 - 2x_1 - 3\left[\frac{2}{3}x_1\right] = 0$$

$$100 - 2x_1 - 2x_1 = 0$$

$$100 = 4x_1$$

$$x_1^* = 25$$

Then we substitute this value into the expression for x_2 to get the optimal value of x_2.

$$x_2 = \frac{2}{3}[25]$$
$$x_2^* = 16\frac{2}{3}$$

The asterisk is used to represent the optimal solution for a choice variable. This consumer should buy 25 units of good 1 and $16\frac{2}{3}$ units of good 2 in order to maximize satisfaction given the budget constraint.

We can use either equation 1 or 2 (from the original first-order conditions) to find the optimal value of lambda. Either way, we get $\lambda^* = 8\frac{1}{3}$.

For many optimization problems, we would be interested in finding the value of the maximum by evaluating the objective function (in this case the utility function) at the optimal solution. But recall that utility is measured only up to an ordinal scale and the actual value of utility is irrelevant. We want to maximize utility, but we do not care about its actual maximum value. The fact that utility is ordinal, not cardinal, also explains why the optimal value of lambda is not meaningful. In general, the Lagrangean multiplier tells us how the maximum value of the objective function changes as the constraint is relaxed. With utility as the objective function, this interpretation is not applicable.

Numerical Approach

Instead of calculus (via the method of Lagrange) and pencil and paper, we can use numerical methods to find the optimal solution.

We have to set up the problem in Excel, carefully organizing things into a goal, endogenous variables, exogenous variables, and constraint; then use Excel's Solver to get the solution.

Step Open the Excel workbook OptimalChoice.xls and read the *Intro* sheet, then go to the *OptimalChoice* sheet to see how the numerical approach can be used to solve this problem.

Figure 1.3.1.2 reproduces the display when you first arrive at the *OptimalChoice* sheet.

Notice how the sheet is organized by the three components of the optimization problem, goal, endogenous and exogenous variables. The constraint cell displays how much of the consumer's budget remains available for buying goods. The consumer in Figure 1.3.1.2 is not using all of the income available so we know satisfaction cannot be maximized at the point 20,10.

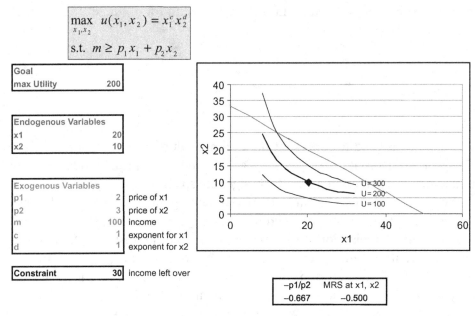

$$\max_{x_1, x_2} u(x_1, x_2) = x_1^c x_2^d$$

$$\text{s.t. } m \geq p_1 x_1 + p_2 x_2$$

Goal	
max Utility	200

Endogenous Variables	
x1	20
x2	10

Exogenous Variables		
p1	2	price of x1
p2	3	price of x2
m	100	income
c	1	exponent for x1
d	1	exponent for x2

Constraint	30	income left over

−p1/p2	MRS at x1, x2
−0.667	−0.500

Figure 1.3.1.2. The initial display in the *OptimalChoice* sheet.
Source: OptimalChoice.xls!OptimalChoice

Step Let's have the consumer buy x_2 with the remaining \$30. At \$3/unit, 10 additional units of x_2 can be purchased. Enter 20 in the x_2 cell (B13) and hit the Enter key. The chart refreshes to display the point 20,20, which is on the budget constraint, and draws three new indifference curves.

Although 20,20 does exhaust the available income, it is not the optimal solution. The display at the bottom reveals the MRS does not equal the price ratio.

In absolute value, the MRS $> p_1/p_2$; in other words, the slope of the indifference curve at that point is greater than the slope of the budget constraint.

The consumer cannot change the slope of the budget constraint, but the MRS can be altered by changing the combination of goods purchased. This consumer needs to lower the MRS (in absolute value) to make the two equal. This can be done by crawling down the budget constraint.

If the consumer buys 10 more of good 1 (so 30 units of x_1 total), consumption of x_2 must fall by $6\frac{2}{3}$ units to 13.33 (repeating, of course).

Step Enter 30 in cell B12 and 13.33 in B13. (You can enter "$= 13 + 1/3$" if you want more precision, but Excel cannot perfectly accurately represent a repeating decimal.) Now you are on the other side of the optimal solution. The MRS is less than the price ratio.

You could, of course, continue adjusting the cells, but there is a faster way.

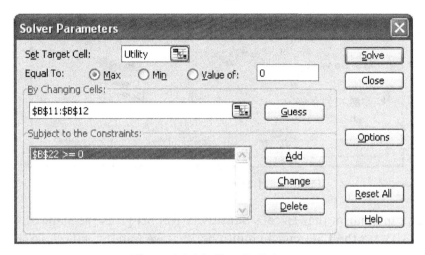

Figure 1.3.1.3. Excel's Solver.

Step Click Data and click Solver (grouped under the Analysis tab) or execute Tools: Solver in older versions of Excel to bring up the Solver Parameters dialog box (displayed in Figure 1.3.1.3).

If you do not have Solver available as a choice, bring up the Add-in Manager dialog box and make sure that Solver is listed and checked. If Solver is not listed, you must install it from the Office CD or download from <www.solver.com>.

Notice how Excel's Solver includes information on the objective function (the target cell), the choice variables (the changing cells), and the budget constraint.

Step All of the information has been entered into the Solver Parameters dialog box so you simply click the Solve button.

Excel's Solver works by trying different combinations of x_1 and x_2 and evaluating the improvement in the target cell, while meeting the constraint. When it cannot improve very much more, it figures it has found the answer and displays a message as shown in Figure 1.3.1.4.

Although Solver gets the right answer in this problem, we will see in future applications that Solver is not perfect and does not deserve blind trust.

Step Click the Sensitivity option under Reports and click OK; Excel puts down the Solver solution into cells B12 and B13. It also inserts a new sheet into the workbook with the Sensitivity Report.

Step Click on cells B12 and B13. Notice that Excel did not get exactly 25 and $16\frac{2}{3}$. It got extremely close and you can certainly interpret the result as confirming the analytical solution, but Solver's output will require interpretation.

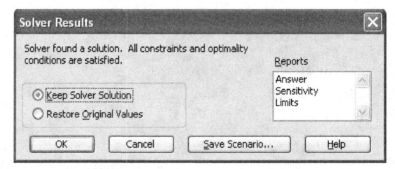

Figure 1.3.1.4. Solver reports success.

You can confirm that Excel's Sensitivity Report gives the same absolute value, 8.33, for the Lagrangean multiplier that we found via the Lagrangean method. In later chapters, we will explain what this means. For now, we simply note that the Excel results agreed with the Lagrangean method.

You might notice that Excel reports a Lagrangean multiplier value of -8.33. It turns out that we ignore the sign of λ^*. If we set up the Lagrangean as the objective function *minus* lambda times the constraint or rewrite the constraint as $0 = 2x_1 + 3x_2 - 100$ (instead of $0 = 100 - 2x_1 - 3x_2$), we would get a negative value for λ^*. The way we write the constraint or whether we add or subtract the constraint is arbitrary, so we ignore the sign of λ^*.

Unlike the sign, the magnitude of λ^* can be meaningful. Because utility is not cardinal, λ^* does not have an interesting economic interpretation in this problem, but we will see applications where the value of λ^* is useful.

Using Analytical and Numerical Methods to Find the Optimal Solution

There are two ways to solve optimization problems.

The traditional way uses pencil and paper, derivatives, and algebra. The Lagrangean method is used to solve constrained optimization problems, such as the consumer's choice problem.

Advances in computers have led to the creation of numerical methods to solve optimization problems. Excel's Solver is an example of a numerical algorithm that can be used to find optimal solutions.

In the chapters that follow, we will continue to use both analytical and numerical approaches. You will see that neither method is perfect and both have strengths and weaknesses.

Exercises

Open Word and answer the following questions. Save the document and print it when you are done.

The utility function, $U = 10x - 0.1x^2 + y$, has a quasilinear functional form. Use this utility function to answer the questions that follow.

1. Suppose the budget line is $100 = 2x + 3y$. Use the analytical method to find the optimal solution. Show your work.
2. Suppose the consumer considers the bundle 0,33.33, buying no x and spending all income on y. Use the MRS compared to the price ratio logic to explain what the consumer will do and why.
3. Consider the parameters in the utility function, a, b, c, and d ($U = ax - bx^c + dy$). If a increases, what happens to the optimal consumption of x^*? Explain how you arrived at your answer.

References

The epigraph is from page 421 of W. W. Rouse Ball's *A Short Account of the History of Mathematics* (first published in 1888). Of course, there are many books on the history of mathematics, but this classic is fun and easy to read. It mixes stories about people with real mathematical content.

This entire book (and many others) is freely available at <books.google.com>. You can read it online or download it as a pdf file.

Appendix: Derivatives and Optimization

A derivative is a mathematical expression that tells you how y in a function $y = f(x)$ changes given an infinitesimally small change in x. Graphically, it is the slope, or rate of change, of the function at that particular value of x.

Linear functions have a constant slope and, therefore, a constant value for the derivative. For the linear function $y = 6 + 3x$, the derivative of y with respect to x is written dy/dx (pronounced "d y d x") and its value is 3. This tells you that every time the x variable goes up, the y variable goes up 3-fold. So, if x increases by 1 unit, y will increase by 3 units. This is easy to see in Figure 1.3.1.5.

For linear functions, the size of the change in x does not affect the rate of change. So, if x increases by 2 units (say from 1 to 3), then y increases by 6 units (from 9 to 15) and the rate of change, defined as the change in y divided by the change in x, remains 3.

Another simple property of linear functions is that the slope remains the same no matter the value of x. In Figure 1.3.1.5, the slope is 3 when you increase x from 1 to 2 or from 3.000 to 3.001.

An easy way to tell whether a function is linear is to compute the derivative and check to see whether x appears in the derivative. With $y = 6 + 3x$, $\frac{dy}{dx} = 3$ and x does not appear in the derivative. A mathematician would say, "In this case, the slope is constant so y is linear in x."

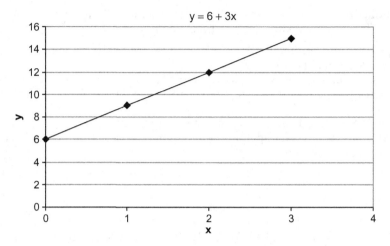

Figure 1.3.1.5. A linear function.

Nonlinear functions have a changing slope and, therefore, a derivative that takes on different values at different values of x. Consider the function $y = 4x - x^2$. Its derivative is $\frac{dy}{dx} = 4 - 2x$. Notice that the derivative has x in it. This means the function is nonlinear.

Because it is nonlinear, the size of the change in x affects the rate of change and the rate of change depends on the value of x. Figure 1.3.1.6 graphs this function.

With a nonlinear function, the size of the change in x leads to different measures of the slope. The change in y from $x = 1$ to $x = 2$ is 1 (because we move from $y = 3$ to $y = 4$ as we increase x by 1). If we increase x by 0.1

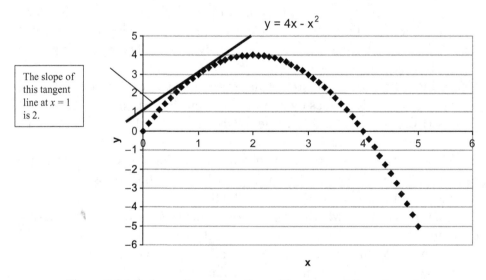

Figure 1.3.1.6. A nonlinear function with a tangent line at $x = 1$.

(from 1 to 1.1), the $\frac{\Delta y}{\Delta x} = \frac{3.19-3}{1.1-1} = 1.9$. By taking a smaller change in x, we get a different measure of the rate of change.

If we compute the rate of change via the derivative, by evaluating $4 - 2x$ at $x = 1$, we get 2. The derivative computes the rate of change for an infinitesimally small change in x. The smaller the change in x, the closer $\frac{\Delta y}{\Delta x}$ gets to $\frac{dy}{dx}$. The derivative is based on the rate of change of the slope of the tangent line, as shown in Figure 1.3.1.6.

Figure 1.3.1.6 makes clear that the slope, or rate of change, of the function varies along the curve. The rate of change is 2 at $x = 1$ and -2 at $x = 3$ (found by plugging 3 into the derivative and computing $4 - 2[3]$). The minus means the function is downward sloping.

Optimizing with the Derivative

An optimization problem typically requires you to find the value of an endogenous variable (or variables) that maximizes or minimizes a particular objective function. We can use derivatives to find the optimal solution. This is called an analytical approach.

Figure 1.3.1.6 shows that the maximum of the function is where the slope is zero. By finding the flat spot, we find the top.

By solving for the value of x where $\frac{dy}{dx} = 0$, we find the optimal solution. For $y = 4x - x^2$, this is easy. We set the derivative equal to zero and solve for x^*:

$$\frac{dy}{dx} = 4 - 2x^* = 0$$
$$4 = 2x^*$$
$$x^* = 2$$

The equation that you make when you set the first derivative equal to zero is called the *first-order condition*. The first-order condition is different from the derivative because the derivative by itself is not equal to anything – you can plug in any value of x and the derivative expression will pump out an answer that tells you whether and by how much the function is rising or falling at that point.

A *reduced form* is the answer that you get when the derivative is set equal to zero and solved for the optimal solution. It may be a number or a function of exogenous variables. It cannot have any endogenous variables in the expression. Sometimes, you cannot solve explicitly for x^*. We say there is no closed form solution in these cases. The solution may exist (and numerical methods may be used to find it), but we cannot express the answer as an equation.

The second derivative is simply the derivative of the first derivative. It tells you the slope of the slope function. For example, if a function has a constant slope, we saw that its first derivative is a constant value (like 3 in the first example). The second derivative of the function tells you how the slope changes when x changes. Well, since the slope is unchanging, the second derivative would be zero.

Second derivatives are useful for the following reason: When you find the value of the endogenous variable that makes the first derivative equal to zero, the point that you have located could be either a maximum or a minimum. If you want to be sure which one you have found, you can check out the second derivative. For $y = 4x - x^2$, the first derivative is $4 - 2x$ and the second derivative is -2. Because the second derivative is negative, we know that our flat spot at $x = 2$ is a maximum and not a minimum.

In summary, derivatives are used to measure the rate of change of a function. If we set a derivative equal to zero, we are trying to find an optimal solution by finding where the function is flat. This appendix concludes with a short list of common rules for taking derivatives and other useful math facts.

Rules for Taking Derivatives

A derivative can be computed by directly applying the definition – i.e., taking the limit of the change in x as it approaches zero and determining the change in y. Fortunately, however, there is an easier way. Differentiation rules have been developed that make it much less tedious to take a derivative. Most calculus books have inside covers that are full of rules. Many students never grasp that these rules are actually shortcuts. Here is a short list, with special emphasis on those used in economics.

Let x be the variable and a be a constant.

General Rule	Example of its Application
$\dfrac{d}{dx}(x) = 1$	
$\dfrac{d}{dx}(ax) = a$	$\dfrac{d}{dx}(4x) = 4$
$\dfrac{d}{dx}(a) = 0$	$\dfrac{d}{dx}(4) = 0$
$\dfrac{d}{dx}(x^a) = ax^{a-1}$	$\dfrac{d}{dx}(x^4) = 4x^3$
$\dfrac{d}{dx}(a \ln x) = \dfrac{a}{x}$	$\dfrac{d}{dx}(4 \ln x) = \dfrac{4}{x}$

Chain Rule: derivative of the whole thing times the derivative of the inside:

$$\frac{d}{dx}((f(x))^a) = a(f(x))^{a-1}f'(x) \qquad \frac{d}{dx}((x^2)^3) = 3x^2 2x$$

Product Rule: derivative of the first times the second plus the first times the derivative of the second:

$$\frac{d}{dx}(f(x)g(x)) = f'(x)g(x) + f(x)g'(x) \qquad \frac{d}{dx}((2x+3)(4x)) = (2)(4x) + (2x+3)(4)$$

When you take a derivative of a function with respect to a variable, you apply the rules to the different parts of the function. For example, if $y = 4x - x^2$, then you apply the $\frac{d}{dx}(ax) = a$ rule to the $4x$ part of the function, getting 4. You apply the $\frac{d}{dx}(x^a) = ax^{a-1}$ rule to the $-x^2$ term and get $-2x$. Thus, the derivative of y with respect to x is $\frac{dy}{dx} = 4 - 2x$.

Laws of Exponents

We end this appendix with a short list of algebra rules relating to legal operations on exponents. We will use these rules often to find optimal solutions and reduce complicated expressions to simpler final answers.

General Rule	Example of its Application
$x^0 = 1$	
$x^{-a} = \dfrac{1}{x^a}$	$x^{-\frac{1}{2}} = \dfrac{1}{\sqrt{x}}$
$x^a x^b = x^{a+b}$	$x^2 x^3 = x^5 \Rightarrow 2^2 2^3 = 2^5 = 32$
$\dfrac{x^a}{x^b} = x^{a-b}$	$\dfrac{x^5}{x^3} = x^2 \Rightarrow \dfrac{2^5}{2^3} = 2^2 = 4$
$(xy)^a = x^a y^a$	$(xy)^2 = x^2 y^2 \Rightarrow (2 \cdot 3)^2 = 2^2 3^2 = 36$
$(x^a)^b = x^{ab}$	$(x^2)^3 = x^6 \Rightarrow (2^2)^3 = 2^6 = 64$

1.3.2

More Practice and Understanding Solver

The methods of mathematics apply as soon as spatial or numerical attributes are associated with our phenomena, as soon as objects can be located by points in space and events described by properties capable of indication or measurement in numbers.

R. G. D. Allen

We know there are two approaches to solving optimization problems:

- Analytical methods using algebra and calculus (conventional, paper and pencil, using the Lagrangean method): The idea is to transform the consumer's constrained optimization problem into an unconstrained problem and then solve it using standard unconstrained calculus techniques – i.e., take derivatives, set equal to zero, and solve the system of equations.
- Numerical methods using a computer (Excel's Solver): Set up the problem in Excel, carefully organizing things into a goal, endogenous variables, exogenous variables, and constraint; then use Excel's Solver (Tools: Solver). Use the Sensitivity Report in the Solver Results dialog box to get λ^*.

We will practice applying the analytical method and begin learning about how Excel's Solver actually works.

Quasilinear Utility Practice Problem

A utility function that is composed of a nonlinear function of one good plus a linear function of the other good is called a quasilinear functional form. It is quasi, or sort of, linear because one good increases utility in a linear fashion and the other does not.

Below are a general example and a more specific example of quasilinear utility.

$$u(x_1, x_2) = v(x_1) + x_2$$
$$u(x_1, x_2) = (x_1)^c + x_2, \text{ where } c < 1$$

52

If $c < 1$, then the quasilinear utility function says that utility increases at a decreasing rate as x_1 increases, but utility increases at a constant rate as x_2 increases.

The optimization problem is to maximize utility subject to the usual budget constraint.

First, we solve the general version of this problem via analytical methods.

1. Rewrite the constraint so that it is equal to zero:

$$0 = m - p_1 x_1 - p_2 x_2$$

2. Form the Lagrangean:

$$\max_{x_1, x_2, \lambda} L = x_1^c + x_2 + \lambda(m - p_1 x_1 - p_2 x_2)$$

Note that the Lagrangean function, L, has the quasilinear utility function plus the Lagrangean multiplier, λ, times the rewritten constraint.

Unlike the concrete problem in the previous chapter, which used numerical values, this is a general problem with letters indicating exogenous variables. General problems, without numerical values for exogenous variables, are harder to solve because we have to keep track of many variables. If the solution can be written as a function of the exogenous variables, however, it is often easy to see how an exogenous variable will affect the optimal solution.

3. Take partial derivatives with respect to x_1, x_2, and λ:

$$\frac{\partial L}{\partial x_1} = c x_1^{c-1} - p_1 \lambda$$

$$\frac{\partial L}{\partial x_2} = 1 - p_2 \lambda$$

$$\frac{\partial L}{\partial \lambda} = m - p_1 x_1 - p_2 x_2$$

Remember that the partial derivative treats other variables as constants. Thus, the partial derivative of the quasilinear utility function with respect to x_1 has no x_2 variable in it.

4. Set the partial derivatives equal to zero and solve the system of equations for x_1, x_2, and λ:

$$\frac{\partial L}{\partial x_1} = c x_1^{c-1} - p_1 \lambda = 0$$

$$\frac{\partial L}{\partial x_2} = 1 - p_2 \lambda = 0$$

$$\frac{\partial L}{\partial \lambda} = m - p_1 x_1 - p_2 x_2 = 0$$

We use the same solution method as before, moving the lambda terms to the right-hand side and then dividing the first equation by the second, which allows us to cancel the lambda terms.

$$cx_1^{c-1} = p_1\lambda$$

$$1 = p_2\lambda$$

$$\frac{cx_1^{c-1}}{1} = \frac{p_1\lambda}{p_2\lambda}$$

$$\frac{cx_1^{c-1}}{1} = \frac{p_1}{p_2}$$

By canceling the lambda terms, we have reduced the three equation, three unknown system to two equations with two unknowns.

$$\frac{cx_1^{c-1}}{1} = \frac{p_1}{p_2}$$

$$m - p_1x_1 - p_2x_2 = 0$$

Remember that not all variables are the same. The endogenous variables, the unknowns, are x_1 and x_2. The other letters are exogenous variables.

From the first equation, we can solve for the optimal quantity of good 1.

$$\frac{cx_1^{c-1}}{1} = \frac{p_1}{p_2}$$

$$cx_1^{c-1} = \frac{p_1}{p_2}$$

$$x_1^{c-1} = \frac{p_1}{cp_2}$$

$$x_1^* = \left(\frac{p_1}{cp_2}\right)^{\frac{1}{c-1}}$$

Notice that we used the rule that $(x^a)^b = x^{ab}$. Because we wanted to solve for x_1, we raised both sides to the $\frac{1}{c-1}$ power so that $c - 1$ times $\frac{1}{c-1}$ would give 1.

Usually, when we have the MRS equal to the price ratio, we need to solve for one of the x variables in terms of the other and substitute it into the budget constraint. However, a property of the quasilinear utility function is that the MRS only depends on x_1; thus by solving for x_1, we get the reduced-form equation. When solving a problem in general terms, the answer must be expressed as a function of exogenous variables alone (no endogenous variables) and this is called a reduced form.

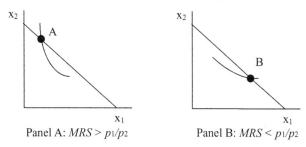

Figure 1.3.2.1. MRS does not equal the price ratio.

To get x_2, we simply substitute x_1 into the budget constraint and solve for x_1.

$$m - p_1 \left[\left(\frac{p_1}{cp_2} \right)^{\frac{1}{c-1}} \right] - p_2 x_2 = 0$$

$$x_2^* = \frac{m}{p_2} - \frac{p_1}{p_2} \left(\frac{p_1}{cp_2} \right)^{\frac{1}{c-1}}$$

It is a bit messy, but it is the answer. We have an expression for the optimal amount of x_2 that is a function of exogenous variables alone.

To get the optimal value of lambda, we can use the second first-order condition, which simply says that $\lambda^* = 1/p_2$. If you use the first condition, substituting in the value for optimal x_1, it will take a little work, but you will get the same result.

Practice with the *MRS* = p_1/p_2 Logic

Economists stress marginal thinking. The idea is that, from any position, you can move and see how things change. If there is improvement, continue moving. The optimal solution is on a flat spot, where improvement is impossible.

When we move the lambda terms over to the right-hand side and divide the first equation by the second equation, we get a crucial statement of the fact that improvement is impossible and we are optimizing.

The familiar MRS equals the price ratio expression, along with the third first-order condition, which says that the consumer must be on the budget line (exhausting all income), is a mathematical way of describing marginal thinking.

The MRS condition tells us that if the MRS is not equal to the price ratio, there are two possibilities, depicted in Figure 1.3.2.1.

In Panel A, the slope of the indifference curve at point A is greater than the slope of the budget line (in absolute value). This consumer should crawl down the budget line, reaching higher indifference curves, until the MRS equals the price ratio. At this point, the slope of the indifference curve will exactly equal the slope of the budget line and the consumer's in-difference curve will just touch the budget line.

In Panel B, the story is the same, but reversed. The slope of the indiffer-ence curve at point B is less than the slope of the budget line. This consumer should crawl up the budget line, reaching higher indifference curves, until the MRS equals the price ratio. At this point, the slope of the indifference curve will exactly equal the slope of the budget line and the consumer's in-difference curve will just touch the budget line.

Numerical Approach to Quasilinear Practice Problem

Step Open the Excel workbook OptimalChoicePractice.xls and read the *Intro* sheet, then go to the *QuasilinearChoice* sheet to see how the numerical approach can be used to solve this problem.

The consumer cannot afford the bundle 5,20. If she buys five units of x_1, what's the maximum x_2 she can buy?

Step Enter this amount in cell B12.

The chart updates and shows that the consumer is now on the budget line. In addition, the constraint cell, B21, is now zero.

Without running Solver or doing any calculations at all, is she maximizing at 5,13? No. It's hard to see on the chart whether the indifference curve is cutting the budget line, but the information below the chart shows that the MRS is not equal to the price ratio. That tells you that the indifference curve is, in fact, not tangent to the budget line so the consumer is not optimizing. Because the MRS is greater than the price ratio (in absolute value) we also know that the consumer should buy more x_1 and less x_2, moving down the budget line until the marginal condition is satisfied.

Step Run Solver. Select the Sensitivity Report to get λ^*.

We can compare Solver's result to our analytical result. Recall that

$$x_1^* = \left(\frac{p_1}{cp_2}\right)^{\frac{1}{c-1}}$$

$$x_2^* = \frac{m}{p_2} - \frac{p_1}{p_2}\left(\frac{p_1}{cp_2}\right)^{\frac{1}{c-1}}$$

Step Create formulas in Excel to compute these two solutions (using cells C11 and C12 would make sense).

Step Create formulas in cells D11 and D12 that compute the difference between the numerical and analytical answers.

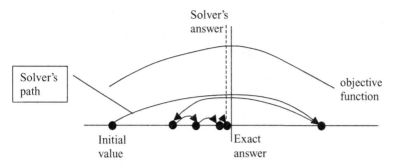

Figure 1.3.2.2. Solver in action.

You should discover that Excel's Solver is slightly off the computed analytical result. There are two reasons for the discrepancy.

1. Excel cannot display the algebraic result to an infinite number of decimal places. If the solution is a repeating decimal or irrational number, Excel cannot handle it. Even if the number can be expressed as a decimal – for example, one-half is 0.5 – precision error may occur during the computation of the final answer.
2. Excel's Solver often misses the exactly correct answer by small amounts. Solver has a convergence criterion (that you can set via the Options button in the Solver Parameters dialog box) that determines when it stops hunting for a better answer. Figure 1.3.2.2 offers a graphical representation of Solver's algorithm in a one-variable case.

The stylized graph (which means it represents an idea without using actual data) in Figure 1.3.2.2 shows that Solver works by trying different values and seeing how much improvement occurs. The path of the choice variable (on the x axis) is determined by Solver's internal optimization algorithm. By default, it uses Newton's method (a steepest descent algorithm), but you can choose an alternative by clicking the Options button in the Solver dialog box.

When Solver takes a step that improves the value of the objective function by very little, determined by the convergence criterion (adjustable via the Options button), it stops searching and announces success. In Figure 1.3.2.2, Solver is missing the optimal solution by a little bit because the objective function is almost flat at the top. Solver cannot distinguish additional improvement.

When we say that the analytical method agrees with Solver, we do not mean that the two methods exactly agree, but simply that they correspond, in a practical sense. If Solver is off the exact answer in the 15th decimal place, that is agreement, for all practical purposes.

In the quasilinear utility function example, we would conclude that Solver and the calculus agree because they are very close.

Now, let's learn that Solver is not perfect.

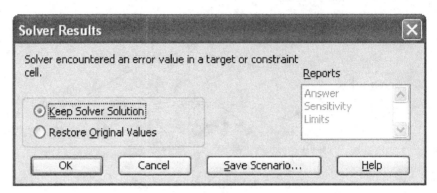

Figure 1.3.2.3. A miserable result.

Step Start from $x_1 = 1$, $x_2 = 20$ to see an example of a miserable result. After setting the cells to 1 and 20, run Solver. What happens?

A *miserable result* (an actual, technical term in the numerical methods literature) occurs when an algorithm reports that it cannot find the answer or displays an obviously erroneous solution. Figure 1.3.2.3 displays an example of a miserable result. Solver is clearly announcing that it cannot find an answer.

If you look carefully at the spreadsheet, you will see that Solver blew up when it tried a negative value for x_1. The objective function cell, B7, is displaying the error #NUM! because Excel cannot take the square root of a negative number.

When Solver can't find an answer, there are three basic strategies to fix the problem:

1. Try different initial values (in the changing cells).

   If you know roughly where the solution lies, start near it.
   Always avoid starting from zero or a blank cell.

2. Add more structure to the problem.

   Include non-negativity constraints on the endogenous variables, if appropriate.
   In the case of consumer theory, if you know the buyer will be on the budget constraint, use an equality constraint.

3. Completely reorganize the problem.

   Instead of directly optimizing, you can put Solver to work on equations that must be met.
   In this problem, you know that $MRS = p_1/p_2$ is required. You could create a cell that is the difference between the MRS and the price ratio and have Solver find the values of the choice variable that force this cell to equal zero.

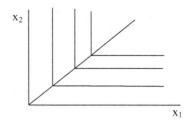

Figure 1.3.2.4. The optimal solution line with perfect complements.

Perfect Complements Practice Problem

Recall that L-shaped indifference curves represent perfect complements, which are reflected via the following mathematical function:

$$u(x_1, x_2) = \min\{ax_1, bx_2\}$$

Suppose $a = b = 1$. Suppose the budget line is $50 = 2x_1 + 10x_2$.

We want to solve this problem analytically.

The first thing to realize is that the Lagrangean method cannot be applied. The function is not differentiable at the corner of the L.

The Lagrangean method, however, is not the only analytical method available. Figure 1.3.2.4 shows that when $a = b = 1$, the optimal solution must lie on a ray from the origin with slope $+1$.

The optimal solution has to be on the corner of the L-shaped indifference curves because a non-corner point (on either the vertical or horizontal part of the indifference curve) implies the consumer is spending money on more of one of the goods without getting any additional satisfaction.

The equation of the optimal solution line is simple: $x_2 = x_1$.

We can combine this equation with the budget constraint to find the optimal solution. The two equation, two unknown system can be solved easily by substitution.

$$\left.\begin{array}{l} x_2 = x_1 \\ 50 = 2x_1 + 10x_2 \end{array}\right\} \Rightarrow 50 = 2x_1 + 10\,[x_1] \Rightarrow 50 = 12x_1 \Rightarrow x_1^* = 4\frac{1}{6}.$$

Of course, we know $x_2 = x_1$ so $x_2^* = 4\frac{1}{6}$.

Step Proceed to the *PerfectComplements* sheet to see that Excel's Solver can also solve this problem. Notice that Excel's Solver can be used to generate a value for the Lagrangean multiplier (via the Sensitivity Report) even though we did not use the Lagrangean method.

As with the previous problem (with quasilinear utility), we find that Solver and the analytical approach substantially agree. The answer is a repeating decimal, so Excel cannot get the exact answer, but it comes extremely close.

Now, let's learn that Solver can really misbehave.

Step Start from $x_1 = 1$, $x_2 = 1$ to see an example of a disastrous result. After setting cells B11 and B12 to 1 and 1, run Solver. What happens?

Solver reports a successful outcome, but the answer is 1,1 and we know the right answer is about 4.167, 4.167.

This is an example of a *disastrous result* which occurs when an algorithm reports that it has found the answer, but it is wrong. There is no obvious error and the user may well accept the answer as true.

Disastrous results include an element of interpretation. In this case, we might notice that 1,1 is way inside the budget constraint and, therefore, the algorithm has failed. A truly disastrous result occurs when there is no way to independently test or verify the algorithm's wrong answer.

Miserable and disastrous results are well defined and understood, technical terms in the mathematical literature on numerical methods. Disastrous results are much more dangerous than miserable results. The latter are frustrating because the computer cannot provide an answer, but disastrous results lead the user to believe an answer that is actually wrong. In the world of numerical optimization, they are a fact of life. Numerical methods are not perfect. You should not completely trust any optimization algorithm.

Understanding Solver – Be Skeptical

This chapter enabled practice solving the consumer's constrained optimization problem with two different utility functions, a quasilinear function and perfect complements. In both cases, we found that Excel's Solver agreed, practically speaking, with the analytical method.

In addition, Excel's Solver was explored in detail. It works by evaluating the objective function for different values of the choice variables. It can fail by reporting that it cannot find a solution (called a miserable result) or – even worse – by reporting an incorrect answer (which is a disastrous result).

It is easy to believe that a result displayed by a computer is guaranteed to be correct. Do not be careless and trusting – numerical methods can and do fail, sometimes spectacularly.

Exercises

Open Word and answer the following questions. Save the document and print it when you are done.

1. In the quasilinear example in this chapter, use the first equation in the first-order conditions to find λ^*. Show your work.
2. Use analytical methods to find the optimal solution for the same perfect complements problem as presented in this chapter, except that $a = 4$ and $b = 1$. Show your work.

3. Draw a graph (using Word's Drawing Tools) of the optimal solution for the previous question.
4. Use Excel's Solver to confirm that you have the correct answer. Take a picture of the cells that contain your goal, endogenous variables, and exogenous variables.

References

As economics became more mathematical, a new course was born, Math Econ. The course needed books and R. G. D. Allen's *Mathematical Analysis for Economists* (first published in 1938) became a classic textbook. As E. Schneider, a reviewer, said, "This book fills a long-felt want. At last we possess a book which presents the mathematical apparatus necessary to a serious study of economics in a form suited to the needs of the economist." See *The Economic Journal*, Vol. 48, No. 191 (September, 1938), p. 515. The epigraph is from page 2 of *Mathematical Analysis for Economists*, as Allen discusses how and why mathematics can be applied to the study of economics.

1.3.3

Food Stamps

Tastes are the unchallengeable axioms of a man's behavior; he may properly (use-fully) be criticized for inefficiency in satisfying his desires, but the desires themselves are *data*.

George J. Stigler and Gary S. Becker

This chapter applies the consumer choice model to a real-world example. We will see that the model can be used to explain why someone would sell food stamps. We also tackle an important policy question: If cash is better than food stamps, why does the Food Stamp Program exist?

About the U.S. Food Stamp Program

The Food Stamp Program is run by the Department of Agriculture (USDA). They say,

The Food Stamp Program serves as the first line of defense against hunger. It enables low-income families to buy nutritious food with Electronic Benefits Transfer (EBT) cards. Food stamp recipients spend their benefits to buy eligible food in authorized retail food stores. <www.fns.usda.gov/fsp>

Before EBT cards, recipients were given a booklet with different denominations of paper food coupons that were torn off and used as bills. Figure 1.3.3.1 shows a typical food stamp booklet on the cover of a USDA publication.

Today, recipients are given an EBT card that is like a debit card. The recipient swipes it and the amount is deducted from the account. Each month, more money is added.

Since the program's inception in 1969, food stamps have been used only to purchase food. You cannot buy alcoholic beverages or tobacco, prepared hot food, or non-food items such as laundry detergent.

Figure 1.3.3.1. Old style food stamps.

Eligibility and Benefits

Step Visit <www.fns.usda.gov/fsp/applicant_recipients/fs_Res_Ben_Elig.htm> to see how eligibility and benefits are determined.

Basically, the amount of food stamps each month is a function of your income and household size.

Food Stamp Participation and Costs

Roughly $30 billion in food stamps are allocated to about 25 million participants.

Step Visit <www.fns.usda.gov/pd/snapmain.htm> for more detailed statistics.

Because there are about 300 million people in the United States, this means almost 10% of the U.S. population relies on food stamps. That is a lot.

Step Open the Excel workbook USGovBudget.xls and read the *Intro* sheet. The sheet has links for excellent sources on U.S. government finance.

Step Proceed to the *TableB-80* sheet.

The sheet shows that, of the federal government's roughly $2 trillion budget in 2002, $300 billion was spent on income security programs.

Step Use the links in the *Intro* sheet to get the current year's budget.

It is easy to access this information. You should notice that the GPO access site has other free data.

The Food Stamp Program is a huge part of the government's efforts to help the poor. Both in numbers of recipients and government expenditures, it is a major federal program.

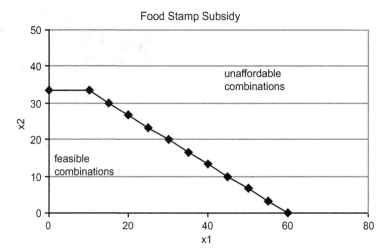

Figure 1.3.3.2. The budget constraint with food stamps.
Source: FoodStamp!BudgetConstraint

Next, we see how the Theory of Consumer Behavior can be applied to the Food Stamp Program.

Food Stamp Theory

We know the consumer decides on the optimal bundle to purchase by maximizing utility subject to the budget constraint.

The constraint for a food stamp recipient is not the usual straight line. We can interpret the x_1 variable on the x axis as units of food and the x_2 variable on the y axis as units of other goods. The budget constraint will have a horizontal segment, as shown in Figure 1.3.3.2, because food stamps can be used to buy only food.

Step Open the Excel workbook FoodStamp.xls and read the *Intro* sheet. Proceed to the *BudgetConstraint* sheet.

Step Change cell E13 from 10 to 20. Notice that the horizontal segment, which is the monetary value of the food stamps divided by the price of food, gets longer. Also notice that the chart on the right, showing the budget constraint if the food stamp amount was treated as cash, has no horizontal segment. In the chart on the right, the value of the food stamp subsidy is computed (*xbar* times price of food) and then added to income as if it were cash; hence the name, cash equivalent subsidy.

It should be quite clear that the cash equivalent subsidy provides consumption possibilities that are unattainable above the horizontal segment of the food stamp budget constraint.

Step Proceed to the *Inframarginal* sheet. It combines a food stamp budget constraint with a Cobb-Douglas utility function.

The word *inframarginal* means below the edge or margin. The edge in this case is the kink in the budget constraint.

This consumer is inframarginal because his optimal solution is on the downward sloping part of the budget line. He will use up his food stamp allotment on food and then spend some of his income to get additional food. The sheet reveals that he buys 35 units of food, 20 of which he obtains with food stamps and the remaining 15 he buys with cash.

We can easily see that he is optimizing because the "MRS equals the price ratio" condition is met. This is reflected in the graph where the highest attainable indifference curve is just touching the budget constraint.

Step Click on cell B25 to see the formula for the budget constraint.

Expressed as an equation, the budget line looks like this:

$$\text{if } x_1 \leq \bar{x}, \quad x_2 = m/p_2$$
$$\text{if } x_1 > \bar{x}, \quad x_2 = m/p_2 - p_1/p_2\,(x_1 - \bar{x})$$

The first equation says that if the consumer buys an amount of food that is less than or equal to *xbar*, that frees up his whole income to spend on good 2. Things are more complicated if the consumer wants more than *xbar* of food. The second equation says that the consumer will have to use cash to buy amounts of x_1 greater than *xbar* and it computes the amount of x_2 that can be purchased as a function of x_1.

The constraint (rewritten to equal zero) has been entered in a single cell with an IF statement:

$$= \text{IF}(x1_- < x1bar, m/p2 - x2, m/p2 - (p1/p2)^*(x1 - x1bar) - x2)$$

From Excel's Help on the IF function:

> Returns one value if a condition you specify evaluates to TRUE and another
> value if it evaluates to FALSE.
> Use IF to conduct conditional tests on values and formulas.
> Syntax: IF(logical_test,value_if_true,value_if_false)

The formula in cell B25 says that if $x_1 < x_1bar$, then the consumer can buy m/p_2 amount of x_2 (this is the horizontal part of the budget constraint), else (i.e., if x_1 is not less than x_1bar) the consumer can buy x_2 along the downward sloping part of the budget line.

This problem shows that Excel can be used to handle complicated examples in the Theory of Consumer Behavior. This food stamp problem has a kinked budget constraint, but using Excel's IF statement allows us to implement the constraint in the workbook and use Solver to find the optimal solution.

This problem also can be solved via analytical methods, but it is cumbersome. We will use the easier numerical approach to conduct our analysis.

Step Proceed to the *Distorted* sheet.

The *Distorted* sheet is exactly the same as the *Inframarginal* sheet with one crucial exception: the preferences, in cells B21 and B22, are different. The consumer in the *Distorted* sheet prefers other goods more and food less than the consumer in the *Inframarginal* sheet.

The change in exponents in the Cobb-Douglas utility function has affected the indifference map. The curves are more horizontal in the *Distorted* sheet compared with the *Inframarginal* sheet.

The *Distorted* sheet opens with the optimal values for food and other goods from the *Inframarginal* sheet. It is obvious that the MRS does not equal the price ratio and the indifference curve is cutting the budget constraint at the current bundle of x_1 and x_2. This consumer is not optimizing at this point.

Introducing the Corner Solution

Step Run Solver on the *Distorted* sheet.

Solver announces it has found the optimal solution, yet the MRS still does not equal the price ratio. Is this really the optimal solution?

Yes, it is the optimal solution.

We have encountered what is called a *corner solution* (or *boundary optimum*). In this special case, the equimarginal condition, $MRS = p_1/p_2$, does not hold because the optimal solution is found at one of the end points (or corners) of the constraint.

Step To see what is happening here, copy the optimal solution from the *Inframarginal* sheet (copy cells B13 and B14) and paste in the *Distorted* sheet (select cells B13 and B14 and then paste).

The graph and MRS information is immediately updated and you can see that the distorted consumer would not select the inframarginal consumer's chosen bundle.

Which way should this consumer move – up or down the budget line?

The graph makes clear that up is the right way to go, but you should notice that the marginal condition, $MRS < p_1/p_2$, tells you the same thing.

Step Click on the `Crawl Up the Budget Line` button. Click a few more times and pay attention to the chart and the MRS in cell H26. Also keep an eye on utility in cell B9. Each click lowers the amount of x_1 by one unit and increases the amount of x_2 by 2/3.

By moving up the budget line, this consumer is improving her satisfaction and closing the gap between the MRS and the price ratio.

Do not be misled by the display – the indifference curves are not shifting. Remember that the indifference map is dense, meaning that every point has an indifference curve through it. We cannot draw in all of the indifference curves because the graph would then be solid black. The consumer is simply moving from one indifference curve to another one that was not previously displayed.

Step Keep clicking the Crawl Up the Budget Line button. Eventually, you will hit the kink in the budget line and you will not be able to move northwest any longer. Instead, you will be on the horizontal segment and as you move strictly west, utility falls. Notice that the price ratio is now showing zero.

On the flat part of the budget line, when the consumer chooses less food than food stamps, it makes sense that additional food is free, in terms of spending *m* on food. The consumer simply has to use the available food stamps to acquire food.

Once you are on the flat part of the budget line, you should see that the graph and marginal condition point you to choosing more food.

Step Click on the Crawl Down the Budget Line button repeatedly to move east and, eventually, down the budget line.

Step Use the crawl up and down buttons to find the best solution for this consumer.

You should end your travels at the kink – and MRS does not equal the price ratio there.

The distorted consumer wishes she could continue crawling up the downward sloping line, consuming less than the food stamp allotment of food and more of other goods, but she cannot do this. Her best, or optimal, solution is at the kink.

But at the kink, the MRS condition is not met. In a corner solution, we accept that the MRS condition is not met. We are maximizing even though the MRS does not equal the ratio. It is the best we can do given the constraints on our choices.

Cash Instead of Food Stamps

Step Proceed to the *Cash* sheet. Notice that cell B24 computes the cash value of the food stamps and that the chart has a linear budget constraint with no kink. Click on cell B25 to see that the constraint is the familiar income minus expenditures, with income equal to the sum of income plus the cash value of the food stamps.

The idea here is that instead of giving the poor food stamps, we give them the cash equivalent value. They are no longer constrained to buy food alone, but can purchase any goods with the cash received.

With $40 in food stamps, the two consumers optimize like this:

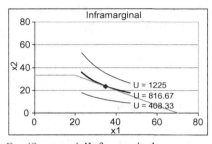

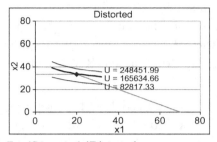

FoodStamps.xls!Inframarginal
Food=35, Expenditure on Food=$70
$40 of food stamps + $30 cash

FoodStamps.xls!Distorted
Food=20, Expenditure on Food=$40
$40 of food stamps; no cash spent on food

Suppose that instead of $40 in food stamps, these two consumers were given $40 cash:

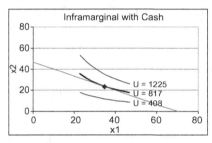

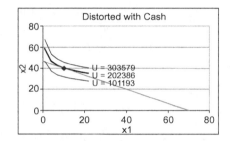

FoodStamps.xls!Cash
Food=35, Expenditure on Food=$70
No change in behavior

FoodStamps.xls!Cash
Food=10, Expenditure on Food=$20
Less Food, More Other Goods Bought

Figure 1.3.3.3. Comparing the two consumers with food stamps versus cash.

The sheet opens with the inframarginal consumer's optimal solution. It is the same as before, when she was given food stamps. Cash or food stamps are the same to this consumer.

Step Click on the [Set to Distorted] button to quickly apply the preferences for the distorted consumer. Run Solver.

With cash, the distorted consumer chooses an optimal bundle that is different from the one chosen under the Food Stamp Program. She finds an interior (as opposed to a corner) solution in the far northwest corner, which means she has opted for little food and more of other goods.

Figure 1.3.3.3 summarizes our work to this point.

If you compare the inframarginal consumer, by looking top left and then bottom left, in Figure 1.3.3.3, you can easily see that there is no change in his behavior: $40 in food stamps versus $40 in cash are the same to this consumer.

On the other hand, comparing the top right and bottom right panels reveals that the distorted consumer chooses less food and more other goods when given cash. This is why we say her choices are distorted by the Food Stamp Program. The distortion results in a decrease in satisfaction for this consumer.

The Carte Blanche Principle and Deadweight Loss

Carte blanche, a term of obvious French origin (literally, "blank document"), means unconditional authority or freedom to act in any way you wish.

In economics, the Carte Blanche Principle means that cash is always as good as or better than in-kind. Cash allows the consumer to buy anything, while food stamps restrict the set of choices.

Figure 1.3.3.3 shows the Carte Blanche Principle in action. Cash dominates food stamps.

If you are an inframarginal consumer, the cash and food stamps are the same. This consumer is going to buy more food than can be purchased with the allotment of food stamps anyway so if you gave him the cash equivalent value, he would spend the cash on food.

If you are a distorted consumer, however, you are better off if you are given cash because you can use the cash to buy more of the other goods that you prefer over food.

In economics, *deadweight loss* is a measure of inefficiency. It is a number that tells you how much a solution differs from the optimal solution.

In this application, deadweight loss is the lost value due to using food stamps instead of cash.

In principle, for every consumer, we could compute the maximum utility with cash minus the maximum utility with food stamps. For the inframarginal consumers, this number would be zero, but it would be positive for the distorted consumers.

Unfortunately, this approach would be impossible to measure and aggregate. Remember, we cannot simply add the utility values for different people.

In practice, we measure deadweight loss in dollars. In this case, we can compute the value of food stamps to recipients and compare that to the cash equivalent value. The next section shows an estimate of total deadweight loss from the Food Stamp Program.

Food Stamp Practice

Distortion is theoretically possible, but is it of practical, real-world importance? In other words, how many distorteds are out there? And how badly are they distorted? Our Excel workbook is of little help here. We need real-world data.

Food Stamps

	San Diego		
	Check	Stamp	P-Value
	(1)	(2)	(3)
Food stamps >=	$49.7	$63.2	0.011
Monthly food spending	[2.4]	[5.2]	
	(24.5)	(43.6)	

Figure 1.3.3.4. Estimating distortion (SEs in brackets; SDs in parentheses).

The empirical work described next comes from Diane Whitmore's working paper titled "What are Food Stamps Worth?" See the references section for source information.

The San Diego Experiment

Whitmore describes two controlled experiments carried out by the USDA in the early 1990s. In the San Diego experiment, around 1000 people who were receiving food stamps were randomly selected to participate in the experiment. Half were given food stamps as usual and the other half were given cash equivalent aid (checks).

Of the roughly 500 people given checks, about 100 were distorted – they bought less food compared to what they bought when they were given food stamps.

Figure 1.3.3.4 reproduces a portion of Whitmore's Table 2A: Weekly Food Expenditures for Distorted Households: Various Measures. Whitmore estimated a roughly 30% distortion in Weekly Food Expenditures = ($63.20 − $49.70)/$49.70 for the distorted consumers.

Figure 1.3.3.4 says that the average weekly food expenditure for the distorted consumers who were given checks was $49.70, with typical dispersion (SD, or standard deviation) of $24.50. The SE (standard error) of $2.40 measures the variability in the sample average. A 95% confidence interval for our estimate of the population average is $49.70 ± $4.80.

The P-value of 1.1% tells us the probability that the distorted check recipients and stamp recipients are actually spending the same on food and the observed difference in the sample of $13.50 was due to chance alone. The low P-value means we can reject the explanation that the observed difference was due to luck. Could it be that many high food purchasers were randomly assigned to the Stamp group and many low food purchasers went to the Check group? The low P-value means this explanation is highly unlikely. We conclude that there is a real difference in spending on food between people who get checks and those who get food stamps.

What Are They Buying Instead of Food?

This is a crucial question. Many people would assume that the distorted consumers would make poor decisions if left free to choose what to buy. They
think distortion is a good thing. Whitmore (p. 3) says this:

> To some, this distortion is the best part of the food stamp program: the govern-
> ment can ensure that needy families get enough to eat and that they don't spend the
> money on other things. To others, this distortion represents a waste of resources –
> it is inefficient to give in-kind transfers instead of cash.*

> *See, for example, Doug Besharov's comments in the November 14, 2001, *New York
> Times*, p. A14. He argues: "in some instances, particularly the elderly, they might
> need money to pay utility bills, rather than more food stamps."

At its most extreme, the case can be stated this way: Taxpayers will support buying food for the poor, but not drugs, alcohol, and other wasteful
consumption.

But exactly how distorted consumers would spend cash is an empirical
question and Whitmore has the data to answer it.

Researchers in the San Diego experiment kept careful food diaries. As
shown in Figure 1.3.3.5, Whitmore compared the purchases of the distorted
check group to the stamp group. She found that the distorted group bought
far less juice and soda.

> Even though spending on food declines for the treatment group, the food diary data
> from San Diego provide no firm evidence that cashing-out food stamps leads to
> declines in nutritional intake, and suggest that it may actually reduce extreme over-
> consumption of calories, an important contributing factor to obesity. (Whitmore,
> p. 35)

Whitmore's surprising result is that cash instead of food stamps may actually
improve nutritional outcomes because consumers are not exhausting their
food stamps by simply buying juice and soda.

Notice also that the data in Figure 1.3.3.5 show virtually no difference
in alcohol consumption. The picture that many have of the indigent as drug
addicts or exceptionally poor decision makers is unsupported by Whitmore's
data.

In the final section, we turn to an interesting unintended consequence of
the Food Stamp Program.

The (Illegal) Sale of Food Stamps

Whitmore conducted a survey and found that distorted consumers may sell
their stamps. She estimated the price at 61 cents on the dollar (Whitmore,
p. 4).

Food Stamps

	Distorted					
	Pounds of Food Per Capita			Per Capita Money Value of Food		
	Stamps (1)	Check (2)	P-value (3)	Stamps (4)	Check (5)	P-value (6)
Vegetables	3.08 (2.44)	2.94 (2.91)	0.728	$2.13 (1.68)	$2.00 (1.61)	0.573
Fruit	2.96 (3.54)	2.88 (3.35)	0.869	$1.61 (1.64)	$1.62 (1.96)	0.992
Grain	2.67 (1.56)	2.88 (3.35)	0.791	$3.36 (1.99)	$3.41 (2.84)	0.888
Dairy	5.95 (4.93)	5.31 (5.22)	0.385	$3.02 (2.65)	$2.75 (4.41)	0.604
Milk & Yogurt	5.42 (5.03)	4.72 (4.62)	0.302	$2.01 (2.15)	$1.80 (3.45)	0.199
Cheese	0.27 (0.33)	0.23 (0.32)	0.347	$0.64 (0.78)	$0.55 (0.75)	0.440
Meat	4.08 (3.40)	3.65 (2.83)	0.339	$6.17 (4.61)	$5.42 (3.96)	0.225
High-quality beef	1.97 (1.88)	1.84 (1.91)	0.617	$3.13 (3.02)	$2.67 (2.56)	0.500
Low-quality beef	1.68 (1.88)	1.43 (1.34)	0.271	$2.63 (2.31)	$2.38 (2.23)	0.533
Chicken	0.92 (0.92)	1.14 (1.43)	0.201	$0.93 (0.88)	$1.16 (1.28)	0.133
Fish	0.42 (1.06)	0.25 (0.50)	0.157	$0.93 (2.02)	$0.53 (1.11)	0.080
Legumes	0.64 (0.75)	0.62 (0.92)	0.882	$1.12 (1.93)	$1.00 (1.54)	0.646
Fats & Sugars	1.10 (0.93)	1.10 (1.26)	0.963	$1.09 (1.10)	$1.08 (1.23)	0.922
Beverages	3.08 (4.00)	2.07 (3.51)	0.065	$1.28 (1.26)	$0.97 (1.09)	0.075
Juice & Soda	3.05 (3.91)	2.02 (3.51)	0.051	$1.12 (1.18)	$0.78 (0.99)	0.028
Alcohol	0.12 (0.33)	0.10 (0.28)	0.664	$0.38 (0.84)	$0.37 (0.80)	0.902
N =	99	101		99	101	

Note: Standard deviations in parentheses. Alcohol consumption is per food consumption unit member aged 16 or older.

Figure 1.3.3.5. Comparing consumption patterns.

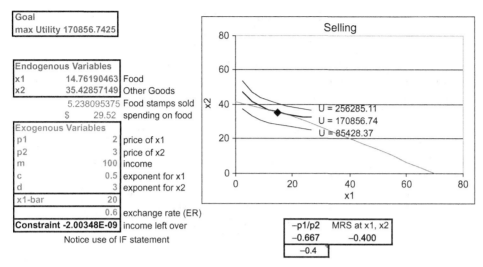

Figure 1.3.3.6. Optimizing by selling food stamps.
Source: FoodStamp.xls!Selling

This behavior is easily understood with the help of the Excel workbook.

Step Proceed to the *Selling* sheet.

The budget constraint has been modified yet again. This time, the segment below the food stamp allotment (x_1bar) is no longer horizontal. The constraint cell shows that we allow the consumer to sell food stamps and move to the northwest. The slope of this portion of the budget constraint is $ER^* p_1/p_2$, where ER is the exchange rate of food stamps for cash. With ER initially set at 0.6 (in cell B24), a seller of food stamps would get 60 cents for every dollar of food stamps sold.

Notice that below the price ratio, cell G27 shows the slope of this portion of the budget constraint.

Step Run Solver. You should get a result like Figure 1.3.3.6.

The consumer reaches a higher level of satisfaction than what is attainable by staying on the kink and not selling the food stamps, but exhausting the food stamp allotment on food.

This explains the unintended consequence of an active illegal trade in food stamps.

Notice also that, once again, the MRS (-0.4) equals the slope of the budget constraint (-0.4) on the relevant part of the budget line.

One Last Question

If the Carte Blanche Principle is true, then why does the government use food stamps instead of cash to help the poor?

Whitmore devotes the conclusion of her paper (pp. 37–38) to answering this question:

On the face of it, paying food stamp benefits in cash seems to be sensible public policy. Based on the method I developed to estimate the cash-equivalent value of food stamps, I calculate that about one-half billion of the 17 billion dollars of annual food stamp spending is deadweight loss. The half-billion in averted deadweight loss could be returned to the government's coffers, or could be transferred back to the food stamp recipients who would then re-optimize their spending patterns. The government and retailers could also save a substantial amount on administration of the program with a cash-out, as seen in Table 7. Evidence suggests that nutritional intakes among food stamp recipients would not suffer. But what are the drawbacks? A crucial aspect of the success of the Food Stamp Program is its political popularity. The Food Stamp Program is not an entitlement program, so its budget must be approved annually in the Farm Bill. The program's budget has always been fully funded, due largely to two factors: its popularity as a targeted welfare program among voters, and its popularity among farmers because they think it increases demand for food.[47]

If indeed the Food Stamp Program's political viability is fundamentally connected to its status as an in-kind transfer program, then it is possible that the half-billion dollar annual deadweight loss is worth the cost in order to maintain the safety net provided by the program.[48] Nonetheless, a full consideration of both the costs and benefits of distributing food stamp benefits in-kind rather than in cash can inform the creation of efficient and viable policies to improve the nutrition of the nation's poor.

Footnotes:

[47] Widely cited food stamp literature estimates that food spending is 15 to 30 percent lower when benefits are provided in cash instead of in-kind. Based on such estimates, some researchers estimate that food spending would have been reduced by approximately $20–40 billion from 1996–2000 if food stamp benefits were cashed out (Kuhn et al, 1996, pp. 193–194). Ohls and Beebout (1993) discuss the politics of food stamps in chapter 7.

[48] Another way to think of the political viability is this: taking away the $500 million in deadweight loss would leave a $16.5 billion pure cash-assistance program. It is virtually inconceivable in today's political climate that such a large pure cash-assistance program would be approved, while the $17 billion food stamp budget is sure to be funded.

Summarizing the Food Stamp Example

This chapter applied the Theory of Consumer Behavior to food stamps. It introduced the idea of a corner solution and defined the Carte Blanche Principle. It also gave a peek into the world of econometrics by using real-world data to answer questions about the prevalence of distortion and the actual behavior of distorted consumers.

As a practical matter, it is not true that, in general, the poor will squander cash subsidies or make terrible buying decisions. Giving aid in the form of food stamps generates a deadweight loss for those distorted consumers who would have been better off with cash. As Whitmore points out, however, it is politically impossible to imagine what is now a $30 billion program being funded annually as a pure cash giveaway.

Exercises

Open Word and answer the following questions. Save the document and print it when you are done.

1. Which parameter in the *Selling* sheet, with the exchange rate set to 0.9, would have to be changed to represent the case of a distorted consumer who decides not to sell food stamps for cash? What would the value of this parameter be?
2. Explain under what condition the MRS equals the price ratio rule (as a condition that the optimal solution has been found) can be violated.
3. A seller of food stamps would obviously prefer a higher price, but what would be the advantage of a higher price in terms of the Theory of Consumer Behavior?

References

The epigraph comes from the first paragraph of Stigler and Becker's "De Gustibus Non Est Disputandum," *The American Economic Review*, Vol. 67, No. 2 (March, 1977), pp. 76–90. As they explain (p. 76), "The venerable admonition not to quarrel over tastes is commonly interpreted as advice to terminate a dispute when it has been resolved into a difference of tastes, presumably because there is no further room for rational persuasion." They offer, however, a second meaning: "Our title seems to us to be capable of another and preferable interpretation: that tastes neither change capriciously nor differ importantly between people." Their key point is this:

> The difference between these two viewpoints of tastes is fundamental. On the traditional view, an explanation of economic phenomena that reaches a difference in tastes between people or times is the terminus of the argument: the problem is abandoned at this point to whoever studies and explains tastes (psychologists? anthropologists? phrenologists? sociobiologists?). On our preferred interpretation, one never reaches this impasse: the economist continues to search for differences in prices or incomes to explain any differences or changes in behavior. (p. 76)

The idea that tastes are stable and differences in behavior are to be found in price or income shocks is a hallmark of Chicago School economics.

Diane Whitmore's working paper, "What Are Food Stamps Worth?," is available from the Industrial Relations Section of working papers from the Department of Economics at Princeton University. It is number 468 and was made available in July, 2002. It is available online at <www.irs.princeton.edu/pubs/pdfs/468.pdf>.

1.3.4

Cigarette Taxes

Taxes upon the necessaries of life have nearly the same effect upon the circumstances of the people as a poor soil and a bad climate.

Adam Smith

The Carte Blanche Principle says that cash is always as good as or better than in-kind. This chapter introduces a corollary: Lump sum taxes are better than quantity taxes.

Quantity taxes are added to the price of the product. There are quantity taxes levied on gasoline, alcoholic beverages, and cigarettes. In addition to the price, the quantity tax is added to the total amount the consumer must pay for each unit. If more is bought, more tax is paid.

A lump sum tax is a fixed amount that must be paid, regardless of how much is purchased.

The Quantity Tax on Cigarettes

Figure 1.3.4.1 shows the state cigarette tax in each state as of January 1, 2007. Visit the web site to see the latest tax rates.

The quantity tax on cigarettes can be quite high (as Figure 1.3.4.1 shows). As of January 1, 2007, New Jersey had the highest quantity tax at $2.575 on each pack of cigarettes.

Figure 1.3.4.2 shows an example calculation of the various taxes applied to a pack of cigarettes in Indiana in 2003. After adding the federal quantity tax of 39 cents and state quantity tax of 55.5 cents, 6% sales tax is added. Total taxes are around 50% of the price.

Federal tax of 39 cents and state tax of 55.5 cents on each pack of cigarettes are quantity taxes. The tax is not on the price of the product (like the sales tax), but on each unit of the product.

You may be tempted to conclude from Figure 1.3.4.2 that the consumer is bearing the entire burden of a quantity tax. In fact, this holds only under

STATE	TAX RATE (¢ per pack)	RANK	STATE	TAX RATE (¢ per pack)	RANK
Alabama (1)	42.5	40	Nebraska	64	31
Alaska (3)	180	7	Nevada	80	26
Arizona	200	4	New Hampshire	80	26
Arkansas	59	33	New Jersey	257.5	1
California	87	24	New Mexico	91	23
Colorado	84	25	New York (1)	150	13
Connecticut	151	11	North Carolina	35	44
Delaware	55	36	North Dakota	44	39
Florida	33.9	45	Ohio	125	16
Georgia	37	41	Oklahoma	103	19
Hawaii (3)	160	10	Oregon	118	18
Idaho	57	34	Pennsylvania	135	15
Illinois (1)	98	22	Rhode Island	246	2
Indiana	55.5	35	South Carolina	7	51
Iowa	36	42	South Dakota	53	38
Kansas	79	28	Tennessee (1) (2)	20	48
Kentucky (2)	30	46	Texas	141	14
Louisiana	36	42	Utah	69.5	30
Maine	200	4	Vermont	179	8
Maryland	100	20	Virginia (1)	30	46
Massachusetts	151	11	Washington	202.5	3
Michigan	200	4	West Virginia	55	36
Minnesota (4)	123	17	Wisconsin	77	29
Mississippi	18	49	Wyoming	60	32
Missouri (1)	17	50	Dist. of Columbia	100	20
Montana	170	9			
			U. S. Median	80.0	

Source: Compiled by FTA from various sources
(1) Counties and cities may impose an additional tax on a pack of cigarettes in AL, 1¢ to 6¢; IL, 10¢ to 15¢; MO, 4¢ to 7¢; NYC $1.50; TN, 1¢; and VA, 2¢ to 15¢.
(2) Dealers pay an additional enforcement and administrative fee of 0.1¢ per pack in KY and 0.05¢ in TN.
(3) Tax rate is scheduled to increase to $2.00 per pack on July 1, 2007 in AK and to $2.00 on Sept. 30, 2007 in HI.
(4) Plus an additional 25.5 cent sales tax is added to the wholesale price of a tax stamp (total $1.485).

Figure 1.3.4.1. Cigarette tax rates.
Source: <www.taxadmin.org/fta/rate/cigarett.html>

special conditions. In general, quantity taxes are not completely passed through to consumers. Using supply and demand, Chapter 3.1.3 offers a more complete analysis of quantity taxes.

A Brief History of Cigarettes

Figure 1.3.4.3 shows that per capita cigarette consumption has dropped precipitously since the mid 1960s.

F&F Mart Crawfordsville, IN Sep-2003			
Final Price	$	3.29	Price with state excise tax
Price before 6% Indiana Sales Tax	$	3.10	Price with federal quantity tax
Price before 39 cent Federal quantity tax	$	2.71	Price with state quantity tax
Price before 55.5 cent Indiana quantity tax	$	2.16	Initial, base price
Total Taxes	$	1.13	
% increase in price due to tax		52%	

Figure 1.3.4.2. Computing the final price after all taxes for one pack of cigarettes.

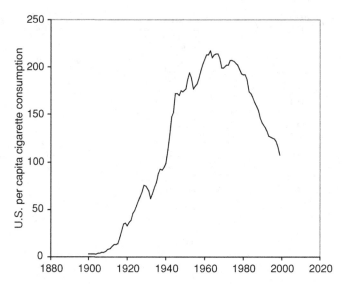

Figure 1.3.4.3. U.S. per capita cigarette consumption.
Source: CigaretteTaxes.xls!HistoricalData

The first half of the 20th century saw a rapid increase in smoking. Today, the government actively discourages smoking, but this was not always the case.

Beginning with World War I, public attitudes toward smoking changed. Congress ordered the War Department to include cigarettes in the rations issued to soldiers and subsidized their sale to soldiers. Some groups that previously had voiced opposition to smoking, such as the YMCA and the Salvation Army, helped supply cigarettes to military personnel. The policy of subsidizing cigarette use in the U.S. armed forces was reinforced in World War II. If anything, during the first half of the century, the U.S. government promoted cigarette consumption. (Sloan et al., p. 149)

More recently, quantity taxes on cigarettes have increased dramatically.
Figure 1.3.4.4 shows that state cigarette taxes, unlike other state taxes, jumped markedly in 2002.

Step Open the Excel workbook StateExciseTaxData.xls and read the *Intro* sheet. Visit the *CigTaxChanges* sheet to see that, starting in 2002, states are applying huge tax increases.

The federal tax on cigarettes was 8 cents/pack from 1951 to 1982, and then it increased to 16 cents in 1990, 20 cents in 1991, 24 cents in 1993, 34 cents in 2001–02, and 39 cents in 2002.

Expect further large increases in cigarette taxes at both the state and federal levels. Proponents point to the decrease in consumption, but the need for tax revenue is also an important factor.

State Averages

Year	Sales Tax (Percent)	Gasoline Tax (Cents Per Gallon)	Cigarette Tax (Cents Per Pack)	Spirits Tax ($ Per Gallon)	Table Wine Tax ($ Per Gallon)	Beer Tax ($ Per Gallon)
1999	4.66	18.96	40.80	3.51	0.72	0.23
2000	4.65	18.98	41.94	3.58	0.73	0.24
2001	4.66	18.66	42.31	3.58	0.74	0.24
2002	4.75	20.21	61.15	3.58	0.74	0.24
2003	4.86	20.25	71.21	3.69	0.79	0.24
2004	4.83	19.91	77.48	3.74	0.78	0.24
2005			84.04			
2006			91.72			

Figure 1.3.4.4. A recent history of state taxes.
Source: StateExciseTaxData.xls!Average

An Alternative to the Quantity Tax: The Lump Sum Tax

An alternative to a quantity tax is a lump sum tax. With this kind of tax, the amount paid by each consumer does not depend on the purchase of particular goods and services.

An income tax can be based on a percentage of income, but lump sum taxes are sometimes called income taxes. To be clear, we will analyze a tax that is a constant, fixed dollar amount.

Comparing Quantity and Lump Sum Taxes

We can compare the effect of a quantity versus a lump sum tax by using the standard consumer theory model.

To make a good comparison, we have to make sure that the taxes are *revenue neutral*. This means that the tax revenues generated by the tax proposals are the same. It would not be fair to compare a quantity tax that generated $50 in revenues to a $100 lump sum tax.

Step Open the Excel workbook CigaretteTaxes.xls and read the *Intro* sheet.

The *HistoricalData* sheet has links to tobacco sources and data.

Step Proceed to the *QuantityTax* sheet.

Cell B21 is the crucial parameter in this example. The sheet opens with cell B21 = 0, which means there is no tax.

The sheet opens with the consumer considering the bundle 20,60. The MRS is greater than the price ratio (in absolute value) and the consumer can move down the budget constraint so we know utility is not being maximized.

Step Utility is maximized at a value of 1250 by consuming 25 units of cigarettes and 50 units of other goods. Run Solver to confirm this result.

Suppose we impose a $1/unit quantity tax on x_1. What effect does this have on the consumer?

Step You can find the consumer's optimal solution under this situation by changing cell B21 to 1 and running Solver.

We can also find the optimal solution using analytical methods by solving the following constrained optimization problem:

$$\max_{x_1,x_2} u(x_1, x_2) = x_1 x_2$$
$$\text{s.t. } 100 = (2 + Q\_Tax)x_1 + x_2$$

The consumer wishes to maximize utility (which is Cobb-Douglas with both exponents equal to 1), subject to the budget constraint, with parameter values for income and prices plugged in. We leave Q_Tax as an exogenous variable so we can find the optimal solution as a function of Q_Tax.

We can apply the Lagrangean recipe:

1. Rewrite the constraint so that it is equal to zero:

$$0 = 100 - (2 + Q\_Tax)x_1 - x_2$$

2. Form the Lagrangean:

$$\max_{x_1,x_2,\lambda} L = x_1 x_2 + \lambda(100 - (2 + Q\_Tax)x_1 - x_2)$$

Notice, as stated earlier, that we are working with a mixed concrete and general problem. We have numerical values for prices, income, and the utility function exponents, but we have the amount of the quantity tax as a variable. We use this strategy whenever we want to find the optimal solution as a function of a particular exogenous variable.

3. Take partial derivatives with respect to x_1, x_2, and λ.

$$\frac{\partial L}{\partial x_1} = x_2 - (2 + Q\_Tax)\lambda$$
$$\frac{\partial L}{\partial x_2} = x_1 - \lambda$$
$$\frac{\partial L}{\partial \lambda} = 100 - (2 + Q\_Tax)x_1 - x_2$$

4. Set the partial derivatives equal to zero and solve the system of equations for x_1, x_2, and λ.

$$\frac{\partial L}{\partial x_1} = x_2 - (2 + Q\_Tax)\lambda = 0$$
$$\frac{\partial L}{\partial x_2} = x_1 - \lambda = 0$$
$$\frac{\partial L}{\partial \lambda} = 100 - (2 + Q\_Tax)x_1 - x_2 = 0$$

We use the usual solution method, moving the lambda terms to the right-hand side and then dividing the first equation by the second, which allows us to cancel the lambda terms.

$$x_2 = (2 + Q\_Tax)\lambda$$

$$x_1 = \lambda$$

$$\frac{x_2}{x_1} = \frac{(2 + Q\_Tax)\lambda}{\lambda}$$

$$x_2 = (2 + Q\_Tax)x_1 \quad \boxed{\text{This is not a reduced-form answer for } x_2 \text{ because it is a function of } x_1.}$$

By canceling the lambda terms, we have reduced the three equation, three unknown system to two equations in two unknowns.

$$x_2 = (2 + Q\_Tax)x_1$$

$$100 - (2 + Q\_Tax)x_1 - x_2 = 0$$

We substitute the first equation into the second and solve for the optimal amount of good 1.

$$100 - (2 + Q\_Tax)x_1 - [(2 + Q\_Tax)x_1] = 0$$

$$100 = 2(2 + Q\_Tax)x_1$$

$$x_1^* = \frac{50}{(2 + Q\_Tax)}$$

Then, we substitute this back to get the optimal amount of good 2.

$$x_2^* = (2 + Q\_Tax)\left[\frac{50}{(2 + Q\_Tax)}\right] = 50$$

We can easily confirm Solver's result by substituting $Q\_Tax = 1$ into the reduced-form solution for the two goods. Because Q_Tax does not appear in the optimal solution for good 2, its value is simply 50 for any value of Q_Tax.

Step Proceed to the *IncomeTax* sheet.

The quantity tax imposed in the *QuantityTax* sheet has been replaced with a revenue-neutral lump sum tax. With a $1/unit quantity tax, the consumer purchases $16\frac{2}{3}$ units of x_1, which means the state generates $16.67 of revenue from the quantity tax. It could have generated the same revenue by taxing the consumer $16.67, regardless of how much x_1 or x_2 the consumer bought. This tax is called a lump sum tax because you pay a fixed amount (that's the "lump sum" part) no matter what you decide to buy.

How would the consumer respond to this tax?

Step Run Solver from the *IncomeTax* sheet to find out.

Once again, we can confirm Solver's numerically based answer by working out the problem analytically.

$$\max_{x_1, x_2} u(x_1, x_2) = x_1 x_2$$

$$\text{s.t.} \, 100 - Lump\_Tax = 2x_1 + x_2$$

We can apply the Lagrangean recipe:

1. Rewrite the constraint so that it is equal to zero:

$$0 = 100 - Lump\_Tax - 2x_1 - x_2$$

2. Form the Lagrangean:

$$\max_{x_1, x_2, \lambda} L = x_1 x_2 + \lambda(100 - Lump\_Tax - 2x_1 - x_2)$$

3. Take partial derivatives with respect to x_1, x_2, and λ.

$$\frac{\partial L}{\partial x_1} = x_2 - 2\lambda$$

$$\frac{\partial L}{\partial x_2} = x_1 - \lambda$$

$$\frac{\partial L}{\partial \lambda} = 100 - Lump\_Tax - 2x_1 - x_2$$

4. Set the partial derivatives equal to zero and solve the system of equations for x_1, x_2, and λ.

$$\frac{\partial L}{\partial x_1} = x_2 - 2\lambda = 0$$

$$\frac{\partial L}{\partial x_2} = x_1 - \lambda = 0$$

$$\frac{\partial L}{\partial \lambda} = 100 - Lump\_Tax - 2x_1 - x_2 = 0$$

We use the usual solution method, moving the lambda terms to the right-hand side and then dividing the first equation by the second, which allows us to cancel the lambda terms.

$$x_2 = 2\lambda$$

$$x_1 = \lambda$$

$$\frac{x_2}{x_1} = \frac{2\lambda}{\lambda}$$

$$x_2 = 2x_1$$

By canceling the lambda terms, we have reduced the three equation, three unknown system to two equations in two unknowns.

$$x_2 = 2x_1$$

$$100 - Lump\_Tax - 2x_1 - x_2 = 0$$

Tax	Revenue	x1*	x2*	Utility*
No tax	$0	25	50	1250
Q_tax = $1/unit	$16.67	$16\frac{2}{3}$	50	$833\frac{1}{3}$
Income_tax=$16.67	$16.67	20.833	$41\frac{2}{3}$	868

Figure 1.3.4.5. Comparing the tax schemes.

We substitute the first equation into the second and solve for the optimal amount of good 1.

$$100 - Lump\_Tax - 2x_1 - [2x_1] = 0$$
$$x_1^* = \frac{100 - Lump\_Tax}{4}$$

Then, we substitute this back to get the optimal amount of good 2.

$$x_2^* = 2\left[\frac{100 - Lump\_Tax}{4}\right] = \frac{100 - Lump\_Tax}{2}$$

To compare the analytical results with Solver, we evaluate the reduced-form expressions at the revenue-neutral value of *Lump_Sum*, 16.67. This confirms Solver's result.

Comparing the Tax Schemes

Figure 1.3.4.5 shows the results of the three scenarios we have considered. The first row shows that the consumer will buy the bundle 25,50 when there is no tax, generating an optimal utility of 1250.

The second row shows that utility falls to $833\frac{1}{3}$ with an optimal solution of $16\frac{2}{3}$,50 with a $1/unit of x_1 quantity tax.

The last row shows that an income tax of $16.67 would induce purchase of the $20\frac{5}{6}$,$41\frac{2}{3}$ combination, which would give a level of utility of 868.

The primary lesson is that, for this consumer, the income tax is better than the quantity tax because utility is higher under the income tax.

Notice that we are not violating the rule against interpreting utility values as being meaningful. We are not comparing two consumers. We are not treating utility as if it were on a cardinal scale by saying, for example, that there is a gain of 868 minus $833\frac{1}{3}$ equals $34\frac{2}{3}$ utils of increased satisfaction. We are merely saying that satisfaction is higher under the lump sum tax scheme. This is a fact and a true statement.

A graph can be used to explain this rather curious result that lump sum taxes enable higher utility than equivalent revenue quantity taxes. It is a complicated graph, so we will build up to it in stages.

The first layer is simply the initial solution. It is shown in Figure 1.3.4.6.

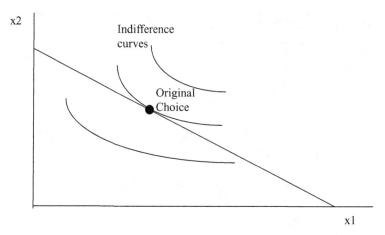

Figure 1.3.4.6. The initial optimal solution.

Figure 1.3.4.7 shows what happens with a quantity tax. The budget constraint rotates in because the price paid by the consumer (composed of the price of the product plus the tax) has increased. The consumer is forced to re-optimize and find a new optimal solution, labeled Quantity Tax.

Then we add another layer to show the income tax. The lump sum tax budget constraint has to go through the optimal choice bundle with the quantity tax so that the lump sum tax is equivalent in value to the quantity tax. It also has to be parallel to the original budget constraint. Because it cuts the indifference curve at the quantity tax point, we know we can move down the budget line and reach a higher indifference curve.

Figure 1.3.4.8 shows the graph with the income tax and enables comparison of the two tax schemes.

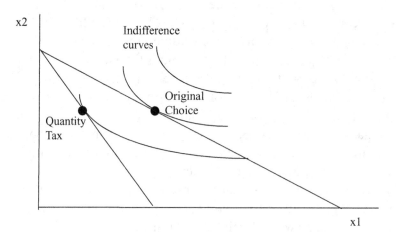

Figure 1.3.4.7. Applying a quantity tax.

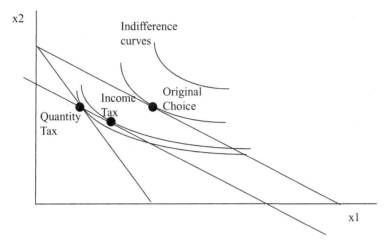

Figure 1.3.4.8. Comparing taxes.

Figure 1.3.4.8 shows that, starting from the Original Choice point, we can compare a quantity tax and a revenue-neutral income tax. Figure 1.3.4.8 makes clear that the income tax enables attainment of a higher level of utility than the quantity tax because the indifference curve attainable under the income tax is higher than the indifference curve that maximizes utility with the quantity tax.

The reason why the income tax is better is due to the fact that it is non-distorting. It leaves the relative prices of the two goods unchanged.

The Lesson and a Question

The lesson is that the Theory of Consumer Behavior has been used to show that income taxes are better than quantity taxes.

This begs a question: Why do we see quantity taxes? Or, in the context of our example, if income taxes are better, then why are cigarettes (and alcohol and gasoline) so heavily quantity taxed?

In the first place, this lesson holds only for each individual consumer. It is a fact that there is a revenue-neutral lump sum tax that leaves each individual consumer better off. The amount, however, of the preferable lump sum tax is different, in general, for each consumer. In other words, the lesson does not hold for all consumers taken as a whole. Thus, a single lump tax for all consumers will not necessarily yield higher utility than a quantity tax for each consumer.

This point is obvious if you consider a consumer who does not buy the taxed product at all. This consumer would prefer any size quantity tax to a lump sum tax. After all, if you do not buy the good, you do not have to pay any quantity tax, while you pay the lump sum tax regardless of how much of the good you buy.

The Theory of Consumer Behavior makes clear that there is a particular revenue-neutral lump sum tax that is preferable to a quantity tax for each individual who purchases the taxed good. The dominance of lump sum taxes does not, however, extend to all consumers.

With respect to the use of quantity taxes for cigarettes, consider the following points: (1) nonsmokers are completely unaffected by these taxes; (2) in the United States today, there are many more nonsmokers than smokers; and (3) cigarette demand is inelastic, so quantity demanded will not fall by much as the total amount paid by the consumer (price + tax) rises – which means government revenue rises as the tax rate on cigarettes rises. Under these conditions, perhaps it is not too surprising that quantity taxes for cigarettes continue to increase.

Other goods that have similar quantity taxes include alcoholic beverages and gasoline. The former is a "sin tax" (like cigarette taxes), but the latter is not. Notice how all three of these products are inelastically demanded, which means that tax increases lead to tax revenue increases.

Lump Sum Corollary to the Carte Blanche Principle

If given the option between a quantity and a revenue-neutral lump sum tax, a consumer who buys the taxed good would prefer the lump sum tax because it will leave the consumer with a higher level of utility. Unlike the quantity tax, the income tax will not distort the relative prices faced by the consumer.

The Theory of Consumer Behavior can be used to demonstrate this claim. Figure 1.3.4.8 is the key graphic. It shows that the consumer can reach a higher indifference curve with the lump sum tax than the quantity tax.

Although the Lump Sum Corollary is true, we see quantity taxes for various products because the Lump Sum Corollary does not apply to all consumers taken as a group. It is not true that there is a single lump sum tax that is preferred to a quantity tax by all consumers.

Exercises

Open Word and answer the following questions. Save the document and print it when you are done.

1. Return to the CigaretteTaxes.xls workbook and apply a \$2/unit quantity tax. Run Solver. Find the solution by evaluating the reduced form. Show your work. Do the two methods agree?
2. Repeat this for the income tax. Find the revenue-neutral solution via Solver, evaluate the reduced-form expression at the new Lump_Tax, and compare the two methods. Do the two methods agree?
3. Would the percentage change in the consumer's consumption of x_1 be more affected by a quantity tax if her indifference curves were flatter, assuming a Cobb-Douglas utility function? Describe your procedure in answering this question.

References

The epigraph is from the online version of *The Wealth of Nations* by Adam Smith, who is well known as the father of economics. You can access *The Wealth of Nations* (and many other texts) online at <www.econlib.org>. If you want the book, used copies abound or you can get a new, inexpensive copy at <www.libertyfund.org>.

The economics literature on cigarette smoking is vast. Frank A. Sloan, V. Kerry Smith, and Donald H. Taylor, "Information, Addiction, and Bad 'Choices': Lessons from a Century of Cigarettes," *Economics Letters*, Vol. 77 (2002), pp. 147–155, is an accessible, informative starting point.

For a broader, historical review, see Allan M. Brandt, *The Cigarette Century: The Rise, Fall, and Deadly Persistence of the Product That Defined America* (2007).

1.4

Comparative Statics

1.4.1

Engel Curves

Of all the empirical regularities observed in economic data, Engel's Law is probably the best established.

Hendrik S. Houthakker

We begin with a quick review of what we know thus far.

The Consumer's Optimization Problem

1. Goal: maximize satisfaction
2. Endogenous variables: x_1, x_2
3. Exogenous variables: m, p_1, p_2, and preference parameters (e.g., if Cobb-Douglas, c and d).

Finding the Initial Solution

There are analytical (Lagrangean) and numerical (Solver) methods available to find the initial solution.

The canonical graph displays indifference curves, the budget constraint, and the optimal solution, as shown in Figure 1.4.1.1.

In this chapter, we introduce the idea and logic behind comparative statics, discuss elasticity, and then apply the ideas to a concrete example.

The focus is on the effects on the optimal solution as we change income. An Engel Curve tells you the quantity demanded as a function of income, ceteris paribus.

Introduction to Comparative Statics – Initial, Shock, New, Compare

When we change an exogenous variable, ceteris paribus, and track the changes in the optimal values of the endogenous variables, we are doing comparative statics analysis.

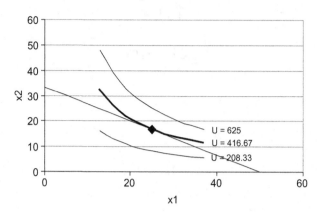

Figure 1.4.1.1. The initial solution.

The idea behind comparative statics is simple: We want to see how the optimizing agent responds to a change in the environment.

To do comparative statics analysis, we follow a four-step procedure.

1. We find the *initial* solution.
2. We change a single exogenous variable, called the *shock*, holding all other exogenous variables constant. Economists use the Latin phrase, *ceteris paribus*, as shorthand. This literally means *with other things held equal* and economists use the phrase to mean *everything else held constant*.
3. We find the *new* optimal solution.
4. Finally, we compare the new to the initial solution to see how the optimal solution responded to the shock.

Comparative statics (not statistics) is the heart and soul of economics as a framework for interpreting observed behavior. This framework has been given many names, including the method of economics, the economic approach, the economic way of thinking, and economic reasoning.

Whereas *comparative* clearly points to the comparison between the new and initial solution, the meaning of *statics* is less obvious. It means that we are going to focus on positions of rest and not worry about the path of the solution as it moves from the initial to the new point.

There are a few complications and additional issues when doing comparative statics analysis.

1. Analytical Versus Numerical Methods

The computation of the response can be via analytical or numerical methods. It can be confusing because sometimes the two methods give the same answer and other times not. We will see why this happens.

2. *Qualitative Versus Quantitative Comparisons*

We have several choices when we compare the new to the initial solution.

A qualitative comparison focuses only on the *direction* of the response. We would say that the shock led to an increase or decrease in a particular endogenous variable.

A quantitative comparison tells us both the *direction* and *magnitude* of the response. In addition to whether the endogenous variable moved up or down, we could report by how much. Our description of the magnitude could use the own units of the variable themselves or we could report the elasticity (which is a ratio of percentage changes).

3. *Underlying Versus Presentation Graph*

Finally, we have an option in displaying the comparative statics results. We can use the *underlying graph* – a graph that shows the initial optimal solution, shock, and new optimal solution. Or, we can use a *presentation graph* – a graph that shows only the relationship between the response and shock variables (hiding everything else).

Elasticity Basics

$$x \text{ elasticity of } y = \frac{\%\,\Delta y}{\%\,\Delta x}$$

Elasticity is a number that measures the sensitivity or responsiveness of one variable when another changes. Elasticity, responsiveness, and sensitivity are synonyms. An elasticity number expresses the impact one variable has on another. The closer the elasticity is to zero, the more insensitive or inelastic the relationship.

Elasticity is often expressed as *the something elasticity of something*. For example, many students are familiar with the price elasticity of demand. The first *something*, in this case price, is always the exogenous variable; the second *something*, in this case demand (the amount purchased), is the response or optimal value being tracked.

A less common, but perhaps easier, way of stating an elasticity is to say, "the elasticity of something with respect to something." That more clearly shows what depends on what.

Unlike the own units way of comparing the initial and new solutions, elasticity is computed as the ratio of percentage changes in the values. The endogenous or response variable always goes in the numerator and the exogenous or shock variable is always in the denominator.

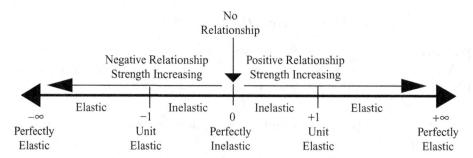

Figure 1.4.1.2. Elasticity on the number line.

The percentage change, $\frac{(new-initial)}{initial}$, is different from just the change, *new − initial*. When we divide by the initial value, the units in the numerator and denominator of the percentage change cancel and we are left with a percent as the unit. If we compute the percentage change in apples from 2 to 3 apples, we get 50%. The change, however, is +1 apple.

If we divide one percentage change by another, the percents cancel and we get a *unitless* number. Thus, elasticity is a pure number with no units.

The lack of units in an elasticity measure is a huge advantage because it means we can compare wildly different things. No matter the underlying units of the variables, we can put the number on a common yardstick and make a statement about its responsiveness.

Figure 1.4.1.2 shows the possible values that an elasticity can take, along with the names we give particular values.

Empirically, elasticities are usually low numbers around zero or one (in absolute value). An elasticity of +2 is extremely responsive. It means that a 1% increase in the exogenous variable generates a 2% increase in the endogenous variable.

The sign of the elasticity indicates direction (a qualitative statement about the relationship between the two variables). Zero means that there is no relationship – i.e., that the exogenous variable does not influence the response variable at all. Thus, −2 is extremely responsive like +2, but the variables are inversely related so a 1% increase in the exogenous variable leads to a 2% *decrease* in the endogenous variable.

One (both positive and negative) is an important marker on the elasticity number line because it tells you whether the given percentage change in an exogenous variable results in a smaller percentage change (when the elasticity is less than one), an equal percentage change (elasticity equal to one), or greater percentage change (elasticity greater than one) in the exogenous variable.

Elasticities are a confusing part of economics. Following are seven points to keep in mind as you compute and interpret this fundamental but easily misunderstood concept.

1. Elasticity is about the relationship between two variables, not just the change in one variable. Thus, do not confuse a negative elasticity as meaning that the response variable (in the numerator) must decrease. The negative means that the relationship or ratio is negative, not the change in the numerator. So, if the age elasticity of time playing sports is negative, that means both that

- Time playing sports falls as age increases
- Time playing sports rises as age falls.

2. Elasticity is a local phenomenon. The elasticity will usually change as the exogenous variable changes. Thus, any one value of elasticity is a local or point value that applies only to the change in the exogenous variable under consideration from a certain point.

You should not think of a price elasticity of demand of −0.6 as applying to an entire demand curve. Instead, it is a statement about the movement in price from one value to another value close by, say $3.00/unit to $3.01/unit. The price elasticity of demand from $4.00/unit to $4.01/unit may well be very different.

There are constant elasticity functions, where the elasticity is the same all along the function, but they are a special case.

3. Elasticity can be calculated for different size changes. Economists are sloppy in their language and do not bother to distinguish elasticity calculated at a point via calculus (for an infinitesimal change) and elasticity calculated for a finite distance from one point to another. If the function is non-linear, these two methods give different results. If an economist mentions a *point elasticity*, it is probably calculated via calculus as an infinitesimally small change.

4. As just mentioned, the measured value of elasticity will generally be different depending upon how big a change in the exogenous variable is considered. How big a movement in the exogenous variable you want to use to measure elasticity depends on the question you are asking.

Economists usually want to know how the optimal value of the endogenous variable will change if there is a small change in the exogenous variable. It is convenient, therefore, to consider infinitesimal changes in the exogenous variable; this produces a formula for the elasticity that utilizes the derivative.

5. Elasticity always puts the response variable in the numerator. Do not confuse the numerator and denominator in the computation. In the x elasticity of y, x is the exogenous or shock variable and y is the endogenous or response variable. Students often compute the reciprocal of the correct elasticity. Avoid this common mistake by always checking to make sure that

the variable in the numerator responds or is driven by the variable in the denominator.

6. Elasticity is unitless. The x elasticity of y of 0.2 is not 20%. It is 0.2. It means that a 1% increase in x leads to a 0.2% increase in y.

Perhaps the single most important thing to remember about elasticity is:

7. Do not confuse elasticity with slope. This may be the most common confusion of all.

The slope is a quantitative measure in the units of the two variables being compared. If $Q^* = P/2$, then the slope, $\frac{\Delta Q^*}{\Delta P}$, is $1/2$. This says that an increase in P of $1/unit will lead to an increase in Q^* of $1/2$ a unit. Thus, the slope would be measured in units squared per dollar (so that when multiplied by the price, we end up with just units of Q).

Elasticity, on the other hand, is a quantitative measure based on percentage changes and is, therefore, unitless. The P elasticity of $Q^* = 1$ says that a 1% increase in P leads to a 1% increase in Q^*. It does not say anything about the actual, numerical $/unit increase in P, but speaks of the percentage increase in P. Similarly, elasticity focuses on the percentage change in Q^*, not the change in terms of number of units.

Thus, elasticity and slope are two different ways to measure the responsiveness of a variable as another variable changes. Elasticity uses percentage changes, $\frac{\%\Delta y}{\%\Delta x}$, whereas the slope, $\frac{\Delta y}{\Delta x}$, does not.

Numerical Comparative Statics Analysis of Changing Income

Step Open the Excel workbook EngelCurves.xls and read the *Intro* sheet. Proceed to the *OptimalChoice* sheet.

Solver has been run and the initial solution, $x_1^* = 25$ and $x_2^* = 16.67$, is displayed.

Our first attempt at comparative statics analysis is straightforward: Compute the response in x_1^* and x_2^* for a given change in income, ceteris paribus.

Step Change cell B18 to 150 (this is the shock) and then run Solver to find the new optimal solution.

Step Compare the initial and new values of x_1^* and x_2^* given the $50 increase in income.

In qualitative terms, we would say that the increase in income has led to an increase in optimal consumption of the two goods.

In quantitative terms, we can compute the response as the change in the own units of the two variables.

The own units statement of comparative statics for x_1^* is simply $\frac{\Delta x_1^*}{\Delta m}$.

Income rose by $50 and optimal consumption of each good went up by 12.5 units. We usually translate this into a per unit rate, so we would divide 12.5 by 50 and say that we get an increase of 1/4 unit for every $1 increase in income.

Often, however, we use elasticity as a way to present the comparative statics result.

Income elasticity of $x_1^* = \frac{\Delta x_1^*}{\Delta m} \cdot \frac{m}{x_1^*} = \frac{12.5}{50} \cdot \frac{100}{25} = 1.$

Notice that the elasticity is unit elastic. This means that a 1% change in income leads to a 1% change in the optimal purchase of good 1.

The formula is easily derived from the definition of the ratio of percentage changes:

$$\frac{\dfrac{new\ x_1^* - initial\ x_1^*}{initial\ x_1^*}}{\dfrac{new\ m - initial\ m}{initial\ m}} = \frac{\dfrac{\Delta x_1^*}{x_1^*}}{\dfrac{\Delta m}{m}} = \frac{\Delta x_1^*}{\Delta m} \cdot \frac{m}{x_1^*}.$$

Numerical Approach via the Comparative Statics Wizard

Although it is certainly possible to do comparative statics analysis by running Solver to find the initial solution, changing a parameter on the sheet, running Solver again to find the new solution, and then comparing the initial and new solutions, the tediousness of this manual approach is obvious.

Fortunately, there is a better way. It involves using the Comparative Statics Wizard Excel add-in.

Step Install the Comparative Statics Wizard add-in (cswiz.xla). Instructions and documentation are available in the CompStatics.doc file in the SolverCompStaticsWizard folder. You can see which add-ins are installed by clicking the Office button, then Excel Options, and then the Add-ins tab. (You can accomplish the same thing in earlier versions of Excel by executing Tools: Add-Ins to bring up the Excel Add-In Manager.)

Step Once the Comparative Statics Wizard add-in is installed, from the *OptimalChoice* sheet, click the Add-ins tab on the ribbon, then click Wizard and Comp Statics (in earlier versions, execute Tools: Wizard: Comp Statics) to bring up the main dialog box of the CSWiz add-in, shown in Figure 1.4.1.3.

Step Click on the Input button and answer the three questions posed. Clearly, the goal is cell B7 so you will click on cell B7 when prompted by the first question. Excel enters the absolute reference to that cell (B7) in the dialog box and you click OK. Follow the same procedure for the next two questions. The endogenous variables are in cells B11:B12 and the exogenous variables are in cells B16:B20.

Engel Curves

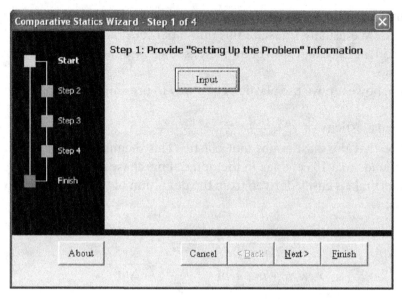

Figure 1.4.1.3. CSWiz main dialog box.

Notice how the Comparative Statics Wizard add-in presumes that you have properly organized and set up the problem on the spreadsheet.

Step Once you have provided the goal, endogenous, and exogenous variable cells, click Next.

Step At the Step 2: Finding the Initial Solution screen, click the Run Solver button to bring up the Solver dialog box. Click Solve to have Solver find the initial solution.

Step Having found the initial solution, click Next.

Step At the Step 3: Providing Shock Information screen, click the Input button. As in the first screen, you are asked three questions. The first question asks for the shock variable itself. In this case, click on cell B18 (the income variable). The second question is the amount of change. Enter 50. The third question is the number of shocks. The default value is 5. Accept this value by clicking the OK button. You have asked Excel to change income, holding the other variables constant, from 100 to 150 to 200 to 250 to 300 to 350 – five jumps of 50 each from the 100 initial value.

Step Having entered the shock information, click Next.

The Step 4: Comparative Statics Calculation screen is the heart of the add-in. You have provided the goal, endogenous and exogenous variable information, Solver found the initial solution, and you have told Excel which variable to shock and how. Excel is ready to run the problem over and over again for each of the shock variable values you provided. It is essentially the manual approach, but Excel does all of the tedious work.

Step Click the Run Comparative Statics button. The bar displays Excel's progress through the repeated optimization problems. It runs Solver at each value of income, but it is very fast.

Step Click Next, read the next screen, and click Finish.

Excel has inserted a sheet into the workbook with all of the comparative statics results. This sheet is similar to the *CS1* sheet.

The results produced by the Comparative Statics Wizard can be further processed.

Step Proceed to the *CS1* sheet. Columns F and G contain slope and elasticity calculations. Click on the cells to see the formulas.

Notice that you have to be careful with parentheses when doing percentage change calculations in Excel. Simply entering "= C14 − C13/C13" will not do what you want because Excel's order of operations rule will divide C13 by C13 and subtract that from C14.

Engel and Income Consumption (Offer) Curves

There are two graphs on the *CS1* sheet. They appear to be the same, but they are not. One graph is an Engel Curve and the other is an Income Consumption Curve (sometimes called an Income Offer Curve or Income Expansion Path).

Ernst Engel (not to be confused with Karl Marx's benefactor and friend, Friedrich Engels) was a 19th-century German statistician who analyzed consumer expenditure data. He found that food purchases increased as income rose, but at a decreasing rate. This became known as *Engel's Law*. A graph of demand for a good as a function of income, ceteris paribus, is called an *Engel Curve*.

The Income Consumption Curve shows the effect of the increase in income in the canonical indifference-curves-and-budget-constraint graph. In other words, it shows the comparative statics analysis on the underlying, canonical graph. Panel A in Figure 1.4.1.4 shows the Income Consumption Curve.

Panel B in Figure 1.4.1.4 shows that the Engel Curve for x_1 is a presentation graph of the relationship between income and optimal x_1. It hides everything else. There is an Engel Curve graph for x_2, but it is not displayed.

The slope of the Engel Curve reveals whether the good is normal or inferior. A *normal* good, as in Figure 1.4.1.4, has a positively sloped Engel Curve: when income rises, so does optimal consumption. An *inferior* good has a negatively sloped Engel Curve: increases in income lead to decreases in optimal consumption of the good. Figure 1.4.1.5 shows this case.

Hamburger is the classic inferior good example. As income rises, the idea is that you eat less hamburger meat and more of better cuts of beef. The

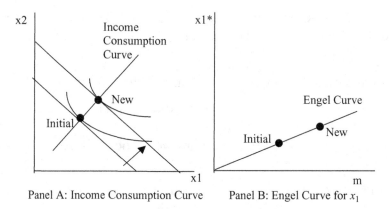

Panel A: Income Consumption Curve   Panel B: Engel Curve for x_1

Figure 1.4.1.4. Displaying the results of a shock in income.

example also serves to point out that goods aren't either normal or inferior as a result of some innate characteristic, but that the relationship is a local phenomenon. Figure 1.4.1.6 shows how a consumer might react across the full range of income.

Figure 1.4.1.6 shows that hamburger is normal at low levels of income (with increasing consumption as income rises), but inferior at higher levels of income.

Analytical Comparative Statics Analysis of Changing Income

We can derive the Engel Curve for the problem in the EngelCurves.xls workbook via analytical methods.

As usual, we rewrite the constraint and form the Lagrangean. We leave m as a letter so that our final answer is a function of income.

$$\max_{x_1,x_2,\lambda} L = x_1 x_2 + \lambda(m - 2x_1 - 3x_2)$$

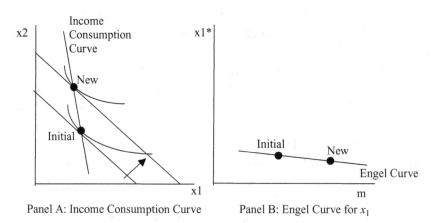

Panel A: Income Consumption Curve   Panel B: Engel Curve for x_1

Figure 1.4.1.5. x_1 as an inferior good.

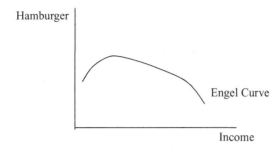

Figure 1.4.1.6. A hypothetical Engel Curve for hamburger.

Take derivatives with respect to each choice variable and set equal to zero:

$$\frac{\partial L}{\partial x_1} = x_2^* - 2\lambda^* = 0$$

$$\frac{\partial L}{\partial x_2} = x_1^* - 3\lambda^* = 0$$

$$\frac{\partial L}{\partial \lambda} = m - 2x_1^* - 3x_2^* = 0$$

Solve for the optimal values of x_1 and x_2. Moving the lambda terms to the right-hand side and dividing the first equation by the second gets rid of lambda (and gives the familiar $MRS = p_1/p_2$ condition), which can then be solved for optimal x_2 as a function of optimal x_1:

$$\frac{x_2^*}{x_1^*} = \frac{2}{3}$$

$$x_2^* = \frac{2}{3}x_1^*$$

Substitute this expression for x_2^* into the third first-order condition and solve for x_1^*.

$$m - 2x_1^* - 3\left[\tfrac{2}{3}x_1^*\right] = 0$$

$$4x_1^* = m$$

$$x_1^* = \tfrac{1}{4}m$$

This agrees perfectly with the numerical approach using the Comparative Statics Wizard to recalculate the optimal solution at given values of income. The numerical method picks individual points off the Engel Curve function that we derived here.

There is an Engel Curve for x_2^*. It is $x_2^* = \tfrac{1}{6}m$.

Of course, these Engel Curves are for this particular consumer, with this particular utility function and set of exogenous variables. Different preferences will give different Engel Curves.

If we make the problem more general, in the sense of substituting letters for numbers in the Lagrangean, then these exogenous variables will appear in the reduced-form expression. In other words, the one-quarter and one-sixth constants in the Engel Curves will be changed into an expression with the exogenous variables. Evaluating that expression at the current values of the exogenous variables will give one-quarter and one-sixth.

If you change an exogenous variable other than income, you will no longer move along the Engel Curve. Instead, you will shift the entire Engel Curve.

To compute an own units response in x_1^* given a change in income, we can take the derivative with respect to m, which is simply $1/4$. This means the slope of the reduced form is constant at any value of m.

The elasticity *at* a given value of m can be computed via the following formula:

$$\frac{dx_1^*}{dm} \cdot \frac{m}{x_1^*}$$

Because it is calculated *at* a particular point (which explains why the *at* is italicized), this is called a point elasticity. Economists usually compute and report point elasticities, but they often omit the adjective and simply call the result an elasticity.

The income elasticity we computed earlier was based on the following formula:

$$\frac{\dfrac{new\ x_1^* - initial\ x_1^*}{initial\ x_1^*}}{\dfrac{new\ m - initial\ m}{initial\ m}} = \frac{\dfrac{\Delta x_1^*}{x_1^*}}{\dfrac{\Delta m}{m}} = \frac{\Delta x_1^*}{\Delta m} \cdot \frac{m}{x_1^*}$$

If we replace the $\frac{\Delta x_1^*}{\Delta m}$ term with the derivative, $\frac{dx_1^*}{dm}$, we get the point elasticity formula. Thus, the point elasticity formula is the same; it is just based on an infinitesimally small change in m.

At $m = 100$, the income elasticity of $x_1^* = (1/4)(100/25) = 1$. Good x_2 also has a constant unit income elasticity. Rays from the origin always have constant, unit elasticities.

Once again, the income elasticity computed via the derivative agrees perfectly with the results from the numerical method. If you use the discrete change in income, then the elasticity is *from* one point to another. If you use the derivative, the elasticity is *at* a point. Either way, the interpretation is usually based on a 1% change in the exogenous variable. So, we would say that a 1% increase in income leads to a 1% increase in consumption of good 1 because the income elasticity of good 1 is $+1$.

The linear Engel Curves and constant unit income elasticities are generated by the utility function. Cobb-Douglas utility functions always yield linear Engel Curves with constant unit income elasticities. We do not believe that Engel Curves are always linear and unit income elastic. Although there are other utility functions with less restrictive results, they are more difficult to work with mathematically. Ease of algebraic manipulation helps explain the popularity of the Cobb-Douglas functional form.

An Engel Curve is an Example of Comparative Statics Analysis

This chapter introduced comparative statics analysis. It focused on tracking the optimal solution as income changes. This is called an Engel Curve.

Comparative statics analysis, including elasticities, can be done via numerical and analytical methods. The Comparative Statics Wizard handles much of the tedious work in the numerical approach.

We can compute elasticity in two ways: *at* a point and *from* one point to another. The former uses the derivative and latter is based on a discrete-size change in the exogenous variable. A point elasticity is one based on the derivative. Both elasticities are based on percentage changes, but the derivative uses infinitesimally small changes in the exogenous variable.

We will often compare the two methods. When shocking income, the two methods agreed perfectly. This will not always be the case.

Exercises

Open Word and answer the following questions. Save the document and print it when you are done.

1. Change the price of good 1 from 2 to 3 in the *OptimalChoice* sheet of the Engel-Curves.xls workbook. From $m = 100$, use the Comparative Statics Wizard to create a graph of the Engel Curve for good 1. Title the graph and label the axes. Take a picture of your graph and paste it in your Word document.
2. Why is the slope of your graph different from the one in the *CS1* sheet?
3. Compute the income elasticity of demand for good 1 from $m = 100$ to 200. Show your work.
4. Compute the income elasticity of demand for good 1 at $m = 100$. Show your work.
5. Why are your answers in question 3 and 4 the same?

References

The epigraph is from H. S. Houthakker, "Engel's Law," in J. Eatwell, M. Milgate, and P. Newman (eds.), *The New Palgrave Dictionary of Economics* (London: McMillan, 1987), pp. 143–144.

The *Palgrave* is really much more than a simple dictionary. It is a reference resource with articles on specific terms or phrases. The 2008 version of the *Palgrave Dictionary* is edited by Stephen N. Durlauf and Lawrence E. Blume. It is available online at <www.dictionaryofeconomics.com>.

1.4.2

More Practice with Engel Curves

I shall also argue that the most secure propositions and the most reliable predictions, even though they are conditional predictions, arise out of comparative statics, and that when we are asked the awkward question "what good is economics to anyone," apart from its usefulness in providing a gainful occupation for economists, the defense rests mainly on the achievements of rather old-fashioned comparative statics.

Kenneth E. Boulding

This chapter derives Engel Curves via numerical and analytical methods for various utility functions. It applies the same logic as the previous chapter.

Comparative Statics Analysis of Changing Income
with Quasilinear Preferences

This example uses a quasilinear utility function, $U = x_1^{1/2} + x_2$. The budget constraint is $140 = 2x_1 + 10x_2$.

We begin with the analytical approach.

Rewrite the constraint and form the Lagrangean, leaving m as a letter:

$$\max_{x_1, x_2, \lambda} L = x_1^{1/2} + x_2 + \lambda(m - 2x_1 - 10x_2)$$

Take derivatives with respect to each choice variable and set equal to zero:

$$\frac{\partial L}{\partial x_1} = \frac{1}{2}x_1^{-1/2} - 2\lambda = 0$$

$$\frac{\partial L}{\partial x_2} = 1 - 10\lambda = 0$$

$$\frac{\partial L}{\partial \lambda} = m - 2x_1 - 10x_2 = 0$$

Solve for the optimal values of x_1 and x_2. Move the λ terms over and divide equations.

$$\frac{1}{2}x_1^{-1/2} = 2\lambda$$

$$1 = 10\lambda$$

$$\frac{\frac{1}{2}x_1^{-1/2}}{1} = \frac{2\lambda}{10\lambda}$$

$$\frac{\frac{1}{2}x_1^{-1/2}}{1} = \frac{2}{10}$$

Notice that the MRS is a function of x_1 alone. This is a property of the quasilinear utility function. We can solve for x_1^* from the MRS equals the price ratio equation.

$$\frac{\frac{1}{2}x_1^{-1/2}}{1} = \frac{2}{10}$$

$$\left[x_1^{-1/2}\right]^{-2} = \left[\frac{4}{10}\right]^{-2}$$

$$x_1^* = 6.25$$

Next, we plug this value into the third first-order condition and solve for x_2^*.

$$m - 2[6.25] - 10x_2 = 0$$

$$10x_2 = m - 12.5$$

$$x_2^* = \frac{1}{10}m - 1.25$$

To compute an own units response in x_1^* given a change in income, we can simply take the derivative with respect to m, which is zero (because m does not appear in the reduced form). Thus, increases in income leave optimal consumption of good 1 unchanged. In other words, the Engel Curve for good 1 is horizontal at 6.25.

The own units response for x_2^* is $\frac{dx_2^*}{dm} = \frac{1}{10}$. This means that an additional dollar in income leads to a 1/10 increase in good 1.

The elasticity at a given value of m can be computed via the following formula:

$$\frac{dx_1^*}{dm} \cdot \frac{m}{x_1^*}$$

At $m = 50$, the income elasticity of $x_1^* = (0)(140/6.25) = 0$, which is perfectly inelastic. This means that changes in m have no effect at all on x_1^*.

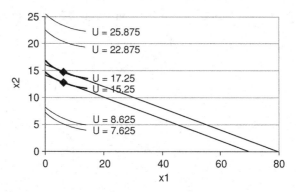

Figure 1.4.2.1. Income shock with quasilinear preferences.

These results seem a little strange. Perhaps the numerical approach can shed some light on what's going on here.

Step Open the Excel workbook EngelCurvesPractice.xls and read the *Intro* sheet, then go to the *QuasilinearChoice* sheet. Change income to 160. As expected, the budget line shifts out.

Step Run Solver to find the new initial solution. The resulting chart looks like Figure 1.4.2.1.

Figure 1.4.2.1 and your screen show that the value of x_1^* remained unchanged as income rose from $140 to $160. This consumer maximizes utility by using all of the extra $20 in income on good 2.

Figure 1.4.2.1 also displays a key property of the quasilinear functional form: the indifference curves are vertically shifted and actually parallel to each other. Thus, when we increase income, the new point of tangency is found directly, vertically up from the original solution.

Step Return income to its initial value of $140. Run the Comparative Statics Wizard, applying five shocks to income in $10 increments.

Your results should look like the *CS1* sheet.

Step Create Engel and Income Consumption Curves. For the Engel Curves, this requires making a chart of x_1^* as a function of m and another chart of x_2^* as a function of m. For the Income Consumption Curve, the chart is x_2^* as a function of x_1^*. Each point on this chart is a point of tangency between the budget line and maximum attainable indifference curve.

Your first attempt at making a chart of x_1^* as a function of m will not yield a horizontal line at 25. Look closely, however, at the y axis scale. The problem is that Solver is reporting numbers very close to, but not exactly, 25 as income changes.

We need to clean up Solver's results. Simply changing the display to fewer decimals will not work. Instead, we have to use Excel's Round function.
From Excel's Help:

ROUND
Rounds a number to a specified number of digits.
Syntax
ROUND(number,num_digits)
   Number is the number you want to round.
   Num_digits specifies the number of digits to which you want to round number.

Step Apply Excel's Round function to your results and then make a chart of the Engel Curve for good 1 using the rounded data. Your final chart should look like the one in the *CS1* sheet.

Step Compute the response to the income changes in own units and income elasticities for x_1^* and x_2^*. Check your work by looking in the *CS1* sheet.

Notice that the results from the numerical method are the same as those via the analytical approach.

Comparative Statics Analysis of Changing Income with Perfect Complements

Step Proceed to the *PerfCompChoice* sheet to practice on another utility function. This utility function reflects preferences in which the two goods are perfect complements.

The problem is to maximize the perfect complements utility function subject to the budget constraint.
The *PerfCompChoice* sheet shows that $p_1 = 2$, $p_2 = 10$, $a = 1$, and $b = 1$. Income remains a letter, m, so we can find $x_1^* = f(m)$ and $x_2^* = f(m)$.
Chapter 1.3.2 showed how to solve this problem. Calculus cannot be used here because the utility function is discontinuous at the corner of the L-shaped indifference curves.
However, because we know the optimal solution must be at a corner, the equation of the optimal solution line must be $x_2 = x_1$. This holds only when $a = b$. If these parameters are not equal, then the optimal solution line would have a different slope, but it would still be a ray out of the origin.
We can combine the equation of the optimal solution line with the budget constraint to find the optimal solution. The two equation, two unknown system can be easily solved by substitution.

$$\left.\begin{array}{l} x_2 = x_1 \\ m = 2x_1 + 10x_2 \end{array}\right\} \Rightarrow m = 2x_1 + 10\,[x_1] \Rightarrow m = 12x_1 \Rightarrow x_1^* = \frac{m}{12}.$$

Of course, we know $x_2 = x_1$ so $x_2^* = \frac{m}{12}$.

To compute an own units response in x_1^* given a change in income, we can take the derivative of x_1^* with respect to m, which is simply $1/12$. This slope is constant and the Engel Curve is linear.

The elasticity at a given value of m can be computed via the following formula:

$$\frac{dx_1^*}{dm} \cdot \frac{m}{x_1^*}$$

At $m = 50$, the income elasticity of $x_1^* = (1/12)(50/4.167) = 1$. This means that a 1% change in m will result in a 1% change in x_1^*.

Step Run the Comparative Statics Wizard on the *PerfCompChoice* sheet (you can make the change in income $10) and create Engel and Income Consumption Curves.

Step Compute the response to the income changes in own units and income elasticities for x_1^* and x_2^*.

Step Check your work with the *CS2* sheet.

As before, the results in Excel are the same as the analytical approach.

The Utility Function Determines the Shape of the Engel Curve

This chapter ran a comparative statics analysis of a change in income on quasilinear and perfect complement utility functions. This enabled practice in deriving Engel Curves and Income Consumption Curves.

The quasilinear function has the peculiar result that the income elasticity of x_1^* is zero. This results from the fact that the indifference map of a quasilinear utility function is a series of vertically parallel curves. Thus, when the budget line shifts out, the new optimal solution is found directly above the initial solution and x_1^* remains unchanged.

With the perfect complements utility function, we were able to find an analytical solution even though we could not use the Lagrangean method. The Engel Curve for x_1^* has a constant slope and a unit income elasticity. This Engel Curve is similar to the one found in the previous chapter by using the Cobb-Douglas functional form.

The shape of the Engel Curve, its slope, and income elasticity are all influenced by the consumer's utility function. Ernst Engel's original interest lay in the consumption of food as income rose. He believed food purchases would increase at a decreasing rate as income increased, as shown in Figure 1.4.2.2.

None of three utility functions we have encountered thus far (Cobb-Douglas, quasilinear, and perfect complements) is capable of generating an

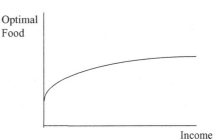

Figure 1.4.2.2. Engel's Law: Food purchases increase at a decreasing rate as income rises.

Engel Curve that conforms to Engel's Law for food purchases. If we were interested in food, we would have to find and use a utility function that was able to produce an Engel Curve that conformed to Engel's Law. Such functions exist, but as you can imagine, they are more complicated than the computationally easy functions used thus far.

Exercises

Open Word and answer the following questions. Save the document and print it when you are done.

1. In the *QuasilinearChoice* sheet, copy cell B11 and paste it in cell C11. Set income to $200 and run Solver to find the new optimal solution. In cell D11, enter a formula to find the difference between cell C11 and B11. Is this tiny difference meaningful? Explain.
2. Having changed income and run Solver in question 1, if you connected the initial and new solutions on the chart, you would get a vertical line. Why is this happening? Will this happen with every consumer?
3. Having changed income and run Solver in question 1, is good 1 a normal or an inferior good? Explain.
4. Use Word's Equation Editor to solve the general version of the perfect complements problem. In other words, find x_1^* and x_2^* for

$$\max_{x_1,x_2} U = \min\{ax_1, bx_2\}$$

$$\text{s.t.} m = p_1 x_1 + p_2 x_2$$

References

The epigraph is from pages 487 and 488 of Kenneth E. Boulding, "In Defense of Statics," *The Quarterly Journal of Economics*, Vol. 69, No. 4 (November, 1955), pp. 485–502. As you can tell from the quotation, Boulding had a well-deserved reputation for witty, biting comments. His defense of comparative statics in the article just cited notwithstanding, he once quipped, "Mathematics brought rigor to Economics. Unfortunately, it also brought mortis."

1.4.3

Deriving an Individual Consumer's
Demand Curve

The first "empirical" demand schedule was published in 1699 by Charles Davenant.

George J. Stigler

In previous chapters, we have seen how to find the initial optimal solution in the Theory of Consumer Behavior and we have explored the comparative statics properties of a change in income.

We are well prepared for the most important comparative statics analysis in the Theory of Consumer Behavior: deriving a demand curve.

Numerical Comparative Statics Analysis of Changing Price

Step Open the Excel workbook DemandCurves.xls and read the *Intro* sheet, then go to the *OptimalChoice* sheet. The problem is set up, but the consumer is not optimizing because the MRS does not equal the price ratio and the consumer can move to higher indifference curves by traveling up the constraint. Run Solver to find the initial solution: $x_1^* = 25$ and $x_2^* = 16.67$.

Next, we explore how the optimal solution changes as the price of good 1 changes, ceteris paribus.

Step Shock: Change cell B16 to 3.

Figure 1.4.3.1 shows how your screen should look. With a higher p_1, the budget constraint rotates in, pivoting on the x_2 intercept. The consumer now has fewer consumption possibilities and needs to re-optimize to find the new optimal solution.

Step New: Run Solver to find the new optimal solution.

Step Compare: Compare the initial and new values of x_1^* and x_2^* given the $1 increase in price. Figure 1.4.3.2 displays the comparative statics results in a table.

In qualitative terms, we can say that x_1^* fell as its price rose and x_2^* did not change as good 1's price rose.

110

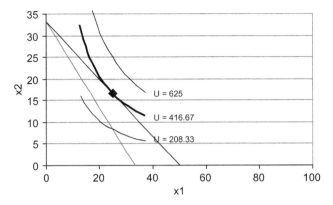

Figure 1.4.3.1. New budget line when p_1 rises.

Quantitatively, we can compute the own units change in x_1^*, the slope $(\Delta x_1^*/\Delta p_1)$, as $25 - 16\frac{2}{3}$ divided by 1, or $-8\frac{1}{3}$.

The price elasticity of x_1^* ($\%\Delta x_1^*/\%\Delta p_1$) from $p_1 = 2$ to 3 is the percentage change in x_1^*, -33%, divided by the percentage change in p_1, 50%, or -0.67.

The same calculations can be performed on x_2^*. The effect of p_1 on x_2^* is called a cross price analysis because we are exploring how the price of one good affects another good's demand.

Comparative statics via numerical methods is easier with the Comparative Statics Wizard (CSWiz) add-in.

If this add-in is unavailable under the Add-ins tab (or, in earlier versions of Excel, Tools: Wizard menu), click the Office button, then Excel Options, and then the Add-ins tab to see which add-ins are installed. (You can accomplish the same thing in earlier versions of Excel by executing Tools: Add-Ins to bring up the Excel Add-In Manager.) If the Comparative Statics Wizard is unchecked, check it and click OK. If it is unlisted, click Browse and navigate to where it is located. See CompStatics.doc in the SolverCompStaticsWizard folder for more detailed instructions.

Step Analyze the effect of a change in p_1 by running the CSWiz and changing the price of good 1 by \$1 increments (for five shocks).

Step The *demand curve* is simply a graph of x_1^* as a function of p_1. Use your results in the *CS* sheet to create such a chart.

p_1	x_1^*	x_2^*	$\Delta x_1^*/\Delta p_1$	$\%\Delta x_1^*/\%\Delta p_1$	$\Delta x_2^*/\Delta p_1$	$\%\Delta x_2^*/\%\Delta p_1$
2	25	$16\frac{2}{3}$				
3	$16\frac{2}{3}$	$16\frac{2}{3}$	$-8\frac{1}{3}$	-0.67	0	0

Figure 1.4.3.2. Comparative statics results of an increase in p_1.

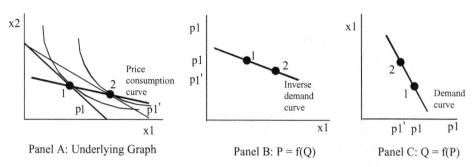

Panel A: Underlying Graph   Panel B: P = f(Q)   Panel C: Q = f(P)

Figure 1.4.3.3. Displaying comparative statics results.

Another way to display the comparative statics results is via the *price consumption (or offer) curve*, as shown in Panel A of Figure 1.4.3.3 for a utility function that is not Cobb-Douglas and not meant to display the increasing price analysis that you just completed. Instead, a price decrease is shown.

Figure 1.4.3.3 shows a price decrease on the graph on the left and plots the corresponding price and optimal quantity values in the graphs on the right. Notice that the axes are switched in the two graphs on the right. Instead of graphing x_1^* as a function of p_1, the exogenous variable (p_1) is on the y axis in the conventional demand curve. This is a backwards but common presentation in economics. The roots of this strange way of presenting the results can be traced back in the history of economics to Alfred Marshall in 1890 and even further.

Modern economists call the graph in Panel B of Figure 1.4.3.3 an *inverse demand curve* because it is $P = f(Q)$. The *demand curve*, the mathematically correct version, is $Q = f(P)$.

When communicating to introductory economics students or non-economists, the inverse demand curve is usually used. As the level of sophistication rises, especially if we are doing empirical work, we use the demand curve. Economists are used to flipping the axes back and forth. It is confusing at first, but you can get the hang of it pretty quickly.

Step Use your comparative statics results to create a *price consumption curve*. To do this, you need to create a chart of x_2^* as a function of x_1^*. This gives the points of tangency between budget lines and highest attainable indifference curves. You will have to use the Round function to correctly plot the price consumption curve. You can check your work by comparing your results to the *CS1* sheet.

Notice that the price consumption curve for changes in p_1 in the Excel workbook is horizontal. This is a property of the Cobb-Douglas utility function and is not especially realistic. This is how we know that the indifference map in Figure 1.4.3.3 is not based on a Cobb-Douglas utility function.

Step Cross price analysis: Explore the effect of changing p_1 on x_2^*. Draw a graph of the cross price relationship. Check the *CS1* sheet to confirm that your chart is correct.

Analytical Comparative Statics Analysis of Changing Price

Rewrite the constraint and form the Lagrangean, leaving all exogenous variables as letters:

$$\max_{x_1, x_2, \lambda} L = x_1^c x_2^d + \lambda(m - p_1 x_1 - p_2 x_2)$$

This is the *general* form of the problem (with a Cobb-Douglas utility function). Although it seems more formidable than when numbers are used in place of letters, we can apply the usual strategies for taking derivatives and solving the first-order conditions to find the optimal solution.

Take derivatives with respect to each choice variable and set equal to zero:

$$\frac{\partial L}{\partial x_1} = c x_1^{c-1} x_2^d - p_1 \lambda = 0$$

$$\frac{\partial L}{\partial x_2} = d x_1^c x_2^{d-1} - p_2 \lambda = 0$$

$$\frac{\partial L}{\partial \lambda} = m - p_1 x_1 - p_2 x_2 = 0$$

Solve for the optimal values of x_1 and x_2. Moving the lambda terms to the right-hand side and dividing the first equation by the second gets rid of lambda (and gives the familiar $MRS = p_1/p_2$ condition), which can then be solved for optimal x_2 as a function of optimal x_1:

$$\frac{c x_2^*}{d x_1^*} = \frac{p_1}{p_2}$$

$$x_2^* = \frac{d}{c} \frac{p_1}{p_2} x_1^*$$

Substitute this expression for x_2^* into the third first-order condition and solve for x_1^*:

$$m - p_1 x_1^* - p_2 \left[\frac{d}{c} \frac{p_1}{p_2} x_1^* \right] = 0$$

$$\left(1 + \frac{d}{c} \right) p_1 x_1^* = m$$

$$x_1^* = \left(\frac{c}{c+d} \right) \frac{m}{p_1}$$

Exogenous Shock Variable	Optimal Objective Function	Optimal Endogenous Variable	Optimal Endogenous Variable		Own Units	Elasticity		Own Units	Elasticity
OptimalChoice!p1_	OptimalChoice!Utility	OptimalChoice!x1_	OptimalChoice!x2_	x2 Rounded	$\Delta x1^*/\Delta P1$	$\% \Delta x1^*/\% \Delta P1$		dx1*/dP1	(dx1*/dP1)(P1/x1*)
2	416.6667	25	16.66667	16.667				-12.5	-1
2.1	396.8254	23.80952	16.66667	16.667	-11.90475792	-0.952380634		-11.33786848	-1
2.2	378.7879	22.72727	16.66667	16.667	-10.8225172	-0.954546001		-10.33057851	-1
2.3	362.3188	21.73913	16.66667	16.667	-9.881417087	-0.956521184		-9.451795841	-1
2.4	347.2222	20.83333	16.66667	16.667	-9.057977236	-0.958333976		-8.680555556	-1
2.5	333.3333	20	16.66667	16.667	-8.333333506	-0.960000033		-8	-1

Figure 1.4.3.4. Comparing two approaches to comparative statics.
Source: DemandCurves.xls!CS1

This expression is a demand curve for x_1. It shows the quantity demanded at a given p_1.

Furthermore, this expression can be evaluated for any combination of exogenous variable values. For example, suppose $c = d = 1$, $p_1 = 2$, and $m = 100$. Then it can be seen easily that optimal $x_1 = 25$. This agrees perfectly with the numerical approach using the Comparative Statics Wizard to recalculate the optimal solution at given values of p_1.

To compute an own units response in x_1^* given a change in price, we can take the derivative with respect to p_1:

$$x_1^* = \left(\frac{c}{c+d}\right)\frac{m}{p_1}$$

$$x_1^* = \left(\frac{c}{c+d}\right)m(p_1)^{-1}$$

$$\frac{dx_1^*}{dp_1} = -1\left(\frac{c}{c+d}\right)m(p_1)^{-2}$$

This expression shows that the slope is not a constant, but a function of p_1.

This formidable-looking expression is the instantaneous rate of change of the demand curve at a particular point. Because x_1^* is a nonlinear function of p_1, the rate of change computed via the derivative will be different from that computed via $\Delta x_1/\Delta p_1$.

Figure 1.4.3.4 displays a portion of the *CS1* sheet, which compares the discrete (Δ) and infinitesimally small (d) approaches to the change in p_1.

The own price elasticity can be computed via the following formula:

$$\frac{dx_1^*}{dp_1}\cdot\frac{p_1}{x_1^*} = -1\left(\frac{c}{c+d}\right)m(p_1)^{-2}\frac{p_1}{\left(\frac{c}{c+d}\right)\frac{m}{p_1}}$$

$$\frac{dx_1^*}{dp_1}\cdot\frac{p_1}{x_1^*} = -1$$

Thus, the own price elasticity of $x_1^* = -1$ and it is constant. This is a property of the Cobb-Douglas utility function and is not especially realistic.

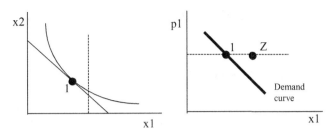

Figure 1.4.3.5. Interpreting a point off the (inverse) demand curve.

Cobb-Douglas is used so often because it is easy to work with, not because it is realistic.

Notice by comparing the two elasticity columns in Figure 1.4.3.4 that the numerical and analytical methods are giving different numbers for the slope and elasticity. The fact that the demand curve under consideration here is a curve, not a line, drives this result.

The numerical method is computing the slope and elasticity as a change *from* two distinct points on the curve while the analytical method is using a slope *at* a single point (based on the slope of the tangent line at that point).

Step You can confirm that the numerical method converges to the analytical method as the discrete change gets smaller by computing slopes and elasticities for your comparative statics results. Because you used $1 changes in p_1 and the *CS1* sheet used smaller, 10 cent changes, you will see that your slope and elasticity results are farther from the analytical method values.

A Point Off the Demand Curve?

If we consider what it means to be at a point off the demand curve, such as point Z in Figure 1.4.3.5, it helps us understand that the demand curve is really like a ridge line across the top of a mountain range.

With a point Z to the right of the demand curve, we know that the consumer is buying too much Z, as shown by the vertical dashed line in the graph on the left of Figure 1.4.3.5. We cannot precisely plot the point Z on the indifference curve graph because we do not know how much good 2 the person is buying at point Z. We do know, however, that she is not optimizing. In other words, at point Z, this consumer is failing to maximize satisfaction and is not on the tangency of the budget line and highest attainable indifference curve.

This means that a demand curve is a geometrical object with a special characteristic – every point on the demand curve is a point of maximum utility given prices and income. If we added an axis for utility, the demand curve would show itself as a 3D object that displayed the maximum utility at each given price.

A Demand Curve Is a Comparative Statics Exercise

Deriving a demand curve is the most important comparative statics analysis in the Theory of Consumer Behavior. Demand and supply (the most important comparative statics analysis in the Theory of the Firm) are at the heart of the market mechanism.

Demand curves can be derived via numerical methods, giving particular points on the demand curve for explicit values of price, ceteris paribus. Slopes and elasticities can be computed.

Demand curves can also be derived via analytical methods by finding the reduced-form expression as a function of price. Slopes and elasticities can be computed by using the derivative.

In the case of a Cobb-Douglas utility function, the numerical and analytical methods yield different values for slopes and elasticities because the demand curve is a curve, instead of a line. The smaller the discrete change used in the numerical method, the closer it gets to the analytical result.

Exercises

Open Word and answer the following questions. Save the document and print it when you are done.

1. In the *OptimalChoice* sheet, click the Reset button and reproduce Figure 1.4.3.2 with a decrease (instead of an increase) in p_1 from \$2/unit to \$1/unit. Use Word's Table feature to create the table and fill in the cells.
2. Use Word's Drawing Tools to create a graph of the Price Consumption Curve and Demand Curve for x_1 (as in Figure 1.4.3.3) that accurately reflects the shock and results from question 1.
3. What is the difference between a demand curve and an inverse demand curve?

References

The epigraph is from page 103 of George J. Stigler, "The Early History of Empirical Studies of Consumer Behavior," *The Journal of Political Economy*, Vol. 62, No. 2 (April, 1954), pp. 95–113.

Most economists do not care who first came up with the concept of a demand schedule. Most of those who do care believe that it was Gregory King, a century after Charles Davenant. Stigler was a winner of the Nobel Prize in Economics and a professor at the University of Chicago. He had a lifelong passion for the intellectual history of economics. In this article, he showed that Davenant actually preceded King.

It took a long time to translate demand (and supply) schedules as tables (with columns for price and quantity) into graphs. Although there were precursors,

Alfred Marshall's *Principles of Economics* (1890) is credited with introducing supply and demand graphs to English-speaking economists. These graphs appeared, however, only in footnotes.

Marshall's *Principles* was the most popular economics book of its era. It is freely available online at <www.econlib.org/library/Marshall/marP.html>.

Marshall put price on the vertical axis because he wanted to show market demand and supply curves on a graph as the horizontal sum of individual demand and supply curves, as in footnote 70 from Book III, Chapter IV. Future generations of introductory economics students became locked in to the Marshallian inverse demand and supply curves.

Although you may conclude that Marshall's violation of accepted mathematical convention (i.e., independent variables belong on the x axis) is confusing, the decision was not based on ignorance. In fact, Marshall was a brilliant mathematician, earning Second Wrangler (to the future Lord Rayleigh) as an undergraduate at Cambridge in the Tripos competition.

To understand how the role of mathematics has changed in economics, consider the recipe Marshall gave a friend for using math in economics: "1) Use mathematics as a shorthand language, rather than as an engine of inquiry. 2) Keep to them till you have done. 3) Translate into English. 4) Then illustrate by examples that are important in real life. 5) Burn the mathematics. 6) If you can't succeed in 4 burn 3. This last I did often" (from A. C. Pigou, *Memorials of Alfred Marshall*, 1925, p. 427).

1.4.4

More Practice Deriving Demand Curves

Quasilinear utility functions are not particularly realistic, but they are very easy to work with.

Hal Varian

This chapter derives the demand curve from two different utility functions, quasilinear preferences and perfect complements, to provide practice deriving demand curves.

Comparative Statics Analysis of Changing Price with Quasilinear Preferences

We begin with the analytical approach.

Rewrite the constraint and form the Lagrangean, leaving p_1 as a letter:

$$\max_{x_1, x_2, \lambda} L = x_1^{1/2} + x_2 + \lambda(140 - p_1 x_1 - 10 x_2)$$

Take derivatives and solve the system of equations for the optimal values of goods 1 and 2:

$$x_1^* = \frac{25}{p_1^2}$$

$$x_2^* = 14 - \frac{2.5}{p_1}$$

Step If needed, revisit Chapter 1.3.2 to see the steps involved in finding the optimal solution for the quasilinear utility function.

The first expression, $x_1^* = \frac{25}{p_1^2}$, is the demand curve for x_1^*. It tells us the optimal amount of x_1^* for a given price of good 1. If we rewrite the equation in terms of $P = f(Q)$ like this, $p_1^2 = \frac{25}{x_1^*} \Rightarrow p_1 = \frac{5}{\sqrt{x_1^*}}$, then we have the inverse demand curve, with price on the y axis and quantity on the x axis.

The derivative of x_1^* with respect to p_1 tells us the slope of the demand curve at a given price.

$$x_1^* = 25p_1^{-2}$$

$$\frac{dx_1^*}{dp_1} = -2 \cdot 25p_1^{-3} = -\frac{50}{p_1^3}$$

The own price elasticity of demand is

$$\frac{dx_1^*}{dp_1} \cdot \frac{p_1}{x_1^*} = -\frac{50}{p_1^3} \frac{p_1}{\frac{25}{p_1^2}} = -2$$

The constant elasticity of demand for good 1 is a property of the quasilinear utility function. Notice that 2 is the reciprocal of $\frac{1}{2}$ (the exponent on x_1 in the utility function). In fact, with $U = x_1^c + x_2$, the price elasticity of demand for x_1 is $-\frac{1}{1-c}$ for values of c that yield interior solutions.

The expression for optimal x_2 is a cross price relationship. It tells us how the quantity demanded for good 2 varies as the price of good 1 changes. The equation can be used to compute a cross price elasticity, like this:

$$\frac{dx_2^*}{dp_1} \cdot \frac{p_1}{x_2^*} = \frac{2.5}{p_1^2} \frac{p_1}{14 - \frac{2.5}{p_1}} = \frac{2.5}{p_1\left(14 - \frac{2.5}{p_1}\right)} = \frac{2.5}{p_1\left(\frac{14p_1 - 2.5}{p_1}\right)} = \frac{2.5}{14p_1 - 2.5}.$$

Unlike the own price elasticity, the cross price elasticity is not constant – it depends on the value of p_1. It is also positive (whereas the own price elasticity was negative). When p_1 rises, optimal x_2 also rises. This means that goods 1 and 2 are substitutes.

Demand can also be derived via numerical methods.

Step Open the Excel workbook DemandCurvesPractice.xls and read the *Intro* sheet, then go to the *QuasilinearChoice* sheet.

The consumer is maximizing satisfaction at the initial parameter values because the marginal condition, $MRS = p_1/p_2$, is met at the point 6.25,12.75 (ignoring Solver's precision errors) and income is exhausted.

We can explore how this initial optimal solution varies as the price of good 1 changes via numerical methods. We simply change p_1 repeatedly, running Solver at each price, while keeping track of the optimal solution at each price. The Comparative Statics Wizard add-in handles the tedious, cumbersome calculations.

Step Run the Comparative Statics Wizard on the *QuasilinearChoice* sheet in DemandCurvesPractice.xls. Increase the price of good 1 by 0.1 (10 cent) increments.

You can qualitatively check your analysis by comparing your results to the *CS1* sheet, which is based on 1 (instead of 0.1) dollar size shocks.

The columns of price and optimal x_1 are points on the demand schedule. The CSWiz approach essentially picks individual points on the demand curve. If you plot these points, you have a graph of the demand curve.

The analytical approach gives the demand function as an equation. You can evaluate the expression at particular prices and generate a plot of the demand curve.

The two approaches, if done correctly, will always yield the same graphical depiction of the demand curve. They may not, however, yield the same slopes or elasticities.

Step Using your results, create Demand and Price Consumption Curves. Compute the own unit changes and elasticities for x_1^* and x_2^*. The *CS1* sheet shows how to do this if you get stuck.

Notice that your own unit changes and elasticities are closer to the instantaneous rates of change in columns I and J of the *CS1* sheet because you have smaller changes in p_1.

Take a moment to reflect on what is going in the calculations presented in the *CS1* sheet. The color-shaded cells invite you to compare those cells.

Step Click on cell F13 to see its formula.

It is computed as the change in optimal x_1 for a \$1 increase in p_1. There is a decrease of about 3.47 units when price increases by 1 unit.

Step Click on cell I12 to see its formula.

It is computed by substituting the initial price, \$2/unit, into the expression for the derivative (displayed as an equation above the cell). The result of the formula, -6.25, is the instantaneous rate of change. In other words, there will be a 6.25-fold decrease in optimal x_1 given an infinitesimally small increase in p_1.

Step Go to your *CSWiz* sheet and compute the change in optimal x_1 for a \$0.1 increase in p_1.

You should find that your slope is about -5.8. The change in optimal x_1 is about 0.58, but you have to divide by the change in price, 0.1, to get the slope. Notice that your answer is much closer to the derivative-based rate of change (-6.25). This is because you took a much smaller change in price, 0.1, than the change in price in the *CS1* sheet and you are working with a curve.

Step Return to the *CS1* sheet and compare cells G13 and J12.

The same principle is at work here. Because the demand curve is non-linear, the two cells do not agree. Cell G13 is computing the elasticity from one point to another, whereas cell J12 is using the instantaneous rate of change (slope of the tangent line) at a point.

If you compute the price elasticity from 2 to 2.1 (using your CS results), you will find that it is much closer to -2.

Finally, you might notice that unlike the Cobb-Douglas utility function, which produced a horizontal price consumption curve (PCC), the quasilinear utility function in this case is generating a downward sloping price consumption curve. In fact, the slope of the price consumption curve tells you the price elasticity of demand: Upward sloping PCC means that demand is inelastic, horizontal PCC yields a unit elastic demand (as in the Cobb-Douglas case), and downward sloping PCC gives elastic demand (as in this case).

Comparative Statics Analysis of Changing Price with Perfect Complements

We begin with the analytical approach.

$$u(x_1, x_2) = \min\{ax_1, bx_2\}$$

For $a = b = 1$, we have seen in earlier chapters (see 1.3.2) that we can find the intersection of the optimal choice and budget lines to find the reduced-form expressions for the endogenous variables, $x_1^* = m/(p_1 + p_2)$ – and, of course, given that the consumer buys the same amount of good 2, $x_2^* = m/(p_1 + p_2)$.

The solution says that when a and b are the same in a perfect complements utility function, the optimal amounts of each good are equal and found by simply dividing income by the sum of the prices.

The optimal solutions are the demand curves for x_1^* and x_2^*. Consider the expression for x_1^*; it tells us the quantity demanded of x_1^* when the price of good 1 changes, ceteris paribus.

As usual, we can find the instantaneous rate of change by taking the derivative with respect to p_1 and the elasticity by multiplying the derivative by p_1/x_1^*.

$$\frac{dx_1^{x^*}}{dp_1} = -\frac{m}{(p_1 + p_2)^2}$$

$$\frac{dx_1^{x^*}}{dp_1} \cdot \frac{p_1}{x_1^{x^*}} = -\frac{m}{(p_1 + p_2)^2} \frac{p_1}{\dfrac{m}{p_1 + p_2}} = -\frac{p_1}{p_1 + p_2}$$

We can also derive demand for a perfect complements utility function via numerical methods.

Step Proceed to the *PerfCompChoice* sheet in DemandCurvesPractice .xls.

Step Run the Comparative Statics Wizard from the *PerfCompChoice* sheet. As before, increase the price of good 1 by 0.1 (10 cent) increments.

Create demand and price consumption curves. Compute the own units changes and elasticities for x_1^* and x_2^*. The *CS2* sheet shows how to do this if you get stuck.

Notice that your own units changes and elasticities are closer to the instantaneous rates of change in columns I and J of the *CS2* sheet because you have smaller changes in p_1.

Notice also that the price consumption curve is upward sloping and the price elasticity is less than one (in absolute value).

Whenever the demand curve is nonlinear, that is, x_1^* is a nonlinear function of price, the analytical, derivative-based and numerical, finite-size change methods of computing slope and elasticities will not agree. As the size of the change in price gets smaller, the numerical method result will approach the result based on the derivative.

Deriving Demand from the Consumer's Utility Maximization Problem

This chapter did not present anything new, except that the slope of the price consumption curve reveals the price elasticity of demand.

The primary purpose of this chapter was to provide additional practice in deriving demand with different utility functions. Clearly, the demand curve is strongly influenced by the utility function that is being maximized given a budget constraint.

In addition, the two examples were used to demonstrate how the analytical and numerical methods are related. Calculus is based on the idea of infinitesimally small changes. You can see calculus in action by using the CSWiz to take smaller changes in price – which drives the numerical method ever closer to the derivative-based result.

Exercises

Open Word and answer the following questions. Save the document and print it when you are done.

1. Return to the *QuasilinearChoice* sheet and click the Reset button. Now change the exponent on good 1 from 0.5 to 0.75. Use the Comparative Statics Wizard to derive a demand curve for this utility function.
2. Working with the same utility function as in the first question, derive the demand curve for x_1^* via analytical methods. Use Word's Equation Editor as needed. Show your work.

3. Use your results from questions 1 and 2, compute the own price elasticity via numerical and analytical methods. Do they agree? Why or why not? Show your work and take screen shots as needed.

References

The epigraph is from page 63 of Hal Varian's best-selling, undergraduate textbook, *Intermediate Microeconomics* (7th edition, 2006). In the preface, Varian tackles head on the issue of calculus. "Many undergraduate majors in economics are students who *should* know calculus, but don't – at least not very well. For this reason, I have kept calculus out of the main body of the text."

The book you are reading at this moment takes a different approach. Calculus is used extensively, but it is made accessible by consistent repetition along with the substantial support of numerical methods. If you are a student who struggles with analytical methods, you will never have a better opportunity to master calculus and algebra. Do the practice problems with care and match the analytical and numerical approaches in each application.

1.4.5

Giffen Goods

To my knowledge, no one has described heroin as a Giffen good. But the description may be appropriate for those users who are addicted.

Neal Kumar Katyal

Demand curves are derived by doing comparative statics on the consumer's optimization problem: Change price, ceteris paribus, and track optimal consumption of a good.

Usually, as every introductory economics student knows, demand is downward sloping so that as price rises, ceteris paribus, quantity demanded falls. Economists have long been intrigued, however, by a weird possibility: quantity demanded rising as price rises. An upward sloping demand curve!

Giffen goods are goods that have upward sloping demand curves.

The Theory of Consumer Behavior can easily handle such a case. We begin with a little history.

The Canonical Example: Robert Giffin and the Irish Potato Famine

The Great Irish Famine took place during 1845–1848.

To put the disaster in proper perspective, the famine killed at least 12 percent of the population over a three-year period. Another 6–8 percent migrated to other countries. In terms of the percentage of population affected, the 1845–48 famine is one of the largest ever recorded. Other famines have killed more people in total because the affected populations were larger, not the percentage of exposure. For instance, the 30 million or more people who perished in the Chinese famine of 1958–62 were 5 percent or 6 percent of the population. (Rosen, footnote 4, p. S303)

Why did so many people die? This is a difficult question to answer comprehensively. The proximate answer is that the Irish ate a *lot* of potatoes and a potato blight destroyed the food source. Rosen (p. S303) says this:

As difficult as it is to imagine today, on the eve of the famine, per capita consumption of potatoes is reliably estimated to have averaged 9 pounds (40–50 potatoes) per person per day (Bourke 1993). Diets were astonishingly concentrated on potatoes,

124

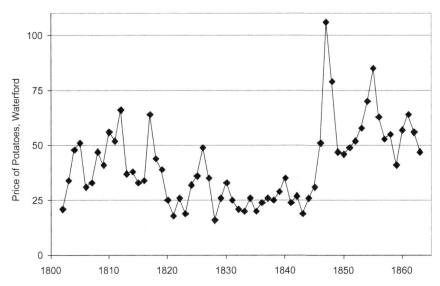

Figure 1.4.5.1. Potato price in Waterford, Ireland.
Source: GiffenGoods.xls!RosenChart

especially in rural areas. Grain was grown in rural Ireland but was either sent to towns or exported abroad.

Why didn't the Irish eat something else? This is harder to explain. Books have been written on the subject. The *Biblio* sheet in GiffenGoods.xls has references.

The story of the Giffen good picks up decades after the famine. Although there is no evidence that he ever said it (see Stigler, "Notes on the History of the Giffen Paradox" in the *Biblio* sheet), Sir Robert Giffen (1837–1910) is credited with using the behavior of potato prices and quantities to support the claim that quantity demanded rose as prices rose.

Figure 1.4.5.1 shows the behavior of potato prices.

Although consumption fell when price spiked in 1847 to more than double the 1846 price, somehow the legend grew that quantity demanded increased as prices rose in this time period. Thus, the Irish potato became the canonical example of a Giffen good – even though it was no such thing.

The question remains, however: Could a Giffen good exist?

Two Common Mistakes in Giffen Good Analysis

Before explaining how we could get a Giffen good, we need to clear up two mistakes in thinking about Giffen goods. Both mistakes involve violating the strict ceteris paribus requirement that underlies a demand curve. The first mistake has a long history in econometrics and the second is easily corrected once we remember that we must hold everything else constant.

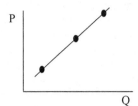

Q   Figure 1.4.5.2. Not a demand curve.

It is quite difficult to estimate demand from observed prices and quanti-ties. It turns out that plotting price and quantity data and fitting a line is no way to estimate a demand curve.

Suppose that the observed quantity of potatoes sold had increased as price rose over time. Would that have been a good way to support the Giffen good claim? Absolutely not.

The problem is that the price and quantity data in different time periods do not fulfill the ceteris paribus requirement. Price and quantity changed over time, but presumably so did other factors that affect demand and supply.

Figure 1.4.5.2 shows the mistaken approach of fitting a line to observed *P, Q* data. Each point represents the price and quantity sold each year. Price is rising, but so is quantity. Is this a Giffen good?

Figure 1.4.5.2 does show that price and output rose over time, but this does not mean we have a Giffen good. The observed pattern of price and quantity data is consistent with another story, displayed in Figure 1.4.5.3.

Figure 1.4.5.3 says that demand is actually downward sloping, as expected, but over time, increases in demand lead to higher observed price and quan-tity values.

Those who believe that a Giffen good exists whenever observed prices and quantities move together over time are making a fundamental error. They are forgetting that a demand curve requires that price change and everything else be held constant.

Estimating a demand curve in the real world is not easy because you can-not simply fit a line to a price–quantity scatterplot. You have to be very care-ful in making sure that while price and quantity vary, everything else remains constant. To correctly estimate a demand (or supply) curve, advanced methods – beyond the mere fitting of a line to observed price and quantity – are needed.

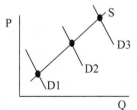

Q   Figure 1.4.5.3. Shifts in demand.

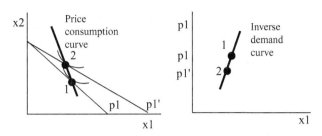

Figure 1.4.5.4. A Giffen good.

The second mistake is less easy to forgive. No complicated issues of estimation are involved. We simply forget that demand requires that the ceteris paribus condition hold. Suppose you notice that a particular brand of jeans has become increasingly popular and suddenly more people want it as its price rises. Have we discovered a Giffen good?

Absolutely not. Once again, we are forgetting about the crucial ceteris paribus part of the definition of a demand curve. In this case, the increased popularity of a particular brand is a shock to the demand curve, shifting it right. This is not a Giffen good because we are not working with a single, fixed demand curve. Instead, as in Figure 1.4.5.3, increases in demand are driving new equilibrium price–quantity combinations.

Having seen two common mistakes in trying to understand Giffen behavior, the natural question then is: Can Giffen goods, meeting the specific requirements of a demand function, exist?

The answer is yes.

Giffen Goods in Theory

Figure 1.4.5.4 shows a canonical graph of a Giffen good. Notice that the indifference curves require a little twisting to make x_1 be a Giffen good. Remember that they cannot cross, but in order for x_1 to be Giffen, point 2 has to lie to the left of point 1 so that the decrease in p_1 leads to a decrease in x_1^*.

Do not be confused. Quantity demanded fell, but so did price. Thus, we have a positive relationship between price and quantity demanded and an upward sloping demand curve. This is a Giffen good.

To be clear, it is not the fact that optimal x_1 decreased, but that it decreased as price fell. If we started at point 2 and raised the price, we would find that optimal x_1 rose. We would be traveling up the upward sloping demand curve.

Figure 1.4.5.4 is depicted in every microeconomics book that discusses Giffen goods. Let us turn to a concrete problem to help you really understand what Giffenness is all about.

Step Open the Excel workbook GiffenGoods.xls and read the *Intro* sheet, then go to the *Optimal1* sheet.

The sheet models a Giffen good. The utility function is admittedly quite complicated.

$$u(x_1, x_2) = \begin{cases} ax_1 - \dfrac{b}{2}x_1^2 + cx_2 + \dfrac{d}{2}x_2^2 & \text{for } 0 \le x_1 \le a/b \\ \dfrac{a^2}{2b} + cx_2 + \dfrac{d}{2}x_2^2 & \text{for } x_1 > a/b \end{cases}$$

Another example of a utility function that exhibits Giffen behavior is in the *Optimal2* sheet. We will work with the *Optimal1* sheet here and use the *Optimal2* sheet for Q&A work.

The *Optimal1* sheet opens with $x_1 = 44$ and $x_2 = 11$. Without running Solver, we know this is the optimal solution because the MRS equals the price ratio.

Step It is hard to see that the budget line is just touching the indifference curve, but if you click the Zoom in button, you will see that the tangency condition is clearly met.

Step Change p_1 to 1.1. What happens?

The budget line pivots around the y intercept. It may look like a parallel shift, but it really is not.

Step Click the Zoom Out button to see that the price increase has, in fact, rotated the budget line in.

The 44,11 initially optimal bundle is no longer affordable. The consumer must re-optimize.

Step Run Solver. What happens?

Figure 1.4.5.5 shows the result. Optimal consumption of good 2 has collapsed from 11 to around 1.5 and the consumer now wants to buy 48.6 units of good 1.

This is amazing. The price of good 1 went *up* by 10 cents (from 1 to 1.1) and the optimal amount of good 1 *increased* by 4.6 units (from 44 to 48.6).

This is a concrete example of a Giffen good.

We can use numerical methods to more carefully explore the demand curve resulting from this bizarre utility function.

Step Use the Comparative Statics Wizard to trace out the demand curve from 0.1 to 3. Set cell B16 to 0.1, then apply 300 shocks by increments of 0.01 with the CSWiz add-in. Finally, create a graph of p_1 as a function of x_1^*.

Your results should look like Figure 1.4.5.6.

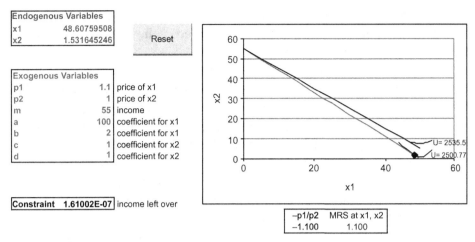

Endogenous Variables	
x1	48.60759508
x2	1.531645246

Reset

Exogenous Variables		
p1	1.1	price of x1
p2	1	price of x2
m	55	income
a	100	coefficient for x1
b	2	coefficient for x1
c	1	coefficient for x2
d	1	coefficient for x2

Constraint	1.61002E-07	income left over

−p1/p2	MRS at x1, x2
−1.100	1.100

Figure 1.4.5.5. A numerical example of Giffen behavior.
Source: GiffenGoods.xls!Optimal1

That is a weird demand curve. It is Giffen in a *range*. In other words, a Giffen good is not intrinsically and everywhere a Giffen good. Giffenness is a local phenomenon. The demand curve pictured in Figure 1.4.5.6 has three different behaviors. As price rises from zero, quantity demanded falls. This continues until a price of about 70 cents. From there, penny increases lead to increased consumption of good 1. In this range, x_1 is a Giffen good. There is a third region, at prices such as \$2 and \$3, where the good is not Giffen.

So, Giffen goods are not only possible, they can be modeled by the Theory of Consumer Behavior. There are utility functions that reflect well-behaved preferences that generate Giffen behavior.

Giffen Goods in Theory and Practice

A Giffen good is a strange creature in economics. The phenomenon of quantity demanded rising as price increases was first purportedly sighted during

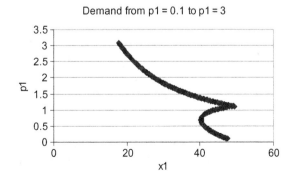

Figure 1.4.5.6. Inverse demand for x_1.
Source: GiffenGoods.xls!CS1

the Irish potato famine and named after Sir Robert Giffen, even though there is no evidence that Giffen actually claimed seeing quantity demanded rise as prices rose, ceteris paribus.

Certainly there are utility functions that give rise to Giffen goods. Certainly individual consumers may have well-behaved preferences that yield Giffen behavior. But has a Giffen good ever been spotted? Do Giffen goods exist in the real world in the sense that a market demand curve is upward sloping? This is the subject of much debate. Ceteris paribus is a difficult thing to guarantee.

The actual sighting of a Giffen good in the real world remains contentious. We know for sure that the original example, potatoes during the Great Irish Famine, was flawed and not a Giffen good.

For a careful yet accessible empirical study attempting to find a Giffen good, see David Mckenzie, "Are Tortillas a Giffen Good in Mexico?" *Economics Bulletin*, Vol. 15, No. 1 (2002), pp. 1–7. Relaxation of price controls and the peso crisis in 1995 triggered a large increase in the price of tortillas, a staple in the Mexican diet. Alas, the author concludes, "We find tortillas to be an inferior good, but not a Giffen Good."

Exercises

Open Word and answer the following questions. Save the document and print it when you are done.

1. Use the results in the *CS1* sheet to find the price range for which we see Giffen behavior. Report your answer and describe your procedure.
2. Use the *Optimal1* sheet utility function and parameter values to find the optimal solution via analytical methods. Show your work. Note that $x_1 < a/b$, so the utility function is

$$U = ax_1 - \frac{b}{2}x_1^2 + cx_2 + \frac{d}{2}x_2^2$$

3. Use Word's Drawing Tools to reproduce Figure 1.4.5.4, depicting x_1 as a Giffen good, but use a p_1 increase (instead of a decrease).

References

The epigraph comes from page 2436 of Neal Kumar Katyal, "Deterrence's Difficulty," *Michigan Law Review*, Vol. 95, No. 8. (August, 1997), pp. 2385–2476.

The *Biblio* sheet in GiffenGoods.xls has a list of references on Giffen goods. Scroll down (if needed) to see suggested readings on the Irish Potato Famine, the history of Giffen goods in economics, and modern-day efforts at finding Giffen goods. Click on a link if it seems interesting to you.

An excellent article on the potato famine and the source of several quotations in this chapter is Sherwin Rosen, "Potato Paradoxes," *The Journal of Political Economy*, Vol. 107, No. 6, Part 2: Symposium on the Economic Analysis of Social Behavior in Honor of Gary S. Becker (December, 1999), pp. S294–S313.

1.4.6

Income and Substitution Effects

Eugene (or Eugen or Yevgeni) Slutsky [1880–1948] intended to become a mathematician, but he was expelled from the University of Kiev for participating in student revolts.

Gonçalo L. Fonseca

Without a doubt, the demand curve is the most important idea in the Theory of Consumer Behavior. We have derived the demand curve analytically and numerically. The demand curve tells us the optimal amount to buy at a given price. It also tells us how quantity demanded will change as price changes, ceteris paribus.

This chapter remains focused on the demand curve, extending the analysis of the consumer's optimal response to a change in price. The core concept is that the total effect on quantity demanded (given by the demand curve) for a given change in price can be broken down into two separate effects, called *income* and *substitution* effects.

You can think of income and substitution effects as delving deeper into the demand curve. The focus is still on the change in quantity demanded as price changes, ceteris paribus, but we now want to understand better how and why the consumer responds according to the demand curve.

Intuition

Before diving into complicated graphs and math, let's review the story behind income and substitution effects. By first getting the big picture down, this improves your chances of really understanding what income and substitution effects are all about.

Suppose that, ceteris paribus, price rises. We know the consumer has to re-optimize. We know the consumer will choose a new optimal combination of goods. If we simply compute the change in the amount purchased of

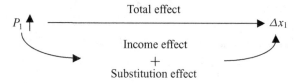

Figure 1.4.6.1. The basic idea behind income and substitution effects.

x_1 before and after the price change, we are comparing two points on the demand curve. This is called the *total effect* of a price change.

The increase in price has two channels by which it affects the consumer. One channel focuses on the fact that a price increase is like a decrease in purchasing power. After all, given an income level, if prices double, then I can buy half of what I bought before. The *income effect* reflects the fact that price changes affect optimal quantity demanded by altering purchasing power.

The second channel is called the *substitution effect*. The idea is that a price change in one good alters the relative prices faced by the consumer and induces substitution of the relatively cheaper good for the relatively more expensive one. When p_1 rises, x_1 is relatively more expensive to x_2 and so I am naturally going to avoid x_1 and be attracted to x_2.

We will see that the income effect can be either positive or negative, but the substitution effect is always negative (assuming well-behaved preferences). When price goes up, the substitution effect says "buy less." Of course, if price falls, the reverse occurs and, according to the substitution effect alone, consumption increases.

The reason the income effect is ambiguous in sign is the fact that there are normal and inferior goods. If the good is normal, the optimal x_1 rises as income increases, but if the good is inferior, then consumption and income are inversely related.

These ideas are expressed in Figure 1.4.6.1. It shows that the total effect, which is all that we actually observe, can be split into income and substitution effects. Neither of these two effects is directly observable, but we know they are there and together they produce the observed total effect.

Finally, it may help to know the underlying motivation behind income and substitution effects. Not only do they help us understand the demand curve and the nature of a consumer's response to a change in price, but they will also help us explain under which conditions Giffen behavior (an upward sloping demand curve) is possible. We will see that if the income and substitution effects work together, then the demand curve is guaranteed to be downward sloping. Understanding income and substitution effects will allow us to give a more refined, precise definition of the law of demand.

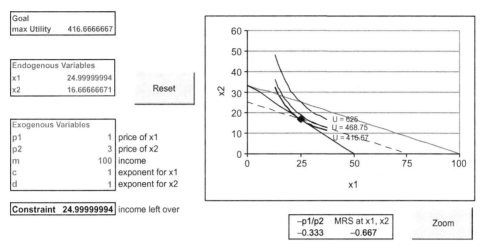

Figure 1.4.6.2. Decreasing p_1.
Source: IncSubEffects.xls!OptimalChoice

Numerical Example of Income and Substitution Effects

Step Open the Excel workbook IncSubEffects.xls and read the *Intro* sheet, then go to the *OptimalChoice* sheet.

Thus far, there is nothing new here. We have the usual Cobb-Douglas utility function with a conventional budget line. The initial optimal solution is $25,16\frac{2}{3}$.

Step Decrease p_1 by 1 to \$1/unit (in cell B17).

Figure 1.4.6.2 displays what is on your screen. The red line on your screen is the familiar new budget line (after the price decrease). There is, however, a dashed line that has not been used before. This dashed line represents the outcome of an imaginary experiment.

Step Click the Zoom button to see a second graph of the situation. It has the axes scale adjusted so you can see better what is going on.

The dashed line has the same slope as the new budget line yet it goes through the initial optimal solution. What we have done is pretend to take away enough income from the consumer to enable him to buy the initial bundle with the new set of prices. Notice that we *took away* income (shifting down the budget constraint relative to the new budget line) because the fall in price implies an increase in purchasing power. Had there been a price rise, we would have had to increase income to compensate for the price increase.

The dashed line will reveal the substitution effect because it is based on the new, lower price and the lower income that just cancels out the increased purchasing power from the lower price.

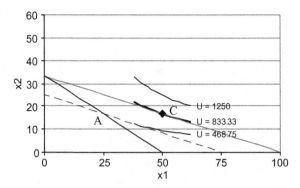

Figure 1.4.6.3. New optimal solution.
Source: IncSubEffects.xls!OptimalChoice

Of course, nothing like this actually happens in the real world. When the price falls, the consumer re-optimizes, buying a new optimal bundle, and that is the end of the story. But for the purposes of understanding the demand curve, we ask the consumer what he would buy at the dashed line and we use that to split the total effect into the substitution and income effects.

How much income do we have to take away to just cancel out the changed purchasing power from the price change? We use the Income Adjuster Equation:

$$\Delta m = x_1^* \Delta p_1$$

Applied to this problem, we know that x_1^* is 25 (from the initial optimal solution) and the change in p_1 is -1 (because the price fell from 2 to 1, so *new – initial* is $1 - 2$); thus

$$\Delta m = x_1^* \Delta p_1$$

$$\Delta m = [25][-1] = -25$$

The minus tells us that we have to take away income. The dashed line is based on an income of \$75, $p_1 = 1$, and $p_2 = 3$.

In summary, we have two new budget constraint lines:

- Initial income with new p_1
- New p_1 with *income adjusted so you can just buy the initial combination.*

We begin by working with the new p_1, income constant budget constraint.

Step Run Solver.

Figure 1.4.6.3 shows that the consumer chooses the $50, 16\frac{2}{3}$ combination. Thus, we have two points to consider:

- Point A: Initial: At $m = 100$, $p_1 = 2$, $x_1^* = 25$; $x_2^* = 16.67$
- Point C: New: At $m = 100$, $p_1 = 1$, $x_1^* = 50$; $x_2^* = 16.67$.

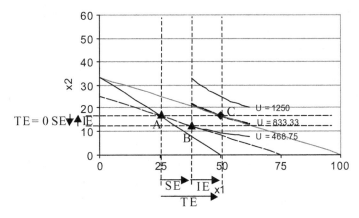

Figure 1.4.6.4. Income and substitution effects.

We have two points on the price consumption curve and two points on the demand curve. The total effect of a \$1/unit decrease in the price of good 1 is +25 units of good 1.

The total effect can be directly observed. With the initial price, we would see the consumer purchase 25 units of good 1. We could see the price fall and the consumer respond by buying 25 units more.

But we are interested in decomposing this observed total effect into its two constituent parts. By finding the optimal solution using the dashed line budget constraint, we can split the total effect into two parts.

Step Change income to \$75 (notice that the budget line now lies on top of the dashed budget line) and run Solver.

The optimal solution is 37.5,12.5. Thus, we have three points to consider, displayed in Figure 1.4.6.4:

- Point A: Initial: At $m = 100$, $p_1 = 2$, $x_1^* = 25$; $x_2^* = 16.67$
- Point B: Unobserved: At $m = 75$, $p_1 = 1$, $x_1^* = 37.5$; $x_2^* = 12.5$
- Point C: New: At $m = 100$, $p_1 = 1$, $x_1^* = 50$; $x_2^* = 16.67$.

With these values, we can compute income and substitution effects for x_1 and x_2.

For x_1:

The total effect (Δx_1) is +25. It is the long horizontal arrow in Figure 1.4.6.4, indicating movement from point A to C.

The substitution effect (Δx_1^s) is +12.5. This is the arrow from A to B.

The income effect is (Δx_1^m) is +12.5. This is the arrow from B to C.

Notice that the effects for x_1 are all computed along the x axis in terms of units of x_1.

There are also cross income and substitution effects for x_2:

1. The total effect (Δx_2) is 0.
2. The substitution effect (Δx_2^s) is -4.167. This is the downward pointing arrow (on the y axis) from A to B.
3. The income effect (Δx_2^m) is $+4.167$. This is the upward pointing arrow from B to C.

You might be wondering how the movement from A to B of $+12.5$ is interpreted as a negative substitution effect. The answer to this apparent puzzle is simple: Given that price fell, an increase in quantity purchased is consistent with a negative effect because it is the relationship between the two variables that is being described as negative.

The sign of the income effect is tricky. The key is to pay attention to which variable is being discussed. The income effect measured as the response to a change in income is positive, in this case, because as I move from B to C, my income is increased and I respond by increasing my optimal consumption of good 1.

Now you might ask, "If the two effects work together, then how is the substitution effect negative and the income effect positive?" This is because we define the income effect as the response to a change in income, like the movement from point B to C in Figure 1.4.6.4. But, if you remember, this example began with a *decrease* in the price of good 1. The decrease in the price of good 1 can be interpreted as an increase in income. If we tie the 12.5 increase in good 1 from the income effect to the *decrease* in price of good 1, we see that this negative effect reinforces the negative substitution effect and gives a negative total effect.

This seemingly contorted logic can be cleared up with the Slutsky Equation.

The Slutsky Equation

In 1915, Eugen Slutsky published a paper that showed how to decompose the total effect of a price change into income and substitution effects. Unfortunately, his work went unnoticed. Twenty years later, John R. Hicks (a Nobel laureate in 1972) and R. G. D. Allen rediscovered the ideas in Slutsky's paper. Sometimes, the idea of income and substitution effects are referred to as Slutsky-Hicks or Slutsky-Hicks-Allen. We will keep it simple and call it the Slutsky Equation.

The Slutsky Equation says, in mathematical terms, something that we already know: The total effect of a price change can be expressed as the sum of a substitution and an income effect. It turns out that there are several ways to express the decomposition. A Slutsky Equation is any equation that splits the total into two parts. Here is one way to write a Slutsky Equation:

$$\Delta x_1 = \Delta x_1^s + \Delta x_1^m$$

In the concrete problem in the Excel workbook, here are the numbers we found for this expression:

$$\Delta x_1 = \Delta x_1^s + \Delta x_1^m$$

$$+25 = [+12.5] + [+12.5]$$

By working with this basic equation, we can explain the confusing sign issue and see how to quickly extract the income and substitution effects from a given demand curve.

First, we divide both sides by the change in the price of good 1. This is another way to write the Slutsky Equation.

$$\frac{\Delta x_1}{\Delta p_1} = \frac{\Delta x_1^s}{\Delta p_1} + \frac{\Delta x_1^m}{\Delta p_1}$$

We can apply this version of the Slutsky Equation to our example.

$$\frac{\Delta x_1}{\Delta p_1} = \frac{\Delta x_1^s}{\Delta p_1} + \frac{\Delta x_1^m}{\Delta p_1}$$

$$-25 = [-12.5] + [-12.5]$$

Because price fell, the delta p_1 terms are negative. Thus, the total effect, $\frac{\Delta x_1}{\Delta p_1}$, is negative because x_1 rose by 25 units as price fell by \$1 unit. The substitution effect, $\frac{\Delta x_1^s}{\Delta p_1}$, is always negative and, in this case, the income effect with respect to price, $\frac{\Delta x_1^m}{\Delta p_1}$, is also negative. Look carefully at the denominator of the income effect in this version of the Slutsky Equation. The income effect with respect to price is negative because when price falls, after adjusting for the increase in purchasing power, the consumer buys more. If we tie buying more to price falling, we get a negative income effect.

However, economists do not define the income effect with respect to price. We usually define the income effect with respect to income; in other words, how much does consumption change as income changes (i.e., an Engel Curve analysis). A third version of the Slutsky Equation is often used to express the income effect in terms of income.

$$\frac{\Delta x_1}{\Delta p_1} = \frac{\Delta x_1^s}{\Delta p_1} - x_1^* \frac{\Delta x_1^m}{\Delta m}$$

This version of the Slutsky Equation uses the fact that $\frac{\Delta x_1^m}{\Delta p_1} = -x_1^* \frac{\Delta x_1^m}{\Delta m}$. In other words, a price decrease can be interpreted as an income increase times the amount of good 1 initially purchased. Notice the minus sign, which picks up the fact that when price falls, that is like an increase in income.

As before, we apply our problem to this version of the Slutsky Equation.

$$\frac{\Delta x_1}{\Delta p_1} = \frac{\Delta x_1^s}{\Delta p_1} - x_1^* \frac{\Delta x_1^m}{\Delta m}$$

$$-25 = [-12.5] - [25][1/2]$$

Expressions that decompose total effects of a price change into substitution and income effects are called Slutsky Equations. We have examined three versions, listed subsequently for easy comparison.

$$\Delta x_1 = \Delta x_1^s + \Delta x_1^m$$

$$\frac{\Delta x_1}{\Delta p_1} = \frac{\Delta x_1^s}{\Delta p_1} + \frac{\Delta x_1^m}{\Delta p_1}$$

$$\frac{\Delta x_1}{\Delta p_1} = \frac{\Delta x_1^s}{\Delta p_1} - x_1^* \frac{\Delta x_1^m}{\Delta m}$$

The sign of the income effect is confusing because it depends on which version of the Slutsky decomposition we are talking about. The income effect usually refers to the third of the Slutksy Equations just given. If price falls, that is like an increase in income. If the good is a normal good, then the income effect is positive and price decreases will lead to increases in consumption via the income effect.

Working with Demand Curves

We can put the Slutsky Equation to work to quickly figure out the total, substitution, and income effects.

With a Cobb-Douglas utility function and $c = d = 1$, the demand curve for x_1 is $\frac{m}{2p_1}$. We can use this demand curve to confirm our work in Excel and show how easy it is to find the income and substitution effects. At $m = 100$ and $p_1 = 2$, we can compute that $x_1^* = 25$.

If price falls to \$1/unit, obviously $x_1^* = 50$. The total effect is a 25 unit increase in response to the \$1/unit decrease in price.

For the substitution effect, as we did when working with the Excel workbook, we use the Income Adjuster Equation to find the level of income that would enable consumption of the initial amount of $x_1^* = 25$ at the new price of good 1.

$$\Delta m = x_1^* \Delta p_1$$

$$\Delta m = [25][-1] = -25$$

Next, we use the new income, $75, and new price of good 1, $1/unit, in the demand curve:

$$x_1^* = \frac{m}{2p_1} = \frac{[75]}{2[1]} = 37.5.$$

The substitution effect is then a 12.5 unit increase in response to a $1/unit decrease.

For the income effect, we use the third version of the Slutsky Equation. Because the Engel Curve is linear, we know that we can simply take the derivative of the reduced-form expression with respect to income. If the Engel Curve is not linear, then this would serve as an approximation to a discrete-size change in price.

$$x_1^* = \frac{m}{2p_1}$$

$$\frac{dx_1^*}{dm} = \frac{1}{2p_1}$$

We evaluate this expression at the new price, $1/unit.

$$\frac{dx_1^*}{dm} = \frac{1}{2p_1} = \frac{1}{2[1]} = \frac{1}{2}.$$

Then we directly compute the income effect from the third version of the Slutsky Equation, using the initial value of $x_1^* = 25$.

$$= -x_1^* \frac{\Delta x_1^m}{\Delta m} = -[25] \left[\frac{1}{2} \right] = -12.5.$$

This says that the income effect with respect to price is a 12.5 unit decrease in good 1 as its price rises by $1/unit.

We can put all of this together to check the arithmetic.

$$\frac{\Delta x_1}{\Delta p_1} = \frac{\Delta x_1^s}{\Delta p_1} - x_1^* \frac{\Delta x_1^m}{\Delta m}$$

$$-25 = [-12.5] + [-12.5]$$

The Slutsky Equation and Giffen Goods

Aside from helping us better understand the nature of demand, the Slutsky Equation makes crystal clear how Giffen behavior could arise. Using the third version of the Slutsky Equation, it is obvious that the only way a good can have positive total effect is if the income effect term is larger than the always negative substitution effect.

Instead of using a numerical example, this idea will be presented in a series of graphs. We begin with the initial solution, displayed in Figure 1.4.6.5. The

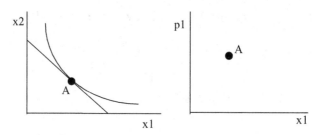

Figure 1.4.6.5. The initial solution.

left side shows the initial optimal solution and the right side displays a single point on the demand curve (which is not shown).

Next, we decrease the price of good 1, which creates a new budget line (with a shallower slope, of course). We know the consumer will re-optimize and choose a new optimal solution along this new budget line, but Figure 1.4.6.6 does not show this new solution quite yet. Instead, it shows with a dashed line the income that would have to be taken away to cancel out the increased purchasing power from the price decrease.

Figure 1.4.6.6 shows what the consumer would have purchased at the unobserved combination of lower price of good 1 and lower income. The SE is the substitution effect, from point A to B on the x axis.

Now, we are ready to use the Slutsky Equation. We have a known negative substitution effect and all that is left is to find the indifference curve tangent to the new budget line (with lower p_1). In terms of the Slutsky Equation, we have the following:

$$\frac{\Delta x_1}{\Delta p_1} = \frac{\Delta x_1^s}{\Delta p_1} - x_1^* \frac{\Delta x_1^m}{\Delta m}$$

$$? = [-] - x_1^*[?]$$

In other words, the total effect depends on the income effect. The consumer's indifference map will produce one of three possibilities:

1. Good 1 is a normal good so the income effect, $\frac{\Delta x_1^m}{\Delta m}$, is positive. Then, the question mark for the income effect is a [+] which, when multiplied by the minus sign,

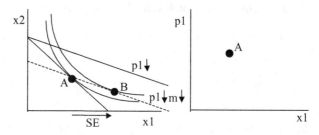

Figure 1.4.6.6. A price decrease and imaginary budget constraint.

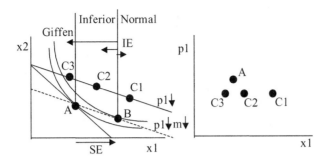

Figure 1.4.6.7. Understanding Giffen behavior.

yields a negative number and reinforces the substitution effect and we have a downward sloping demand curve. This is point C1 on Figure 1.4.6.7.

2. Good 1 is an inferior good so the income effect, $\frac{\Delta x_1^m}{\Delta m}$, is negative. Then, the question mark for the income effect is a $[-]$ which, when multiplied by the minus sign, yields a positive number and opposes the substitution effect. If the substitution effect is bigger than the income effect, we still get a downward sloping demand curve. This is point C2 on Figure 1.4.6.7.

3. Good 1 is an inferior good so the income effect, $\frac{\Delta x_1^m}{\Delta m}$, is negative. Then, the question mark for the income effect is a $[-]$ which, when multiplied by the minus sign, yields a positive number and opposes the substitution effect. If the income effect is bigger than the substitution effect, we end up with a positive number and an upward sloping demand curve. This is a Giffen good. This is point C3 on Figure 1.4.6.7.

There is a lot going on in Figure 1.4.6.7. It is trying to show that the interplay between income and substitution effects determines what the demand curve ends up looking like. The substitution effect is the same for all of the cases. If the good is normal, the demand curve is guaranteed to be downward sloping. If the good is inferior, it may still have a downward sloping demand curve because we may be at a point like C2. For the good to be Giffen, it has to have a large opposing income effect.

Figure 1.4.6.7 also makes clear that it is the indifference curves, which come from the utility function, that determine how quantity demanded responds to a change in price. How a good generates utility (i.e., whether utility is Cobb-Douglas, quasilinear, or perfect complements) determines whether it is normal, inferior, or Giffen.

The Slutsky Equation tells us how we can get a Giffen good. The key is the $-x_1^* \frac{\Delta x_1^m}{\Delta m}$ part of the expression. Obviously, if the good is extremely inferior, so that $\frac{\Delta x_1^m}{\Delta m}$ is much smaller than zero, we might get a Giffen good.

But the income effect term in the Slutsky Equation reveals another way to get Giffen behavior. A large opposing income effect can be obtained by the good being inferior, $\frac{\Delta x_1^m}{\Delta m} < 0$, and by the consumer buying a large amount of it, x_1^*. If the good is merely inferior, but the consumer buys little of it, then it is less likely to be Giffen.

This explains why economists look for Giffen behavior in staple goods purchased by poor consumers. Examples (other than potatoes in Ireland) include tortillas in Mexico and rice in Asia. These goods are more likely to play a large role in a person's budget, although whether such goods are inferior or Giffen is unclear.

Getting the Law of Demand Exactly Right

Every Economics 101 student is taught that the Law of Demand says that quantity demanded rises as price falls, ceteris paribus. In other words, holding everything else constant, quantity demanded and price are inversely related and demand is always downward sloping. This is fine, at the introductory level, where we do not want to confuse beginning students, but we know that an upward sloping demand curve is possible – it is called a Giffen good.

The Slutsky decomposition of the total effect into income and substitution effects enables us to more precisely define the Law of Demand. By inserting a qualifying clause, we can get the Law of Demand to be exactly right: *If the good is normal, then quantity demanded falls as price rises, ceteris paribus.*

Figure 1.4.6.7 makes clear how the restriction that the good be normal guarantees a downward sloping demand curve. The figure shows that for a good to be Giffen, it has to have an income effect in the opposite direction of the substitution effect and the income effect must be bigger than the substitution effect so that we end up to the left of A (after p_1 falls).

But a normal good will have an income effect that will produce a final point C to the right of point B. Thus, there is no way to get a Giffen good from a normal good.

Of course, it is not true that all inferior goods are Giffen. To be Giffen, a good has to be inferior and have an income effect that swamps the substitution effect.

$$TE = SE + IE$$

Income and substitution effects are used by economists to better understand the demand curve and to explain Giffen behavior. By decomposing the total effect of a price change, the Slutsky Equation shows how a Giffen good can arise if the income effect opposes and swamps the substitution effect (which generates an upward sloping relationship between price and quantity demanded).

Given a reduced form of $x^* = f(p, m)$, in other words, a demand function, the Income Adjuster and Slutsky Equations can be used to decompose the total effect into its income and substitution effect components.

Finally, believe it or not, there are even more ways to express the Slutsky Equation than the three used in this chapter. Instead of altering income to allow the consumer to buy the initial bundle of goods, you can change income to allow the consumer to be on the initial indifference curve. This is sometimes referred to as the Hicks substitution effect.

Exercises

Open Word and answer the following questions. Save the document and print it when you are done.

1. Reproduce, using word's Drawing Tools, Figures 1.4.6.5, 1.4.6.6, and 1.4.6.7, explaining each graph in your own words.
2. Repeat question 1, with one key change: apply a price *increase* in good 1 (instead of a price decrease).
3. In stating the Law of Demand, some economists choose to include a condition that the good is normal, like this: If the good is a normal good, then price and quantity demanded are inversely related, ceteris paribus. Why is the normal good clause needed?
4. Given the demand function, $x_1^* = 20 + \frac{m}{20p_1}$, compute the total, income, and substitution effects when price falls from \$5 to \$4, with income of \$1000. Show your work.

References

The epigraph is from the biography of Slutsky available at the New School's History of Economic Thought (HET) web site, <homepage.newschool.edu/het>. The site was created and is maintained by Gonçalo L. Fonseca. There are sketches of hundreds of economists, links to other HET resources, and descriptions of various schools of thought in economics. The intellectual history of economics is fascinating and this Web site is a wonderful place to browse.

1.4.7

More Practice with Income and Substitution Effects

I never saw Slutsky's work until my own was very far advanced. . . . Slutsky's work is highly mathematical, and he does not give much discussion about the significance of his theory.

J. R. Hicks

This chapter uses a quasilinear utility function to provide practice working with income and substitution effects. There is an interesting twist when using the quasilinear functional form.

Income and Substitution Effects with Quasilinear Preferences

Step Open the Excel workbook IncSubEffectsPractice.xls and read the *Intro* sheet, then go to the *OptimalChoice* sheet.

Notice that the absolute value of the MRS is less than the price ratio. Because the slope of indifference curve at 16.25,10.75 is less than the slope of the budget constraint, we know the consumer should travel northwest along the budget constraint, buying more x_2 and less x_1, until the $MRS = p_1/p_2$.

Step Run Solver to find the initial optimal solution. Figure 1.4.7.1 shows this result.

Step Proceed to the *CS1* sheet. It shows a comparative statics analysis of an increase in the price of good 1 from \$2/unit to \$7/unit in \$1 increments. It also charts the results as an inverse demand curve.

The demand curve tracks the total effect of a price change. When price rises from \$2 to \$3, the quantity demanded falls from $6\frac{1}{4}$ to $2\frac{7}{9}$. By subtracting the new from the initial value, we see that the total effect is a decrease of $3\frac{17}{36}$ units.

Income and substitution effects explain how this total effect came to be by decomposing the total effect into two parts that add up to the total.

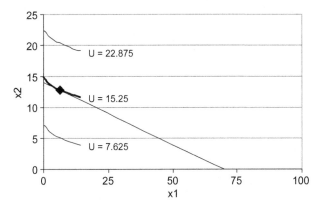

Figure 1.4.7.1. Initial optimal solution.
Source: IncSubEffectsPractice!OptimalChoice

The substitution effect tells us how much less the consumer would have purchased when price rises strictly from the fact that the relative prices of the two goods have changed. We compute how much income we have to give the consumer to cancel out the reduced purchasing power caused by the price increase to focus exclusively on the relative price change.

Figure 1.4.7.2 shows this manipulation with indifference curves suppressed to highlight the budget lines under consideration. From point A, price rose and the consumer will now be at point C on the new budget line (labeled $p_1\uparrow$). The dashed line is the result of a hypothetical scenario in which the consumer has been given enough income to purchase the initial bundle A. Notice how the original budget line and the dashed line go through point A. The dashed line has a higher price, but also a higher income. Thus, the movement from point A to point B reflects solely the different relative prices in the goods, without any change in purchasing power. This is the substitution effect.

While the substitution effect is focused on relative prices, the income effect is that part of the response in quantity demanded when price changes that is due to changed purchasing power. From point B, a decrease in income from the dashed to the new budget line leads to a decrease in x_1 (at point C). Thus, x_1 is a normal good from point B to C and the two effects are working in tandem. The demand curve is guaranteed to be downward sloping for this price change.

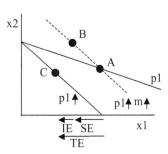

Figure 1.4.7.2. The substitution effect.

In the *CS1* sheet, we have seen that the demand curve is downward sloping because quantity demanded falls when price rises. Do the income and substitution effects work as in Figure 1.4.7.2?

We know point A, the initial optimal solution, is $x_1^* = 6.25$ when $p_1 = 2$ and point C, the new optimal solution, is $x_1^* = 2\frac{7}{9}$ when $p_1 = 3$.

To find point B, we need to use the Income Adjuster Equation to compute how much income to give the consumer in order to cancel out the effect of the reduced purchasing power.

$$\Delta m = x_1^* \Delta p_1$$

$$\Delta m = [6.25][1] = 6.25$$

Step On the *OptimalChoice* sheet, set cell B16 to 3 and cell B18 to 146.25. This applies the dashed line budget constraint to this problem. Run Solver to find point B.

Surprisingly, we find $x_1^* = 2\frac{7}{9}$ when $p_1 = 3$ and $m = 146.25$.
What is going on?
We turn to analytical work to shed light on this mysterious result.

Using the Slutsky Equation

In 1.4.4, we derived a demand curve with this same quasilinear utility function. We solved the constrained optimization problem by first writing the Lagrangean,

$$\max_{x_1, x_2, \lambda} L = x_1^{1/2} + x_2 + \lambda(m - p_1 x_1 - 10 x_2)$$

Then we found that

$$x_1^* = \frac{25}{p_1^2}$$

$$x_2^* = m - \frac{2.5}{p_1}$$

We can apply the Slutsky Equation to this demand function.

$$\frac{\Delta x_1}{\Delta p_1} = \frac{\Delta x_1^s}{\Delta p_1} - x_1^* \frac{\Delta x_1^m}{\Delta m}$$

The left-hand-side term, the total effect, is easy. When $p_1 = 2$, $x_1^* = 25/4 = 6.25$. When $p_1 = 3$, $x_1^* = 25/9 = 2\frac{7}{9}$. The total effect is $-3\frac{17}{36}$, which agrees exactly with our earlier work.

To find the substitution effect, we use new price and adjusted income in the demand function. We see that m does not appear in the demand function – this is the source of the surprising result. We can, of course, continue

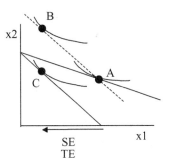

Figure 1.4.7.3. No income effect with quasilinear preferences.

our work, using just new price in the substitution effect term of the Slutsky Equation. We find that $x_1^* = 25/9 = 2\frac{7}{9}$ at $p_1 = 3$, $m = 146\frac{1}{4}$. Thus, the substitution effect is $6\frac{1}{4}$ (point A) minus $2\frac{7}{9}$ (point B) equals minus $3\frac{17}{36}$.

The income effect requires that we take the derivative of x_1^* with respect to m. There is no m in the demand function, so this is zero. The income effect is zero! Thus, the total effect is equal to the substitution effect and the income effect is zero.

$$\frac{\Delta x_1}{\Delta p_1} = \frac{\Delta x_1^s}{\Delta p_1} - x_1^* \frac{\Delta x_1^m}{\Delta m}$$

$$\left[-3\frac{17}{36}\right] = \left[-3\frac{17}{36}\right] - [0]$$

Figure 1.4.7.3 shows how this works. As usual, the substitution effect is the move from point A to B. It is negative because x_1^* falls as its own price rises. The income effect is the movement from B to C. It is zero because C is directly below B. The total effect is A to C.

It is the utility function that is driving this result. A utility function with the functional form $U = f(x_1) + x_2$ has no income effect because the indifference curves are vertically parallel. If you shift the budget line via an income shock, the new tangency point will be directly above or below the initial point. In other words, the income consumption curve is vertical. Thus, the total effect is composed entirely of the substitution effect.

Notice also that we now know that quasilinear preferences cannot yield Giffen behavior. After all, if the substitution effect is always negative and the income effect is zero, there is no way for the total effect to ever be positive.

Quasilinear Preferences Yield Zero Income Effects

Decomposing a total effect into income and substitution effects works for any utility function. After finding the total effect, the Income Adjuster Equation can be used to determine the income needed to cancel out the change in purchasing power from the price change (i.e., locating the imaginary, dashed budget line). Finding the optimal solution with the new price and adjusted income budget constraint determines point B and allows us to split the total effect in two parts.

Of course, the parts need not be equal. We know that Giffen goods arise when the income effect opposes and swamps the substitution effect.

In the case of quasilinear preferences, we have a situation where there is no income effect. The Slutsky decomposition still applies, however, with the total effect being entirely composed of the substitution effect.

Exercises

Open Word and answer the following questions. Save the document and print it when you are done.

1. Click the Reset button on the *OptimalChoice* sheet and apply a price decrease for good 1 from $2/unit to $1.90/unit. Compute the total, substitution, and income effects. Show your work.
2. Use Word's Drawing Tools to draw a graph similar to Figure 1.4.7.3 that shows the total, substitution, and income effects from the 10 cent decrease in price from question 1.
3. In 1.4.2, it was shown that the Income Consumption (and Engel) Curve has a kink for low levels of income. Click the Reset button on the *OptimalChoice* sheet and set income to 10. Compute the total, substitution, and income effects from a 10 cent price increase in good 1 (from $2 to $2.10). Show your work.
4. Use Word's Drawing Tools to draw a graph depicting your results for question 3.

References

The epigraph comes from page 19 of the second edition of *Value and Capital: An Inquiry into Some Fundamental Principles of Economic Theory* by John R. Hicks. This remarkable book was explicitly cited in the press release announcing that Hicks had won the Nobel Prize in Economic Science in 1972 (with Kenneth Arrow). "In his most well-known work, the monograph, *Value and Capital*, published in 1939, Hicks abandoned this [formal] tradition and gave the [general equilibrium] theory an increased economic relevance." See <nobelprize.org/nobel_prizes/economics/laureates/1972/press.html>.

As mentioned in the previous chapter, the history of income and substitution effects is complicated. Hicks (and Allen) figured out that the total effect could be decomposed into income and substitution effects in the 1930s, two decades after Slutsky's work. Once Slutsky was rediscovered, they gave him credit and made the economics profession aware of his contribution. Hicks wrote in *Value and Capital* that "The present volume is the first systematic exploration of the territory which Slutsky opened up" (p. 19).

1.4.8

A Tax/Rebate Proposal

Usually the first question anyone asks about a proposed new tax is "Who pays?" and about a tax cut is "Who benefits?"

Joel Slemrod and Jon Bakija

This chapter examines a tax/rebate policy via income and substitution effects. This provides further practice with the logic of income and substitution effects and shows that they are more than an intellectual curiosity.

A Tax/Rebate Proposal

Government's goal: To reduce consumption of a particular good, for example, gasoline, without hurting the consumer.

Proposal: By taxing the good and then turning around and rebating (giving back) the tax revenues to the consumer, we can alter the consumer's choices without lowering satisfaction. After all, the government isn't making any money (all of the tax revenue raised is refunded back) so the consumer isn't going to be hurt. (We ignore administrative costs of collecting the tax and rebating it.)

Critics: This scheme will have no effect because the rebated tax will immediately be spent on the taxed good and we'll end up right where we started.

Who is right?

We use the Theory of Consumer Behavior to find out. Along the way, income and substitution effects will come into play.

A Concrete Example of the Tax/Rebate Proposal

Step Open the Excel workbook TaxRebate.xls and read the *Intro* sheet, then go to the *QuantityTax* sheet.

We have a Cobb-Douglas utility function with an option to apply a per unit (quantity) tax on good 1. The workbook opens with no tax and

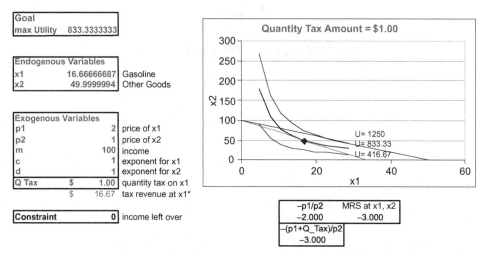

Figure 1.4.8.1. Optimal solution with a per unit tax.
Source: TaxRebate.xls!QuantityTax

the consumer maximizing satisfaction by buying the bundle 25,50, yielding $U^* = 1250$.

Our first step in analyzing the tax/rebate proposal is to apply a \$1/unit tax on x_1.

Step Change cell B21 to 1. Notice that the new budget line appears. The consumer cannot afford the original bundle and must re-optimize. Run Solver to find the new optimal solution.

Figure 1.4.8.1 shows the result. The consumer will now buy the bundle $16\frac{2}{3},50$ and get a maximum utility of $833\frac{1}{3}$. Because the consumer buys $16\frac{2}{3}$ units of x_1 and there is a \$1/unit tax on the amount of x_1 purchased, the government collects \$16.67 in tax revenue.

The idea behind the tax/rebate proposal called for rebating the tax revenue so that the consumer would not be hurt by the tax. We need to implement the rebate part of the proposal.

Step Change cell B18 to 116.67. This shifts the budget constraint out. Run Solver to find the optimal solution.

You will find that the consumer optimizes by purchasing 19.445 units of x_1 and 58.335 units of x_2.

This result presents us with a problem. This is not the tax/rebate scheme the government envisioned. After all, the government is collecting more tax revenue (\$19.445) than the consumer is getting as a rebate (\$16.67).

Instead of giving the consumer \$16.67, let's give her \$19.445. What does the consumer do in this case?

Step Change cell B18 to 119.445. This shifts the budget constraint out a little bit more. Run Solver to find the optimal solution.

Now the consumer buys 19.9075 units of x_1.

We have to change cell B18 again. This process of repeatedly doing the same thing is called *iteration*.

Step Change cell B18 to 119.9075. This shifts the budget constraint out a teeny little bit more. Run Solver to find the optimal solution.

Now the consumer buys 19.9846 units of x_1.

You can see that we are converging because the increases to income keep getting smaller and smaller. There is a tax rebate that yields an x_1^* that generates a tax revenue that exactly equals the tax rebate. The value of this tax rebate is $20.

Step Change cell B18 to 120. Run Solver to find the optimal solution.

Solver might not get the exact optimal solution. You can see, however, that the optimal solution is 20,60.

Step Force Excel to show the exact optimal solution by setting cell B11 to 20 and B12 to 60. Notice that maximum utility is 1200.

Now the consumer buys 20 units of x_1, which generates $20 in tax revenue, which is equal to the $20 rebated to the consumer.

We are (finally!) ready to judge the tax/rebate scheme.

Evaluating the Tax/Rebate Proposal

Supporters of the tax/rebate proposal claimed that "By taxing the good and then turning around and rebating (giving back) the tax revenues to the consumer, we can alter the consumer's choices without lowering satisfaction. After all, the government isn't making any money (all of the tax revenue raised is refunded back) so the consumer isn't going to be hurt."

Clearly the supporters of the tax/rebate proposal are wrong. The consumer had an initial $U^* = 1250$ and has a new $U^* = 1200$. While we cannot meaningfully say that utility has fallen by 50 (because utility is measured on an ordinal, not cardinal scale), we can say that utility has fallen. Thus, in fact, the consumer is hurt by the tax/rebate proposal.

On the other hand, the critics said, "This scheme will have no effect since the rebated tax will immediately be spent on the taxed good and we'll end up right where we started."

Because the consumer went from an initial bundle of 25,50 to 20,60 after the $20 tax/rebate, it is obvious that critics are wrong also. This consumer has altered purchasing plans and is, in fact, buying less x_1.

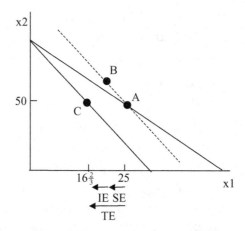

Figure 1.4.8.2. Income and substitution effects.

So, who's right – the critics or the supporters of the scheme? Neither. They are both wrong. Income and substitution effects will help us explain why.

The Income and Substitution Effects of a Price Increase

We return to the original problem without a tax or rebate and the initial solution of 25,50.

The $1/unit tax is just like a price increase. We can compute the substitution effect from such a price change.

We first use the Income Adjuster Equation.

$$\Delta m = x_1^* \Delta p_1$$

$$\Delta m = [25][1] = 25$$

This result says that a $25 increase in income to $125 will allow us to buy the initial bundle.

Step Set income in cell B18 to 125 (and confirm that there is a $1/unit tax in cell B21) and run Solver.

The optimal solution is $20\frac{5}{6}, 62\frac{1}{2}$.

The total effect of the $1/unit price increase (due to the tax without any rebate) is $16\frac{2}{3}$ minus 25 equals minus $8\frac{1}{3}$. The substitution effect is $16\frac{2}{3}$ $-20\frac{5}{6} = -4\frac{1}{6}$. The income effect is $20\frac{5}{6} - 25 = -4\frac{1}{6}$. Figure 1.4.8.2 displays these results with each point signifying a tangency between the budget line and an indifference curve (that is not drawn in to make it easier to read the graph).

The tax/rebate proposal is closely related to Figure 1.4.8.2. The tax is like a price increase that moves the consumer from A to C and the rebate is like an income effect that moves the consumer from C to B.

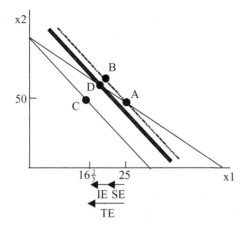

Figure 1.4.8.3. Understanding the tax/rebate proposal.

However, if you look carefully, the changes in income are not the same. In the tax/rebate proposal, the revenue-neutral rebate is $20, whereas in our income and substitution effect work we gave the consumer $25 to be able to purchase the original bundle. A $25 rebate is not revenue neutral because the consumer buys only $20\frac{5}{6}$ units of x_1 so the government ends up losing revenue. The rebate has to be $20 to be consistent with the break-even logic of the proposal.

In addition to the income and substitution effects, Figure 1.4.8.3 adds point D, which shows the optimal solution given the tax/rebate proposal. Point D (at coordinate 20,60) has utility of 1200, which is, of course, lower than point B (the combination $20\frac{5}{6},62\frac{1}{2}$ yields just over 1300 units of utility). More importantly for the purposes of evaluating the proposal, utility at point D is less than utility at point A (where 25,50 generates $U^* = 1250$).

The key to the analysis lies with point D in Figure 1.4.8.3. It has to be on the initial budget line to fulfill the revenue-neutral condition of the proposal. Because point A was the initial optimal solution, we can deduce that the consumer prefers point A to point D and will suffer a decrease in satisfaction if the tax/rebate proposal is implemented.

Tax/Rebate Schemes Do Alter Consumption Patterns, but Lower Utility

Simultaneously taxing a good and rebating the tax revenue periodically appears as a policy proposal (often with regard to gasoline). The scheme is related to income and substitution effects. The tax is like a price increase and the rebate is like an income effect.

Although similar, there is one important difference: The revenue-neutral rebate does not return enough income to allow the consumer to buy the pre-tax bundle or to reach the pre-tax level of satisfaction. Thus, the consumer cannot reach the initial level of satisfaction. Whether the loss in utility is compensated by the changed consumption pattern is a different question.

Exercises

Open Word and answer the following questions. Save the document and print it when you are done.

1. Analytically, we can show that the demand curves for goods 1 and 2 with a Cobb-Douglas utility function (where $c = d$) are $x_1^* = \frac{m}{2(p_1 + Q\_tax)}$ and $x_2^* = \frac{m}{2p_2}$. Use these demand functions to compute the income, substitution, and total effects for x_1 for a \$1/unit tax. Show your work.
2. We know that the tax/rebate scheme gives back too little income to return the consumer to the initial level of utility (1250 units). With a \$1/unit tax, find that level of rebate where the consumer is made whole in the sense that $U^* = 1250$. Describe your procedure in answering this question.
3. At point D in Figure 1.4.8.3, is the MRS greater or smaller in absolute value than the price ratio before the tax/rebate scheme is implemented? How do you know this?

References

The epigraph is from page 56 of the third edition of *Taxing Ourselves: A Citizen's Guide to the Debate over Taxes* published in 2004 by Joel Slemrod and Jon Bakija. The book does not discuss the tax/rebate proposal covered in this chapter, but it is an excellent, user-friendly guide to the ever-present debate over taxes. This topic is part of the subdiscipline of economics called Public Finance. If you are interested in tax reform (including flat or consumption tax proposals), the history of the income tax in the United States, or how economists evaluate and judge taxes, this book is a good place to start.

1.5
Endowment Model

1.5.1

Introduction to the Endowment Model

Our consumers could simply sit down and consume their endowments. But one consumer might, for example, be endowed with a lot of some good that she is not particularly fond of. She may wish to exchange some of that good for something she likes more.

David M. Kreps

This chapter introduces a wrinkle to the standard consumer theory model that greatly enhances its applicability. Instead of treating income as a given cash amount, we model the consumer as having a given initial endowment of goods that can be traded for other goods. This transforms the consumer into a combined consumer and seller.

Although the power of this approach may not be immediately obvious, we will see that a wide variety of examples such as saving/borrowing, charitable giving, and much more can be handled with this modification.

The Budget Constraint in an Endowment Model

Instead of the usual income (m) variable, an Endowment Model is Characterized by a budget constraint that equates expenditures and revenues from sales out of the initial endowment.

$$p_1 x_1 + p_2 x_2 = p_1 \omega_1 + p_2 \omega_2$$

The right-hand-side term says that the consumer has a given amount of each good, ω_1 (omega-one) and ω_2 (omega-two). Because the initial amounts of each good are given, ω_1 and ω_2 are exogenous variables.

The starting amount of each good, the coordinate pair ω_1, ω_2, is called the *initial endowment*. If we multiply the initial amount of each good by the price of that good, as done in the right-hand side of the budget constraint equation, we get a dollar-valued amount that represents the total income that can be raised by selling the entire endowment.

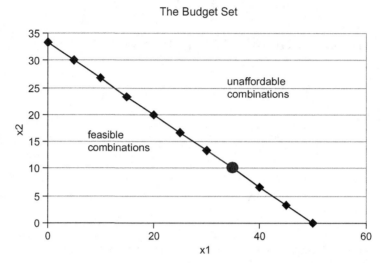

Figure 1.5.1.1. The budget constraint in an Endowment Model.
Source: EndowmentIntro.xls!Properties

The classic example to illustrate the concept of an endowment is a farmer who goes to market with his output. He sells his produce and, with the revenue obtained by selling, buys other goods. The core idea is that the farmer is a buyer *and* a seller.

Perhaps a more modern example is eBay. People sell all kinds of products and turn around and buy different products. Once again, the core idea is that eBayers sell *and* buy.

In an Endowment Model, what the agent can buy depends on how much revenue is generated by sales. High prices for goods to be sold are a good thing from the agent's point of view.

Because Endowment Models transform the consumer into a buying/selling agent, we can get different results than we saw in the Standard Model. The most important difference is that price increases lead to decreases in quantity demanded (assuming the good is normal), but if price rises high enough, the agent will switch from being a buyer to being a seller. This is a key idea.

An easy way to understand the idea of an initial endowment in a budget constraint is through a concrete numerical example.

Step Open the Excel workbook EndowmentIntro.xls and read the *Intro* sheet, then go to the *Properties* sheet.

The brown circle in the graph (reproduced as Figure 1.5.1.1) represents the initial endowment. From the initial allocation of 35,10, the agent can move northwest, selling x_1 and buying x_2. Or, the agent can decide to acquire even more x_1 by selling x_2 and buying x_1, which means traveling in a southeasterly direction. The slope of the constraint is the usual price ratio.

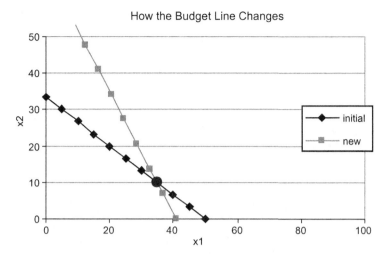

Figure 1.5.1.2. Increasing p_1 in an Endowment Model.
Source: EndowmentIntro.xls!Properties

What will the consumer do? We do not know because we do not have any information on this agent's preferences. Before we tackle that problem, however, we need to see how the budget constraint changes when an exogenous variable is shocked.

Step Proceed to the *Changes* sheet. Change p_1 (in cell K9) from 2 to 5.

Instead of the budget constraint pivoting about the x_2 intercept (as in a standard, cash income model), your screen should look like Figure 1.5.1.2. The budget constraint has pivoted, but the rotation is around the initial endowment.

The way the budget constraint has changed reveals important information. The price increase has improved the agent's consumption possibilities if she is planning on traveling northwest on the constraint. This makes sense because she would be a seller of good 1 and, with the higher price, she would have more money with which to buy good 2.

On the other hand, if she is a buyer, then we get the usual result that the budget line has rotated in and reduced the consumption possibilities.

Step Click the Reset button and change p_1 (in cell K9) from 2 to 1. Notice how the budget line has swiveled around the endowment again, but this time the agent is worse off if she is a seller and better off if she is a buyer.

Step Click the Reset button and change p_2 (in cell K10) from 3 to 6. The result is exactly the same as when you changed p_1 (in cell K9) from 2 to 1.

There is a lesson here: All that matters are relative prices, p_1/p_2.

Finally, we consider shifts in the budget constraint. We cannot shift m (cash income), but we can shift the initial endowment quantities of goods.

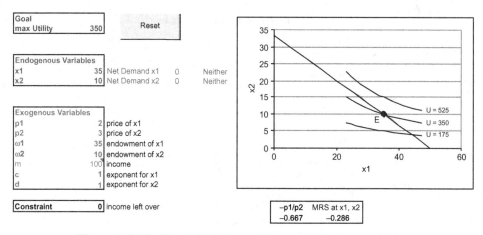

Figure 1.5.1.3. The initial view of the optimization problem.
Source: EndowmentIntro.xls!OptimalChoice

Step Click the Reset button and change ω_1 (in cell K13) from 35 to 50. This looks like the usual increase in income in the standard model.

Step Click the Reset button and change ω_2 (in cell K14) from 10 to 2. This generates a downward shift in the budget constraint.

The budget constraint in an Endowment Model plays the same role as the budget constraint in the Standard Model. It describes the agent's consumption possibilities. Unlike the Standard Model, however, where price changes caused rotation around the x or y intercept, price shocks in the Endowment Model lead to swiveling around the initial endowment. If the initial endowment is unchanged, it makes sense that no matter the price, the initial endowment is going to remain the same.

To get shifts in the budget constraint, we will have to change either ω_1 or ω_2.

Now that you understand the budget constraint, we are ready to use the Endowment Model.

The Initial Solution in an Endowment Model

The rest of the Endowment Model is the same as the Standard Model. The agent's preferences are represented by indifference curves that are represented mathematically by a utility function.

The agent seeks to maximize utility given the budget constraint. We can solve this problem numerically and analytically.

Step Proceed to the *OptimalChoice* sheet. Figure 1.5.1.3 reproduces this sheet when you first arrive.

Notice how the organization is the same as a standard consumer model. The agent seeks to maximize utility, represented by a Cobb-Douglas functional form, by choosing the amounts of x_1 and x_2 to consume subject to the budget constraint.

The graph is also similar, although point E, representing the initial endowment, has been added.

Although much is similar, Figure 1.5.1.3 and your computer screen do have, however, some notable innovations. Cells B18 and B19 have been added to the list of exogenous variables. They represent the given initial endowment. Cell B20 has a formula that computes m, which is not bolded to indicate that it is derived from other exogenous variables.

In addition, cells C11:E12 are new.

Step Click on cell D11 to see its formula, = x1_-w1_.

Gross demand is the optimal amount of the good the agent wishes to end up with, that is, the values of x_1 and x_2. *Net demand* is how much of the good the agent wants to buy or sell. We subtract the initial endowment from gross demand to get net demand.

There is a gross and net demand for each good.

On open, the net demand is zero because cell B11 is set at 35, which is equal to the agent's initial endowment of good 1.

Suppose the agent decided to buy three more units of good 1.

Step Change cell B11 to 38.

Net demand for good 1 is now plus three. That makes sense because the consumer started with 35 units of good 1, but wants to have 38, so three more must be purchased.

Of course, the combination 38,10 is unattainable. The consumer must sell some x_2 in order to be able to buy x_1. How much needs to be sold? Two units.

Step Change cell B12 to 8.

The agent is back on the budget line and net demand for good 2 is negative. Cell E12 reports that the agent is a seller of good 2. Clicking on cell E12 reveals an IF formula that displays Buyer or Seller depending on whether net demand is positive or negative.

Step Compare the MRS on your screen to the MRS at the initial position from Figure 1.5.1.3. Was buying three units of good 1 with the proceeds from the sale of two units of good 2 a smart move?

No. The MRS is farther away from the price ratio. The graph reveals that we moved to a lower indifference curve.

The agent needs to travel up the budget line, selling good 1 and buying good 2. How much should be sold and bought?

Step Run Solver to find the initial solution.

Utility is maximized when gross demands are 25 and $16\frac{2}{3}$ of goods 1 and 2, respectively. Net demands are -10 and $6\frac{2}{3}$. This means the agent sells 10 units of good 1 and uses the \$20 in revenue to buy $6\frac{2}{3}$ units of good 2.

We can easily confirm this result with analytical methods. We follow the recipe for the Lagrangean method of solving constrained optimization problems.

Rewrite the constraint and form the Lagrangean, leaving all exogenous variables as letters:

$$\max_{x_1, x_2, \lambda} L = x_1^c x_2^d + \lambda(p_1\omega_1 + p_2\omega_2 - p_1 x_1 - p_2 x_2)$$

This is the *general* form of the problem (with a Cobb-Douglas utility function).

Take derivatives with respect to each choice variable and set equal to zero:

$$\frac{\partial L}{\partial x_1} = cx_1^{c-1} x_2^d - p_1\lambda = 0$$

$$\frac{\partial L}{\partial x_2} = dx_1^c x_2^{d-1} - p_2\lambda = 0$$

$$\frac{\partial L}{\partial \lambda} = p_1\omega_1 + p_2\omega_2 - p_1 x_1 - p_2 x_2 = 0$$

Solve for the optimal values of x_1 and x_2. Moving the lambda terms to the right-hand side and dividing the first equation by the second gets rid of lambda (and gives the familiar $MRS = p_1/p_2$ condition), which can then be solved for optimal x_2 as a function of optimal x_1:

$$\frac{cx_2^*}{dx_1^*} = \frac{p_1}{p_2}$$

$$x_2^* = \frac{d}{c}\frac{p_1}{p_2}x_1^*$$

Substitute this expression for x_2^* into the third first-order condition and solve for x_1^*:

$$p_1\omega_1 + p_2\omega_2 - p_1 x_1^* - p_2\left[\frac{d}{c}\frac{p_1}{p_2}x_1^*\right] = 0$$

$$\left(1 + \frac{d}{c}\right) p_1 x_1^* = p_1\omega_1 + p_2\omega_2$$

$$x_1^* = \left(\frac{c}{c+d}\right)\frac{p_1\omega_1 + p_2\omega_2}{p_1}$$

This expression is a demand curve for x_1. It shows the quantity demanded at a given p_1, ceteris paribus. There is, of course, a similar expression for good 2.

Furthermore, this expression can be evaluated for any combination of exogenous variable values. For example, if we use the parameter values in the *OptimalChoice* sheet, we can compute that optimal $x_1 = 25$. This agrees perfectly with the numerical approach.

With an Endowment Model, we can subtract the initial amount of good 1 to obtain a net demand curve.

$$nd_1 = x_1{}^* - \omega_1 = \left(\frac{c}{c+d}\right)\frac{p_1\omega_1 + p_2\omega_2}{p_1} - \omega_1$$

Comparative Statics with an Endowment Model

The reduced-form expression just discussed makes analytical comparative statics analysis straightforward. We explore the rate of change of x_1^* with respect to a given exogenous variable.

For example, if own price changes, then we take the derivative with respect to p_1. The actual mechanics of this derivative requires use of the Product Rule because p_1 appears in two places.

$$x_1^* = \left(\frac{c}{c+d}\right)\frac{p_1\omega_1 + p_2\omega_2}{p_1} = \left(\frac{c}{c+d}\right)(p_1\omega_1 + p_2\omega_2)p_1^{-1}$$

$$\frac{dx_1^*}{dp_1} = -\left(\frac{c}{c+d}\right)(p_1\omega_1 + p_2\omega_2)p_1^{-2} + \left(\frac{c}{c+d}\right)\frac{\omega_1}{p_1}$$

We can evaluate this expression at the initial values of the exogenous variables to get an instantaneous rate of change in x_1^* as p_1 changes.

We can also use numerical methods to explore the comparative statics properties of an own price change.

Step Use the Comparative Statics Wizard to *decrease* p_1 by 0.1 (10 cents) for 15 shocks (from 2 to 0.5). Be sure to keep track of net demands and the buyer/seller position in the endogenous variables as depicted in Figure 1.5.1.4.

The *CSP1* sheet shows what your results should look like.

There are several notable points in the comparative statics results.

When the price fell from 90 cents to 80 cents, the agent switched from selling x_1 and buying x_2 to buying x_1 and selling x_2. The price of x_1 got so

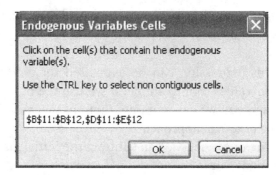

Figure 1.5.1.4. Selecting endogenous variables in the Comparative Statics Wizard.

low that even though the agent starts with a lot of x_1 (compared to x_2), it is better to buy more x_1.

Notice the behavior of maximum utility as price falls. The agent was a seller at first so falling prices hurt. Below 90 cents, however, the agent is a buyer of x_1 and falling prices help.

In addition, we compute the point elasticities and see that unlike the standard model, where a Cobb-Douglas utility function gives a unit price elasticity, we get non-unitary elasticity. This is due to the fact that a change in p_1 appears in the denominator and numerator in the reduced form. In the numerator, the change in price is affecting the value of the agent's endowment whereas in the standard model, income is fixed.

Finally, you can use the results to compute discrete-size changes in p_1 in terms of slopes and elasticities. The *CSP1* sheet shows the calculations. If you compare the changes based on 0.1 decreases in p_1 to the derivative, you find slight differences. This is due to the fact that $x_1^* = f(p_1)$ is non-linear.

The Endowment Model Extends the Standard Model

The Endowment Model is the Standard Model of the Theory of Consumer Behavior with an initial endowment of goods instead of cash income. This transforms the consumer into a seller and buyer of goods. The driving force in the agent's decision making remains utility maximization. Many of the ideas behind the standard model (such as equating the MRS and price ratio) carry over to the endowment model. Of course, the framework for presenting and understanding the model, comparative statics analysis, remains the same.

It may seem that replacing income with an initial endowment is a minor twist, but we will see that the Endowment Model enables analysis of a wide range of choice problems.

Exercises

Open Word and answer the following questions. Save the document and print it when you are done.

1. Perform a comparative statics analysis of c, the exponent on x_1, using the Comparative Statics Wizard. Use increments in c of 0.1. State the effect of changing c on x_1^*. Describe your procedure and take screen shots of your results as needed.
2. Use your comparative statics results to find the c elasticity of x_1^* from 1 to 1.1. Show your work.
3. Use the reduced form expression in this chapter to find the c elasticity of x_1^* at $c = 1$. Show your work.
4. Compare your answers from questions 2 and 3. Explain why they are the same or differ.

References

The epigraph is from page 188 of David M. Kreps, *A Course in Microeconomic Theory* (1990). If you are interested in graduate study in economics, this book is worth browsing. In the preface, Kreps says, "The primary target for this book is a first-year graduate student who is looking for an introduction to microeconomic theory that goes beyond the traditional models of the consumer, the firm, and the market." Kreps allows that it could be used for undergraduate majors taking an "advanced theory" course or "mathematically sophisticated students," but he warns that, "The book presumes, however, that the reader has survived the standard intermediate microeconomics course" (p. xv).

Google "graduate micro theory" for more advanced micro books. To learn more about Masters and PhD programs in economics, search for "graduate economics rankings" and be sure to visit <www.vanderbilt.edu/AEA/gradstudents>.

1.5.2

Intertemporal Consumer Choice

The term impatience carries with it the presumption that present goods are preferred. But I shall treat the two terms (impatience and time preference) as synonymous.

Irving Fisher

Suppose the government wants to stimulate savings by workers so they won't be poor when they retire. Individual Retirement Accounts (IRAs) enable savings to grow tax free, so the interest rate earned is higher than if returns were taxed. This should stimulate more savings. But how much more?

Suppose the interest rate elasticity of savings is positive, but quite small, say 0.15.

Two Questions

1. Will attempts to stimulate savings by increasing the interest rate be effective?

Not really, because the low interest rate elasticity of savings means that saving is not responsive to changes in the interest rate. Suppose the interest rate doubles so we have a huge 100% change. Because the elasticity is 0.15, that means we will see only a 15% increase in savings. A more realistic 10% increase in the interest rate would generate a small 1.5% increase in savings.

Elasticity with a variable that is expressed as a percent can be tricky. We need to distinguish between percentage and percentage point changes. Say the interest rate rises from 4% to 5%. That is a one percentage point (or, in the financial literature, 100 basis points) change and a 25 percent change.

2. What would make the interest rate elasticity of savings be so small?

The rest of this chapter offers an application of an endowment model to answer this question. In addition, income and substitution effects are used in the explanation.

The Intertemporal Choice Model

Intertemporal choice means the consumer is choosing across time periods. We collapse the many time periods into two: present and future. In the present you work and in the future you are retired.

Instead of having two goods x_1 and x_2, we have consumption of a single good in the present, c_1, and the future, c_2. The initial endowment is the amount of present and future consumption you start with.

You can think of the agent as having an income while working and an income while retired, and income while working is greater than while retired. The price of the single good that is consumed in either the present or future is $1 (assume no inflation) so the amount of income you have buys that same amount of the good.

Notice the usual modeling technique at work here – realistic details are simply assumed away. Most people's lives unfold as follows: Childhood becomes teenaged years, and then a long period of working adult life eventually turns to retirement years and death. The Intertemporal Choice Model collapses all of that into two time periods. It also assumes away complications from not knowing exactly when we die.

Faced with criticisms about the unrealistic nature of the model, economists respond by saying that we are not interested in realism. We reduce the complex real world to a model that can be analyzed with comparative statics to produce testable predictions. For economists, the goal is not to describe reality, but to predict via comparative statics.

We follow the usual approach, modeling the budget constraint, then satisfaction, then putting the two together to find the initial solution. Of course, after finding the initial optimum we will do comparative statics analysis, where we will find the answer to this question: What causes the interest rate elasticity of savings to be so small?

The Budget Constraint

Step Open the Excel workbook IntertemporalChoice.xls and read the *Intro* sheet, then go to the *MovingAround* sheet.

The consumer begins at the initial endowment point, 80,20, where 80 represents her income and consumption in time period 1 (remember that the price of the good is $1/unit). Twenty is her lower consumption in time period 2 (given that she is not working).

She does not have to accept this initial position. She can move by *saving* or *borrowing*. Saving means you consume less in the present and carry over the unconsumed portion into the future. Saving is like selling present consumption and buying future consumption.

Suppose she saves 30 units of consumption. What would be her position in time period 2?

Step Change cell B19 to 50. This implements the plan to increase future consumption, but look at cells B21 and B22. Instead of simply reallocating from 80,20 to 50,50, by saving 30 units, she got an extra 6 units in *interest* on her savings.

If you save $30 for one year at 20%, you end up with $56. The $30 you saved (called the principal) and interest earned of $30*20% = $6 makes your savings worth $36 in the future and we add the $20 of future income to get the grand total of $56.

There is an equation that gives us the value of c_2 for any chosen value of c_1.

$$c_2 = m_2 + (m_1 - c_1) + r(m_1 - c_1)$$

The equation says that the amount of consumption in time period 2 equals the initial endowment amount in time period 2 plus the principal saved $(m_1 - c_1)$ plus the interest earned on the amount saved, $r(m_1 - c_1)$.

We can rewrite this in a simpler form by collecting the savings term.

$$c_2 = m_2 + (1 + r)(m_1 - c_1)$$

This is the equation of the budget constraint in this model.

What would be the maximum consumption possible in time period 2?

Step Change cell B19 to 0. She consumes nothing now and ends up with 116 in the future.

"But she will starve." That would be another constraint that is not being modeled. Of course, we are not saying she will consume nothing in the present time period, we are merely exploring the budget line. Saving everything gives us the y intercept. It tells us the future value of the agent's initial endowment.

The *future value* measures the total income in terms of time period 2.

Suppose the agent decided to consume more than 80 in time period 1. How could she do this? Easy: use her time period 2 income to borrow.

Step Change cell B19 to 90. She borrows 10 from her future income.

Does she end up with 90,10? No way. She has to *pay* interest on the borrowed funds. If she borrows 10, she ends up with only 8 in the future because she has to pay back the principal (10) and the interest (2).

What is the most she could consume in time period 1?

Step Change cell B19 to 100. She cannot do this. She does not have enough future income to enable 100 units of time period 1 consumption.

The Budget Set

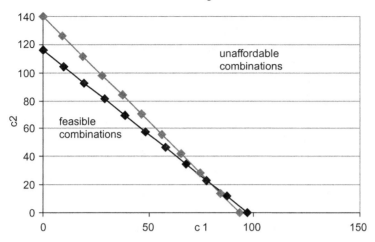

Figure 1.5.2.1. Increasing r.
Source: IntertemporalChoice!Changes

Continue entering numbers in cell B19 until you drive c_2 (in cells B23 and B24) to zero.

The x intercept is 96 and 2/3. It is the present value of her endowment. The *present value* measures all income from the standpoint of time period 1.

Step Proceed to the *Properties* sheet.

Our work in the *MovingAround* sheet makes it easy to understand the budget line displayed in the *Properties* sheet. Clearly, given an initial endowment, movement up the budget line is savings and down is borrowing.

These are just consumption possibilities. We do not know what this person will do until we incorporate her preferences.

The *Properties* sheet shows that the slope of the budget line is $-(1 + r)$. Saving \$1 will yield $1 + r$ dollars in time period 2.

The slope of the budget line is negative because to save \$1 you have to *reduce* consumption in time period 1. We can easily rewrite the budget constraint to show this.

$$c_2 = m_2 + (1 + r)(m_1 - c_1)$$
$$c_2 = m_2 + (1 + r)m_1 - (1 + r)c_1$$

So, $m_2 + (1 + r)m_1$ is the intercept and $-(1 + r)$ is the slope.

Step Proceed to the *Changes* sheet. Change the interest rate, cell L8, to 50%. Your screen will look like Figure 1.5.2.1.

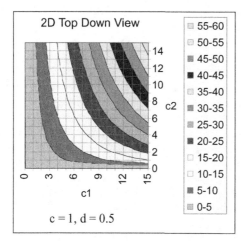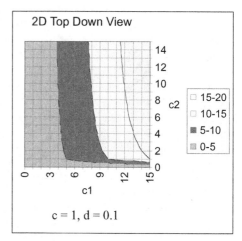

Figure 1.5.2.2. Modeling rates of time preference.
Source: IntertemporalChoice!Preferences

Our work with endowment models in the previous chapter enables us to easily interpret the result. Above the initial endowment point, the increase in r is a good thing, increasing consumption possibilities. If the agent is a saver, the shock is welcome.

Borrowers, however, are not happy. The increase in r is a price increase to present consumption and reduces consumption possibilities.

Step Click the Reset button. Change m_1 and m_2 to see how this shock is like an income shock. It maintains the slope, but shifts the budget constraint.

Now that the budget constraint is clear, we are ready to turn to the agent's goal, maximizing utility.

Preferences

The agent has preferences over present and future consumption that can be captured by the indifference map.

We use the usual Cobb-Douglas function form to express preferences as a utility function.

Step Proceed to the *Preferences* sheet. Compare the utility functions with $d = 0.5$ and $d = 0.1$. The utility function allows us to model different preferences.

Figure 1.5.2.2 shows two different agents with different *rates of time preference* for future consumption.

The consumer on the right of Figure 1.5.2.2 is more of an immediate gratification personality. We would say this person is more impatient – he does

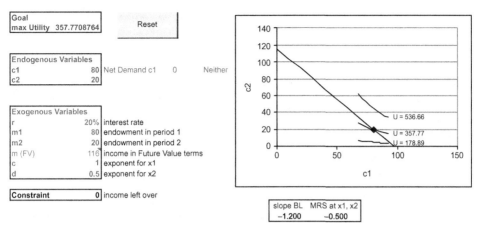

Figure 1.5.2.3. An inefficient position.
Source: IntertemporalChoice.xls!OptimalChoice

not like to wait to consume. The steep parts of his indifferences curves reveal that he is willing to trade a great deal of future consumption for a just a little more present consumption. His MRS at a given point is higher than the MRS of the person on the left.

Economists take preferences as given. We do not judge them as right or wrong. A person with preferences that substantially ignore the future is treated the same as someone who does not like broccoli. There is a complication here, however, in that a person's rate of time preference almost certainly changes over time. A young person may not save much because she does not value the future, but she may regret her decision when she gets older.

Finding the Initial Solution

Step Proceed to the *OptimalChoice* sheet. Figure 1.5.2.3 shows the initial display. The current bundle is 80,20 – the initial endowment point. The agent is not maximizing satisfaction subject to the budget constraint. The indifference curve is clearly cutting the budget line and, therefore, the agent should move northwest up the budget line to maximize utility.

Step Run Solver to find the initial solution.

The agent opts for the point $64\frac{4}{9}, 38\frac{2}{3}$. This means she has decided to save $15\frac{5}{9}$ of her present consumption.

She does this because this maximizes utility subject to the budget constraint.

Notice that the negative net demand in this case is interpreted as the amount of saving.

Comparative Statics

We focus on r.

Step Run the Comparative Statics Wizard, changing the interest rate by 10 percentage point (0.1) increments. Keep track of c_1, c_2, net demand, and whether the person is a saver or borrower.

Your results should be similar to those in the *CSr* sheet.

Step Compute the interest rate elasticity of savings from $r = 20\%$ to 30%.

We find that the interest rate elasticity of savings from $r = 20\%$ to 30% is about 0.11.

This elasticity is similar to the 0.15 elasticity at the very beginning of this chapter. Why is this happening? Why is savings so unresponsive to changes in the interest rate?

It is all about the income and substitution effects. For savings the income and substitution effects work in opposite directions (when c_1 is a normal good).

Step To see how the income and substitution effects apply to this problem, return to the *OptimalChoice* sheet. Suppose r increases to 300%. This huge change enables us to see clearly what is happening on the graph.

Step After changing cell B16 to 300%, run Solver to find the new initial solution.

Savings has increased from $15.56 to $23.33, but this is a pretty weak response to the massive increase in the interest rate from 20% to 300%.

Figure 1.5.2.4 shows the initial solution (point A) and the new optimal solution (point C). It also includes a dashed line that is parallel to point C's budget line, but goes through point A. This, of course, is the line that is used to separate the total effect into income and substitution effects.

How much income (m_1) did we have to take away to cancel out the income effect of the higher interest rate? We can use Excel to display this information.

Step With $r = 300\%$, enter the initial solution $c_1^* = 64\frac{4}{9}$ and $c_2^* = 38\frac{2}{3}$, then start decreasing m_1 (in cell B17). Your goal is to find that value of m_1 so that the initial solution is on the budget line – i.e., the constraint cell is zero.

A little experimentation should convince you that $m_1 = 69\frac{1}{9}$ is the value that puts the dashed budget line through the initial solution.

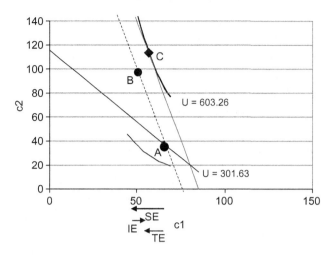

Figure 1.5.2.4. Income and substitution effects.
Source: IntertemporalChoice.xls!OptimalChoice: cell F52

Of course, you could use the budget constraint to find an analytical value. Simply plug in the initial optimal solution along with the new value of r (and initial m_2) and solve for m_1. You are finding the value of m_1 that would enable you to buy the initial optimal combination with the higher interest rate. The analytical answer agrees with the numerical approach.

Step Now, with $r = 300\%$ and $m_1 = 69\frac{1}{9}$, run Solver to find the value of point B.

Be careful with the interpretation of savings for point B. Remember that income is not really $69\frac{1}{9}$, but 80. This means that at point B, the agent would save \$30.59, not \$19.07 as displayed in cell D11.

Figure 1.5.2.5 shows the results in a table. You can see Figures 1.5.2.4 and 1.5.2.5 side by side by scrolling down to row 50. Look at how the substitution effect leads to a large increase in savings, but the income effect cancels out part of this increase.

The income and substitution effects provide an explanation for the low interest rate elasticity of savings. What is happening is that the two effects are working against each other when r rises and the agent is a saver.

Point	Description	c1*	c2*	Savings*
A	Initial solution	64.44	38.67	15.56
B	Imaginary	49.41	98.81	30.59
C	New solution	56.67	113.33	23.33

Effect	Movement	Amount
SE	A to B	15.03
IE	B to C	-7.26
TE	A to C	7.77

Figure 1.5.2.5. Results of the comparative statics analysis.
Source: IntertemporalChoice.xls!OptimalChoice: cell M51

Does this mean c_1 is an inferior good? No. The reason why the effects are opposing each other is because, for savers, an increase in the interest rate is like a decrease in the price of future consumption so the effects on c_1 and savings are actually cross effects. Look carefully at Figure 1.5.2.4. In the region of the graph with points A, B, and C, it is as if we decreased p_2, and rotated the budget line up (with a steeper slope).

Saving and Borrowing with the Theory of Consumer Behavior

The Intertemporal Choice Model is an application of an Endowment Model in the Theory of Consumer Behavior. The model says that the agent chooses the amount to consume in time periods 1 and 2 in order to maximize satisfaction given a budget constraint.

The model can explain why the interest rate elasticity of savings is often estimated as positive, but a small number, which means that savings is quite unresponsive to the interest rate. The explanation rests on the fact that the income effect opposes the substitution effect for c_1 and savings (for those with negative net demand for c_1).

Exercises

Open Word and answer the following questions. Save the document and print it when you are done.

1. Solve the problem in the *OptimalChoice* sheet using analytical methods. In other words, find the reduced-form expressions for c_1^*, c_2^*, and *savings** from

$$\max_{c_1, c_2} u(c_1, c_2) = c_1^c c_2^d$$
$$\text{s.t. } c_2 = m_2 + (1 + \text{r})(m_1 - c_1)$$

   Show your work.
2. Use the parameter values in the sheet (with $r = 20\%$) to evaluate your answers for question 1. Provide numerical answers for the optimal combination of consumption in time periods 1 and 2 and for optimal savings.
3. Do your answers from question 2 agree with Excel's Solver results? Is this surprising? Explain.
4. Use your reduced-form solution from question 1 to compute the interest rate elasticity of savings as $r = 20\%$.
5. In working through this chapter, you found the interest rate elasticity of savings from $r = 20\%$ to 30%. Why is the elasticity computed at a point (in question 4 above) different from this elasticity?

References

The epigraph is on page 66 of Irving Fisher, *The Theory of Interest: As Determined by Impatience to Spend Income and Opportunity to Invest It* (first edition, 1930; reprinted 1977 by Porcupine Press).

Joseph Schumpeter had high praise for Fisher: "[S]ome future historian may well consider Fisher as the greatest of America's scientific economists up to our own day" (*History of Economic Analysis*, 1954, p. 872). Schumpeter chose to ignore Fisher's "propagandist activities (temperance, eugenics, hygiene, and others)," but he did point out that Fisher's reputation as an economist was negatively affected: "Fisher, a reformer of the highest and purest type, never counted costs – even those most intensive pain costs which consist in being looked upon as something of a crank – and his fame as a scientist suffered correspondingly" (*History of Economic Analysis*, 1954, p. 873).

A classic defense of unrealistic assumptions in a model is "The Methodology of Positive Economics," the first chapter in Milton Friedman's *Essays in Positive Economics* (1953).

For more on this, see the references in the introduction to the Theory of the Firm.

The empirical evidence on the interest rate elasticity of savings is mixed (which is actually evidence that it is not large). Irwin Friend and Joel Hasbrouck, "Saving and After-Tax Rates of Return," *The Review of Economics and Statistics*, Vol. 65, No. 4. (November, 1983), pp. 537–543, find a low elasticity.

Jonathan McCarthy and Han N. Pham, "The Impact of Individual Retirement Accounts on Savings," *Current Issues in Economics and Finance* (Federal Reserve Board of New York), Vol. 1, No. 6 (September 1995), conclude that "recent economic research suggests that the effect of the [IRA] accounts on savings is in fact quite small." This paper is available from the Social Science Research Network online at <papers.ssrn.com/sol3/papers.cfm?abstract_id=1001447>.

1.5.3

An Economic Analysis of Charitable Giving

The Prophet said: "Charity is a necessity for every Muslim." He was asked: "What if a person has nothing?" The Prophet replied: "He should work with his own hands for his benefit and then give something out of such earnings in charity."

Prophet Muhammed

The phrase "an economic analysis of" is code for "using the framework of optimization and comparative statics to study observed behavior." In this case, we use an Endowment Model from the Theory of Consumer Behavior to study charitable giving.

Figure 1.5.3.1 shows the breakdown of the $260 billion that were contributed to charities in the United States in 2005.

The Giving USA Foundation keeps track of charitable donations. For example, in 2002, they reported that although Americans gave $240 billion to charities, inflation-adjusted giving went down by 2.3% in 2001 and 0.5% in 2002, the first declines in seven years. Giving USA estimates that individuals gave 1.8% of their income in 2001, a decline from 1.9% in 2000.

The Internal Revenue Service is another source of data. The IRS releases data on giving with a two-year delay. IRS data show that people who itemized their deductions in 1997 claimed they donated about 3% of their income. About 90% of itemizers said they gave something (money or property) to charity.

There are many interesting questions we can ask about charitable giving: Why do people give to charity? What determines how much they give? How can charitable giving be stimulated?

Because this is an economic analysis of charitable giving, we are going to answer these questions by using the method of economics. We will set up and solve an optimization problem. This will provide the economic explanation for why people give and what determines how much they give. We will see that charitable giving can be stimulated by changing exogenous variables, ceteris paribus.

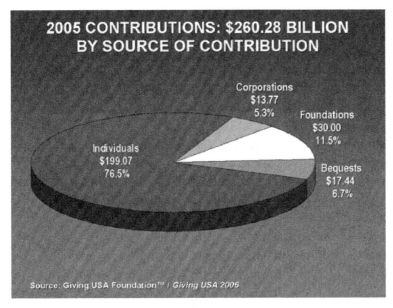

Figure 1.5.3.1. Charitable giving by source of contribution.
Source: <www.aafrc.org>

An Endowment Model of Charitable Giving

As usual, we begin with the budget constraint, then we model preferences, and we conclude by finding the initial solution to the problem of maximizing satisfaction subject to the budget constraint.

The Budget Constraint

Figure 1.5.3.2 depicts the budget constraint in this application. The initial endowment is the coordinate pair that represents the donor's consumption and the beneficiary's (or recipient's) consumption. There is only one good (which represents consumption of all goods) and its price is $1/unit. So, if the donor has $100 and the beneficiary only $10, we know the initial endowment is at the point 10,100.

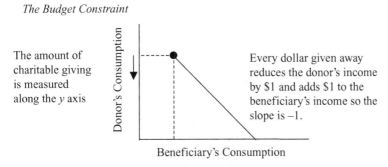

Figure 1.5.3.2. The budget constraint.

Giving is modeled as moving down the budget line in Figure 1.5.3.2. If the donor gives $20 away, then she will have $80 and the beneficiary will have $30. Of course, the donor could give all of her money away, choosing to be at the *x* intercept.

Thus, at any point on the budget line, we can compute the amount of giving as simply the vertical distance (along the *y* axis) from the initial endowment to the point on the budget line.

The slope of the budget line is −1 because there is a dollar-for-dollar exchange from the donor to the beneficiary.

Notice that this budget line does not extend left from the initial endowment because that would imply taking money from the beneficiary. The donor cannot do that.

The donor decides how much, if any, to give and decides where on the budget line the donor and beneficiary will end up.

Finally, because we will (of course) be doing comparative statics analysis, we point out that a tax break for those who donate money means that the budget line will have a shallower slope. If the donor gives $1 and is rewarded, for example, with a 30¢ decrease in taxes, then the recipient gets $1, but the donor actually gave only 70¢. The slope is not −1, but −(1 − *TaxBreak*). By adjusting the tax break, we can see how the agent responds.

Step Open the Excel workbook Charity.xls and read the *Intro* sheet, then go to the *BudgetConstraint* sheet.

Initially, the donor gives nothing and there is no tax break.

Step Change cell C5, the amount the donor gives, to 20. The beneficiary gets the 20 and the slope of the constraint is −1.

Step Change cell E5, the amount of the tax break, to 40%. The beneficiary still gets 20, but because of the tax break on charitable donations, the beneficiary really gave up only 12 and the slope of the constraint is −0.6.

Who pays the difference? The government does. The beneficiary gets the full donation, but the donor pays less tax to the government. Clearly, by manipulating the tax break, the government can make charitable giving less expensive to donors.

Preferences

The usual Cobb-Douglas function will represent the donor's satisfaction derived from her own consumption and the beneficiary's consumption.

$$\max U = BeneficiaryCon^c DonorCon^d$$

If the exponents, *c* and *d*, are equal, the donor gets as much satisfaction from her own consumption as the beneficiary's consumption. Although possible,

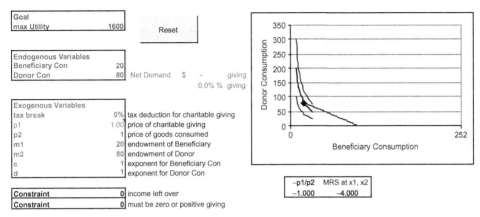

Figure 1.5.3.3. Initial display of the donor's optimization problem.
Source: Charity.xls!OptimalChoice

this is unlikely. Most people get more satisfaction from their own consumption and, thus, d is greater than c.

The shape of the indifference map reflects the person's preferences. With donor consumption on the y axis, steep indifference curves mean that the donor cares a great deal about the beneficiary's welfare.

Preferences are not right or wrong. We take them as given and we model the agent as maximizing based on given preferences.

Finding the Initial Solution

The donor's optimization problem is the following:

$$\max_{BeneficiaryCon, DonorCon} U = BeneficiaryCon^c DonorCon^d$$

$$\text{s.t. } (1 - TaxBreak)\, BeneficiaryCon + p_2 DonorCon \leq m_1 + m_2$$

$$\text{for } BeneficiaryCon \geq m_1$$

Step Proceed to the *OptimalChoice* sheet to see how this constraint can be handled in Excel.

Figure 1.5.3.3 shows the initial display. The endogenous variables are consumption by beneficiary and donor. These are chosen by the donor to maximize utility subject to the budget constraint.

The exogenous variables include the amount of the tax break (initially set at zero so the slope of the budget constraint is −1), the price of the good consumed by the donor and the beneficiary, the initial endowment, and the impact of donor and beneficiary consumption on the donor's utility.

The first constraint cell handles the downward part of the budget line and the second says that income cannot be taken from the beneficiary. The

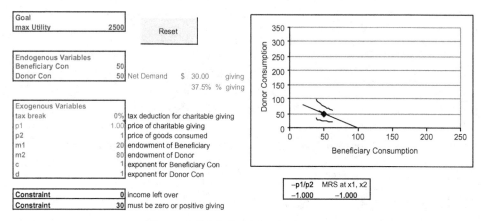

Figure 1.5.3.4. Initial solution.
Source: Charity.xls!OptimalChoice

second constraint is used to model the fact that the budget line ends at the initial endowment.

Because the $MRS > p_1/p_2$, we know the agent can increase satisfaction by traveling down the budget line. For example, suppose the agent decided to donate $10. How would this affect the chart?

Step Change cell B11 to 30 and cell B12 to 70.

The MRS is now closer to the price ratio and utility has risen. The agent has moved down the budget line and is on a higher indifference curve.

Step Run Solver to find the initial optimal solution.

Figure 1.5.3.4 shows the optimal solution after running Solver.

The agent chooses the point 50,50, which means she donates $30 to the beneficiary. The net demand is the amount of giving and we express it as a dollar amount and as a percentage of the donor's income.

This is one mighty nice donor. Because $c = d$, she cares as much about the beneficiary as she does herself.

Comparative Statics

Step Change the exponent for the beneficiary's consumption to 0.2.

The indifference curves become much flatter reflecting the fact that the donor's preferences have changed. This agent is not optimizing at 50,50.

Step Run Solver. Figure 1.5.3.5 displays the result.

Notice that this is a corner solution. There is a second constraint that says the donor can decide not to give any of her income away, but she cannot travel northwest along the budget constraint because that would imply taking income from the beneficiary.

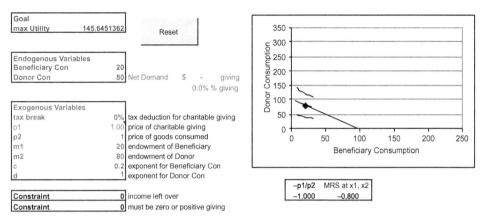

Figure 1.5.3.5. A corner solution.
Source: Charity.xls!OptimalChoice

The best the agent can do is to donate nothing so that is what she does. Even though the MRS does not equal the price ratio, this agent is optimizing.

Our work thus far provides answers to two of the three questions we initially asked.

Why do people give to charity? To maximize satisfaction. A donor gives because the consumption of others affects his or her utility.

Notice that giving is perfectly compatible with self-interest. The economic model says that the donor feels good when she gives and that is why she gives.

What determines how much they give? Clearly preferences matter. The impact of how others are doing (the exponent c in the donor's utility function) plays a major role. Of course, the constraint also matters. Donor's income, beneficiary's income, and the slope of the constraint affect the amount of giving.

How can charitable giving be stimulated? We could try to convince people to care more about others (certainly this is a primary goal of religion), but we can also manipulate the tax break variable to alter the slope of the constraint.

One way to stimulate giving is to lower the price of giving. As we saw earlier, dollars given to charity reduce the donor's adjusted gross income and reduce tax liability. If the donor is in a 30% tax bracket, every dollar donated to charity saves the donor 30 cents in taxes. Thus, the beneficiary receives the dollar, but the donor is actually paying only 70 cents – with Uncle Sam picking up the remaining 30 cents.

What effect will a 30% tax break have on the budget constraint and charitable giving? Apply the shock in Excel and find out.

Step Change the tax break cell to 30% and note that p_1 becomes 0.70.

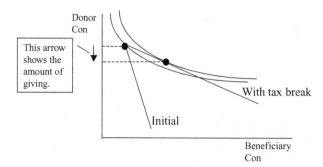

Figure 1.5.3.6. The total effect of a tax break.

A new budget line appears. It has a shallower slope. The MRS is greater than the slope of the new budget line. This agent can improve her utility by traveling down the new budget line.

Step Run Solver.

In this case, the tax break has induced charitable giving. It is hard to see on the graph, but the $MRS = p_1/p_2$ condition tells you the indifference curve is now tangent to the budget line.

Figure 1.5.3.6 shows a rough sketch of what happened.

We can also explore the responsiveness of charitable giving to tax incentives.

Step Change the tax break cell to 40%. That's a 10 percentage point change in the tax break and a rather hefty 33% change.

Step Run Solver.

Charity increased from $1.67 to $3.33. That is a big response – a 100% increase in giving was generated from a 33% increase in the tax break.

A more detailed comparative statics analysis is contained in the *CS1* sheet.

Of course, we do not know whether these preferences and other exogenous variables are representative of many donors. That is an empirical question that requires data and empirical analysis. For example, with $c = 0.5$, tax break increases are much less effective in stimulating more giving.

Step Click the Reset button, change c to 0.5 and the tax break to 30%, and run Solver. Charitable giving is at $17.33.

Step Change the tax break cell to 40% and run Solver. Charitable giving rises to $18.67.

The percentage change in charitable giving, $(18.67 - 17.33)/17.33 = 7.7\%$, resulting from the 33% increase in the tax break yields an elasticity of only about 0.23. That means, for this donor, the tax break won't be very effective in stimulating a lot more giving.

The Theory of Consumer Behavior can explain a wide variety of giving outcomes. Unfortunately, theory alone does not tell us about the magnitude of a particular effect in the real world. By changing c, we saw that the elasticity was drastically affected. We must gather data and employ econometric techniques to estimate the responsiveness of giving as the tax break changes. Theory does, however, give us a framework for analyzing the problem.

The Economic Approach Is Widely Applicable

Charitable giving can be viewed through the lens of an Endowment Model in the Theory of Consumer Behavior. The initial endowment is the consumption of the donor and the beneficiary. The donor can choose to give to the beneficiary. The amount she gives is determined by that point that maximizes her satisfaction subject to the budget constraint.

We can stimulate giving by lowering the price of giving. This rotates the budget line and yields a new optimal solution. The amount of the increase in giving is an empirical question that cannot be answered by theory alone.

If we view giving as the solution to an optimization problem, we are doing an economic analysis of giving. "An economic analysis" is a phrase often used to communicate that the behavior under consideration will be cast in the framework of optimization and comparative statics.

Many people think economics is about stocks, unemployment, and money. This content-based definition of economics is too limited. Economics, defined as a method of analysis, can be applied to such "noneconomic" issues as charity, not to mention marriage, war, and many, many other areas.

Exercises

Open Word and answer the following questions. Save the document and print it when you are done.

1. The total change in charitable giving can be explained via the income and substitution effects for giving. For $c = 0.5$, compute the income and substitution effects when the tax break changes from 30% to 40%. Describe your procedure.
2. Use Word's Drawing Tools to draw a rough sketch of the income and substitution effects for giving, labeling points A, B, and C and using arrows to show the income, substitution, and total effects. Do not include the indifference curves to reduce clutter.
3. Income and substitution effects were originally used to explain Giffen goods. If the tax break increase leads to a decrease in charitable giving, is this Giffen behavior? Why or why not?

References

The epigraph is a hadith, which the web site <www.uga.edu/islam/hadith.html> explains is "a saying of Muhammad or a report about something he did." It would have been easy to find a quotation on charity from any religion because a primary purpose of religion is to encourage us to treat each other with kindness.

If you are thinking of giving to a charitable organization, you can do some background research at <www.guidestar.org> (free registration required to access basic reports). Kiva.org is a micro credit organization that allows you to make loans to low-income entrepreneurs in the developing world.

1.5.4

An Economic Analysis of Insurance

During the early 1960s, Kenneth Arrow and Karl Borch published several important articles that can be viewed as the beginning of modern economic analysis of insurance activity.

Georges Dionne and Scott E. Harrington

Why do people buy insurance?

Because it makes them better off. They solve an optimization problem and it turns out that those who buy insurance reach greater satisfaction than if they did not buy insurance.

We will use an Endowment Model version of the Theory of Consumer Behavior to explain how and why insurance increases utility. The really deep lesson is that Consumer Choice Theory is amazingly flexible and can answer questions from a wide range of problems.

First, we will set up the situation as a constrained utility maximization problem. There's the usual constraint, indifference curves, and initial optimal solution (with MRS equal to the slope condition). The presence of risk, a probability that an event occurs, throws a curveball into the analysis, but we will convert things into our usual framework.

Second, we will do comparative statics. For example, we derive a demand curve for insurance. We can explore the effects of a higher premium (the price of insurance) on the quantity of insurance demanded. We are searching for the premium elasticity of insurance.

An Endowment Model of Insurance

There are always three parts to an optimization problem. In this case, we have the following:

1. Goal: maximize satisfaction (as represented by the utility function).

Exogenous Variables

InitialAssets	$	35,000
PotentialLoss	$	10,000
ProbLoss		1.00% π
InsurancePremium	$	1.00 γ (per $100 of insurance payout)

$\gamma = 0.01$ if you do this problem analytically

Endogenous Variables

InsuredAmount	$	-	K dollars of insurance purchased
InsuranceCost	$	-	γK

Results

Consumption Bad	25000 with 1% probability
Consumption Good	35000 with 99% probability

State of Nature

RandomDraw	0.41429095
Outcome	0 1 if Loss Event Happened
FinalAssets	$ 35,000

Figure 1.5.4.1. The initial setup.
Source: Insurance.xls!Constraint

2. Endogenous variables: consumption in two states of nature, good and bad; by choosing the amount of insurance, we control two choice variables at once.
3. Exogenous variables: initial assets, potential loss, probability of loss, insurance premium, and preferences over the states of nature.

As usual, we start with the constraint, then turn to preferences, and finally use the constraint and preferences to find the initial solution.

The Budget Constraint

Step Open the Excel workbook Insurance.xls and read the *Intro* sheet, then go to the *Constraint* sheet.

Figure 1.5.4.1 reproduces what is on your screen. The idea is that you have an asset, say your house, which may suffer a given amount of damage from an accident (*PotentialLoss*) with a known probability (π). You can buy *K* dollars of insurance (*InsuredAmount*) by paying a price (called a premium) of γ (gamma) per $100 of insurance coverage.

After you decide how much insurance to buy, there are two possible outcomes (or states of nature). Your consumption in the bad outcome (which means the accident actually occurred) is *InitialAssets − PotentialLoss + K −*

γK. You subtract the loss that occurred and the amount you paid for insurance, but you add the amount K that the insurance company pays you because you suffered the accident. You could be fully covered, but you do not have to be. You decide how much insurance to buy.

Step Click on cell B18 to see the formula for the bad outcome.

Your consumption in the good state of nature is simply *InitialAssets* $- \gamma K$. In this case, you do not suffer the accident, but you still have to pay for the insurance.

Step Click on cell B19 to see the formula for the good outcome.

Cells B23:B25 display which state of nature you end up in. Cell B23 has the formula "=RAND()." This draws a number from a uniform distribution on the interval [0,1].

Step Hit the F9 key on your keyboard repeatedly to understand how RAND() works.

Each time you hit the F9 key, Excel draws a random number from 0 to 1 in cell B23. The number drawn is never smaller than zero or bigger than one.

Cell B24 converts the random draw in the cell above it into a 0 or a 1. It uses an IF statement to display a "1" (which means the accident happened) when the random draw is less than 0.01.

It is hard to see that anything is really happening in cell B24 because the probability of the accident occurring is so small.

Step Change π to 50%, then hit F9 a few times. You should be able to see cell B24 flip from 0 to 1 and back again as the random draw is less than 0.5 and greater than 0.5.

Notice that the Final Assets, cell B25, depend on whether or not the accident occurred.

Next, we can buy some insurance.

Step Click the Reset button and set cell B13 to $1000. This will cost you $10.

Notice the values for the good and bad states of nature. You have altered both. If the accident occurs, your consumption is $25,990, which is $990 better than the $25,000 for the bad outcome when you didn't buy insurance. Of course, the good outcome is $10 lower (at $34,990) in the good outcome because you have to pay for the insurance even when the accident does not occur.

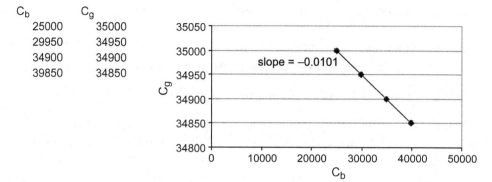

C_b	C_g
25000	35000
29950	34950
34900	34900
39850	34850

Figure 1.5.4.2. The budget line.
Source: Insurance.xls!Constraint

Step Click the |Graph the Constraint| button. Click OK to four points and read each text box as it appears. At the end, the budget line is displayed (see Figure 1.5.4.2).

From your initial endowment (c_b, c_g without insurance), you can move down the budget line by buying insurance. You lower your consumption in the good state of nature (c_g is on the y axis), but raise it in the bad state of nature (c_b is on the x axis).

The terms of trade (the slope of the budget line) are determined by gamma (the insurance premium). The slope is $-\frac{\gamma}{1-\gamma}$, which with $\gamma = 0.01$ is $-\frac{1}{99} = -0.\overline{01}$ (the "01" keeps repeating forever). The graph rounds the slope to four decimal places.

Changes in initial assets, potential loss, or insurance premium shift or pivot the budget constraint. Figure 1.5.4.3 shows an example of what happens if the insurance premium rises to $1.20 per $100 of insurance coverage.

Step To reproduce Figure 1.5.4.3, simply change the premium to $1.20.

The slope value displayed on the chart is for the original budget line. The slope of the new (red) budget line is clearly greater (in absolute value). The new budget line shows that the agent's consumption possibilities have been diminished. It is as if the price of the good on the x axis has been increased.

Preferences

In this application, we model utility as preferences over the two states of nature. The fact that there is uncertainty in which state of nature occurs complicates things.

Instead of having utility simply depend on the amount of consumption in the good and bad outcomes, we have to include the agent's beliefs about the

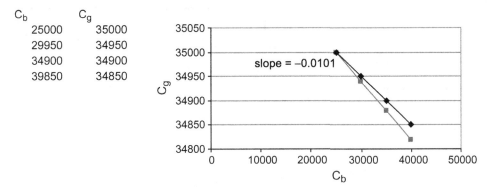

C_b	C_g
25000	35000
29950	34950
34900	34900
39850	34850

Figure 1.5.4.3. The budget line when insurance premium rises.
Source: Insurance.xls!Constraint

chances of each outcome occurring. Fortunately, our usual Cobb-Douglas functional form can incorporate this new information.

We use the exponents in the Cobb-Douglas functional form to represent the agent's beliefs about the probability of the accident occurring. There are two simplifying assumptions. The first is that the agent accurately gauges the probability of loss, which means we can use π as the exponent in the utility function. The second assumption uses the fact that there are only two mutually exclusive outcomes so the bad outcome occurs with probability π and the good outcome has likelihood $1-\pi$.

The utility function is then

$$u(c_b, c_g, \pi, 1 - \pi) = c_b^\pi c_g^{1-\pi}$$

The idea behind the utility function is simple: The higher the probability of loss, the more the agent will care about the bad outcome. In terms of the indifference map, the higher π, the steeper the indifference curves. This means the agent cares more about consumption in the bad state of nature as risk rises.

Unlike the standard model where the exponents in the Cobb-Douglas utility function can be used to represent changes in preferences, changes in the exponents do not really indicate a change in preferences for the choice-under-uncertainty utility function. To get a change in preferences, we would need an entirely different utility function.

The choice-under-certainty utility function is often represented as a weighted average of the probabilities of being in each state of nature:

$$u(c_b, c_g, \pi, 1 - \pi) = \pi f(c_b) + (1 - \pi) f(c_g).$$

In this form, the utility function is called the *expected utility function.*

Endogenous Variables			Dead Utility	Live Utility		Dead MRS	Live MRS
Consumption Bad	25000	C_b	34882.43	34882.43		-0.01414	-0.01414
Consumption Good	35000	C_g					

Exogenous Variables		
ProbLoss	1%	π
1-ProbLoss	99%	$1-\pi$

Figure 1.5.4.4. The utility function.
Source: Insurance.xls!Preferences

Our Cobb-Douglas utility function can be written as an expected utility function by simply taking the natural log:

$$u(c_b, c_g, \pi, 1 - \pi) = \pi \ln c_b + (1 - \pi) \ln c_g.$$

Different preferences are represented by different expected utility functions. The Cobb-Douglas expected utility function reflects a risk averse attitude.

Step Proceed to the *Preferences* sheet to see an implementation of the Cobb-Douglas utility function.

Figure 1.5.4.4 reproduces what is initially on your screen. It shows consumption in the bad and good states of nature, $25,000 and $35,000, respectively, without insurance. This is the initial endowment point. With $\pi = 1\%$, we can compute the level of utility for the initial endowment combination of consumption in the bad and good states of nature.

Figure 1.5.4.4 (and your screen) shows dead and live utility and MRS. The dead cells are numbers. They will not change when we change the cells in column B. The live cells contain formulas. They will update when you change the values of c_b, c_g, and π.

Suppose the agent buys $5000 of insurance. That would mean that consumption in the bad state of nature would rise to $29,950 (if the accident happens, he gets $5000, but he has to pay a $50 premium). In the good state of nature, consumption would fall to $34,950 (because he has to pay the $50 premium).

Step Enter the values 29,950 and 34,950 in cells B13 and B14.

Notice that the live utility and MRS cells change. Utility is higher and the MRS is lower.

Buying $5000 of insurance is a move down the budget line that yields higher satisfaction.

Notice that at both the initial endowment and with $5000, the MRS does not equal the price ratio. You should have a mental picture in your mind of what is happening.

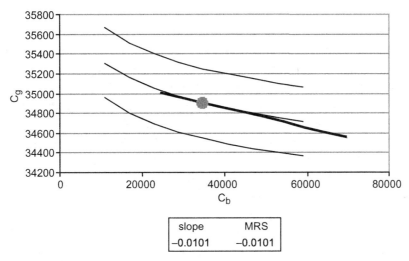

Figure 1.5.4.5. The initial optimal solution.
Source: Insurance.xls!Preferences

Step You can see if your mental picture is correct by going to the *OptimalChoice* sheet.

Initial Solution

The *OptimalChoice* sheet reproduces the *Constraint* sheet, but it adds the indifference map to the chart and displays the slope of the budget line and the MRS at the bottom of the chart. This is the mental picture you should have been considering in the work just described evaluating the purchase of $5000 of insurance.

The *OptimalChoice* sheet also displays the utility in cell B20 from the consumption in the two states of nature.

Step Enter 5000 in cell B13 to see where the agent stands when buying $5000 of insurance.

The chart shows movement down the budget line to a higher level of utility. Of course, there are other points on the budget line available to the agent.

Step Run Solver to find the optimal solution and you get Figure 1.5.4.5.

The Solver dialog box is notable for the fact that there were no constraints. The way we implemented the problem in Excel enabled us to directly maximize the utility cell.

At the optimal solution, the consumer decides to buy $10,000 of insurance.

In the bad state, if the accident occurs, the agent is fully covered, so is consumption $35,000? No, because the agent has to pay $100 for the insurance, so consumption would be $34,900.

In the good state, where there is no accident, consumption is also $34,900.

This is interesting. Insurance has removed the effect of risk. Consumption is the same in both states. This is an extreme example of diversification.

Diversification is a strategy to lower risk by spreading your wealth over different states of nature. By moving $100 from the good state of nature (buying insurance), the agent has a guaranteed level of utility regardless of whether the accident happens. Without insurance, the expected return is $34,900 since 99%*35,000 + 1%*25,000 = $34,900. But the agent has to put up with the risk of every 1 in 100 times getting $25,000. By diversifying, the expected return is the same, 34,900, with absolutely no risk.

Such a perfect result – the complete elimination of risk – relies on the fact that the two states of nature are perfectly correlated. In the real world, when states of nature are not perfectly correlated (such as the stock market), diversification can lower risk while maintaining the same expected return, but it cannot completely eliminate it.

People buy insurance because it increases satisfaction. They will buy that amount of insurance that maximizes utility subject to the budget constraint.

Comparative Statics

We will focus on the insurance premium, γ, in order to derive a demand curve for insurance.

We consider numerical methods and leave the analytical work for the exercises.

Step Change γ (the insurance premium) to $1.30 per $100 of insurance. What happens?

The budget line (displayed in red on your screen) gets steeper. The agent needs to re-optimize.

Step Run Solver to find the new optimal solution.

It is hard to see on the chart, but the cells below the chart confirm that the MRS equals the slope of the budget line when the agent buys $1847 of insurance.

We can conclude that demand for insurance is downward sloping when the premium rises from $1.00 to $1.30.

But how responsive is it?

Step Click the Reset button and use the Comparative Statics Wizard to explore the effect of the insurance premium on the amount of insurance purchased. You can use 0.1 (10 cent) increases in γ and apply 10 shocks. Keep track of K^*, γK^*, C_b^*, and C_g^* as γ changes.

The *CSgamma* sheet shows the results you should obtain. It also charts $K^* = f(\gamma)$, the demand curve for insurance, and computes its slope and elasticity.

Notice the curious behavior of the model as γ rises: at \$1.40, K^* becomes negative. This is an Endowment Model. When premium prices get high enough, the agent switches from buying insurance to selling insurance!

If this option is not allowed, you can impose the constraint in Excel that K^* be greater than or equal to zero. Then, with high premiums, the consumer is at a corner solution and buys no insurance.

Modeling Insurance via the Endowment Model

Insurance is another application of an Endowment Model in the Theory of Consumer Behavior. The usual ideas are applied: the budget constraint, preferences, and MRS equals slope of budget line at the optimal solution. In addition, the usual recipe of the economic approach, finding the initial optimum and then comparative statics, is followed.

But the application does have its own twists. We used a Cobb-Douglas functional form to model satisfaction where the exponents reflect the probabilities of the states of nature. We also used Excel's Solver without a budget constraint because of the way we implemented the problem in Excel. To be clear, this problem can be solved via the Lagrangean method (see the first exercise question) and we could have implemented a "max U subject to a constraint" model in Excel. We would get, of course, the same answer.

Exercises

Open Word and answer the following questions. Save the document and print it when you are done.

1. Use analytical methods to derive a general reduced-form solution for K^*. Show your work.

   Although you can use the Lagrangean method, it is easier to maximize the utility directly, substituting in the values for each state of nature.

$$\max_{K} U = c_b^{\pi} c_g^{1-\pi}$$

The key is that consumption in the good and bad states of nature depends on K:

$$c_b = InitialAssets - PotentialLoss + K - \gamma K$$
$$c_g = InitialAssets - \gamma K$$

We can simply substitute these equations into the utility function and maximize.

$$\max_{K} U = [InitialAssets - PotentialLoss + K - \gamma K]^{\pi} [InitialAssets - \gamma K]^{1-\pi}$$

2. Compare the analytical versus numerical approaches by evaluating your answer to question 1 at the initial parameter values in the *OptimalChoice* sheet. (Click the Reset button if needed.) Do you find that $K^* = \$10,000$?
3. Use your reduced form for K* to find the probability of loss elasticity of insurance demand at $\pi = 1\%$. Show your work. If you cannot find the reduced form, use

$$K^* = \frac{[\pi - \gamma]\, InitialAssets + [1 - \pi][\gamma]PotentialLoss}{[\gamma][1 - \gamma]}.$$

4. Use the Comparative Statics Wizard to find the probability of loss elasticity of insurance demand from $\pi = 1\%$ to 1.1%. Take a picture of your results, including the elasticity calculation.
5. Compare your answers in question 3 and 4. Do these elasticities differ? Why or why not?

References

The epigraph is from the first page of *Foundations of Insurance Economics* by Georges Dionne and Scott E. Harrington, published in 1990. Insurance economics as an organized subfield is quite young, but rapidly growing. It focuses economics, probability, and computer science on applied problems in the world of risk and insurance.

In their wildly popular *Freakonomics: A Rogue Economist Explores the Hidden Side of Everything* (2005), Steven D. Levitt and Stephen J. Dubner include this example from the world of insurance markets:

> In the late 1990s, the price of term life insurance fell dramatically. This posed something of a mystery, for the decline had no obvious cause. Other types of insurance, including health and automobile and homeowners' coverage, were certainly not falling in price. Nor had there been any radical changes among insurance companies, insurance brokers, or the people who buy term life insurance. So what happened? The Internet happened. In the spring of 1996, Quotesmith.com became the first of several websites that enabled a customer to compare, within seconds, the price of term life insurance sold by dozens of different companies. (p. 66)

Levitt and Dubner's blog at <freakonomics.blogs.nytimes.com> says, "This blog, begun in 2005, is meant to keep the conversation going."

1.6
Bads

1.6.1

Risk Versus Return: Optimal Portfolio Theory

One of the best-documented propositions in the field of finance is that, on average, investors have received higher rates of return for bearing greater risk.

Burton Malkiel

A *portfolio* is a briefcase, but it also means the total holdings of stocks, bonds, and other securities of an individual (or other entity, such as a trust or foundation).

Because the investor can decide which securities to hold in her portfolio, in other words, because choices are made, we can apply the method of economics.

An important stop on the road is shown in Figure 1.6.1.1. The indifference curves in Figure 1.6.1.1 are upward sloping because risk (on the *x* axis) is a bad (not a good).

Of course, Figure 1.6.1.1 is just the initial optimal solution. There is more to do than simply finding the initial solution. We want to explore how the optimal solution changes as one of the exogenous variables changes, ceteris paribus. This is called comparative statics analysis.

The strategy is clear: constraint, preferences, find initial solution, then comparative statics to make statements about how a shock variable affects an optimal choice variable. The short way of saying all of this is to just say that we are going to do an economic analysis of portfolio choice.

Optimal Portfolio Theory

Constraint

The *Constraint*, *Compare*, and *Mix* sheets demonstrate that an investor can mix two assets, a risk-free and a risky asset, to create a portfolio that has a particular combination of risk and return.

Step Open the Excel workbook RiskReturn.xls and read the *Intro* sheet, then go to the *Constraint* sheet. The sheet has some variables and a chart

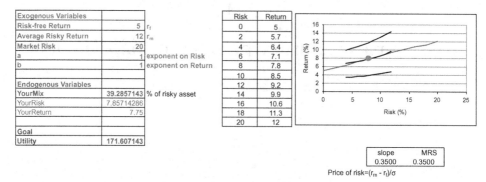

Figure 1.6.1.1. The initial optimal solution.
Source: RiskReturn.xls!OptimalChoice

of the constraint for this problem. In explaining where this constraint line comes from, we use the *Compare* and *Mix* sheets.

The idea is that you have a fixed amount of money, say $10,000, to allocate across two assets.

The risk-free asset, say a U.S. Treasury Bill, has a certain (practically speaking) 5% rate of return. Thus, you are sure to get 5% of $10,000, or $500, along with your initial investment of $10,000 at the end of the year.

The risky asset, say a mutual fund of stocks, has a greater average return, but also uncertainty in the actual realized return. To be even more concrete, say that our risky asset is the S&P 500, a group of 500 large companies.

We will suppose that the actual return will be drawn from a normal distribution centered on 12%, but with a variability of 20%. This means that the typical realized value will be around 12% ± 20%. It also means you will actually lose money (suffering a negative rate of return) about a quarter of the time.

Step Go to the *Compare* sheet to see how the risk-free and risky assets stack up.

The sheet allows you to race the two alternatives and shows how the variability impacts the return.

Step Click the ⟨Invest One Year⟩ button.

For the risk-free asset, cells I3 and L3 show 5% and $500. In other words, if you place $10,000 in the risk-free asset, these are the returns on that investment.

The risky asset is different. Cells J4 and M4 show a number that is taken from the normal distribution on the left of your screen. Cells A2 and C2 have the parameters that control the shape of the distribution.

Step Click the ⟨Invest One Year⟩ button a few times.

You can clearly see what is happening here. The return from the risk-free asset is always the same, but the risky asset bounces around.

Step Click the `Invest One Year` button repeatedly, many times (say 20 or so).

Notice what is happening to the returns of the risky asset: They are converging to 12% (the average return from the normal distribution). In other words, over the long haul, the risky asset will outperform the risk-free asset. However, in any one year, the risky asset can do pretty badly. Look at your screen to confirm that this is true.

Step Click the `Reset` button and change the risk-free asset return to 12% (in cell F2). Repeatedly (many times) click the `Invest One Year` button.

The risk-free asset outperforms the risky asset because, although they both tend to a 12% return, the risky asset has a lot of variability.

Step Click the `Reset` button and change the variability of the risky asset to 6% (in cell C2). Repeatedly (many times) click the `Invest One Year` button.

The SD of the normal distribution controls the variability. The lower SD makes the normal distribution much more spiked. In other words, the draws from the distribution are much more concentrated at the average and it is much less likely that you will see values far from the center of the distribution.

As you get one yearly return after another, it is easy to see that the returns are much more concentrated around 12%. You will rarely lose money in this case.

In finance, the variability or fluctuations in returns is captured by the Greek letter, σ. It represents risk – the risk that you will have a bad year. Risk itself is bad. The lower the risk, the better. In finance, risk is called volatility and it is measured by the SD.

What determines the amount of risk in the risky asset? That depends on the asset. In our example, the risky asset is a mutual fund of the S&P 500.

Step Proceed to the *Data* sheet to see a history of annualized returns from the S&P 500.

You can see that the average return is about 12% and the SD is about 20%. That is where the parameters from the normal distribution originated.

You can see that the histogram of the realized values is not particularly normal looking. We are using the normal distribution as a convenient assumption.

Although we raced risk-free and risky assets in the *Compare* sheet, in fact, your choice isn't simply between the risk-free and the risky asset. You can combine the two in varying proportions.

For example, you can put $5000 in the risk-free and $5000 in the risky asset. In this case, your return would be halfway between the risk-free and risky assets:

$$(r_f + r_m)/2 = 8.5\%$$

Although the return is lower than using the risky asset alone, your risk would be cut in half also.

Step Proceed to the *Mix* sheet to see this idea in action.

The *Mix* sheet is the same as the *Compare* sheet, except it has a scroll bar in cell H1 that enables you to control the allocation of your $10,000 across the two assets.

Step After you set the scroll bar value (any value will do; pick the one you think makes the most sense for you), click the ⌷Invest One Year⌷ button many times.

You should be able to see that the average return for your mix (or portfolio) converges on a return that is in between the risk-free and risky assets. In other words, you can choose the return and risk that you get. You must, however, trade them off – more return requires accepting more risk.

Your work in the *Compare* and *Mix* sheets makes understanding the constraint much easier because you have seen that there are two assets that can be mixed to form a portfolio with a continuous range of risk and return possibilities. This constitutes the constraint for the investor. He or she is free to choose combinations of risk and return, trading higher risk for greater return.

Step Go back to the *Constraint* sheet.

There are two endogenous variables in this problem, *YourRisk* and *YourReturn*, in cells B14 and B15. These are the risk and return you have chosen. However, we can create a single variable, *YourMix* (just like in the *Mix* sheet) that controls the proportion of your investment in the two assets and, therefore, the values of risk and return you select.

Clearly, you can mix the risk-free and risky assets in any combination from 0 to 100%.

Zero means you buy just the risk-free asset and 100% means you buy only the mutual fund.

Do not confuse the exogenous variable *Market Risk* with the endogenous variable *YourRisk*. The riskiness of the risky asset, sigma, is exogenous to the agent. But the agent determines how much risk to take and, therefore, the chosen amount of risk is endogenous.

Step Change cell B13 to 20%, 50%, and 90%.

As you change the cell, the red dot moves on the constraint. You can put the red dot wherever you like (along the line). At 50%, you are setting *YourRisk* to 10% (this is the variability in the 50/50 portfolio) and *YourReturn* to 8.5%.

The equation of the line for the constraint (derived in the *Constraint* sheet) is

$$YourReturn = r_f + \left(\frac{r_m - r_f}{\sigma}\right) YourRisk$$

Clearly, if you choose a risk of zero, then your return is the risk-free return. As you accept more risk, your return grows with a slope given by $\left(\frac{r_m - r_f}{\sigma}\right)$.

Notice that combinations under the budget constraint are feasible, but will not be selected because more return can always be obtained at the same risk by going straight up. Points to the northwest of the line are more desirable, but are unattainable.

Which mix do you like the best? Would your answer change if, say, you needed $10,500 for your education at the beginning of next year?

Of course, we cannot answer the question of which mix is best for a particular individual without knowing the agent's preferences.

Preferences

Step Proceed to the *Preferences* sheet to see how we easily handle risk as a *bad*.

Here is our usual Cobb-Douglas functional form with risk as a bad:

$$U(Risk, Return) = (30 - Risk)^a\ Return^b$$

By having a constant, 30, which is a bigger number than the relevant range for risk (from zero to 20), as we increase the chosen amount of risk, $30 -$ risk falls. This gives us a bad because utility falls as risk rises (for risk < 30). Return is a *good* – as return rises, so does utility.

The chart on your screen (reproduced as Figure 1.6.1.2) shows the indifference map for this utility function.

Step The agent is free to choose any combination of risk and return that is on the budget line. Change cell B12 to 50.

This means the agent chooses a risk of 10 and a return of 8.5. Is this better than the 75% mix?

Yes. The chart on your computer screen shows the original (at 75%) and new chosen value (at 50%). Clearly, the agent is on a higher indifference curve. Notice that the more northwest the indifference curve, the higher satisfaction. The higher return and lower risk, the more utility is obtained.

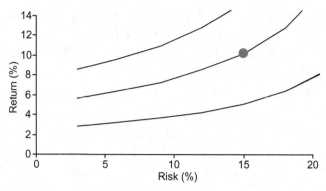

Figure 1.6.1.2. The indifference map.
Source: RiskReturn.xls!Preferences

Step Look at the MRS information at the new position (cell B12 = 50). Compare it to the slope of the budget line. The agent improved by closing the gap between the MRS and the slope of the budget line.

Of course, different people have different preferences. We can compare, for example, the preferences of a person willing to take risk versus that of a very conservative investor.

Step Change cell B12 back to 75 and change cell B19 to 4.

The chart now displays the original indifference curves (with $b = 1$) and a set of three new indifference curves, for a different person, with $b = 4$. The new indifference curves are much flatter and the MRS is much lower. (Utility is much higher, but remember that this means nothing because you cannot make interpersonal utility comparisons.)

The flatter indifference curves reflect the preferences of an aggressive investor. She is willing to take on a lot of risk for a little more return.

Step With cell B12 at 75, change cell B19 to 0.4.

The indifference curves are now steeper. This is the conservative investor. She does not place as much value on return and risk is relatively more important to her.

Step You can also model a conservative investor with cell B18 = 4 and B19 = 1.

The absolute values of the exponents do not matter. The key lies in which exponent is bigger and by how much.

Notice once again that we do not judge preferences. An aggressive investor is not in any sense better than a conservative investor. Some people like risk and others do not in the same way that some people like broccoli and others do not.

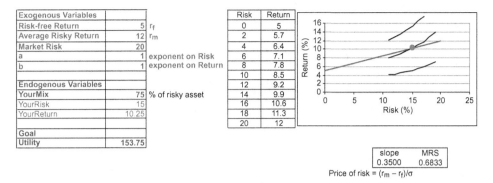

Exogenous Variables		
Risk-free Return	5	r$_f$
Average Risky Return	12	r$_m$
Market Risk	20	
a	1	exponent on Risk
b	1	exponent on Return
Endogenous Variables		
YourMix	75	% of risky asset
YourRisk	15	
YourReturn	10.25	
Goal		
Utility	153.75	

Risk	Return
0	5
2	5.7
4	6.4
6	7.1
8	7.8
10	8.5
12	9.2
14	9.9
16	10.6
18	11.3
20	12

slope	MRS
0.3500	0.6833

Price of risk = (r$_m$ − r$_f$)/σ

Figure 1.6.1.3. A nonoptimal solution.
Source: RiskReturn.xls!OptimalChoice

Preferences can be affected by the environment. A short time horizon, such as needing funds for college in a year, will rotate the indifference map, reflecting an investor who is more conservative.

Initial Optimal Solution

We can solve the portfolio choice problem via numerical and analytical methods.

Step Proceed to the *OptimalChoice* sheet to see the numerical method in action.

The *OptimalChoice* sheet opens with an inefficient solution, as shown in Figure 1.6.1.3. The MRS is greater than the slope of the budget line so the indifference curve cuts the line. The agent should move down the line, accepting less return for less risk. This increases satisfaction.

But how far down to travel? We can run Solver to find the answer to this question.

Step Run Solver.

At the optimal solution, MRS equals the slope of the budget line and the agent is on the highest attainable indifference curve.

For this agent (with these attitudes toward risk and return) and the given market trade-off between risk and return (captured by the equation of the budget constraint), the optimal solution is found with a mix of about 39% of funds invested in the risky asset. Thus, the optimal risk to accept is $7\frac{6}{7}$ and the optimal return is $7\frac{3}{4}$.

Via analytical methods, we can use the usual approach to solve the constrained optimization problem.

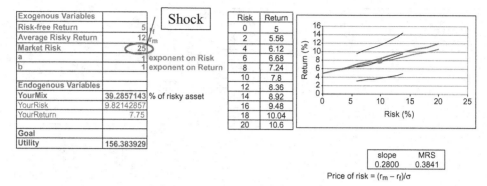

Exogenous Variables		
Risk-free Return	5	r_f
Average Risky Return	12	r_m
Market Risk	25	
a	1	exponent on Risk
b	1	exponent on Return
Endogenous Variables		
YourMix	39.2857143	% of risky asset
YourRisk	9.82142857	
YourReturn	7.75	
Goal		
Utility	156.383929	

Risk	Return
0	5
2	5.56
4	6.12
6	6.68
8	7.24
10	7.8
12	8.36
14	8.92
16	9.48
18	10.04
20	10.6

slope	MRS
0.2800	0.3841

Price of risk = $(r_m - r_f)/\sigma$

Figure 1.6.1.4. Increasing sigma, Solver yet to be run.
Source: RiskReturn.xls!OptimalChoice

Write the Lagrangean and solve for *Risk** (x_1) and *Return** (x_2).

$$\max_{x_1,x_2,\lambda} L = (30 - x_1)x_2 + \lambda\left(x_2 - \left(\frac{r_m - r_f}{\sigma}\right)x_1 - r_f\right)$$

The *Q&A* sheet has a question that asks you to solve a similar problem and the solution is available in the Answers folder. There is an exercise question that asks you to solve this problem in more general terms.

Comparative Statics

As usual, there are a number of comparative statics exercises to consider and they can be done via numerical or analytical methods.

Let's explore the effect of an increase in sigma, the amount of risk the market forces you to bear in return for better performance.

Step Increase σ from 20 to 25; what happens?

Figure 1.6.1.4 and your screen show a new budget line with a shallower slope. This is bad for the agent because consumption possibilities have been reduced. The market says that for a given amount of return, you must accept more risk.

How will the investor respond to this shock?

Step Run Solver to find out.

You will see that the agent chooses less risk and less return.

What elasticity is under consideration here?

There are several. There is the sigma elasticity of *YourRisk*, the sigma elasticity of *YourReturn*, and the sigma elasticity of *YourMix*.

Of course, these elasticities can also be computed at a point, using the derivative. One of the exercises asks you to do exactly that.

Because the change in sigma is a change in the slope of the budget line, we can use the Slutsky decomposition approach to break down the total effect into income and substitution effects. This work is left for you as an exercise.

Asset Allocation is an Optimization Problem

Optimal Portfolio Theory is yet another application of the Theory of Consumer Behavior. The twist here is that one of the choices, risk, is a bad. The agent cannot simply ignore risk. She is forced to accept more risk in order to secure greater return.

The core concepts of the Theory of Consumer Behavior remain easily visible: a budget constraint describing consumption possibilities, preferences translated into an indifference map, maximization of utility given a budget constraint, and MRS equals slope of budget line.

Perhaps most importantly, once we cast the problem as a choice, how to allocate assets among stocks, bonds, and other financial instruments, we are firmly in the land of Economics. This particular optimization problem is different from previous applications in that individuals are keenly interested in getting the optimal solution right. There is often a lot of money at stake and mistakes can prove costly (for example, with a retirement portfolio).

As economists, we remain interested in comparative statics. Changing preferences are an important shock variable in this application. We do not shake our heads at the conservative investor who finds an optimal solution (given conservative preferences) at a low risk, low return point.

Exercises

Open Word and answer the following questions. Save the document and print it when you are done.

1. Use the equation that follows to solve for *YourRisk** (x_1) and *YourReturn** (x_2) in terms of the exogenous variables. Show your work.

$$\max_{x_1,x_2,\lambda} L = (30 - x_1)x_2 + \lambda \left(x_2 - \left(\frac{r_m - r_f}{\sigma} \right) x_1 - r_f \right)$$

2. Use your reduced-form solution to find the sigma elasticity of *YourRisk* at $\sigma = 20\%$ (and the values of the other exogenous variables from the initial position of the *OptimalChoice* sheet – click the reset button if needed). Show your work.
3. Use Word's Drawing Tools to draw a well-labeled graph that depicts the total, income, and substitution effects for *YourRisk*. Make the substitution effect greater than an opposing income effect.
4. Compute the total, income, and substitution effects for *YourRisk* for the change in sigma from 20% to 25%. Show your work and describe your procedure.

References

The epigraph is from page 184 (9th edition) of a classic, excellent book on personal finance and the stock market. *A Random Walk Down Wall Street* by Burton Malkiel was originally published in 1973 by W. W. Norton & Company and the 9th edition came out in 2007. This is not one of those silly books with a scheme to beat the market. Malkiel is sober and reliable. On page 26, he says, "Let me make it quite clear that this is not a book for speculators; I am not going to promise you overnight riches. I am not promising you stock-market miracles. Indeed, a subtitle for this book might well have been *The Get Rich Slowly but Surely Book.*"

For a much deeper analysis of finance with an Excel-based presentation style, see *Principles of Finance with Excel* by Simon Benninga (New York: Oxford University Press, 2006).

1.6.2

Automobile Safety Regulation

Minivans have the lowest fraction of driver fatalities that are men under 26 years old (4 percent); sports cars have the highest (39 percent). So we suspect that differences in the behavior of their drivers account in large measure for why these two classes of vehicles pose such different risks to the people who operate them.

Thomas P. Wenzel and Marc Ross

Cars are much, much safer today than in the past. Everyone knows how seat belts, airbags, and antilock brakes have made cars safer. The future holds great promise: guidance and avoidance systems, fly-by-wire technology that will eliminate steering columns, and much more.

Figure 1.6.2.1 shows United States traffic fatalities from 1994 to 2006. The data show an improving traffic fatality picture. Given that the numbers of people, drivers, vehicles, and miles driven have increased at a *faster rate* than the total number of fatalities, the bottom part of the table, which shows various fatal accident *rates,* demonstrates that driving is safer today than ever before. The circled row shows that the number of fatalities per 100 million miles traveled has fallen from 1.73 to 1.41, which is almost a 20% decrease during this time period. That is wonderful.

But the data beg some questions. First, the data in Figure 1.6.2.1 are based on the Fatal Accident Reporting System (FARS) and, thus, say nothing about *nonfatal* accidents. It turns out we are doing better here also – injury rates and severity of injury have also declined.

So, all is well? Actually, not exactly.

Although it may seem greedy, one should ask, "We're doing better because fatal accident rates are falling, but shouldn't we be doing *much, much* better?" After all, the car you drive today is *much, much* safer than a car from 20 years ago.

So, what is going on – why aren't we doing *much, much* better in reducing traffic fatalities and injuries? Economics can help answer this question. We will apply the remarkably flexible Theory of Consumer Behavior to driving a car. Any problem that can be framed as a choice given a set of exogenous

	2006	2005	2004	2003	2002	2001	2000	1999	1998	1997	1996	1995	1994
Fatal Crashes	38,588	39,252	38,444	38,477	38,491	37,862	37,526	37,140	37,107	37,324	37,494	37,241	36,254
Drivers	27,323	27,491	26,871	26,779	26,659	25,869	25,567	25,257	24,743	24,667	24,534	24,390	23,691
Passengers	9,473	10,069	10,355	10,458	10,604	10,469	10,695	10,521	10,530	10,944	11,058	10,782	10,518
Unknown	106	86	78	104	112	102	86	97	109	114	103	119	109
Sub Total1	36,902	37,646	37,304	37,341	37,375	36,440	36,348	35,875	35,382	35,725	35,695	35,291	34,318
Nonmotorist													
Pedestrians	4,784	4,892	4,675	4,774	4,851	4,901	4,763	4,939	5,228	5,321	5,449	5,584	5,489
Pedalcyclists	773	786	727	629	665	732	693	754	760	814	765	833	802
Other/Unknown	183	186	130	140	114	123	141	149	131	153	154	109	107
Sub Total2	5,740	5,864	5,532	5,543	5,630	5,756	5,597	5,842	6,119	6,288	6,368	6,526	6,398
Total*	42,642	43,510	42,836	42,884	43,005	42,196	41,945	41,717	41,501	42,013	42,065	41,817	40,716
National Rates: Fatalities per													
100-Million Vehicle Miles Traveled	1.41	1.46	1.44	1.48	1.51	1.51	1.53	1.55	1.58	1.64	1.69	1.73	1.73
100,000 Population	14.24	14.67	14.59	14.75	14.93	14.79	14.86	15.3	15.36	15.69	15.86	15.91	15.64
100,000 Registered Vehicles	16.96	17.71	18	18.59	19.06	19.07	19.33	19.61	19.95	20.64	20.86	21.22	21.15
100,000 Licensed Drivers	21.03	21.7	21.54	21.86	22.1	22.06	22	22.29	22.45	22.99	23.43	23.68	23.21

*Total fatalities for 1996 include 2 fatalities of unknown person type.

Figure 1.6.2.1. U.S. traffic fatality data.
Source:

variables can be analyzed via the economic approach. There are certainly choices to be made while driving – what route to take, how fast to drive, and what car to drive are three of many choices drivers make. We will focus on a subset of choices that involve how carefully to drive.

Theoretical Intuition

The crucial idea is that the driver makes choices about how to drive, given a set of exogenous variables.

The key article that spawned a great deal of further work in this area was written in 1975 by University of Chicago economist Sam Peltzman. The abstract for "The Effects of Automobile Safety Regulation" (p. 677) says,

Technological studies imply that annual highway deaths would be 20 percent greater without legally mandated installation of various safety devices on automobiles. However, this literature ignores offsetting effects of nonregulatory demand for safety and driver response to the devices. This article indicates that these offsets are virtually complete, so that regulation has not decreased highway deaths. Time-series (but not cross-section) data imply some saving of auto occupants' lives at the expense of more pedestrian deaths and more nonfatal accidents, a pattern consistent with optimal driver response to regulation.

Technological studies by engineers are based on extrapolation. Cars with seat belts, airbags, antilock brakes, and so on are assumed to be driven in exactly the same way as cars without these safety features. This will give maximum bang for our safety buck.

Economics, however, tells us that we won't get this maximum return on improved safety features because there is a driver response to being in a safer car. As Peltzman points out (p. 681), more intense driving offsets some of the gains from the safety devices:

The typical driver may thus be thought of as facing a choice, not unlike that between leisure and money income, involving the probability of death from accident and what for convenience I will call "driving intensity." More speed, thrills, etc., can be obtained only by forgoing some safety.

This claim sounds rather outrageous at first. Do I suddenly turn into an Indy 500 race car driver upon hearing that my car has airbags? No, but consider some practical examples in your own life:

- Do you drive differently in the rain or snow than on a clear day?
- Do speed bumps, if you can't avoid them, lead you to reduce your speed?
- Would you drive faster on a road in Montana with no cars for miles around versus on the Dan Ryan Expressway in Chicago? In which case, Montana or Chicago (presuming you are actually moving on the Dan Ryan), would you pay more attention to the road and your driving?

- If your car had some magic repulsion system that prevented you from hitting another car, would you drive faster and more aggressively?

Economists believe that agents change their behavior to find a new optimal solution when conditions change. In fact, many believe this is the hallmark of economics as a discipline. Many noneconomists either do not believe this or are not aware of how this affects us in many different ways.

If you do not believe that safer cars lead to more aggressive driving, consider the converse: Do more dangerous cars lead to more careful driving? Here is how Steven Landsburg puts it:

> If the seat belts were removed from your car, wouldn't you be more cautious in driving? Carrying this observation to the extreme, Armen Alchian of the University of California at Los Angeles has suggested a way to bring about a major reduction in the accident rate: Require every car to have a spear mounted on the steering wheel, pointing directly at the driver's heart. Alchian confidently predicts that we would see a lot less tailgating. (Landsburg, p. 5)

Consider the tax on cars over $30,000 passed by Congress in 1990. By adding a 10% tax to such luxury cars, staffers computed that the government would earn 10% of the sales revenue (price × quantity) generated by the number of luxury cars sold the year before the tax was imposed. They were sadly mistaken. Why?

People bought fewer luxury cars! This is a response to a changed environment.

This idea has far-reaching application. Consider, for example, its relevance to the field of macroeconomics. Robert Lucas won the Nobel Prize in Economics in 1995. His citation reads, "for having developed and applied the hypothesis of rational expectations, and thereby having transformed macroeconomic analysis and deepened our understanding of economic policy." See <www.nobel.se/economics/laureates/1995/>.

What exactly did Lucas do? He pointed out that if policy makers fail to take into account how people will respond to a proposed new policy, then the projections of what will happen will be wrong. This is called the *Lucas Critique*.

The Lucas Critique is exactly what is happening in the case of safety features on cars. Economists argue that you should not assume that agents are going to continue to behave in exactly the same way before and after the advent of technological improvements.

What we need is a model of how drivers decide how to drive. Consumer Choice Theory gives us that model.

Finding the Initial Solution

The driver chooses how intensively to drive, which means how aggressively to drive. Faster starts, not coming to a complete stop, and passing slower cars

Figure 1.6.2.2. The budget constraint.

are all more intensive types of driving, as are searching for a better radio station and talking on your cell phone. More intensive driving saves time and it is more fun. Unfortunately, it isn't free. As you drive more intensively, your chances of having an accident rise. Your accident risk, the probability that you have an accident, is a function of how you drive.

The driver chooses a combination of two variables, *Driving Intensity* and *Accident Risk*, that maximize utility, subject to the budget constraint.

The Budget Constraint

The equation of the budget constraint ties the two choice variables together.

Driving Intensity = Safety Features*Accident Risk*

Safety Features represents safety technology and provides a relative price at which you can trade risk for intensity.

When cars get safer, the constraint gets steeper because you can get the same driving intensity at a much lower accident risk, as the dashed arrow in Figure 1.6.2.2 shows.

You can also read the graph vertically. For a given accident risk, a safer car gives you a lot more driving intensity (follow the solid arrow in Figure 1.6.2.2).

After finding the initial solution, comparative statics is sure to follows.

Figure 1.6.2.2 shows that safer technology can be interpreted as a decrease in the price of *Driving Intensity*.

The constraint is only half of the story. We need prefences to find out how drivers will decide to maximize satisfaction.

Preferences

We use a Cobb-Douglas function form to model the driver's preferences for risk (x_1) and intensity (x_2), subtracting risk from a constant so that increases in risk lead to less utility.

$$U(x_1, x_2) = (1 - x_1)^c x_2^d$$

Risk (x_1) is chosen on the interval from 0 to 100%. As risk increases in this interval, utility falls. The indifference curves will be upward sloping because x_1, *Accident Risk,* is a *bad.*

Finding the Initial Solution

We can solve the model via numerical and analytical methods. We begin with Excel's Solver.

Step Open the Excel workbook SafetyRegulation.xls and read the *Intro* sheet, then go to the *OptimalChoice* sheet.

The sheet shows the goal, endogenous variables, and exogenous variables. On open, the driver has chosen 25%, 0.25, which is a point on the budget line (because the constraint cell shows zero). We will use percent points for risk because it is a probability (and has to be between 0% and 100%, inclusive) and decimal points (such as 0.5) for the driving intensity variable, which we interpret as an index number on a scale from 0 to 1.

We know the opening point is feasible, but is it an optimal solution?

You can figure this out by comparing the slope of the budget line to the MRS at this point.

The slope is easy. It is simply the *Safety Features* exogenous variable, which is +1.

The MRS requires only a little more work. It is minus the ratio of marginal utilities. With $c = d = 1$, we have

$$MRS = -\frac{\dfrac{dU}{dx_1}}{\dfrac{dU}{dx_2}} = -\frac{-x_2}{1 - x_1} = \frac{x_2}{1 - x_1}$$

We evaluate this expression at the chosen point, 25%, 0.25, and get

$$\frac{x_2}{1 - x_1} = \frac{[0.25]}{1 - [25\%]} = \frac{1}{3}$$

We immediately know the driver is not optimizing.

In addition, we know he needs to take more risk and more intensity, traveling up the budget line because the indifference curve is flatter than the budget line at that point.

You should be able to form a mental picture of this situation.

Step When you are ready (after you have formed the mental picture of the situation), click the Show Chart button to see what is going on at the 25%, 0.25 point.

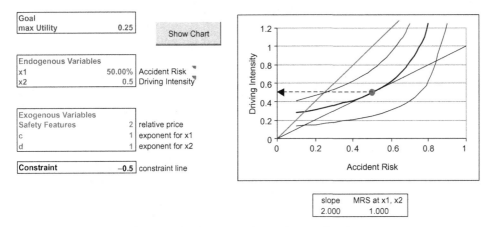

Figure 1.6.2.3. Improving safety technology.
Source: SafetyRegulation.xls!OptimalChoice

The canonical graph (with a bad) appears and the cells below the chart show the slope and MRS at the chosen point.

Step Next, run Excel's Solver to find the optimal solution.

With $c = d = 1$ and a *Safety Features* value of 1, it is not surprising that the optimal solution is at 50%,0.50. Of course, at this point, the slope = MRS.

To implement the analytical approach, the Lagrangean looks like this:

$$\max_{x_1, x_2, \lambda} L = (1 - x_1)x_2 + \lambda(x_2 - Sx_1)$$

An exercise asks you to find the reduced-form solution.

Comparative Statics

Suppose we get safer cars so the terms of trade between *Driving Intensity* and *Accident Risk* change.

Step Change cell B16 to 2.

How does the engineer view the problem? To her, the driver keeps acting the same way, driving just like before. There will be a great gain in lower accident risk. This is shown by the left-pointing arrow in Figure 1.6.2.3. Intensity stays the same and risk falls by a great deal.

For the engineer, because intensity remains constant, if it was 0.5, then improving *Safety Features* to 2 makes the accident risk fall to 25%. We simply travel horizontally along a given driving intensity to the new budget constraint.

The economist doesn't see it this way at all. She sees *Driving Intensity* as a choice variable and as the solution to an optimization problem. Change the

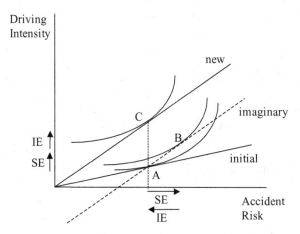

Figure 1.6.2.4. Income and substitution effects.

parameters and you change the consumer's behavior. It is clear from Figure 1.6.2.3 that the driver is not optimizing because the slope does not equal the MRS.

Step With new technology changing the budget line, we must run Solver to find the new optimal solution.

The result is quite surprising. The accident risk has remained exactly the same! What is going on? In Peltzman's language, this is *completely offsetting behavior*. The optimal response to the safer car is to drive much more aggressively and this has completely offset the gain from the safety equipment.

How can this be? By decomposing the zero total effect on risk into its income and substitution effects, we can better understand this curious result.

Figure 1.6.2.4 shows what is happening. The improved safety features lower the price of driving intensity, so the driver buys more of it. On the *y* axis, the substitution and income effects work together to increase the driver's speed, lane changes, and other ways to drive more intensively. On the *x* axis, which measures risk taken while driving, the effects oppose each other, cancelling each other out and leaving no gain in accident safety.

As driving intensity gets cheaper, the substitution effect (the move from A to B in Figure 1.6.2.4) leads the driver to choose more intensity and pay for it with more risk. The income effect leads the driver to buy yet more intensity and (because risk is a normal bad) less risk. The end result, for this utility function, is perfectly offsetting behavior.

Of course, this is not necessarily what we would see in the real world. We do not know whether these preferences represent the majority of drivers. The income effect for risk could outweigh the substitution effect, leaving point C to the left of A in Figure 1.6.2.4.

As usual, theory alone cannot answer the question. Empirical work in this area does confirm that offsetting behavior exists, but there is disagreement as to its extent.

The Economics of Driving

Choices abound when it comes to cars and driving. Should I take the highway or stay on a surface street? Change the oil now or wait a while longer? Pass this slow car or just take it easy and get there a few minutes later? Because there are choices, we can apply economics. This chapter focused on applying the Theory of Consumer Behavior to the choice of how aggressively to drive. The agent is forced to trade off a bad (the risk of having an accident) for getting there faster and greater driving enjoyment.

Yes, teenagers make different choices than older drivers and everyone drives differently on a congested, icy road than on a sunny day with no traffic, but that is not the key comparative statics question. We focus instead on how improved automobile technology impacts the optimal way to drive.

Offsetting behavior is another name for the Lucas Critique. It says that we should not extrapolate. Instead, we should recognize that agents change their behavior when the environment changes. Of course, theory can't tell us *how much* offsetting behavior we will get. This question requires data and econometric analysis.

Economists believe that we have not had as great a reduction in automobile fatalities and injuries as our *much, much* safer cars would enable because drivers have chosen to maximize satisfaction by trading some safety for driving intensity. Offsetting behavior explains why we aren't doing much, much better in traffic fatalities. But do not despair – we are maximizing satisfaction given our new technology.

Exercises

Open Word and answer the following questions. Save the document and print it when you are done.

1. Use the equation that follows to solve for x_1^* and x_2^* in terms of S (safety features). Show your work.

$$\max_{x_1, x_2, \lambda} L = (1 - x_1)x_2 + \lambda(x_2 - Sx_1)$$

2. Use your reduced-form solution to find the S elasticity of x_1^* at $S = 1$. Show your work.
3. If the utility function was such that driving intensity were a Giffen good, describe where point C would be located on Figure 1.6.2.4.
4. If the utility function was such that driving intensity were a Giffen good, would this raise or lower traffic fatalities? Explain.

References

The epigraph is from page 125 of Thomas P. Wenzel and Marc Ross, "Safer Vehicles for People and the Planet," *American Scientist*, Vol. 96, No. 2 (March–April, 2008), pp. 122–128. They claim that the conventional wisdom that we need cars to be heavy to be safe is wrong. Heavier cars waste more fuel. How much more? "If a typical car could somehow drop 10% of its mass, its fuel economy would increase by anywhere from 3% to 8%. (The larger value applies if the size of the engine is also reduced to keep acceleration performance the same.)" (p. 124). The authors are not economists, but notice how they frame the result with percentage changes.

For an excellent review of empirical work on traffic safety, see *Traffic Safety* by Leonhard Evans, online at <www.scienceservingsociety.com>.

The original article from which this application is taken is Sam Peltzman, "The Effects of Automobile Safety Regulation," *The Journal of Political Economy*, Vol. 83, No. 4 (August, 1975), pp. 677–726.

For a simple (that is, no math or graphs) explanation of the idea behind offsetting behavior, see "The Power of Incentives: How Seat Belts Kill," which is the first chapter in Steven E. Landsburg, *The Armchair Economist* (New York: The Free Press, 1993).

Russell S. Sobel and Todd Nesbit find strong support for offsetting behavior from improved safety in professional auto racing. "Automobile Safety Regulation and the Incentive to Drive Recklessly: Evidence from NASCAR" is forthcoming in the *Southern Economic Journal*. A working paper version is available online at the Social Science Research Network, <papers.ssrn.com/Sol3/papers.cfm?abstract_id= 986359>.

Tom Vanderbilt's *Traffic: Why We Drive the Way We Do (and What It Says About Us)* (New York: Alfred A. Knopf), 2008, touches on a variety of issues about cars and driving.

1.6.3

Labor Supply

In the past it was futile to double the wages of an agricultural worker in Silesia who mowed a certain tract of land on a contract, in the hope of inducing him to increase his exertion. He would simply have reduced by half the work expended.

Max Weber

We began the Theory of Consumer Behavior with income (m) given. The Endowment Model replaced given cash income with an initial endowment of two goods, $m = p_1\omega_1 + p_2\omega_2$. We then focused on choices with bads – risky assets and accidents.

The application in this chapter is another example using a bad. As always, our eventual goal is comparative statics and elasticity. In this case, we will derive a supply curve for labor and concentrate on the wage elasticity of labor supply.

An innovation in this chapter is that the accompanying Excel workbook is less finished than usual. This enables you to practice implementing the model in Excel.

Setting Up the Problem

Instead of a mere consumer, the agent in this application is a combined consumer and worker.

Although an initial amount of nonlabor income is given, total income can be increased by working. More work means more income and greater consumption of goods and services. Consumption is good, but work is bad. Therein lies the problem.

Our consumer/worker can buy a single good, G, representing all consumer goods, at price p. Utility increases as she consumes more G.

The 24 hours in a day are divided into two types: work and leisure. The number of hours spent working in one day, H, is chosen by the agent. Earned income is simply wH, where w is the wage rate in \$/hr. Although work

217

generates income, our agent does not like to work. H is a bad in the utility function.

With this background, we are ready to organize the information into the three areas that comprise an optimization problem:

1. Goal: maximize utility, which is a function of goods consumed, G, and work, H, where H is a bad
2. Endogenous variables: G, the amount of goods consumed, and H, the number of hours worked
3. Exogenous variables: p, the price of the composite good; w, the wage rate; m, unearned, nonlabor income; and parameters in the utility function.

The solution to this constrained optimization problem is depicted on a graph with a budget constraint and set of indifference curves. We consider each of these elements separately and then combine them.

Budget Constraint

The budget constraint is $m + wH \geq pG$. This equation says that total income is composed of unearned income (m) and earned income (wH). The inequality means that the consumer/worker cannot spend more on goods and services (pG) than the total income available.

Because we assume a one-time, single optimization problem, there is no reason for the agent to save (i.e., spend less than available) and we can make the constraint a strict equality, $m + wH = pG$. This allows us to use the Lagrangean method to solve the problem analytically.

In terms of a graph, it is easy to see that we can write the constraint as the equation of a line (with G on the y axis and H on the x axis) by dividing by p:

$$m + wH = pG$$
$$G = \frac{m}{p} + \frac{w}{p}H$$

Suppose $w = \$10/\text{hr}$, $m = \$40$, and $p = \$1/\text{unit}$. What would the constraint look like?

Step Open the Excel workbook LaborSupply.xls and read the *Intro* sheet, then go to the *YourConstraint* sheet.

Your task is to fill in the G column and create a chart of the constraint. There are three steps.

Step Click on cell B12 and enter a formula equal to the equation for G. The cells w, p, and m are not named so you should use absolute references

($ in front of column letters and row numbers) to enable easy filling down of the formula.

When finished, the formula in B12 should look like this: $= \$B\$4/\$B\$3+(\$B\$2/\$B\$3)^*A12$.

Step Now fill down the formula.

Step Finally, create a chart with H and G as the source data. Be sure to label the axes of your chart.

The chart is based on hour intervals of work, but fractions of hours are possible. Thus, your chart should be a scatter chart with points connected by lines.

Step Click the Reveal the Constraint button to see a finished version of the budget constraint.

The agent is free to choose any point on the constraint. The y intercept, 40 (equal to m/p), yields a small value of consumption, but the agent does not have to work. Movement up the line yields more G but requires more H.

Points to the northwest of the line are unattainable. For example, the consumer/worker cannot afford the 10, 200 combination. Working 10 hours adds $100 to the $40 nonlabor income. This is not enough to buy $200 worth of goods.

What shock would enable our consumer/worker to buy the 10, 200 combination?

There are three possibilities, one for each exogenous variable in the constraint.

Step From the *Constraint* sheet (click the Reveal the Constraint button from the *YourConstraint* sheet if needed), change the wage to 16 in cell B2.

The constraint rotates up, with a steeper slope and the same intercept, and the combination 10, 200 is now feasible, which is easily confirmed by looking at the chart and row 22.

Changes in wages, ceteris paribus, rotate the constraint around the unearned income intercept.

Step Return the wage to 10 in cell B2 (the constraint returns to its initial position when you hit the Enter key) and set p (in cell B3) to 0.7.

The constraint appears to simply rotate up again, but look more carefully at the chart and underlying data. The slope is steeper, but the intercept has also changed. The $40 of unearned income now buys a little more than 57 units of G. As before, it is easy to see that the combination 10, 200 is now feasible.

Changes in price (p), ceteris paribus, rotate and shift the constraint.

Step Return the price to 1 in cell B3 (the constraint returns to its initial position when you hit the Enter key) and set m (in cell B4) to 100.

This time, the constraint shifts vertically up. With $100 of unearned and $100 of earned income (from working 10 hours), the combination 10, 200 is now feasible.

Changes in unearned income (m), ceteris paribus, shift the constraint.

Changes in w, p, and m affect the constraint. The initially unattainable combination of 10, 200 can be made feasible by appropriately changing any of one of these three exogenous variables.

Preferences

In previous applications with bads, we used a Cobb-Douglas utility function and subtracted the bad from a constant. The same approach is adopted here.

Because the time period under consideration is a day, which has 24 hours, preferences can be represented by $U(H, G) = (24 - H)^c G^d$.

With $H = 0$, the agent gets the maximum value from the first term of the utility function, but remember that earned income will then be low and, therefore, G will be small.

Like the budget constraint, we need a visual representation of the utility function.

Step Proceed to the *YourIndiffCurve* sheet to implement the utility function in Excel.

The sheet is unfinished. You need to fill in column B and draw a graph of the indifference curve. The indifference curve is initially based on $c = d = 1$ and a level of utility of 1960.

To fill in column B, you need to solve for the value of G that yields a utility level of 1960, given H. In other words, rewrite the utility function in terms of G, like this:

$$U(H, G) = (24 - H)^c G^d$$

$$G^d = \frac{U(H, G)}{(24 - H)^c}$$

$$G = \left[\frac{U(H, G)}{(24 - H)^c} \right]^{1/d}$$

Step Use the expression just shown to enter a formula in cell B12 that computes the value of G necessary to produce a utility of 1960 when $H = 2$.

Your formula should look like this: $= (\$B\$5/((24 - A12)^{\wedge}(\$B\$3)))^{\wedge}(1/\$B\$4)$. It evaluates to a value of $G = 89.09$. This makes sense because when $H = 2$, $24 - 2 = 22$ and $22*89.09$ equals a utility value of 1960.

Notice again the use of absolute references.

Step Fill down the formula.

Step Draw a chart with H and G as the source data. Label the axes.

Your chart is a graph of a single indifference curve. In fact, the entire quadrant is full of these upward sloping indifference curves and utility increases as you move in a northwesterly direction (taking less of the bad, H, and more of the good, G). This is the usual indifference map when we have a bad on the x axis.

Step Click the Reveal the Indiff Curve button to check your work or if you need help.

Finally, remember that changes in the exponents make the indifference curves flatter or steeper. A Q&A question explores this point.

Finding the Initial Optimal Solution

Having explored the constraint and preferences, we are ready to find the initial solution.

The numerical approach is covered here; the analytical method is an exercise question.

Step Proceed to the *YourOptimalChoice* sheet.

It is blank! You need to implement the problem in this sheet and run Solver to find the initial solution.

You need to organize the problem into a goal (maximize utility), endogenous variables (H and G), exogenous variables (w, p, m, c, and d), and a cell for the constraint.

The utility function is $U(H, G) = (24 - H)^c G^d$. The wage rate is $10/hr, the price of G is $1/unit, unearned income is $40, and $c = d = 1$.

Step Click the Reveal the Optimal Choice button once you are finished or if you get stuck and need help.

Figure 1.6.3.1 shows the canonical graph of the initial optimal solution for the consumer/worker's choice problem.

This consumer/worker maximizes utility by working 10 hours, thereby earning $100 and then buying 140 units of G. There is no better solution. Traveling up or down the budget constraint is guaranteed to lower utility

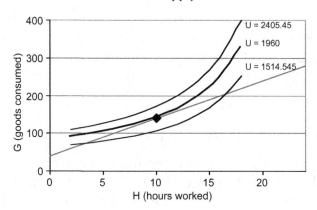

Figure 1.6.3.1. The initial solution.
Source: LaborSupply.xls!OptimalChoice

because the indifference curve is just touching the constraint at 10, 140. The mathematical way of saying this is that the $MRS = w/p$ at 10, 140.

Comparative Statics: Deriving Labor Supply

How does H^* respond as the wage rate changes, ceteris paribus?

This comparative statics question yields the labor supply curve.

We concentrate on the numerical approach and leave the analytical method for an exercise question.

Step From the *OptimalChoice* sheet, (click the Reveal the Optimal Choice button from the *YourOptimalChoice* sheet if needed), use the Comparative Statics Wizard to pick a few points off of the labor supply curve. Make the size of the change in the wage rate 10 and apply the default five shocks.

Step Proceed to the *CS1* sheet and scroll down (if needed) to check your work.

Notice the labor supply and inverse labor supply curves (scroll down if needed). The shape of the curve is intriguing. As wage rises and rises, H^* seems to level off – it continues to increase, but ever more slowly.

Notice also that the computed wage elasticity of labor supply from $w = 10$ to 20 in cell E14 is quite small at 0.1. This means that H^* is unresponsive to changes in wages.

Labor supply has been extensively studied and extremely small elasticities with respect to wage are commonly found. Income and substitution effects explain the result.

Decomposing the Total Effect into Income and Substitution Effects

Step Return to the *OptimalChoice* sheet and click the Reset button.

Step Change the wage rate (in cell B16) from 10 to 20.

The budget constraint rotates up in the chart. The initial optimal solution, 10, 140, is no longer optimal. The consumer/worker needs to re-optimize.

Step Run Solver (with $w = 20$).

The new optimal solution is $H^* = 11$. A 100% increase in the wage (from 10 to 20) has produced a total effect of a 1 hour, or 10%, increase in hours worked.

We can decompose this total effect into income and substitution effects. We need to shift down the budget line to cancel out the increased purchasing power of the wage increase. In other words, we need to draw in an imaginary, dashed line that goes through the initial solution, with a steeper slope caused by the higher wage.

We can use a modified version of the Income Adjuster Equation to determine the amount of income we need to take away. Recall that we determine how much income to change via $\Delta m = x_1^* \Delta p_1$. In the labor supply model, x_1 is obviously H, and the price is now the wage, but we also need a sign change. An increase in the wage increases consumption possibilities in the labor supply model so we need a minus sign to show that wage increases must be offset by income decreases. Below is our modified Income Adjuster Equation with values substituted in:

$$\Delta m = (H^*)(-\Delta w)$$
$$\Delta m = (10)(-10) = -100$$

This says that we must lower unearned income by $100 to cancel out the increased purchasing power from the $10/hr wage increase.

Step Confirm that $w = 20$ (in cell B16) and change m to $-60 (= 40 - 100)$ in cell B17.

Notice that the budget line goes through the initial combination, 10, 140. The line is not dashed, but it should be. Remember that this budget line does not actually exist. No one is going to take $100 from the agent. We are doing this to decompose the total effect of the wage increase into the income and substitution effects.

Step Run Solver with $w = 20$ and $m = -60$.

The optimal solution is $H^* = 13.5$ hours of work. With this solution, we have the information needed to decompose the total into the two separate effects. Figure 1.6.3.2 shows the total (TE), income (SE), and substitution (SE) effects on hours worked.

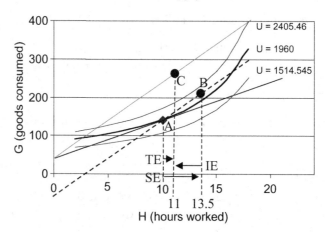

Figure 1.6.3.2. Income and substitution effects of a wage increase. *Source:* LaborSupply!OptimalChoice

The substitution effect is +3.5, the movement from $H = 10$ (the initial optimal solution) to 13.5 (the optimal solution with the higher wage, but lower m). It is the horizontal movement from point A to B.

The income effect is −2.5, the movement from $H = 13.5$ (point B) to $H = 11$ (point C). The negative sign is important. It says that when income rises, the agent buys less of the bad.

The total effect is, of course, the observed movement from point A to point C, a 1-hour increase in hours worked. This is what would actually be observed as the wage rose from $10/hr to $20/hr.

Figure 1.6.3.2 makes clear why the response of hours worked to a wage increase is inelastic – the income and substitution effects are working against each other. The fact that the relative price of goods for an hour of work is cheaper drives the agent to work and consume more (this is the substitution effect, from A to B). But the increase in purchasing power encourages the agent to work less (from B to C, the income effect). The total effect on hours worked is small when the two effects are added together.

In fact, the income and substitution effects can explain an even more curious phenomenon that has been observed in the real world – hours worked actually falling as wage rises. Figure 1.6.3.3 shows the underlying graph and derived labor supply curve for an unknown utility function. Unlike the labor supply derived from the Cobb-Douglas utility function, which was always positively sloped, the labor supply curve in Figure 1.6.3.3 is said to be backward bending. At low wages, increases in wage lead to more hours worked (such as from point 1 to 2), but the supply curve becomes negatively sloped when wages rise from point 2 to 3.

We have already seen that the small wage elasticity from point 1 to 2 is caused by the income effect's working against the substitution effect. The

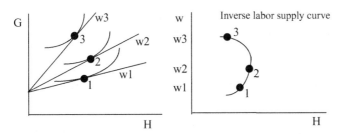

Figure 1.6.3.3. A backward bending labor supply.

same explanation underlies the negative response in hours worked as wages rise from point 2 to 3. In this case, not only does the income effect oppose the substitution effect, it actually swamps it.

Figure 1.6.3.4 shows what happens when we are on the backward bending portion of the labor supply curve. The substitution effect always induces more hours worked as wages rise. This is the movement from A to B. The income effect, however, counters some of this increase in hours worked. We can afford to work less (from B to C) because the wage is higher. When we are on the backward bending portion of the labor supply curve, the income effect actually overcomes the substitution effect so that the total effect (A to C) is a reduction in hours worked as the wage rises. In Figure 1.6.3.4, any point C to the left of A yields a point on the backward bending portion of the labor supply curve.

Wage rises and I work less sounds just about as weird as price rises and I buy more. Is this Giffen behavior?

No because the wage change is not an own price effect. Figure 1.6.3.5 shows p_1 and p_2 changes in the standard model where two goods are purchased given fixed income. On the left, the change in p_1 produces an own effect on x_1 and a cross effect on x_2. If x_1 rises as p_1 rises, then x_1 is Giffen. If x_2 rises as p_1 rises (notice the cross effect), however, that does not make x_2 a Giffen good. We use the cross effect to say that the goods are substitutes (instead of complements). To determine whether x_2 is Giffen, we have to use the graph on the right of Figure 1.6.3.5. If x_2 rises as p_2 rises (notice the

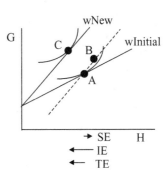

Figure 1.6.3.4. Income and substitution effects when H^* falls as w rises.

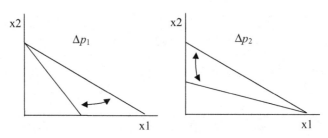

Figure 1.6.3.5. Understanding own and cross effects.

own effect), then x_2 is Giffen. In other words, we need an own price change to determine Giffenness.

Figure 1.6.3.5 makes clear that a change in the wage in the labor supply model is like a change in the price of x_2 in the standard model. The wage change is like the graph on the right, with an upward sloping budget constraint. The rotation is around a fixed y value – zero in the standard model and unearned income in the labor supply model. Thus, the change in wage is an own price effect for G (on the y axis) and a cross price effect for H (on the x axis).

Because a change in the wage exerts a cross effect on hours worked, we cannot say anything about Giffenness for hours worked. We could, however, say that G was Giffen if it fell when wage rose. That would really be weird. Look at the figures of income and substitution effects in this chapter and you will never find a final point C that lies below an initial point A. In fact, leisure (work's counterpart) is usually treated as a normal good: higher income leads to more leisure (and less work).

Modeling Labor Supply: Work as a Bad

Labor Economics is a major subfield within Economics. As a course, it is usually offered as an upper-level elective, with Intermediate Micro-economics as a prerequisite. Labor supply and demand are fundamental concepts. The former is based on a model in which work is a bad (the opposite of leisure, which is a good) and a consumer/worker maximizes satisfaction subject to a budget constraint.

By changing the wage, ceteris paribus, we can derive a labor supply curve. Economists are well aware that labor supply is often quite insensitive to changes in wages. This is explained by the opposing substitution and income effects. The backward bending portion of the labor supply curve is observed when the income effect swamps the substitution effect. This is not Giffen behavior, however, because we are dealing with a cross (not own) price effect.

This chapter used numerical methods to find optimal solutions and do comparative statics analyses. The Q&A and exercise questions are more focused on analytical methods.

Exercises

Open Word and answer the following questions. Save the document and print it when you are done.

1. Use the Lagrangean method to solve this consumer/worker's constrained optimization problem:

$$\max_{H,G} U = (24 - H)G$$

$$\text{s.t. } 40 + wH = G$$

Show all of your work.

2. Do your results for H^* and G^* agree with the numerical approach in the text? Is this surprising?

3. Using the Comparative Statics Wizard, the wage elasticity of labor supply using a wage increase from \$10/hr to \$20/hr is 0.1. Use your reduced-form solution for H^* to find the wage elasticity of labor supply at $w = $10/hr. Show your work.

4. Does your point wage elasticity from the previous question equal 0.1 (the elasticity based on a \$10 wage increase)? Why or why not?

5. Whether the labor supply curve is upward sloping or backward bending has nothing to do with the Giffenness of work. If labor supply is positively sloped, G and H are substitutes or complements, but which one? Draw a graph that helps you explain your answer.

References

The epigraph comes from page 355 of Max Weber's classic, *General Economic History*, originally published in German in 1923 and translated to English by Frank H. Knight in 1927. If you are unfamiliar with Weber (pronounced vay-ber), he was interested in the way capitalism changed people's minds and values.

With respect to labor supply, the consumer/worker's goals and attitudes are a critical issue. In this chapter, labor supply was derived as the solution to an optimization problem. The agent, however, might not be an optimizer, but a target earner, working only enough hours to make a certain amount of money. If wages double, hours worked are cut in half.

Consider this abstract from Henry Farber's 2003 NBER working paper, "Is Tomorrow Another Day? The Labor Supply of New York Cab Drivers":

> I model the labor supply of taxi drivers as the result of optimization based on an inter-temporal utility function. Since income effects in response to temporary fluctuations in daily earnings opportunities are likely to be small, cumulative hours will be much more important than cumulative income in the decision to stop work on a given day. However, if these income effects are large due to very high discount and interest rates, then labor supply functions could be backward bending, and, in the extreme case where the wage elasticity of daily labor supply is minus one, drivers could be target earners. Indeed, Camerer, Babcock,

Lowenstein, and Thaler (1997) and Chou (2000) find that the daily wage elasticity of labor supply of New York City cab drivers is substantially negative and conclude that it is likely that cab drivers are target earners. I conclude from my empirical analysis, based on new data, of the stopping behavior of New York City cab drivers that, when accounting for earnings opportunities in a reduced form with measures of clock hours, day of the week, weather, and geographic location, cumulative hours worked on the shift is a primary determinant of the likelihood of stopping work while cumulative income earned on the shift is weakly related, at best, to the likelihood of stopping work. This is consistent with there being inter-temporal substitution and inconsistent with the hypothesis that taxi drivers are target earners.

See <http://www.nber.org/papers/w9706>.

The responsiveness of labor supply to changes in wage will undoubtedly continue to attract research effort.

1.7
Search Theory

1.7.1

Fixed Sample Search

Price dispersion is a manifestation – and, indeed, it is the measure – of ignorance in the market.

George Stigler

The Theory of Consumer Behavior is based on the idea that buyers choose how much to buy based on preferences, income, and given prices. We know, however, that buyers do not face a single price – there is a distribution of prices. Consumers do not know the prices charged by each firm. We simplify the problem by assuming that the product is identical (i.e., homogeneous) so the consumer wants to buy at the lowest price. Unfortunately, finding that lowest price is costly so the buyer has to solve an optimization problem.

Search Theory is an application of the economic approach to the problem of how long to shop in a world of many prices. Search is a productive activity because it enables one to find lower prices, but it is costly. One can search too little, ending up paying a high price, or oversearch – spending hours to find a price that is a few pennies lower does not make much sense.

This chapter introduces the consumer's search optimization problem and is based on the idea that consumers decide in advance how many price quotes to obtain, according to an optimal search rule. This type of search procedure is known as a *fixed sample search*.

Describing the Search Optimization Problem

Step Open the FixedSampleSearch.xls workbook and read the *Intro* sheet, then proceed to the *Setup* sheet.

The first task is to create the distribution of prices faced by the consumer. We assume that prices remain constant during the search process.

Histogram of Population Prices

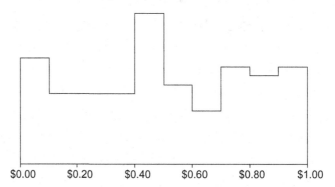

$0.00 $0.20 $0.40 $0.60 $0.80 $1.00

Figure 1.7.1.1. An example distribution of prices.
Source: FixedSampleSearch.xls!Setup

Step Click the Create the Population button.

You will be asked a series of questions that will establish the distribution of prices.

Step Type in 100 and hit OK when asked the number of stores selling the product. Choose Uniform for the distribution and then type in 0.5 when asked for the average price. Enter 0.2887 (which is approximately one over the square root of 12) when prompted for the SD. This creates a uniform distribution in the interval zero to one. Finally, enter 5 when prompted for the number of draws from the population.

After you hit Enter, you will see a column of red numbers in column A that represent the prices charged by each of the 100 stores selling the product. The consumer knows that stores charge different prices, but cannot immediately see each individual store price.

Step Scroll down to see the prices charged at each store.

It is difficult to see by simply scrolling down and looking at the prices, but the uniform distribution you used means that prices are scattered equally from zero to one. The normal distribution, on the other hand, would concentrate prices near the average, with fewer low and high prices (like a bell-shaped curve). The log-normal is the most realistic of the three – prices have a long right-hand tail (with some stores charging very high prices). The primary advantage of the uniform distribution is that it is the easiest to work with.

Figure 1.7.1.1 shows a histogram of 100 prices from a uniform distribution with an average of 0.5 and an SD of 0.2887.

The prices are not exactly evenly distributed on the interval from zero to one. They are drawn from a uniform distribution, but each realization of 100 prices deviates from a purely rectangular distribution due to randomness in sampling from the uniform distribution. You can see a histogram of your prices by scrolling over to column AA of the *Setup* sheet.

Consumers know that the distribution of prices is uniform with a given mean and standard deviation, but they do not know which firm is charging what price, so they cannot immediately go to the firm that has the lowest price. Instead, the fixed sample search model says that the consumer chooses a number of prices to sample (which you set as 5) and then chooses the lowest of the observed prices.

Step Click the `Draw a Sample One Price at a Time` button. A price will appear in the sample column, and a pop-up box tells you where that price came from. Hit OK each time the display comes up. You will hit OK five times because you chose to sample from five stores.

The consumer chooses among the 100 stores randomly and ends up with five observed prices. Column L reports the sample average price, the SD of the sampled prices, and the minimum price in the sample (in cell L7). The consumer will purchase the product at the minimum price observed in the sample.

Why doesn't the consumer visit every store and then pick the lowest price? Because it is costly to obtain the price information, as shown in cell L11. To sample 100 stores would cost the consumer $4. On average, the consumer would pay $0.54 (the average of the price distribution plus the cost of obtaining one price) by buying the product at the very first store visited. Clearly, it is better to buy immediately, $n = 1$, than to sample every store, $n = 100$, but what about other fixed sample sizes? How much will the consumer pay, on average, when sampling five stores?

Step Hit the `Draw a Full Sample` button repeatedly to draw more samples of size five. Keep your eye on the total price paid in cell L22.

There is no doubt about it – the total price the consumer ends up paying is a random variable. We need to figure out what the consumer will pay on average. The next section shows how.

Monte Carlo Simulation

The plan is to alter the spreadsheet so a new sample can be drawn simply by recalculating the sheet, which is done by hitting the F9 key. After this is done, the Monte Carlo simulation add-in will be installed and used to repeatedly draw new samples, tracking the lowest price in each sample.

Step Select cell range J2:J6. You should have five cells highlighted. In the formula bar, enter the following formula:

$$= \text{drawsamplearray}()$$

and then hit Ctrl + Shift + Enter (hold down and continuing holding down the Ctrl key, then hold down and continue holding down the Shift key, and then hit the Enter key). Your sample of five prices will appear in the sample column.

Do not simply hit the Enter key. This will put the formula only in the first cell. You want the formula in all five cells that you selected.

You have used an array function (built into the workbook) that spans the five cells you selected. You cannot individually edit the cells. If you mistakenly try to do so and get stuck, hit the ESC key to return to the spreadsheet.

When using this array function, it may display #VALUE. Simply hit the F9 key when this happens to refresh the function.

When using the drawsamplearray() function, you must be sure to set the number of draws in cell C15 to correspond to the number of cells used by the function. If there is a discrepancy, a warning will be displayed.

Step Hit F9 a few times and keep your eye on cells L7, the minimum price, and L22, the total price paid.

These cells update each time you hit F9. A new sample of five prices is drawn and the minimum price and total price paid are recalculated for the new sample.

The drawsamplearray() function enables Excel to display the minimum (best) price random variable, but we need to figure out the average minimum price when five price quotes are obtained. This can be done by repeatedly resampling and tracking each outcome – this is called *Monte Carlo simulation*.

Step Install the Monte Carlo simulation Excel add-in, available freely from <www.wabash.edu/econometrics>. Full documentation is available at this web site. This powerful add-in enables sophisticated simulations with the click of a button.

Once installed, you can use the add-in to determine the average minimum price and total price paid for the product when five prices are sampled.

Step Run the Monte Carlo simulation add-in on cell L7 with 1000 repetitions.

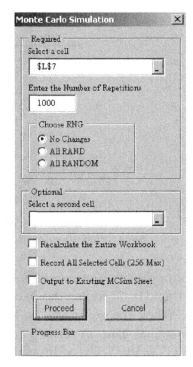

Figure 1.7.1.2. Configuring the MCSim dialog box.

Your MCSim add-in dialog box should look like Figure 1.7.1.2. Click the Proceed button to run the add-in.

Your simulation results will look something like Figure 1.7.1.3, but of course your results will be slightly different. The average of the minimum

Summary Statistics		Notes
Average	0.152	
SD	0.1295	
Max	0.712	
Min	0.010	

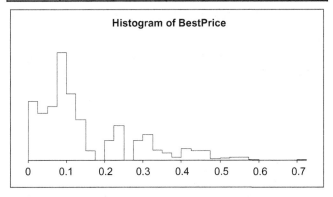

Figure 1.7.1.3. Monte Carlo simulation results with $n = 5$.
Source: FixedSampleSearch!MCSim4

Sample Size	Average Best Price	Search Cost	Total Price Paid
1	0.500	0.04	$ 0.54
2	0.333	0.08	$ 0.41
3	0.250	0.12	$ 0.37
4	0.200	0.16	$ 0.36
5	0.167	0.2	$ 0.37
6	0.143	0.24	$ 0.38
7	0.125	0.28	$ 0.41
8	0.111	0.32	$ 0.43
9	0.100	0.36	$ 0.46
10	0.091	0.4	$ 0.49

Figure 1.7.1.4. Optimal Search with a Uniform Distribution on [0,1].
Source: FixedSampleSearch!Summary

price distribution should be near $1/6$. Thus, the consumer will usually pay around 0.37 (adding the 20 cents in search cost) for the product.

When the consumer searches five stores instead of one, the expected marginal gain, in terms of a lower expected minimum price, is $0.50 − $0.17 = $0.33. The additional cost of searching for five prices instead of one is $0.16. Clearly, searching five stores is better than one because the consumer captures an additional net benefit of $0.33 − $0.16 = $0.17.

But we want to know more than just that searching five stores is better than buying at the first store; we want to find the best sample size – the one that gives the lowest total price paid.

Step Hit the `Clear the Sample` button. Change the number of draws in cell C15 to 10. Select cell range J2:J11, type in the formula bar "=drawsample array()" and hit the Ctrl + Shift + Enter combination to input the array formula. Your sample of 10 prices will appear in column J.

Hit F9 a few times and watch what happens to cell L7, the minimum price. It bounces, but with 10 prices instead of five, it bounces around a different, lower mean.

To figure out what the expected value of that distribution is, we need to run another Monte Carlo simulation.

Step Run a Monte Carlo simulation of the minimum price when 10 prices are obtained.

What did you find?

Figure 1.7.1.4 shows the exact average minimum price as a function of the sample size for this price distribution. Your simulation results for $n = 10$ should be close to 0.091. This means that the price that will be paid for the product will be pretty low when 10 prices are obtained, but notice that it isn't worth it. The cost of obtaining 10 prices is so high that the total price paid is higher than getting just five prices. In fact, getting four prices is the optimal sample size.

Analytical Methods

The optimal search optimization problem can be solved via analytical methods.

For the uniform price distribution on the interval from zero to one, the average minimum price in the consumers' hands after visiting n firms is

$$AverageP_{\min} = \frac{1}{n+1}$$

The equation for the average minimum price shows that it is decreasing as n rises and it does so at a decreasing rate. In other words, there are diminishing returns to searching for low prices.

The consumer's optimization problem is to minimize the total cost of acquiring the product:

$$\min_{n} TC = P(n)q + cn$$

$$\min_{n} TC = \frac{1}{n+1}q + cn$$

To find n^*, take the derivative with respect to n and set it equal to zero:

$$\frac{dTC}{dn} = -\frac{1}{(n+1)^2}q + c = 0$$

$$\frac{1}{(n+1)^2}q = c$$

This equimarginal condition says that the optimal sample size is found where marginal savings equals marginal cost. As long as the savings from searching an additional firm exceeds the cost of collecting one more price, the consumer will continue to search. The marginal savings is just the drop in the expected price, times the number of units that the consumer wants to purchase.

Stigler (1961) pointed out that the exact amount of the savings is the reduction in price times the quantity that would have been purchased at the higher price, plus the average savings on any purchases that would have been induced by the lower price. In line with Stigler, we will ignore this second source of savings as it is likely to be of a much smaller magnitude.

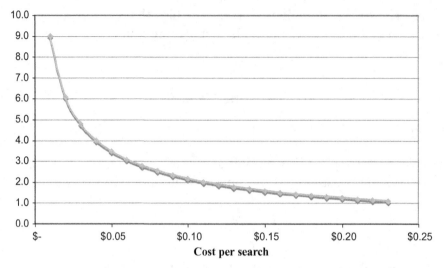

Figure 1.7.1.5. Optimal search with changing search cost for $q = 1$.

From the equimarginal condition, we can solve for n^*:

$$\frac{q}{(n+1)^2} = c$$

$$\frac{q}{c} = (n+1)^2$$

$$\sqrt{\frac{q}{c}} = (n+1)$$

$$n^* = \sqrt{\frac{q}{c}} - 1$$

With $q = 1$ and $c = \$0.04$, we have

$$n^* = \sqrt{\frac{1}{0.04}} - 1 = \sqrt{25} - 1 = 4$$

Of course, this agrees with the optimal solution obtained from Figure 1.7.1.4.

Comparative Statics

The reduced form makes comparative statics analysis straightforward. It is obvious that higher c, search cost, leads to lower optimal sample size, as shown in Figure 1.7.1.5.

Search cost is not the same for each consumer. Time is an important element of search cost. Those with more valuable time and, therefore, higher search cost will optimize by obtaining fewer price quotes.

The availability of information is another component of search cost. Informational advertising is simply firms letting consumers know where they are

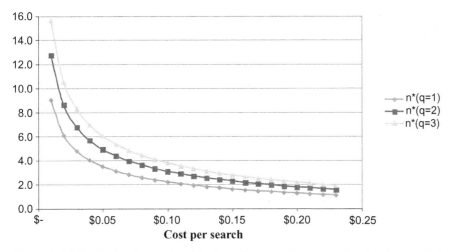

Figure 1.7.1.6. Optimal search with changing search cost and units demanded.

and what prices are being charged. We can model this as a decrease in search costs – now all the consumer has to do is pick up a newspaper or flyer to see what prices are being offered. Search costs are still positive (we do not know, for example, whether all firms advertise or just some), but lower than without advertising. Consumers obtain the product for a lower total price when advertising lowers search costs.

If we allow for multiple purchases – that is, a value of $q > 1$ – then the returns to search increase and, other things equal, the optimal number of searches increases. The effect of increasing q on the relationship between the cost of search and the optimal number of searches is shown in Figure 1.7.1.6.

For example, the driver of an 18-wheel truck that carries two 200-gallon diesel tanks is going to search more than someone looking to fill her car with gas. But this example leads to the next chapter, where it is shown that there is a better way to search than the fixed sample procedure used thus far.

Results of Fixed Sample Search

What are the implications of incomplete price information? Because consumers will not search every store, there will be price dispersion.

In other words, the law of one price will fail to hold. Some consumers will end up paying higher prices than others because the minimum price in their particular information set is different than the minimum price in another consumer's set.

Because lower search costs induce more search, a reduction in search costs would have the effect of reducing (but not eliminating) price dispersion. Price dispersion will not be eliminated because optimizing consumers will choose not to canvass every store for prices. This is the key result of the fixed sample search model.

Exercises

Open Word and answer the following questions. Save the document and print it when you are done.

Suppose the price distribution of 100 firms is uniform, with an average price of \$50 and an SD of \$28.87. Search cost, c, is \$1 per price.

1. On what interval (from the minimum to the maximum) are prices equally likely to fall?
2. Implement this problem in the *Setup* sheet and run a Monte Carlo simulation with a sample size of 20. Take a picture of your results (like Figure 1.7.1.3) and paste it in your Word document. What's good about obtaining 20 prices? What's bad?
3. Use the equation for the average minimum price as a function of n for this distribution, $AverageP_{min} = \frac{100}{n+1}$, to find the optimal sample size. Show your work.
4. Find the c elasticity of n^* at $q = c = 1$. Show your work.

References

The epigraph is from page 214 of George J. Stigler, "The Economics of Information," *The Journal of Political Economy*, Vol. 69, No. 3 (June, 1961), pp. 213–225. This paper is recognized as the beginning of the economics of search. Stigler was trying to explain price dispersion, but search theory has expanded far beyond this and is especially important in labor economics. For a review of recent developments, see Richard Rogerson, Robert Shimer, and Randall Wright, "Search-Theoretic Models of the Labor Market: A Survey," *Journal of Economic Literature*, Vol. 43, No. 4 (December, 2005), pp. 959–988.

1.7.2

Sequential Search

Job offers are independent random selections from the distribution of wages. These offers occur periodically and are either accepted or rejected. Under these conditions it is easy to show that the optimal policy for the job searcher is to reject all offers below a single critical number and to accept any offer above this critical number.

J. J. McCall

We introduced search theory with a Fixed Sample Search Model. A consumer samples from the population of stores and gets a list of n prices for a product, then chooses the minimum price. The bigger n, the lower the minimum price in the list, but the price paid to obtain the price quotes increases as n rises. The consumer has to decide how many prices to obtain.

This chapter explores the properties of a Sequential Search Model. Unlike the fixed sample search model where the consumer obtains a set of price quotes and then picks the lowest price, sequential search proceeds one at a time. The consumer samples from the population and gets a single price, then decides whether or not to accept it. As the epigraph shows, the sequential search model is easily applied to job offers, but it will be applied in this chapter to another common search problem – buying gas.

Setting Up the Model

Imagine you are driving down the road and you need fuel. As you drive, there are gas stations (say $N = 100$) to the left and right (taking a left does not bother you too much) and you can easily read the price per gallon as you drive up to each station. If you drive past a station, turning around is out of the question (there is traffic and you have a weird phobia about U-turns). There is a lowest price station and the stations can be ranked from 1 (lowest, best price) to 100 (highest, worst price). You do not know the prices of the stations ahead. The stations are randomly distributed on the road so the lowest price station might be 18th or 72nd or even 1st. Figure 1.7.2.1 sums it all up.

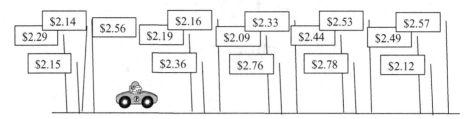

Figure 1.7.2.1. Deciding where to buy gas.

Suppose you focus on the following question: How do you maximize the chances of finding the cheapest station?

You might argue that you should drive by all of the stations, and then just pick the best one. This is a terrible idea because you cannot go back (remember, no U-turns). Once you pass a station, you cannot return to it. So, this strategy will only work if the cheapest station is the very last one. The chances of that are 1 in a 100.

You have developed a strategy for choosing a station: Pick some number $K < N$ where you reject (drive by) the first K stations, then choose the first station that has a price lower than the lowest of the K stations.

Perhaps $K = 50$ is the right answer? That is, drive by the first 50 stations, then look at the next (51st) station and if it is better than the lowest of the first 50 stations, pull in. If not, pass it up and consider the 52nd station. If it is cheaper than the previous 51 (or first 50 since we know the 51st station isn't lower than the lowest of the first 50), get gas there.

Continue this process until you get gas somewhere, pulling into the last (100th) station if you get to it (it will have a sign that says, "Next gas station 1000 miles").

This strategy will fail if the lowest price station is in the group of the K stations you drove by, so you might want to choose K to be small. But if you choose K too small, you won't get much of a sample and the first station with a price lower than the lowest of the K stations won't give you a very low price.

So, $K = 3$ is probably not going to work very well because you probably won't get a super low price in a set of just 3 so you probably won't end up choosing the lowest price. For example, say the first three stations are ranked $41, 27,$ and 90. Then as soon as you see a station better than 27, you will pull in there. That might be 1, but with 26 possibilities, that's not likely.

On the other hand, a high value of K, say 98, suffers from the fact that the lowest price station is probably in that group and you've already rejected it! Yes, this problem is certainly tricky.

This model can be used for much more than buying gas – it has extremely wide applicability. In hiring, it is called the optimal interview model. A firm picks the first K applicants, interviews and rejects them, then picks the next applicant that is better than the best of the K applicants. It also applies to many other areas, including marriage – you can fill in the details.

Step Open the Excel workbook SequentialSearch.xls and read the *Intro* sheet, then proceed to the *Setup* sheet.

Column A has the 100 stations ranked from 1 to 100. The lowest priced station is 1, and the highest priced station is 100.

Step Click the [Randomly Assign] button. It essentially shuffles the stations, distributing them along the road you are traveling.

Cell B7 reports where the lowest priced station (#1) is located. Columns C and D report the location of each station. Column D changes every time you click the [Randomly Assign] button because the stations are shuffled.

Cell F2 sets the value of K. This is the choice variable in this problem. Our goal is to determine the value of K that maximizes the probability that we get the lowest priced station.

On open, $K = 10$. We pass up the first 10 stations, then take the next station that is better than the best of the 10 stations we rejected.

Step Click the [How Did I Do?] button.

Cell F5 reports the best of the K stations (that were rejected).
Cell F7 displays the station you ended up at.

Step Scroll down to see why you ended up at that station.

Cell F7 always displays the first station that is better (lower) than the best of the K stations in cell F5.

Step Repeatedly click the [How Did I Do?] button. After every click, see how you did. Is 10 a good choice for K?

Step Change K to 60 (in cell F2) and repeatedly click the [How Did I Do?] button. Is 60 better than 10?

Solving the Problem via Monte Carlo Simulation

The *Setup* sheet is a good way to understand the problem, but it is not very helpful for figuring out the optimal value of K. Presumably, we could manually keep track of the number of times we get the best station at a given value of K, but that is a lot of work.

Fortunately, the *MCSim* sheet does this hard work for us.

Step Proceed to the *MCSim* sheet.

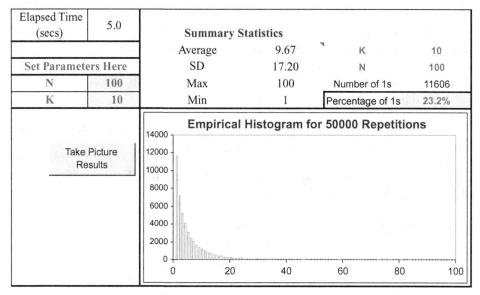

Figure 1.7.2.2. Monte Carlo simulation results.
Source: SequentialSearch.xls!MCSim

With $N = 100$ (we can change this parameter later), we set the value of K (in cell D7) and run a Monte Carlo simulation to get the approximate chances of getting the best station (reported in cell H7).

Unlike the MCSim add-in used in the previous chapter, this Monte Carlo simulation is hard wired into this workbook. Thus, it is very fast.

Step With $N = 100$ and $K = 10$, click the `Run Monte Carlo Simulation` button. The default number of repetitions is 50,000, which seems high, but a modern computer can do the simulation in a matter of seconds.

Figure 1.7.2.2 shows our results. Choosing $K = 10$ gives us the best station about 23.2% of the time. Your results will be slightly different.

Notice that we are using Monte Carlo simulation to approximate the exact probability histogram. Monte Carlo simulation cannot give an exact right answer. By increasing the number of repetitions, we improve the approximation, but we can never get the exact truth.

Can we do better than getting the best station 23% of the time?

We can answer this question by exploring how the chance of getting the lowest price varies with K. By changing the value of K to a different number and running a Monte Carlo simulation, we can evaluate different values of K.

Step Explore different values of K and fill in the table in cells J3:M10.

Step Create a chart of the chance of getting the lowest price station as a function of K.

Number of Repetitions	Value of K	Percentage of 1s	Average
100,000	30	35.84%	17.06
100,000	31	36.54%	17.41
100,000	32	36.59%	17.76
100,000	33	36.81%	18.24
100,000	34	36.60%	18.99
100,000	35	36.61%	19.30
100,000	36	36.93%	19.58
100,000	37	36.73%	20.21
100,000	38	36.62%	20.56
100,000	39	36.55%	21.38
100,000	40	36.52%	21.57

Figure 1.7.2.3. Zooming in on the value of optimal K.

What do you conclude?

One problem with Monte Carlo simulation is the variability in the approximation. It seems pretty clear that optimal value of K is between 30 and 40, but exactly where is it?

Figure 1.7.2.3 displays our results of series of Monte Carlo experiments. Notice that we doubled the number of repetitions to increase the resolution. The best value of K appears to be 36, but there seems to be a lot of noise.

With Monte Carlo simulation, we can continue to increase the number of repetitions. Figure 1.7.2.4 shows more zooming in. It looks like the answer might be 36 or 37, but it is hard to tell.

An Exact Solution

Perhaps you are wondering whether this problem can be solved analytically.

In fact, it can. The solution is implemented in Excel. For the details, see the Ferguson citation at the end of this chapter.

Step Proceed to the *Analytical* sheet to see the exact probability of getting the cheapest station for a given K-sized sample from N stations.

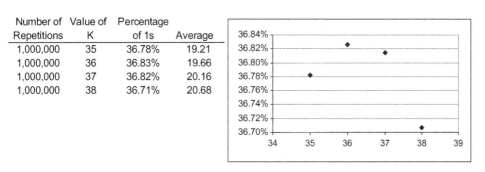

Number of Repetitions	Value of K	Percentage of 1s	Average
1,000,000	35	36.78%	19.21
1,000,000	36	36.83%	19.66
1,000,000	37	36.82%	20.16
1,000,000	38	36.71%	20.68

Figure 1.7.2.4. Further zooming in on the value of optimal K.

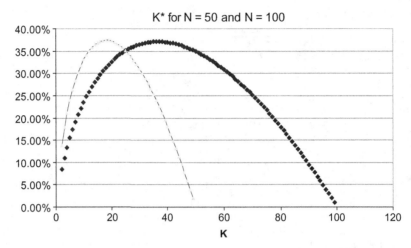

Figure 1.7.2.5. Exact probabilities of finding the cheapest station.
Source: SequentialSearch.xls!Analytical

For example, cell G10 displays 32.74%. This means you have a 32.74% chance of getting the cheapest station out of 10 stations if you drive by the first six stations and then choose the next station that has a price lower than the cheapest of the K stations you drove by.

For $N = 10$, is $K = 6$ the best solution?

No. The probability of choosing the cheapest station rises if you choose $K = 5$. The 3 and 4 choices are close, but clearly, $K^* = 3$ (with a 39.87% likelihood of getting the cheapest station) is the best choice.

In our initial example, we had $N = 100$. Monte Carlo simulations showed K^* around 36 or 37, but we were having trouble locating the exact right answer.

Step Scroll down to see the probabilities for $N = 100$. Click on cells AL100 and AM100 to see the exact value. The display has been rounded to two decimal (percentage) places, but the computation is precise to more decimal places.

$K^* = 37$ just barely beats out $K = 36$. This explains why we were having so much trouble zooming in on the right answer with Monte Carlo simulation.

Step Create a chart that shows the probability of getting the cheapest station from 100 stations for given K.

Step Add the case of $N = 50$ to your chart.

Our results are displayed in Figure 1.7.2.5. It shows that as N rises, so does optimal K. It can be shown (see the Ferguson source in the References section) that optimal K is N/e, giving a probability of finding the cheapest station of $1/e$. It is unclear why the transcendental number e, the base of natural logarithms, plays a role in the solution.

Optimal Sequential Search

Unlike the Fixed Sample Search Model (where you obtain a set of prices and choose the best one), the Sequential Search Model says that you draw sample observations one after the other. This could apply to a decision to choose a gas station. As you drive down the road, you decide whether to turn in and get gas at Station X or pass up that station and proceed to Station Y.

Faced with price dispersion, a driver deciding where to get gas can be modeled as solving a Sequential Search Model. The goal can be to maximize the chances of getting the lowest price or the lowest average price. We focused on the lowest price goal and found that as N rises, so does optimal K. The more stations, the more driving you should do before picking a station.

Like the Fixed Sample Search Model, the Sequential Search Model does not have any interaction between firms and consumers. Price dispersion is given and the model is used to analyze how consumers react in the given environment.

Ferguson points out that our Sequential Search Model (which mathematicians call the secretary problem) is part of a class of finite-horizon problems. "There is a large literature on this problem, and one book, *Problems of Best Selection* (in Russian) by Berezovskiy and Gnedin (1984) devoted solely to it." (Ferguson, Chapter 2).

Fixed Sample and Sequential Search Models are merely the tip of the iceberg. There is a vast literature and many applications in the economics of search, economics of information, and economics of uncertainty.

Exercises

Open Word and answer the following questions. Save the document and print it when you are done.

1. Use the results in the *Analytical* sheet to compute the N elasticity of K^* from $N = 10$ to $N = 11$. Show your work.
2. Use the results in the *Analytical* sheet to draw a chart of K^* as a function of N. Copy and paste your graph in your Word document.
3. Run a Monte Carlo simulation that supports one of the N-K^* combinations in the *Analytical* sheet. Take a picture of your simulation results and paste it in your Word document.
4. Explain why the Monte Carlo simulation was unable to exactly replicate the percentage of times the lowest priced station was found.

References

The epigraph is from pages 115 and 116 of J. J. McCall, "Economics of Information and Job Search," *The Quarterly Journal of Economics*, Vol. 84, No. 1 (February, 1970), pp. 113–126. This paper shows that sequential search (with recall) dominates fixed sample search. For more on this point, see Robert M. Feinberg and William R. Johnson, "The Superiority of Sequential Search: A Calculation," *Southern Economic Journal*, Vol. 43, No. 4 (April, 1977), pp. 1594–1598.

Thomas Ferguson, *Optimal Stopping and Applications*, online at <www.math.ucla.edu/~tom/Stopping/Contents.html>, offers a technical presentation of search theory.

C. J. McKenna, *The Economics of Uncertainty* (New York: Oxford University Press, 1986), is a concise, nontechnical introduction to imperfect information models.

John Allen Paulos, *Beyond Numeracy* (New York: Alfred A. Knopf, 1991), p. 64, discusses the optimal interview problem with an easy, intuitive style.

1.8

Behavioral Economics

1.8.1

Behavioral Economics

14.127 Behavioral Economics and Finance

This course surveys research which incorporates psychological evidence into economics. Topics include: prospect theory, biases in probabilistic judgment, self-control and mental accounting with implications for consumption and savings, fairness, altruism, and public goods contributions, financial market anomalies and theories, impact of markets, learning, and incentives, and memory, attention, categorization, and the thinking process.

MITOpenCourseware

The subfield of Behavioral Economics (and Behavioral Finance) is a growing research area that focuses on how decisions are actually made. It is closely tied to psychology and neuroscience. Behavioral economists reject the idea of utility maximization as an assumed black box. Both experimental methods and sophisticated procedures (such as fMRI brain scans) are used to examine how real-world problems are actually solved. A number of results have emerged that challenge the conventional wisdom in mainstream economics.

One area of long-standing interest in psychology involves repeated choice problems. This chapter focuses on a particular kind of repeated choice in which the satisfaction obtained currently depends on past decisions. This is called distributed choice.

Suppose you are deciding whether to watch TV or play a video game. You face this choice repeatedly. The satisfaction gained from watching TV or playing a video game depends on how often that choice has been made in the past. What is the optimal combination of TV and video games over a period of time and, more importantly, how well do people handle this kind of repeated decision?

Instead of explaining why the repeated choice optimization problem is difficult and presenting results from human trials, it is more fun to let you first participate in an experiment.

Choice Number	Pause Time A	Pause Time B	Choice Made
1	2.00		A
2	2.40		A
3	2.80		A
4	3.20		A
5	3.60		A
6	4.00		A
7		8.00	B
8	4.40		A
9	4.80		A
10		7.60	B

Figure 1.8.1.1. A portion of results.
Source: Melioration.xls!MyResults

The Choice Game

Step Open the Excel workbook Melioration.xls and read the *Intro* sheet, then go to the *Choice Game* sheet to play this simple game.

Your goal is to make as many choices as possible in 10 minutes. When you make a choice, by clicking on one of the buttons, you are forced to wait. Waiting is costly because you cannot click (make another choice) while waiting.

Step Click the Practice option button (near the top left corner of the screen) to see how the game works.

You get up to 100 practice trials. In practice mode, time is not kept. You can take as long as you want between button clicks. Practice now.

Are you ready to play? Unlike practice, when you play, a timer will be running. You will not use the buttons on the sheet like you did in practice mode. The buttons will be on a dialog box, right next to each other. You will have 10 minutes to make as many choices as possible. The time remaining will be displayed as you play.

Step Click the Play option button. Good luck!

After you finish the game, a message box displays your score and a *Results* sheet shows a record of your picks.

Figure 1.8.1.1 shows the first 10 choices made by another player. The player went with choice A at first, then switched to B with his 7th choice, but switched back.

Step You can see the full record of yet another player by clicking the Show MyResults Sheet button (near cell G9 in the *Results* sheet, which was revealed when you finished playing the choice game – yet another reason to play and complete the game).

Allocation to A	Average Delay	#Choices
0.45	4.7	128
0.53	5.2	115
0.58	5.4	111
0.61	5.5	109
0.68	5.2	115
0.71	5.5	109
0.79	5.4	111
0.83	5.8	103
0.86	5.7	105
0.87	6	100
0.92	5.65	106
0.93	6.1	98
0.94	5.7	105
0.95	6.1	98
0.97	6.05	99
0.98	6.9	87
0.99	6.1	98

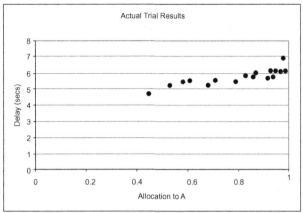

Figure 1.8.1.2. Actual results from a single session of the choice game. *Source:* Melioration.xls!Data

This player tried streaks of A and B.

Your *Results* sheet also compares the number of choices you made to the maximum possible and computes your score as a percentage of the maximum.

Having played this game – and if you have not played yet, please do so before continuing – you are ready to learn how most people play this game and why they usually fail.

Actual Empirical Results

This experiment was actually conducted by Herrnstein and Prelec (1991) and you can compare how you did to the average result (and to the player in the *MyResults* sheet).

Step Click the `Show Data Sheet` button (near cell I9 in the *Results* sheet).

The *Data* sheet shows how 17 subjects played the choice game that you just played. Each dot in the chart, reproduced as Figure 1.8.1.2, shows the fraction of times that a player chose A (on the *x* axis) and the corresponding average delay endured by that player (on the *y* axis). The player with the shortest delay, the first one in the table, also has the most choices (number of choices = 600/average delay) and is the winner in this set of players. How did you do?

Step To add your result to the chart, copy your results from cells J2 and K2 of the *Results* sheet, select cells A23 in the *Data* sheet, and Paste Special (Values) (or simply type in the two numbers). A red dot will appear in the chart. This shows how you did.

Did you beat the best player out of the 17 in the chart? We know you could have because the best player failed to optimize. The next section reveals how the game works and it is followed by an explanation of why most people fail to optimize.

Deconstructing the Choice Game

The heart of the choice game is the wait time between choices. The duration of the pause is a function of the previous 10 choices (including the current choice). For choice A, the wait time, in seconds, is $2 + 0.4 \times$ Proportion of A choices in the last 10 choices. So, if the last 10 choices had been B, then A would have a very short pause time of just 2 seconds. As you click on A, however, the pause time for choice A rises by 0.4 seconds until it hits a maximum of 6 seconds.

Choice B's wait time is determined by $8 - 0.4 \times$ Proportion of B choices in the last 10 choices. As you click on B, the duration of the pause gets lower and lower until reaching a minimum of 4 seconds.

Step Confirm that the wait times were determined as described by returning to the *Results* sheet and examining the pause times in columns B and C.

You can check to see that the first clicks of A and B had pause times of 2 and 8 seconds, respectively. You can also check that each pause time is following the functions described above.

Choice A exhibits increasing marginal cost – every time you click on A, you are penalized and forced to wait longer. Choice B rewards you with a decrease in wait time when it is clicked, but the wait time starts very high so you have to be persistent and stick to it. Plus, choice A is always 2 seconds lower than choice B so you are constantly being lured toward choice A.

Step Check your results to see if you clicked B after A forced you to wait too long. Did you switch back to A after one or two long pauses from B?

Now that you know the rules of the game, how do you actually optimize with this game? Simple – start with choice B and never deviate.

Step Go to the *Solution* sheet and click the `Show Solution Sheet` button (below the chart).

Column B shows what happens when you exclusively choose A. It starts well, but you end up with many 6 second pauses.

Step Scroll down to see that you make 103 choices in 600 seconds, yielding an average delay of 5.8 seconds. This is a poor outcome.

Column F displays what happens when B is exclusively chosen. The first few wait times are long, but each choice of B lowers the wait time until the minimum, 4 seconds, is reached.

Step Scroll down to see that clicking choice B every time lets you make 144 choices (with an average delay of 4.167 seconds).

The strategy of choosing B exclusively cannot be beat (except for an endgame correction, which is one of the exercise questions). If the player switches from B to A, the temporary gain is swamped by higher wait times when the inevitable switch back to B occurs.

To be sure that this point is clear, consider switching after having reached the 4 second minimum pause time for choice B. What would happen?

Step Change cell K15 (in the *Solution* sheet) to A.

Five consecutive A choices are made and each one has a pause time less than or equal to four seconds, as shown in column L. Thus, we have saved time. But when we switch back to B (since we know A's pause time will continue to rise and we can get to 4 seconds with B), we have to suffer higher pause times. The trade-off is not worth it. We end up making fewer choices (142 instead of 144) and suffering a longer average delay.

The *Solution* sheet makes clear the following key point: The optimal strategy is to choose B exclusively and never deviate. If you failed to do this, do not worry; you have plenty of company.

Melioration

Herrnstein and Prelec (1991) designed the experiment to test for the presence of something called melioration (pronounced mee-lee-uh-RAY-shun). To meliorate (or ameliorate) means to make better or more tolerable. Melioration says that we are drawn to choices with higher immediate satisfaction. We do a poor job of maximizing when there is a trade-off between short- and long-run returns. We are shortsighted and look to make immediate improvements. In fact, melioration has been found in other animals besides humans.

The attraction of switching to A and having the pause time fall is melioration at work. The immediate pain of waiting is lessened and, thus, players are drawn toward choice A.

In addition to the actual choices from the 17 players, Figure 1.8.1.3 shows wait times for choices A and B given the proportion of A choices in the previous 10. It is easy to see, once again, that the optimal solution is to choose B exclusively because that lets you travel down the solid line to the intercept

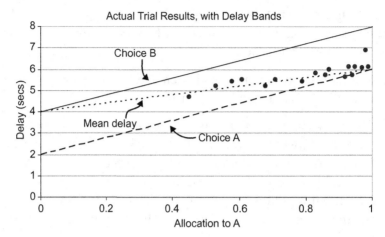

Figure 1.8.1.3. Understanding melioration.
Source: Melioration.xls!Data

at 4 seconds. If you ever jump on the A train, you are swept upwards toward a 6-second wait time.

Figure 1.8.1.3 shows that if the last 10 choices were B and then A was chosen, the player would immediately gain a reduction in wait time from 4 to 2 seconds. For a few choices, the player would be better off, but after the 5th consecutive A choice, the wait time would be greater than 4 seconds. The player would be forced to endure longer wait times than would have been obtained by sticking with B.

Furthermore, it will be hard to switch to B because wait time immediately jumps by 2 seconds. The player will have to suffer through the ride down the B line, with choice A promising a 2-second decrease with every click. The immediate attraction of the 2-second decrease is the core of the melioration process that guides subjects to choose A.

Implications of Melioration

Figure 1.8.1.3 makes clear that the 17 human subjects who played the choice game failed to optimize. The fraction of allocation to A should be zero, but most players do not do this. This begs the question, so what?

Herrnstein and Prelec (1991) argue that the lack of optimization is a big deal. For them, choice is often not a single, isolated decision, but a series of many decisions, distributed over time. Frequency of athletic exercise, buying lottery tickets, choices of restaurants, and rate of work in freelance occupations are some of the examples offered.

For all of these distributed choice problems, melioration is common and this means people systematically fail to optimize. "This would imply that preferences as revealed by the marketplace may be a distortion of the true underlying preferences" (Herrnstein and Prelec, 1991, p. 137). Melioration helps explain complaints about one's own behavior (such as exercising too little), which is part of a growing literature on self-control. It also may contribute to the study of impulsiveness and addiction.

Of course, this presumes that the laboratory findings carry over to real-world settings. This is often an Achilles' heel of experimental economics. Results are often criticized as having little external validity because they are based on fake scenarios played by college students. Herrnstein and Prelec (1991) acknowledge that little money was at stake (they paid their players based on performance), but they rely on two other motivating factors. "First, delays are genuinely annoying and the difference between two and four seconds is not trivial, as any computer user will appreciate. Second, the 'puzzle' nature of the experiment presents a challenge that is presumably satisfying to solve" (Herrnstein and Prelec, 1991, p. 144).

Others have tried to nail down exactly what causes melioration and how it can be overcome:

We hypothesized that frequent and informative feedback about optimal performance might be the key to enable people to overcome the documented tendency to meliorate when choices are rewarded probabilistically. Much to our surprise, this intuition turned out to be mistaken. Instead of maximizing, 19 out of 22 participants demonstrated a clear bias towards melioration, regardless of feedback condition. (Neth, Sims, and Gray, 2005, p. 357)

The Future of Behavioral Economics

With faculty, courses, conferences, and specialized journals, there is no doubt that Behavioral Economics is here to stay. In 2002, the Nobel Prize in Economics Science was awarded to Daniel Kahneman and Vernon Smith for work incorporating psychology and laboratory methods in the study of decision making. Unlike conventional economics, which simply assumes optimizing behavior and rationality, behavioral economists seek to determine under what conditions agents struggle to optimize and find persistently suboptimizing behavior. They work with psychologists and neuroscientists to devise tests and laboratory experiments.

Melioration is but one simple example of the work in this area. Melioration means that decision makers fail to optimize because they focus on the small (immediate, single choice) instead of the large (future, many choices).

A person does not normally make a once-and-for-all decision to become an exercise junkie, a miser, a glutton, a profligate, or a gambler; rather, he slips into the pattern through a myriad of innocent, or almost innocent choices, each of which carries little weight. Indeed, he may be the last one to recognize "how far he has slipped," and may take corrective action only when prompted by others. (Herrnstein and Prelec, 1991, p. 149)

According to the behavioral economists, the list of examples where humans struggle to optimize is actually quite long. Evaluating probabilities (such as risk), choice over time, and misperception of reality are all areas being actively studied.

It remains unclear whether the results being generated by behavioral economists are simply a series of interesting puzzles that will extend the boundaries of economics or more serious anomalies that will one day bring down the paradigm of rationality and optimizing behavior that is the hallmark of modern, mainstream economics.

Exercises

Open Word and answer the following questions. Save the document and print it when you are done.

If you did the Q&A problems and changed the parameters, set them back to the original values (2 and 0.4 for A and 8 and −0.4 for B).

1. With your observation included, copy and paste the chart titled *Actual Trial Results* in your Word document. Comment briefly on how you did.
2. What endgame correction could be implemented to increase the total number of choices? What is the true, exact maximum number of choices? Explain. Note: "In fact, the subjects showed no evidence of having been influenced by the endgame contingency." See Herrnstein and Prelec (1991), p. 142.
3. With columns Q:U in the *Solution* sheet, use Solver to find the optimal solution to the choice game. Notice how the choice variables have been constrained. How does Solver do? Explain.
4. Training someone to touch type does not guarantee continued touch typing in the workplace. How would melioration explain this result?

References

The epigraph is from a course available freely at <ocw.mit.edu>. The course description in the epigraph was from the Spring 2004 version of Behavioral Economics and Finance (see <ocw.mit.edu/OcwWeb/Economics/14-127Spring2004/CourseHome>). The readings for this course include introductory and more advanced work.

The repeated choice problem in this chapter is based on Richard J. Herrnstein and Dražen Prelec, "Melioration: A Theory of Distributed Choice," *The Journal of Economic Perspectives*, Vol. 5, No. 3 (Summer, 1991), pp. 137–156 and Herrnstein and Prelec's "Melioration," pages 235–263 in *Choice Over Time*, edited by George Loewenstein and Jon Elster (1992).

Herrnstein, a psychologist, teamed up with Charles Murray, a political scientist, to write a controversial book titled *The Bell Curve: Intelligence and Class Structure in American Life* (1994). The book argued that nature (IQ) is more important than nurture (socioeconomic status) in explaining a wide range of outcomes.

Hansjörg Neth, Chris R. Sims, and Wayne D. Gray, "Melioration Despite More Information: The Role of Feedback Frequency in Stable Suboptimal Performance," *Proceedings of the Human Factors and Ergonomics Society 49th Annual Meeting*, 2005.

Richard Thaler, *The Winner's Curse: Paradoxes and Anomalies of Economic Life* (1994), is a good place to start learning about behavioral economics.

Thaler and Cass Sunstein's *Nudge: Improving Decisions About Health, Wealth, and Happiness* (2008) focuses on how "choice architecture" can be designed to promote good decisions. For their blog and more, visit the book's web site at <www.nudges.org>.

Part II

The Theory of the Firm

For Friedman, lack of realism of assumptions is not a virtue. It is a necessary evil: to base theories on absolutely realistic assumptions is like drawing a map on a one-to-one scale.

Mark Blaug

Consumer Theory focuses on the buyer. It models a consumer's optimization problem and emphasizes deriving a Demand Curve as an important result.

The Theory of the Firm is about the seller. Firm decisions about inputs and outputs are modeled as optimization problems. A key result will be deriving a Supply Curve.

The Theory of the Firm is made up of three interrelated optimization problems.

1. Input cost minimization: Choose inputs to minimize the cost of producing a given level of output. Derive the cost function by changing q and tracking the minimum total cost.
2. Output profit maximization: Choose output to maximize profits. Derive the supply curve by changing the price and tracking the optimal output.
3. Input profit maximization: Choose inputs to maximize profits. Derive an input demand curve by changing an input price and tracking optimal input use.

The economic approach (optimization and comparative statics) will play a key role, but there are three crucial innovations in the Theory of the Firm.

1. Market structure: The Theory of the Firm includes the market environment as an important consideration in the model. The firm can be a *price taker*, a perfectly competitive firm, or a *price maker*, a monopolist. Other market structures include oligopoly (where there a few firms) and monopolistic competition.

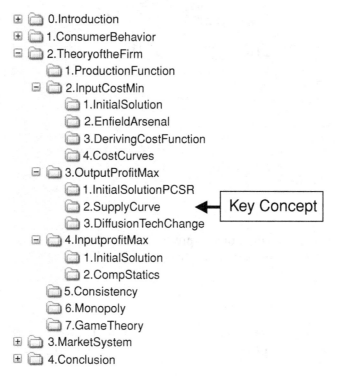

Figure II.1. Content map with focus on the Theory of the Firm.

2. Time period: The Theory of the Firm distinguishes between long-run and short-run decision-making horizons. In the long run, all factors are freely variable and firms may enter or exit the industry. In the short run, at least one input (usually capital) is fixed and the firm may cease production (shut down), but it must pay fixed costs whether it produces or not.
3. Output is cardinally measurable: Unlike utility, the output produced by a firm and the resulting revenues, costs, and profits can be directly observed and measured on a cardinal scale.

The chapters are organized as shown in Figure II.1. Notice that the production function is the first idea presented. It plays a role in every optimization problem faced by the firm. Figure II.1 also provides a broad overview of the entire landscape. We have completed the Theory of Consumer Behavior and, once we finish our work in the Theory of the Firm, we will be ready to analyze the behavior of consumers and firms together in the Market System.

References

The epigraph is from page 703 of the third edition (1978) of Mark Blaug's *Economic Theory in Retrospect* (originally published in 1962). Blaug's concluding chapter, "A Methodological Postscript," is a good review of how theories develop and knowledge grows.

Part of methodology revolves around the rules for determining truth and acceptable procedures in each discipline. For example, economics utilizes highly abstract models. The assumptions of these models are plainly unrealistic and false. Milton Friedman's defense in "The Methodology of Positive Economics," the first chapter in *Essays in Positive Economics* (1953), was initially controversial but became conventional thinking in economics. Basically, Friedman urged economists to ignore unrealistic assumptions and focus on the predictive power of a model. If you want to predict how billiard balls will move when hit by an expert pool player, vectors and complicated mathematics are involved.

> It seems not at all unreasonable that excellent predictions would be yielded by the hypothesis that the billiard player made his shots *as if* he knew the complicated mathematical formulas that would give the optimum directions of travel, could estimate accurately by eye the angles, etc., describing the location of the balls, could make lightning calculations from the formulas, and could then make the balls travel in the direction indicated by the formulas. (Friedman, 1953, p. 21)

The Theory of the Firm (like the Theory of Consumer Behavior) is built on the idea of rationally calculating optimizing agents. This is plainly unreal, but the point is not to describe how firms actually make decisions. Instead, we want a model that makes predictions about changes in output, for example, as product price changes.

It is quite easy to forget this basic idea and find oneself wondering how economists can believe such a ridiculously unreal and abstract model of a firm. Remember, economists do not test theories via the assumptions – it is the implications that matter.

2.1

Production Function

2.1.1

Production Function

Let us choose that function $P' = bL^k C^{k-1}$ and find such numerical values of b and k that P' will "best" approximate P [product or output] in the sense of the Theory of Least Squares.

Then relative to the indices and the period we have the norm $P' = 1.01 L^{3/4} C^{1/4}$.

Charles W. Cobb and Paul H. Douglas

The production function is the backbone of the Theory of the Firm. It describes the current state of technology and how input can be transformed into output.

The production function can be displayed in a variety of ways, including product curves and isoquants. In every optimization problem faced by the firm, the production function is included.

Key Definitions and Assumptions

Inputs, or *factors of production*, are used to make *output*, or *product*. As shown in Figure 2.1.1.1, the firm is a highly abstract entity – a black box – that simply transforms inputs into output.

Inputs are often broken down into large categories: land, labor, raw materials, and capital. Capital can be confusing. Capital, K, as a factor of production means physical capital goods such as machinery, tools, or equipment. That is different from financial or venture capital that is a fund of money.

Like labor, capital is rented. The firm does not own any of its machines. This is extremely unrealistic but allows us to avoid complicated issues involving depreciation, financing of machinery purchases (debt versus equity, for example), and so on.

Like the consumer, the firm exists only for a nanosecond. It makes decisions about how much to produce to maximize profits with no time horizon. It produces the output in an instant.

Another simplifying assumption is that the firm produces only one product. That makes revenues simply price times quantity sold.

Figure 2.1.1.1. The black box nature of the firm.

The reason why we make these unbelievably unrealistic assumptions is because our primary goal is to derive a supply curve. We want to know how a firm responds to a change in price, ceteris paribus. By assuming away many real-world complications, we can model the problem, solve it, and do comparative statics to get the supply curve.

We distinguish between a production set and function:

Production set: describes *all* of the technologically feasible outputs from a given amount of inputs

Production function: describes the *maximum output possible* from a given amount of inputs

A general function: $y = f(x_1, x_2)$

A Cobb-Douglas functional form: $y = A L^\alpha K^\beta$

Step Open the Excel workbook ProductionFunction.xls and read the *Intro* sheet, then go to the *Technology* sheet to see an example of the production function.

In Figure 2.1.1.2, the production set is the surface and everything inside; the production function is just the surface.

The production function implicitly includes an already solved engineering optimization problem – it gives the maximum output from any given combination of inputs. In other words, we are assuming that the inputs are organized in their most productive configuration and nothing is wasted.

Step Notice that the Cobb-Douglas function on the *Technology* sheet has been set up so it can be controlled by a single parameter, α (alpha), by making the exponents α and $(1 - \alpha)$. Use the scroll bar to change alpha and

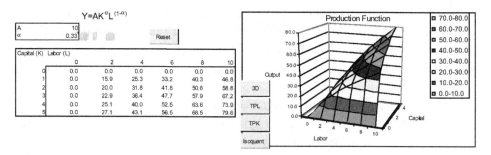

Figure 2.1.1.2. The production function.
Source: ProductionFunction.xls!Technology

Total Product Curves: Slices of the production function at given values of one input.

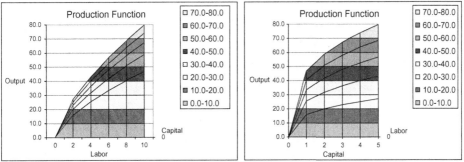

Figure 2.1.1.3. Total product curves.
Source: ProductionFunction.xls!Technology

notice how the shape of the production function surface changes. Alpha is a parameter that takes values between zero and one.

Step Click the Reset button to return the sheet to its default, initial position.

Product Curves

In addition to the 3D view, the production function can be displayed in other ways. To graph the production function in two dimensions, we need to suppress an axis. If we keep output and suppress one of the input axes we get a *total product curve*. If we suppress output and keep the two inputs, we get an *isoquant*.

Product and output mean the same thing. Total product is the number of units of output produced.

Step Click the TPL and TPK buttons to see the product curves displayed in Figure 2.1.1.3.

In addition to the total product curves, there are marginal product curves. The marginal product curves can be computed based on finite-size changes in an input, ceteris paribus, or via the derivative.

Via calculus, the marginal product is simply the derivative of the production function with respect to the input.

$$MP_L = \frac{\partial f(L, K)}{\partial L}$$

$$MP_K = \frac{\partial f(L, K)}{\partial K}$$

Step Scroll down to row 50 or so in the *Technology* sheet to see the marginal product of labor curve. The display on your screen resembles Figure 2.1.1.4.

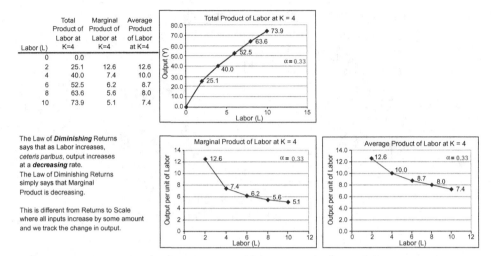

The Law of *Diminishing* Returns says that as Labor increases, *ceteris paribus*, output increases at a *decreasing* rate. The Law of Diminishing Returns simply says that Marginal Product is decreasing.

This is different from Returns to Scale where all inputs increase by some amount and we track the change in output.

Figure 2.1.1.4. Total, marginal, and average product of labor curves. *Source:* ProductionFunction.xls!Technology

Marginal product is the additional output generated by additional input, ceteris paribus. The average product is the output per input, ceteris paribus.

Notice how the product curves are drawn based on a given amount of capital. If the amount of capital changes, then the product curves shift.

Marginal and average product can be graphed together because they share a common *y* axis scale, output per unit of input. The total product curve can never be graphed with the marginal and average product curves because the total product curve uses output as its *y* axis scale.

Figure 2.1.1.4 demonstrates that when total product increases at a decreasing rate, marginal product is decreasing. When output increases at a decreasing rate as more input is applied, ceteris paribus, we are obeying the *Law of Diminishing Returns*. As long as alpha is between zero and one, our Cobb-Douglas production function exhibits diminishing returns.

The Law of Diminishing Returns does not deny that there can be ranges of input use where output increases at an increasing rate. It says that, *eventually*, continued application of more input along with a fixed factor must lead to diminishing returns in the sense that output will increase, but it will do so at a decreasing rate. Thus, the Law of Diminishing Returns is simply a statement that marginal productivity is falling.

As with utility, the Cobb-Douglas functional form is convenient, but there are many, many other functional forms available.

Step Proceed to the *Polynomial* sheet to see a different functional form.

Unlike the Cobb-Douglas functional form, which always shows diminishing returns, the polynomial production function has three different kinds of

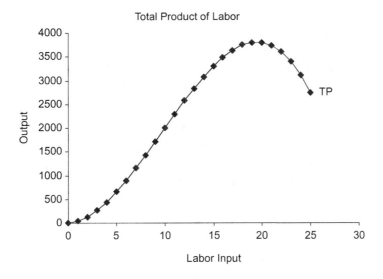

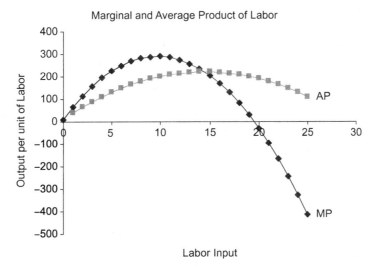

Figure 2.1.1.5. Product curves for a polynomial production function.
Source: ProductionFunction.xls!Polynomial

returns: increasing, diminishing, and negative returns. Figure 2.1.1.5 shows the total, marginal, and average product curves.

At low levels of labor use, output is increasing at an increasing rate so the total product curve is curved upward and marginal product is increasing. In this range, as long as marginal product is rising and output is increasing at an increasing rate, we have increasing returns. The *Polynomial* sheet is color coded, and tan-backgrounded cells are the range where labor yields increasing returns.

When the marginal product curve reaches its peak, the total product curve is at an inflection point. From here, additional labor leads to increases in output, but at a decreasing rate. We say that diminishing returns have set in. The cells with yellow backgrounds signal the range of labor use where diminishing returns apply.

Remember that the Law of Diminishing Returns does not say that we always have diminishing returns for every level of labor use. Instead, the law says that, eventually, diminishing returns will set in.

As more and more labor is used, total product reaches its maximum point (where marginal product is zero). Beyond this point, we are in a range of negative returns. This is a theoretical possibility, but not a practical one. No profit-maximizing firm would ever operate in this region because you can get the same amount of output with fewer workers. The range of negative returns is denoted by the values of L that have light-green backgrounds.

Notice the relationship between the marginal and average product curves. It is no coincidence that the marginal product curve intersects the average product curve at the maximum value of the average product curve. There is a guaranteed relationship between marginal and average curves: Whenever the marginal is greater than the average, the average must be rising and whenever the marginal is less than the average, the average must be falling. Thus, the only time the two curves can meet is when the marginal equals the average. Figure 2.1.1.5 clearly shows this to be the case.

Step Change the parameter for the b coefficient from 30 to 40.

Notice that the S shape becomes much more linear. The range of increasing returns is larger and we do not hit negative returns over the observed range of L from 0 to 25.

Step Set the parameter for the b coefficient to 80.

Over the observed range of L from 0 to 25, we see only increasing returns.

Step Change the ΔL parameter from 1 to 2. This makes L increase by 2 and the range goes from 0 to 50.

You can see that diminishing returns do kick in; it just takes more labor for the law of diminishing returns to be observed when the b coefficient is set to 80.

One confusing thing about the Law of Diminishing Returns has to do with another concept called *returns to scale*. Unlike the Law of Diminishing Returns – which is based on applying more and more of a particular input while holding other inputs constant – returns to scale focuses on the effect on output of changing all of the inputs by the same proportion.

There is no law for returns to scale. A production process may exhibit increasing, decreasing, or constant returns to scale. For example, the Cobb-Douglas function on the *Technology* sheet has constant returns to scale because if you double L and K, you are guaranteed to double output.

You can see this is true by comparing the points 2,2 and 4,4 in the table in the *Technology* sheet. A more complete demonstration uses a little algebra.

$$A K^\alpha L^{(1-\alpha)}$$

$$A(2K)^\alpha (2L)^{(1-\alpha)}$$

$$A 2^\alpha K^\alpha 2^{(1-\alpha)} L^{(1-\alpha)}$$

$$A 2^{(\alpha+1-\alpha)} K^\alpha L^{(1-\alpha)}$$

$$A 2 K^\alpha L^{(1-\alpha)}$$

Doubling the inputs from any input levels leads to doubling the output, and this is called *constant returns to scale*. If the exponents in the Cobb-Douglas function do not sum to 1, then the function does not exhibit this property.

Notice that the Cobb-Douglas function in the *Technology* sheet obeys the Law of Diminishing Returns for each input (as long as $0 < \alpha < 1$), yet it has constant returns to scale. Do diminishing returns imply decreasing returns to scale? No, absolutely not. The two concepts are distinguished by virtue of the fact that they ask different questions. The Law of Diminishing Returns is about what happens to output when a particular input is increased, ceteris paribus, and decreasing returns to scale says that output will less than double when all inputs are doubled.

Isoquants

In addition to product curves, another way to represent the production function uses the isoquant. The prefix "iso," meaning equal or the same (as in isosceles triangle), is combined with "quant" (obviously referring to the quantity of output) to convey the idea that the isoquant displays the combinations of L and K that yield the same output.

Step From the *Technology* sheet, click the |Isoquant| button to see the isoquant displayed in Figure 2.1.1.6.

Isoquants are combinations of inputs that yield the same (iso) output (quant).

Your screen (and Figure 2.1.1.6) makes clear that an isoquant is simply a 2D, top down view of the 3D production function. Unlike the product curves, where we kept the q axis and suppressed one of the inputs, the isoquant shows L and K on the x and y axes and suppresses output. Notice that Excel 2007 cannot correctly draw the isoquant map, putting garbled characters in the bottom left-hand corner of the chart. This is due to the new way charts are drawn in Excel 2007 and was not a problem in earlier versions.

There are strong parallels between isoquants and indifference curves. Both are top-down views of a 3D object and, therefore, both are level curves

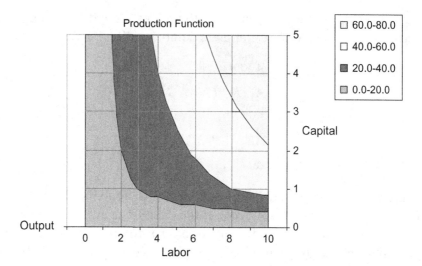

Figure 2.1.1.6. Isoquants for a Cobb-Douglas technology.
Source: ProductionFunction.xls!Technology

or contour plots. Both are used to find and display the solution to an optimization problem.

However, there is one critical difference: Unlike an indifference curve, each isoquant is, in principle, directly *observable* and the isoquants can be compared on a cardinal scale. With indifference curves, the utility function is a convenient fiction and we do not worry about the actual values of the indifference curve. No one cares that a particular indifference curve yields 28 utils of satisfaction. This is not the case for isoquants, given that the suppressed axis, output, is measurable. You can certainly say that one isoquant gives twice the output as another or that one isoquant gives 17 more units of output than another.

Finally, we define the *technical rate of substitution*, TRS, as the slope of an isoquant at a point. With labor on the x axis and capital on the y axis, the TRS tells us how much capital we can save if one more unit of labor is used to produce the same level of output.

Like the MRS, the TRS can be computed from one point to another as the rise over the run, $\Delta K/\Delta L$, from two points on the isoquant or with calculus via the ratio of the first derivatives:

$$Y = f(L, K)$$

$$TRS = -\frac{MP_L}{MP_K} = -\frac{\dfrac{\partial f(L, K)}{\partial L}}{\dfrac{\partial f(L, K)}{\partial K}}$$

Whereas MRS is universally used for the slope of an indifference curve, MRTS (marginal rate of technical substitution) is sometimes used instead of TRS. MRTS and TRS are perfect synonyms. We will use TRS.

The TRS (like the MRS) is a number that expresses the substitutability of labor for capital at a point on an isoquant. So, a comparison of the TRS of two different L and K combinations on the same isoquant might yield -100 and -2. The $TRS = -100$ value says that I can replace 100 units of capital with 1 unit of labor and still produce the same output. At the TRS $= -2$ point on the isoquant, 1 unit of labor can replace 2 units of capital to get the same output. The TRS tells me how steep the isoquant is at a point. The steeper the isoquant the more capital can be replaced by a unit of labor.

Technological Progress

Over time, technology – our ability to transform inputs into output – improves. Electric power and computers are examples of technological progress that enables more output to be produced from the same input.

There are two kinds of technological change. The Cobb-Douglas functional form can be used to illustrate each type.

A new production method or increased education, for example, that improves the productivity of labor, but not capital, would be modeled as an increase in the exponent for labor. Small changes, say from 0.75 to 0.751, lead to large responses (e.g., in output or labor use) because we are working with an exponent.

We could also have a situation where the coefficient A in the function $A K^\alpha L^\beta$ increased over time. As A rises, the same number of inputs can make more output. This technological progress is said to be neutral (in terms of the utilization of L and K) because it leaves the marginal productivities of the inputs unchanged:

$$MP_L = \frac{\partial f(L, K)}{\partial L} = \beta A K^\alpha L^{\beta-1}$$
$$MP_K = \frac{\partial f(L, K)}{\partial K} = \alpha A K^{\alpha-1} L^\beta \Rightarrow \frac{MP_L}{MP_K} = \frac{\beta A K^\alpha L^{\beta-1}}{\alpha A K^{\alpha-1} L^\beta} = \frac{\beta K}{\alpha L}$$

The A terms cancel out, which means that the ratio of the marginal productivities of each input depends only on each input's exponent and the amount of the input used.

As we shall see, technological progress, modeled as changes in exponents or the A parameter in the Cobb-Douglas functional form, impacts the optimal solution.

The Production Function (or Technology) Is the Core of the Firm

The production function is the starting point for the Theory of the Firm. As with utility, many, many functional forms can be used to represent real-world production processes.

Economists represent the production function not as a 3D object but in two dimensions. We get product curves (total, marginal, and average product curves) by focusing on output as a function of an input, holding all other inputs constant. An isoquant suppresses the output and shows the different combinations of L and K that produce a given level of output.

The TRS is similar to the MRS, and it will play an important role in the understanding the firm's cost minimizing input choice.

Remember to keep straight the difference between the Law of Diminishing Returns and idea of returns to scale. The former applies more and more of an input, holding all other inputs constant; the latter reports what happens to output when all inputs are changed by the same proportion.

Exercises

Open Excel and answer the following questions. Save the workbook when you are done.

1. Starting from a blank workbook, with $K = 100$, draw total, marginal, and average product curves for $L = 1$ to 100 by 1 for the Cobb-Douglas production function, $Y = L^{\alpha} K^{\beta}$, where $\alpha = 3/4$ and $\beta = 1/2$. Use the derivative to compute the marginal product of labor. Hint: Label cells in a row in columns A, B, C, and D as L, Q, MPL, and APL. For L, create a list of numbers from 1 to 100. For the other three columns, enter the appropriate formula and fill down. For MPL, do not use the change in Q divided by the change in L; instead use the derivative for the MPL at a point.

2. For what range of L does the Cobb-Douglas function in question 1 exhibit the Law of Diminishing Returns? Put your answer in a text box in your workbook.

3. Determine whether this function has increasing, decreasing, or constant returns to scale. Use the workbook for computations and include your answer in a text box.

4. From your work in question 3 and the comment in the text that you cannot have constant returns to scale "if the exponents in the Cobb-Douglas function do not sum to 1," provide a rule to determine the returns to scale for a Cobb-Douglas functional form.

5. Is it possible for a production function to exhibit the Law of Diminishing Returns and increasing returns to scale at the same time? If so, give an example. Put your answer in a text box in your workbook.

6. Draw an isoquant for 50 units of output for the Cobb-Douglas function in question 1.
   Hint: Use algebra to find an equation that tells you the K needed to produce 50 units given L. Create a column for K that uses this equation based on L ranging from 20 to 40 by 1 and then create a chart of the L and K data.

7. Compute the TRS of the Cobb-Douglas function at $L = 23$, $K = 312.5$. Show your work on the spreadsheet.

References

The epigraph comes from page 152 of "A Theory of Production" by Charles W. Cobb and Paul H. Douglas, *The American Economic Review*, Vol. 18, No. 1, Supplement, Papers and Proceedings of the Fortieth Annual Meeting of the American Economic Association (March, 1928), pp. 139–165. Douglas, an accomplished professor and US Senator from Illinois, explained how he and Cobb used the functional form that would be named after them: "I was then temporarily lecturing at Amherst College, and consulted with my friend and colleague, Charles W. Cobb, a mathematician. At the latter's suggestion, the formula $P = bL^k C^{k-1}$ was adopted, a form that had also been used by Wicksteed and Wicksell." See p. 904 in Paul H. Douglas, "The Cobb-Douglas Production Function Once Again: Its History, Its Testing, and Some New Empirical Values," *The Journal of Political Economy*, Vol. 84, No. 5 (October, 1976), pp. 903–916.

2.2

Input Cost Minimization

2.2.1

Initial Solution for Input Cost Minimization

The term "isoquant" was introduced by R. Frisch but originally for a different concept, for which it should have been reserved.

Joseph Schumpeter

Input cost minimization is one of the three optimization problems faced by the firm. It revolves around the question of choosing the best combination of inputs, L and K, to produce a given level of output, q.

The best combination is defined as the cheapest one. The idea is that many combinations of L and K can produce a given q. We want to know the amounts of labor and capital that should be used to produce a given amount of output.

Of course, we answer this question by setting up and solving an optimization problem; then we do comparative statics.

Setting Up the Problem

The economic approach organizes optimization problems by answering three questions: (1) What is the goal? (2) What are the choice variables? (3) What are the given variables?

The goal is to minimize total cost, TC, which is simply the sum of the amount paid to the workers, wL, and the amount spent on renting machines, rK.

The endogenous variables are L and K. Labor is measured in hours and capital is the number of machines. The firm can decide to produce the given output by being labor intensive, using lots of labor and little capital, or roughly equal amounts of both, or by renting a lot of machinery and using little labor.

The exogenous variables are the input prices, wage (w), and the rental price of capital (r). The wage is measured in $/hour and the rental price of

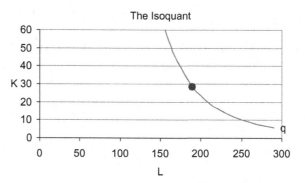

Figure 2.2.1.1. An isoquant from a Cobb-Douglas production function. *Source:* InputCostMin!Isoquant

capital is $/machine. We assume that the firm is price taker in the markets for labor and capital. The amount to produce, q, is also an exogenous variable in this problem. We are not considering how much should be produced, but what is the best way to produce any given amount of output. Finally, the firm's technology, the production function, $f(L, K)$, is also given.

Because the firm has to produce a given amount of output, we know this is a constrained optimization problem. Our work in the Theory of Consumer Behavior has made us expert at solving this kind of problem. As you will see, the analysis is similar, but there are some striking differences.

The Constraint

The menu of options available to the firm is given by the isoquant. The isoquant will serve as the constraint because the firm must produce the assigned level of output. The equation for the constraint is simply the production function, $q = f(L, K)$.

Step Open the Excel workbook InputCostMin.xls and read the *Intro* sheet, then go to the *Isoquant* sheet to see an example.

The isoquant displayed in Figure 2.2.1.1 (and on your screen) tells the firm the feasible input options. All combinations below and left of the isoquant are ruled out. There is no way to produce 100 units of output with the L,K combination of 100,20. The technology is simply not advanced or powerful enough.

The points above and to the right of the isoquant are feasible, but they are clearly wasteful. In other words, the firm could produce 100 units of output with 250,50, but the isoquant tells the firm it does not need that much labor and capital to make 100 units. At 250,50, it could travel straight down to $K = 10$ and still produce $q = 100$ or straight left until it hit the isoquant and use a lot less labor. The firm could also travel in a diagonal, southwest direction until it hit the isoquant to economize on both inputs.

Points off the isoquant to the northeast (such as 250,50) are said to be *technically inefficient*. The "inefficient" part tells you that the firm is not minimizing its total cost at that point; "technical" describes the fact that the firm is not using its inputs to maximize output. In other words, it is not correctly solving the engineering optimization problem represented by the production function. Making 100 units of output with 250 hours of labor and 50 machines means that you are not getting the most out of your labor and capital.

Step Use the scroll bar next to cell B11 to see the input mixes available to the firm. As you change cell B11, the cell below changes also. It has a formula that computes the amount of K needed to produce the required output when you choose a value for L.

The idea is quite clear: The firm will roll around the isoquant in search of the best combination. Because we do not have the input prices, we cannot find the optimal solution with the isoquant alone.

Step Change the exogenous variables to see how the isoquant is affected. Increases in A, c, and d pull the isoquant down. That makes sense given that these shocks are all productivity enhancing and the firm will need less L and K to make the given q.

Lowering q has the same effect, but this is not a productivity shock. You are simply telling the firm it does not have to produce as much so it makes sense that it can use less labor and capital.

Goal

With the constraint in hand, we are ready to model the goal.

In this problem, the goal is represented by a series of *isocost* (equal cost) lines.

Total cost is simply $TC = wL + rK$. If we solve this equation for K (in order to graph it in L-K space), we get $K = \frac{TC}{r} - \frac{w}{r}L$. The K (or y axis) intercept is TC/r and the slope is $-w/r$.

Step Proceed to the *Isocost* sheet to see how the isocost lines are used to find the optimal solution.

Each point on the same isocost line has the exact same total cost. So, the point on Figure 2.2.1.2 (and on your screen) has a cost of $500 (given that $2 \times 190 + 3 \times 40 = 500$).

Step If you increase L by 30 and decrease K by 20, you will be at another point on the same isocost line.

Clearly, all points on the TC $= 500$ isocost line have a total cost of $500. It is also obvious that the slope of each isocost line is $-2/3$.

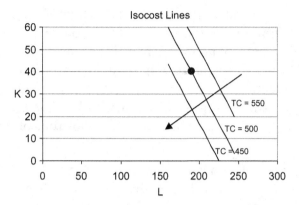

Figure 2.2.1.2. Three isocost lines.
Source: InputCostMin!Isocosts

Because the firm can choose the input mix, it can choose any combination of L and K, provided that the chosen combination can produce the given amount of output.

The Initial Optimal Solution

Step Proceed to the *OptimalChoice* sheet.

The idea is to be on the lowest isocost line (i.e., the one with the smallest intercept) that is just touching the isoquant because that means the firm will be minimizing the total cost of producing the given level of output.

Clearly, this initial position is not optimal. You can see that the isocost is intersecting the isoquant. This information is also revealed by the slope and TRS information below the chart. The TRS, which is the slope of the isoquant at a point, is greater (in absolute value) than the slope of the isocost line at that point.

At the initial position, the firm is said to suffer from *allocative inefficiency* because it is on the isoquant, but it fails to choose the cost minimizing input mix. Because it is on the isoquant, we know it is not technically inefficient – it is using the combination of L and K to get the maximum output. The problem is that it is using the wrong combination of inputs in the sense that there is a cheaper way to produce the given output.

We know there are two ways to solve optimization problems: analytically and numerically. Because we have Excel and the problem implemented on the sheet, we begin with the numerical approach.

Step Run Solver. The optimal solution is depicted by the canonical graph displayed in Figure 2.2.1.3.

As expected, Solver has found the optimal combination, the isocost of which just touches the isoquant. There is no cheaper combination that can

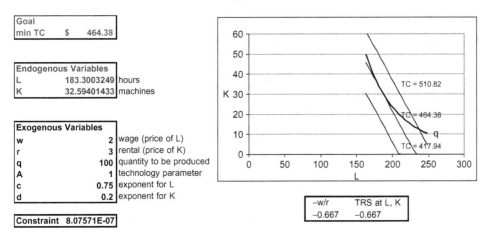

Goal		
min TC	$	464.38

Endogenous Variables		
L	183.3003249	hours
K	32.59401433	machines

Exogenous Variables		
w	2	wage (price of L)
r	3	rental (price of K)
q	100	quantity to be produced
A	1	technology parameter
c	0.75	exponent for L
d	0.2	exponent for K

Constraint	8.07571E-07

−w/r	TRS at L, K
−0.667	−0.667

Figure 2.2.1.3. Initial optimal solution.
Source: InputCostMin!OptimalChoice

produce 100 units with the existing technology (given by the production function).

We can confirm Solver's result by applying the Lagrangean method to solve this constrained optimization problem.

We start by writing down the problem, using the parameter values from the *OptimalChoice* sheet.

$$\min_{L,K} TC = 2L + 3K$$

$$\text{s.t. } 100 = L^{0.75} K^{0.2}$$

The first step is to rewrite the constraint so that it is equal to zero.

$$100 - L^{0.75} K^{0.2} = 0$$

Next, we form the Lagrangean (using a larger L to distinguish it from the input L) by adding lambda times the rewritten constraint to the original objective function.

$$\min_{L,K,\lambda} L = 2L + 3K + \lambda(100 - L^{0.75} K^{0.2})$$

We find the optimal solution by taking the derivative of the Lagrangean with respect to each endogenous variable and setting each first-order condition to zero.

$$\frac{\partial L}{\partial L} = 2 - 0.75\lambda L^{-0.25} K^{0.2} = 0$$

$$\frac{\partial L}{\partial K} = 3 - 0.2\lambda L^{0.75} K^{-0.8} = 0$$

$$\frac{\partial L}{\partial \lambda} = 100 - L^{0.75} K^{0.2} = 0$$

We need to solve this system of equations for L^*, K^*, and λ^*. The most common approach is to move the terms with lambda in the first two equations to the right-side hand and then divide the first equation by the second. The strategy here is to cancel the lambdas and get an expression for $L = f(K)$, which, in conjunction with the third first-order condition, reduces the system to two equations with two unknowns. Notice how the Cobb-Douglas production function is easy to work with because the exponents of L and K sum to -1 and 1, respectively.

$$\frac{2}{3} = \frac{0.75\lambda L^{-0.25} K^{0.2}}{0.2\lambda L^{0.75} K^{-0.8}}$$

$$\frac{2}{3} = \frac{0.75 L^{-0.25} K^{0.2}}{0.2 L^{0.75} K^{-0.8}}$$

$$\frac{2}{3} = \frac{3.75 K}{L}$$

$$L = 5.625 K$$

We substitute this expression into the constraint (the third first-order condition) and solve for K^*.

$$100 - [5.625 K]^{0.75} K^{0.2} = 0$$

$$100 = 3.6525 K^{0.75} K^{0.2}$$

$$27.3784^{\frac{1}{0.95}} = (K^{0.95})^{\frac{1}{0.95}}$$

$$27.3784^{\frac{1}{0.95}} = (K^{0.95})^{\frac{1}{0.95}}$$

$$K^* = 32.588$$

Then, substituting back into the expression for $L = f(K)$, we get L^*.

$$L = 5.625[32.588]$$

$$L^* = 183.31$$

Substituting L^* and K^* into the original objective function, we can compute the minimum cost of producing 100 units.

$$TC^* = 2[183.31] + 3[32.588] = \$464.38$$

This agrees with Solver's result.

Notice also that the work just done in dividing the first equation by the second yields the familiar "input price ratio must equal the TRS" condition.

$$\frac{2}{3} = \frac{3.75 K}{L}$$

Characteristic	Theory of Consumer Behavior	Isoquant Side of the Theory of the Firm
Goal	maximize utility ($U = f(x_1, x_2)$)	minimize total cost ($TC = wL + rK$)
Canonical Graph of Initial Solution	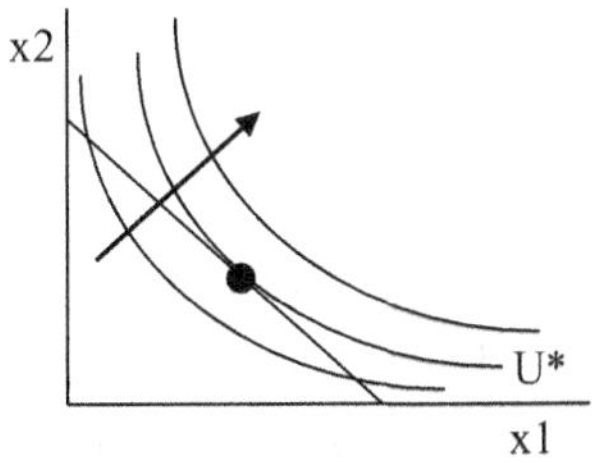 The line is the constraint. The curves are the goal. One line and several (representative) curves.	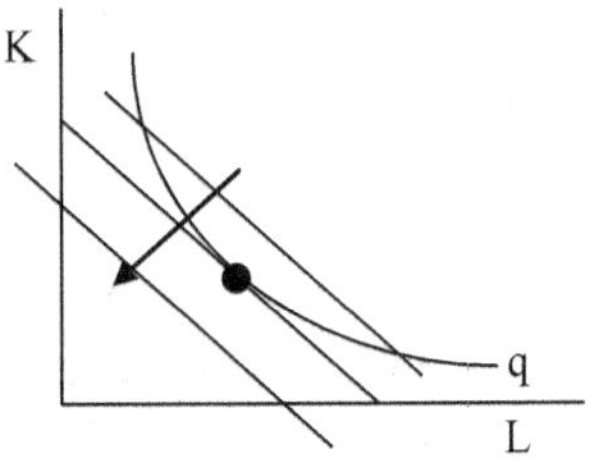 The curve is the constraint. The lines are the goal. One curve and several (representative) lines.
Function Properties	Utility is a fiction that represents preferences. The actual value of the utility function has no meaning.	The production function gives q as a measurable, cardinal quantity.
Maximum Value Function	The numerical value of maximum utility (U^*) is not important.	The numerical value of minimum total cost (TC^*), measured in dollars, is the *highest* priority.
Key Comparative Statics Exercise	Demand Curve $x_1^* = f(p_1)$, ceteris paribus	Cost Function $TC^* = f(q)$, ceteris paribus
Interpreting λ^*	No real economic meaning because utility is merely ordinal.	λ^* is marginal cost, the additional cost of producing more output.

Figure 2.2.1.4. Comparing two constrained optimization problems.

This equation says that the optimal solution is found at the point of tangency between the isocost and the isoquant. If this condition is not met, but the firm is on the isoquant (i.e., it is technically efficient), then we have allocative inefficiency.

Comparing the Theory of Consumer Behavior and Input Cost Minimization

Figure 2.2.1.3 bears a striking resemblance to the canonical graph used in the Theory of Consumer Behavior, but there are some critical differences. Figure 2.2.1.4 presents a side-by-side comparison of the two optimization problems in order to highlight the differences between them.

Of course it makes sense to use the knowledge and skills learned from the Theory of Consumer Behavior, but do not fall into a false sense of security. The input cost minimization problem has its own characteristics and terminology.

Cost Minimization is One of Three Optimization Problems

The Theory of the Firm is actually a set of three interrelated optimization problems. The initial solution to the firm's isoquant side problem focuses attention on the cheapest combination of inputs to produce a given level of output.

The canonical graph is quite similar to the standard graph from the Theory of Consumer Behavior, but as Figure 2.2.1.4 shows, there are substantial differences.

Perhaps the most important similarity is the continued use of the comparison of a price ratio to the slope of a curve in order to determine whether the optimal solution has been found. In the case of the constrained cost minimization problem, the firm will choose that combination of inputs where $\frac{w}{r} = TRS$.

Exercises

Open Word and answer the following questions. Save the document and print it when you are done.

1. The *Q&A* sheet asks you to change r to 30 and use Solver to find the initial solution. Find the initial solution to this same problem via analytical methods and compare the two results. Are they the same? Show your work.
2. The fixed proportions production function, $Y = \min\{\alpha L, \beta K\}$ is analogous to the perfect complements utility functional form. Suppose $\alpha = \beta = 1$, $w = 10$, $r = 50$, and $q = 100$. Find L^*, K^* and TC^*. Show your work. Use Word's Drawing Tools to draw a graph of the optimal solution.
3. Given the quasilinear production function, $Y = \sqrt{L} + K$, and input prices $r = 2$ and $w = 5$, find the cheapest way to produce 1000 units of output. Use analytical methods and show your work.
4. Set up the problem in question 3 in Excel and use Solver to find the optimal solution. Take a screen shot of the solution on your spreadsheet and paste it into your Word document.
5. Can isoquants intersect? Explain why or why not.

References

The epigraph is from page 1044 of Joseph Schumpeter's *History of Economic Analysis* (published in 1954, shortly after his death). This classic traces the intellectual history of economics from Aristotle to the 20th century.

Ragnar Frisch, credited by Schumpeter with inventing the term *isoquant*, had a knack for inventing words, e.g., *macroeconomics* and *econometrics*. Luckily, "substitumal cost flexibility" did not catch on. A Norwegian, Frisch was part of an exceptionally strong quantitative and empirical tradition in Scandinavian economics that remains alive to this day.

2.2.2

Enfield Arsenal

Several hundred years ago, an unknown inventor combined charcoal, sulfur and saltpeter and lit it afire.

When the dust settled the world was changed forever.

The Story of the Gun

This chapter departs from the usual presentation style employed in this book. There is no Excel workbook associated with this application. Instead, you will be given the opportunity to answer questions and the answers are provided at the end of the chapter. Each question is highlighted by the usual "Step" marker. Try to work out each question on your own before looking at the answer.

Goals

1. To understand cost minimization with isoquants and isocosts
2. To provide an example of how theory can be applied to real-world problems
3. To illustrate how economics can help us understand what we observe
4. To see that economics is fun and interesting.

Source

Edward Ames and Nathan Rosenberg, "The Enfield Arsenal in Theory and History," *The Economic Journal* (Vol. 78, No. 312, December, 1968), pp. 827–842.

Rifling

Rifles are a relatively recent innovation in firearms.

Figure 2.2.2.1 shows the famous Enfield rifle with labels for the three main parts: the lock, stock, and barrel.

It is the barrel that distinguishes rifles from smooth-bore muskets. The barrel of a rifle has a striated pattern that spins the bullet, increasing velocity

Figure 2.2.2.1. Rifle produced at the Enfield Arsenal.
Source: US government photo from about.com

and accuracy compared with a ball from a musket. But the Enfield rifle was important not because it rifled, but because of how it was made.

The Enfield Arsenal Versus the Springfield Armory

Ames and Rosenberg explain what the Enfield Arsenal was in the introduction to their paper:

This paper analyses a particular historical event, the establishment of the Enfield Arsenal, in the context of the literature cited. The British Government committed itself to the construction of the Enfield Arsenal in 1854 because it wished to be able to make large numbers of rifles for an impending war with Russia (now known as the Crimean War). The event is important because it marked the beginning of the movement of mass production techniques from the United States to Europe. Technical changes in gunmaking in the nineteenth century were a major source of new machine techniques; and industrialisation in the nineteenth century is overwhelmingly the history of the spread of machine making and machine using. (p. 827)

Enfield is a town in Britain and the Enfield Arsenal is literally a building constructed by the British government in 1854 that would be used to store rifles made with mass production techniques. Up to this point, the British had made guns by hand in the small shops of thousands of skilled artisans in the area around Birmingham. The stock was carefully carved by an experienced craftsman who fitted the stock with the lock and barrel.

Ames and Rosenberg point out that making the stock by hand was slow and expensive:

The gunstock was one of the most serious bottlenecks in firearms production. In England, at the time of the Parliamentary hearings, out of about 7,300 workmen in the Birmingham gun trade, the number of men employed in making gunstocks totalled perhaps as many as 2,000. Its highly irregular shape for long seemed to defy mechanical assistance, and the hand-shaping of the stock was a very tedious operation. Furthermore, the fitting and recessing of the stock so that it would properly accommodate the lock and barrel were extremely time-consuming processes, the proper performance of which required considerable experience. With Birmingham methods, it required 75 men to produce 100 stocks per day. Using the early (1818) version of the Blanchard lathe, 17 men could produce 100 stocks per day. (p. 832, footnotes omitted)

Eighteen fifty-four is a crucial date in this story because until this time, the British used Birmingham methods, which means an experienced craftsman made each entire gun by hand. Guns produced for the Enfield Arsenal, however, were made with interchangeable parts that could be put together in an assembly line.

Try to answer the question below. You can check your answer at the back of the chapter.

Question What are the tremendous advantages of interchangeable parts in a rifle (or anything else for that matter)?

In the new country of the United States of America, guns were not made with Birmingham methods. The United States used mass production techniques to make the guns stored in the Springfield Armory, which was built in 1794 in Springfield, Massachusetts.

The history of gun-making is closely tied to the rise of precision manufacturing. In a video titled *The Story of the Gun*, produced by the A&E Network, the narrator says, "Prior to the Blanchard Lathe, it took one to two days to make a rifle stock by hand. Now, a twelve-year-old boy could turn out a dozen stocks in a single day."

In an interview in that same video, William Ruger cites an idea from French philosopher Denis Diderot (1713–1784). Ruger says Diderot's theory at that time was that "It would be possible to make all of the individual parts alike and then at the last minute assemble them, rather than fitting them together as you went, which was the customary thing up to that time." By applying this theory, the Springfield Armory was able to enjoy a huge increase in productivity compared with Birmingham methods.

The Puzzle

Ames and Rosenberg sum up the situation like this:

As of 1785, neither the British nor the Americans could make guns with interchangeable parts. As of 1815, Americans could make guns with interchangeable metal parts, but could not make interchangeable gunstocks. As of 1820, they could make interchangeable gunstocks. At any date, presumably, they could use not only current methods but earlier methods which these had displaced. (pp. 839–840, footnotes omitted)

The United States had been mass-producing guns with interchangeable parts since 1815. The British waited until 1854 to use the superior, mass production techniques. This gives rise to two big questions:

1. Why did the British *wait so long* to use mass production techniques to make rifles with interchangeable parts?
2. Why did the British *switch* to mass production techniques in 1854?

Why Did the British *Wait so Long* to Use Mass Production Techniques to Make Rifles with Interchangeable Parts?

Possible Answer:
Information: The British didn't know about it.

Question What do you think of this possible answer?

Another Possible Answer:
Massive managerial failure: British rifle manufacturers were lazy, stupid, and careless.

Question What do you think of this possible answer?

Step Check your answers with those at the end of the chapter before continuing.

Another Possible Answer:
An economic historian's explanation: Look for differences in the environment that would lead to different optimal solutions.

In other words, stop searching for why the British made a mistake and accept the fact that their refusal to adopt mass production techniques was actually smart and right. Look for reasons that justify their decision.

There are two important ways in which England and the United States differed before 1854:

1. Labor force: Skilled versus unskilled labor: The British had a cohort of skilled rifle craftsmen and the United States did not.
2. Endowment of wood: Wood was cheap in the United States and expensive in Britain. Ames and Rosenberg offer the following footnote (p. 831) to help explain why wood plays a critical role:

Report of the Small Arms Committee, op. cit., Q. 7273–81 and Q. 7520–7521; G. L. Molesworth, "On the Conversion of Wood by Machinery," Proceedings of the Institution of Civil Engineers, Vol. XVII, pp. 22, 45–6. In the discussion which followed Mr. Moleworth's paper Mr. Worssam, a prominent English dealer in woodworking machinery, made some interesting comparative observations which were summarised as follows: "He had seen American machines in operation, and he found that, although they might be adapted for the description of work required in that country, they were not so suitable for English work, in which latter high finish and economy of material were of greatest importance. In America the saws were much thicker than those used in the English saw-mills, so that they consumed more power, wasted more material, and did not cut so clean, or so true, though there was less care required in working them" (ibid., pp. 45–6).

Step Draw graphs that show how the different resource endowments affected the optimal input mix. Use the detailed instructions that follow as a guide.

One graph, representing the British situation, should have *skilled labor* on the *y* axis and *unskilled labor* on the *x* axis. Draw in an isoquant. Create another graph exactly like the first one. Your second graph represents the U.S. case. The fact that both isoquants are the same means that the two countries had access to the same technology.

The key idea concerns the isocost lines. We know the British have skilled labor and the United States does not – immigrants to the United States were not typically skilled, well-paid workers, but young, unskilled males. That means the price of skilled labor is much higher in the United States. How is that reflected in the isocosts for your two graphs?

Next, draw a pair of graphs, one for the British and the other for the United States, with *machinery* on the *y* axis and *labor* on the *x* axis. Include the isoquants. Once again, the isoquants are the same (meaning that the British were aware of and could have used American methods) and the key lies in the isocosts. Remember the quotation that pointed out that early versions of the Blanchard Lathe used a lot of wood. This affects the price of machinery.

Step Proceed to the end of this chapter to check your graphs. How did you do?

We now turn to the second question.

Why Did the British Switch to Mass Production Techniques in 1854?

In other words, why did the British build the Enfield Arsenal in 1854 and give up on the Birmingham method? The Birmingham method, as defined by Ames and Rosenberg, is the old way of producing guns:

Before 1854, British gunmaking was concentrated in a large but complicated structure of handicraft firms, mainly located in Birmingham, and producing firearms to individual order or in very small batches. (pp. 827–828)

For Ames and Rosenberg, "'Enfield' is shorthand for 'guns made with interchangeable parts by American methods.'" (p. 829)

So, why did the British switch from Birmingham to Enfield?

Possible Answer:
Information: They finally heard about the Springfield Armory 40 years after it was founded.

Question What do you think of this possible answer?

Possible Answer:
Massive managerial improvement: They wised up.

Question What do you think of this possible answer?

Step Check your answers with those at the end of the chapter before continuing.

Possible Answer:

An Economic Historian's Explanation: Look for changes in the environment that would lead to changes in optimal behavior.

Once again, do not search for events that changed a mistake into the right answer. Instead, accept that the answer to not use mass production was right for, say, 1830, but the new right answer, in 1854, was to switch to the American system.

The search is on for shocks that would change the right answer from "reject" to "accept" interchangeable parts.

There are two ways in which England before 1854 differed from England after 1854:

1. Labor force: Changes in the structure of the British labor force.

   Question What happened to the British labor force?

2. Endowment of wood: Changes in technology.

   Question How did technology improve?

Step Check your answers with those at the end of the chapter before continuing.

Step Draw graphs that show how the changes mentioned affected the optimal input mix. The two pairs of graphs are the same as before (unskilled and skilled labor on one and machinery and labor on the other), but this time we vary time. Compare the optimal mix of unskilled and skilled labor for Britain in 1820 versus 1854. Remember that the skilled craftsmen died and were not replaced. In the machinery and labor graphs, we know that machinery got better and better (wasting less and less wood) over time.

Step After trying to draw graphs to answer this question, check the answers at the end of the chapter. How did you do?

Evaluating the Application of the Economic Approach to the Enfield Arsenal

Our goals for this application were as follows:

1. To understand cost minimization with isoquants and isocosts
2. To provide an example of how theory can be applied to real-world problems
3. To illustrate how economics can help us understand what we observe
4. To see that economics is fun and interesting.

You decide to what extent the goals were met. At the very least, you learned a little about American manufacturing in the 19th century and rifles (including where the phrase "lock, stock, and barrel" comes from).

This application should help you understand the conventional isoquant–isocost graph as a cost minimization problem. Remember that the higher the price of the input on the x axis, the steeper the isocost.

But the real deep learning and big picture idea concerns how economists view the world. This is called economic reasoning or the economic approach. The phrase "an economic analysis of" communicates that the economic approach is being applied.

The idea is that economics is not a discipline organized around content (the stock market or money, for example), but a way of thinking. Economists often interpret observed behaviors as optimal solutions to optimization problems and they see change as driven by a shock that takes us from one optimal solution to another.

Thinking like an economist is difficult, but it can provide an interesting perspective on the world.

Exercises

Open Word and answer the following questions. Save the document and print it when you are done.

1. Explain why the endowment of wood affects the price of machinery used in producing rifles in the 19th century.
2. What could have caused the British to switch to mass production techniques before 1854? Give a concrete example.
3. Ames and Rosenberg include additional differences between America and Britain, such as the fact that the British consumer liked fancier gunstocks:

American machine processes could not produce guns of the kind favoured by English civilians. The Blanchard lathe produced stocks of a standard size, whereas English buyers did not want standard gunstocks. The English methods were suited to catering to the idiosyncratic needs of individual users. (p. 836)

How would this information change the comparison of the isoquant–isocost graph in the two countries?

References

The epigraph comes from the *Story of the Gun's* Web site, <store.aetv.com/html/product/index.jhtml?id=70772>. This entertaining video mixes the history of firearms with military history and technological change.

Ames and Rosenberg's article is an excellent example of economic history. The Cliometric Society is online at <eh.net/Clio>. In Greek mythology, Clio is the muse of history. Cliometricians use economic theory and econometrics to analyze economic history.

Enfield Arsenal Answers

Here are the answers to the questions posed in this chapter.

Question What are the tremendous advantages of interchangeable parts in a rifle (or anything else for that matter)?

Answer: There are two types of advantages:

1. Fixing broken rifles: You can quickly repair a mass produced rifle if one of its pieces (lock, stock, or barrel) breaks. A rifle built by hand is useless once one of its individual parts fails.
2. Productivity: Breaking production into a series of steps and then assembling the parts enables many more rifles to be produced. This is called the division of labor. It also enables machines to be used on individual parts.

Adam Smith recognized the advantages of the division of labor. He emphasized several reasons for greater productivity with his famous pin-making example:

1. Practice makes perfect: focusing on a single task makes you very good at it,
2. Saves time: no need to move to a new position and set things up, and
3. Innovation: adjustments are made by workers who are expert in a particular task.

Responses to the Possible Answers to Why the British Did Not Use Mass Production Techniques

Information: The British didn't know about it.

Question What do you think of this possible answer?

Answer: Granted there is an ocean, but given the common language and communication, this is not a satisfying explanation. In fact, there is lots of evidence that British knew about the American methods.

Massive managerial failure: British Rifle Manufacturers were lazy, stupid, and careless.

Question What do you think of this possible answer?

Answer: That's not very satisfying either. There is no reason to believe this.

Economists are wary of this type of answer. We believe agents are self-interested and respond to incentives.

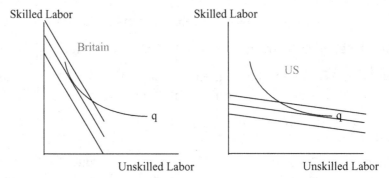

Figure 2.2.2.2. The effect of different wages for skilled labor.

Question Draw graphs that show how the different resource endowments affected the optimal input mix.

Answer: Two ways in which England and the United States differed before 1854:

1. Labor force: The isoquant is exactly the same in each graph in Figure 2.2.2.2. U.S. skilled labor wages were very high because there were few experienced craftsmen migrating to the United States. The United States had lots of young, unskilled workers. This makes the U.S. isocost lines flatter than Britain's and leads to a different cost-minimizing input mix.

2. Endowment of wood: The price of machinery included the wasted wood. The early versions of the Blanchard Lathe were quite wasteful, but this didn't matter in the heavily forested United States. In Britain, on the other hand, wood was expensive. This makes the isocost lines steeper in Figure 2.2.2.3. Once again, factor prices help determine the input mix. The different resource endowments

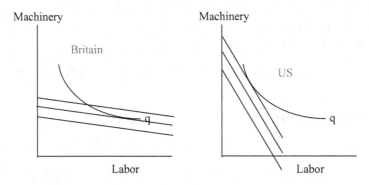

Figure 2.2.2.3. The effect of different prices for machinery.

lead to different input prices, which in turn lead to different cost-minimizing solutions.

Responses to the Possible Anwers to Why the British Switched

Information: In 1854, the British heard that mass production techniques were available and immediately moved to adopt the new production methods.

Question What do you think of this possible answer?

Answer: This makes little sense. American and British citizen and entrepreneurs moved freely across the Atlantic and were well aware of production methods in each country. The claim that a new technique was suddenly made known to the British is wrong.

Massive managerial improvement: British firearms manufacturers recovered from their slumber and moved quickly to modernize their industry.

Question What do you think of this possible answer?

Answer: Again, this is difficult to swallow. The answer requires an explanation for the sudden change from stupid, lazy producers of firearms to smart, energetic ones. There is no evidence of an explosion in managerial aptitude or a burst in managerial education.

The possible answers to why the British switched in 1854 are pretty silly. There is no evidence of a sudden increase in communication or an improvement in managerial decision making.

Question What happened to the British labor force?

Answer: The skilled craftsmen died off and were not replaced. No skilled rifle artisan would suggest that his son follow him into the trade. They could see the writing on the wall. As the supply of these workers dwindled, the wages of skilled rifle artisans in England rose.

Question How did technology improve?

Answer: The Blanchard Lathe was continually improved over time; more modern versions of the lathe wasted a lot less wood. Today, a lathe uses a laser sight to precisely cut the wood.

As the lathe wasted less wood, the price of machinery fell. This is a nice example of how the price of an input can represent more than simply the out-of-pocket cost paid for the input. In this example, the price of a lathe is not simply the price paid for the machine itself; it includes the price of the wood used.

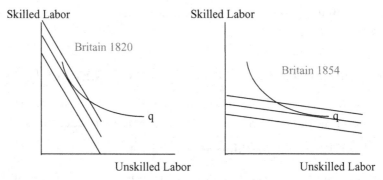

Figure 2.2.2.4. The effect of changes in the British skilled labor force.

Question Draw graphs that show how the changes in labor and machinery affected the optimal input mix.

Answer: Two ways in which England before 1854 differed from England after 1854:

1. Labor force: Notice how the comparison in Figure 2.2.2.4 now is across time periods. A high price of skilled labor makes the isocost lines flat and leads to a more unskilled-labor intensive decision. As skilled craftsmen disappeared and their wages rose, there was greater incentive to use unskilled labor.
2. Endowment of wood: The price of machinery fell and fell, making the isocost lines steeper and steeper as shown in Figure 2.2.2.5, and leading to the adoption of mass production techniques in England – the Enfield Arsenal was born.

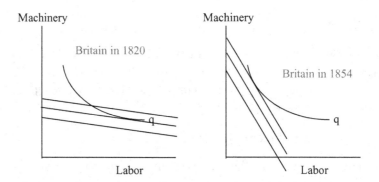

Figure 2.2.2.5. The effect of improvement in the Blanchard Lathe.

2.2.3

Deriving the Cost Function

There are reasons to hope that another type of production function, more diversified than Douglas's, may soon be available, and from these it would be possible to derive cost functions typical for particular industries.

Hans Staehle

While we can explore the effects on L^*, K^*, and TC^* of changes in w, r, q, and technology, the most important comparative statics question is the relationship between TC^* and q. This is called the *cost function*, $TC = f(q,$ ceteris paribus).

As usual, we will explore both ways to do comparative statics:

- Analytical methods using algebra and calculus – conventional paper and pencil
- Numerical methods using a computer – Excel's Solver and the Comparative Statics Wizard.

In addition, because total cost is the objective function and, unlike utility, can be cardinally measured, we will be able to interpret the Lagrangean multiplier.

Numerical Methods: Deriving the Cost Function
with the Comparative Statics Wizard

Step Open the Excel workbook DerivingCostFunction.xls and read the *Intro* sheet, then go to the *OptimalChoice* sheet. The organization is the same as in the InputCostMin.xls workbook.

The cost-minimizing way of producing 100 units of output is to use about 183.3 hours of labor with 32.6 machines, which costs $464.38.

What happens if the firm needs to produce more, say, 110 units of output?

Step Change cell B18 to 110.

301

The chart updates, showing a new (red) isoquant. The initial combination is not a viable option because it cannot produce 110 units.

Step Run Solver to find the new optimal solution.

The cost-minimizing amounts of labor and capital increase in order to produce the increased output and the minimum total cost is now $513.39. It is the minimum total cost that we are especially interested in. We want to know the cheapest way of producing any given output. This is called the cost function.

If we connected the points of tangency of isoquants and isocosts, we would get the *least cost expansion path*.

But the cost function does not use the underlying, isoquant graph. Instead, the cost function is shown on its own graph, tracking minimum total cost as a function of output. We can derive the cost function with the Comparative Statics Wizard.

Step Run the Comparative Statics Wizard, changing q, to get several points on the cost function. Return cell B18 to 100, then apply 10 q shocks in increments of 10.

The *CS1* sheet shows what your results should look like. The *CS1* sheet includes two graphs, the cost function, and the least cost expansion path (without displaying the isoquants and tangent isocosts).

Is the cost function linear? The chart seems to show a linear relationship between total cost and output, but the way to find out for sure is to compute the slope at different points on the function. If the slope is changing, you know the function is not linear.

Step Use your comparative statics results to compute the change in total cost divided by the change in output from $q = 100$ to 110. Fill your formula down.

Compare your results to column E in the *CS1* sheet. It is clear that the slope changes as output changes. This means that the cost function is nonlinear.

Analytical Methods: Finding the Cost Function via the Lagrangean

We can use the Lagrangean method to find $TC^* = f(q)$. The problem is

$$\min_{L,K} TC = wL + rK$$

$$\text{s.t.} \ q = AL^c K^d$$

We can rewrite the constraint so that it is equal to zero, then form the Lagrangean (with a larger font L to distinguish the Lagrangean from the variable labor, L), including parameter values from the *OptimalChoice* sheet – except for q, which we leave as a letter in order to get a reduced form in terms of output.

$$\min_{L,K,\lambda} L = 2L + 3K + \lambda(q - L^{0.75} K^{0.2})$$

Then we find the three first-order conditions.

$$\frac{\partial L}{\partial L} = 2 - 0.75\lambda L^{-0.25} K^{0.2} = 0$$

$$\frac{\partial L}{\partial K} = 3 - 0.2\lambda L^{0.75} K^{-0.8} = 0$$

$$\frac{\partial L}{\partial \lambda} = q - L^{0.75} K^{0.2} = 0$$

We solve for L^*, K^*, and λ^*. Moving the λ terms to the right and dividing the first by the second equation gives $L = 5.625K$. Then we substitute this equation for L into the third first-order condition and solve for K^*, followed by L^*.

$$q - [5.625K]^{0.75} K^{0.2} = 0$$
$$q = 3.6525 K^{0.75} K^{0.2}$$
$$\frac{q}{3.6525} = K^{0.95}$$
$$\left[\frac{q}{3.6525}\right]^{\frac{1}{0.95}} = \left(K^{0.95}\right)^{\frac{1}{0.95}}$$
$$K^* = 0.25574 q^{\frac{1}{0.95}} \Rightarrow L^* = 1.43854 q^{\frac{1}{0.95}}$$

Finally, we substitute the optimal solutions for L and K in the total cost function.

$$TC = wL + rK$$
$$TC^* = 2\left[1.43854 q^{\frac{1}{0.95}}\right] + 3\left[0.25574 q^{\frac{1}{0.95}}\right]$$
$$TC^* = 2.877 q^{\frac{1}{0.95}} + 0.767 q^{\frac{1}{0.95}}$$
$$TC^* = 3.644 q^{\frac{1}{0.95}}$$

This expression is the total cost function. It gives the cheapest cost of producing any given amount of output. If $q = 100$, $TC = \$464.38$. Not surprisingly, this agrees with the Solver result.

Notice also that the cost function is clearly nonlinear. It is increasing at an increasing rate because the exponent on q is greater than one.

Interpreting Points Off the Cost Function

When we derived the demand curve from the "maximize utility subject to a budget constraint optimization" problem, we explored what it meant to

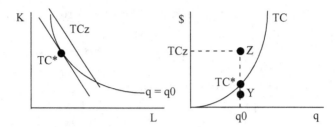

Figure 2.2.3.1. Understanding points off the cost function.

be off the demand curve. We learned that points to the left or right of the inverse demand curve (with price on the y axis) mean that the consumer is not optimizing, i.e., the consumer is not choosing a point of tangency between the indifference curve and budget constraint.

We can conduct the same kind of inquiry with the cost function, asking this question: What does it mean to be off the cost curve?

Unlike the inverse demand curve, where the exogenous variable is on the y axis, the cost function is graphed with the exogenous variable, output, on the x axis. Thus, points off the curve are interpreted vertically above or below the cost function.

More specifically, what does it mean if a point is above the cost curve? Figure 2.2.3.1 helps us answer this question. On the left is the familiar isoquant/isocost graph. The cheapest way to produce $q0$ units of output is with the L and K combination at the point labeled TC^*. The graph on the right of Figure 2.2.3.1 shows that TC^* is a point on the cost function at an output of $q0$.

Point Z, a point above the cost function, reveals that the firm is producing the level of output $q0$ at a total cost above the minimum total cost. Then we can deduce that the firm is choosing an input mix that is not cost minimizing. Point Z on the graph on the left of Figure 2.2.3.1 must lie on an isocost above the tangent isocost. We do not know exactly where point Z is on the graph on the left (so we do not know if there is technical or allocative inefficiency), but we do know it has to be somewhere on the isocost that has a total cost the same as the cost of producing point Z (on the graph on the right).

Point Y on the right side of Figure 2.2.3.1 is below the cost function. How can this point be generated by the graph on the left? It cannot. There is an isocost with a total cost equal to that at point Y, but it is below the isoquant and, therefore, unattainable. In other words, point Y does not actually exist. The firm cannot produce $q0$ units of output at any cost less than TC^*.

The fact that there are no points below the cost function means that we certainly could never fit a line to a cloud of points to estimate a cost function. Instead of fitting a line through the observed points, techniques in the

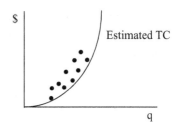

Figure 2.2.3.2. Estimating a cost function.

stochastic frontier literature are based on fitting a curve around the observed points, as in Figure 2.2.3.2.

Shifts in the Cost Function

Step Proceed to the *CostFn* sheet.

The sheet shows a cost function charted from the data above it. The data in columns L and M are actually formulas for the reduced-form expressions for L^* and K^*. Column N has the minimum total cost for the benchmark problem and will not change because the cells are merely numbers. Column O, however, has the reduced-form expression for TC^* and will update if any of the underlying parameters are changed.

Step Change cell B20, the exponent on L, to 0.8.

Your screen looks like Figure 2.2.3.3. The increase in labor productivity has shifted down the total cost curve. This makes sense. The increase in c has made it cheaper to produce any given output.

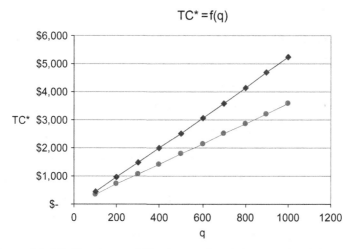

Figure 2.2.3.3. Total cost shifts down when labor productivity rises.
Source: DerivingCostFunction!CostFn

You can experiment with other shocks to the cost function. Change input prices, input exponents, or A to see how the cost function shifts. Changes in q have no visible effect because you simply move along the cost function.

Interpreting λ^*

We end this chapter by demonstrating that there is an easier way to derive a cost function than by solving the constrained cost minimization problem and finding $TC^* = f(q)$.

The shortcut uses the fact that the Lagrangean multiplier, λ^*, tells you the instantaneous rate of change in the optimum value of the objective function as the constraint varies. The objective function in this case is minimum total cost and the constraint depends on q.

If we vary the constraint by having the firm produce one more unit of output, we know total cost would rise as we moved to a higher isoquant. The Lagrangean multiplier, λ^*, tells you by how much minimum total cost would rise.

For example, at $q = 100$, λ^* is about \$4.89. You can find λ^* by numerical methods (using Excel's Solver and getting the Sensitivity Report) or by analytical methods, solving for λ^* from the three first-order conditions. Either way, you will get (approximately) the same answer.

The \$4.89 value means that if we increase output by a small amount, minimum total cost will go up by \$4.89-fold.

Step Click the Reset button in the *CostFn* sheet and take a look at the highlighted cell (P7). Its value is \$4.99. That is close to the value of λ^*, but not quite exactly the same.

What is going on?

Step Proceed to the *CS1* sheet and take a look at the highlighted cell (E15). Its value is \$4.90.

This is much closer to λ^*. Why? Because the change in q is much smaller in the *CS1* sheet. As the change in q approaches zero, the change in TC^* divided by the change in q will approach λ^*.

Of course, this is nothing more than a demonstration of the idea of the derivative. If you are puzzled as to how $\Delta TC^*/\Delta q$ can be that close to λ^* in the *CS1* sheet, given that the change in q is 10 units (which is hardly infinitesimally small), the answer lies in the total cost function: It simply is not very curvy. Because TC^* follows almost (but not quite) a straight line, computing the slope from $q = 100$ to $q = 110$ is almost the same as the slope of the tangent line at $q = 100$.

What can we do with the knowledge that λ^* tells you the rate of change in total cost with respect to output? We can easily derive the cost function. After all, the rate of change in total cost as output changes is marginal cost. Thus, $\lambda^* = MC(q)$. Because $MC(q) = dTC(q)/dq$, we can easily get the total cost function by simply integrating λ^* with respect to q.

Actually, as we will see when we solve the output profit maximization problem, we usually want marginal revenue and marginal cost, so knowing that $\lambda^* = MC$ is a real shortcut. If we have λ^*, then we do not have to find $TC^* = f(q)$ and take the derivative to get MC.

Step You can confirm the claim that $\lambda^* = MC$ by changing the parameters in the *CostFn* sheet and keeping your eye on the rose-backgrounded cell (H31). It computes the difference between λ^* and MC obtained by finding $dTC(q)/(dq)$. The difference is always zero.

Notice that the general versions of the reduced forms for the Cobb-Douglas production functions are provided and entered in cells. The expressions look daunting (and they are tedious to derive), but the derivation is straightforward: Leave every exogenous variable as a letter and find the optimal solution for L^*, K^*, λ^*, and TC^*.

Conclusion

Although we are often interested in the response of an endogenous variable to a shock, comparative statics in the input cost minimization problem is focused on how the objective function, minimum total cost, is affected by a shock. This is called the cost function.

By explaining what it means to be above or below the cost function in terms of the isoquant–isocost graph, we emphasized the idea that the cost function shows the cheapest way to produce any given output.

Of course, changes in other parameters besides output will cause the entire cost function to shift, but the interpretation of the cost function as the minimum total cost of producing a given output remains the same.

Finally, we explained a mathematically sophisticated idea: λ^* provides information on the rate of change of the optimum value of the objective function as the constraint is relaxed. This interpretation holds for every constrained optimization problem. We did not take advantage of this in the Theory of Consumer Behavior because utility (the objective function) cannot be cardinally measured. In the old days, when utility was believed to be cardinally measured, λ^* was the marginal utility of money. λ^* would tell you the rate of change in maximum utility if you gave the consumer an infinitesimal increase in income.

Because total cost is cardinally measured, we applied the definition of λ^* to this problem, $\lambda^* = MC$, and this can be used as a shortcut or a check on a cost function derived by the comparative statics, $TC^* = f(q)$, approach.

Exercises

Open Word and answer the following questions. Save the document and print it when you are done.

1. With the production function, $Y = L^{0.75} K^{0.5}$, and exogenous variables $w = 2$, $r = 3$, use Excel to create a graph of the cost function for the same q values as the one in the *CS1* sheet. Copy and paste your graph in your Word document.
2. How is the cost function you just derived different from the one in the *CS1* sheet? Which variable is responsible for generating this difference?
3. From the cost functions in the *CS1* sheet and question 1, what can you deduce about cost functions derived from Cobb-Douglas production functions?
4. If someone solves an input cost minimization problem and finds that $\lambda^* = 50$, what does this mean?

References

The epigraph is from page 333 of Hans Staehle, "The Measurement of Statistical Cost Functions: An Appraisal of Some Recent Contributions," *The American Economic Review*, Vol. 32, No. 2, Part 1 (June, 1942), pp. 321–333. Unfortunately, it is fair to say that Staehle's dream of the discovery of flexible functional forms that would enable derivation of cost functions for particular industries remains unfulfilled. Empirical work on cost functions usually finds that firms face linear (or nearly linear) total costs (yielding horizontal average and marginal costs) over large ranges of output.

2.2.4

Cost Curves

Only 11 percent of firms report that their MC curves are rising. By contrast, about 40 percent claim that their MC curves are falling.

Alan Blinder, Elie Canetti, David Lebow, and Jeremy Rudd

On the output side, the firm maximizes profits by choosing the amount of output to produce. Because profits are revenues minus costs, the cost function plays an important role in the firm's profit maximization problem.

The cost function, derived from the input cost minimization problem, can be broken down and graphed a variety of ways. This chapter is devoted to the terminology of cost curves and an exploration of their geometric properties.

Cost Curve Terminology

We know that if we explore the comparative statics properties of TC^*, minimum total cost, as a function of q, we find the cost function.

A basic idea that is easy to forget is that there are many shapes of cost functions. Our work on deriving the cost function used a Cobb-Douglas production function and that gives rise to a particular cost function. A different production function would give a different cost function.

No matter the shape of the cost function, there are three kinds of cost curves: total, average, and marginal.

Total Costs

The total cost, TC, curve is simply the cost function, $TC = f(q)$. It has units of dollars ($) on the y axis (for total cost).

We can divide total costs into two parts, total variable costs, TVC, and total fixed costs, TFC.

$$TC(q) = TVC(q) + TFC$$

If the firm is in the short run, it has at least one fixed factor of production (usually K) and the total fixed costs are the dollar value spent on the fixed inputs (rK). Notice that the total fixed costs do not vary with output. *TFC* is a constant and does not change as output changes.

The total variable costs are the costs of the factors that the firm is free to adjust, usually L. As output rises, so does total variable cost.

In the long run, defined as a planning horizon in which there are no fixed factors, there are no fixed costs and, therefore, $TC(q) = TVC(q)$.

Average Costs

The firm has average costs associated with each level of output. The average is simply the total divided by the amount produced.

Average total cost, *ATC* (also known as *AC*), is total cost divided by output.

$$ATC(q) = \frac{TC(q)}{q}$$

Average variable cost, *AVC*, is total variable cost divided by output.

$$AVC(q) = \frac{TVC(q)}{q}$$

Average fixed cost, *AFC*, is total fixed cost divided by output.

$$AFC(q) = \frac{TFC}{q}$$

Notice that $AFC(q)$ is a function of q even though *TFC* is not because *AFC* is *TFC* divided by q. Because the numerator is a constant, $AFC(q)$ is a rectangular hyperbola ($y = c/x$) and is guaranteed to fall as q rises. This can be confirmed by a simple example. Say $TFC = \$100$. For very small q, such as 0.0001, *AFC* is extremely large. But *AFC* falls really fast as q rises from zero (and *AFC* is undefined at $q = 0$). At $q = 1$, *AFC* is \$100, at $q = 2$, *AFC* is \$50, and so forth. The larger the value of q, the closer *AFC* gets to zero (i.e., it approaches the x axis).

It is easy to show that the average total cost must equal the sum of the average variable and average fixed costs:

$$TC(q) = TVC(q) + TFC$$
$$\frac{TC(q)}{q} = \frac{TVC(q)}{q} + \frac{TFC}{q}$$
$$ATC(q) = AVC(q) + AFC(q)$$

Unlike the total costs, which are simply dollars, the average costs are a rate, dollars per unit of output. You cannot graph the total and average costs on the same graph because the y axes are different.

We often omit $AFC(q)$ from the graphical display of the firm's cost structure because we know it is a rectangular hyperbola and it can be easily determined by simply measuring the vertical distance between ATC and AVC at a given q.

The fact that AFC falls as q rises means that AVC must approach ATC as q rises. In a graph, you should always draw AVC as getting closer to ATC as q increases.

Marginal Costs

When the firm chooses q to maximize profit, it can find the optimal q by equating marginal revenue to marginal cost. Thus, marginal cost is a crucial cost curve.

Marginal cost tells you the additional cost of producing more output. If the change in output is discrete, then we are measuring marginal cost from one point to another on the cost curve and the equation looks like this:

$$MC(q) = \frac{\Delta TC(q)}{\Delta q}$$

If, on the other hand, we treat the change in output as infinitesimally small, then we use the derivative and we have

$$MC(q) = \frac{dTC(q)}{dq}$$

Like the average costs, marginal cost is a rate, dollars per unit of output. It is often graphed together with the average curves.

Because TFC does not vary with q, it is easy to see that marginal cost can be found by using the total cost, $TC(q)$, or total variable cost, $TVC(q)$, function.

$$MC(q) = \frac{dTC(q)}{dq} = \frac{dTVC(q)}{dq}$$

A Key Relationship between Average and Marginal Curves

Whenever an average curve is above the marginal curve, the marginal curve must be rising. Conversely, whenever the average is below marginal, the marginal must be falling.

For example, consider the average score on an exam. After the first 10 students are graded, there is an average score. The 11th student is now graded.

312   *Cost Curves*

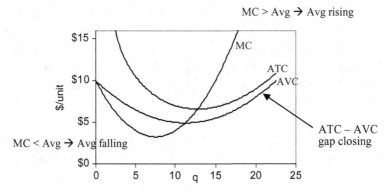

Figure 2.2.4.1. Marginal and average relationships.

Suppose she gets a score above average. Hers is the marginal score and we know it is above the average so it has to pull the average up. The next student bombed. His marginal score is below the average and it pulls the average down. So, we know that whenever a marginal score is below the average, the average is falling and whenever a marginal score is above the average, the average is rising. The only time the average stays the same is when the marginal score is exactly equal to the average score.

This relationship between the average and marginal means that the marginal cost curve must intersect the average variable and average total cost curves at their respective minimums, as shown in Figure 2.2.4.1. From $q = 0$ to the intersection of AVC or ATC, the average curve falls. To the right of the intersection of MC and AVC or ATC, the average curve rises.

Figure 2.2.4.1 also shows a property that was highlighted earlier: The gap between ATC and AVC must fall as q rises.

You will understand these abstract ideas better by exploring concrete examples. Three cases are offered.

Step Open the Excel workbook CostCurves.xls and read the *Intro* sheet, then go to the *CobbDouglas* sheet to see the first example.

Cobb-Douglas Cost Curves

The *CobbDouglas* sheet is the *CostFn* sheet from the DerivingCostFunction.xls workbook with the ATC and MC curves plotted below the TC curve.

Column I has data for the TC curve, from which we can compute ATC and MC in columns J and K. Click on an MC cell, for example, cell K4, to see that the cell formula is actually for λ^*, not dTC^*/dq. We are using the shortcut that $\lambda^* = MC$.

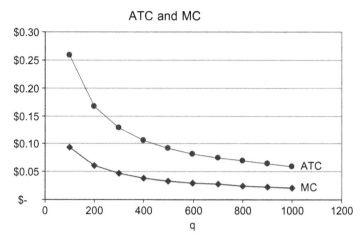

Figure 2.2.4.2. Cost curves with increasing returns to scale.
Source: CostCurves.xls!CobbDouglas

Because L and K are variable, there are no fixed factors of production. This means we are in the long run and there are no fixed costs. Thus, $TC = TVC$ and $ATC = AVC$.

It is immediately obvious that the marginal and average curves do not look at all like Figure 2.2.4.1. In fact, a Cobb-Douglas production function cannot give U-shaped average and marginal cost curves as in Figure 2.2.4.1.

It is important to remember that there are many shapes for cost curves and the shape depends on the production function. In other words, the production function is expressed in the cost structure of a firm.

Step Change the exponent on capital, d, from 0.2 to 2.

Figure 2.2.4.2 displays the average and marginal cost curves.

Because average cost is falling as q rises, it means that total cost is increasing less than linearly as output rises. The total cost graph confirms that this is the case. It costs \$33 to make 200 units, but only \$43 to make 400 units. Double output again to 800. How much does it cost? Cell I9 tells you, \$55. This is crazy. If input prices remain constant, how can we double output and not at least double costs?

The answer lies in the production function. You changed the exponent on capital, d, from 0.2 to 2. Now the sum of the exponents, $c + d$, is greater than 1. This means that we are operating under increasing returns to scale. This means that if we double the inputs, we get more than double the output. Or, put another way, we can double the output by using less than double the inputs.

314 *Cost Curves*

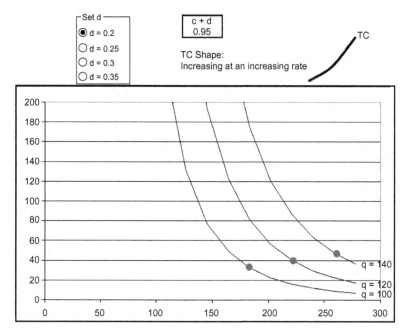

Figure 2.2.4.3. Understanding how isoquants determine the shape of the cost function.
Source: CostCurves.xls!CobbDouglas

We can make 400 units cheaper *per unit* than 200 units. We can make 800 units even cheaper *per unit* because we are taking advantage of the increasing returns to scale.

Increasing returns are a big problem in the eyes of some economists because they lead to a paradox: One firm should make all of the output. There are situations in which increasing returns seem to be justified, such as the case of *natural monopolies*, in which a single firm provides the output for an entire industry because the production function exhibits increasing returns to scale. The classic examples are utility companies, e.g., electric, water, and natural gas companies.

Tying the Isoquant Map to the Cost Function

We can emphasize the crucial connection between the production function and the cost function via the isoquant map.

Step Scroll down to row 100 or so in the *CobbDouglas* sheet.

Figure 2.2.4.3 shows the information displayed on your screen. The three isoquants are based on a Cobb-Douglas production function with parameter values from the top of the sheet, except for d, which can be manipulated from the "Set d" radio buttons. The three dots (red on your screen) are the cost-minimizing input combinations. Above the graph, the sheet shows the value of the sum of the exponents, initially 0.95, a description of the shape of the total cost function, and a small picture of that shape.

Step Click on the $d = 0.25$ option.

The isoquants shift in because it takes fewer inputs to make the three levels of output depicted. Notice also that the distance between the isoquants has been decreased and the *TC* shape is now linear.

Step Click on the $d = 0.3$ option.

Once again, the isoquants shift in and the distance between them decreases. Now the total cost function is increasing at a decreasing rate.

Step Click on the $d = 0.35$ option.

The isoquants shift in and the gap between them continues to fall.

The distance between the isoquants reflects the production function. If the distance is increasing as constant increases in quantity are applied, the total cost function will increase at an increasing rate. If the gaps remain constant, the cost function will be linear. If the gaps get smaller as output rises, the firm has costs that rise at a decreasing rate.

Many students do not realize that the shape of the cost function is dependent on the production technology. Repeatedly cycle through the radio buttons, keeping your eye on the isoquants and resulting total cost function, to cement the relationship between the production and cost functions.

Canonical Cost Curves

Step Proceed to the *Cubic* sheet.

This sheet displays what we might call the canonical cost structure, in other words, the most commonly used cost function.

Notice that the cost function has a cubic polynomial functional form:

$$TC = aq^3 + bq^2 + cq + d$$

The *d* coefficient represents the fixed cost. Because there are fixed costs, we know the firm is in the short run.

Once we have the cost function, the top curve on the top graph, we can apply the definitions to get all of the other cost curves. The other total curves are

$$TVC = aq^3 + bq^2 + cq$$
$$TFC = d$$

Step Click on each of the three curves in the top graph to see the data that are being plotted.

The curves in the bottom graph are all derived from the top graph.

Step Click on each of the three curves in the bottom graph to see the data that are being plotted.

Special formatting has been applied to the numbers in the average and marginal cost cells to display "$/unit" in each cell. It should be clear that average and marginal cost curves cannot be plotted on the same graph as total cost curves because the y axes are different.

Marginal cost is defined as the additional cost of producing more output. "More" can be 1 unit, 10 units, or an infinitesimally small change in the number of units.

There are two basic ways to get the marginal cost function.

The first, more straightforward way, is to get the cost function, then apply the definition given earlier, computing the change in total cost for a given change in output.

Using calculus makes this easy, but you have to have the cost function available. We do have the cost function and we can easily take the derivative with respect to q.

$$TC = aq^3 + bq^2 + cq + d$$
$$MC = \frac{dTC}{dq} = 3aq^2 + 2bq + c$$

Notice that the d coefficient, *TFC*, disappears. The expression for *MC* is entered in column G.

Column H has *MC* for a discrete-size change. You can vary the size of the change by adjusting the "step" size in cell B3.

Step Make the step size smaller and smaller. Try 0.1, 0.01, and 0.001.

Clearly, as the step size gets smaller, *MC* based on discrete-size changes in column H approaches *MC* based on the derivative in column G.

The second way to get the cost function is to use the neat result from Lagrangean method. We can simply use $\lambda^* = MC$ and we have the *MC* curve. Of course, if we really wanted the total cost function, then we would have to integrate the *MC* function with respect to q. The constant of integration is the fixed cost, which would be zero in the long run.

The family of cost curves in the *Cubic* sheet (shown in Figure 2.2.4.1) are the canonical cost curves displayed in every introductory economics and intermediate micro textbook. You might wonder, if not Cobb-Douglas, then what production function could produce such a cost function. That is not an easy question to answer. In fact, the functional form for technology that would give rise to the canonical cost curves is quite complicated and it is not worth the effort to painstakingly derive the usual U-shaped average and marginal cost curves from first principles.

It is sufficient to know that a production function underlies the cost curves. Of course, if input prices rise, we know the cost curves shift up and, if technology improves, they shift down.

Quadratic Cost Curves

Step Proceed to the *Quadratic* sheet to see a final example of cost curves.

You immediately see that the quadratic is a special case of the cubic cost function, with coefficients a and c equal to zero.

Notice the manifestation of the properties emphasized earlier in this chapter. The MC curve (actually, MC is linear) intersects AVC and ATC at their minimums. In the case of AVC, they both start from zero. When MC is below ATC, ATC is falling, but beyond the point at which MC intersects ATC (at the minimum ATC), MC is above ATC and ATC is rising.

MC is easily found when TC is known.

$$TC = bq^2 + d$$
$$MC = \frac{dTC}{dq} = 2bq$$

The shapes of the cost curves are not the usual U-shaped average and marginal curves, but this is another of the many possible cost structures that could be derived from a firm's input cost minimization problem.

The Role of Cost Curves in the Theory of the Firm

Cost curves are not particularly exciting, but they are an important geometric tool. When combined with a firm's revenue structure, the family of cost curves is used to find the profit-maximizing level of output and maximum profits.

Cost curves can come in many forms and shapes, but they all share the basic idea that they are derived by minimizing the total cost of producing output, where output is represented by the firm's production function. Different production functions give rise to different cost functions.

The shape of the cost function, rising at an increasing, constant, or decreasing rate, is determined by the production function. With increasing returns to scale, for example, a firm can more than double output when it doubles its input use. That means, on the cost side, that doubling output will less than double total cost. Returns to scale can be spotted by the spacing between the isoquants. With increasing returns to scale, for example, the gaps between the isoquants get smaller as output rises.

No matter the production function, it is always true that for output levels at which marginal cost is below an average cost, the average must be falling and *MC* above *AVC* or *ATC* means *AVC* or *ATC* is rising. It is also true that *AVC* approaches *ATC* as output rises.

Exercises

Open Word and answer the following questions. Save the document and print it when you are done.

1. A Cobb-Douglas production function with increasing returns to scale yields a total cost function that increases at a decreasing rate. Use Word's Drawing Tools to draw the underlying isoquant map for such a production function.
   Hint: The spacing between the isoquants is crucial.

A commonly used specification for production functions in empirical work is the translog functional form. There are several versions. When applied to the cost function, you get a result like this:

$$\ln TC = \alpha_0 + \alpha_1 \ln Q + \alpha_2 \ln w + \alpha_3 \ln r + \alpha_4 \ln Q \ln w + \alpha_5 \ln Q \ln r$$
$$+ \alpha_6 \ln w \ln r$$

Notice that the function is a modification of the log version of a Cobb-Douglas function. In addition to the individual log terms there are combinations of the three variables, called interaction terms.

Click the Exercise Questions button at the bottom of the *Q&A* sheet in the CostCurves.xls workbook to reveal a sheet with translog cost function parameters. Use this sheet to answer the following questions.

2. Enter a formula in cell B18 for the *TC* of producing 100 units of output, given the alpha coefficient and input price values in cells B5:B13. Fill your formula down and then create a chart of the total cost function (with appropriate axes labels and a title). Copy and paste your chart in your Word document.
   Hint: $TC = e^{\ln TC}$ and Exp(number) in Excel returns e raised to the to the power of number.
3. Compute *MC* via the change in output from 100 to 110 in cell C19. Report your result.
4. Compute *MC* via the derivative at $Q = 100$ in cell D18. Report your result.
   Hint: $\frac{d}{dx}\left(e^{f(x)}\right) = e^{f(x)} \frac{d}{dx}(f(x))$.
5. Compare your results for *MC* in questions 3 and 4 – are your answers the same or different? Explain.

References

The epigraph is from page 218 of Alan Blinder, Elie Canetti, David Lebow, and Jeremy Rudd, *Asking About Prices: A New Approach to Understanding Price Stickiness* (Russell Sage Foundation, 1998). This book reports the results of interviews with more than 200 business executives. The authors explain that asking about a firm's marginal cost "turned out to be quite tricky because the term 'marginal cost' is not in the lexicon of most business people; the concept itself may not even be a natural one" (p. 216). The question was, therefore, phrased in terms of "variable costs of producing additional units."

The results confirmed what many who have attempted to estimate cost curves know: The canonical, U-shaped family of cost curves makes for nice theory, but it is not common in the real world. Do not lose sight, however, of the purpose of the Theory of the Firm. It is not designed to realistically describe a living firm. The Theory of the Firm is a severe abstraction with a primary goal of deriving a supply curve.

2.3
Output Profit Maximization

2.3.1

PCSR Output Initial Solution

There are many occasions, therefore, when several explorers are surprised, and somewhat pained, on meeting each other at the Pole. Of such an occasion the history of the "marginal revenue curve" presents a striking example. This piece of apparatus plays a great part in my work, and my book arose out of the attempt to apply it to various problems, but I was not myself one of the many explorers who arrived in rapid succession at this particular Pole.

Joan Robinson

This chapter works with a perfectly competitive, PC, firm in the short run, SR.

With a cost function, $TC^* = f(q, w, r,$ and production functions parameters), we are ready to solve the PCSR firm's output side profit maximization problem. This is the second of three optimization problems that make up the Theory of the Firm.

The firm chooses the amount of output that maximizes profit, defined as total revenue minus total cost.

The firm's market structure impacts its revenue function. The simplest case is a perfectly (or purely) competitive firm. A PC firm takes price as given and, therefore, revenues are simply price times quantity. Total cost comes from the cost function (choosing the input mix that minimizes the cost of any given level of output).

The *short run* is defined by the fact that at least one input (usually K) is fixed and cannot be varied. In the *long run*, the firm is free to choose how much to use of each factor. K is fixed not because it is immovable (like a pizza oven or a building), but because the firm has contracted to rent a certain amount. It cannot increase or decrease the amount of K in the short run.

Market Structure

A perfectly competitive firm sells a product provided by many other firms selling that homogeneous (which means identical) product to perfectly informed consumers. Because the product is homogeneous, there are no quality differences or other reasons for consumers to care about who they buy from. Because consumers are perfectly informed, they know the price of every seller. This leads to the following fundamental concept for a perfectly competitive firm:

Price taker: The PC firm sells its product at the market price. The price is exogenous to the firm, which means it cannot be chosen by the firm.

In addition to price taking, the market structure of the PC firm is characterized by an assumption about the movement of other firms into and out of the industry:

Free entry and exit: Firms can enter or leave the market, selling the same good as everyone else, at any time.

These two ideas, price-taking behavior and free entry, distinguish the PC firm from its polar opposite, monopoly. A monopolist chooses price and has a barrier to entry.

The combination of a homogeneous product sold by many firms to perfectly informed buyers means that an individual PC firm does not worry about what other firms are doing. The PC firm simply chooses its own output to maximize profit and does not watch the other firms to gain a strategic advantage. In this sense, there is no rivalry in perfect competition.

A truly perfectly competitive firm does not exist in the real world. The concept is an abstraction that enables derivation of the supply curve.

Setting Up the Problem

1. Goal: maximize profits (π), which equal total revenues (TR) minus total costs (TC)
2. Endogenous variable: output (q)
3. Exogenous variables: price (of the product), input prices (the wage rate and the rental rate of capital), and technology (parameters in the production function).

The optimization problem is unconstrained because the firm can choose any level of output from zero to any positive number.

Finding the Initial Solution

Suppose the cost function is

$$TC = aq^3 + bq^2 + cq + d$$

Then we can form the PC firm's profit function and optimization problem like this:

$$\max_{q} \pi = TR - TC$$

$$\max_{q} \pi = Pq - (aq^3 + bq^2 + cq + d)$$

As usual, we have two ways to solve this optimization problem: numerically and analytically.

Numerical Approach

Step Open the Excel workbook OutputProfitMaxPCSR.xls and read the *Intro* sheet.

This sheet prints as one landscaped page and provides a compact summary of the optimal solution of the output side profit maximization problem for a perfectly competitive firm in the short run.

Step Proceed to the *OptimalChoice* sheet to find the initial solution.

The sheet is organized into the components of an optimization problem, with goal, endogenous, and exogenous variable cells.

On open, the firm is producing nine units of output and making $11.74 of profit. Is this the optimal solution?

No. The marginal cost of the ninth unit is $3.52 (as shown in cell B22). The firm would make a mistake (we would say it is inefficient) if it produced just nine units. We can see that the additional revenue produced by the last unit, $7 (the price), is greater than the additional cost, $3.52 (cell B22). Thus, the firm should produce more.

How much should the firm produce?

Step Run Solver to find the optimal solution.

Notice that at the optimal solution, $MC = \$7$ per unit.

$P = MC$ is the equimarginal condition in this problem, analogous to $MRS = p_1/p_2$ and $TRS = w/r$.

Analytical Approach

After doing constrained optimization problems using the Lagrangean method, this optimization problem is trivial. It is a single-choice variable (q), unconstrained maximization problem.

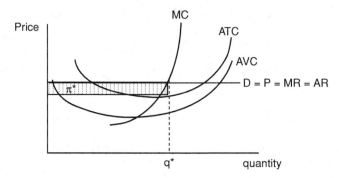

Figure 2.3.1.1. The canonical output profit maximization graph.

You simply take the first derivative of the profit function with respect to q, set it equal to zero, and solve for q^*. There is the complication that you have to use the quadratic formula.

Step Click the Show the Analytical Solution button to see how to solve this problem with calculus.

As usual, Solver and calculus agree (not exactly, but they give effectively the same answer).

Representing the Optimal Solution with Graphs

The firm's output side profit maximization problem is usually represented by a graph that depicts the family of cost curves along with marginal and average revenue. Figure 2.3.1.1 shows this canonical graph for a perfectly competitive firm (signaled by the fact that firm demand is horizontal, so marginal revenue equals demand).

Step Proceed to the *Graphs* sheet to see why Figure 2.3.1.1 is so common. Figure 2.3.1.2 displays the initial view.

The four graphs in Figure 2.3.1.2 can be used to show the firm's optimization problem and its solution. The top left graph has *TR* and *TC*. The firm wants to choose q to maximize the difference between revenues and costs. The top right graph shows the profit function. The firm wants to choose q so that it is at the highest point on the profit function. The bottom right graph displays marginal profit. The firm can find the maximum profit by choosing q so that marginal profit is zero (and the second-order condition is met so the flat spot on the profit function is a max and not a min). Finally, the bottom left graph is the way the firm's problem is usually displayed. The firm chooses q where *MR* (which equals *P* given that the firm is a price taker) equals *MC*.

The *Graphs* sheet opens with $P = 7$ and an inefficient output level.

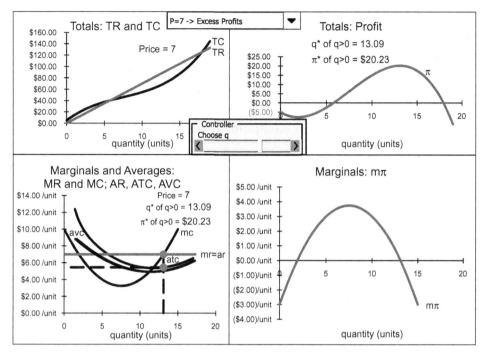

Figure 2.3.1.2. Four views of output profit maximization.
Source: OutputProfitMaxPCSR.xls!Graphs

Step Move the output with the slider control to find the profit-maximizing solution. The bottom left graph shows the profit rectangle, $(AR - ATC)q$, at each level of q. When you find the point where $MR(= P) = MC$, you get the maximum area of the profit rectangle.

The profit rectangle is an area, length times width, with units in dollars. Because the y axis is a rate, $/unit, and the x axis is in units of the product, multiplying the two leaves dollars. In other words, say the product is milk in gallons. Then price, average total, and average variable cost are all in $/gallon. Suppose that at a price of $2/gallon, $MR = MC$ at an optimal output of 7000 gallons and $ATC = \$1.50$/gallon at this output. Clearly, profits are ($2/gallon $- \$1.50$/gallon) $\times$ 7000 gallons, which equals $3,500.

You can compute profits from the profit rectangle at any level of output. The height of the rectangle is always average revenue (which equals price) minus average total cost. This vertical distance is average profit. When multiplied by the level of output, we get profits, in dollars, at that level of output.

The bottom left graph in Figure 2.3.1.2 (and on your screen) is the conventional display of the initial solution because it is easy to find optimal output (where $MR = MC$) and the family of cost curves provides information about the firm's cost structure. It is easy to see whether the cost curves are U shaped or if there are increasing returns to scale. Also, the gap between

ATC and *AVC* reveals the amount of fixed costs. Finally, as you will see later, the graph enables us to apply a simple rule to determine whether the firm should shut down or continue production.

Although the bottom left graph is the most common way to show the firm's profit maximization problem, it should be clear that the other three graphs are displaying different features of the same profit maximization problem. It is easy to see that the optimal output is the same in each of the four graphs.

The Shutdown Rule

The primary message here is that the firm has an option when profits are negative: It can simply shut down, close its doors, and produce nothing. The *Shutdown Rule* says the the firm will maximize profits by producing nothing ($q^* = 0$) when $P < AVC$.

The key to whether the firm shuts down or continues production in the face of negative profits lies in its fixed costs. If the firm can do better by shutting down and paying its fixed costs instead of producing and choosing the level of output where $MR = MC$, then it should produce nothing.

There are four profit positions in the short run.

- Excess or positive profits ($\pi > 0$)
- Zero or normal profits ($\pi = 0$)
- Negative profits, but continuing production ($\pi < 0$, but $P > AVC$)
- Negative profits, shutdown ($\pi < 0$ and $P < AVC$).

Case 1, excess profits, occurs whenever maximum profits are positive. With $P = 7$, we know that $q^* = 13.09$ and $\pi^* = \$20.23$.

Step Click on the pull down menu (over cell R5) and select the Zero Profits option.

Your screen now looks like Figure 2.3.1.3.

Notice that the price (\$5.373) just touches the minimum of the average total cost curve. The profit rectangle has zero area. The firm is earning zero profits. In the top left graph, you can see that *TR* just touches *TC*. In the top right graph, the top of the profit hill just touches the *x* axis. If the firm increases or decreases output, then it is quite clear that profits will fall and become negative.

Zero profits are sometimes called *normal profits*. This can be quite confusing. After all, what can be normal about not making any money? In fact, the firm is making money when profits are zero. It is making exactly the amount it would make in its next best alternative business.

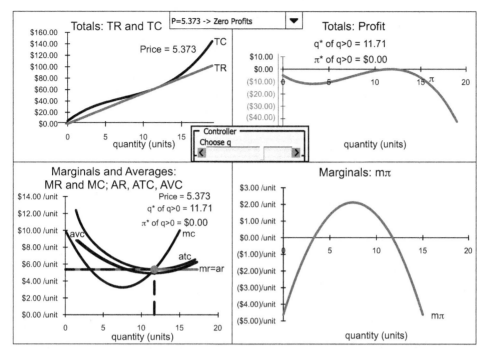

Figure 2.3.1.3. Zero profits.
Source: OutputProfitMaxPCSR.xls!Graphs

Perhaps a pair of definitions would clear things up:

Accounting profits = revenues − explicit costs

Economic profits = revenues − explicit costs − opportunity costs

Without an adjective, profits means economic profits. So, when profits are zero that means it is economic profits that are zero. An accountant would subtract explicit (out-of-pocket) costs and announce that the firm is making money. The economist would then subtract the cost of the profits that could be made by the next best alternative industry that the firm could be in. Because profits are zero, we know the opportunity costs are exactly equal to the accounting profit.

Although this may seem incredibly confusing at first, there is a nice interpretation of economic profits: If positive, the firm will stay in the industry and new firms will enter in the long run; if negative, the firm will exit in the long run; and if zero, there will be neither exit nor entry in the long run. Economists are not concerned with how much money the firm made, but with profits as a signal to entry and exit. Defining economic profit as accounting profit minus opportunity cost gives us a profit measure that tells us whether the firm will stay or leave in the long run.

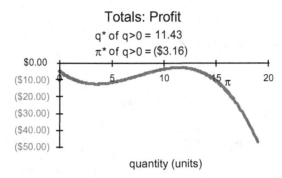

Figure 2.3.1.4. Negative profits, continuing production.
Source: OutputProfitMaxPCSR.xls!Graphs

The distinction between economic and accounting profits also explains why positive profits are excess profits. It is not meant as a pejorative term, but to indicate that the firm is earning greater profits than are needed to keep it in production.

You can use this sheet to explore different prices and watch how the four graphs change. As you follow the steps below, keep your eye on the profit function in the top, right-hand corner.

Step Click on the pull down menu (over cell R5) and select the Neg Profits, Cont Prod option.

With $P = 5.10$, the firm produces $q^* = 11.43$ and suffers negative profits of $-\$3.16$. Notice that price is below ATC in the bottom left graph, so that the profit rectangle, $(AR - ATC)q$, will be a negative number. (The area is not negative, but it is interpreted as a negative amount since revenues are below costs.) In the top left graph, the TR line is below the TC curve. In the top right graph, the profit function is below the x axis.

Keep your eye on the top right graph, reproduced as Figure 2.3.1.4. Notice that the top of the profit function is higher than the intercept (where $q = 0$). It is better for the firm to continue production, even though it is earning negative profits of $-\$3.16$ at the optimal output level, because it would make an even lower negative profit of $-\$5$ (the fixed cost) if it shut down.

The canonical graph can be used to compare negative profits for the best output if the firm produces versus negative profits if the firm shuts down. The Shutdown Rule is easy: Shut down if $P < AVC$.

Step Look at the bottom left graph on your screen. It confirms that the Shutdown Rule works. Profits are negative because price is below average total cost, but the firm will continue production because $P > AVC$.

The Shutdown Rule   331

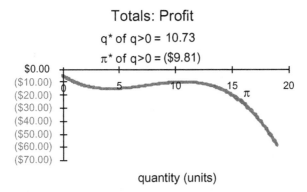

Figure 2.3.1.5. Negative profits, shutdown.
Source: OutputProfitMaxPCSR.xls!Graphs

Because $P > AVC$, we know that the top of the profit function is higher than the y intercept in Figure 2.3.1.4.

Step Click on the pull down menu (over cell R5) and select the Neg Profits, Shutdown option. Figure 2.3.1.5 displays the top right graph.

In this case, the top of the profit function is actually below the y intercept. In other words, the maximum profit if the firm produces, −$9.81, is worse than the negative profit incurred if the firm shuts down, −$5. The firm optimizes by choosing $q^* = 0$, that is, shutting down.

Step Look at the bottom left graph on your screen. Once again, we have confirmation of the Shutdown Rule. With $P = 4.5$, $P < AVC$ and the firm should shut down.

Carefully watching the canonical (bottom left) and profit function (top right) graphs makes clear that the Shutdown Rule works. As long as $P > AVC$, you know that the top of the profit hill is above the y intercept. If $P = AVC$, the two are exactly equal. $P < AVC$ means that the top of the hill is below the y intercept, the negative profit suffered if the firm produces nothing, and the firm's best choice is to produce nothing.

If you multiply the Shutdown Rule by q, you get

$$(P < AVC)q$$
$$Pq < AVCq$$
$$TR < TVC$$

This version of the Shutdown Rule says that the firm should produce nothing if total revenue cannot cover total variable costs. This makes sense. Why produce if you can't even pay for the variable expenses? You are better off

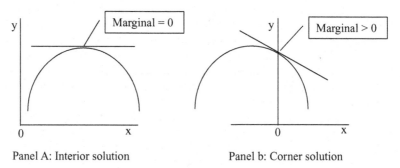

Figure 2.3.1.6. Understanding the corner solution.

not producing at all. If $TR > TVC$, however, then production makes sense because you will be able to reduce some of the fixed costs you have to pay no matter what you do.

Finally, we return to the issue of economic versus accounting profit. It should be clear that negative economic profit does not necessarily mean that the firm is losing money. It could be that the firm is earning an accounting profit (and making money), but when you subtract the opportunity cost, profits are negative. The firm cannot leave the industry yet because we are in the short run and it has contracts to honor for fixed factors of production. We know, however, that when those contracts expire and the firm considers its long-run planning horizon, it will exit this industry.

The Corner Solution Revisited

In the Theory of Consumer Behavior, we know that there are situations in which the MRS does not equal the price ratio, yet the solution is optimal. We called this a corner solution. Figure 2.3.1.6 depicts the difference between an interior and a corner solution. In panel b, the agent cannot choose negative values of the x variable and, therefore, the function is cut off by the y axis.

Shutting down is another example of a corner solution because, once again, the equimarginal condition is not met, yet producing nothing is the optimal solution. Shutting down is an interesting example of a corner solution because there is a place where the marginal condition is met (there is an output where $MR = MC$), but it is not optimal. The profit function bends and twists in such a way (see Figure 2.3.1.5) that profit is decreasing as output increases from zero. This means that profits would rise if we were able to produce negative output. Since we are not, we have a corner solution.

The complexity of the profit function should increase your sensitivity to lurking problems with analytical and numerical methods. We know neither is perfect so there may be glitches in applying the methods to the firm's profit maximization problem. The *Q&A* sheet provides an example.

Finding and Displaying the Initial Solution

The output side profit maximization problem is a single-variable (q) uncon-strained problem. It can be solved with numerical and analytical methods. The equimarginal rule applied is that $MR (= P) = MC$.

You can think of the firm as walking through a series of three steps when solving its profit maximization problem:

1. Choose q where $MR (= P) = MC$.
2. Compute profits at q^* via $TR - TC$ or $(AR - ATC)q$ (the profit rectangle).
3. If profits are negative at q^*, check to determine whether shutting down is a better option by comparing the negative profits at q^* to minus TFC. A shortcut is to use the Shutdown Rule, which says that the firm should shut down if $P < AVC$.

The solution is displayed by a canonical graph that superimposes the firm's revenue side (average and marginal revenue) over its cost structure (aver-age and marginal costs). Optimal output is easily found where $MR = MC$ (as long as $P > AVC$) and maximum profit is displayed in the area of the appropriate rectangle.

Exercises

Open Word and answer the following questions. Save the document and print it when you are done.

1. Use Excel's Solver to find the optimal output and profit for a firm with cost func-tion $TC = 2q^2 + 10q + 50$ and $P = 40$. Take a screen shot of your optimal solu-tion (including output and profits).
2. Use analytical methods to solve the problem in the previous question.
3. For what price range will the firm in questions 1 and 2 shut down? Explain.
4. If fixed costs are higher, will this influence the firm's shutdown decision? Explain.

References

The epigraph is from the foreword (p. vi) of Joan Robinson, *The Economics of Imperfect Competition* (first edition, 1933, followed by many reprints). In a male-dominated profession, Joan Robinson established herself as a well-known, important economist. She helped create the Theory of the Firm, including the canonical graph with average and marginal revenue and cost that is used to this day.

Ironically, however, much of her work was critical of mainstream economics. Her famous Richard T. Ely lecture at the 1971 American Economics Association conference pulled no punches:

For once the president of the AEA was a dissident. This was the veteran institutionalist and Keynesian John Kenneth Galbraith, a longtime friend of Robinson's and celebrated critic of US capitalism and its apologists in academic economics. Galbraith now offered her the most important platform she had ever occupied. Robinson took full advantage of it, delivering an abrasive, challenging, deliberately provocative indictment of neoclassical economics that was designed to polarize her audience between the old and conservative and the young and progressive. (John Edward King, *A History of Post Keynesian Economics Since 1936* (2002), p. 123)

2.3.2

Deriving the Supply Curve

As all the functions $\phi'_k(D_k)$ are supposed to increase with D_k, the expression for D_k derived from the equation $p = \phi'_k(D_k)$ is itself a function of p, increasing with p. [Translation: The supply curve, $Q^* = f(P)$, is derived from $P = MC$ and it is upward sloping because MC is upward sloping.]

Augustin Cournot

The most important comparative statics analysis of the firm's output side profit maximization problem is based on tracking q^* (quantity supplied) as price changes, ceteris paribus. This gives us the firm's supply curve.

The important thing to remember is that the supply curve has two parts:

- MC when $P > \min AVC$
- Zero otherwise (this is the shutdown case).

We begin with a comparative statics analysis via numerical methods.

Numerical Approach

Step Open the Excel workbook DerivingSupply.xls and read the *Intro* sheet, then go to the *OptimalChoice* sheet to find the initial solution.

The sheet looks like the *OptimalChoice* sheet in the OutputProfitMax-PCSR.xls workbook, but it has a few additional cells.

The IF statements in cells C4 and C8 of the *OptimalChoice* sheet are a convenient way to incorporate the firm's shutdown option.

Step Click on cell C8 to reveal its formula: =IF(max_profit>−d,q,0). We will use this cell as the correct optimal solution in all cases, including the shutdown case.

Notice that cells B8 and B4 display a disastrous solution. The correct solution, shutting down, is displayed in C8 and C4. Thus, we can use C8 and C4 to track the optimal solution as price changes, ceteris paribus.

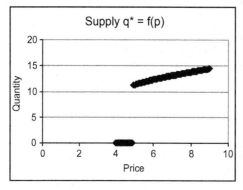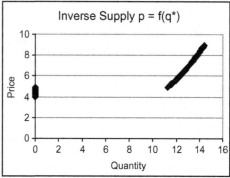

Figure 2.3.2.1. Supply functions.
Source: DerivingSupply.xls!CS1

Solver will find the best of the positive levels of output in cell B8 and the IF statement in cell C8 checks to make sure that the best solution (of the $q > 0$) is better than shutting down and producing nothing ($q = 0$).

With $P = 4$, the best of all of the positive levels of output, $q = 10$, provides a profit of minus \$15. Of course, producing nothing yields a profit of minus \$5 and is the correct optimal solution.

There is one glitch with using cells C8 and C4: if you set the initial price from which Solver begins searching low enough, Solver will give a miserable result.

Step Set $P = 2$ and run Solver to see an example of this.

The correct answer is to shut down, but Solver cannot find this answer because it requires leaving the first quadrant. We could add a constraint to prevent Solver from considering negative output.

Step Set cell B8 back to 10 and $P = 4$ so Solver will converge to the local max at $q = -15$.

Step Run the Comparative Statics Wizard from $P = 4$ with 0.05 sized shocks 100 times. Of course, you will want to track the C4 and C8 cells as endogenous variables. You can safely ignore the warning – you are using the CSWiz to keep track of these cells, but will not include them as changing cells in the Solver dialog box.

Your results will look like those in the *CS1* sheet. Notice that at low prices, the firm is producing nothing. This is the part of the supply curve where the firm shuts down to maximize profits.

The supply curve and inverse supply curves easily can be graphed with these data, as shown in Figure 2.3.2.1 and the *CS1* sheet. Of course, the tail runs along the quantity axis all the way to zero.

The supply function in the short run has a discontinuity at the point where the price falls below the AVC curve.

You can confirm this discontinuity by running another CSWiz analysis.

Step Return P to 4. Run the Comparative Statics Wizard from $P = 4$ with 0.05 sized shocks 100 times and track the Solver solution, B4 and B8, the correct solution, C4 and C8, and the MC, AVC, and ATC cells.

The results show quite clearly what is going on. As long as $P < AVC$, the firm can do better by producing nothing because revenues do not cover variable costs.

Analytical methods can be used to find the discontinuity. First we find AVC; then we find its minimum.

$$TC = 0.04q^3 - 0.9q^2 + 10q + 5$$

$$TVC = 0.04q^3 - 0.9q^2 + 10q$$

$$AVC = \frac{TVC}{q} = 0.04q^2 - 0.9q + 10$$

$$\min_{q} TVC \Rightarrow \frac{dAVC}{dq} = 0$$

$$\frac{dAVC}{dq} = 0.08q - 0.9 = 0$$

$$0.08q = 0.9$$

$$q = 11.25$$

By plugging this minimum value of output into the AVC function, we know the price at which the discontinuity kicks in.

$$AVC = 0.04[11.25]^2 - 0.9[11.25] + 10 = 4.9375$$

In the *CS1* sheet, the discontinuity occurs when price rises from \$4.90 to \$4.95. The analytical work tells us that the discontinuity is exactly at \$4.9375.

Analytical Approach

Let us consider a different cost function and derive the supply curve via analytical methods.

$$TC^* = q^2 + 20$$

Set up and solve the profit maximization problem. The firm seeks to maximize profits, which is simply total revenue minus total cost. Because it is a perfectly competitive firm, we know price is given and $TR = Pq$. Thus, the optimization problem is

$$\max_q \pi = Pq - q^2 - 20$$

We proceed by taking the derivative with respect to q, setting the first-order condition equal to zero, and solving for q^*.

$$\frac{d\pi}{dq} = P - 2q$$

$$P - 2q = 0$$

$$q^* = \frac{1}{2}P$$

This is the supply function. It reports the quantity supplied by a firm at every given price.

Notice that this firm will never shut down. We can construct the firm's canonical graph by figuring out the cost curves. We know $TVC = q^2$ and $TFC = 20$. Then we can find the average and marginal curves.

$$AVC = \frac{TVC}{q} = \frac{q^2}{q} = q$$

$$ATC = \frac{TC}{q} = \frac{q^2 + 20}{q} = q + \frac{20}{q}$$

$$MC = \frac{dTC}{dq} = \frac{d(q^2 + 1)}{q} = 2q$$

Step Proceed to the *Graphs* sheet to see the four graph display of the optimal solution for this problem.

Clearly, with $P = 20$, $q^* = 10$. In fact, for any P, q^* is simply $P/2$. There is no positive price at which this firm will shut down because AVC is simply a ray with slope $+1$ out of the origin. Thus, price can never fall below AVC.

In this example, the supply curve is $q^* = P/2$ and the inverse supply curve is $P = 2q$, which is the MC curve.

Points Off the Supply Curve

As we did with the demand curve, we can explore the meaning of being off the supply curve.

Step Proceed to the *CS1* sheet and notice the point off the supply and inverse supply curves. Use the scroll bar to the left of the supply curve graph to move the point.

Notice how the point off the curve moves in a vertical fashion in the supply curve graph and horizontally on the inverse supply curve graph. The idea is that price is constant (at $P = 6.25$) so you can be off the supply curve above or below and off the inverse supply curve to the right or left.

As you move the scroll bar, you are moving output in both graphs. The number next to the point is profits at that output level.

Step Scroll down to row 58 to see the optimal solution for $P = 6.25$. At this price, the maximum profit of $10.63 is obtained by producing 12.5 units of output.

Step Return to the two graphs and use the scroll bar to set output to five units. Profits are minus $6.25. Increase output by one unit at a time (by clicking on the up arrow of the scroll bar). Keep your eye on the profits associated with each output level. Keep going past the supply curve so that you end up above the supply curve.

Seeing the value of profit as the point climbed through the supply curve makes clear what a point off the curve means: The firm is failing to maximize profits. Like the demand curve, the supply curve is a ridge line and points off it are associated with lower values of the objective function.

On the inverse supply curve, the inefficiency of being off the curve is obvious because output levels off the inverse supply curve are off the MC curve and this means the firm is not choosing a point where MR ($= P$) $= MC$.

Supply is $q^* = f(P,$ ceteris paribus$)$

The supply curve is a comparative statics analysis of the effects on optimal quantity as price changes, ceteris paribus.

Unlike the demand curve, the supply curve has a discontinuity because the firm will shut down if price falls below AVC.

The supply curve depends critically on the firm's cost function. The inverse supply curve is simply MC above AVC and zero otherwise. The firm will choose that level of output where $P = MC$ as long as $P > AVC$.

Like the demand curve, points off the supply curve are interpreted as inefficient solutions to the optimization problem. Although possible, no optimizing agent would choose a point off the supply (or demand) curve.

Exercises

Open Word and answer the following questions. Save the document and print it when you are done.

1. What happens to the short-run supply curve if wages rise? Explain. Use Word's Drawing Tools to create a graph depicting your answer.

2. What happens to the inverse short-run supply curve if wages rise? Explain. Use Word's Drawing Tools to create a graph depicting your answer.
3. What happens to the short-run supply curve if the rental rate of capital increases? Explain.
4. What happens to the short-run supply curve if the price increases? Explain.
5. Suppose a firm is off its short-run supply curve, but at a point where $MR = MC$. Use Word's Drawing Tools to a draw the profit function for this situation and label a point Z that meets the supposed conditions.

References

The epigraph comes from page 92 of the 1897 English translation of Augustin Cournot's *Researches into the Mathematical Principles of the Theory of Wealth*. The book was originally published in French in 1838. It is a remarkable work – truly far ahead of its time. Cournot (pronounced coor–no) solves profit maximization problems for monopoly, unlimited (today called perfect) competition, and intermediate cases of small numbers of firms. He uses derivatives and integrals with numerous supporting figures, including supply and demand with price on the x axis. The mathematical exposition was simply beyond the grasp of many economists and the book languished in obscurity until the rise of mathematics in economics.

2.3.3

Diffusion and Technical Change

Why was the spread of crops from the Fertile Crescent so rapid? The answer depends partly on that east-west axis of Eurasia.

Jared Diamond

The Theory of the Firm is a highly abstracted model of a real-world firm, but there are fundamental ideas that can be applied to observed firm behavior.

The core concept used in this application is that of the Shutdown Rule, $P < AVC$. In this case, the negative profits generated by producing the best of the positive output choices (at $MR = MC$) are less than the negative profits suffered by shutting down and producing nothing.

Setting the Table

Consider two thoughts that are both wrong:

- Always upgrade to have the best equipment or "best practice"
- Never throw working machinery away

The first statement is wrong because you would always be throwing away almost new equipment in order to have the very latest equipment. The second statement is the polar opposite of the first: Now you keep using ancient machinery that was long ago superseded by better technology.

There has to be a middle ground between these two extremes and a logical way to determine when to replace equipment.

There are several definitions that will prove to be important:

- *Outmoded*: machinery that is not the best at the time but is still used.
- *Obsolete*: machinery that is scrapped (thrown away) yet still functions.

These definitions sharpen this question: When does machinery go from being outmoded to obsolete?

- *Labor productivity*: the ability of labor to make output and it is measured in two ways, output per hour or labor required to produce one unit of output.

The output per hour version is simply the average product of labor, q/L. The bigger this ratio, the more productive is labor. You can take the reciprocal and ask, "How much labor is needed to make one unit of output?" This measure, called the *unit labor requirement*, gets smaller as labor productivity improves.

There are basically two ways of increasing labor productivity:

- Better labor
- Better machinery – technical (or Technological) change.

More educated and skilled labor obviously will be more effective in translating input into output. But holding labor quality constant, if you provide workers with better technology, then labor productivity rises.

So, if you want to improve the speed at which a worker can dig a ditch, you can improve the worker or you can improve the technology used: A worker with a backhoe digs a ditch a lot faster than one with a shovel.

The final definition underlies this fundamental question:

- *Rate of diffusion*: how rapidly do the latest, best machinery and methods spread?

The mere existence of a new machine (e.g., a backhoe) is not enough to spur economywide increases in labor productivity. If the machine is not adopted rapidly, it will have little effect.

The rate of diffusion is like adding a drop of red dye in a bucket of water. How rapidly will the water turn red? What factors affect the rate of diffusion?

This application revolves around two crucial questions:

1. Why is a machine that works sometimes kept and other times scrapped?
2. What determines the rate of diffusion of technical change?

The two questions are obviously interrelated. If machines are scrapped and replaced with the latest technology fairly quickly, then the rate of diffusion of technical change will be very fast. If old technology is kept online and in production for a long time, then the rate of diffusion of technical change will be slow.

The next section presents some data used by W. E. G. Salter (1960) to support the claim that the rate of diffusion varies across industries.

Table 5. Methods in use in the U.S. blast-furnace industry, selected years, 1911–26

Year	Gross tons of pig-iron produced per man-hour		Percentage of plants using the following methods		
	Best-practice plants	Industry average	Hand-charged and sand-cast %	Mixed types %	Machine charged and cast %
1911	0.313	0.14	50.0	22.7	27.3
1917	0.326	0.15	41.9	34.9	23.2
1919	0.328	0.14	42.0	28.0	30.0
1921	0.428	0.178	22.2	44.3	33.5
1923	0.462	0.213	20.7	39.7	39.6
1925	0.512	0.285	7.2	25.5	67.3
1926	0.573	0.296	6.1	24.5	69.4

Figure 2.3.3.1. Slow diffusion in pig-iron production.
Source: DiffusionTechChange.xls!Data

On the Variation of Methods Used in a Variety of Industries

Salter presents data on the methods of production used at any point in time. It is quite obvious that there is always a mix of technologies being used. As new plants come online and new machinery is installed, older plants with older machinery remain in operation.

Salter's Table 5, reproduced as Figure 2.3.3.1, shows this mix of technologies in terms of pig-iron production. Notice that the labor productivity of the best-practice plants (the latest technology) rises from 1911 to 1926. The industry average, however, lags behind because the latest technology is not immediately adopted by every manufacturer. The machine charged and cast method (the right most column) is the best technology, but even by 1926, 30% of the firms are not using it. These firms remain in operation with older technology. This slow diffusion hampers the industrywide labor productivity.

Figure 2.3.3.2 focuses on the production of five-cent cigars. Salter focuses on a particular quality and type of cigar, the five-cent variety, to focus on an apples-to-apples comparison of production methods. Because the measure

Table 6. Approximate labour requirements per thousand five-cent cigars
for different manufacturing methods, Unites States, 1936

Manufacturing methods in use in 1936	Man-hours per thousand cigars
Hand made	33.38
Machine bunched, hand rolled	27.38
Four-operator machine	15.96
Two-operator machine	11.94

Figure 2.3.3.2. Various methods of producing five-cent cigars.
Source: DiffusionTechChange.xls!Data

Table 8. Variation in labour content per unit of output in selected industries

Industry, time and place	No. of plants	Unit of Output	Man-hours per unit of output			Ratio of range to mean	
			Mean	Range of all plants	Range of middle 50% of plants	All plants	Middle 50%
Bricks, UK, 1947	17	1000 bricks	1.36	2.12–0.64	1.75–0.93	1.16	0.61
Houses, UK, 1948	160	Standard house	3080	4300–2150	3520–2630	0.66	0.29
Men's shoes, UK, 1949	12	Dozen pairs	9.70	12.34–7.30	11.02–8.53	0.53	0.26
Cement, US, 1935	60	100 barrels	46.7	86.0–25.3	57.9–39.3	1.30	0.40
Beet sugar, US, 1935	59	Ton of beet sliced	1.46	2.81–0.88	1.98–1.20	1.32	0.53
Sole leather, US, 1949	8	1000 lb.	48	–	61–39	–	0.47

Figure 2.3.3.3. Variation in labor productivity across six industries.
Source: DiffusionTechChange.xls!Data

of productivity is the labor required to make 1000 five-cent cigars, the lower the hours required, the greater the labor productivity. The two-operator machine is the best practice, but three other methods are also used. Once again, the point is that a mix of methods are used and their combination determines industrywide productivity.

Figure 2.3.3.3 offers a final example of Salter's point that an economy's labor productivity depends on the technology actually used to make output. The Range of all plants column shows substantial variation in output from the best-practice firms (the lowest number given that we are measuring hours per unit of output) to the least productive methods still being used. For bricks, with 17 plants in operation, the middle 50% range from a best 0.93 hours to make 1000 bricks to 1.75 hours. The Ratio of range to mean columns (which are slightly off) measure the rate of diffusion. If somehow every plant adopted the best-practice method, this ratio would be zero. Thus, houses and men's shoes are industries with faster diffusion than the others.

Salter used an interesting graph to show how an industry incorporated various technologies in production. Figure 2.3.3.4 (Salter's original Fig. 5) uses rectangles to indicate each method or vintage of machinery. The greater

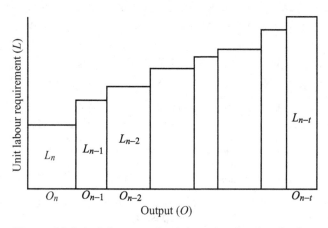

Figure 2.3.3.4. Salter graph of the mix of technologies.

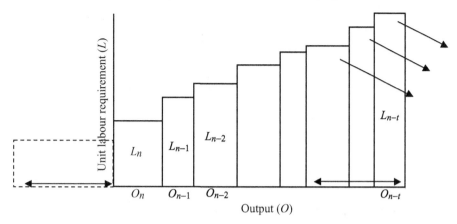

Figure 2.3.3.5. Salter graph as time goes by.

the base of the rectangle, the greater share of the industry's output for that particular technology. The lower the height (because the y axis shows the labor required to make one unit of output), the greater labor productivity for that technology. The Salter graph has to have the stair-step structure because the rectangles are ordered according to when they came online. The oldest technology is to the right and the newest is the left most rectangle. The left most rectangle is the best-practice technology at that time and all of the other rectangles are in different levels of outmodedness.

The graph is actually a single frame of a motion picture. As time goes by, and new techniques are invented and brought online, some of the right most rectangles will "fall over" and be replaced by a new shorter rectangle coming in from the left. Figure 2.3.3.5 shows a possibility for the next frame in the movie.

The base of the rectangle of the newest technology in Figure 2.3.3.5 equals the sum of the widths of the three rectangles representing obsolete technologies, which fall off the graph because they are no longer used. The wider the base of the newest technology, the better in terms of fast diffusion of technological change and rapid increases in industrywide productivity.

Another, less favorable possibility is that the newest technology has a small width. This would mean that few firms have adopted the best-practice method and industrywide productivity will not improve by much. The industry will remain dominated by outmoded methods.

Consider the two Salter graphs in Figure 2.3.3.6 (Salter's original Fig. 12). They are enhanced by a strip in the middle, the height of which represents the industry average productivity.

The two industries in Figure 2.3.3.6 are drawn so the best-practice productivity is the same and the most outmoded plant's productivity is the same. They also share eight different practices in producing the total output for the industry.

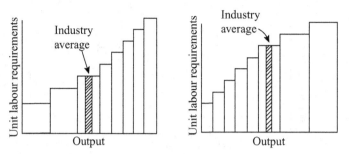

Figure 2.3.3.6. Comparison of two industries.

We would much prefer, however, the industry on the left of Figure 2.3.3.6 because it has a lower industry average productivity. This is a result of much more rapid diffusion of newer, higher productivity technology.

The industrywide productivity is a *weighted average* of all of the technologies in existence at any point in time.

Step Open the Excel workbook DiffusionTechChange.xls and read the *Intro* sheet, then go to the *IndustryAverage* sheet to see how a weighted average is computed and how the Salter graph works.

Cells C9 and C10 show how two technologies contribute to the industry output. On open, Methods A and B produce 50% of the total output. Because A (the superior, best-practice technology) requires only 1 hour of labor to make a unit of output, whereas B (an outmoded technology) requires 2 hours, the industry average productivity is 1.5 hours per unit of output.

Step Click on the scroll bar to increase A's share of total output to 90%. Notice how the Salter graph changes as you manipulate the scroll bar.

The Salter graph now shows A's share as a much wider rectangle (indicating much faster diffusion) and the red industry (weighted) average marker is much shorter. Although the simple average does not change, the weighted average falls because more of the output is being generated by the more productive A technology. The weighted average computation (implemented in the formula for cell M10) is

$$WeightedAverage = \frac{A'sOutput}{TotalOutput}A'sUnitLReq + \frac{B'sOutput}{TotalOutput}B'sUnitLReq$$

Step Click on the scroll bar to decrease A's share of total output to 10%.

Notice how the Salter graph changes as you manipulate the scroll bar.

Now, the industry (weighted) average is 1.9 because only 10% of the output is produced with the best-practice technology. This would be an example of slow diffusion.

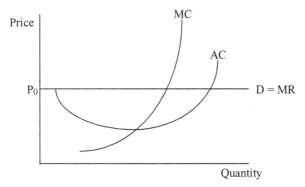

Figure 2.3.3.7. A new plant earns positive profits.

The weighted average of the contributions of each technology to industry output is a good way to show that the rate of diffusion affects industrywide productivity.

Having seen that there is substantial variation in the rate of diffusion and that a Salter graph displays this variation, we are ready to explain why industries use mixes of technologies.

Question 1: Why is a Machine that Works Sometimes Kept and Other Times Scrapped?

We can answer this question by reviewing the life cycle of a factory.

When first built, the factory reflects the best practices and technology available at that point in time. Figure 2.3.3.7 shows the canonical output side graph. This firm will produce where $MR (= P) = MC$ and earn positive profits.

As time goes by, the factory loses its place at the top of the heap, but it is still functioning and generating positive profits. Figure 2.3.3.8 shows the same firm with the same cost curves, but the price (in real terms) has fallen. The decrease in price is driven by newer technologies with lower costs.

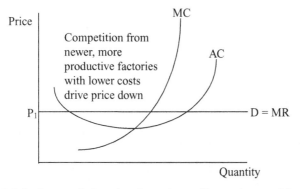

Figure 2.3.3.8. Outmoded technology, but still earning positive profits.

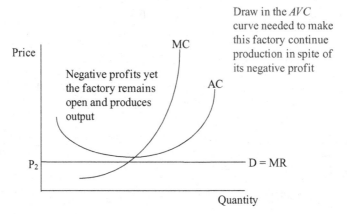

Figure 2.3.3.9. Suffering negative positive profits, but continuing production.

More time goes by and price keeps falling as newer technologies, incorporated in newly built factories, continue driving costs down – again, both prices and costs are measured in real terms.

The price will eventually fall below the factory's AC curve, but the factory remains online, producing even though it suffers negative profits, as shown in Figure 2.3.3.9. Why?

The AVC curve (which was not included in the earlier figures) must be drawn so that price is above average variable cost (where $MR = MC$) in order to meet the condition that firm will continue production.

The plant is quite old at this point; it is a tall rectangle to the right in the Salter graph, but it stays in production because shutting down would mean suffering even more negative profits.

More time goes by, and, eventually, finally, the factory shuts down. It has been *outmoded* since the day a newer factory came online, but it has now become *obsolete*.

If the firm produces where $MR (= P) = MC$ in Figure 2.3.3.10, it finds the best profit position for the best of the positive levels of output. In other

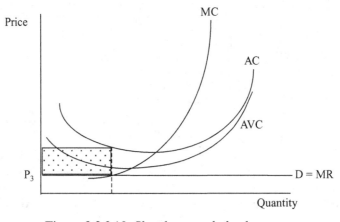

Figure 2.3.3.10. Shutdown and obsolescence.

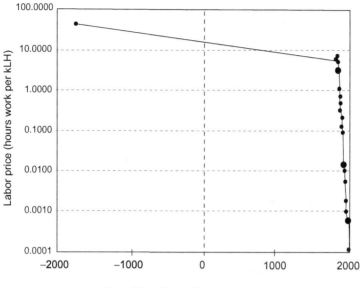

Figure 2.3.3.11. Labor price of light: 1750 B.C. to present.
Source: Bresnahan and Gordon (eds.), 1997, p. 54

words, this is a local maximum on the profit function. However, shutting down is a better option. The firm should not produce at all and simply pay its fixed costs.

So, to directly answer the question, why is a factory that works sometimes kept and other times scrapped, we use the Shutdown Rule, $P < AVC$. Old plants that are kept, using outmoded machines, operate in an environment in which $P > AVC$. Even if profits are negative, these plants will remain in operation as long as revenues cover variable costs. Once $P < AVC$, we know the machines will be scrapped and become obsolete.

Aside: Price Falling over Time?

You might be thinking that prices do not fall, they rise, as time goes by. Of course this is usually true in nominal terms. The price of a light bulb is definitely higher today than 10 years ago and much higher than 100 years ago.

But in this application, the correct price to consider is the real price, in terms of actual input use. In real terms, the price of lighting is incredibly lower today. Figure 2.3.3.11, created by William Nordhaus, tells an amazing story. In terms of the number of hours of work needed to buy 1,000 lumen hours, the price of light went from expensive for thousands of years to a freefall since the 1800s. In terms of input use, as technology improves, costs and, therefore, price of the output fall over time.

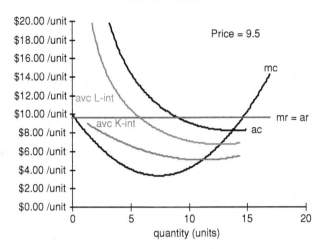

Figure 2.3.3.12. Comparing diffusion in *L*- and *K*-intensive firms.
Source: DiffusionTechChange.xls!Data

Nordhaus argues that "price indexes can capture the small, run-of-the-mill changes in economic activity, but revolutionary jumps in technology are simply ignored by the indexes" (Bresnahan and Gordon, eds., 1997, p. 55). Thus, the real price of lighting, in terms of the labor used, keeps falling and falling as time goes by.

Question 2: What Determines the Rate of Diffusion of Technical Change?

Obviously, the rate at which new technologies are developed is a crucial factor, but Salter's work pointed to an easily overlooked element: *the cost structure of the firms in an industry.*

Step Proceed to the *Output* sheet. The opening situation is depicted in Figure 2.3.3.12. The graph shows two firms, one that is labor intensive and the other capital intensive. They both have the same average and marginal costs, but the capital intensive firm has a larger gap between *ATC* and *AVC* because it has higher fixed (capital) costs.

Both firms are making the same output (because *MC* is the same) and the same profits (because average costs are the same).

Step Use the scroll bar to decrease the price of the product. As price falls, profits are lowered and eventually eliminated. As you continue to lower the price (as new methods of production continually shift down the cost curves of brand new plants and competition leads to lower prices), eventually, prices will fall below the *AVC* of the *L*-intensive firm, but remain above the *AVC* of the *K*-intensive firm. At *P* = $6/unit, for example, the labor intensive firm will shut down and this technology will become obsolete. The capital intensive firm, however, will continue using its outmoded technology because price remains above its *AVC*.

As the price falls from the competition of newer technologies, the labor intensive methods will disappear much faster than the heavily *K* dependent industries. Thus, we would expect steel plants to remain online long after the factories have ceased to generate economic profits.

A second factor in this story is the speed at which price falls. If the government protects an industry from foreign competition, preventing price from falling, the rate of diffusion of new technology and growth of labor productivity are retarded.

We are ready to answer the second question: What determines the rate of diffusion of technical change?

The rate of diffusion of technical change depends on three factors:

1. New ideas and innovations from research and development (R&D): This is the inventiveness of the society.
2. The cost structure of the firm: Capital intensive industry retards diffusion of new technology.
3. The speed at which price falls: If it is slow, we get slow diffusion.

The first factor is the obvious one that everyone thinks of when explaining why technology affects labor productivity and economic growth. But Salter identified another crucial factor: Even if new technology exists, it will be mixed with existing technology and the rate at which it is adopted will depend on the Shutdown Rule.

Highly *K*-intensive industries will feel the drag of old technology for a long time because the gap between *ATC* and *AVC* will be great. Steel is an obvious example of this.

In addition to the gap between *ATC* and *AVC*, the movement in price also plays an important role. If the steel industry is protected by tariffs and quotas, price will not fall as rapidly and the rate of diffusion of new technology will be slowed. Although economists usually defend free trade policies on the basis of comparative advantage, this analysis points to another reason for allowing foreign competition in domestic markets.

It Is Diffusion, not Discovery, that Really Matters

Wilfred Edward Graham Salter was an Australian economist born in 1929. He passed away in 1963 after battling heart disease. See <www.adb.online .anu.edu.au/biogs/A160198b.htm>. His dissertation, finished in 1960, was published by Cambridge University Press as *Productivity and Technical Change* and was met with wide acclaim.

Salter focused on the amazing ability of markets to generate new technology and improve output per person. He realized that scientific knowledge, technology "on the shelf," is not the sole reason behind rapid growth. The technology has to be implemented, actually used in production, and the faster it is adopted, the faster the economy grows.

Salter's work goes well beyond the idea that firms will keep old technology online as long as $P > AVC$, but this is a key point. If the $ATC - AVC$ gap is huge, meaning the firm produces with a great deal of fixed capital, this firm will continue producing for years and years. At first, it will be a best-practice plant, but as the years roll by, it will drag down labor productivity because it will remain online.

Exercises

Open Word and answer the following questions. Save the document and print it when you are done.

1. Sometimes a best-practice investment is quickly leapfrogged by newer technology. Google "fiber optic overinvestment" to see an example. Briefly describe what happened and cite the web sources used.
2. Automobile emissions requirements are stricter in Japan than in the United States (where many areas have no vehicle inspection at all). In both countries, newer cars pass inspection (if required) easily, but older cars are more likely to fail inspection and be removed from the operating car fleet. Draw hypothetical Salter Graphs, with emissions on the *y* axis, for the car fleets of Japan and the United States that reflect the stricter emissions standards in Japan.
3. What happens to a late model year Toyota or Honda that has failed an emissions inspection in Japan and, therefore, cannot be used there? Google "japan used engines" to find out. What effect does this have on the U.S. Salter Graph that you drew earlier?
4. The National Highway and Traffic Safety Administration maintains a database of car characteristics by model year. For miles per gallon (MPG) performance, they show the following:

NEW PASSENGER CAR FLEET AVERAGE CHARACTERISTICS																												
MODEL YEAR	1977	1978	1979	1980	1981	1982	1983	1984	1985	1986	1987	1988	1989	1990	1991	1992	1993	1994	1995	1996	1997	1998	1999	2000	2001	2002	2003	2004
FUEL ECONOMY STANDARD, MPG	N/A	18.0	19.0	20.0	22.0	24.0	26.0	27.0	27.5	26.0	26.0	26.0	26.5	27.5	27.5	27.5	27.5	27.5	27.5	27.5	27.5	27.5	27.5	27.5	27.5	27.5	27.5	27.5

Source: <www.nhtsa.gov/cars/rules/CAFE/NewPassengerCarFleet.htm>

These data cannot be used to show a Salter Graph (with MPG on *y* axis) of the U.S. car fleet. Why not? What additional information is needed?

References

The epigraph is from page 183 of Jared Diamond, *Guns, Germs, and Steel: The Fates of Human Societies* (originally published in 1997). Diamond argues that geography determines historical development. It is not the people, but fortunate geographical circumstances that guaranteed that western Eurasian societies would become disproportionately powerful. It is geography that enabled the rapid diffusion of technology and knowledge. Diamond, like Salter, is concerned with a point that is easily missed – diffusion is more important than discovery. The video version, available at <www.pbs.org/gunsgermssteel>, is also recommended.

The primary source for the application in this chapter is W. E. G. Salter, *Productivity and Technical Change* (Cambridge: Cambridge University Press; 1st edition, 1960; 2nd edition, 1966; 1st paperback edition, 1969).

For more on technological change and the spread of new ideas, see Timothy F. Bresnahan and Robert J. Gordon, *The Economics of New Goods* (Chicago: The University of Chicago Press), 1997 and David Warsh, *Knowledge and the Wealth of Nations: A Story of Economic Discovery* (New York: W. W. Norton & Company), 2006.

Richard Preston's *American Steel* (1991) tells the story of a mini-mill in rural Indiana that uses German cold-casting technology. It is an entertaining tale of entrepreneurship – a billion dollar gamble – and an introduction to the exciting world of business management.

2.4
Input Profit Maximization

2.4.1

Initial Solution for Input Profit Maximization

Most would agree that the excess of a college player's marginal revenue product over actual in-kind payment stays in the athletic department. But "talent collectors" also receive some of that value.

The Sports Economist Blog

Recall that the firm's backbone is the production function, shown in Figure 2.4.1.1.

Inputs, or factors of production, are used to make output, or product.

Market structure is an important element of the firm's optimization problem. The extremes are perfect competition and monopoly. A PC firm takes price as given and there is free entry, whereas a monopolist can choose P and enjoys a barrier to entry.

The Theory of the Firm is actually a group of three different optimization problems. Each one has its own interesting comparative statics analysis.

Input Cost Min: Choose inputs to minimize cost of a given output level
                        Key comparative statics: Cost function
Output Profit Max: Choose output to maximize profits
                        Key comparative statics: Supply curve
Input Profit Max: Choose inputs to maximize profit
                        Key comparative statics: Demand for an input

We have explored the first two optimization problems and seen how the cost function derived from the input cost minimization problem is used in the output side profit maximization problem.

Before we set up and find the initial solution for the input profit max problem, we need to discuss the market structure for each input. The firm has the same price-taking versus market power issue in hiring inputs. If the firm is a small buyer of inputs with many other buyers, it is an input price taker. It

Inputs ⟶ 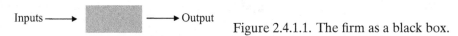 ⟶ Output   Figure 2.4.1.1. The firm as a black box.

only chooses the amount of input to hire, not how much to pay each unit. If it is a big buyer, then the firm not only determines how much to hire but also gets to choose the input price. In this case, we say the firm has *monopsony* power.

A perfectly competitive firm is an output and input price taker. It can hire as much L and K as it wants at the market wage and rental price of capital.

Setting Up the Problem

1. Goal: Maximize profits (π), which equal total revenues minus total costs. To distinguish the input from the output side, we use the terms *total revenue product* (*TRP*) and *total factor cost* (*TFacC*). The idea is that labor and capital are used to make product that is sold so price times the number of units produced is the *TRP*.
2. Endogenous variables: labor (L) and capital (K), in the long run; only L in the short run
3. Exogenous variables: price (of the product), input prices (the wage rate and the rental rate of capital), and technology (parameters in the production function).

As usual, we will start with a Cobb-Douglas production function.

The optimization problem is usually cast as an unconstrained problem because the firm can choose any level of inputs to hire from zero to any positive number.

You can, however, model it as a constrained problem, in which the production function serves as the constraint.

Finding the Initial Solution

The profit function on the input side is formed by subtracting costs from revenues.

Revenues are the output price (P) multiplied by the output produced (q). In the unconstrained version of the problem, we substitute the production function for output produced in order to get total revenue product, $PAK^{\alpha}L^{\beta}$, the units of which are dollars (just like total revenue). Revenue product indicates that we are considering the revenue produced by the input.

Exogenous variables		
Price (P)	$	2.00 $/loaf of bread
Wage (W)	$	20.00 $/hr
Rental (R)	$	50.00 $/machine
alpha		0.20
beta		0.75
technology (A)		30
Prod Fn (q)		19,086 loaves of bread

Endogenous Variables	
Labor (L)	1,431 hours
Capital (K)	153 machines

Goal		
Profit (π)	$	1,908.55 dollars
Revenue	$	38,171 dollars
Cost	$	36,262 dollars

Calculating Distribution of Revenues

	Dollar Payments	Percentage of Total
Labor Share	$ 28,628	75%
Capital Share	$ 7,634	20%
Profit Share	$ 1,909	5%

Figure 2.4.1.2. The initial optimal solution.
Source: [InputProfitMax.xls]!TwoVar

The costs are simply labor and capital costs, $wL + rK$.

First the problem is solved using Excel, and then the analytical approach is used.

Step Open the Excel workbook InputProfitMax.xls and read the *Intro* sheet, then go to the *TwoVar* sheet to find the initial solution for long-run profit maximization (when both inputs are freely variable).

As usual, the sheet is organized into the components of an optimization problem, with goal, endogenous, and exogenous cells.

Notice that the firm is using a Cobb-Douglas technology and it chooses L and K to maximize profits.

On open, the sheet has 500 hours of labor hired and 100 units of capital rented, yielding a profit of $936. Is this the best this firm can do? Cells B48 and B49 show the marginal revenue product of labor and marginal factor cost. By hiring one more hour of labor, revenues would rise by more than costs, so profits would increase. Clearly, therefore, this firm is not optimizing.

Step Run Solver to find the initial solution. Your screen should look like Figure 2.4.1.2.

We can also solve this problem via the analytical approach. First, we form the objective function:

$$\max_{L,K} \pi = PAK^\alpha L^\beta - wL - rK$$

Substitute in the exogenous variable values from the *TwoVar* sheet (and Figure 2.4.1.2) to make it a concrete problem:

$$\max_{L,K} \pi = 2 \cdot 30\, K^{0.2} L^{0.75} - 20L - 50K$$

Take derivatives with respect to L and K, then use algebra to find L^*, K^*, and π^*.

$$\frac{\partial \pi}{\partial L} = 0.75 \cdot 2 \cdot 30\, K^{0.2} L^{-0.25} - 20 = 0$$

$$\frac{\partial \pi}{\partial K} = 0.2 \cdot 2 \cdot 30\, K^{-0.8} L^{0.75} - 50 = 0$$

These first-order conditions show that, at the optimal solution, for every input, the optimal amount of the input can be found where marginal revenue product equals the input price. In other words, we can find L^* where $MRP_L = w$ and K^* where $MRP_K = r$.

The MRP_L is the additional revenue generated by hiring more labor and MFC is the additional cost. If $MRP_L > MFC$ (as it was before you ran Solver and found the optimal solution), the firm can increase its profits by hiring more labor. It should continue doing so until $MRP_L = MFC$. This is what the two first-order conditions require. You can confirm that the equimarginal condition for labor is met at Solver's optimal solution by taking a look at cells B48 and B49.

Setting the derivatives of the profit function with respect to L and K equal to zero gives two equations that the optimal solution must satisfy, but it does not directly yield L^* and K^*. The two equation, two unknown system must be solved. The most straightforward approach is via substitution.

Solve the first equation for L.

$$45K^{0.2} L^{-0.25} = 20$$

$$2.25 K^{0.2} = L^{0.25}$$

$$\left[2.25 K^{0.2} = L^{0.25}\right]^4$$

$$L = 2.25^4 K^{0.8}$$

Substitute this expression into the second equation and solve for K.

$$0.2 \cdot 2 \cdot 30\, K^{-0.8} \left[2.25^4 K^{0.8}\right]^{0.75} = 50$$

$$12 K^{-0.8} 2.25^3 K^{0.6} = 50$$

$$K^{-0.2} = 0.365798$$

$$K^* = 152.6842$$

Compute optimal labor use.

$$L = 2.25^4[152.6842]^{0.8}$$
$$L^* = 1431.414$$

Compute maximum profits.

$$\pi^* = 2 \cdot 30 \cdot 0[152.6842]^{0.2}[1431.414]^{0.75} - 20[1431.414] - 50[152.6842]$$
$$\pi^* = \$1908.552$$

This solution is quite close to Excel's solution. Practically speaking, the two solutions are the same.

In addition to the optimal solution, we can compute *factor shares* – the payments received by each input – and the profits (a residual) made by the firm:

- Labor share: wL
- Capital share: rK
- Profit: $PQ - wL - rK$.

Figure 2.4.1.2 shows that, at the optimal solution, factor shares as a percentage of total revenue equal each input's exponent in the production function. This is not a coincidence, but a property of the Cobb-Douglas functional form.

The Short Run

By putting a bar over K, we highlight that capital is fixed.

$$\max_{L} \pi = PA\bar{K}^{\alpha} L^{\beta} - wL - r\bar{K}$$

The analytical solution is easy so it is presented first, in general form. There is only one derivative and we can solve for the optimal labor use with a little algebra.

$$\frac{\partial \pi}{\partial L} = \beta PA\bar{K}^{\alpha} L^{\beta-1} - w = 0$$
$$\beta PA\bar{K}^{\alpha} L^{\beta-1} = w$$
$$L^{\beta-1} = \frac{w}{\beta PA\bar{K}^{\alpha}}$$
$$L^* = \left[\frac{w}{\beta PA\bar{K}^{\alpha}}\right]^{\frac{1}{\beta-1}}$$

Step To see the numerical version of this problem, proceed to the *OneVar* sheet.

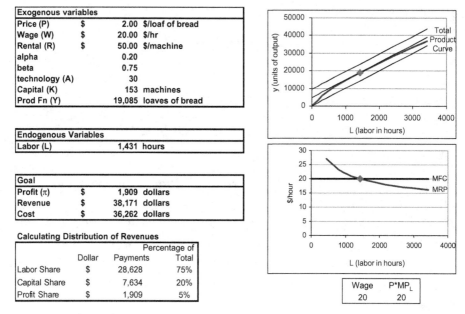

Exogenous variables		
Price (P)	$	2.00 $/loaf of bread
Wage (W)	$	20.00 $/hr
Rental (R)	$	50.00 $/machine
alpha		0.20
beta		0.75
technology (A)		30
Capital (K)		153 machines
Prod Fn (Y)		19,085 loaves of bread

Endogenous Variables	
Labor (L)	1,431 hours

Goal		
Profit (π)	$	1,909 dollars
Revenue	$	38,171 dollars
Cost	$	36,262 dollars

Calculating Distribution of Revenues

	Dollar	Payments	Percentage of Total
Labor Share	$	28,628	75%
Capital Share	$	7,634	20%
Profit Share	$	1,909	5%

Wage	P*MP$_L$
20	20

Figure 2.4.1.3. The initial optimal solution in the short run.
Source: [InputProfitMax.xls]!OneVar

Notice that there is only one endogenous variable, L. Capital has been moved to the exogenous list because we are in the short run.

Notice also that there are two graphs. Each one can be used to represent the initial solution.

Below the graph, you can see that the marginal revenue product of labor does not equal the wage. As you know, this means you need to run Solver because the firm is not optimizing.

Step Run Solver to find the initial solution. Your screen should look like Figure 2.4.1.3.

The bottom graph on your screen (and in Figure 2.4.1.3) shows that the optimal labor use can be found where the marginal revenue product of labor (the curve) equals the wage (at $20/hr). This is the canonical graph for the input side profit maximization problem. The top graph is a different way of viewing the exact same problem. It is using the production function as a constraint (the curve is the total product of labor) and the straight lines are "isoprofit" lines. In other words, the problem is viewed as a constrained optimization problem:

$$\max_{L} \pi = Pq - wL - r\bar{K}$$
$$\text{s.t.} \ q = A\bar{K}^{\alpha} L^{\beta}$$

Naturally, the exact same solution is obtained whether we use the unconstrained or constrained versions of the input side profit maximization problem.

Another Short-Run Production Function

Step Proceed to the *Graphs* sheet to see a set of four graphs that can be used to represent the firm's input profit maximization problem.

The first thing to notice is that these graphs mirror the four graphs we used to describe the firm's output side profit maximization problem. The two top graphs show total revenue and total cost on the top left, along with total profits on the top right. The bottom graphs display a series of marginal and average curves on the bottom left and marginal profit on the bottom right.

If you look carefully, you will notice that things are switched around a bit. Instead of total cost being a curve (as it is in the output side), it is a straight line because total cost on the input side is $wL + r\bar{K}$. On the other hand, total revenue product (so named to distinguish it from total revenue on the output side) is a curve (instead of a straight line).

Unlike the canonical output side profit maximization graph (with U-shaped MC, ATC, and AVC curves and a horizontal $P = MR$ line), most presentations of the input side profit maximization solution show only wage and MRP. There are, however, average revenue product and average cost curves that can be used to compute profit as a profit rectangle (just like in the output side).

The length of the profit rectangle ranges from zero to the chosen amount of labor hired. The height is the difference between average revenue product, ARP_L, and average factor cost, AFC. The area of this rectangle is profit because $ARP_L - AFC$ is profit per hour so multiplying by L, measured in hours, yields profits. Another way to think about this is that multiplying L by ARP_L (which is TRP/L) yields total revenues and multiplying L by AFC (which is $TFacC/L$) gives total costs. Subtracting the total cost rectangle from the total revenue rectangle leaves the profit rectangle.

Step Use the pull down menu to change the firm's output price and place the firm in any of the four profit positions. Select "Neg Profits, Shutdown" option to see that the firm will shut down when the $w > ARP_L$. This is analogous to the $P < AVC$ Shutdown Rule.

The firm shuts down when the wage is greater than the average revenue product because such a situation means that variable costs are greater than revenues. By hiring labor, the firm has variable cost of w times L. Its total revenue is ARP_L times L. If $w > ARP_L$, then multiplying by L reveals that

$wL > ARP_L L$, which means that variable costs are greater than revenues. In this case, the firm is better off not producing at all and suffering negative profits equal to its fixed costs. After all, the minute it opens its doors, produces output, and sells it, it suffers even bigger negative profits.

Step Compare the two negative profit positions to confirm that the firm will continue production in the face of negative profits as long as it can cover its variable costs (wL) and eat into some of its fixed costs ($r\bar{K}$).

Input Profit Maximization Highlights

Like every optimization problem, the input side profit maximization problem can be organized into a goal, endogenous, and exogenous variables. This problem has a canonical graph (with w and MRP_L as the key elements) and an equimarginal rule (derived from the first-order conditions), $w = MRP_L$.

Because the input profit maximization problem is the flip side of the output side profit maximization problem, it should not be surprising that we can represent the initial solution with a set of four graphs. The parallelism carries through all the way to the Shutdown Rule, where $w > ARP_L$ is equivalent to $P < AVC$.

Exercises

Open Word and answer the following questions. Save the document and print it when you are done.

1. Use the *TwoVar* sheet to compute the long-run beta elasticity of L^* from beta = 0.75 to beta = 0.74. Show your work.
2. In the *Q&A* sheet, question 4 asks you to find short-run beta elasticity of L^* from beta = 0.75 to beta = 0.74. The InputProfitMaxA.doc file in the Answers folder shows that the answer is about 28. Explain why the short-run elasticity (which is admittedly quite large) is much smaller than the long-run elasticity that you computed in the previous question.
3. Use Excel to set up and solve (with Solver, of course) the constrained version of the input profit maximization problem in the *OneVar* sheet. Take a screenshot of your solution (including the constraint cell) and paste it in your Word document.
4. In the *Graphs* sheet, select the "Neg Profits, Shutdown" case. Does the top, right graph support the $w > ARP_L$ Shutdown Rule? Explain.

References

The epigraph, from <thesporteconomist.com/2007/02/rents-accrue-rents-get-collected.htm>, points to two avenues for further reading: sports economics and blogs.

The worlds of economics and sports are increasingly intertwined. There are courses, conferences, and journals dedicated to the economics of sports. For a classic paper on baseball, see Simon Rottenberg's "The Baseball Players' Labor Market," *The Journal of Political Economy*, Vol. 64, No. 3 (June, 1956), pp. 242–258.

There are, of course, many blogs dedicated to economics. The Marginal Revolution and Café Hayek are often fun and interesting. For macroeconomics and contemporary policy issues, see Greg Mankiw's and Brad DeLong's blogs. Google "economics blogs" for many more.

2.4.2

Deriving Demand for Labor

To be sure, we are living in a dessert age. We want things to be sweet; too many of us work to live and live to be happy. Nothing wrong with that; it just does not promote high productivity. You want high productivity? Then you should live to work and get happiness as a by-product.

David S. Landes

A profit-maximizing firm with Cobb-Douglas technology and given prices in all markets (P, w, and r) in the short run can be modeled as solving the following optimization problem:

$$\max_{L} \pi = PA\bar{K}^{\alpha}L^{\beta} - wL - r\bar{K}$$

How will this firm respond to a change in one of its exogenous variables, ceteris paribus?

Although there are several exogenous variables from which to choose, we are often interested in the responsiveness of L^* to a change in the wage. This comparative statics analysis will give us the short-run demand for labor.

We can relax the assumption of fixed capital to derive the long-run demand for labor.

We apply numerical and analytical methods.

Demand for Labor in the Short Run

Step Open the Excel workbook DerivingDemandL.xls and read the *Intro* sheet, then go to the *OneVar* sheet.

Step Change the wage in the *OneVar* sheet to $19/hr from the initial value of $20/hr.

It is difficult to see anything in the top graph, but the bottom graph clearly shows that the red diamond (at $L = 1431$ hours) has a marginal revenue product greater than the marginal factor cost (equal to the wage). Cells H40

366

and I40 show that the wage is less than P^*MP_L (which is marginal revenue product).

In other words, when the wage falls to \$19/hr, the initial solution of 1431 hours is no longer the profit-maximizing amount of labor. We need to find the new optimal solution.

Step Run Solver.

To maximize profits, the firm will hire 1757 hours when the wage falls to \$19/hr, ceteris paribus. At this level of labor use, the marginal revenue product once again equals the marginal factor cost.

Although we have only two data points, it should be clear that the firm will hire that amount of labor where the marginal revenue product equals the wage. This means that the marginal revenue product curve is the firm's (inverse) demand for labor curve. Quote the firm a wage and it will look to its MRP_L curve to decide how much labor to hire.

We have two points on the demand for labor curve; at $w = \$20/\text{hr}$, $L^* = 1431$ hours and at $w = \$19/\text{hr}$, $L^* = 1757$ hours. Can we pick more points off of the demand for labor curve?

Step Use the Comparative Statics Wizard to derive the demand for labor. Set the initial wage back to \$20/hr and apply \$1/hr decreases in the wage.

Step Create charts of the demand for labor and the inverse demand for labor.

Your results should look like those in the *CS1* sheet.

The demand for labor can also be derived via analytical methods by solving for L^* as a function of w.

$$\max_{L} \pi = PA\bar{K}^{\alpha} L^{\beta} - wL - r\bar{K}$$

We can find the solution for the general case or substitute in exogenous values – except for w, given that we want L^* as a function of w. We take the derivative of profits with respect to labor, set the derivative equal to zero, and solve for L^*.

$$\frac{\partial \pi}{\partial L} = \beta PA\bar{K}^{\alpha} L^{\beta-1} - w = 0$$

$$\beta PA\bar{K}^{\alpha} L^{\beta-1} = w$$

$$L^{\beta-1} = \frac{w}{\beta PA\bar{K}^{\alpha}}$$

$$L^* = \left[\frac{w}{\beta PA\bar{K}^{\alpha}} \right]^{\frac{1}{\beta-1}}$$

This expression is the demand curve for labor. If we substitute in values for all exogenous variables except w, we can plot L^* as a function of w.

We can compare the numerical and analytical methods.

Step Proceed to the *CS1* sheet. Click on cell C16. This is Solver's answer for L^* when the wage is $20/hr.

Do not be misled by all of the decimal places. That is false precision.

Step Look at cell E26. It represents L^* when the wage is $20/hr based on the reduced-form solution.

Do not be misled by the number displayed in cell E26. This is Excel's display for the formula entered into that cell.

Step Widen column E to see that Excel can display more decimal places.

We proceed slowly because things can get confusing here.
Consider this hierarchy of truth:

1. The exact right answer for L^* when $w = $20/hr is $\left[\frac{w}{\beta P A \bar{K}^\alpha}\right]^{\frac{1}{\beta-1}}$.
2. Excel is representing the exact right answer as a decimal in cell E26.
3. Solver is giving a number close to the exact right answer in cell C16.

Step To see that cell E26 is not the exact right answer, make column E really wide, select cell E26, and click the Increase Decimal ($\overset{+.0}{.00}$) button repeatedly. You will see that, eventually, Excel will start reporting zeroes. Excel has finite memory and, therefore, it cannot compute an infinite number of decimal places for the exact answer.

Thus, neither cell E26 nor cell C16 is the exact right answer. They are both close to the right answer and, in practical terms, they are both correct.

We can use the analytical approach to reinforce the idea that the short-run (inverse) demand for labor is the marginal revenue product of labor.

The first-order condition gives the equimarginal rule.

$$\frac{\partial \pi}{\partial L} = \beta P A \bar{K}^\alpha L^{\beta-1} - w = 0$$

$$\beta P A \bar{K}^\alpha L^{\beta-1} = w$$

$$MRP_L = w$$

Evaluating the $\beta P A \bar{K}^\alpha$ term at the initial values of the exogenous variables gives 123.0187 (as shown in cell K26 of the *CS1* sheet). Thus,

$$MRP_L = 123.0187 L^{\beta-1} = 123.0187 L^{-\frac{1}{4}}.$$

The *CS1* sheet has an inverse demand for labor chart. Is the relationship in this chart the same as the MRP_L function that we just found? Let's find out.

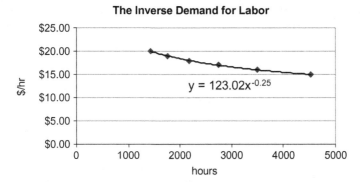

Figure 2.4.2.1. Finding the function for the inverse demand curve for labor.
Source: DerivingDemandforL!CS1

By finding the function that fits the data in the inverse demand for labor chart, we can compare this relationship to the MRP_L function.

Step Right-click on the series in the inverse demand for labor chart and select the Add Trendline option. Select the Power fit, click on the Options tab and check the "Display equation on chart" option. Click OK. Move the equation (if needed) and increase the font size to see it better. Your results should look like Figure 2.4.2.1.

The result is clear: The fitted curve that reveals the function for the inverse demand curve for labor is the marginal revenue product of labor curve.

With either the numerical or analytical result, we can find the wage elasticity of labor demand.

Elasticity at a point is based on the derivative of the reduced-form expression. We can use the Chain Rule.

$$L^* = \left[\frac{w}{123.0187}\right]^{-4}$$

$$\frac{\partial L}{\partial w} = -4\left[\frac{w}{123.0187}\right]^{-5} \frac{1}{123.0187} = -4\frac{w^{-5}}{123.0187^{-4}}$$

If we first rewrite the reduced form to separate out the constant, we get the same result.

$$L^* = \left[\frac{w}{123.0187}\right]^{-4} = \frac{w^{-4}}{123.0187^{-4}} = \frac{1}{123.0187^{-4}} w^{-4}$$

$$\frac{\partial L}{\partial w} = -4\frac{w^{-5}}{123.0187^{-4}}$$

This expression is merely the slope or rate of change of optimal labor hired as a function of the wage. To find the elasticity, we must multiply the derivative by the ratio w/L.

$$\frac{\partial L}{\partial w} \cdot \frac{w}{L} = -4 \frac{w^{-5}}{123.0187^{-4}} \cdot \frac{w}{\dfrac{w^{-4}}{123.0187^{-4}}} = -4$$

As usual, the Cobb-Douglas functional form is a computational breeze – everything cancels out and we get a constant wage elasticity of short-run labor demand.

Of course, if we compute the elasticity from one point to another, say from a wage of $20/hr to $21/hour, we will get a different answer than -4. As the change in the wage approaches zero, the elasticity computed from one point to another approaches -4.

This elasticity is rather large. This is a consequence of the use of the Cobb-Douglas production function and the value of β in this particular problem. We would not expect to find such a large wage elasticity of short-run labor demand in the real world.

Demand for Labor in the Long Run

If we relax the assumption that capital is fixed, we change the firm's planning horizon from short to long run.

The *TwoVar* sheet implements the firm's long-run input profit maximization problem. Notice that there are two endogenous variables, Labor and Capital, and no fixed factors of production.

Step To derive the firm's long-run demand for labor, use the Comparative Statics Wizard from the *TwoVar* sheet. As you did in the short-run analysis, apply $1 decreases in the wage.

Step Proceed to the *CSCompared* sheet to see a comparison of the short- and long-run demand for labor. The wage elasticities in the short and long run are highlighted. The difference is remarkable – the long-run elasticity is much higher.

Unlike your comparative statics analysis, the *CSCompared* sheet is based on $1 increases in the wage.

Step Use your results to compare the short- and long-run wage elasticity when the wage falls from $20/hr to $19/hr.

Once again, the long-run elasticity is much higher. What is going on?

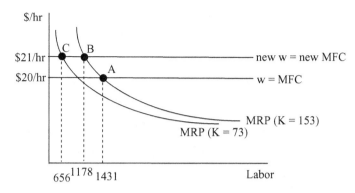

Figure 2.4.2.2. Why L^* is more responsive to Δw in the long run than in the short run.

Figure 2.4.2.2 provides an answer to this question. The movement from point A to B is the short-run response. As the short-run results in the *CSCompared* sheet show, when the wage rises from \$20/hr to \$21/hr, L^* falls from 1431 to 1178 hours.

In the short run, capital stays fixed and the firm moves along its marginal revenue product curve (which as we already know is the firm's short-run demand for labor) as the wage changes.

In the long run, however, the adjustment is different. The data in the *CSCompared* sheet show clearly that the firm will change both labor and capital as the wage rises. Notice that capital falls from 153 machines to 73 machines as the wage rises from \$20/hr to \$21/hr.

This change in capital shifts labor's marginal revenue product curve. As shown in Figure 2.4.2.2, the firm's long-run response to the change in the wage is from A to C, not simply A to B. This is the reason why the wage elasticity of labor demand is more responsive in the long run.

Figure 2.4.2.3 shows the firm's long-run demand for labor. The demand curve for labor is no longer the MRP_L curve. Because capital falls as wage

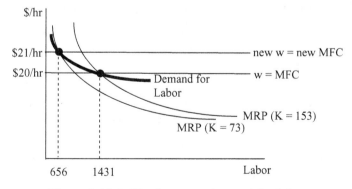

Figure 2.4.2.3. The long-run demand for labor.

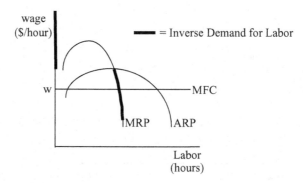

Figure 2.4.2.4. The complete inverse demand for labor curve.

rises, the firm is much more responsive to changes in the wage. It is clear that the inverse labor demand curve is flatter in the long run than the MRP_L curve (which is the short-run inverse demand for labor).

The Effect of the Shutdown Rule on the Demand Curve for Labor

On the output side, the supply curve is the MC curve when $P > AVC$. If $P < AVC$ where $MR = MC$, then the firm shuts down and $q^* = 0$. The supply curve has a tail where the quantity supplied is zero when the price falls below average variable cost.

There is a similar tail on the demand curve for labor. The previous chapter showed that if $w > ARP_L$, the firm will shut down. Let's review this concept.

Step Proceed to the *Graphs* sheet. Use the pull down menu to change the firm's output price and place the firm in any of the four profit positions. Select "Neg Profits, Shutdown" to see that the firm will shut down when the $w > ARP_L$. This is analogous to the $P < AVC$ Shutdown Rule.

The Shutdown Rule means that we have to change our definition of the demand curve for labor to get it exactly right. In the short run, the inverse demand curve is the MRP_L curve, as long as $w > ARP_L$; otherwise it is zero, as shown in Figure 2.4.2.4.

The Shutdown Rule is usually presented from the output side as $P < AVC$. This version of the rule is perfectly compatible with the input side version of the shutdown rule, $w > ARP_L$. Remember that as wage rises, cost curves on the output side shift up. At the precise point at which a higher wage triggers the decision to not hire any labor, AVC will have inched above P and the firm will decide to not produce any output.

The Shutdown Rule can also be applied via decreases in P. On the output side, this is easy: When the horizontal price line falls below AVC, the firm shuts down. What is happening on the input side?

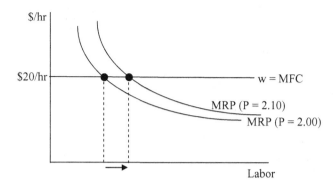

Figure 2.4.2.5. Changing the product price.

As output price falls, the *MRP* and *ARP* curves in Figure 2.4.2.4 shift down. At the precise moment when *P* falls below *AVC* and the firm decides to produce no output, the *ARP* will fall below the horizontal wage line and the firm will decide to hire no labor.

More Comparative Statics

Change *P*, ceteris paribus. How does the firm react? There are short-run and long-run responses. We consider the short run here and leave the long run for an exercise.

Step Return to the *OneVar* sheet. Return the wage to $20/hr. Run Solver.

Step Change the price of bread from $2.00 to $2.10/loaf. Undo the change (CTRL-z). Redo the change (CTRL-y). Toggle back and forth from $2.00 to $2.10 and keep your eye on the charts.

What happens in the two graphs that show the optimal solution as you change the price?

We focus on the bottom graph. From our analytical work, we know that $MRP_L = \beta P A \bar{K}^\alpha L^{\beta-1}$ so it is obvious that an increase in *P* will shift the MRP_L curve up.

Step With $P = \$2.10$/loaf, run Solver. What happens to L^*?

The effect on labor hired from an increase in product price is obvious: L^* rises as *P* rises.

Figure 2.4.2.5 shows what happens as you increase the product price. The MRP_L curve shifts and a new solution is found where the new $MRP_L = w$.

Because the optimal input use depends on the product price, we say that input demands are *derived demands* – derived from the price in the output market. If the demand for a firm's output is high, the price will be high, and this will induce an increased demand (rightward shift) for labor.

It is easy to see that labor is a derived demand by considering professional sports. Pro athletes in major sports make a lot of money because the price of the good they produce (including TV revenue) is very high. The output side is most definitely reflected in the input side via the product price.

Marginal Productivity Theory of Distribution

In addition to determining the optimal rates of input use, the input side profit maximization problem also explains the distribution of the firm's revenues. The basic idea is that shares are a function of an input's productivity: The more productive the input, the greater its share.

Step From the *TwoVar* sheet, run a comparative statics experiment that changes the exponent on labor from 0.75 to 0.755 (5 shocks of 0.001). In the endogenous variables input box, be sure to track not only L and K, but also the shares received in cells C44:C46.

Step Check your results with the *CS3* sheet.

By increasing the exponent on labor in the Cobb-Douglas production function, labor's productivity rises. In other words, labor can make more output, ceteris paribus, as the exponent on labor increases. The firm maximizes profit by using more labor and labor's share of firm revenues rises.

It is (yet another) convenient property of the Cobb-Douglas functional form that we can immediately determine the percentage share of revenues gained by each input by the input's exponent in the production function. Although a different production function may not have this simple shortcut to determine the percentage share of revenues accruing to each input, it remains true that an input's share will depend on its marginal productivity.

Whereas algebraic convenience and simplicity are often invoked as a rationale for utilizing the Cobb-Douglas functional form, in the case of factor shares, a strong empirical regularity supports the use of $AK^\alpha L^\beta$. About 2/3 of national income goes to labor and 1/3 to capital. "In fact, the long-term stability of factor shares has become enshrined as one of the "stylized facts" of growth" (Gollin, 2002, pp. 458–459).

Labor Demand Highlights

The most important comparative statics exercise on the input side is to derive the demand for inputs. This chapter focused on labor demand and showed that the short-run demand for labor is the marginal revenue product of labor curve. In the long run, however, the demand for labor is not the MRP_L curve because K^* changes as w changes. For this same reason, labor demand is more responsive to changes in the wage in the long run.

Whether in the long or short run, the demand curve for labor is subject to the same Shutdown Rule qualification as the supply curve for output. If the wage is higher than the ARP at the point at which $MRP = MFC$, the firm will hire no labor. This coincides perfectly with the firm's decision to shut down on the output side, producing no output.

In addition to changes in the wage, this chapter explored the effects of a change in product price. As P increases, L^* rises. In terms of the graph, an increase in P shifts the MRP_L and leads to a new optimal solution. We say that labor demand is a derived demand because the price of the product influences labor demand.

The chapter ended by pointing out that an input's productivity determines its share of firm revenues. As productivity rises, so does the percentage share accruing to that input. Productivity is a key variable in determining input use and distribution of revenues.

Exercises

Open Word and answer the following questions. Save the document and print it when you are done.

1. Derive the wage elasticity of short-run labor demand for the general case where $L^* = \left[\frac{w}{\beta PA K^\alpha}\right]^{\frac{1}{\beta-1}}$. Show your work, using Word's Equation Editor.
2. Does your result from the previous question agree with the -4 value obtained in the text?
3. Use the Comparative Statics Wizard to analyze the effect of an increase in the product price in the long run. Compute the P elasticity of L^* from $P = 2.00$ to $P = 2.10$. Copy and paste your results in your Word document.
4. Is L^* more responsive to changes in P in the short run or long run? Explain why.

References

The epigraph is from page 523 of David S. Landes, *The Wealth and Poverty of Nations: Why Some are So Rich and Some So Poor* (paperback edition, 1999; originally published, 1998). Landes is an economic historian interested in economic development. He asks really difficult, fascinating questions: "How and why did we get where we are? How did the rich countries get so rich? Why are the poor countries so poor? Why did Europe ('the West') take the lead in changing the world?" (p. xxi). His answers are opinionated and clear.

The idea that a profit-maximizing firm will use and reward factors according to productivity has a normative or ethical dimension. John Bates Clark, an American economist, argued in *The Distribution of Wealth* (1899) that the equimarginal principle was not only efficient, but also fair. Paying factors according to productivity showed that capitalism was just. For more modern reading on

morality or ethics in economics, from one end of the spectrum to the other, see
Robert Nozick, *Anarchy, State, and Utopia* (1974) and John Rawls, *A Theory of
Justice* (1971).

You are undoubtedly familiar with the Nobel Prize in Economic Sciences, but the
John Bates Clark Medal is given every two years "to that American economist
under the age of forty who is adjudged to have made the most significant
contribution to economic thought and knowledge." See <www.vanderbilt.edu/
AEA/clark_medal.htm> for a complete list of winners – you will immediately
notice that it is peppered with Nobel Prize winners.

In his paper reconciling time series and cross section data, Douglas Gollin,
"Getting Income Shares Right," *The Journal of Political Economy*, Vol. 110, No. 2
(April, 2002), pp. 458–474, points out that Cobb and Douglas "were among the
earliest authors to point out that, for the United States, the labor share of income
appeared to be roughly constant over time, regardless of changes in factor prices"
(pp. 460–461).

2.5

Consistency in the Theory of the Firm

2.5.1

Consistency in the Theory of the Firm

[That long-run responses are more elastic than short run responses] is commonly believed to be empirically true, simply as a matter of assertion. It is interesting and noteworthy that this type of behavior is in fact mathematically implied by a maximization hypothesis.

Eugene Silberberg

We have considered three separate optimization problems in our study of the perfectly competitive firm.

Figures 2.5.1.1, 2.5.1.2, and 2.5.1.3 provide a snapshot of the initial solution and the key comparative statics analysis from each of the three optimization problems.

Key Idea

These three problems are tightly integrated and are actually different views of the same firm and same optimal solution. Change an exogenous variable and all three optimization problems are affected. The new optimal solutions and comparative statics results are *consistent* – i.e., they tell you the same thing and are never contradictory.

The idea of consistency in the Theory of the Firm can be demonstrated by example.

Perfect Competition in the Long Run

Step Open the Excel workbook Consistency.xls and read the *Intro* sheet; then proceed to the *TheoryoftheFirmLongRun* sheet. Use the Zoom In button to fill your screen with graphs.

Figure 2.5.1.4 displays what is on your screen.

Gray-backgrounded cells are dead (click on one to see that it has a number, not a formula) – they will serve as benchmarks for comparisons when we do comparative statics.

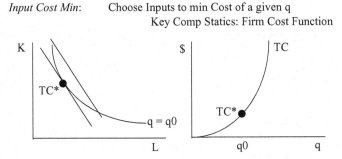

Figure 2.5.1.1. Initial solution and cost function from the Input Cost Min problem.

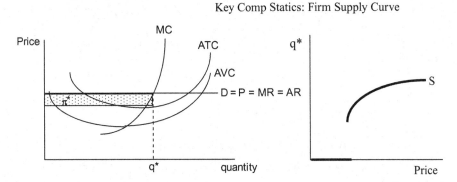

Figure 2.5.1.2. Initial solution with a supply curve.

The Output Profit Max graph (on the right) is not the usual U-shaped family of cost curves because the production function from which the cost curves are derived is Cobb-Douglas. This functional form cannot generate conventional U-shaped MC and AC curves. There is no separate AVC curve because we are in the long run, so $AC = AVC$.

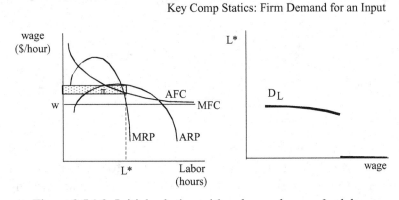

Figure 2.5.1.3. Initial solution with a demand curve for labor.

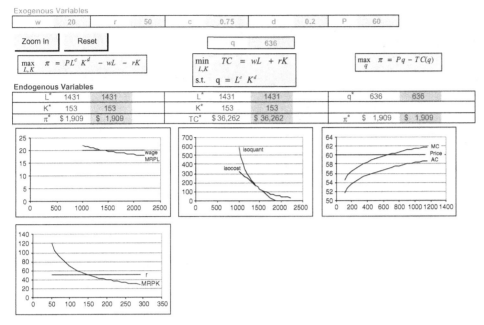

Figure 2.5.1.4. Initial solution in the long run.
Source: Consistency.xls! TheoryoftheFirmLongRun

When we speak of the Theory of the Firm, many students think of the output profit maximization graph (on the right in Figure 2.5.1.4). But the Theory of the Firm is really the set of three optimization problems and you need to understand that they are tightly integrated. Figure 2.5.1.4 is a strong visual presentation of the entire, or overall, Theory of the Firm.

Compare the initial solutions for each of the three problems. There are several ways in which they agree.

L^* and K^* are the same in the Input Profit Max and Input Cost Min graphs. If you use these amounts of L and K, you will produce 636 units of output, as shown in the Output Profit Max graph.

π^* is the same in the Input and Output Profit Max graphs. There is no profit in the Input Cost Min graph because there is no price and, therefore, no revenue in that optimization problem.

Step Find TC from each optimization problem and compare. Are they the same?

Total cost from each side is exactly the same. You can find TC from the Input Profit Max by creating a cell that computes $wL^* + rK^*$. This will equal \$36,262. From the Output Profit Max side, calculate TC by subtracting revenue, P^*q, from profit. Again, you get \$36,262.

A further demonstration of consistency uses comparative statics effects on each problem. As you would expect, the results are identical.

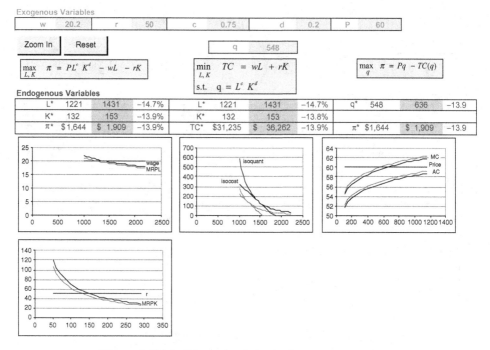

Figure 2.5.1.5. Wage shock in the long run.
Source: Consistency.xls! TheoryoftheFirmLongRun

Change the light-green-backgrounded exogenous variable cells in row 2 and follow the results in the graphs.

Step Wage increase of 1%. Change cell B2 to 20.2. Use the Zoom In button if needed to see more clearly how the graphs have changed.

Figure 2.5.1.5 shows the results of this shock.

On the Input Profit Max graph, we see that optimal labor use has fallen by 14.7% as wage rose by 1% (so the wage elasticity of labor from wage = $20/hr to $20.20/hr is −14.7). Labor demand collapsed because the horizontal wage line shifted up and because the MRP_L schedule shifted left. The latter effect is due to the fact that K^* fell.

On the Input Cost Min graph, we see that the firm is minimizing the cost of producing a lower level of output. In other words, we are on a new isoquant. Notice that the changes in L^* and K^* are consistent with the decreases reported from the Input Profit Max results.

The wage increase in the Output Profit Max graph is felt via the shifting up of the cost curves. The firm decreases q^* because MC shifted up and therefore the intersection of MR and MC occurs to the left of the initial solution.

Step Click the Reset button, and then implement a labor productivity increase to 0.751 by changing cell F2.

Figure 2.5.1.6 shows the dramatic results of this shock. Input use and output produced have increased by about 18% in response to this tiny change in *c*.

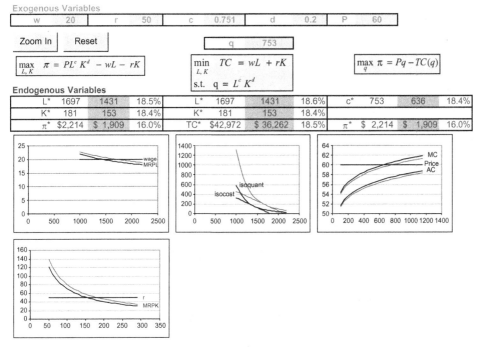

Figure 2.5.1.6. Labor productivity shock in the long run.
Source: Consistency.xls! TheoryoftheFirmLongRun

As before, comparison of the effects of the change in c on the three optimization problems shows consistency. The two input side problems show that input use is the same and the inputs used will make the desired output on the output side. Profits on the input and output sides are the same. The productivity increase has shifted *MRP* right and cost curves down.

We leave other shocks for Q&A and Exercise questions. Suffice it to say that shocks are felt throughout the three optimization problems and the results are always consistent.

Perfect Competition in the Short Run

Step Proceed to the *TheoryoftheFirmShortRun* sheet to explore the comparative statics properties of the firm in the short run.

Figure 2.5.1.7 shows the initial position.

This sheet has several differences, compared to the previous overall view of the firm in the long run.

- There is an extra exogenous variable, K, because we are in the short run. Its value is set to the long-run optimal solution for the given set of parameters.
- There is a missing graph in the Input Profit Max problem. With K fixed, we no longer need to depict its optimal solution.

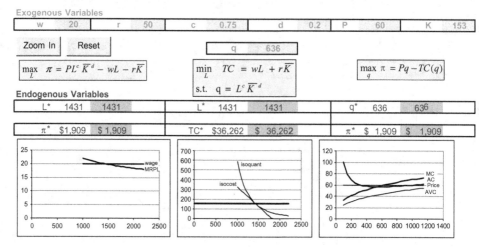

Figure 2.5.1.7. Initial solution in the short run.
Source: Consistency.xls! TheoryoftheFirmShortRun

- There is a straight, horizontal line in the isoquant side graph. With K fixed, the firm will not be able to roll around the isoquant to find the cost-minimizing input mix. It must use the given amount of K.
- There is an extra cost curve in the Output Profit Max. Having K fixed means there is a fixed cost so we now have separate average total and average variable costs.

Compare the initial solutions for each of the three problems. As we would expect, they agree in input use, output produced, and profits generated.

Change the light-green-backgrounded exogenous variable cells in row 2 and follow the results in the graphs.

Step Apply a wage increase of 1%. Change cell B2 to 20.2. Use the Zoom In button if needed to see more clearly how the graphs have changed.

Figure 2.5.1.8 shows the results of this shock.

The usual consistency properties are readily apparent. We observe the same change in L^*, q^*, and π^* across the board. Notice that the Input Profit Max problem does not show a shift in MRP_L because K is fixed.

If we compare the short (Figure 2.5.1.8) to the long run (Figure 2.5.1.5), we see that the responsiveness of the changes in endogenous variables is greater in the long run. Labor and output fall by more in the long run. Profits, however, fall by less in the long run.

Step Click the Reset button, then implement a labor productivity increase to 0.751 by changing cell F2.

Figure 2.5.1.9 displays the results.

As expected, Figure 2.5.1.9 shows consistency in the results and, once again, the long-run (Figure 2.5.1.6) changes in L and K are more responsive

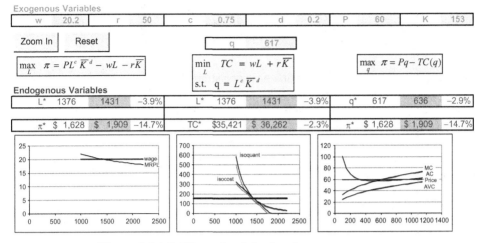

Figure 2.5.1.8. Wage shock in the short run.
Source: Consistency.xls! TheoryoftheFirmShortRun

than in the short run (Figure 2.5.1.9). The increase in profits is also higher in the long run.

Comparing Long- and Short-Run Results

When we compared the short- and long-run results for shocks in w and c, the long run exhibited greater responsiveness in labor and output. Is there a general principle at work?

Yes. The general principle is that long-run responses are always at least as or more elastic than in the short run. This is known as the *Le Chatelier Principle.*

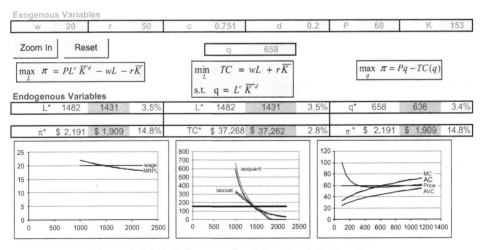

Figure 2.5.1.9. Labor productivity shock in the short run.
Source: Consistency.xls! TheoryoftheFirmShortRun

Le Chatelier's idea, which he originally applied to the concept of equilibrium in chemical reactions, was introduced to economics by Nobel laureate Paul Samuelson in 1947.

The Le Chatelier principle explains how a system that is in equilibrium will react to a perturbation. It predicts that the system will respond in a manner that will counteract the perturbation. Samuelson, following the methods of the hard sciences, has transported this principle of chemist Henri-Louis Le Chatelier to economics, to study the response of agents to price changes given some additional constraints. In his extension of this principle, Samuelson uses the metaphor of squeezing a balloon to further explain the concept. If you squeeze a balloon, its volume will decrease more if you keep its temperature constant than it will if you let the squeezing warm it up. This principle is now considered as a standard tool for comparative static analysis in economic theory. (Szenberg, et al., 2005, p. 51, footnote omitted)

In the context of the short- and long-run responses to shocks by a firm, the Le Chatelier Principle says that long-run effects are greater because there are fewer constraints.

When the wage rises, a firm in the short run is stuck with its given quantity of K. In the long run, however, it will be able to adjust both L and K and it is this additional freedom that guarantees at least as great or a greater response in input use and output produced.

For increasing c, the Le Chatelier Principle is reflected in the fact that labor demand is much more responsive in the long run than the short run. In the long run, the firm is able to take greater advantage of the labor productivity shock by renting more machines and hiring even more labor. This is, of course, reflected in the greater profits obtained in the long run in response to the increased c.

The Theory of the Firm *in toto*

Figures 2.5.1.1, 2.5.1.2, and 2.5.1.3 are fundamental graphs for the Theory of the Firm. They represent the three optimization problems that, in unison, comprise the theory.

The Input Cost Min (isoquants and isocosts that can be used derive the cost function), Output Profit Max (horizontal P with the family of cost curves that yield a supply curve), and Input Profit Max (horizontal w with MRP generating a demand curve for an input) are all intertwined. Not only do they all yield consistent answers for the initial solution, they all provide consistent comparative statics responses.

If we compare short- and long-run effects of shocks, we see that the firm responds more in the long run. The wage elasticity of labor is greater (in absolute value) in the long run and, via consistency, so is the wage elasticity of output. Similarly, the c elasticities of labor and output are also greater in the long run. This is an application of the Le Chatelier Principle: With fewer constraints, responsiveness increases.

The supply curve, the key comparative statics exercise on the Output Profit Max problem for a perfectly competitive firm, forms the foundation of future work on markets and how they function.

Exercises

Open Word and answer the following questions. Save the document and print it when you are done.

1. What happens in the long run when price increases by 1%? Implement the shock and take a picture of the results, then paste it in your Word document. Comment on the changes in optimal labor, capital, output, and profits.
2. Compute the long-run output price elasticity of labor demand. Show your work.
3. Apply the same 1% price increase in the short run. Take a picture of the results, then paste it in your Word document. Comment on the changes in optimal labor, capital, output, and profits.
4. Compute the short-run output price elasticity of labor demand. Show your work.
5. Compare the price elasticities of labor demand in the long (question 2) and short run (question 4). Is the Le Chatelier Principle at work here? Explain why or why not.
6. With output price 1% higher, increase the wage by 1% in the long and short run. Do these two shocks cancel each other out in either case? Explain.

References

The epigraph is from page 116 of Eugene Silberberg, *The Structure of Economics: A Mathematical Analysis* (1978). This is a classic Math Econ book that was a popular graduate-level text.

Michael Szenberg, Aron Gottesman, and Lall Ramrattan, *Paul Samuelson On Being an Economist* (2005), explore the life and contributions of one of the most important economists of the 20th century.

2.6
Monopoly

2.6.1

Monopoly

Instead of using marginal conditions as Cournot had done, Marshall used total ones. Perhaps for that reason, Cournot's marginal-revenue concept was forgotten and had to be rediscovered in the 1930s.

Hans Brems

Like the perfectly competitive firm, a monopolist has three interrelated optimization problems. Attention is focused on the Output Profit Max problem because that is where the essential difference lies between a PC firm and a monopoly. Of course, we know that via consistency, monopoly power manifests itself on the input side also. A monopoly will produce less than a PC firm and, in turn, hire less labor and capital.

Definition and Issues

A *monopoly* is defined as a firm that is the sole seller of a product with no close substitutes. The definition is inherently vague because there is no clear demarcation for what constitutes a close substitute.

Consider this example: Your local cable provider may have an exclusive agreement to provide cable TV in your community. You could argue that your cable provider is a monopoly because it is the sole seller of cable TV. But what are the substitutes for cable TV?

Years ago, cable TV was the only way to access subscription channels such as ESPN and HBO. Commercial broadcasts (with national broadcasters such as ABC, NBC, and CBS and local channels) were a poor substitute for cable TV. In this environment, cable TV would be a good example of a monopoly.

Today, however, cable TV has strong competition from satellite services and, increasingly, the web. Even if a firm has an exclusive franchise to deliver cable TV in a community, satellite providers (such as DirecTV or Dish Network) are free to sell essentially the same package of channels. Today, cable TV is not a monopoly.

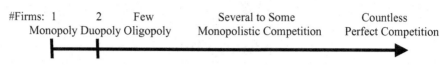

Figure 2.6.1.1. A continuum of market structures.

Of course, cable TV is not a good example of perfect competition either. The cable company does not accept price as a given variable. It is in the middle, somewhere between perfect competition and monopoly. Markets served by a few firms are called *oligopolies*. Add more firms and you eventually get *monopolistic competition*. The study of how firms behave under a variety of market structures is part of the subdiscipline of economics called Industrial Organization. Figure 2.6.1.1 sums things up.

Barrier to Entry

To remain a monopoly, the firm must have a *barrier to entry* to prevent other firms from selling its product. In the cable TV example, the barrier to entry was provided by the exclusive agreement with the community. Such governmental restriction is a common form of a barrier to entry.

Another way to erect a barrier to entry is control over a needed input. ALCOA (the Aluminum Corporation of America) had a monopoly in the aluminum market in the early 20th century because it owned virtually all bauxite reserves.

If a product requires entry on a large scale, like automobile manufacturing, this is considered a barrier to entry.

Like the concept of a close substitute, a barrier to entry is not a simple yes or no issue. Barriers can be weak or strong and they can change over time. Cable TV's barrier was eroded not by changes in legal rules, but by technological change – the advent of satellite TV and the web.

Monopoly's Revenue Structure

We know that the firm's market structure impacts its revenue function. The simplest case is a perfectly (or purely) competitive firm. Such a firm takes price as given and, therefore, revenues are simply price times quantity. For a perfect competitor, even though market demand is downward sloping, the firm's own individual demand curve is perfectly elastic at the given, market price. Because the *PC* firm can sell as much as it wants at the given price, selling one more unit of output makes total revenue increase by the price of the product. *MR* is defined as the change in *TR* when one more unit is sold. Thus, for a PC firm, $MR = P$. This is not true for a monopoly. A critical implication of monopoly power is that *MR* diverges from the demand curve.

Step Open the Excel workbook Monopoly.xls and read the *Intro* sheet, then go to the *Revenue* sheet to see how monopoly power affects the firm's revenue structure.

The sheet opens with a perfectly competitive revenue structure. Total revenue (TR) is a linear function of output and, therefore, $P = MR$ in the bottom graph.

Unlike a PC firm, a monopoly faces the market's downward sloping demand curve. We can model a linear inverse demand curve simply as $P = p_0 - p_1 q$. Obviously, because the slope parameter, p_1, is initially zero, TR is linear and MR is horizontal.

Step To show how monopoly power affects the firm's revenue structure, click on the Price Slope scroll bar.

Notice that as you increase the slope parameter, MR diverges more from D.

The smaller (in absolute value) the price elasticity of demand, the greater the divergence of MR from D and the stronger the monopoly power.

The monopolist uses the divergence of MR from D to extract higher profits than would be possible if there were other sellers of the product.

When drawing MR and D in the case of a linear inverse demand curve, keep in mind these two basic rules:

- MR and D have the same intercept
- MR bisects the y axis and D

We can derive these properties easily. With $P = p_0 - p_1 q$, we can do the following:

$$TR = Pq$$
$$TR = (p_0 - p_1 q)q$$
$$MR = \frac{dTR}{dq} = p_0 - 2p_1 q$$

Clearly, both D and MR share the same intercept, p_0, and because the slope of MR is $-2p_1$, it is twice the slope of D, which is simply $-p_1$.

Thus, when you draw a linear inverse demand curve and then prepare to draw the corresponding MR curve, remember the two rules: (1) the intercept is the same and (2) MR has twice the slope so at every y axis value, MR is halfway between the y axis and the D curve.

Figure 2.6.1.2, with an inverse demand curve slope of -1, shows the monopoly's revenue structure. Unlike the PC firm, TR is a curve and MR diverges from D. Notice that MR bisects the y axis and D. At a value of $10/unit, for example, MR's q value is 15 and D's q value is 30.

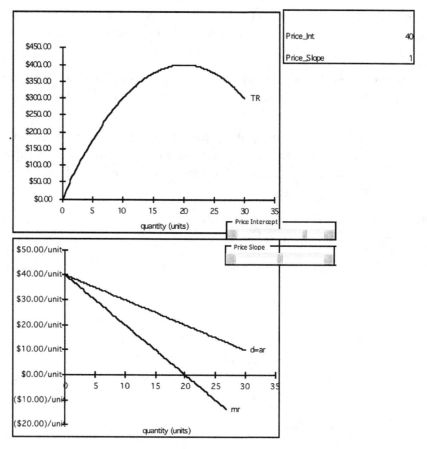

| Price_Int | 40 |
| Price_Slope | 1 |

Figure 2.6.1.2. *TR*, *D*, and *MR* for a monopolist.
Source: Monopoly.xls!Revenues

Notice that where $MR = 0$ at $q = 20$, TR is at its maximum. At this quantity, the price elasticity of demand is exactly -1.

Figure 2.6.1.2 shows that MR can be negative. This can happen because there are two opposing forces at work. Increasing quantity increases TR, which is Pq. However, the only way to sell that extra product is to lower the price (by traveling down the demand curve) so TR falls. When the increase to TR by selling additional output outweighs the effect of the drop in the price, MR is positive. Eventually, however, with a linear demand curve, the monopolist will reach a point at which the increase in revenue for selling one more unit is negative. In the range of output ($q > 20$ in Figure 2.6.1.2) where $MR < 0$, the effect of the decreased price outweighs the positive effect of selling more output.

When $MR > 0$, the price elasticity of demand is greater than 1 (in absolute value). When MR is negative, demand is inelastic. The monopolist will never produce on the negative part of *MR*, which is the same as the inelastic portion of the demand curve.

There is a neat formula that expresses the relationship between *MR* and *P*. With an inverse demand curve, $P(Q)$, we know that $TR = P(Q)Q$. From the *TR* function we can take the derivative with respect to output to find the *MR* function:

$$MR = \frac{dTR}{dQ} = P + \frac{dP}{dQ}Q.$$

If we factor out *P* from this expression, then *MR* can be rewritten as

$$MR = P + \frac{dP}{dQ}Q = P\left(1 + \frac{dP}{dQ}\frac{Q}{P}\right) = P\left(1 + \frac{1}{\varepsilon}\right)$$

where ε is the price elasticity of demand.

$MR = P\left(1 + \frac{1}{\varepsilon}\right)$ shows that $MR = P$ under perfect competition because an individual firm faces a perfectly elastic demand curve ($\varepsilon = \infty \rightarrow 1/\varepsilon = 0$). It also shows that the more inelastic the demand curve (the closer ε is to 0), the greater the separation between *MR* and the demand curve (*P*).

If $\varepsilon = 0$, then *MR* is undefined. With $\varepsilon = 0$, inverse demand is a vertical line. The monopoly would charge an infinite price.

Setting Up the Problem

1. Goal: maximize profits (π), which equal total revenues (*TR*) minus total costs (*TC*)
2. Endogenous variable: output (q) and price (*P*)
3. Exogenous variables: input prices (the wage rate and the rental rate of capital), and technology (parameters in the production function).

The only difference between this problem and the perfectly competitive firm's Output Profit Max problem is that price is now endogenous. The cost structure is the same. The monopoly has an Input Cost Min problem and it is used to derive a cost function. Increases in input prices shift cost curves up and increases in technology shift cost curves down. The monopolist has a long and short run, just like a PC firm, and in the short run there is a gap between *ATC* and *AVC* that represents the fixed costs.

Finding the Initial Solution

We will show the conventional approach to solving the monopoly problem first, then turn to an alternative formulation based on constrained optimization.

The conventional approach is to find q^*, then get p^* from the demand curve, then compute π^* as a rectangle. This is the standard approach and there is a canonical graph that goes along with this approach. Its primary virtue is that it can be easily compared to the perfectly competitive case.

A Concrete Problem

Suppose the cost function is $TC = aq^3 + bq^2 + cq + d$. Suppose the market (inverse) demand curve is $P = p_0 - p_1 q$.

With this information, we can form the firm's profit function and optimization problem, like this:

$$TR = Pq = (p_0 - p_1 q)q$$

$$\max_q \pi = TR - TC$$

$$\max_q \pi = (p_0 - p_1 q)q - (aq^3 + bq^2 + cq + d)$$

As usual, we can solve the problem numerically and analytically.

Numerical Solution

Step Proceed to the *OptimalChoice* sheet.

Figure 2.6.1.3 displays what is on your screen. The profit function has been entered into cell B4. Quantity and price are displayed as endogenous variables, but q is bolded to indicate that it is the primary endogenous variable. In other words, Solver will search for the profit-maximizing output and, having found it, will compute the highest price that can be obtained from the demand curve.

On open, the firm is making $245 in profits by producing 10 units of output (and charging $34.50 per unit), but this is not the profit-maximizing solution. We know this because the marginal revenue of the 10th unit is $29/unit, whereas the marginal cost of that last unit is only $4/unit. Clearly, the firm should produce more because it is making more in additional revenues from the last unit produced than the additional cost of producing that unit.

Step Run Solver to find the optimal solution.

At the optimal solution, the equimarginal condition, $MR = MC$, is met.

The analytical solution to this problem is straightforward. This is a single variable unconstrained problem because $P = p_0 - p_1 q$ has been substituted into the profit function. Take the derivative with respect to q and solve for q^*.

$$\max_q \pi = (40 - 0.55q)q - 0.04q^3 + 0.9q^2 - 10q - 50$$

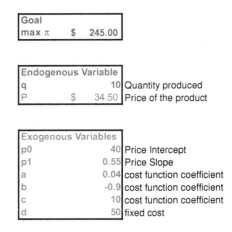

Goal		
max π	$	245.00

Endogenous Variable			
q		10	Quantity produced
P	$	34.50	Price of the product

Exogenous Variables		
p0	40	Price Intercept
p1	0.55	Price Slope
a	0.04	cost function coefficient
b	-0.9	cost function coefficient
c	10	cost function coefficient
d	50	fixed cost

Figure 2.6.1.3. An inefficient solution.
Source: Monopoly.xls!OptimalChoice

MR		MC	
$	29.00	$	4.00

Check your work by clicking the Show Analytical Solution button.

The numerical and analytical solutions give essentially the same answers.

Step Proceed to the *OutputSide* sheet, which is reproduced as Figure 2.6.1.4.

The bottom left-hand corner graph in Figure 2.6.1.4 is the standard graph for a monopolist. It can be used to quickly find q^* (where $MR = MC$), then p^* (from the demand curve), then maximum profit (as the rectangle, $AR - ATC$ by q^*).

Here's how to read and use the conventional monopoly graph:

1. Finding q^*: Choose q where $MR = MC$. This gives the biggest the difference between TR and TC.
2. At q^*, read p off of the demand curve. This is the highest price that the monopolist can get for the chosen level of output.
3. Draw in the usual profit rectangle as $(AR - ATC)$ times q^*.

The *OutputSide* sheet has several slider controls you can use to depict different situations.

Step Changes in fixed costs do not affect the monopolist's optimal quantity and price solution. This is just like the perfectly competitive case.

Step Click the Reset button; explore changes in the price intercept to see how the firm responds. At a low enough price intercept, you can even get the monopolist to shut down.

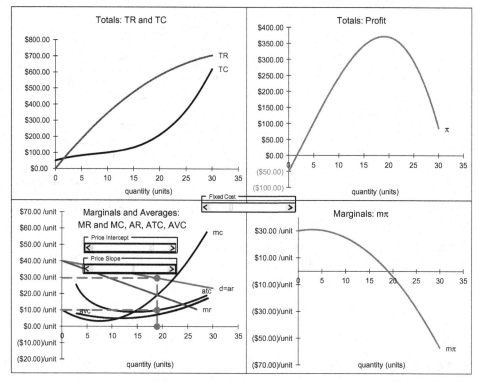

Figure 2.6.1.4. Representing the initial optimal solution.
Source: Monopoly.xls!OutputSide

Monopoly and the Supply Curve

It is impossible to derive a supply curve for a monopolist.

Because a PC firm is a price taker, it is possible to shock p and see how the optimal output changes. We can derive $q^* = f(p$, ceteris paribus) and this is called a supply curve.

Unlike a perfectly competitive firm, for which price is exogenous, a monopoly chooses the price. Thus, we cannot ask, "Given this price, what is the optimal quantity supplied?" With price as an endogenous variable, it cannot serve as a shock variable in a comparative statics analysis.

Thus, a monopolist has no supply curve.

Measuring Monopoly Power: Lerner and Herfindahl Indexes

Step Proceed to the *Lerner* sheet.

The more inelastic the demand faced by a monopolist, the greater the monopoly power. In other words, from a profit-maximizing point of view, it is better to have a monopoly over a product that everyone desperately needs

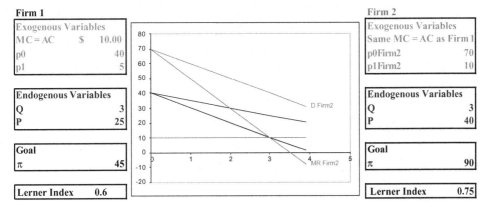

Figure 2.6.1.5. The Lerner Index in action.
Source: Monopoly.xls!Lerner

(i.e., very inelastic) than to be the sole seller of a product that has a highly elastic market demand curve.

Abba Lerner formalized this idea in a mathematical expression that bears his name, the Lerner Index. "If P = price and MC = marginal cost, then the index of the degree of monopoly power is $\frac{P-MC}{P}$" (Lerner, 1934, p. 169). The Lerner Index takes advantage of the fact that a monopolist will choose that quantity where $MR = MC$, then charge the highest price possible for that quantity. The higher the price that can be charged, the more inelastic is demand and the greater the monopoly power.

Figure 2.6.1.5 compares two monopolies with the exact same cost structure (assumed for simplicity to have a constant $MC = AC$). Firm 2 faces a more inelastic demand curve than Firm 1 and, therefore, it has a bigger gap between price and marginal cost.

Step Click on cells B16 and I16 to see the simple formulas for the Lerner Index.

The idea is that the bigger the divergence between price and marginal cost, the greater the monopoly power. Firm 2 has more monopoly power than Firm 1 and more monopoly profits. The Lerner Index for each firm reflects this.

Notice that a perfectly competitive firm that sets $MC = P$ will have a Lerner Index of zero. As the index approaches one, monopoly power rises.

Step Change Firm 2's demand parameters to 6010 and 1000. The graph is hard to read, but notice that $Q^* = 3$. This firm produces the same output as Firm 1. Its Lerner Index is close to one. It cannot rise above one, but the closer it gets, the greater the monopoly power.

The Lerner Index can be derived by expressing *MR* in terms of the price elasticity:

$$MR = P + \frac{dP}{dQ}Q = P\left(1 + \frac{dP}{dQ}\frac{Q}{P}\right) = P\left(1 + \frac{1}{\varepsilon}\right)$$

At the optimal solution, *MR* must equal *MC*:

$$P\left(1 + \frac{1}{\varepsilon}\right) = MC$$

Rewriting this equation yields the Lerner Index:

$$MC = P\left(1 + \frac{1}{\varepsilon}\right)$$

$$\frac{MC}{P} = 1 + \frac{1}{\varepsilon}$$

$$\frac{MC}{P} - 1 = \frac{1}{\varepsilon}$$

$$\frac{MC - P}{P} = \frac{1}{\varepsilon}$$

$$\frac{P - MC}{P} = \frac{1}{-\varepsilon} = \frac{1}{|\varepsilon|}$$

In other words, because we know *MR* = *MC* at the profit-maximizing level of output, the Lerner Index equals the absolute value of the reciprocal of the price elasticity of demand.

Step Set Firm 2's demand parameters back to 70 and 10, and then click the Show Elasticity button. The price elasticity of demand for the two firms is displayed. If you click in the cells, you can see the formula. Notice that the reciprocal of the inverse demand curve's slope is used to compute the price elasticity of demand correctly.

Firm 2's price elasticity of demand at the profit-maximizing price is lower than Firm 1's. The lower the price elasticity, the greater the firm's monopoly power (as measured by the Lerner Index).

Step Proceed to the *Herfindahl* sheet for a quick look at another way to measure monopoly power.

Instead of measuring the markup of price over marginal cost, we can see how big the firms are in an industry. Strictly speaking, a monopoly is one firm so it would have a 100% market share, but in practice, firms have monopoly power even though they aren't technically monopolies. Any firm that faces a downward sloping demand curve and has the ability to set its price is said to have monopoly power.

If an industry has many firms, each with the same share of the market, we can expect competition to prevail. If, on the other hand, a few firms dominate, we know they will exercise monopoly power to increase profits. Thus, it is of some interest to determine whether an industry is competitive or monopolistic.

We can sort the firms in an industry from highest to lowest share and then add the shares of the four biggest firms. This gives the four firm concentration ratio in cell D5. It turns out this is not a very good way to distinguish between concentrated and unconcentrated industries.

The problem is that the four firm concentration ratio tells you nothing about the sizes of the top four firms or the rest of the industry. The four firm concentration ratio is 70%, which seems pretty highly concentrated.

Step Click on the Distribution A button. The four firm concentration ratio is the same as before (70%), but this industry is clearly more concentrated.

Step Click on the Distribution B button. The four firm concentration ratio is the same as before (70%), but this industry is clearly less concentrated.

Because we have three scenarios with wildly different concentrations yielding the same four firm concentration ratio, we can conclude that this ratio is a poor way to determine whether firms in an industry are in a competitive or monopolistic environment.

A better way to judge concentration is via the *Herfindahl Index*. Unlike the Lerner Index, there is confusion about who invented it. Hirschman concludes, "The net result is that my index is named either after Gini who did not invent it at all or after Herfindahl who reinvented it. Well, it's a cruel world" (Hirschman, 1964, p. 761). It is sometimes called the Herfindahl-Hirschman Index (HHI).

Fortunately, its computation is simpler than its paternity. The idea is to square each share and sum, like this:

$$H = \sum_{i=1}^{n} s_i^2$$

The index ranges from $1/n$ to 1 (when using decimal values of shares). The higher the index, the greater the concentration.

The *Herfindahl* sheet shows the computation. Notice how each value in column B is squared in column G. The sum of the squares is in cell G15 and it is the value of the Herfindahl Index.

Step Click on the three buttons one after the other to cycle through them. Notice how the Herfindahl Index changes.

For Distribution A, the value is 0.325. This is quite high.

The 0.1375 value with Distribution B means there is more competition in this scenario than the other two.

In fact, the Justice Department uses 0.18 (or 1800 when integer instead of decimal values of share are used) to determine whether mergers are allowed without legal challenge.

The Herfindahl index or HHI is not perfect, but it is better than the four firm concentration ratio.

An Unconventional Approach to the Monopolist's Profit Maximization Problem

The optimization problem can also be solved by choosing p and q simultaneously subject to the constraint of the demand curve. This enables practice with the Lagrangean method of solving constrained optimization problems and reading isoprofit curves.

The analytical solution is based on forming the Lagrangean, setting derivatives equal to zero, and solving the system of equations for the optimal solution.

$$\max_{p,q} L = Pq - (aq^3 + bq^2 + cq + d) + \lambda(P - (p_0 - p_1q))$$

$$\frac{dL}{dP} = q + \lambda$$

$$\frac{dL}{dq} = P - 3aq^2 - 2bq - c + \lambda p_1$$

$$\frac{dL}{d\lambda} = P - (p_0 - p_1q)$$

Set each first-order condition equal to zero and solve for q^*, P^*, and λ^*.

From the first equation, $\lambda = -q$, substitute into equation 2:

$$P - 3aq^2 - 2bq - c + [-q]\, p_1 = 0$$

From the third first-order condition, $P = p_0 - p_1q$, so

$$(p_0 - p_1q) - 3aq^2 - 2bq - c - qp_1 = 0$$

Rearrange the terms to prepare for using the quadratic formula.

$$-3aq^2 - 2(b + p_1)q + (p_0 - c) = 0$$

$$\frac{-b + \sqrt{b^2 - 4ac}}{2a}$$

$$\frac{2(b + p_1) \pm \sqrt{4(b + p_1)^2 - 4(-3a)(p_0 - c)}}{2(-3a)}$$

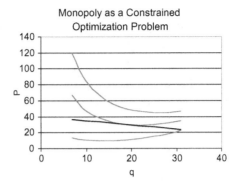

Figure 2.6.1.6. The constrained optimization version of the monopoly problem. *Source:* Monopoly.xls!ConOpt

Step Proceed to the *ConOpt* sheet to see formulas based on the Lagrangean solution. It is not surprising that we get the same, correct answer as the unconstrained version.

The *ConOpt* sheet shows that monopoly as a constrained optimization problem can be depicted with a graph, reproduced in Figure 2.6.1.6.

The demand curve (or, in this example, line) is interpreted as a constraint. The *MR* curve is not drawn because it is not used.

The three isoprofit curves represent the goal. The monopolist wants to reach the highest (farthest to the northeast) isoprofit line.

The point of tangency provides the optimal q and p solution, whereas the value of the isoprofit curve at that point is the level of profits.

The *ConOpt* sheet also shows how Solver can be used to find the optimal solution to the constrained version of the monopoly problem.

Step Run Solver from the *ConOpt* sheet to see how the dialog box is set up. Note that the constraint cell (B20) is the demand curve.

Do not be confused. The constrained version is rarely used. The conventional approach can be described as: (1) choose q (from $MR = MC$), (2) read p from the demand curve, and (3) draw a profit rectangle to find the max profits.

Monopoly Basics

A monopoly differs from a perfectly competitive firm in that a monopolist faces the downward sloping market demand curve whereas a perfect competitor is a price taker. In addition, a monopolist has a barrier to entry that enables it to maintain positive economic profits even in the long run.

The two are the same, however, in the cost structure (like a perfect competitor, the monopolist derives its cost function from the input cost minimization problem) and the fact that it seeks to maximize profits (where $MR = MC$). We depict the monopolist's optimal solution with a graph that superimposes D and MR over the family of cost curves (MC, ATC, and AVC). Like a perfectly competitive firm, a monopolist can suffer negative profits in the short run and it will shut down when $P < AVC$.

The Lerner Index measures monopoly power. The greater the gap between price and marginal cost, the greater the monopoly power. The Herfindahl Index measures industry concentration. Unlike the four firm concentration ratio, it uses all the market shares of all the firms to create a single number that reflects the concentration of an industry. The Herfindahl magic number is 0.18 (or 1800) – mergers that produce values above this level will trigger scrutiny by the Department of Justice because it is presumed that the market will not be competitive.

The monopoly's profit maximization problem can be cast as a constrained problem. In addition to providing practice with constrained optimization, this version makes quite clear that the monopolist must obey the demand curve. It is not true that a monopolist will charge the highest price possible. It is true, however, that monopoly leads to lower output and higher prices compared with perfect competition. This important comparison will be analyzed in detail when we judge the market system in the last part of this book.

Exercises

Open Word and answer the following questions. Save the document and print it when you are done.

1. DeBeers is an internationally famous company that has a monopoly over diamonds.
   A) What is their barrier to entry?
   B) Google "synthetic diamonds" (using the quotation marks in your search) to learn about this threat to DeBeers. Based on your search results, do you think DeBeers will be able to maintain its monopoly? Include web citations for supporting evidence.
2. Use Word's Drawing Tools to depict a monopoly shutting down in the short run. Explain the graph.
3. In the *ConOpt* sheet, set the demand intercept (cell B13) to 9 and the fixed cost (B18) to 180. Run Solver. Why is Solver generating a miserable result? What is the correct answer?
4. Use Word's Drawing Tools to depict the effect of monopoly from the input side profit maximization perspective. Explain the graph.
   Hint: With perfect competition, L^* is found where $w = MRP_L$ (where MRP_L is based on the given, constant price, $PxMP_L$). With monopoly, however, P and MR diverge.
5. Is the effect of monopoly on the input side consistent with the effect of monopoly on the output side? Explain.

References

The epigraph is from page 149 of Hans Brems, *Pioneering Economic Theory, 1630–1980: A Mathematical Restatement* (1986). This book recasts ideas in the history of economics in mathematical terms. Seeing the thoughts of Smith, Ricardo, Marx, and others presented as mathematical models provides an interesting, uncommon perspective.

See Abba P. Lerner, "The Concept of Monopoly and the Measurement of Monopoly Power," *The Review of Economic Studies*, Vol. 1, No. 3 (June, 1934), pp. 157–175.

Also see Albert O. Hirschman, "The Paternity of an Index," *The American Economic Review*, Vol. 54, No. 5 (September, 1964), p. 761.

"Horizontal Merger Guidelines," U.S. Department of Justice and the Federal Trade Commission, Issued: April 2, 1992, Revised: April 8, 1997, is online at <http://www.usdoj.gov/atr/public/guidelines/horiz_book/hmg1.html>.

2.7
Game Theory

2.7.1

Game Theory

Von Neumann hovered for a moment by two rather sloppily dressed graduate students who hunched over a peculiar-looking piece of cardboard. It was a rhombus covered with hexagons. It looked like a bathroom floor. The two young men were taking turns putting down black and white go stones and had very nearly covered the entire board.

Later that evening, at a faculty dinner, he buttonholed Tucker and asked, with studied casualness, "Oh, by the way, what was it they were playing?" "Nash," answered Tucker, allowing the corners of mouth to turn upwards ever so slightly, "Nash."

Sylvia Nasar

Perfect competition: Firms are price takers with no power to affect the market price; optimize by choosing q to equalize MC and P.

Monopoly: the sole seller of a product with no close substitutes; optimize by choosing q to equalize MC and MR and then charge the highest price that clears the market (given by the demand curve).

In both market structures, the profits of the individual firm are not affected by what any other firm does. In perfect competition, there are so many other firms that Firm i does not care about what Firm j is doing. In monopoly, there is no other firm to worry about.

What about market structures between the extremes of perfect competition and monopoly?

Oligopoly is a market dominated by a few firms that are interdependent. In other words, what each individual firm chooses *does* affect the profits of the other firm. Firms optimize by trying to anticipate what their rivals will do and then choosing their best options. This is clearly a more realistic model than that of perfect competition and monopoly, which rely on idealized, abstract descriptions of firms that have no real-world counterparts.

How do oligopolies behave? We know that, like other firms, they optimize given the economic environment, but because of interdependence, it is much

Table 2.7.1.1. *The Payoff Matrix*

		Firm 2	
		High Output	Low Output
Firm 1	High Output	$300 profits, $300 profits	$1000 profits, $200 profits
	Low Output	$200 profits, $1000 profits	$800 profits, $800 profits

more difficult to analyze. We will consider a few basic ideas from the field of *game theory*.

Interdependence and Nash Equilibrium

How can firms be interdependent? Consider two firms that generate and sell electricity. (Notice that this is a homogenous product.) To keep it simple, suppose that each firm can choose either a high level of output or a low level of output. Market price is a function of the output decisions of the two firms. Each firm's profits are functions of their own decision to produce and the market price.

Table 2.7.1.1 displays a *payoff matrix*, which shows the possible choices and outcomes. You read the payoff matrix like coordinate pairs on a graph, (*x, y*). The top left corner says that Firm 1 chose high output and Firm 2 chose high output. Each firm ends up with low profits. If Firm 2 had chosen Low output, Firm 1 would end up with high profits (because it made a lot of output and price rose when Firm 2 decided to cut back).

This particular game is a one-shot, simultaneous-move game known as the *Prisoner's Dilemma*.

The outcome that is best for both firms together is $1600 total, with $800 for each firm. Suppose that both firms agree beforehand that they are going to collude and both choose low output. Unless they can write a binding agreement that is enforceable (so a cheater can be punished), there is an incentive for each firm to change its decision and choose high output if it thinks that the other firm will stick with low output. As a result, both firms end up with low profits.

If you think the other firm is going to cheat, your best move is to also cheat. It looks like cheating, producing high output, is the best move no matter what the other firm does.

This result illustrates the reason why *cartels* – groups of firms that get together to charge the monopoly price and split the monopoly profits – are unstable. It is difficult for oligopolistic firms to get together and act like a monopoly because there is an incentive for individual firms to cheat on the agreement and produce more to take advantage of high prices.

Because of the interdependence of firms' decision making, competition among oligopolistic firms may resemble military operations involving tactics, strategies, moves, and countermoves. Economists model these sophisticated decision-making processes using *game theory*, a branch of mathematics that was developed by John von Neumann (pronounced noy-man) and Oskar Morgenstern in the 1930s. One of the most important contributors to game theory is John Nash, a mathematician who shared the Nobel Prize in Economics.

A game-theoretic analysis of oligopoly is based on the assumption that each firm's manager assumes that its rivals are optimizing agents. That is, managers act as though their opponents or rivals will always adopt the most profitable countermove to any move they make. The manager's job is to find the optimal response.

Nash's most important and enduring contribution is the concept of Nash equilibrium. Once we are in a world where firms are interdependent and one firm's profits depends on what other firms do, we are out of the world of exogenously given price that we used for perfect competition and out of the isolated world of the monopolist. John Nash invented an equilibrium concept that describes a state of rest in this new world of interdependence.

A *Nash equilibrium* exists when each player, observing what her rivals have chosen, would not choose to alter the move she herself chose. In other words, this is a *no regrets* equilibrium: After observing the outcome, the player does not wish she would have done something else instead.

We will explore in detail a concrete example of a duopoly with a single Nash equilibrium. Remember, however, that this is simply one example. Some games have one Nash equilibrium, some have many, and some have none.

Introducing the Cournot Model

Augustin Cournot (pronounced coor-no) was a remarkably creative 19th-century French economist (see the References section of chapter 2.3.2). Cournot originally set up a model of duopolists who produce the same good and optimize by choosing their own output levels based on assumptions about what the rival will do.

Here is the setup:

- Two firms
- Each produces the exact same product
- The unit cost of production is constant for each firm
- Firms choose output levels at the same time
- Both know the market demand for the product.

The profit of each firm depends on how much it sells and how much its rival sells because the more its rival sells, the lower the market price will be.

What strategy should each firm use to choose its output level? The answer depends on its beliefs regarding its rival's behavior.

Step Open the Excel workbook GameTheory.xls and read the *Intro* sheet, then go to the *Parameters* sheet. Market demand is given by the linear inverse demand curve and, for simplicity, we assume a linear total cost function. This means that $MC = AC$.

Step Proceed to the *PerfectCompetition* sheet. Under PC, the industry will produce where demand intersects supply (which is the sum of the individual firm's MCs).

The homogenous output is electricity. The perfectly competitive market will produce 15,000 kwh at a price of 5 ¢/kwh.

What happens if a single firm takes over the entire market?

Step Proceed to the *Monopoly* sheet. Use the Choose Q slider control to determine the profit-maximizing quantity. Keep your eye on cell B18 as you adjust output. The optimal output is found where $MR = MC$.

The monopolist will produce 7500 kwh and charge a price of 12.5 ¢/kwh. This solution nets a maximum profit of 56,250 ¢.

Not surprisingly, compared to the perfectly competitive results, monopoly results in lower output and higher prices.

Cournot was the first to ask the question, "What happens if the industry is shared by two firms?"

To understand the answer, the concept of *residual demand* is crucial because it enables us to solve the firm's optimization problem. The reaction function for each firm is derived from a comparative statics analysis. The two reaction functions are then combined to yield the Nash equilibrium, which is the answer to Cournot's question.

Residual Demand

Step Proceed to the *ResidualDemand* sheet. It shows how Firm 1 decides what to do, given Firm 2's output decision. Think of the chart as belonging to Firm 1. It will use this chart to decide what to do, given different scenarios.

Conjectured Q2, in cell B14, is the key variable. A conjecture is a guess. It is based on incomplete information. Firm 1 does not know and cannot control what Firm 2 is going to do. Firm 1 must act, however, so it treats Firm 2's output decision as a conjecture and proceeds based on that guess.

Conjectured Q2 is an exogenous variable for the analysis. The conjectured output of Firm 2 may be different from Firm 2's actual output. In that case,

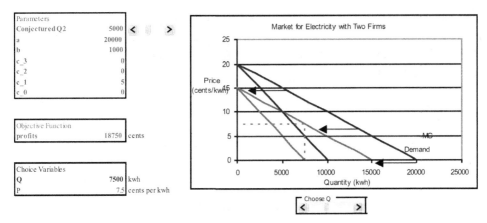

Figure 2.7.1.1. Residual *D* and *MR* with *Conjectured Q2* = 5000.
Source: GameTheory!ResidualDemand

presumably Firm 1 would have made a mistake and it would re-optimize based on a new *Conjectured Q2*.

The *ResidualDemand* sheet opens with *Conjectured Q2* = 0. In this scenario, Firm 2 produces nothing and Firm 1 behaves as a monopolist, producing 7500 kwh and charging a price of 12.5 ¢/kwh.

Step Click five times on the scroll bar in cell C14. With each click, *Conjectured Q2* rises by 1000 units and the red lines in the graph shift left.

The red lines are the critical factor for Firm 1. They represent residual demand and residual marginal revenue.

The idea behind residual demand is that Firm 2's output will be sold first, leaving Firm 1 with the rest of the market. The residual refers to the fact that Firm 2 will supply a given amount of the market and then Firm 1 is free to decide what to do with the demand that is left over.

With each click, Firm 2 was producing more and so the demand left over for Firm 1 was falling. This is why the residual demand shifts left when Firm 2 produces more.

As the *Parameters* sheet shows, the inverse demand curve for the entire market is given by the function $P = 20 - 0.001Q$. If *Conjectured Q2* = 5000, then the residual inverse demand curve is $P = 20 - 0.001Q - 0.001*5000$. In other words, we subtract the amount supplied by Firm 2. Thus, the residual inverse demand curve is $P = 15 - 0.001Q$.

Figure 2.7.1.1 shows how the residual demand is shifted left by 5000 kwh when *Conjectured Q2* is 5000. The key idea is that Firm 2's output is subtracted from the demand curve and what is left over, the residual, is the demand faced by Firm 1.

Once we have residual demand for Firm 1, we can find the profit-maximizing solution. Firm 1 derives residual *MR* from its residual demand curve and uses this to maximize profits by setting residual $MR = MC$. In Figure 2.7.1.1, Firm 1 is not maximizing profits by producing 7500 units and charging 7.5 / c/kwh. Notice that the price is read from the residual demand curve, not the full market demand curve.

Step Use the scroll bar to find Firm 1's optimal solution when *Conjectured Q2* is 5000.

You should have found that optimal quantity is 5000 kwh, $P^* = 10 ¢$/kwh and maximum profits are at 25,000 $¢$.

Deriving Firm 1's Reaction Function

We can track Firm 1's optimal output as a function of *Conjectured Q2*. This is called the reaction (or best response) function.

Step Fill in the table in the *Residual Demand* sheet. You already have two of the rows. In addition to the optimal solution at *Conjectured Q2 = 5000* which we just found, when *Conjectured Q2 = 0*, optimal output is 7500 and optimal price is 12.5 $¢$/kwh. Fill in the rest of the table.

Step Check your work by clicking the Check Table button.

Deriving Firm 1's reaction function is an important step in figuring out how two firms will interact. The reaction function gives us Firm 1's optimal response to Firm 2's output decision. We do not know, however, what Firm 2 will actually do. It has a reaction function just like Firm 1. The two firms must interact to determine what will happen in the market.

Finding the Nash Equilibrium

Step Proceed to the *Duopoly* sheet.

Instead of using the residual demand graph to find the optimal output given a conjecture about the other firm's output, this sheet uses the analytical solution.

Step Note that *Conjectured Q2* (in cell B13) is zero. Click the Choose q₁* button.

The optimal solution is displayed. Not surprisingly (given our work with the residual demand graph), Firm 1 chooses to produce 7500 kwh.

Step Click the Firm 1's Reaction Function button.

Excel changes *Conjectured Q2* and finds the optimal output after each change, then provides a table and chart of the comparative statics results.

The chart has the exogenous variable *q2* on the *y* axis so it is an inverse reaction function. The table and chart give Firm 1's optimal response to Firm 2's output decision.

If Firm 2 decides not to produce at all, then Firm 1 maximizes profits by producing 7500 units.

But what will Firm 2 decide to do? That depends on what Firm 1 does. The next few steps are critical for understanding the concept of a Nash equilibrium. Proceed carefully. We will be switching back and forth from one firm's perspective to the other.

Step Note that *Conjectured Q2* (in cell B13) is once again zero and that *Conjectured Q1* (in cell G13) is also zero. Click the Choose q₁* button.

Step As we know, Firm 1 optimizes by producing 7500 units, but look at cell G13. It now displays Firm 1's output and Firm 2 has a decision to make based on Firm 1's output.

Step Click the Choose q₂* button. This finds the optimal output for Firm 2, based on Firm 1's output.

Firm 2's optimal output is 3750 units when Firm 1 produces 7500 units.

Step But look at cell B13. *Conjectured Q2* is now 3750 – Firm 2's output.

Firm 1 has to re-optimize based on this new level of Firm 2 output.

Step Click the Choose q₁* button.

Firm 1 re-optimizes. Now it's Firm 2's turn.

Step Click the Choose q₂* button.

Firm 2 has changed its output level, so we go back to Firm 1.

Step Click the Choose q₁* button.

Will this ever end?
Yes.

Step Repeatedly click the Choose q₁* and Choose q₂* buttons.

You should see convergence. Clearly, the two optimal output levels are closing in on 5000 – this is the Nash equilibrium solution to this problem!

Step Instead of manually optimizing each firm in turn, click the Nash Equilibrium button. This button does all of the hard work for you. It alternately solves one firm's problem given the other firm's output many times. It also displays the individual firm's reaction functions (scroll down if needed).

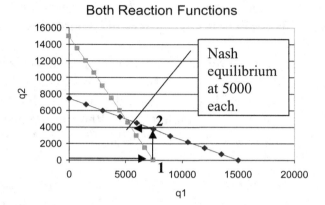

Figure 2.7.1.2. Graphing the Nash equilibrium.
Source: GameTheory.xls!Duopoly

Step Look carefully at the axes labels on the two charts in row 46. For Firm 1, the reaction function is $q_1^* = f(q_2)$ and for Firm 2, we get the reverse: $q_2^* = f(q_1)$. For Firm 1, q_2 is given, but for Firm 2, q_1 is given.

Step Scroll back up and right (if needed) to see a new graph, reproduced as Figure 2.7.1.2, with a top left corner at cell I6. This graph contains both reaction functions. It has q_2 on the y axis and q_1 on the x axis. Firm 1's inverse reaction function was graphed previously to enable display of both reaction functions on the same graph.

In Figure 2.7.1.2, the steeper line is Firm 1's reaction function. It is read horizontally, then down. For example, if Firm 2 produces nothing, then Firm 1 produces 7500. This is point 1 on Firm 1's reaction function (and it is labeled 1 on Figure 2.7.1.2).

Of course, the industry will not stay at this point. This is not a Nash equilibrium because Firm 2 would regret its decision to produce nothing. If Firm 1 makes 7500, Firm 2 can do better than zero output.

In Figure 2.7.1.2, the flatter line is Firm 2's reaction function. It is read vertically, then left. From point 1, when Firm 1 produces 7500 units, we proceed up until we hit Firm 2's reaction function and read off the value on the y axis, 3750 units. This is Firm 2's optimal response to Firm 1's decision to produce 7500.

Point 2 in Figure 2.7.1.2 is not a Nash equilibrium. This time, it is Firm 1's turn to regret. If Firm 2 produces 3750, Firm 1 is not optimizing producing 7500. It takes Firm 2's 3750 as *Conjectured Q2* and optimizes by producing on its reaction function.

This process continues until the Nash equilibrium is reached.

Remember: A Nash equilibrium exists when each player, observing what her rivals have chosen, would not choose to alter the move she herself chose. Nash equilibrium is a no regrets point for all players.

Figure 2.7.1.2 shows that the Nash equilibrium is at the intersection of the two reaction functions. Only there will both firms refuse to change their optimal decisions. This is a position of rest.

Evaluating the Nash Equilibrium

Step In cell D16 in the *Duopoly* sheet, enter a formula that adds the profits of the two firms. What are the joint profits at the Nash equilibrium? In other words, enter 5000 in cells B20 and G20 and note the value in cell D16.

Step Now, suppose each firm produced half, 3750, of the monopoly output (7500). What would their joint profits be? In other words, enter 5000 in cells B20 and G20 and note the value in cell D16.

Why don't the two firms produce 3750 units each and make greater joint profits than the Nash equilibrium solution?

Step To answer this question, click the Choose q_1* button.

When each firm's output is 3750 units, joint profits are maximized, but each firm has an incentive to produce more in order to increase its profits.

Yes, if they *both* do this then they end up at the Nash equilibrium with 5000 units each and lower joint profits, but unless they can collude, competition will force them to the Nash equilibrium solution.

Step Proceed to the *Summary* sheet to see a comparison of the three market structures. Duopoly falls between perfect competition and monopoly.

Interdependence is the Foundation of Game Theory

Game theory is an exciting, growing area of economics. Its primary appeal lies in the realistic modeling of agents as strategic decision makers playing against each other, moving and countering. This is obviously what a real-world firm does.

The Cournot model is an extremely simple game matching two firms against each other. It illustrates nicely the notion of interdependence and how one firm moves, and then the other responds, and so on. Whereas some games do not have a Nash equilibrium, the Cournot duopolists do settle down to a position of rest.

We have just scratched the surface. There are many, many more games. The file RockPaperScissors.xls lets you play this child's game in Excel. For another application of game theory, see the chapter on cartels and dead-weight loss.

Exercises

Open Word and answer the following questions. Save the document and print it when you are done.

1. If *Conjectured Q2* is 15,000, why does Firm 1 decide to produce nothing? Use the *ResidualDemand* sheet (with B11 = 5) to support your explanation.
2. Firm 1 produces 4500 and Firm 2 produces 6000. Does Firm 1 have any regrets? Does Firm 2 have any regrets? Enter these two values in the *Duopoly* sheet (with B11 = 5) and click the Choose q buttons. Which firm changed its mind? Why?
3. Click the Reset All button in the *Duopoly* sheet. Explore the effect of changing Firm 1's cost function so that c_2 (cell B10) is 0.001 (with B11 = 5). How does this affect the Nash equilibrium?

References

The epigraph is from page 75 of Sylvia Nasar, *A Beautiful Mind* (1998). This biography of Nash has won countless awards and was made into an Academy Award-winning motion picture, with Russell Crowe starring as John Nash. Although much of the book is devoted to Nash's personal struggle with schizophrenia, Nasar gives a clear and engaging review of game-theoretic concepts before Nash and of the Nash equilibrium.

On the game Nash invented, Nasar writes, "That spring, Nash astounded everyone by inventing an extremely clever game that quickly took over the common room. Piet Hein, a Dane, had invented the game a few years before Nash, and it would be marketed by Parker Brothers in the mid-1950s as Hex. But Nash's invention of the game appears to have been entirely independent" (p. 76).

The PBS program *American Experience* did a documentary on Nash in 2002 and it is available online at <www.pbs.org/wgbh/amex/nash>.

In 1994, Nash, John C. Harsanyi, and Richard Selten shared the Nobel Prize in Economics "for their pioneering analysis of equilibria in the theory of non-cooperative games." See <nobelprize.org/nobel_prizes/economics/laureates/1994/press.html>.

The first edition of *The Theory of Games and Economic Behavior* by John von Neumann and Oskar Morgenstern was published in 1944.

Thinking Strategically: The Competitive Edge in Business, Politics, and Everyday Life by Avinash K. Dixit and Barry J. Nalebuff (originally published in 1991) explains and applies game theory to a variety of interesting examples and situations.

Part III

The Market System

The Butterfly Effect acquired a technical name: sensitive dependence on initial conditions.

James Gleick

This is the third (and last) part of this book.

The first part was the Theory of Consumer Behavior. It modeled a consumer's optimization problem and emphasized deriving a Demand Curve as an important result.

The Theory of the Firm comprised the second part. Firm decisions about inputs and outputs were modeled as optimization problems. The key result was deriving a Supply Curve from the perfectly competitive firm's output profit maximization problem.

This third part will put together consumers' demand and firms' supply in an equilibrium model in order to show how individual markets solve society's resource allocation problem. In addition, we will introduce an equilibrium model that incorporates all markets simultaneously.

Unlike the introduction to the first two parts, which were brief and simple, there are three important ideas that need to be clear before we begin:

- Optimization versus equilibrium
- Society's resource allocation problem
- Partial and general equilibrium.

Optimization Versus Equilibrium

Equilibrium models are similar to optimization problems in many respects, especially in that they both rely heavily on comparative statics, but there are important differences.

Equilibrium means no tendency to change. Optimal means best (from the decision maker's point of view).

Optimization: superscript $* \rightarrow Q^*$
Equilibrium: subscript $e \rightarrow Q_e$

Figure III.1. Labeling optimal and equilibrium solutions.

Unlike optimization problems, equilibrium models do not have an agent directly controlling or setting values of a variable. Instead, forces within the model drive variables to positions of rest. No agent actually picks the solution in an equilibrium model.

Figure III.1 shows the notation used to distinguish optimization and equilibrium solutions.

Unlike optimization problems, an equilibrium solution says nothing about the desirability of the solution. In other words, we cannot conclude that an equilibrium solution is a good one simply because it is the equilibrium solution. We could be at rest at a bad place. Confusing equilibrium with optimal is common, but bad practice.

Unlike optimization problems, we are often interested in the equilibration process, that is, the path followed to the final resting place. The type of convergence, direct or oscillatory, can be studied.

Society's Resource Allocation Problem

The equilibrium models in this third and final part are devoted to explaining how markets function in solving a particularly fundamental optimization problem. It is so important that is it often referred to as "The Economic Problem."

Figure III.2 depicts the problem. Given scarce resources of labor and capital (representing all inputs), society must decide what to produce, how much of each product to make, and how to distribute the output.

Production: Which goods and services to produce with limited resources?
                How much of each kind?
Distribution: How much does each person get of the goods and services produced?

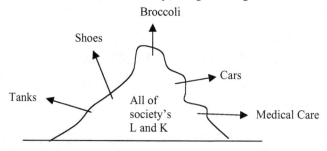

Figure III.2. Society's resource allocation problem.

This problem can be solved in three basic ways:

- Tradition
- Authority
- Markets.

Most people do not realize that the last way, markets, is a brand new approach. Of the 200,000 years that humans have been on this planet, traditional and authoritarian arrangements are by far the usual ways to solve society's resource allocation problem. Markets have been utilized only in the last couple of hundred years.

This may seem an outlandish claim given that money and prices have been around for a long, long time. A moment's reflection should convince you that trading is not a sufficient condition to determine whether a market system is being used to solve society's resource allocation problem. After all, societies in Biblical times had bazaars where people bought and sold goods and the former Soviet Union had stores where people paid rubles for groceries, but neither of these societies had market economies.

The key to the market system is that each person decides how to use his or her labor and other privately owned resources. In a market system, individual resource owners respond to incentives. Unlike traditional and authoritarian systems, which rely on custom and command to get work done and products made, markets use the lure of gain to attract effort and capital.

Because they are based on incentives, markets require that individuals be self-interested. Whether self-interest is innate or learned is a deep philosophical question, but there is no doubt that players in a market system are driven to succeed and they calculate (and maximize, as they see it) before deciding what to do.

Although market system, or simply markets, is the usual terminology today, other names have been used, such as capitalism, private property, free enterprise, price system, and laissez-faire. Adam Smith's *An Inquiry into the Nature and Causes of the Wealth of Nations* (1776) is the first attempt at a comprehensive explanation of how a decentralized system that allows individual resource owners to decide where and how to use society's inputs can give a reasonable solution to society's economic problem.

This is not a history book, but you should be aware that the market system first evolved in Europe and, even more specifically, England, in the 1700s. From close up, focusing on the 15th to the 20th centuries, it was a long, gradual transformation of society that took a few hundred years. From far away, on a scale of centuries stretching back thousands of years, it was a sudden, explosive societal change. For an excellent, brief review of the rise of markets, see the second chapter, "The Economic Revolution," in Robert Heilbroner's classic book, *The Worldly Philosophers*.

The intellectual history of research on capitalism and markets is also quite fascinating. A great deal of work revolves around the idea of patterns emerging without direct, top-down control. Smith invoked the image of an "invisible hand" and Nobel Prize winning economist Friedrich Hayek coined the term "spontaneous order." In mathematics today, nonlinear dynamics and chaos theory focus on self-organizing behavior. Many have noticed that birds fly in a V, ants can form long chains and never seem to get stuck in traffic, and many animals (bees, locusts, and fish) swarm – they seem to act as if they had a collective mind. How do they do it? They do not rely on a single command center to direct each animal. Instead, each animal follows simple rules that, taken together, produce a pattern or coherent order.

In computer science, the Game of Life is an artificial world that produces unbelievable patterns from trivially simple rules. Google "game of life" to see the latest and visit these two web sites to play the Game of Life:

- <www.math.com/students/wonders/life/life.html>
- <www.ibiblio.org/lifepatterns/>.

Supply and demand analysis is more than two intersecting lines. It is a model used by economists to explain how multitudes of interacting agents in markets can solve society's incredibly complicated resource allocation problem.

For the purposes of understanding how the market system works, an individual market will be defined by the commodity bought and sold. Thus, there is a market for broccoli and a market for engineers and a market for TVs. As mentioned earlier, the fundamental questions revolving around society's resource allocation problem include what to produce, how much of each product, and how to distribute the output. By having a market for each product, we can use the market's equilibrium output as the market's answer to the resource allocation problem.

This may sound simple enough, but remember that defining the market can be difficult. In 1956, the U.S. government sued DuPont for monopolizing the cellophane (i.e., plastic wrap) market. DuPont sold more than 75% of the cellophane produced in the United States. It argued, however, the relevant market was "flexible packaging materials," including, for example, aluminum foil. DuPont had only a 20% market share of this more broadly defined market. The U.S. Supreme Court agreed with DuPont and found that there was no monopoly.

Figure III.3. Content map with focus on the market system.

Partial and General Equilibrium

There are two fundamental approaches to studying how the market system operates:

1. Partial equilibrium: Focus on a single good or service, in isolation.
2. General equilibrium: Consider all of the goods or services together.

General equilibrium analysis is superior, but more complicated. We will first analyze individual markets using conventional supply and demand graphs, then we turn to general equilibrium analysis via a new graph called the Edgeworth Box.

In both partial and general equilibrium analyses, we first determine the equilibrium solution and then judge it by comparing it to an optimal solution.

Even a casual observer would notice that the market system exhibits high rates of innovation and technological change, but we will limit our analysis to exploring how the market system functions in a static environment in which the only issue is resource allocation (given constant technology).

Organization

The chapters in this final part are organized as shown in Figure III.3.

References

The epigraph is from page 23 of James Gleick, *Chaos: The Making of a New Science* (New York: Penguin Books, 1987). This serves as an excellent, friendly introduction to nonlinear dynamics and chaotic systems.

Adam Smith's *An Inquiry into the Nature and Causes of the Wealth of Nations* (1776) is available online at <www.econlib.org/library/Smith/smWN.html>.

Robert Heilbroner, *The Worldly Philosophers: The Lives, Times, and Ideas of the Great Economic Thinkers* (New York: Touchstone, 1999, 7th edition, originally published 1953), remains one of the best summaries of the history of economics.

3.1
Partial Equilibrium

3.1.1

Supply and Demand

Credit for the ubiquitous demand and supply diagrams in principles texts is usually given to Fleeming Jenkin [1870]. ... For the first time, a real visual sense of the market is located. Pride of place goes to the equilibrium price.

Judy Klein

We begin our analysis of the market system by making an obvious, but necessary point: A market demand (or supply) curve is the sum of individual demand (or supply) curves.

Step Open the Excel workbook SupplyDemand.xls and read the *Intro* sheet, then go to the *SummingD* sheet.

The sheet has three consumers, with three different utility functions and different incomes. We assume the consumers face the same prices for goods 1 and 2. We set $p_2 = 10$, but leave p_1 as an unknown in order to derive the individual demand curve for each consumer.

Step Confirm, by clicking on a few cells in the range B18:D22, that the formulas in these cells represent the individual demand curves for each consumer. Notice that the graphs below the data represent the individual demand ($x_1^* = f(p_1)$) and inverse demand ($p_1 = f(x_1^*)$) curves.

Given individual demands, market demand can be found by simply summing the optimal quantity demanded at each price.

Step Confirm, by examining the formula in cell E18, that market demand has been computed by adding the individual demands at $p_1 = 1$. The same, of course, holds true for the other points on the market demand curve.

Because we often display demand schedules as inverse demand curves, with price on the y axis, the arrow (see your screen and Figure 3.1.1.1) shows that market demand is the result of a horizontal summation. At $p_1 = 5$, we

427

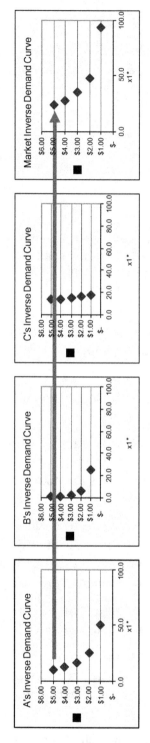

Figure 3.1.1.1. The market inverse demand curve is a horizontal sum.
Source: SupplyDemand.xls!SummingD

428

read off each of the individual quantities demanded and add them together to obtain the market quantity demanded of 24.3 units.

Because market demand is the sum of individual demands, we know that points off the market demand curve represent a failure of individual consumers to maximize utility subject to the budget constraint.

Supply works just like demand. We add individual supply curves (horizontally if we are working with inverse supply curves) to get the market supply curve. Because individual supply curves are MC above AVC, we know that the market supply curve is simply the sum of the marginal costs above AVC of all the firms producing the particular good or service sold in this market.

Points off the market supply curve represent positions where firms are failing to maximize profits. We do not expect to find points off the market demand or supply curve, but understanding what such points mean serve to reinforce the crucial concept that both curves are actually the reduced-form solutions from underlying optimization problems.

Solving Society's Resource Allocation Problem for a Single Commodity

In a nutshell, supply and demand are combined to generate an equilibrium solution that determines the quantity produced and consumed. This equilibrium solution is the market's answer to society's resource allocation problem.

The basic story is that price adjusts, responding to surpluses and shortages, until it settles down at its equilibrium level, where quantity demanded equals quantity supplied.

It is worth restating that equilibrium means no tendency to change. When applied to the model of supply and demand, equilibrium means that price (and therefore quantity demanded and supplied) has no tendency to change. A price that does have a tendency to change (because there is a surplus or shortage) is a disequilibrium price.

As with optimization problems, there are two ways to solve for an equilibrium solution:

- Analytical methods using algebra – conventional paper and pencil
- Numerical methods using a computer – for example, Excel's Solver.

Numerical Approach

We set up the problem in Excel, carefully organizing things into three main areas: endogenous variables, exogenous variables, and an equilibrium condition. Excel's Solver is then used to find the values of the endogenous variables that meet the equilibrium condition.

Step Proceed to the *EquilibriumSolution* sheet to see how the equilibrium model has been implemented in Excel.

As usual, green represents exogenous variables, the coefficients on the demand and supply curves.

Although price and quantity are endogenous variables, price is bolded to indicate that the model will be solved by finding the equilibrium price and then the equilibrium quantity (demanded and supplied) is determined.

Finally, the equilibrium condition is represented by the difference between quantity demanded and supplied.

Every first-year economics student learns that prices above the equilibrium price generate surpluses (where $Q_D < Q_S$) and, therefore, price is pushed down (as firms seek to unload unsold inventory).

Step Use the scroll bar next to the price cell to set the price below the intersection of supply and demand. The dashed line (representing the current price) responds to changes in the price cell (B12).

The quantity demanded and supplied cells also change when price changes, which makes the equilibrium condition cell (B17) change.

With a low price, the market experiences a shortage ($Q_D > Q_S$) and price is pushed up. The force in the market model is the pressure generated by surpluses (excess supply) or shortages (excess demand).

Obviously, the equilibrium price is found where supply and demand intersect. At this price, there is no tendency to change. The forces of supply and demand are balanced. We can find this price by adjusting the price manually and keeping our eye on the chart or by using Excel's Solver.

Step Open Solver. The Solver dialog box appears, as shown in Figure 3.1.1.2.

Notice that the objective is not to Max or Min, but to set an equilibrium condition equal to zero.

Notice also that *P*, price, is being used to drive the market to equilibrium.

Step Click Solve to find the equilibrium solution.

The chart reflects the correctness of Solver's result. At $P = 100$, $Q_D = Q_S = 125$. Without a surplus or shortage, there is no tendency for the price to change and we have found the equilibrium resting point.

The equilibrium quantity, 125 units, is the market's answer to society's resource allocation problem. It says that we should apply enough resources from the scarce, finite amount available to produce 125 units of this product.

You should envision a supply and demand diagram for every product and the equilibrium quantity is the market's answer to how much we should have of each commodity.

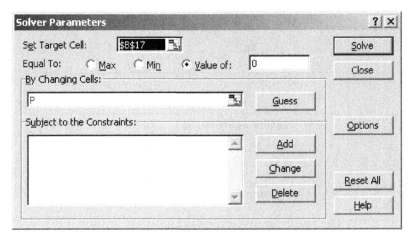

Figure 3.1.1.2. Solver dialog box.
Source: SupplyDemand.xls!EquilibriumSolution

Analytical Approach

Given either market supply and demand curves $Q = f(P)$ or inverse supply and demand functions, $P = f^{-1}(Q)$, we can easily find the equilibrium solution by setting supply and demand equal to each other.

Given the inverse functions,

$$P = 350 - 2Q_d$$
$$P = 35 + 0.52Q_s$$

the supply and demand functions are

$$P = 350 - 2Q_d \Rightarrow 2Q_d = 350 - P \Rightarrow Q_d = 175 - \frac{1}{2p}$$

$$p = 35 + 0.52Q_s \Rightarrow 0.52Q_s = P - 35 \Rightarrow Q_s = \frac{1}{0.52P} - \frac{35}{0.52}$$

Setting the inverse functions equal to each other, $350 - 2Q_e = 35 + 0.52Q_e$, we can find $Q_e = 125$, and substituting this solution into either function yields $P_e = 100$. If we set demand equal to supply, $175 - \frac{1}{2}P = 1/0.52\ P - 35/0.52$, we find $P_e = 100$, and plugging this price into either function gives $Q_e = 125$.

Not surprisingly, the numerical and analytical approaches agree.

Elasticity

We can compute the price elasticity of demand and supply at the equilibrium price by simply applying the formula for elasticity, $\frac{dQ}{dP}\frac{P}{Q}$.

Step Click the Show Point Elasticity button to see the calculation.

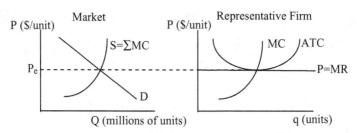

Figure 3.1.1.3. Long-run equilibrium.

Long-Run Equilibrium

In the long run (when there are no fixed factors of production), a competitive market has another adjustment to make. In addition to responding to pressure from surpluses and shortages, the market will respond to the presence of non-zero profits.

The story is simple. Excess profits (economic profits greater than zero) will lead to the entry of more firms. This will shift the inverse supply curve right, lowering the price until all excess profits are competed away. Of course, if the long-run price is too low, firms suffering negative profits will exit, shifting the inverse supply curve left and raising prices. Thus, a long-run competitive equilibrium has to look like Figure 3.1.1.3.

In essence, the long-run adjustment process endogenizes the number of firms. Forces within the model determine the number of firms in an industry. This is not true in the short run, where the number of firms is assumed fixed and the only adjustment is that surpluses and shortages are eliminated by price movements.

There are several noteworthy aspects of Figure 3.1.1.3.

1. The market supply curve is the sum of the individual firm supply curves and because we know MC above AVC is the individual firm's supply curve, we know that market supply is the sum of individual marginal costs (above AVC).
2. The market x axis is labeled "Q (millions of units)" whereas the firm's x axis is simply "q (units)." The idea is that there are many firms, each producing small amounts of the same output. In the aggregate, they make millions of units, but one individual firm produces only a tiny amount of the total.
3. Notice that the long-run equilibrium price meets two equilibrium conditions:
   A. Quantity demanded equals quantity supplied so there is no surplus or shortage in the market.
   B. Economic profits are zero so there is no incentive for entry or desire to exit.

Previous chapters discussed long-run optimization by the firm but did not include the idea of zero profit in the long run because equilibrium via supply and demand had yet to be introduced. Now that buyers and sellers are part of an equilibrium model, attention can be focused on the fact that a position of rest in the long run can be found only when profits are zero (which means firms earn positive accounting profits exactly equal to their next best alternative). Remember that the long run indicates that all inputs are freely variable and long-run equilibrium means, in addition to the absence of fixed factors, that exit and entry adjustments have driven the system to a position of rest, as shown in Figure 3.1.1.3.

Comparative Statics

Comparative statics analysis with the supply and demand equilibrium model is easy. Most introductory economics courses emphasize shifts in supply and demand. Here is a quick review.

A change in any variable that affects supply or demand, other than price, causes a shift in the inverse supply or demand curve. (Of course, a change in price causes a movement along stationary supply and demand curves.) For demand, the shift factors are income, prices of other goods related in consumption (i.e., complements and substitutes), tastes, consumers' expectations, and the number of buyers. The usual shift factors for supply include input prices, technology, firms' expectations, and the number of sellers.

As usual, comparative statics analysis consists of determining the initial solution, applying the shock, finding the new solution, and comparing the initial to the new solution. In the case of supply and demand, we want to make statements about the changes in equilibrium price and quantity.

For example, suppose the wage fell. What would that do to equilibrium price and quantity?

Step From the *EquilibriumSolution* sheet, run Solver if needed to establish the initial equilibrium position of $P_e = 125$ and $Q_e = 100$.

Next, we must apply the shock. We know that input prices affect supply. A decrease in the wage will cause the firm's cost curves (including marginal cost) to shift down. We can represent this by decreasing the intercept of the supply curve.

Step Use the scroll bar over cell F7 to decrease *s0* to 15.

The graph immediately updates and shows the shift in supply with a new, red supply curve.

Step Run Solver to find the new equilibrium solution.

Figure 3.1.1.4 shows the result. The equilibrium price falls (from 100 to roughly 84) and the equilibrium quantity rises from (from 125 to about 133).

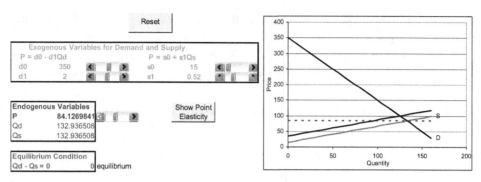

Figure 3.1.1.4. Comparative statics analysis of a decrease in the wage.
Source: SupplyDemand.xls!EquilibriumSolution

   Notice that we do not examine the equilibration process from the initial to the new solution when doing comparative statics analysis. The focus is entirely on comparing the new to the initial solution. We may, in fact, be interested in the path to the new equilibrium, but that would take us into comparative dynamics and is beyond our scope.

Supply and Demand as a Resource Allocation Mechanism

This chapter showed how an individual market settles down to its equilibrium solution. Much of this material is familiar because most introductory economics courses emphasize supply and demand analysis.

   There are two concepts, however, that are critical in gaining a deep understanding of supply and demand.

1. Supply and demand curves do not materialize out of thin air. They are the result of comparative statics analyses on consumers and firms. In other words, supply and demand must be interpreted as the reduced-form solutions from profit- and utility-maximizing agents. Figure 3.1.1.5 drives this point home.
2. It is the equilibrium quantity that is of greatest importance because this is the market's answer to society's resource allocation problem. The price is the variable that drives a market to equilibrium, but it is Q_e that represents how much of society's scarce resources are to be allocated to the production of each commodity, according to the market system.

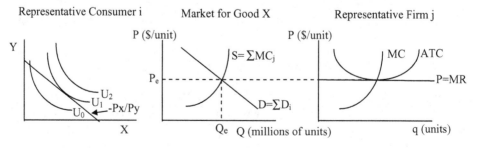

Figure 3.1.1.5. The market's resource allocation solution for one good.

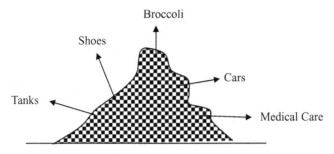

Figure 3.1.1.6. Society's resource allocation problem.

Introductory economics students are taught supply and demand, but they do not understand that the market demand and supply curves are reduced forms from individual optimization problems. The D line in the middle graph in Figure 3.1.1.5 is the sum of the individual demand curves that come from each consumer (depicted on the left panel). The same goes for supply – it is the outcome of a comparative statics experiment on each firm, in which price is varied and optimal quantity is tracked. Each panel in Figure 3.1.1.5 is presented with its usual labels, which are not consistent. In other words, X in the left panel is the number of units of the same good that is produced by the firm in the right panel with label q (units). Likewise, P in the middle and right panels equals P_x in the left panel.

The interaction of many optimizing buyers and sellers in a market (the middle panel) results in movements in price until an equilibrium (position of rest) is found. The equilibrium quantity is the market's answer to how much of society's scarce resources should be devoted to this particular commodity. There are pictures like Figure 3.1.1.5 for every good or service allocated by the market.

One way to think of the market system is to view the total of society's scarce, finite resources as being individually owned and controlled. In Figure 3.1.1.6, the mountain has been filled in with a checkerboard pattern. Each square represents the resources controlled by each person. Every person owns a tiny piece of the mountain and decides what do with that labor and capital.

Of course, the checkerboard pattern makes it seem like everyone controls equal shares, yet there is no question that some people own more resources than others. Inequality in the distribution of resources can be a serious obstacle facing the market system. It will not work well if resources are grossly unequally distributed.

Can we conclude that by virtue of the fact that the market is in equilibrium it has correctly solved society's optimization problem? Absolutely not. Equilibrium does not automatically equal optimal.

We need to set up and solve society's resource allocation problem in order to judge the market system's solution. This is the task of the next chapter.

Exercises

Open Word and answer the following questions. Save the document and print it when you are done.

1. Use the scroll bar in cell C7 of the *EquilibriumSolution* sheet to set the intercept of the inverse demand curve to 375. Use Excel's Solver to find the equilibrium solution. Take a picture of the answer and paste it in your Word document.
2. Solve the equilibrium model with $d0 = 375$ via analytical methods. Show your work, using Word's Equation Editor as needed.
3. Because the intercept increased compared with the initial values of the parameters, we know there has been an increase in demand. How has the market responded to this shock? Is the market's response reasonable?

References

The epigraph is from page 111 of Judy Klein, "The Method of Diagrams and the Black Arts of Inductive Economics," published in Ingrid Hahne Rima, *Measurement, Quantification and Economic Analysis: Numeracy in Economics* (1995). Although credit for the supply and demand graphical apparatus is often given to Fleeming (pronounced flem-ming) Jenkin, Klein reviews precursors and the fascinating history of graphs in economics.

The basic questions that must be answered by society can be traced to Paul Samuelson's dominant *Introductory Economics* textbook (first published in 1948) and Frank Knight's *The Economic Organization* (1933). "Samuelson boiled Knight's five functions down to three: i) What commodities shall be produced and in what quantities?, ii) How shall they be produced?, and iii) For whom are they to be produced? 'These three questions,' Samuelson adds, paraphrasing Knight, 'are fundamental and common to all economies.'" See Ross B. Emmett, "Frank H. Knight and *The Economic Organization*," Working Paper No. 0405–01, p. 16.

Michael Lewis, *The Blind Side: Evolution of a Game* (New York: W. W. Norton & Company, 2006), inspired the appendix to this chapter.

Appendix: An Empirical Application of Supply and Demand

This appendix uses National Football League, NFL, salary data from the 2005 season to show the effect of the market system on the salaries of different positions.

Step Open the Excel workbook NFLSalaryData.xls and read the *Intro* sheet, then go to the *Data* sheet. Scroll around a bit to familiarize yourself with the data set.

There is information on the salaries of 1973 players from the 2005 season.

Step Proceed to the *PTData* sheet. The table reports the average salary for each position. It is not shocking that quarterbacks (QB) are the highest paid, but it is surprising to see defensive ends and offensive tackles in second and third place on the salary scale.

Linemen	$398,000
Wide receiver	$504,000
Defensive end	$551,000
Running back	$620,000
Quarterback	$1,250,000

Figure 3.1.1.7. NFL salaries in 1990.
Source: Lewis (2006), p. 227

The table suffers from mixing right and left end and tackle positions along with starters and substitutes. Separating these out tells a different story.

Step Scroll right to see the table displayed starting in column R.

Whereas the QB remains the highest paid, the blind side (or left) tackle is the second highest paid player on the field at the start of a game. That is stunning. The average football fan is totally unaware of this.

Why is the blind side tackle position so highly paid?

In his entertaining book, *The Blind Side: The Evolution of a Game* (2006), Michael Lewis explains that it is a simple application of supply and demand. First, there is low supply:

The ideal left tackle was big, but a lot of people were big. What set him apart were his more subtle specifications. He was wide in the ass and massive in the thighs: the girth of his lower body lessened the likelihood that Lawrence Taylor, or his successors, would run right over him. He had long arms: pass rushers tried to get in tight to the blocker's body, then spin off it, and long arms helped to keep them at bay. He had giant hands, so that when he grabbed ahold of you, it meant something.

But size alone couldn't cope with the threat to the quarterback's blind side, because that threat was also fast. The ideal left tackle also had great feet. Incredibly nimble and quick feet. Quick enough feet, ideally, that the idea of racing him in a five-yard dash made the team's running backs uneasy. He had the body control of a ballerina and the agility of a basketball player. The combination was just incredibly rare. And so, ultimately, very expensive. (Lewis, p. 33)

In addition to low supply, there is high demand. The left tackle is charged with protecting the QB's blind side, the direction from which defensive ends and blitzing linebackers come shooting in, causing sacks, fumbles, and worst of all, injuries. Because the QB is the team's most prized asset, the left tackle position is a highly sought-after bodyguard.

But even more surprising than the fact that blind side tackles are the second highest paid players in the NFL is that this was not always the case. Lewis reports that for many years, linemen were low paid, as shown in Figure 3.1.1.7.

So, why do blind side tackles make so much money today?

NFL players did not enjoy free agency until the 1993 season. Up to that time, players were drafted or signed by teams and could move only by being traded.

The players' union and team owners signed a contract that enabled free agency for players and in return the players agreed to a salary cap that was a percentage of leaguewide team revenue. Free agency meant that a player could sell himself to the highest bidder – in other words, the market would operate to establish player salaries.

At first, everyone was shocked. Teams spent unheard of amounts on unknown linemen. Players that most fans never heard of made millions. Then a starting left tackle for the Bills, Will Wolford, announced his deal: $7.65 million over three years to play for the Colts. No one had ever paid so much money for a mere lineman. Not only that, his contract stipulated that Wolford was guaranteed to be the highest paid player on offense for as long as he was on the team.

The NFL threatened to invalidate the outlandish contract. In the end, the contract was allowed, but the commissioner decreed that such terms in a contract could not be used again.

Lewis eloquently states what happened.

The curious thing about this market revaluation is that nothing had changed in the game to make the left tackle position more valuable. Lawrence Taylor had been around since 1981. Bill Walsh's passing game had long since swept across the league. Passing attempts per game reached a new peak and remained there. There had been no meaningful change in strategy, or rules, or the threat posed by the defense to quarterbacks' health in ten years. There was no new data to enable NFL front offices to value left tackles – or any offensive linemen – more precisely. *The only thing that happened is that the market was allowed to function.* And the market assigned a radically higher value to the left tackle than had the old pre-market football culture. (Lewis, pp. 227–228, emphasis added)

This chapter has stressed that markets are a resource allocation device. Supply and demand are used to answer society's resource allocation problem. The equilibrium quantity is the market's answer to how much of society's scarce resources should be devoted to production of a particular commodity. This appendix shows that markets also correctly value commodities, in the sense that they reflect the underlying demand and supply conditions. Blind side tackles are worth a lot of money in the NFL. Before markets were used, they were grossly underpaid. There were (and still are) no statistics for linemen and they could not differentiate themselves. The market system, however, expressing the desires of general managers and reflecting the true importance of the blind side tackle, correctly values the position.

3.1.2

Consumers' and Producers' Surplus

It follows that consumer's surplus is not a concept which can be attributed to Marshall as something rather peculiarly his own. All that belongs *exclusively* to him is the name.

R. W. Houghton

Society's resource allocation problem is an especially important optimization problem. It is an easy problem to envision. Figure 3.1.2.1 shows that decisions about how to allocate society's scarce productive resources must be made. More tanks mean less of other goods and services.

The previous chapter showed how the market system uses supply and demand for each good to solve society's resource allocation problem.

This chapter changes the focus from how the market works to an evaluation of the market's solution. The approach is simple: We first consider what an optimal allocation would look like, and then check to see whether the market's allocation conforms to the optimal solution.

Finding an Optimal Quantity in a Single Market

Suppose you had special powers and could allocate resources any way you wanted? Your official title might be *Omniscient, Omnipotent Social Planner*, or OOSP, for short. You are omniscient, or all knowing, so you know everyone's desires and every firm's costs of production. Because you are omnipotent, or all powerful, you can decide how much to produce of each good and service and how it is produced.

Because this is partial equilibrium analysis, we focus on just one good or service. The question for you, OOSP, is, "How much should be produced of this particular commodity?"

One way for you to answer this question is to measure the total gain obtained by the consumers and producers of the good (when we compute the gain to producers, we subtract the costs of production). We will compute

Production: Which goods and services to produce with limited resources?
                     How much of each kind?
Distribution: How much does each person get of the goods and services produced?

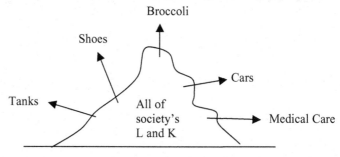

Figure 3.1.2.1. Society's resource allocation problem.

the total gain for different quantities and pick that quantity at which the total gain is maximized.

This is the fundamental idea behind consumers' and producers' surplus.

Producers' Surplus

At any given price, if sellers get that price for all of the units sold, they get a surplus from the sale of each unit except the last one. The sum of these surpluses is the producer's surplus. The sum of all of the producer's surpluses in the market is the producers' surplus, *PS*.

The location of the apostrophe matters. *Producer's* surplus is the surplus obtained by one firm. If the focus is on all of the firms, we use *producers'* surplus.

Step Open the Excel workbook CSPS.xls and read the *Intro* sheet, then go to the *PS* sheet.

The sheet displays an example with an inverse supply curve given by $P = 35 + 0.52Qs$.

The area of the green triangle is the *PS*. To see why, consider the situation when output is 75 units and the price is $74/unit.

The very last unit sold added $74 to total cost (given that we know that the supply curve is the marginal cost curve). Thus, the 75th unit sold yielded no surplus. In general, the marginal unit yields no surplus.

But what about the other units? All of the other units are inframarginal units. In other words, these are units below the marginal (last) unit and, in general, the inframarginal units generate surplus. The firm is receiving a price in excess of marginal cost for these units and, therefore, it is reaping a surplus.

Consider the 50th unit. The marginal cost of the 50th unit is given by 35 + 0.52*50 = $61. The firm would have been willing to sell the 50th unit for $61, but instead it was paid $74 for that 50th unit. So, the producer made $13 on the 50th unit.

Step Look at cell Q28. It reports the surplus generated by the 10th unit, $33.80. Cell R19 adds the surpluses from all of the inframarginal units. Cell R19 differs from cells B19 and B21 because cell R19 is based on an integer interpretation of output. If output is continuous, then we can compute the *PS* as the area of the triangle above the supply curve.

Note that cell B19 offers another way to understand *PS*. If supply is marginal cost, then the area under the marginal cost curve is total variable cost. Because marginal cost is linear, the computation is easy. If *MC* was a curve, we would have to integrate. Total revenue is simply price times quantity. Cell B19 computes *TR – TVC*, the excess over variable cost, which is the producers' surplus.

Step If $Qs = 95$, what is *PS*? Simply move the scroll bar in cell C12 to set quantity equal to 95.

Step Confirm that as quantity rises, so does *PS*.

Consumers' Surplus

The idea is the same. At any given price, if a buyer pays that price for all of the units bought, she gets a surplus from the purchase of each unit except the last one. The sum of these surpluses is the consumer's surplus. The sum of all of the consumer's surpluses is the consumers' surplus, *CS*.

Step Proceed to the *CS* sheet.

Given the inverse demand curve, $P = 350 - 0.2Qd$, we can easily compute *CS* for a given quantity.

If $Qd = 95$, what is *CS*?

At $Qd = 95$, the price is 190. The last unit purchased provides no surplus, but the inframarginal units generate *CS*. The area under the demand curve, but above the price, is a measure of the net satisfaction enjoyed by consumers.

Note that consumers would have paid more for each inframarginal unit than the price they actually paid so they get a surplus for each marginal unit.

If we interpret the demand curve as a marginal benefit curve, then the area under the curve up to a given quantity is the total benefit from consuming that amount. Price times quantity is the total cost to the consumers so the triangle above the price is the net benefit. This is an interpretation of *CS* that is similar to the view of *PS* as *TR* − *TVC*.

Step Use the scroll bar in cell C12 to adjust the output and display the *CS* for any given level of output.

Maximizing CS + PS

Producers' surplus is the amount by which the total revenue exceeds variable costs. Consumers' surplus is the amount by which the total satisfaction provided by the commodity exceeds the total costs of purchasing the commodity.

Both parties, consumers and producers, gain from trade. This is why a trade is made – because both buyer and seller are better off. When you buy something, you part with some money in exchange for the good or service. If the purchase is voluntary, you must value what you are getting more than what you paid for it – or else you would not have bought it. Similarly, the seller values the money you pay more than the good or service – or else she would refuse to sell at that price. The gains from voluntary trade are captured in the terms consumers' and producers' surplus.

Casting the problem in terms of surplus benefits received by buyers and sellers leads naturally to this question: What is the level of output that maximizes the total surplus? After all, it is clear that as quantity changes the *CS* and *PS* also change.

Thus, OOSP is faced with the following optimization problem:

$$\max_q CS(q) + PS(q)$$

The idea is to maximize the gains from trade for all buyers and sellers. This problem can be solved analytically and numerically. We focus on the latter.

Step Proceed to the *CSandPS* sheet. This sheet combines the surpluses enjoyed by producers and consumers into a single chart.

Figure 3.1.2.2 shows the *CS* and *PS* when *Q* = 95. Cell J20 shows the sum of the two surpluses when *Q* = 95.

In Figure 3.1.2.2 (and on your computer screen), it is presumed that producers receive a price of $84.40 for each of the 95 units, yet consumers pay $160.00 per unit. Remember that you are the OOSP so it is easy for you to charge one price to consumers and give a different price to producers. By adding the values in cells E18 and B21, we get the value in cell J20.

Can we increase the sum of *CS* and *PS*? Of course we can.

Step Click on the slider control (over cell C12), to increase output in increments of five units.

As output increases, *CS* and *PS* both rise.

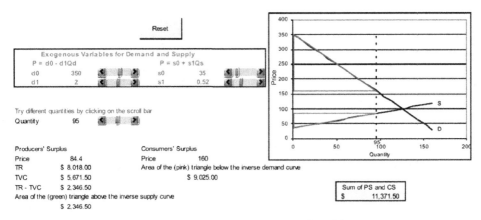

Figure 3.1.2.2. *CS* and *PS* at $Q = 95$.
Source: CSPS.xls!CSandPS

Step Continue clicking on the slider control. As you do, observe that $CS + PS$ is maximized at $Q^* = 125$. As output increases beyond this point, $CS + PS$ decreases.

In other words, the OOSP should order the production and sale of 125 units of output at a price of $100 unit. This level of output maximizes the sum of *CS* and *PS*.

Deadweight Loss

If the OOSP chooses an output level below 125 and charges a price to consumers based on the inverse demand curve and pays producers a price based on the inverse supply curve, it will generate a smaller value of $CS + PS$.

How much smaller? The amount of surplus not captured is given by the trapezoid between the consumers' and producers' surpluses. This area is called deadweight loss. It is a fundamental concept in economics and merits careful attention.

Step Enter 95 in cell B12 and click the Show DWL button.

Not only do data appear below the button, but the chart has been modified to include a red trapezoid. The area of the trapezoid is displayed in cell D30.

To see how deadweight loss is calculated, you can view the formulas in the cells.

Step First, click on cell D26. The formula is simply the solution of the intersection of the supply and demand curves. We know this quantity is the solution to the problem of maximizing *CS* and *PS*.

Step Next, click on cell D28. This seemingly complicated formula is not really that hard. It displays the maximum possible total surplus.

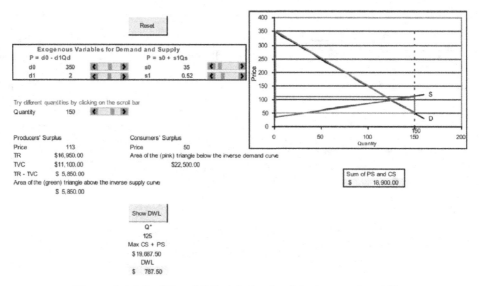

Figure 3.1.2.3. *CS* and *PS* with deadweight loss at $Q = 150$.
Source: CSPS.xls!CSandPS

Two things are being added, *CS* and *PS*. The first part of the formula is *PS*: 0.5*(((s0_+s1_*D26)-s0_)*D26). It is half the height of the *PS* triangle times the length (or quantity produced). The second part of the formula computes the *CS*: 0.5*((d0_ − (d0_ − d1*D26))*D26). The area of this triangle is also half its height times its width.

Step Last, click on cell D30. This is the formula: = D28 − J20.

This formula makes crystal clear that *deadweight loss* is maximum total surplus minus the sum of *CS* and *PS* at any value of output. In other words, it is a measure of the inefficiency of producing the wrong level of output in a particular market.

Step Click on the slider control (over cell C12) to increase output in increments of five units.

As you increase output, note that the deadweight loss falls as the output approaches the optimal quantity. There is no deadweight loss when the output is at 125 because this is the optimal level of output.

Step Set output above the optimal level, for example, $Q = 150$.

Your screen should look like Figure 3.1.2.3.

It is tempting to think that the OOSP could choose very high levels of output in order to create huge consumers' and producers' surpluses. After all, both *CS* and *PS* increase as output rises. In Figure 3.1.2.3, *CS* is extremely high because the output of 150 is sold at a low price of $50 per unit. Similarly, *PS* is large because the price received by firms is $113.

The green triangle and positive deadweight loss value in cell D30, however, give a hint that $Q = 150$ is not a good solution. The problem is that the OOSP is going to have to finance this scheme. It is possible (by appropriately subsidizing buyers or sellers) to have sellers receive $113 per unit sold yet have buyers pay only $50 per unit sold, but someone is going to have to make up that $63 per unit difference. The total value of the subsidy, 63*150 = $9340, must be subtracted from the sum of *CS* and *PS*. When you do this, you get a total surplus of $18,900, which is lower than the maximum total surplus. Cell J20 uses an IF statement to get the calculation right. The deadweight loss from producing 150 units is $787.50 (cell *D*30).

The deadweight loss at $Q = 150$ is given by the red triangle. The geometry is easy. We must subtract a rectangle with height 63 and length 150 from the sum of the pink *CS* and green *PS* triangles. This leaves the red triangle as a measure of the inefficiency caused by producing too much output.

Optimal Resource Allocation

In the previous chapter, we saw that the equilibrium quantity, Qe, generated by a properly functioning market is located at the intersection of supply and demand. The market uses a good's price to send signals to buyers and sellers. Prices above equilibrium are pushed down, whereas prices below equilibrium are pushed up. At the equilibrium solution, the price has no tendency to change and output is also at rest. The equilibrium level of output is the market's answer to how much of society's resources will be devoted to producing this particular good.

Our work with consumers' and producers' surplus in this chapter takes a much different perspective on the problem. Instead of examining how the market works, we have created a thought experiment, giving an imaginary social planner awesome powers. Given the goal of maximizing total surplus, the OOSP would choose an optimal quantity, Q^*, that should be produced. If we produce less or more than this socially optimal amount, society would forego surpluses that would make producers and consumers better off.

If we compare the market's equilibrium quantity to the socially optimal quantity, we are struck by an amazing fact: $Qe = Q^*$. This is a powerful result. It says that the socially optimal amount is found where demand and supply intersect. You do not need a dictator, benevolent or otherwise, to optimally allocate resources. The market, using prices, will settle down to a position of rest where all gains from trade are completely exploited and the sum of producers' and consumers' surplus is maximized.

Observing that a properly functioning market has no deadweight loss is another way of expressing the result that the market generates an output that is socially optimal.

The procedure followed – comparing the market's quantity (or answer to society's resource allocation problem) to the socially optimal quantity – will be used over and over again. It is a common way of evaluating allocation schemes.

Price Controls

Price controls are legally mandated limits on prices. A price ceiling sets the highest price at which the good can be legally sold. A price floor does the opposite: The good cannot be sold any lower than the given amount. To be effective, a price ceiling has to be set below and a price floor has to be set above the equilibrium price.

Most introductory economics students are taught that price ceilings generate shortages and price floors lead to surpluses. For most students, the take-home message is that market forces cannot push the price above the ceiling or below the floor so the market cannot clear and this is why price controls are undesirable.

It turns out that this is not exactly right. Although it is true that ceilings lead to persistent excess demand and floors prevent the market from eliminating excess supply, the real reason behind the unpopularity (among economists) of price controls is the fact that they cause a misallocation of resources.

Step Proceed to the *PriceControls* sheet.

Suppose there is a price ceiling on this good at $84.40. At this price, there is a shortage of the good because quantity demanded at $84.40 is 181.2 units (cell B13) while quantity supplied is only 95 (cell B12).

The price cannot be bid up because $84.40 is the highest price at which the good can be legally sold. Thus, with this price ceiling, the output level is 95. We know this is an inefficient result because we know $Q^* = 125$. This is the real reason why this price ceiling is a poor policy, not because it causes a shortage. The price ceiling fails to maximize total surplus.

The amount of the surplus with the price control and the deadweight loss depends on the particular story behind the price control. Suppose that there is no black market (illegal selling of the good above the legally set limit) associated with this ceiling. In other words, producers do not violate the law. Suppose further that the good is allocated via lottery so there are no lines of buyers or resources spent waiting.

This means that consumers' surplus is now a trapezoid instead of a triangle. As shown in Figure 3.1.2.4 (and on your screen), in addition to the usual

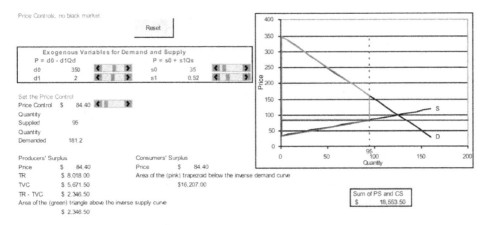

Figure 3.1.2.4. Evaluating a price ceiling of $84.40.
Source: CSPS.xls!PriceControls

CS triangle, consumers enjoy the area of the rectangle computed by multiplying a price of $160 (which is the price consumers are willing to pay for 95 units of the good) minus $84.40 (the price consumers actually pay) times 95 units.

The good news behind this price ceiling is that the deadweight loss is much smaller than in the *CSandPS* sheet because the lucky consumers who can purchase the good do not have to pay $160. The bad news is that there is still a deadweight loss of $1134. This is a measure of the inefficiency of the price ceiling with no black market.

Suppose instead that the sellers cheat and illegally sell the product at the black market price, $160. Then the producers get the rectangle. With a black market, the rectangle is transferred from consumers to producers, but the deadweight loss stays the same. The *Q&A* sheet asks you to demonstrate this.

This result illustrates an interesting point about *CS* and *PS* analysis – we do not care who gets the surplus. A dollar of surplus to a consumer is the same as a dollar of surplus to a producer. We care only about potential surpluses that no one gets, which we call deadweight loss.

Consider two other possibilities. The price ceiling is set and a limited set of buyers are given coupons. To buy the good (at the legal price), you must have a coupon. If a rationing coupon scheme is used, the sellers of the coupons get the rectangle. The deadweight loss remains the same.

Suppose finally that a price ceiling is set and the good is allocated on a first-come-first-serve basis. In other words, buyers have to wait in line. Now no one gets the rectangle. The resources buyers waste standing in line (or paying others to stand in line for them) must be subtracted from the total surplus. The deadweight loss rises. If the entire rectangle is lost, then the deadweight loss is the same as that in the *CSandPS* sheet when 95 units of output are produced.

You might think these different descriptions of how price ceilings might be implemented are of merely theoretical interest, but in fact every one of these scenarios has been used. Price controls are a popular way to modify market results. Unfortunately, from a resource allocation standpoint, price controls suffer from the fact that they fail to maximize total surplus.

Do not be confused by the many ways price controls are implemented. The take-home message is that any deviation from Q^* means that the allocation scheme has failed. Deadweight loss, which gives a measure of the inefficiency in monetary units, depends on the specific implementation of the price control.

Caveat Emptor

Deadweight loss is a common way that economists measure inefficiency. It is based on the idea that the maximum total surplus is not attained from a particular output level. Unfortunately, it has two glaring weaknesses.

The first has to do with our calculation of consumers' surplus. For technical reasons, restrictive assumptions about the utility function must be imposed. For example, a Cobb-Douglas utility function for individual consumers will not work because it has an income effect. A quasilinear utility function will work (no income effect), but it is unlikely that all consumers have quasilinear utility.

The second weakness stems from the use of partial equilibrium analysis. We are calculating deadweight loss based on the impact in a single market of a deviation in output from its optimal level. The focus on one market is too limited. If we apply too many or too few resources to the production of one good, we will cause deviations from optimal output for other goods and services. So, the deadweight loss computation based on one market is a lower bound. To get it exactly right, we would have to analyze effects on other markets and do a general equilibrium analysis.

Regarding deadweight loss, it is caveat emptor – buyer beware. Remember that deadweight loss measures inefficiency, but it is not exactly right. The best way to think of deadweight loss is as an approximation.

Choose *Q* to Max *CS* + *PS*

This is an important chapter. It introduced producers' and consumers' surpluses, which are key elements in the omnipotent, omniscient social planner's objective function.

The idea that there is an optimal level of output for each good and service is fundamental. From this idea we get the procedure for evaluating any allocation scheme or government policy: We compare an observed result to the optimal answer.

It is obvious that quantities below the intersection of supply and demand cannot be optimal because both *CS* and *PS* rise as Q increases. The situation with quantity above the intersection of supply and demand is more subtle. To get the calculation right, whenever quantity is above the intersection point, we must subtract from the sum of *CS* and *PS* a rectangle that is the difference between prices multiplied by quantity.

One remarkable result from this chapter is that $Qe = Q^*$. This says that in a properly functioning market, the equilibrium quantity (which is the answer to society's resource allocation problem) yields the socially optimal level of output.

Price controls lead to inefficient allocation of resources. The output generated does not match the optimal output. The deadweight loss associated with a price control depends on the particular implementation of the price control.

There is no question that deadweight loss is a linchpin of policy analysis. Countless cost–benefit studies have been conducted. Because of technical complications, real-world applications of deadweight loss should be seen as an approximation to the exact answer.

Exercises

Open Word and answer the following questions. Save the document and print it when you are done.

1. From the *CSandPS* sheet, use Solver to find the optimal quantity. Take a picture of the cells that contain your answer and paste it in your Word doc.
2. With linear supply and demand, *PS* and *CS* are given by the following functions:

$$CS = \frac{1}{2}\left(d_0 - (d_0 - d_1 q)\right) q$$

$$PS = \frac{1}{2}\left((s_0 + s_1 q) - s_0\right) q$$

Use these functions to set up and solve the OOSP's optimization problem. Show your work.
Hint: Remember that if Q is greater than the intersection of supply and demand, we must subtract the rectangle given by (supply price minus demand price) times quantity.
3. Do the answers to questions 1 and 2 agree? Is this surprising? Explain why or why not.
4. Use the *PriceControls* sheet to set a price floor at $120 per unit. Click the Show DWL button. Take a picture of the chart with this price floor. Explain the deadweight loss triangle.

References

The epigraph is from the first page of R. W. Houghton, "A Note on the Early
History of Consumer's Surplus," *Economica*, New Series, Vol. 25, No. 97
(February, 1958), pp. 49–57. A French engineer, Jules Dupuit (pronounced
doo-pwee) presented the idea of *utilité relative* in 1844, but Alfred Marshall
independently rediscovered and popularized the notion of consumer's surplus.

Almost immediately after Marshall introduced consumers' surplus, the concept
came under attack. It has survived the move from a cardinal to an ordinal
perspective on utility and a variety of other criticisms. Economists know that CS is
built on shaky foundations, but they often use it in practical, policy-oriented,
real-world discussions. In a review of the state of CS, Abram Bergson concludes,
"Despite theoretic criticism, practitioners have continued to apply consumer's
surplus analysis through the years. As some have argued, that must already say
something about the usefulness (as well as the use) of such analysis, but just what it
says has remained more or less in doubt." See "A Note on Consumer's Surplus,"
Journal of Economic Literature, Vol. 13, No. 1 (March, 1975), pp. 38–44.

3.1.3

Taxes: Incidence and Deadweight Loss

Harberger triangles, now common fare, were once rare delicacies.... While the theory of deadweight loss measurement was well-established by the 1950s, economists very rarely estimated deadweight losses prior to the appearance of Harberger's work.

James R. Hines, Jr.

Many goods and services are taxed. Sales taxes (also called value added or *ad valorem* taxes) are a percentage of the monetary amount spent; quantity taxes are levied per unit bought. Quantity taxes are applied to gasoline, alcohol, and cigarettes.

In Chapter 1.3.4, it was shown that, for a particular consumer, lump sum (fixed amount) taxes are better than quantity taxes. Our perspective now turns from the individual to the market.

Supply and demand analysis can be used to evaluate the effects of taxes on goods and services allocated by the market. We work with quantity taxes because our linear supply and demand curves will shift vertically as the tax is applied. Sales taxes are harder to analyze, but the qualitative results we derive for quantity taxes carry over to sales taxes.

The chapter focuses on two basic issues:

- Incidence, determining how the burden of the tax is split between consumers and producers
- Deadweight loss, evaluating the inefficiency generated by the tax.

Our work on tax incidence will demonstrate a counterintuitive proposition: It does not matter whether consumers or producers pay the quantity tax. In the end, the tax burden does not depend on who sends tax revenue to the government.

Our approach to evaluating the effects of a quantity tax relies on comparing the output after the tax is imposed to the socially optimal output (based on maximizing consumers' and producers' surplus). Deviations from optimality are said to be inefficient solutions to society's resource allocation problem. Deadweight loss is used to measure the inefficiency.

It Does Not Matter Who Collects the Tax

Suppose you rent an apartment for $700 a month. Suppose further that property taxes rise $100. If your landlord raises the rent to $800 a month and you agree, it is easy to see that you are paying for the entire tax increase. The landlord pays the property tax to the government, but you are bearing the burden of the tax.

Suppose you refuse to pay the $100 increase and move out. The landlord cannot find anyone to rent the apartment at $800 and, eventually, agrees to rent the apartment for $725 a month to a new tenant. The computation of the tax burden is easy. The tenant is bearing the burden of $25 or 25% of the tax increase, while the landlord's burden is $75 or 75%.

Tax incidence is the analysis of who bears the burden of a tax. In a moment, we will be shifting demand and supply curves and drawing complicated graphs, but the analysis is basically the same as the story of the tenant and the landlord.

Case 1: Supplier Pays

Suppose that the supplier is responsible for collecting the tax when the good is purchased and for sending in the tax payments to the government. This is what is meant by "supplier pays." Of course, we know that who collects and pays the tax is different from the tax incidence because anywhere from 0 to 100% of the tax may be shifted.

Step Open the Excel workbook Taxes.xls and read the *Intro* sheet, then go to the *SupplierPays* sheet.

The sheet has parameters for linear demand and supply curves. On open, there is no tax so the equilibrium price is $100 and the equilibrium quantity is 125. Cell B17 shows that the government collects no revenue and cell E17 shows that there is no deadweight loss (because the market's equilibrium quantity equals the socially optimal quantity).

Step In the *SupplierPays* sheet, click on the scroll bar next to the Tax cell five times. A red line appears on the chart and it shifts with each click. Five clicks will set the tax at $50 and the spreadsheet will look like Figure 3.1.3.1.

The inverse supply curve has shifted up by $50 because in order for the suppliers to offer any given quantity, they have to receive $50 more than the

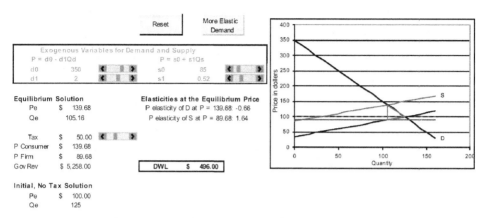

Figure 3.1.3.1. Supplier pays a $50 quantity tax.
Source: Taxes.xls!SupplierPays

original supply curve (without the tax). They will not get to keep the extra $50 per unit – they have to send it to the government.

The spreadsheet displays the information we need to compute the tax incidence. We can easily see that the consumer is bearing the majority of the tax. In fact, we can compute the fraction of the tax actually paid by the consumer: 39.68/50 ≈ 80%. The supplier has managed to pass along all but 20% of the tax to the consumer.

Notice that demand is more inelastic than supply at the equilibrium point. It turns out that the price elasticities of demand and supply play a critical role in determining the tax incidence.

With respect to our second issue, deadweight loss, we see that cell E17 is reporting a value of $496. The deadweight loss can be calculated by finding the difference of the maximum possible surplus minus the surpluses enjoyed by the consumers, producers, and government. This is equivalent to the (red) triangle on the chart, which is also known as a *Harberger triangle*. The height of the triangle is the price the consumer pays minus the price received by the firm, which is called the tax wedge. This distance is the amount of the tax. The length is the distance from the new equilibrium quantity after the tax to the original equilibrium quantity. The bigger this distance, the greater is the distortion of the tax in terms of resource allocation.

Step Click on cell E17 to see the formula. It simply computes the area of the red, Harberger triangle.

Deadweight loss is a dollar measure of the distortion caused by the tax – the "market with a tax" scheme is no longer producing the optimal quantity. Deadweight loss represents gains from trades that are not being exploited. There is $496 in value that no one is getting. It is simply vaporized and disappears into thin air.

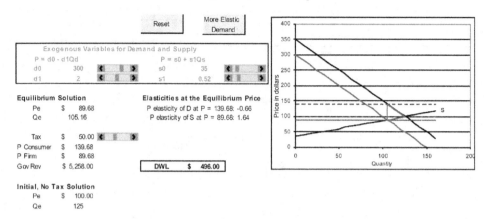

Figure 3.1.3.2. Consumer pays a $50 quantity tax.
Source: Taxes.xls!DemanderPays

The rectangle formed by the tax times the equilibrium quantity (after the tax is imposed) is a transfer from consumers and producers to the government. It does not count as deadweight loss because someone (the government) is getting it. The key to understanding deadweight loss is that it accrues to no one – it is unclaimed surplus and, therefore, pure waste.

Case 2: Demander Pays

Suppose instead that the consumer is responsible for collecting the tax when the good is purchased and for sending in the tax payments to the government. This may seem a little strange at first, but there are cases where this occurs. For example, if you buy cigarettes or wine on the Internet (and have it shipped to your home), you are supposed to pay the taxes (federal and state).

For the purposes of this exercise, forget about administrative costs or the fact that firms are much better tax collectors than consumers. We assume that consumers and firms will both pay the tax even though that is obviously not true.

Step Go to the *DemanderPays* sheet and impose a $50 tax. Figure 3.1.3.2 shows the result.

This time, it is the demand curve that is shifting. Instead of the firm paying the tax, it is the consumer who must collect the tax and send in the payments. A $50 tax will shift the inverse demand curve down by $50 because each consumer is willing to buy any given quantity for $50 less than before since she will have to pay an additional $50 to the government for the good.

As before, a deadweight loss triangle arises when you impose the $50 tax. The equilibrium quantity is driven down by the tax and, therefore, it no longer equals the socially optimal quantity. The tax causes an inefficient allocation of resources. The deadweight loss of $496 is a measure of the inefficiency caused by the tax.

The area of the Harberger triangle is the deadweight loss. The rectangle that represents government revenue is a transfer and is not included in the deadweight loss.

Comparing Supplier and Demander Pays Cases

Step We will compare the results in the two sheets by toggling back and forth. Click the *SupplierPays* sheet tab, then click the *DemanderPays* sheet tab. Repeat this several times while keeping your eye on the screen. What do you notice?

Careful comparison of the *SupplierPays* and *DemanderPays* sheets reveals that many of the results are exactly the same!

The chart is different, of course, and the *d0* and *s0* parameters are different because the demand and supply intercepts do change based on who collects the tax for the government. But the price paid by the consumer, the price received by the firm, government revenue, and, most importantly, equilibrium quantity and deadweight loss are all exactly the same.

This demonstrates a fundamental principle in tax analysis: *it doesn't matter who actually pays the tax* (assuming the two parties are equally likely to collect and send the payments to the government). The tax incidence does not depend at all on who physically collects the tax. Just like the tax incidence, the deadweight loss is the same regardless of who actually sends the government the tax.

If it does not matter who collects the tax for the government, then what do tax incidence and deadweight loss depend on?

Price Elasticities of Demand and Supply Determine Tax Incidence and Deadweight Loss

The actual distribution of the tax burden, i.e., the tax incidence, depends only on the elasticities of demand and supply. The more inelastic the demand curve, given a supply curve, the more the consumer will bear the burden of the tax. The more inelastic the supply curve, given a demand curve, the more the supplier bears the burden of the tax.

Price elasticities of demand and supply also play a crucial role in determining the deadweight loss of a tax.

To consider an extreme case, we return to the apartment example. If you agree to a $100 increase in rent, your demand for apartments is perfectly

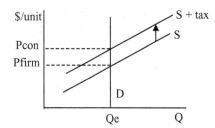

Figure 3.1.3.3. Tax effects with perfectly inelastic demand.

inelastic in this price range. The price increase from $700 to $800 has no effect on the quantity demanded. In this case, the consumer bears the entire burden of the tax and there is no deadweight loss. The situation is depicted in Figure 3.1.3.3.

Suppose the situation was reversed and supply was perfectly inelastic. If we shift up a vertical line, the line remains unchanged. Figure 3.1.3.4 shows that now firms bear the entire burden of the tax. Producers receive the same price as before, but they have to pay the tax. Once again, however, there is no deadweight loss because the equilibrium output remains unchanged and equal to the socially optimal level of output.

Of course, the main result that price elasticities determine tax incidence and deadweight loss applies in general and not just to these extreme cases. Figure 3.1.3.5 offers an example. The product is inelastically demanded and elastically supplied. Imposing a tax yields the following results:

• Buyers will bear more of the burden of the tax because price will rise substantially.
• There will be a small DWL because Q will fall only slightly.

Figure 3.1.3.5 shows that the price paid by the consumer rises almost by as much as the amount of the tax and the price received by the firm is only a tiny bit lower. This is obviously a direct consequence of the extremely steep demand and flat supply curve.

Figure 3.1.3.5 also shows that the deadweight loss, Harberger triangle is small because output does not decrease by much. Once again, the steep demand curve is responsible for this outcome.

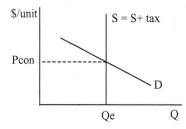

Figure 3.1.3.4. Tax effects with perfectly inelastic supply.

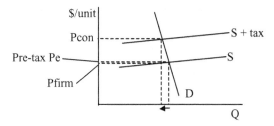

Figure 3.1.3.5. Inelastic D and elastic S.

We conclude our analysis of the effects of taxes by returning to the Excel workbook.

Step Return to the *SupplierPays* sheet. With a tax of $50, we know that the consumer bears 80% of the tax and the deadweight loss is $496. The government collects $5258 in tax revenues. Note that the price elasticity of demand (at the equilibrium solution) was −0.4 before the tax and is −0.66 after the tax.

Step Click the Reset button. Click the More Elastic Demand button. Notice that the demand curve is flatter, yet it goes through the initial equilibrium solution. The button simply sets the intercept and slope to 225 and 1, respectively. The price elasticity of demand has risen (in absolute value) to −0.8.

The idea is to compare the effects of the same tax with this new, more price elastic demand curve versus the original, more price inelastic demand curve, ceteris paribus.

Step Impose the $50 tax. Figure 3.1.3.6 shows the result.

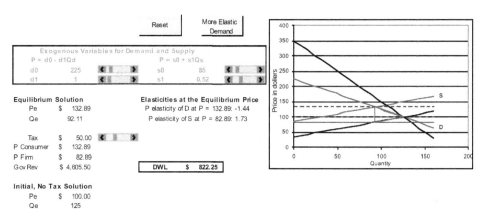

Figure 3.1.3.6. Tax incidence and deadweight loss with more elastic demand.
Source: Taxes.xls!SupplierPays

The result is clear: The tax incidence is lower on the consumer and higher on the producer and the deadweight loss is greater.

Before, the consumer bore 80% of the tax; after, the consumer pays about 66% (32.89/50) of the tax. Figure 3.1.3.6 and your computer screen show that the equilibrium price did not increase by as much as before because the demand curve is flatter.

The deadweight loss increased from $496 to $822.25. Although the red triangle that represents the deadweight loss is shorter (because the new equilibrium price is lower than before), it is much wider. In other words, quantity has fallen by much more after the imposition of the tax. With more elastic demand, ceteris paribus, a tax causes a greater deviation from the socially optimal output and, therefore, more deadweight loss.

Finally, note that government tax revenue fell from $5528.00 to $4605.50. The government continues to get $50 per unit sold, but because demand is more elastic, output has fallen by more and, therefore, the government's revenue falls.

Clearly, it is better, ceteris paribus, to tax goods with low price elasticities of demand or supply. In the introduction to this chapter, gasoline, cigarettes, and alcohol were mentioned as goods that carry quantity taxes. It is no surprise that these goods are relatively inelastically demanded.

There is no quantity tax on Milky Ways, a scrumptious chocolate candy. Obviously, the government could never generate the same tax revenue from Milky Ways as gasoline, but even if it could, with so many substitutes, Milky Ways must be very price elastic. A tax on Milky Ways would lead to a great fall in equilibrium output. Government revenue would be quite low and deadweight loss very high.

Optimal Taxation

Public Finance (also known as Public Economics) is a subdiscipline of Economics that includes the study of government tax policy. The theory of optimal taxation focuses on the best way to tax. The analysis in this chapter says that quantity taxes should not be applied to goods that are relatively price elastic because the deadweight loss will be high. Instead, by taxing goods with steep demand or supply curves, the government can raise needed revenue with a minimum of distortion.

The chapter also focused on the issue of tax incidence, i.e., who really bears the burden of a tax. It does not matter who collects the tax for the government because that party may be able to shift the tax onto someone else. Like deadweight loss, the tax incidence depends on the elasticities of demand and supply. The more inelastic one of the curves is versus the other, the more that party will bear the burden of the tax.

Exercises

Open Word and answer the following questions. Save the document and print it when you are done.

1. Do we get the same result as Figure 3.1.3.4 if we have consumers pay the tax to the government with a perfectly inelastic supply curve? To support your answer, use Word's Drawing Tools to draw a graph like Figure 3.1.3.4, except the demander pays. Explain the graph and the result.
2. Use Word's Drawing Tools to draw a graph like Figure 3.1.3.5, except supply is more inelastic than demand. Comment on the tax incidence and deadweight loss.
3. In 1937, when Congress set up the Social Security system, it was decided that firms and workers each pay half of the total tax so the burden is equally shared. Do you think this is true? Draw a graph to support your answer.

References

The epigraph comes from page 168 of James R. Hines, Jr., "Three Sides of Harberger Triangles," *The Journal of Economic Perspectives*, Vol. 13, No. 2 (Spring, 1999), pp. 167–188. Hines explains that the theory of deadweight loss dates back to Dupuit, Jenkin, and Marshall, but Harberger's papers in the 1950s and 1960s "illustrated the techniques, the usefulness, and the realistic possibility of performing such calculations, and in so doing, ushered in a new generation of applied normative work" (p. 168). For this reason, argues Hines, "Welfare loss triangles are 'Harberger triangles' because Harberger's papers measured them, did so in a consistent manner, and assisted and encouraged a host of others to do likewise" (p. 185).

Arnold C. Harberger published a number of papers, but perhaps his key contribution was "The Measurement of Waste," *American Economic Review*, Vol. 54, No. 3 (May, 1964), pp. 58–76.

3.1.4

Inefficiency of Monopoly

Marginal cost pricing as a policy is largely without merit. How then can one explain the widespread support that it has enjoyed in the economics profession? I believe it is the result of economists using an approach which I have termed "blackboard economics."

Ronald Coase

We know that a properly functioning market correctly solves society's resource allocation problem (depicted in Figure 3.1.4.1). Each good and service has supply and demand curves. Prices signal quantities demanded and supplied and are pushed toward equilibrium by market forces. The equilibrium quantity is the market's answer to society's resource allocation problem.

If an omniscient, omnipotent social planner, OOSP, were to maximize the consumers' and producers' surplus of an individual good or service, he would explicitly order the production of the socially optimal amount of each good and service.

A properly functioning market's equilibrium quantity equals the socially optimal quantity. This is what we mean when we say that a properly functioning market correctly solves society's resource allocation problem. There is no deadweight loss because the correct output is produced.

This chapter focuses on the following question: What happens if one of the goods is produced by a single seller (instead of the many individual firms that define perfect competition)?

In other words, we explore the welfare effects of monopoly. Our analysis is based on partial equilibrium and uses the tools of consumers' and producers' surplus. We evaluate monopoly by figuring out what a monopolist would produce, and then compare the monopoly output to the socially optimal output.

Production: Which goods and services to produce with limited resources?
How much of each kind?

Distribution: How much does each person get of the goods and services produced?

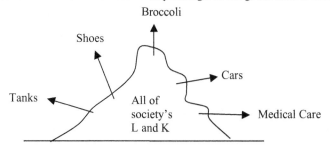

Figure 3.1.4.1. Society's resource allocation problem.

The Perfectly Competitive Solution

Step Open the Excel workbook MonopolyDWL.xls and read the *Intro* sheet; then go to the *PC* sheet.

The linear demand and supply curves have the same parameter values used in previous examples. The equilibrium price is $100, which yields an equilibrium output of 125 units. Because the socially optimal level of production is also 125 units, the market yields an efficient allocation of resources.

Notice that at the socially optimal and competitive market solution, industrywide marginal cost (which is the supply curve) equals demand. This is called *marginal cost pricing* and is indicative of a socially optimal solution.

The Monopoly Solution

Suppose a good is supplied via a perfectly competitive market. Then the equilibrium price is determined by the forces of supply and demand and an equilibrium quantity is established.

Now suppose all of the firms that produce that product merge into a giant, single firm. We assume that the cost structure stays exactly the same. In other words, the supply curve, which was the sum of the individual marginal cost curves, now becomes the monopolist's marginal cost curve.

Assuming that the industrywide costs of many firms would be the same costs faced by a single firm is a bit farfetched. After all, the monopolist needs only one CEO and one customer service hotline. In other words, there may be economies of scale in administration, distribution, and other areas. We assume this away in our comparison of perfect competition and monopoly.

This monopoly will behave differently than the many firms did because there is no competition. Unlike the competitive result, where price is determined by the interaction of many buyers and sellers, the monopolist will find and set the profit-maximizing price and quantity. We want to evaluate the performance of the monopoly market structure.

There are two ways to do this:

- Analytical methods using algebra – conventional, paper and pencil
- Numerical methods using a computer, e.g., Excel's Solver.

Analytical Approach

The monopoly will seek to maximize profit. It can do so by finding that quantity where $MR = MC$.

The MC function is given by the supply curve parameters in the PC sheet. Once a monopoly takes over, it doesn't have a supply curve, but it does have a marginal cost function, which is the same as the supply curve (because of our assumption that there is no difference in costs between a competitive industry and a monopoly).

Thus, $MC = 35 + 0.52Q$.

The MR function can be found from the demand curve.

$$TR = PQ = (d_0 - d_1 Q)Q = d_0 Q - d_1 Q^2$$

$$dTR/dQ = MR = d_0 - 2d_1 Q$$

As expected, we see that MR has twice the slope of the demand curve.

Thus, for this example, using the parameter values from the PC sheet, we have:

$$MC = 35 + 0.52Q \quad \text{and} \quad MR = 350 - 2{*}2Q$$

To find Q^*, we set $MR = MC$ and solve for Q^*.

$$35 + 0.52Q = 350 - 2{*}2Q$$

$$4.52Q = 315$$

$$Q^* \approx 69.7$$

To find P^*, we use the demand curve to compute the highest price obtainable for that quantity.

$$P^* = 350 - 2Q^* = 350 - 2(69.7)$$

$$P^* \approx 210.6$$

Numerical Approach

Step Proceed to the *Monopoly* sheet. The graph has been augmented with the MR curve and the supply curve is now labeled MC. The MR curve was always there, but perfectly competitive firms cannot exploit it.

The sheet shows the monopoly solution in cells B15 and B16. Before we examine the deadweight loss and surplus information, we confirm that the monopoly solution is correct. When you run Solver, notice that the Solver dialog box is set up to choose that quantity that sets cell B20 to zero. The initial output of 50 units is too low. The fact that $MR - MC$ is $89 means that the 50th unit of output adds $89 more in profits and, therefore, more should be produced.

Step Run Solver to find the Q that sets $MR - MC$ equal to zero.

After running Solver, you should see that cell B20 equals zero and that the Solver solution agrees (not exactly, but practically speaking) with the analytical method.

Evaluating Monopoly

Now that we know the monopoly solution – it will produce roughly 70 units of output – we are ready to judge it.

The evaluation is based on computing the consumers' surplus, *CS*, and producers' surplus, *PS*, generated by the monopoly, and then comparing it to the socially optimal result.

We begin with the socially optimal result, which is the same as the perfectly competitive solution.

Step Cell F19 displays $15,625 of consumers' surplus. Click on the cell to see its formula: $= 0.5*(d0\_ - P)*Q$. P and Q are named cells for the perfectly competitive solution of 100 and 125, respectively.

Cell F20 has producers' surplus at $Q = 125$. Cell F21 adds *CS* and *PS*. The total surplus of $19,688 is the maximum and it is obtained when 125 units are produced.

Now, consider what happens under monopoly.

Step Cell I19 shows a dramatic drop in *CS*. Click on the cell to see its formula: $= 0.5*(d0\_ - Pm)*Qm$. Pm and Qm are named cells for the monopoly price and output.

The monopolist has lowered output and raised the price, relative to the competitive solution.

Cell I20 shows a producers' surplus. Its formula is $= (Pm - I18)*Qm + 0.5*(I18 - s0\_)*Qm$. The first part of the formula is a rectangle. The height is the monopoly price minus the *MR* (or *MC* given that they are equal). The length is the monopoly output. A large part of this rectangle – from the monopoly price to the perfectly competitive equilibrium price – used to belong to the consumers. It has been taken by the monopolist and helps explain why *CS* and *PS* have changed so dramatically.

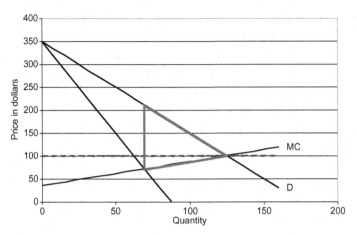

Figure 3.1.4.2. Deadweight loss from monopoly.
Source: MonopolyDWL.xls!Monopoly

Cell I21 adds *CS* and *PS* under monopoly. The total surplus of $15,833 is lower than the maximum possible surplus of $19,688. The difference, $3855 (in cell I23), is the lost surplus due to monopoly. This is also known as the deadweight or welfare loss.

Step Click the [Show DWL in Chart] button to see a visual presentation in the monopoly graph of the deadweight loss, or DWL, of monopoly.

Figure 3.1.4.2 is a canonical graph in microeconomics. It shows that the monopoly output is too low and the deadweight loss or Harberger triangle is used to indicate the inefficiency caused by monopoly.

Because the monopoly solution does not equal the socially optimal output, we say there is a *market failure*. It is a failure in the sense that resources are not optimally allocated from society's point of view.

Inframarginal thinking can be applied to Figure 3.1.4.2. The basic idea is that all of the output from the monopoly solution, roughly 70 units, up to the socially optimal output level of 125 units, exhibits unrealized gains from trade. For example, the marginal cost of producing the 100th unit is 35 + 0.52*100, which equals $87. The demand curve tells us that consumers are willing to pay up to $150 for the 100th unit. Clearly, the 100th unit should be produced because the additional satisfaction (as measured by willingness to pay) is greater than the additional costs of production.

The monopolist refuses to produce and sell the 100th unit, however, because selling the 100th unit at a price of $150 means that all units must be sold at this price. Doing this lowers monopoly profit.

But the critique of monopoly does not ride on the fact that monopoly forces consumers to pay higher prices than under a competitive market. The real problem with monopoly is that it produces too little output – it produces less than the socially optimal level. This causes too few resources to be allocated to the production of the monopolized good or service. We measure the amount of this inefficiency in resource allocation by the deadweight loss.

Yet another way to frame the inefficiency of monopoly is to focus on the fact that the monopolist produces where $MR = MC$ and this differs from $P = MC$ because MR diverges from the demand curve. A competitive market yields a socially optimal output because output is produced up to the point at which marginal cost equals the price (i.e., marginal cost pricing). Figure 3.1.4.2 makes clear that the monopolist does not do this. $MR = MC$ yields the output that maximizes profits, but $P = MC$ (where demand intersects supply or the aggregate marginal cost curve) is the socially optimal output. The monopolist is not interested in social optimality and, therefore, does not obey marginal cost pricing.

Monopoly DWL Is a Function of the Elasticities of Supply and Demand

In the previous chapter, we saw that the deadweight loss from a quantity tax depended on the price elasticities of supply and demand. The same holds true for monopoly.

Step Click the ⎹D More Elastic⎸ button. Demand is flatter, while going through the same competitive equilibrium point, $Q = 125$, $P = 100$. Thus, demand is more elastic in this case.

The button is actually a toggle. By clicking it repeatedly, you can switch back and forth from the original, more inelastic demand (price elasticity of -0.4 at $Q = 125$) to the more elastic demand (price elasticity of -0.8 at $Q = 125$).

Step Click the button a few times to convince yourself that the deadweight loss from monopoly is in fact larger when demand is more inelastic. It is easier to see this if you are displaying the red deadweight loss triangle. Click the ⎹Show DWL in chart⎸ button if needed. Figure 3.1.4.3 compares the two situations.

In Figure 3.1.4.3, the filled-in triangle is the deadweight loss of $3855 in the initial case, with a price elasticity of demand of -0.4 at $Q = 125$. The triangle with thick (red, on your screen) lines is the DWL when the price elasticity is -0.8. The DWL is lower, falling to $1870, when demand is more elastic. The DWL falls when demand is more elastic because the output does not deviate as much from the socially optimal result and the monopoly price is much lower.

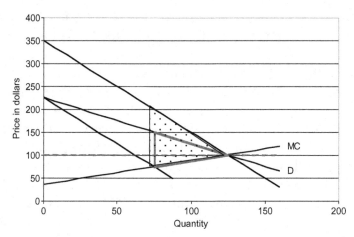

Figure 3.1.4.3. Comparing DWL with different price elasticity of demand.
Source: MonopolyDWL!Monopoly

Intuitively, the more inelastic the demand curve, the greater is the monopoly power. A monopolist who enjoys an extremely inelastic demand is able to charge very high prices and the gap from marginal cost to demand for the inframarginal units will be large. This is the primary reason why the deadweight loss from monopoly increases as demand becomes more inelastic.

Monopoly and Price Discrimination

Sometimes a seller can charge different prices for the same product. This is known as *price discrimination* and it enables profits to be even greater than when a single price is charged to all customers.

Charging different prices to see a movie in the afternoon versus the evening, different prices for coach versus first-class on a plane, and different tuition to students (in the form of differing amounts of financial aid) are all examples of price discrimination. In each case, the firm is able to increase its profits by separating consumers into different groups and charging them different prices.

There are three requirements for price discrimination to work:

- Some degree of monopoly power (facing a downward sloping demand curve).
- The firm must be able to segregate customers into groups (splitting the overall demand curve into subgroup demands).
- There must be a way to prevent resale from the low-price to the high-price market, which is called *arbitrage*.

Assuming these requirements are met, we can construct a simple example that illustrates the essential logic of price discrimination.

Step From the *Monopoly* sheet, click the Reset button and change cell E8 to 0 (zero).

Step With *MC* constant at $35/unit, run Solver to find the monopolist's optimal solution.

Step Confirm that your screen shows that the monopolist will produce 78.75 units of output and charge a price of $192.50. *CS* under monopoly is $6202 and *PS* is $12,403.

Step Click the Show DWL in chart button to see the Harberger triangle. The area is the DWL of $6202.

The fact that *CS* equals the DWL is a property of linear demand and constant *MC*.

Suppose that this monopolist can separate the overall market demand, given by the inverse demand function of $P = 350 - 2Q$, into two separate subdemands. For example, the two subdemands could be given by

$$\text{Market 1: } P = 450 - 6Q$$

$$\text{Market 2: } P = 300 - 3Q$$

The coefficients in the two separate markets have to be consistent with the coefficients in the overall market inverse demand curve. Notice that if the price is zero, quantity demanded in market 1 is $75 (= 450/6)$, while market 2's quantity demanded would be $100 (= 300/3)$. The sum of the two is 175, which equals the quantity demanded at $P = 0$ using the overall inverse demand curve. At $P = 300$, market 1's quantity demanded is 25 and market 2's is zero, and this sum equals the quantity demanded using the overall demand curve.

How can a monopolist take advantage of the ability to separate the overall market into two sealed, separate subdemands?

The intuitive answer is simple: Instead of charging the same price, $192.50, to all customers, increase the price in the market with more inelastic demand and reduce it in the other market. The customers in market 1 can be charged a higher price than those in market 2. This will lead to greater profits.

Step Proceed to the *TwoPriceDisc* sheet to see this plan in action.

Unlike the *Monopoly* sheet, there is no need to run Solver. The analytical solution has been entered and will instantly respond to changes in parameter values.

The chart in the sheet is reproduced in Figure 3.1.4.4. It shows the conventional monopoly graph for market 1 on the right and uses the left side as a mirror for market 2. Although the *x* axis shows output as negative on the

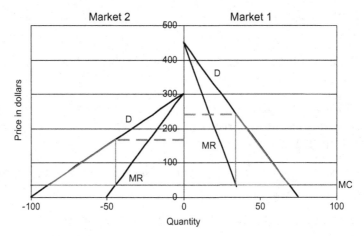

Figure 3.1.4.4. The optimal solution and DWL with price discrimination.
Source: TwoPriceDisc!Monopoly

left side, that is just a consequence of using Excel to draw the chart. Read the output as a positive number.

Figure 3.1.4.4 shows that the price discriminating monopolist will choose output where $MR = MC$ in each market, then charge the highest price obtainable for that output in each market. The price in each market is indicated by the dashed line and it is clear that price is higher in market 1. This makes sense because demand is more inelastic in market 1. Those consumers are much less price sensitive and the monopolist takes advantage of this to generate higher profits.

Step Compare the results of the single-price monopolist in the *Monopoly* sheet to the price discriminator in the *TwoPriceDisc* sheet by clicking the Show Single Price Monopoly button.

The price discriminator has the same total output, but it splits the single price into two prices. Cell B34 in the *TwoPriceDisc* sheet computes a weighted average of the two prices and it is higher than the single price of $192.50 charged by the conventional monopolist. This enables the two-price monopolist to make greater profits, as shown by the increase in PS from $12,403 to $13,028.

Comparing cells L38 and H34 shows that the DWL has increased from $6202 to $6514 when the monopolist separated the markets and charged different prices. Of course, the monopolist does not care about DWL; she is focused on maximizing profits.

Unfortunately, these results are guaranteed only for linear demand functions. In general, with nonlinear demands, we cannot state with certainty the effects on output and welfare. In other words, it is possible for output to rise and DWL to fall with a two-price discriminating monopolist. The effect on output and DWL depends on the shapes of the individual market demand curves.

For a concrete scenario of price discrimination improving welfare, consider the following:

> It is possible, for instance, that no physician would be attracted to a small town if he were required to charge the same fee to rich patients as to poor. Since profits can be increased by discriminating, the added revenue attainable through discrimination may be sufficient to make the difference between having a service provided and not having it. (Scherer, p. 259)

There is a special case of price discriminating monopoly power that is interesting and yields a definitive result. The *perfectly price discriminating monopolist* has the ability to charge different prices for different output levels and to each individual consumer. This remarkable power enables the monopolist to sell every unit of output at the highest price the market will bear. The first unit goes for $348, the 100th for $150, and the 125th is priced at $100. The perfectly price discriminating monopolist takes every bit of consumers' surplus, but does produce the socially optimal level of output. Thus, he has no deadweight loss.

A Final Note

Economists do not believe monopolists are inherently bad folks. The monopolist, like the perfectly competitive firm and consumer, is optimizing. Monopolies are in a position to improve their individual outcome and they take advantage. According to the economists, put anyone of us in the same position and we do the same thing. Do not blame the monopolist; blame the market structure for the deadweight loss.

Also, you should know that there is another line of thinking concerning monopoly that is based on the work of Joseph Schumpeter. He argued monopoly was actually a good thing because he had an evolutionary, dynamic view of capitalism. Striving for monopoly drives capitalism and monopolies are toppled by new firms in a process he named *creative destruction*.

Schumpeter's perspective is not that of solving society's resource allocation problem. He considered this static optimization problem to be uninteresting because it did not apply to the real world and it had been already solved. For Schumpeter, the serious open problem was how and why markets generated so much innovation and growth.

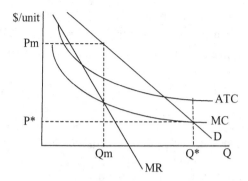

Figure 3.1.4.5. Monopoly with decreasing average costs.

Exercises

Open Word and answer the following questions. Save the document and print it when you are done.

1. In order to punish a monopolist, your friend suggests applying a quantity tax on the monopoly's commodity. Is this a good idea? Explain why or why not, using the initial values of the parameters for supply and demand in the *Monopoly* sheet for a concrete example.
2. Another friend suggests a quantity subsidy to eliminate the deadweight loss caused by monopoly. The idea would be to shift down *MC* via the subsidy until output equaled the socially optimal output. Does this make sense?
3. Consider a monopoly that sells its output in two completely separated markets. Marginal cost is constant at \$35 per unit. Inverse demand in the two markets is given by

$$P_1 = 100 - 2Q_1$$

$$P_2 = 300 - 2Q_2$$

   a. Solve this problem via analytical methods. Report optimal quantity and price in each market. Use Word's Equation Editor as needed.
   b. Solve this problem with the *TwoPriceDisc* sheet. Enter the appropriate coefficients on the sheet. Take a picture of the results and paste it in your Word doc.
   c. Which market has a higher price?
   d. How does the price elasticity of demand in each market affect the price?
   e. Which market has greater deadweight loss? How do you know?
   f. How does the price elasticity of demand affect the deadweight loss?
   g. The overall market demand is given by $P = 200 - Q$. Enter the overall market demand coefficients in the *Monopoly* sheet and run Solver to find the optimal solution. How does price discrimination affect welfare loss?
4. Suppose that, in the long run, average cost is decreasing throughout and marginal cost is below average cost, as shown in Figure 3.1.4.5. The profit-maximizing level of output for the monopolist is where $MR = MC$. The socially optimal result is where $D = MC$.
   a. What is the problem with using competitive markets to achieve the socially optimal result in this situation?
   b. What government policy could be used to help the market reach the social optimum?

References

The epigraph is from page 19 of Ronald Coase, *The Firm, the Market and the Law* (paperback edition, 1990 – originally published in 1988). Coase, a Nobel Prize winner for his work on transactions costs and property rights, criticized economics for its simplified, mathematical models that were completely stripped of real-world nuance and complexity. In "The Marginal Cost Controversy" (originally published in *Economica* in 1946 and reprinted in *The Firm, the Market and the Law*), Coase rejected the standard view that everywhere decreasing average cost (as in Figure 3.1.4.5) implied government intervention was the only solution.

Like Schumpeter, Coase has a broader, less mathematical view of economic analysis. Coase says, "Blackboard economics is undoubtedly an exercise requiring great intellectual ability, and it may have a role in developing the skills of an economist, but it misdirects our attention when thinking about economic policy. For this we need to consider the way in which the economic system would work with alternative institutional structures. And this requires a different approach from that used by most modern economists" (Coase, *The Firm, the Market and the Law*, pp. 19–20).

For more on Schumpeter, visit <homepage.newschool.edu/het/profiles/schump .htm>. His most accessible work is *Capitalism, Socialism and Democracy.*

F. M. Scherer's *Industrial Market Structure and Economic Performance* (1970) was a popular Industrial Organization book. Most IO courses and books begin with a review of competition and monopoly, and then cover the complicated, interesting, and vast area between pure competition and monopoly.

3.1.5

Sugar Quota

We apply nonparametric regression models to estimation of demand curves of the type most often used in applied research. From the demand curve estimators we derive estimates of exact consumers' surplus and deadweight loss, which are the most widely used welfare and economic efficiency measures in areas of economics such as public finance.

Jerry A. Hausman and Whitney K. Newey

This chapter applies the tools of partial equilibrium analysis and deadweight loss to analyze the U.S. sugar quota. In addition to theory, an empirical estimate of the size of the deadweight loss (i.e., the Harberger triangle) is computed.

Before analyzing this government program, we take a crash course on sugar – production, pricing, and how the U.S. sugar quota works.

Facts about Sugar

The source for the data and explanation of the sugar program is <www.ers .usda.gov/briefing/sugar/data.htm>.

Step Open the Excel workbook SugarQuota.xls and read the *Intro* sheet, then go to the *Table24* sheet, of which a part is reproduced in Figure 3.1.5.1. The data show how the United States gets and uses sugar.

Consider the 2005/06 column in Figure 3.1.5.1. This is for the year from October 1, 2005 to September 30, 2006. The numbers come in units of short tons, raw value, or STRV. A short ton is 2000 pounds. Raw value means the dry weight of raw sugar. You get 1 ton of refined sugar (the white crystals you buy in the store) from 1.07 tons of raw sugar.

Notice that there are two main types of plants used to produce sugar, beet and cane. Sugarcane is grown in warmer areas, whereas beets come from cooler climates. Figure 3.1.5.1 breaks out the four states that produce

Items	2000/01	2001/02	2002/03	2003/04	2004/05	2005/06	2006/07 Estimate May-07	2007/08 Projection May-07
Beginning stocks 2	2,216	2,180	1,528	1,670	1,897	1,332	1,698	1,715
Total production 3,4	8,769	7,900	8,426	8,649	7,876	7,399	8,503	8,255
Beet sugar	4,680	3,915	4,462	4,692	4,611	4,444	5,014	4,520
Cane sugar	4,089	3,985	3,964	3,957	3,265	2,955	3,489	3,735
Florida	2,057	1,980	2,129	2,154	1,693	1,367	1,713	1,870
Louisiana	1,585	1,580	1,367	1,377	1,157	1,190	1,335	1,430
Texas	206	174	191	175	158	175	198	206
Hawaii	241	251	276	251	258	223	244	229
Puerto Rico	0	0	0	0	0	0	0	0
Total imports	1,590	1,535	1,730	1,750	2,100	3,443	2,034	1,789
Tariff-rate quota imports 5	1,277	1,158	1,210	1,226	1,408	2,588	1,574	1,284
Other Program imports	238	296	488	464	500	349	400	425
Non-program imports	76	81	32	60	192	506	60	80
Mexico 6								75
Total Supply	12,575	11,615	11,684	12,070	11,873	12,174	12,235	11,759
Total imports/Total supply	13%	13%	15%	15%	18%	28%	17%	15%

Figure 3.1.5.1. U.S. sugar supply and use by fiscal year.
Source: SugarQuota!Table24

cane sugar. Beets are grown in many states, but half of U.S. beet production comes from the Red River Valley in Minnesota and North Dakota. Cane is more productively efficient than extracting sugar from beets, but cane requires a warm climate. You can't tell the difference between refined sugar made from cane or beets.

Step Proceed to the *Table01* sheet to see where sugar is produced around the world. Brazil is a huge producer and exporter, but some of the smaller countries (such as Guatemala) certainly produce a great deal of sugar relative to their size. Brazil uses cane to make ethanol and has a fleet of flex-fuel cars that run on ethanol or gasoline. This frees Brazil from having to import oil.

Figure 3.1.5.1 shows that the United States started with 1332 thousand STRV in fiscal 2005 and produced 7399 thousand STRVs during the year. The United States ended up with a total supply of 12,174 thousand STRVs for 2005/06 because there were 3443 thousand STRVs imported. Sugar is imported under several categories, the most important of which is the tariff-rate quota, TRQ.

A TRQ is a type of import restriction where a split tariff (or tax on imported goods) is employed. There is an extremely low tariff (zero or a nominal charge) applied to imports under a given amount (called the in-quota tariff) and a really high tariff applied to quantities imported beyond the given amount (so little is imported after the in-quota tariff is exhausted). The TRQ was created in 1990 after multilateral trade agreements forced elimination of traditional quotas. In Europe, the EU Sugar Protocol is similar to the U.S. system. The U.S. Department of Agriculture (USDA) runs the TRQ. The overall allotment is established by multilateral trade agreements and the USDA decides on the country allocations, which are based on the pattern of sugar importing from 1975 to 1981.

Step Proceed to the *Table23c* sheet to see how the TRQ works. In August, the United States announces the country-by-country allocations for the coming fiscal year. Brazil is highlighted in red. Brazilian sugar producers were allowed to ship 152,691 metric tons of raw sugar to the United States each fiscal year from 2001 to 2003. Once this in-quota tariff is exceeded, as it was in 2001, imported sugar from that country is heavily taxed. Column N shows high balances because the data are based on August of 2004 (cell M5).

The next step is to explore world and U.S. sugar prices (provided by the USDA).

Step Proceed to the *Table03* sheet to see world raw sugar price data. Go to the next sheet, *Table04*, to see the price paid for raw sugar in the United States over the same time period.

U.S. and World Nominal Raw Sugar Prices

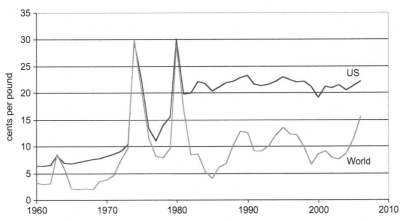

Figure 3.1.5.2. Comparing U.S. and world raw sugar prices.
Source: SugarQuota!Table04

Figure 3.1.5.2 was created from the calendar price data in the *Table03* and *Table04* sheets. It shows that since the turbulent 1970s, the U.S. raw sugar price has been roughly double, 20 cents per pound, the world raw sugar price of 10 cents per pound.

Both sheets have the Consumer Price Index (CPI) from 1960 to 2006 and it is used to compute the real price. Because the U.S. raw price has hovered just over 20 cents per pound, the real price has been falling. Of course, this is also true of the world price, except for the upsurge in the past few years.

Step See the data in the *Table06* sheet to see the effect of the sugar quota on retail refined sugar prices in the United States.

We have ended our whirlwind tour of sugar production, the U.S. TRQ system, and prices. Obviously, the sugar quota is causing higher prices for U.S. consumers and it benefits U.S. producers. But can we say more? Can we evaluate the inefficiency generated by the U.S. sugar quota?

Supply and Demand for U.S. Sugar

To analyze the effects of the sugar quota, we need estimates of demand and supply curves for sugar in the United States. Because we will work with linear functions, we need to estimate intercept and slope parameters for demand and supply of sugar.

The data provided by the USDA shows that U.S. sugar use is roughly 10,000 thousand STRVs. United States consumers pay about 20 cents per pound for raw sugar. We assume the market is in equilibrium so we interpret these values as the equilibrium quantity and price.

There are many studies of the demand for sugar (in the United States and other countries). A few are listed at the bottom of the *DerivingDandS* sheet.

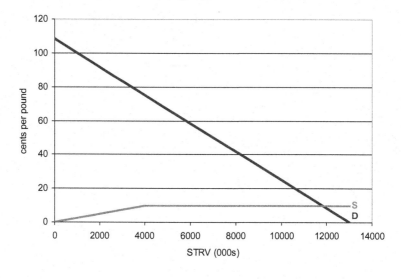

CS	$	11,603,333,333
PS	$	400,000,000
sum CS+PS	$	12,003,333,333

Figure 3.1.5.3. Supply and demand with free trade in sugar.
Source: SugarQuota!FreeTrade

We will use −0.3 as a reasonable estimate of the price elasticity of demand at the equilibrium point.

The price elasticity of the supply of sugar, on the other hand, is much less studied and there is much less agreement in the results. We will use a unit elastic, linear supply curve.

Step Proceed to the *DerivingDandS* sheet. It contains the calculations used to derive the inverse demand and supply curves for U.S. raw sugar.

Demand is $Q = -120P + 13{,}000$ and inverse demand is $P = -\dfrac{1}{120}Q + 108\dfrac{1}{3}$

Supply is $Q = 400P$ and inverse supply is $P = \dfrac{1}{400}Q$

Free Trade

We begin our analysis of the U.S. sugar quota in Fantasyland – we assume that there is no restriction of any kind on the importation of sugar.

Step Proceed to the *FreeTrade* sheet to see how the market would work under free trade. Figure 3.1.5.3 reproduces the graph. The demand curve is straightforward, but the supply curve merits special attention.

The first part of the supply curve (from the origin to the kink at the $Q = 4000$, $P = 10$ coordinate) is U.S. produced sugar. As long as the price is below 10 cents per pound, U.S. cane and beet producers are cheaper than the world raw sugar price and, therefore, U.S. production will supply the market.

Beyond 4000 units (measured in thousands of STRVs for consistency with USDA TRQ units), world suppliers take over. It is assumed that the United States has access to as much sugar as it wants at the world raw sugar price of 10 cents per pound. Thus, the market would not continue to use U.S. produced sugar beyond 4000 units. Instead, supply would come from the perfectly elastic world supply curve.

The U.S. consumer would enjoy a 10 cent per pound price for raw sugar and the equilibrium quantity would be 11,800 in thousands of STRVs or 23.6 billion pounds (as shown in cells J6 and J7). Roughly 2/3 of sugar consumed would be imported.

The sum of U.S. consumers' and producers' surplus is more than $12 billion. Click on cells G33 and G34 to see the formulas used to compute *CS* and *PS*. In this properly functioning market, this is the maximum possible total surplus.

Notice that U.S. producers would earn $400 million in producers' surplus under a free trade regime. As will be clear in a moment, this is an important number to keep in mind.

Analyzing the U.S. Sugar Quota

Step Proceed to the *SugarQuota* sheet to see what happens under the TRQ system.

As before, we focus on the supply curve. It is crucial to understanding the analysis.

In Figure 3.1.5.4 and on the *SugarQuota* sheet, the supply curve has an upward sloping part, then a flat part, and then it starts sloping up again. The first part is the same as before – it shows that U.S. producers will supply the market when the price is below the 10 cents per pound world price. The flat part is the amount of imported sugar allowed (as determined by multilateral trade negotiations). In the *SugarQuota* sheet in cell H6, this amount is 1750 units, so the flat segment is 1750 units long. The last, rising part of the supply curve is, once again, the U.S. supply curve. Because, effectively, no more sugar is allowed into the United States, domestic producers once again supply the market.

What is the equilibrium quantity and price with a TRQ of 1750 thousand STRVs?

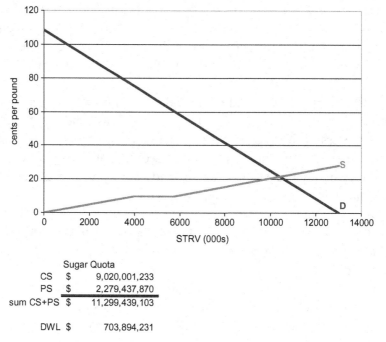

	Sugar Quota	
CS	$	9,020,001,233
PS	$	2,279,437,870
sum CS+PS	$	11,299,439,103
DWL	$	703,894,231

Figure 3.1.5.4. Supply and demand with the U.S. sugar quota.
Source: SugarQuota!SugarQuota

Consumers do not get to enjoy cheap sugar at the 10 cents per pound world price. Instead, supply and demand intersect at a price of 21.6 cents per pound. The equilibrium quantity falls from 11,800 (under free trade) to just over 10,400.

Under the TRQ system, we get too little output. This is also known as an inefficient allocation of resources.

We measure the inefficiency by the deadweight loss. Under the quota, the total surplus is almost $11.3 billion. Because the maximum total surplus is $12 billion, we say there is a $700 million deadweight loss. This is value that no one gets.

Just as with price ceilings, price floors, taxes, and monopoly, the supply and demand graph can be used to visually highlight *CS*, *PS*, and DWL.

Step In column C of the *SugarQuota* sheet, there are four check boxes. Click the Show CS check box to display the *CS* under the TRQ system and show the points that outline the displayed shape.

Under the sugar quota, the *CS* no longer extends to the world price of 10 cents per pound and quantity is smaller than under free trade. Consumers lose more than $2.5 billion.

Step Click the Show US PS check box.

United States producers gain surplus from two distinct areas. The first one is a trapezoid with length from zero to 4000 units of output. This is the same length as the *PS* triangle under free trade, but the shape is taller now because the price is 21.6 instead of 10 cents per pound. United States producers also get a second area of surplus, the triangle after the quota is reached.

If the U.S. sugar quota is inefficient, it seems natural to ask why it exists. The answer lies in the producers' surplus. Under free trade, U.S. producers made $400 million in surplus. With the TRQ system, they make more than $2 billion.

Step Click the Show Foreign PS check box.

Foreign producers share in the feast. They earn a surplus on the sugar they sell in the U.S. market at 21.6 cents per pound instead of the world price of 10 cents per pound.

Step Finally, click the Show DWL check box.

The DWL triangle is not the usual bowtie shape (as in the price ceiling, price floor, tax, and monopoly applications). In this case, the DWL is a triangle under supply and demand.

Consumers have lost a strip of surplus (to be exact, a trapezoid) with height 21.6 – 10 cents per pound. United States and foreign producers have taken most of the surplus lost by consumers, but the DWL triangle is a piece that is enjoyed by no one.

Figure 3.1.5.5 shows the situation with all four boxes checked.

Obviously, consumers are hurt the most by the TRQ system. They lose a lot – more than $2.5 billion. But they do not notice and they are not well organized. Visit <www.opensecrets.org> to see how the powerful U.S. sugar lobby influences Congress.

Comparative Statics

We conclude by exploring the effect of changing the level of the quota.

Step Click on the scroll bar, [IMPORT 1750   Pe 21.63462], twice to increase the total amount of imported sugar allowed to 2750 units.

The length of the orange rectangle expands and the rising part of the U.S. supply curve is pushed right. Equilibrium price falls and output rises. *CS* and foreign *PS* rise. Deadweight loss falls. This is better for U.S. consumers and foreign sugar producers than the initial quota of 1750 units.

United States *PS*, however, falls. Domestic sugar producers are not happy with this. They prefer a lower import quota.

480   *Sugar Quota*

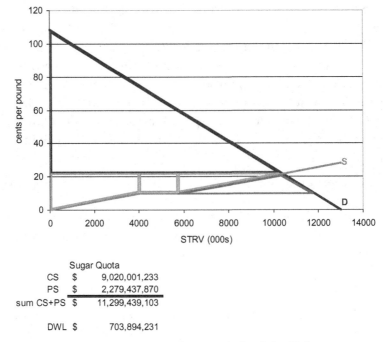

	Sugar Quota	
CS	$	9,020,001,233
PS	$	2,279,437,870
sum CS+PS	$	11,299,439,103
DWL	$	703,894,231

Figure 3.1.5.5. Partial equilibrium analysis of the U.S. sugar quota.
Source: SugarQuota!SugarQuota

Do as I Say, Not as I Do

Developed countries talk a lot about free trade, especially to lesser developed countries, but it is clear that powerful special interests can and do dominate individual markets in the rich countries of the world. The tools of partial equilibrium analysis can be used to (approximately) evaluate the results of protectionist policies.

In the case of the U.S. sugar quota, data provided by the USDA can be used to estimate the size of the deadweight loss. With a total import level of 1750 thousand STRVs (the total amount of imports in the 2003/04 fiscal year), assuming price elasticities of demand and supply of −0.3 and 1.0, the deadweight loss is $700 million. United States consumers bear the brunt of the costs of the TRQ system because consumers' surplus falls by about $2.5 billion.

The SugarQuota.xls workbook can be used to explore the effects of other scenarios. Try your hand at a few from the exercises that follow or invent your own.

Remember that partial equilibrium deadweight loss analysis is a rough, back-of-the-envelope calculation. Although progress has been made in estimating deadweight loss (see the references to this chapter), focusing on a single market ignores the ramifications of the sugar quota on other goods and services.

Exercises

Open Word and answer the following questions. Save the document and print it when you are done.

1. Use the *SugarQuota* sheet to Figure 3.1.5.1 to figure out what happens if all imports are banned. Explain your procedure and take screenshots as needed. Would you support a ban of all imports? Explain.
2. The deadweight loss estimates in the text are sensitive to the demand and supply curve parameters. Suppose that the supply curve had a slope of 1/100 instead of 1/400. (Be sure to change this parameter in the *SugarQuota* and *FreeTrade* sheets.) What effect would this have on the TRQ system? Explain your procedure and take screenshots as needed.
3. Search the web to learn about CAFTA. What is CAFTA and what effect does it have on the U.S. sugar quota?

References

The epigraph is from the abstract of Jerry A. Hausman and Whitney K. Newey, "Nonparametric Estimation of Exact Consumers Surplus and Deadweight Loss," *Econometrica*, Vol. 63, No. 6 (November, 1995), pp. 1445–1476. This paper has a nice explanation of developments in estimating deadweight loss and an example application to gasoline demand.

For further reading on correctly estimating deadweight loss, see Pascal Lavergne, Vincent Réquillart, and Michel Simioni, "Welfare Losses Due to Market Power: Hicksian Versus Marshallian Measurement," *American Journal of Agricultural Economics*, Vol. 83, No. 1 (February, 2001), pp. 157–165.

The *DerivingSandD* sheet has several references on sugar demand and the sugar industry.

3.1.6

Externality

When the beekeeper's bees fly into the adjoining apple orchard and pollinate the apple-grower's apple blossoms, they are conferring a positive benefit on the apple-grower that the beekeeper cannot take advantage of directly (i.e., a positive externality).

Eric S. Maskin

This chapter is devoted to explaining the concept of externality, why it causes a market failure, and how the inefficiency can be corrected.

The core idea is that externalities cause markets to fail – too much or too little is produced. Society's resources are inefficiently allocated. The reason why markets fail in the presence of externalities is that decision makers (consumers or firms) fail to incorporate the full costs or benefits of an action so they make a bad decision (from society's point of view).

Things to know about externality:

1. What is it?
2. Why does it break the market?
3. How does command and control fix it?
4. How do decentralized solutions correct the market?

What Is an Externality?

An *externality* is a cost or benefit not taken into account by the decision maker.

The decision maker takes an action that impacts others, but she does not incorporate this "external impact" into her optimization problem. The decision maker considers only personal (also known as private) cost and benefit, not the full cost and benefit.

Figure 3.1.6.1 offers a visual definition of externality and introduces the conventional language of private and social values. Externalities can arise

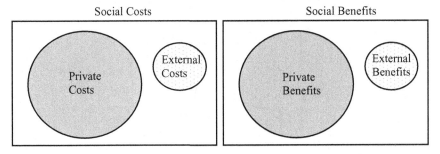

Figure 3.1.6.1. Understanding externalities.

on the cost or benefit side of an optimization problem. The private costs or benefits are included in the agent's calculations. The external costs or benefits are ignored. The full or total costs or benefits are called social costs or benefits.

Pollution can be an externality when the cost of pollution is not taken into account by the firm. This is called a *negative production externality*. A steel firm deciding how much steel to produce factors into its choice of output level the revenue from making steel and a whole series of costs: labor, raw materials, and equipment. The costs that are counted are private costs.

If the firm pollutes the air through a smokestack, but does not have to pay for polluting the air, this is an external cost. The social cost includes the private costs and the external cost. It is a negative externality because costs are imposed on others that are not taken into account by the decision maker. It is a production externality because the decision is made by a firm deciding how much to produce.

Education is often used as an example of a *positive consumption externality* because there are benefits to education that are not taken into account by the student. The choice variable is how many years of schooling to acquire. The costs are huge – out-of-pocket costs of a 4-year college degree include tuition and books – but opportunity costs are even greater. The benefits include access to better jobs, higher pay, and greater quality of life. These private benefits are considered when high school students decide whether or not to go to college.

But society benefits from education also. College-educated people have lower unemployment rates, smoke less, and are more likely to vote. These benefits are ignored by individuals making a decision about whether or not to acquire a college education. It is a positive externality because benefits flow to others that are not taken into account by the decision maker. It is a consumption externality because the decision is made by a consumer deciding how much to purchase.

Many studies attempt to estimate the gap between the social rate of return and private rate of return to a college degree. Social rates of return to

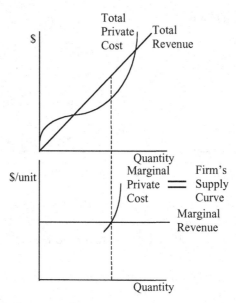

Figure 3.1.6.2. Profit maximization for a perfectly competitive firm.

education are usually several percentage points higher than the private return. This gap is an estimate of the external value generated by education.

Externalities are clearly everywhere. To the extent that you ignore the impact on others, your decision about which shirt to wear contains an externality. When you decide to take the freeway, you ignore the additional congestion your car will cause. That is an externality.

The examples offered thus far make it easy to see why externalities are also known as *spillover effects*.

Why Do Externalities Cause Market Failure?

Suppose we have an individual, perfectly competitive producer who is not taking into account the costs of pollution created as a by-product of manufacturing.

She decides how much to produce by solving a profit maximization problem that looks like Figure 3.1.6.2. The information in the figure is standard except for the labeling of the cost curves. Instead of total cost and marginal cost, we have total private cost and marginal private cost.

Each firm in this perfectly competitive industry is doing the same thing so the market is depicted by Figure 3.1.6.3. Prices will respond to shortages and surpluses and eventually settle down to the equilibrium price. The equilibrium quantity is the market's solution to society's resource allocation problem.

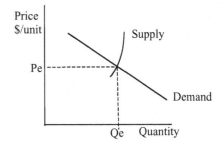

Figure 3.1.6.3. Supply and demand.

Can we conclude that the equilibrium output equals the socially optimal output? No. In fact, this market suffers from a big problem and it leads to a market failure.

The Big Problem

The market supply curve is wrong – because of the externality, it does not tell us the marginal cost to society from producing one more unit of output.

Suppose we knew the marginal social cost of producing one more unit and we added it to the familiar supply and demand graph, as shown in Figure 3.1.6.4.

Q^* in Figure 3.1.6.4 shows the optimal output for society. The socially optimal level of output is based on the full, social cost of production. Q_e shows the (broken) market's output. The market's equilibrium output is based only on the private cost of production.

The market fails in the presence of a negative externality because it produces too much output.

We can easily implement this example in Excel.

Step Open the Externality.xls workbook and read the *Intro* sheet, then proceed to the *Externalities* sheet.

Let's take a quick tour of the screen (reproduced in Figure 3.1.6.5). On the left are the total and marginal graphs for a single firm. We ignore the

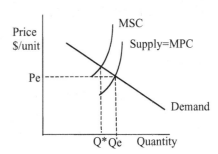

Figure 3.1.6.4. Understanding why externality causes a market failure.

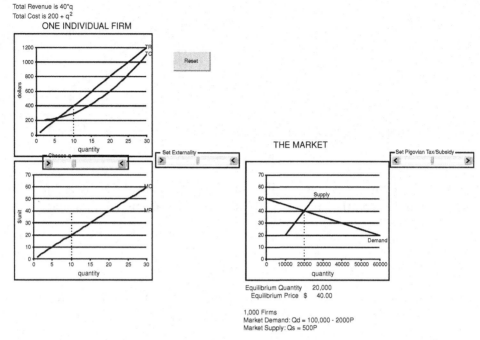

Figure 3.1.6.5. Initial view.
Source: Externality.xls!Externality

average cost curves (ATC and AVC) because we are not interested in this firm's profit position. All we care about is how much it will produce. The cost function is a simple quadratic and the market price is \$40/unit so the revenue function is $40q$.

On the right is the conventional supply and demand graph. Notice that the *y* axes of the marginal and supply and demand graphs are the same. The *x* axes, however, are different. There are 1000 firms and, combined, they produce tens of thousands of units of output.

On open, this particular firm is producing 10 units of output. What would you advise this firm to do? Why?

Step Use the firm's scroll bar control to adjust its output level. To maximize profits, this firm will choose output where $MR = MC$. This output level will generate the maximum difference between the total revenue and total cost curves in the top graph.

The problem is easily solved via analytical methods.

$$\max_{q} \pi = 40q - (200 + q^2)$$

$$\frac{d\pi}{dq} = 40 - 2q = 0 \Rightarrow q^* = 20$$

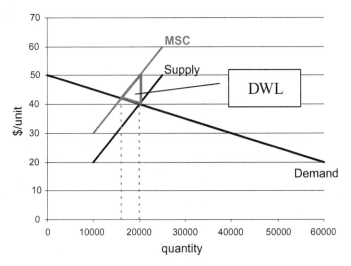

Figure 3.1.6.6. Deadweight loss.
Source: Externality.xls!Externality

Step To implement the externality, slide the Set Externality control all the way to the right (so the red lines are above the black lines in the three graphs).

Step The red lines are not labeled. Label the red curve in the top graph, the red line in the bottom graph, and the red line above the supply curve.

The correct labels must include the word "social." The red line in the top graph is the *TSC*, or total social cost, and its marginal counterpart is the *MSC*, or marginal social cost. The divergence between the red, social cost curves and the black, private cost curves signals the presence of an externality. The distance between the curves are costs not taken into account by the firm.

Note that neither the firm's profit-maximizing output level nor the market's equilibrium solution changes in the presence of the externality. We have imposed an added cost, yet the firms and market do not respond because the cost is ignored.

The dashed line from the intersection of *MSC* and demand is the socially optimal level of output. An omniscient, omnipotent social planner, OOSP, would incorporate the full costs of production in determining the optimal solution to society's resource allocation problem.

We could measure the inefficiency caused by the externality by the deadweight loss. This would be the area of the triangle shown in Figure 3.1.6.6. The market in the presence of a negative externality has produced too much output. Units beyond 16,000 have greater marginal social cost than marginal benefit (as given by the demand curve) and should not be produced. The market produces an extra 4000 units because it ignores the external costs of production.

Correcting the Market Failure

There are several regulatory approaches the government can take to fix the market failure caused by externality.

Perhaps the most obvious is a quota on pollution. Firms are allowed to pollute only a certain amount. Because they cannot pollute past a certain amount, they cannot produce as much as they want.

In other words, the OOSP could tell the producers, "You are only allowed to produce Q^*." This is called *command and control*, a term borrowed from the military, where top down decision making is the norm.

But this approach suffers from a serious drawback. It requires massive amounts of information to set the total amount of pollution and output.

Furthermore, if everyone is forced to reduce pollution by, say 20%, this doesn't take advantage of the fact that some firms (say with more modern plants) can reduce pollution more cheaply than older firms. In other words, the government not only has to determine the total amount of pollution and output, it has to tell each individual firm exactly what and how to produce.

The Environmental Protection Agency (EPA) still uses effluent restrictions, but the EPA is moving toward other regulatory strategies.

Decentralized Solutions

There are two varieties of decentralized solutions. Both are based on letting firms decide how much to produce. Economists believe both to be big improvements over command and control.

The first approach is based on the work of Arthur C. Pigou (rhymes with zoo). He argued that the government could offer incentives to align individual optimal solutions with socially optimal levels of output. Thus, we call this solution a Pigovian tax or subsidy.

Pigou's approach dominated economics for many years. Then, in 1960, Ronald Coase offered an ingenious alternative: Define property rights over all resources (such as clean air) in order to internalize the externality. It took some time, but Coase's approach caught on.

Pigovian Taxes

By imposing a tax on polluting firms, producers are forced to consider the full costs of production in a roundabout way – the tax takes the place of the external cost.

The tax shifts the supply curve up so that, if properly calibrated, the amount of the tax reflects the external cost not taken into account. Figure 3.1.6.7

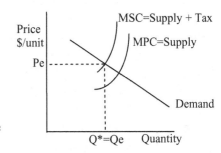

Figure 3.1.6.7. Pigovian tax correcting the inefficiency from a negative externality.

shows how a Pigovian tax fixes the market failure caused by externality. Notice that the Supply + Tax curve equals the *MSC*. This enables the market equilibrium solution to equal the socially optimal solution.

Unlike regular taxes that distort markets, Pigovian taxes are used to correct market failure.

The Excel workbook Externality.xls enables you to correct the externality with a Pigovian incentive.

Step With a negative externality in place (i.e., the externality scroll bar is set to the right and the red social costs are above the black private costs in all three graphs), click the Set Pigovian Tax/Subsidy scroll bar to fix the inefficiency.

With every click, the market supply curve shifts up because you are imposing a greater tax. A Pigovian tax works like a regular tax – it shifts the supply curve up. Obviously, you want to set the tax so that the black supply curve is coincident with and covers the red *MSC* curve.

The Pigovian tax fixes the externality when the amount of the tax takes the place of the divergence between marginal social and private cost. You know you have the right tax when the market's equilibrium output equals the socially optimal level of output (at 16,000 units).

Because a Pigovian tax shifts the supply curve up just like a regular tax, why do we bother giving this tax a special name? In other words, what's the difference between Pigovian taxes and regular taxes?

Unlike regular taxes, which are applied to generate revenue for the government and cause the equilibrium quantity to be less than the optimal quantity, Pigovian taxes are actually applied to correct a market failure. They do generate revenue, but the primary purpose of a Pigovian tax is to change the market's equilibrium output to allocate resources optimally.

Marketable Permits and the Coase Theorem

A different decentralized approach to curing market failure relies on *creating more markets* to internalize the externality.

In recent years, this approach has gained widespread acceptance. The idea won Ronald Coase a Nobel Prize in Economics.

In fact, the history of the idea of creating more markets is fascinating. Frank Knight (an economist at the University of Chicago) disagreed with Pigou (who succeeded Marshall as a professor at Cambridge) in an article way back in 1926. Pigou had claimed that externalities cause market failure and this can be remedied by the appropriate tax (just like in Figure 3.1.6.7). He used too much traffic as an example.

Knight said that, far from this being a market failure, the problem created by the externality was that there was a missing market! He maintained that you cannot blame the market system for a *lack* of markets. In Knight's view, a properly functioning market system would force firms to pay for all the resources used. A negative externality meant that firms would treat some resources as free and it is no surprise that they would overuse those resources.

Pigou removed the traffic congestion externality example from the next edition of his book. He left, however, the overall framework of corrective taxes and subsidies intact and it became part of the paradigm of economics.

In 1960, Coase wrote his most famous article, "The Problem of Social Cost," in which he explained how markets would operate to cure externalities. Instead of command and control or a government tax, Coase advocated establishing property rights to clean air (or whatever the missing market was) and letting the market work its magic.

There is no Excel implementation of Coase's solution. The idea is simply that unpriced resources be priced. This happens when unowned resources are assigned owners. This directly internalizes the externality.

A theorem bears Coase's name and a brief explanation of its content is in order. The Coase Theorem arises out of the idea that more finely delineated property rights enable the market to solve the problem of externality. The word *theorem* is loosely used here and Coase never claimed to have found or proved the Coase Theorem. Coase wanted to show that by settling property rights disputes, courts played a key role in enabling markets to work. He argued that it was not important who won the case because the resource would end up with whoever valued it more. By giving one party the property right, the court established ownership and enabled the resource to be traded. If the winner valued the resource more, the loser would be unwilling to buy it. If the winner valued it less, the loser would buy the resource. Either way, said Coase, once the judge ruled, the resource would end up at its most highly valued use. This idea is now known as the Coase Theorem.

Coase Versus Pigou

Although Coase and Pigou can be grouped as providing alternative types of decentralized solutions in the sense that individual agents can decide what to buy or sell (as opposed to the more authoritarian command and control approach), Coase was a strong critic of Pigou.

Coase saw Pigou's tax/subsidy plan as hopelessly idealistic and impossible to implement in the real world. It is easy to draw Figure 3.1.6.7 and a snap to show that the correct tax or subsidy enables the market to hit the socially optimal output. Unfortunately, this blackboard economics (as Coase derisively called it) is far removed from reality. The government regulator will know neither the demand nor the supply functions and changes over time imply constant tweaking of optimal taxes or subsidies.

Furthermore, the two differ radically in their view of government. Pigou's vision of a dedicated, educated British civil servant figuring out the optimal tax or subsidy clashes with Coase's libertarian view of minimal government. For Coase, direct government intervention in markets should be avoided. Coase sees the court as a referee and arbiter, with buyers and sellers having full freedom to trade without government interference.

Coase argued that Pigovian taxes and subsidies are merely one option and not necessarily the best solution. He preferred that individuals be allowed to bargain because this type of negotiation would be most likely to find the truly cost-minimizing solution to the problem of externality. According to Coase, Pigovian taxes and subsidies should be a last resort – intervention of this kind requires strong evidence that other, less draconian, remedies are ineffective.

Finally, Coase believed Pigou fundamentally misunderstood the problem of externality. In Pigou's view, the emitter had to be identified so that the corrective tax or subsidy could be determined. Coase argued that this wrong. "We are dealing with a problem of a reciprocal nature. The real question that has to be decided is: should A be allowed to harm B or should B be allowed to harm A?" (Coase, 1960, p. 2)

The EPA and Acid Rain

Although Pigovian taxes and subsidies are a decentralized approach to correcting a market failure caused by externality, in recent years, market-based strategies relying on Coase's logic have gained popularity.

For example, by creating a market for the right to pollute, firms are forced to take into account the full costs of their production decisions. They must buy a permit in order to pollute and this forces them to internalize the externality.

The EPA maintains two emissions trading programs, one for sulfur dioxide (SO_2) and the other for nitrogen oxides (NOx). These programs were established in the 1980s to decrease pollutants that cause acid rain. Instead of command and control or taxes, the EPA set a total emissions constraint, or bubble, then allowed firms to buy and sell pollution permits. This cap and trade scheme is equivalent to setting up a market for pollution.

There are many details to be worked out when setting up a market. For example, the government can give each firm an initial allocation of permits or they can auction off the permits. See <www.epa.gov/airmarkets/trading/basics.html> for more information on how the EPA's program works.

Some environmentalists remain strongly opposed to market-based solutions to pollution abatement. They see such programs as "licenses to pollute." But using the market to price resources correctly and enable socially optimal resource allocation is a powerful factor in favor of the market.

The EU Emissions Trading Scheme advertises itself as "the largest multi-country, multi-sector Greenhouse Gas emission trading scheme worldwide." See <ec.europa.eu/environment/climat/emission.htm>.

Other countries (including such different places as Costa Rica and China) have started emissions trading programs. The idea of creating a market for pollution in order to correct the market failure caused by externality is most definitely a real, practical solution that continues to grow in popularity.

Externalities, Market Failure, and Corrective Action

Externalities are costs or benefits not taken into account by the decision maker (consumer or producer). Externalities cause inefficiency because the socially optimal level of output is not produced. As usual, we can measure the inefficiency caused by an externality by computing the deadweight loss.

Externalities can be corrected by command and control, but this approach is not popular because it requires micromanagement by government regulators. Pigovian taxes and subsidies are a decentralized solution in the sense that individual agents decide what to do. A firm, for example, would decide how much to pollute and produce, given a tax or subsidy. The government, however, does intervene because it imposes a tax or subsidy on the market.

A second decentralized approach, suggested by Coase, relies on market-based solutions to the inefficiency created by externality. Instead of taxing or subsidizing buyers or sellers, property rights for resources are established and then the market is left to work its magic. The Coase Theorem expresses confidence that private negotiation can correct inefficiency caused by externalities.

Exercises

Open Word and answer the following questions. Save the document and print it when you are done.

1. Give an example of a positive externality in consumption.
2. Analyze the welfare effects of a positive externality in consumption. Use Word's Drawing Tools to support your answer with a demand and supply graph.

3. In each case that follows, describe the regulatory strategy to correct the market failure caused by a positive externality in consumption.
   a. Command and control
   b. Pigou
   c. Coase

References

The epigraph is from the first page of Eric S. Maskin, "The Invisible Hand and Externalities," *The American Economic Review*, Vol. 84, No. 2, Papers and Proceedings of the Hundred and Sixth Annual Meeting of the American Economic Association (May, 1994), pp. 333–337.

Ronald H. Coase published "The Problem of Social Cost" in the *Journal of Law and Economics*, Vol. 3 (October, 1960), pp. 1–44. For an interesting transcript of a conversation about Coase's article and the Chicago School in general, see Edmund W. Kitch, "The Fire of Truth: A Remembrance of Law and Economics at Chicago, 1932–1970," *Journal of Law and Economics*, Vol. 26, No. 1 (April, 1983), pp. 163–234. George Stigler describes the presentation by Coase to a "collection of superb theorists" as "one of the most exciting intellectual experiences of my life":

> My recollection is that Ronald didn't persuade us. But he refused to yield to all our erroneous arguments. Milton would hit him from one side, then from another, then from another. Then to our horror, Milton missed him and hit us. At the end of that evening the vote had changed. There were twenty-one votes for Ronald and no votes for Pigou. (Kitch, p. 221)

Arthur Cecil Pigou's *The Economics of Welfare* was first published in 1920 and is available online at <www.econlib.org/library/NPDBooks/Pigou/pgEW.html>.

Frank H. Knight's criticism of Pigou's traffic congestion example is in "Some Fallacies in the Interpretation of Social Cost," *The Quarterly Journal of Economics*, Vol. 38, No. 4 (August, 1924), pp. 582–606.

3.1.7

Cartels and Deadweight Loss

Lack of legal sanctions means that loyal members of the cartel must exact penalties against deviants in the market place. Unless such disciplinary actions (mainly price cuts) can be localized, every member of the cartel, loyalist and defector alike, suffers. That is a very severe (if little remarked) limitation on the efficiency of cartels.

Oliver E. Williamson

We know that the equilibrium output of a competitive market equals the output that maximizes consumers' and producers' surplus. We also know that monopoly produces too little output and the resulting deadweight loss is a measure of the inefficiency of monopoly. But competition and monopoly mark opposite ends of a spectrum that includes a wide range of other market structures.

A *cartel* is a type of market structure in which a group of firms cooperate to control output and price. Perhaps the most famous international cartel is the Organization of the Petroleum Exporting Countries, OPEC. Cartels are not monopolies because there are several independent firms in the syndicate or trust, but they hope to act like a monopolist, restricting output and raising price, to earn monopoly profits. Cartels are inherently unstable because it is in the interest of each member to cheat and sell more than the agreed amount.

This chapter explores the welfare properties of a specific type of cartel. The application is based on the workings of the Norwegian cement cartel as explained by Röller and Steen (2006). Analyzing the cartel involves solving a two-stage game and the cartel result is compared to monopoly and non-cooperative, Cournot competition. This material is advanced and it is recommended that the chapter on Game Theory be completed before proceeding.

A Brief History of Norwegian Cement

Cement output in Norway (and in other countries that use the metric system) is measured in tonnes (pronounced tons). This is not simply a foreign

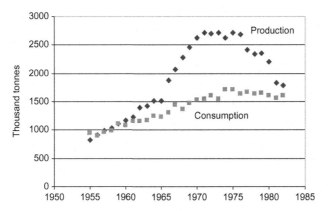

Figure 3.1.7.1. Norwegian cement production and consumption from 1955–1982. *Source:* CartelDWL.xls!Data

spelling for a ton. A ton is 2000 pounds. A tonne, sometimes called a metric ton, is 1000 kilograms. Given there are roughly 2.2 kilos in a pound, a tonne is about 2200 pounds. Thus, a tonne is bigger than a ton.

Figure 3.1.7.1 shows that production rose dramatically during the second half of the 1960s, greatly outpacing demand. This excess output was exported. A balance between production and consumption was restored by the early 1980s.

Production rocketed because of the sharing rule adopted by the Norwegian cement industry. A *sharing rule* determines how the monopoly rent is to be distributed among the firms in the cartel. Each firm's share of the domestic market was based on its fraction of total industry capacity. We will see that this gives each firm an incentive to expand plant capacity and led to the explosion in output shown in Figure 3.1.7.1.

In 1968, the three firms in the cement industry abandoned the cartel market structure and merged to form a monopoly. By then, however, plant capacity had been expanded and it took years to reduce output.

Röller and Steen explain that there are few empirical studies of cartels because they are illegal in many places (including the United States) so obtaining data is difficult. Such is not the case in Norway. "Given the legality of the Norwegian cement cartel, we have a large amount of primary data allowing us to do a complete welfare analysis." (Röller and Steen, 2006, p. 321)

Monopoly Review

Step Open the Excel workbook CartelDWL.xls and read the *Intro* sheet, then go to the *Monopoly* sheet.

Given the linear inverse demand curve and constant marginal cost, finding the monopolist's profit-maximizing solution is easy.

Step Use the scroll bar under the chart to find Q^*. As you change the quantity, you can see the corresponding price in the chart and in cell B11. You can also see the producers' surplus (also known as profits) change in cell B19 as you set Q.

You can choose Q^* by watching cell B19, but you could also find Q^* by choosing the intersection of *MR* and *MC*.

Step Excel's Solver offers yet another alternative to finding the profit-maximizing level of output. Execute Tools: Solver and configure the Solver dialog box to solve the monopolist's profit maximization problem.

Step Finally, click on cells B18, B19, and B21 to show the consumers' surplus (*CS*), producers' surplus (*PS*), and deadweight loss (*DWL*) from the monopoly solution in the chart.

Having found the monopoly solution, we turn to output (and price) under a noncooperative, Cournot environment.

Cournot Review

Step Proceed to the *CournotFirm* sheet.

Chapter 2.7 on game theory presented the material reviewed here, which assumes a basic understanding of the Cournot model and Nash equilibrium.

Instead of a single firm, we suppose there are three firms making a homogeneous product. They do not collude or combine forces. Instead, they compete. Unlike perfect competition, however, there are so few firms that they impact each other's decision making. If one firm decides to produce a lot, this will lower the price for all three firms.

How will an individual firm decide how much to produce? The core idea is that each firm will make profit-maximizing output decisions based on conjectures about what the other firms will do. The output level at which each firm's decision is consistent with the output chosen by the other firms is the solution, called a Nash equilibrium.

The *CournotFirm* sheet opens with cell B10 set equal to zero. This means that Firm 1 is exploring what its best option is if the other firms produce nothing.

Step Use the scroll bar under the chart to find the profit-maximizing output for the conjecture that the other firms produce nothing.

If the other firms decide to produce zero output, Firm 1 will produce 2.3 million units of output. But this is not an equilibrium solution because the other firms would not choose to produce zero units of output when this firm produced 2.3 million tonnes. How much would the other firms produce?

Step Click the Set Exo Q button to copy Firm 1's optimal solution (in cell B15) to the conjectured output in cell B10.

Notice how the chart shows new, red *D* and *MR* curves. These are the residual demand and residual marginal revenues curves for Firm 2, given that Firm 1 produces 2.3 million and Firm 3 produces nothing.

Step Use Excel's Solver to find the profit-maximizing output for the conjecture that the other firms produce 2.3 million units.

You should find that Firm 2 will produce 1,150,000 units when the other two firms produce 2.3 million. We have stumbled upon the Nash equilibrium solution! If each firm produces 1.15 million units, then none of them will regret its output decision. In other words, each firm's optimizing decision (1.15 million) is consistent with the conjectured output (2.3 million).

Notice that the Nash equilibrium is not Firm 1 = 2.3 million, Firm 2 = 1.15 million, and Firm 3 = 0. Both Firms 1 and 2 would regret their decisions and would opt for different output choices. It should be clear, however, that if each firm makes 1.15 million, then none of the firms would regret or wish to change its chosen output level.

The Cournot solution can be found via iteration (which was easy in this example) or by analytical methods. Analytical methods (see work starting in cell A28) can be used to show that the industry's Nash equilibrium output in this Cournot model (linear demand and cost function and *n* firms) is

$$Q_e = \frac{n}{n+1} \frac{(d_0 - MC)}{d_1}$$

Price, of course, is simply read from the inverse demand curve.

Step Proceed to the *Cournot* sheet to see the welfare implications of the Cournot solution.

Step Click on cell B14 to see that the formula for the Nash equilibrium has been entered.

Notice that the Cournot output level is between the perfectly competitive ($D = MC$) and monopoly ($MR = MC$) output levels.

Step Click on cells B18, B19, and B21 to highlight *CS*, *PS*, and *DWL* in the chart.

Once again, notice that the *DWL* for the Cournot solution is between the monopoly (highest *DWL*) and perfect competition with many firms (no *DWL*) extremes.

Step Finally, increase the number of firms in cell B10 to 5, 10, and 20.

Obviously, as *n* rises, *DWL* falls, because as *n* rises, we are approaching the ideal solution of competition with many firms. Thus, perfect competition is simply an *n*-firm Cournot model with an infinite number of firms. You can confirm that at $n = 1$, the monopoly solution is found.

Having covered the monopoly and competitive Cournot models, you are ready to tackle yet another market structure: the cartel.

Cartel Behavior

Suppose an industry, made up of several firms, organized into a cartel. In other words, the firms would join forces and cooperate in making decisions. The cartel would decide the total domestic output and price for the product. In addition, the cartel would have to determine how much each firm would produce. This is called the sharing rule. Different sharing rules yield different results. Suppose that the sharing rule applied is that each firm's output reflects its share of total industry capacity. There are no limits on each firm's capacity and any output not sold domestically could be exported at the world price.

Although each firm chooses capacity first and then the cartel chooses total output (and price), we solve the two-step optimization problem recursively. This means we start at the second stage, then work backwards to the first stage.

Stage 2: Choosing Total Domestic Output (and Price)

Step Proceed to the *CartelStage2* sheet.

The information is laid out as in the *Monopoly* sheet, but there are additional variables. The world price (below marginal cost) has been added in cell F8 and to the chart. Individual firm parameters start in row 26. The three firms have chosen their capacities (cells B30:B32), determining total capacity (B28) and shares of domestic output (C30:C32).

Step Use the scroll bar under the chart to explore different quantities of domestic output. This is the cartel's key choice variable. It can choose anywhere from no output to the vertical, total capacity, line (which is determined by the firm's capacity decisions in stage 1 and is now an exogenous variable to the cartel).

Step Click on cell B19, which is the *PS* and also the profit generated by a given output level, to highlight the *PS* in the chart. The formula and the chart reveal that *PS* has two parts: $=(P-s0_-)^*Q-(s0_--R_-)^*(B28-Q)$.

The first part is a rectangle with height from *MC* to price and width from zero to the chosen output. This would be the *PS* under monopoly.

But the cartel has a second component to *PS*. This is the smaller rectangle on the chart and it is subtracted from the bigger rectangle. This second part is the excess output that is exported and sold at the world price. It is subtracted from profits because the world price is below *MC*. Thus, these units are sold at a loss.

Step Use the scroll bar to find the cartel's Q^*. Notice that you can find the optimal output by keeping an eye on *PS* (in cell B19) or by setting $MR = R$. You can also use Excel's Solver to find the optimal output.

Cell B13 shows the optimal output and your cell B12 should equal this solution. The cartel will produce 3,150,000 units and charge $1725 per unit. This is a higher output (and lower price) than the monopoly solution.

R is an important variable. It plays the role of *MC* in the cartel's optimization problem. What effect does changing *R* have on Q^* and P^*? What welfare effect does changing *R* have? We can figure out the answers to these questions with Excel.

Step Change *R* to 500 in cell F8. Solve the cartel's optimization problem again.

You should see that optimal domestic quantity is lower and price is higher.

Step With the new optimal solution for $R = 500$ in B12 ($Q^* = 2.8$ million), click the Compare Surplus button. It displays the initial *CS*, *PS*, and *DWL* values (for $R = 150$) and computes the difference between the new and initial values.

As *R* rises, *CS* falls and *PS* rises. Total *DWL* is bigger by $136 million, with both parts of *DWL* (the traditional triangle that represents domestic *DWL* and the export loss) rising.

Step Click the Reset button (or reset *R* to 150).

We conclude our analysis of the cartel's first stage of the optimization problem by examining the effect on the individual firms. Cells D30:G32 show how the sharing rule is applied to determine how much each firm produces, given the cartel's total domestic output decision. The blue text color means these variables are endogenous: They are determined by the cartel's domestic output decision.

Step Adjust Q via the scroll bar under the chart and keep your eye on cells D30:G32. As Q changes, so do the individual firm variables in blue.

Because the firms have equal capacities, each sells a third of the domestic output and exports the rest. Domestic and export sales for each firm are displayed.

Step Enter 3,150,000 in cell B12 (the value of Q^* at the initial values of the exogenous variables) to see the PS earned by each firm at the cartel's optimal output.

From the cartel's point of view, the individual firm capacities are given. But would profit-maximizing firms choose these particular capacities? This question is at the heart of the first stage of the cartel's two-stage optimization problem.

Stage 1: Choosing Capacity

Now that we know how the cartel is going to decide how much domestic output to produce and the sharing rule, we can tackle the question facing each firm: How much capacity?

At any point in time, firms have a given maximum total production, or capacity, determined by factory size. To increase capacity, firms must expand factory size and this takes time.

Notice that the marginal cost of cement production is different from the marginal cost of capacity. The former is assumed to be low and it does not play a role in this analysis. In fact, it is assumed that firms always produce up to capacity.

The capacities of each firm and hence total capacity are given to the cartel but are chosen by each firm. Each firm would pick that capacity that would maximize its profits.

The profit function has revenue from two sources: domestically sold output at price P (chosen by the cartel) and the excess output that is exported and sold at the world price, R. The cost of capacity function is linear, with constant marginal cost.

Step Proceed to the *CartelStage1* sheet and click on cell B11 to see that the formula reflects the firm's profit function.

Cells B19:B23 have the exogenous variables. Each firm chooses capacity (q_i) in order to maximize profits.

The file opens with the firm having a capacity level of 1,200,000 units, the same as the other two firms, so the total industry capacity is 3,600,000 units.

Step Click on the scroll bar (next to cell B27) to increase the firm's chosen capacity.

Notice that the larger the chosen capacity, the greater the share of the domestic sales (Q), which is chosen by the cartel, and thus domestic revenues (B13) rise. As capacity increases, exports also rise (because only a share of the firm's output is sold domestically) and this is bad because the world price is below marginal cost. Of course, increasing output is going to increase costs because the firm has to build a bigger plant.

Given these trade-offs, what level of capacity should this firm select?

Step Keep your eye on cells F27:H27 as you adjust the scroll bar to select the profit-maximizing output. As usual, the firm can equate $MR = MC$ to find the optimal solution.

Step Check your work by using Excel's Solver to find q^*.

The optimal capacity, 1,342,758 units, differs from the original 1.2 million units. This means that the optimizing firm would choose to make 1,342,758 units when the other two firms make a total of 2.4 million.

Step Copy the optimal capacity in cell B27 and paste it in cell K9 (or enter 1,342,758 units in cell K9).

We are not done yet because if this firm wants to make 1,342,758 units, it stands to reason that the other firms (with identical cost structures) will also want to do this.

Step Return to the *CartelStage2* sheet, select cell B30, and paste (or type in) 1,342,758.

Notice that cells B31 and B32 change to the value of cell B30. Cell B28, Total Capacity, is now higher and, thus, the vertical line in the chart has shifted right.

We do not need to run Solver again because the cartel's optimal output and price combination in the domestic market is unaffected by the total industry capacity. The extra output is simply exported and sold at the world price.

Step Return to the *CartelStage1* sheet and notice that *MR* no longer equals *MC*. Click on cell B20 to see that it is a formula. Cell B20, Other Capacity, has changed because the other two firms have selected different capacities.

Step Copy cell B20, select cell J10, and paste as value (Paste: Paste Values or, in older versions, Paste Special: Values).

Step Run Solver to find the new optimal solution. Copy the optimal Q (cell B27) and paste it in cell K10.

Stage 1 and Stage 2 Consistency

Iteration	Other Capacity	qi*	Starting Total Capacity	Ending Total Capacity	Difference
1	2,400,000	1,342,758	3,600,000	3,742,758	(142,758)
2	2,685,515	1,273,616	4,028,273	3,959,131	69,142
3	2,547,232	1,308,620	3,820,848	3,855,852	(35,004)
4	2,617,240	1,291,240	3,925,860	3,908,480	17,380
5	2,582,480	1,299,959	3,873,719	3,882,438	(8,719)
6	2,599,917	1,295,607	3,899,876	3,895,524	4,352
7	2,591,213	1,297,784	3,886,820	3,888,997	(2,178)
8	2,595,569	1,296,696	3,893,353	3,892,265	1,088
9	2,593,392	1,297,240	3,890,088	3,890,632	(544)

Nash eq q_i 1,297,059

Nash eq Total Q   3,891,176

Figure 3.1.7.2. Nash Equilibrium capacity.
Source: CartelDWL.xls!CartelStage1

Notice that we still do not have an internally consistent solution between the two optimization problems. The firm capacity optimal solution is different from the total capacity used by the cartel. We must iterate.

Step Return to the *CartelStage2* sheet, select cell B30, and paste the value of optimal capacity.

Step Return to the *CartelStage1* sheet and copy cell B20, select cell J11, and paste as values.

Step Run Solver to find the new optimal solution. Copy the optimal Q (cell B27) and paste it in cell K11.

We still do not have a situation in which the optimal capacity decision of Firm 1 agrees with the total capacity parameter used by the cartel.

Step Fill in the Stage 1 and Stage 2 Consistency table. You will need to iterate, repeating the process of solving for Firm 1's optimal capacity, pasting that result in the *CartelStage1* sheet, then returning to the *CartelStage2* sheet to see if the two solutions coincide.

Step When you have finished completing the table, click the ⬚Show Data⬚ button. This reveals results in columns L, M, and N that are based on your iterations. It also shows the Nash equilibrium solution for q_i^*. As with our work in the Cournot model earlier, there is an analytical solution to each firm's optimal and consistent capacity and we entered it in cell K19.

Figure 3.1.7.2 shows what your screen should look like. The total capacity, the vertical line in the *CartelStage2* chart, is driven to an equilibrium value of 3,891,176 units. The total capacity line bounces right and left until settling down at a value that is consistent with the optimal solution to the individual firm's profit maximization problem. In equilibrium, each firm will have a capacity of 1,297,059 units. This is consistent in the sense that each firm would choose this capacity if it knew the sharing rule adopted by the cartel.

Given the demand curve parameters, marginal cost, and the world price, we know the cartel's profit-maximizing domestic output and price. Because we know the equilibrium solution to each firm's capacity decision, we can compute the total output produced and export loss. Thus, we can compute *CS*, *PS*, and *DWL*.

Step Copy cell K19 from the *CartelStage1* sheet and paste as values in cell B30 of the *CartelStage2* sheet.

Step Click on cells B18, B19, and B21 to display the *CS*, *PS*, and *DWL* generated by the cartel solution.

Cartel Model Summary

Determining the cartel's output is not easy. One has to solve a two-stage game. The cartel's sharing rule means that each profit-maximizing firm is willing to trade off export losses in order to get a share of high-priced domestic output.

The vertical total capacity line in the *CartelStage2* chart is actually an equilibrium solution to the first stage of the game. There is only one value of total capacity that is internally consistent with individual firm capacity decisions.

The cartel game-theoretic model also can be solved via analytical methods. The mathematics is not easy, but if you are interested in seeing the solution, click the Show Analytical button near cell M5 of the *CartelStage1* sheet.

Having determined the output and price solutions to each of the three market structures, we are ready for the welfare analysis.

Comparing Monopoly, Cournot, and Cartel Solutions

Step Proceed to the *Compare* sheet.

Given the parameter values (in the shaded cells), the table displays the output, price, *CS*, *PS*, and *DWL* associated with perfect competition, monopoly, cartel (with the sharing rule), and Cournot market structures.

Cells B18:B21 are connected to the market structure currently displayed on the chart. On open, the perfectly competitive result is displayed. *DWL* will be computed against this standard.

Step Click the Monopoly option.

Cell range B18:B21 is updated and the chart displays the monopoly result. Notice that the monopolist ignores the world price and does not export cement. She maximizes profits by choosing output where $MR = MC$.

Compared to perfect competition (in cells B10:B14), the monopoly generates much lower CS, higher PS, and a substantial DWL.

Step Click the Cartel option.

The chart displays the total capacity vertical line and the exports are highlighted. We can compare the cartel to the monopoly and PC results by looking at the cells in columns B, C, and D, in rows 10 to 14.

Note that for the Cartel option, cell D13 shows the value of *profits* for the cartel. This is domestic PS less export loss. Cell B19, also labeled PS, shows domestic producers' surplus (and leaves out the export loss). This is confusing, but it allows separation of the two sources of total DWL, domestic DWL, given in B21, and export loss, shown in cell B22, and ensures that domestic DWL plus total surplus will sum to total surplus in the perfect competition case. Total DWL, the sum of domestic DWL and the export loss, is reported in cell D14.

Vis-à-vis perfect competition, the cartel generates lower output and higher prices, but it is better than monopoly. Cells G10:G14 show what happens when you move from cartel to monopoly.

Step Click on cells G10 to G14 to see their formulas.

If the Norwegian cement industry merged to monopoly from a cartel, we would see the following: Output falls, price rises, CS falls, PS rises, and DWL rises.

The increase in DWL would enable to us to judge such a move as a failure in terms of resource allocation in the Norwegian economy.

Step Click the Cournot option.

Comparing cartel and monopoly to perfect competition is not particularly useful, because we are not going to get a perfectly competitive cement industry. There are only three firms. If we had competition, it would be Cournot competition. The three firms would not collude, but they would behave strategically.

If the industry went from cartel to Cournot, cells F10:F14 show what would happen. As with cells G10:G14, these cells report the difference from the cartel to the Cournot market structure. Notice that output rises, price falls, CS rises, PS rises, and DWL falls.

Of these effects, PS rising is surprising at first, but remember that under Cournot, the export losses are eliminated.

	Exogenous Variables for Demand and Marginal Cost						
P = d0 - d1Qd				MC = s0		World Price	
d0	953.7203057			s0	288.6596342	(R)	
d1	0.000252144					235.0740945	

	Perfect Competition	Monopoly	Cartel	Cournot	Cartel to Cournot	Cartel to Monopoly
Q (domestic)	2,637,622	1,318,811	1,425,071	1,978,217	553,146	(106,260)
P	kr 288.66	kr 621.19	kr 594.40	kr 454.92	(kr 139.47)	kr 26.79
CS (millions)	kr 877	kr 219	kr 256	kr 493	kr 237.332	(kr 36.758)
PS (millions)	kr 0	kr 439	kr 391	kr 329	(kr 61.745)	kr 47.891
DWL (millions)	kr 0	kr 219	kr 230	kr 55	(kr 175.587)	(kr 11.133)

Figure 3.1.7.3. Welfare analysis.
Source: CartelDWL.xls!CompareActual

This completes the theoretical welfare analysis. The results are clear: To maximize surplus, the Norwegians should have moved from a cartel to Cournot competition. Of the three market structures, Cournot has the lowest *DWL*.

There is, however, one important issue left unresolved: These results apply only to the parameter values on the sheet. We do not know the intercept or slope of the Norwegian demand curve for cement, nor do we know *R* or *MC*. We need to get these parameter values, and then do the analysis based on these real-world parameter values.

Welfare Analysis for 1968

Step In the *Compare* sheet, scroll to the right of the graph and click the Show Actual button (over cell N1).

After clicking the button, a new sheet appears, populated with key parameters for 1968, the last year of the cartel.

Figure 3.1.7.3 shows the results for the various market structures for the estimated demand curve for 1968. The conclusion is clear – Cournot is the best of the three market structures. It produces the highest output, lowest price, highest *CS*, and lowest *DWL*.

Figure 3.1.7.3 also makes clear why the industry went to monopoly instead of Cournot after the cartel collapsed (under the weight of overproduction and export losses). *PS* would rise when moving from Cartel to monopoly (by 47,891,000 kroner), but fall (by 61,745,000 kroner) if the industry had adopted a noncooperative Cournot arrangement.

Thus, it is clear that the cement industry chose to maximize its own *PS* instead of *CS* + *PS*. This is not surprising.

In fact, Röller and Steen build an even stronger case by exploring the welfare effects over several years. Scroll to column AE and read the text box if you are interested.

Step Click the Monopoly option to display the monopoly solution in the graph.

The monopolist would choose output where $MR = MC$ and charge the highest price possible for that level of output. Monopoly profit in 1968 would have been 439 million kroner. Consumer surplus would be much smaller than under perfect competition and Norway would suffer a deadweight loss from monopoly of 219 million kroner.

But the Norwegians did not have a monopoly before 1968, they had the cement cartel.

Step Click the Cartel option.

The cartel chooses output where $MR = R$, allocates the domestic output to the three firms based on capacity shares, and exports the excess output.

Notice, however, that Röller and Steen do not use the predicted capacity based on the demand curve parameters. Instead, they use actual exports. The story here is that capacity takes time to build. The cartel puts persistent pressure on expansion, but the firms do not actually reach their goal of vast capacity because the cartel collapses.

Step You can check the theoretical cartel solution for the estimated parameters by simply copying the range A5:F8 from the *CompareActual* sheet and pasting in the same range in the *Compare* sheet. Click Yes if prompted to replace the destination cells.

Step Click the Cartel option to refresh the screen.

Figure 3.1.7.4 shows the result. Capacity is huge and export losses are staggering. This is the capacity that would have been installed in the long run under the cartel. Röller and Steen do not use this capacity value. Instead, they use actual exports, based on the actual capacity in 1968.

Step Return to the *CompareActual* sheet. Focus on columns F and G.

We know the firms merged to monopoly and the cartel to monopoly column (G) shows the welfare implications of this move for just 1968. As expected, output falls and price rises, *CS* falls and *PS* rises. The net welfare effect can be computed as the sum of the changes in *CS* and *PS*, which is an 11 million kroner increase (in cell G15).

Alternatively, the net welfare effect can be determined by looking at the reduction in *DWL* in cell G14. Because *DWL* falls as we move from cartel to monopoly, this number is negative. But notice that the absolute values are the same.

Our standard models tell us that merger to monopoly is the worst possible outcome – monopoly generates the greatest *DWL* of any market

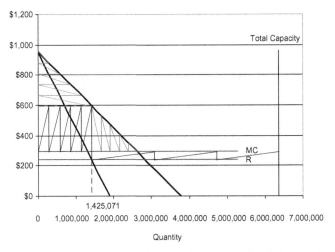

Figure 3.1.7.4. Cartel results with capacity determined theoretically.
Source: CartelDWL.xls!Compare using estimated parameters for 1968

structure. However, because of the sharing rule, welfare actually increases when the cartel merges to monopoly because monopoly does not suffer export loss.

Step Compare the values in Table 3 for the cartel to monopoly in 1968 to the values in column G.

The slight differences are due to rounding and precision differences.

Although monopoly beats the cartel, this is a poor argument for supporting monopolization. After all, the cartel could have dissolved into a noncooperative, Cournot competition. We must examine the welfare effects of this move and compare it to moving to monopoly to find the better option.

Step Compare the red circled value of the change in *PS* when moving from Cartel to Cournot in Table 3 to cell F13. These numbers should be the same, but they are not.

Röller and Steen made a mistake in computing the net welfare effect for the move from cartel to Cournot in Table 3. They report the change in domestic *PS* in the table, not the change in total *PS*, which includes the export loss. As a result, the net welfare effect for cartel to Cournot in Table 3 is also incorrect. By failing to include the export loss in the reported *PS*, they underestimated the welfare gain from adopting a Cournot noncooperative market structure.

Notice that this error does not change Röller and Steen's conclusion. In fact, if anything, their results are strengthened once the export loss is accounted for. The loss in *PS* that the cement industry undergoes in moving to Cournot competition is not as bad as Table 3 suggests because of the elimination of the export loss. The true net change in welfare is some 45 million kroner higher than Table 3 estimates.

Consequences of Using Actual Versus Theoretical Total Capacity

Now that we understand how net welfare effects for 1968 are computed, we turn to the issue of how the export loss is measured.

Cell D20, the export loss in 1968, is based on actual exports – the difference between actual capacity (total production) and domestic output.

Figure 3.1.7.4 and your *Compare* sheet show that the Nash equilibrium, long-run capacity is much higher than the actual capacity (based on actual total production). How does this impact the analysis? This is an interesting question with a surprising answer.

Step Compare the formulas in cells G16 and G17. Both display the same number, but the formulas are different.

G16 computes the net welfare gain from going to Cournot instead of monopoly (from the cartel, of course) by taking *DWL* from cartel to Cournot minus the *DWL* from cartel to monopoly. Cournot beats monopoly by about 165 million kroner.

G17 computes the same net welfare gain, but does so by subtracting the net welfare effect from going to monopoly from the net welfare effect from going to Cournot. Once again, the move to Cournot beats the move to monopoly by roughly 165 million kroner.

Step Copy the two cells, G16:G17, and go to the *Compare* sheet, pasting these cells in the same range.

The result is surprising – the superiority of Cournot over the cartel remains exactly the same, even though the *Compare* sheet is using theoretical, long-run total capacity and the export losses are huge.

If you compare the values in columns F and G in both sheets, you will find that for both the move to monopoly and the move to Cournot, the change in *PS* and the change in net welfare are much higher if the theoretical capacity is used. This makes sense because the export loss is much greater.

However, the relative improvement in Cournot over monopoly remains the same because both Cournot and monopoly avoid export losses. Thus, the size of the export loss does not matter.

Had Röller and Steen used the theoretical, long-run total capacity level based on the estimated parameters in 1968, their qualitative and quantitative conclusion regarding the superiority of Cournot over monopoly would remain completely unaffected.

Lessons from the Norwegian Cement Cartel

Röller and Steen (2006) evaluate the effectiveness of the (legal) cement cartel in Norway over the period 1955 to 1968. They solve monopoly, Cournot, and cartel models and compare the results. They find that because of the sharing rule adopted by the cartel, consumers actually did better (in terms of consumer surplus) than they would have if the industry had been monopolized. Producers, on the other hand, lose in the domestic market with the cartel compared to a monopoly. Producers suffer an additional export loss under the cartel and this leads to a key result: The merger to monopoly that occurred in 1968 actually improved net welfare relative to the cartel outcome. This is certainly a surprise, given that we expect monopoly to be the worst market structure. The authors point out, however, that simply breaking up the cartel and allowing Cournot competition would have improved welfare even more.

The fact that Röller and Steen used actual exports instead of estimated exports makes no difference to their final conclusion that Cournot competition would have been the first-best choice. The reason it does not matter is that both monopoly and Cournot competition result in the elimination of the export loss, so in comparing a move to either Cournot competition or monopoly, the actual size of the export loss does not matter.

Röller and Steen (2006) give an excellent example of how economists use *CS*, *PS*, and *DWL* in policy analysis. It is also enables deeper understanding of game theory by examining the two-stage game played by members of the cartel.

Exercises

Open Word and answer the following questions. Save the document and print it when you are done.

Suppose the inverse demand curve is $P = 1000 - 0.5Q$, marginal cost is constant at \$100 per unit, and the world price is \$50. Enter these parameter values in the *Compare* sheet and answer the questions below. Enter the demand slope as a positive number, 0.5, and click one of the market structure options to refresh the chart.

The math theory prep section showed two surprising results. First, consumers' and producers' surplus under the cement cartel do not depend on the marginal cost of capacity. Second, as the number of firms in the cartel rises, the likelihood a merger to monopoly will be welfare enhancing rises.

To answer the questions that follow, taking pictures is helpful. You can select cells (e.g., A1:M25) and copy as a picture, then paste.

1. Increase *MC* from 100 to 200 and determine the impact on the cartel's *Q*, *P*, *CS*, *PS*, DWL, and export loss. What happens to each of these variables as *MC* rises?
   Be sure to click the Perfect Competition and then Cartel option button to refresh the data below the buttons.
2. Which changes, if any, in the variables are surprising? Why?

3. At what value of *MC* will there be no exports? Take a picture of this situation and paste it in your Word document.
4. Increase the number of firms from 3 to 5 (with *MC* at the no export loss value). What effect does this have on the cartel's *Q*, *P*, *CS*, *PS*, DWL, and export loss?
5. What can you conclude about the effect of the number of firms on *PS* from a merger to monopoly (from the cartel)?

References

The epigraph is from page 278 of Oliver E. Williamson, *The Economic Institutions of Capitalism: Firms, Markets, Relational Contracting* (1985). Williamson applies the standard tools of economic reasoning (optimization and comparative statics) to transactions and argues that the institutions we observe are the evolutionary product of selection based on optimization. Google "transaction cost economics" to learn more.

The cartel theory example is based on the excellent paper by Lars-Hendrik Röller and Frode Steen, "On the Workings of a Cartel: Evidence from the Norwegian Cement Industry," *American Economic Review*, Vol. 96, No. 1 (January, 2006), pp. 321–338.

3.1.8

Signaling Theory

The presence of people in the market who are willing to offer inferior goods tends to drive the market out of existence – as in the case of our automobile "lemons." It is this possibility that represents the major costs of dishonesty – for dishonest dealings tend to drive honest dealings out of the market.

George A. Akerlof

We all want to live in a world in which every buyer and seller is always completely honest, dependable, and trustworthy. In such a world, no one would lie, cheat, or steal. No one would misrepresent a product or hide a defect to make a sale, and the buyer would always alert the cashier when receiving too much change. Even politicians and children would always tell the truth.

Plainly, we do not live in such a world. Cigarette manufacturers swear under oath that their products are safe and that there is no proof that tobacco causes lung cancer. Management lies to labor about the true profitability of the firm and the size of the wage increase that the firm can really afford. It seems that we live in the midst of lies and deceit. Few can be trusted and few trust us.

This then is the problem: How can we make our world – the one full of distrust and scams – more like the world we all agree is better – the one in which individuals are sincere and open? How can we get people to tell the truth?

Three Approaches to Honest Behavior

We consider utopian and authoritarian solutions, and then focus on a third way that most people rarely consider.

If somehow it were possible to create a perfectly honest person, we could attain our goal of living in an honest world. People could be counted on, with

511

no doubt or reservation whatsoever, to be completely clear and forthright. This is the utopian solution.

Karl Marx believed private property, money, and the capitalist system created an all-encompassing greed that generated fraud, deception, and a variety of other reprehensible individual behaviors. For Marx, the solution to the problem was quite simple: Replace vicious capitalism with its superior evolutionary offspring, communism, and replace the money-hungry *homo economicus* with the noble *new socialist man*.

Although seemingly hopelessly idealistic, in certain cases, reliance on people's good qualities is, in fact, possible. We all have close friends and family whom we can trust to be sincere and truthful. In our daily lives, however, we deal with countless strangers, and we cannot rely on personal relationships to ensure honest behavior. In a modern society that incorporates the actions and decisions of millions of individuals, it is simply impractical to expect trustworthiness from everyone.

To protect against dishonesty, many people think immediately of monitoring. This second approach can be called the authoritarian solution.

If a store owner thinks customers are going to steal, valuable merchandise can be put under a glass counter, security cameras installed, and guards can watch the customers. If the government knows that citizens will cheat on their taxes, a sample of tax returns will be audited carefully to check for full compliance and severe penalties will be imposed on those caught cheating.

In general, the authoritarian approach to solving the problem of dishonesty requires a powerful judge who can check the truthfulness of statements and punish those who are caught violating the rules. This can work well when it is clear what constitutes a lie, and it is easy to observe the dishonest behavior.

Unfortunately, in many cases, it is quite difficult to determine dishonest behavior because there are shades of dishonesty, ambiguities in truthfulness, and inherent uncertainty in the world. For example, if I sell you an expensive product, promising that it is of high quality, and then it breaks, am I a liar? It may very well be a high-quality good that just happened to break. Of course, I may have known that it was really shoddy merchandise and I just tricked you.

In addition to that rather large subset of cases in which detecting dishonesty is difficult, every application of the authoritarian approach suffers from a much larger drawback. In order to be effective, the powerful judge must be able to monitor individuals, including investigating alleged wrongdoing, determining guilt, and meting out punishment accordingly. This raises a serious concern: Who watches the watcher?

The inescapable paradox is that the stronger the authority, the more it will be able to control the individual, but also the more dangerous it becomes to the individual. Secret police, neighbors spying on friends, and severe control of individual behavior via strict rules and regulations seem the destiny of authoritarian schemes to coerce honesty from unwilling individuals.

There is little doubt that the authoritarian approach to the problem of dishonesty is the most common solution contemplated and applied. Faced with severe cheating, our first instinct is to call the referee and demand that force be applied to ensure truthfulness. There is, however, another alternative – one that does not suffer from the dangers inherent in the authoritarian solution.

Transforming humans to excise the driving force of self-interest or imposing authoritarian control to repress behavior driven by greed is like swimming against a powerful tide. The third approach is completely different. It is based on accepting self-interest and greed as immutable forces and using them to get desired behavior. We can harness the power of self-interest in favor of our desired end. Individuals are free to decide to lie or not, but lying leaves them worse off. If honesty is the best choice from a self-interested point of view, then honesty is what we will get.

Signaling theory shows how this approach works.

An Economic Model of Used Cars

Suppose that there are only two kinds of used cars: high-quality A cars and low-quality B cars (called *lemons* in the United States). To keep things simple, suppose that there are equal numbers of each and that the high-quality A car is worth $10,000 while the low-quality B car is worth only $5000.

The seller knows whether his or her car is of low or high quality, but the buyer does not. This is called *asymmetric information* because one party has knowledge and the other does not. The general problem of honesty, in this case, is reduced to figuring out a way to get sellers to tell the truth about the quality of the cars they are selling.

It is important to emphasize that, as illustrated in Figure 3.1.8.1, the buyer has no easy way to tell the cars apart. The underlying distribution of cars is on the left, but what the buyer actually sees is on the right.

In such a world, buyers would expect to get a car worth $7500 on average. Half of the time they would get a $10,000 car and the other half a $5000 car. Thus, on average, a used car would be worth $7500 and this is the amount buyers would be willing to pay for a used car.

Whereas sellers of low-quality cars would be quite happy getting $7500 for their low-quality cars, sellers of high-quality cars would be upset. After all, owners of A cars have a product worth $10,000. They might try to convince buyers to pay $10,000 by making claims about the high quality of the car. Declarations about high quality, however, are likely to be ignored because

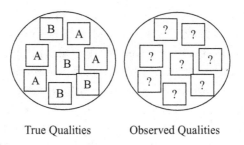

True Qualities   Observed Qualities

Figure 3.1.8.1. The problem of incomplete information.

the buyer has no way of knowing if the seller is telling the truth. After all, the seller might actually have a low-quality car worth $5000 and is lying to make an extra $5000. The buyer would worry that the seller's self-interest would dominate any desire to be honest.

The frustrated sellers of high-quality used cars simply leave the market. This phenomenon is an example of Gresham's Law, "bad money drives out good." It was first stated in the 16th century, when monarchs would debase coinage (by adding filler) to get more coins out of a given amount of gold. People would exchange the less valuable coins (bad money) and hoard the pure gold ones (good money). With more bad money in circulation, prices would rise.

Applied to the used car market, the low-quality used cars can be seen as driving out the high-quality cars. Left alone, we would not expect to see high-quality used cars for sale. In fact, that is not what happens – high-quality used cars are sold.

Instead of fixing the problem by attempting to correct the unethical behavior of the sellers of low-quality used cars (whose dishonesty is causing the trouble here) or imposing authoritarian control over the used car sellers, an alternative scheme has arisen that has certain appealing properties – not the least of which is that car sellers truthfully reveal the qualities of their cars without any central, controlling authority.

Before explaining signaling theory, it is worth pointing out that what is happening here is actually an externality problem. The low-quality sellers fail to take into account the full cost of their lying and, therefore, they lie too much. No individual seller is aware, or would care, that his or her lying is contributing to the elimination of high-quality goods.

Signaling Theory

Developed by Spence (1973), the idea behind signaling theory is simple: The sellers of high-quality cars, frustrated by their inability to convince the buyers of the true quality of their cars, will look for ways to offer evidence that they are telling the truth.

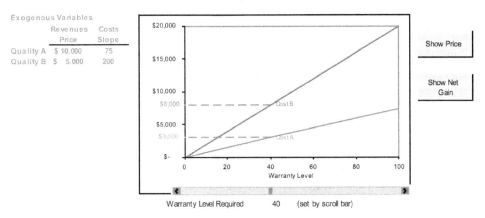

Figure 3.1.8.2. Seller's cost of warranty for each type of car.
Source: SignalingTheory.xls!Optimizing

Buyers cannot directly observe the quality of the car, but there are other observable characteristics bundled with the car and seller. *Indices* are attributes that cannot be changed, such as the age or gender of the seller. *Signals*, on the other hand, are observable markers that can be acquired.

The signal, however, must have some special properties to be effective. The signal must be correlated with the underlying, unobservable characteristic. It must be something the A car owner is willing to do, but the B car owner is not, so that it is not immediately copied by unscrupulous sellers of low-quality cars.

In the case of used cars, a common signal is a warranty. Suppose that high-quality cars will have low warranty costs to the seller because they are unlikely to break, but the sellers of low-quality cars would face high warranty costs for these cars that will probably require many repairs.

Step Open the Excel workbook SignalingTheory.xls and read the *Intro* sheet, then go to the *Optimizing* sheet.

A graph of the cost of the warranty to the sellers of A and B cars is depicted in Figure 3.1.8.2. With no warranty at all, at a warranty level of zero, a seller has no warranty costs – if something breaks after the car is sold, it is the buyer's problem. As the amount of warranty coverage increases, however, the seller of the B car incurs higher warranty costs as more and more repairs are covered. At a warranty level of 40 (this might be repairs covered by the seller for the first 12 months or 12,000 miles), sellers of high-quality cars expect to incur costs of about $3000, whereas the sellers of low-quality cars will pay around $8000 for repairs.

The warranty cost functions are determined by the slopes in cells C6 and C7. It is easy to see that a seller's warranty cost is simply the slope parameter times the warranty level.

The Signal

Now, suppose that buyers said, "We will believe sellers who claim that their cars are high quality and pay the $10,000 price if and only if the car comes with a warranty level of 40."

Step Click the Show Price button.

Anyone buying a car with a warranty level below 40 will be willing to pay, at most, $5000 because it is assumed that the car is of low quality. Even if the car is actually a high-quality car, if it fails to come with the warranty level for high-quality cars, no buyer will pay $10,000 for it because the claim that the car is of high quality is unbelievable without the warranty. On the other hand, a buyer would be willing to pay $10,000 for any car with a warranty level of 40, even if it is actually a low-quality car.

It is now up to the sellers of used cars to make a decision of whether or not to lie. Sellers of low-quality used cars can claim that their cars are high quality and thereby receive the $10,000 high-quality price.

They will not misrepresent the quality of the car, however, because they would end up worse off. Their individual self-interest will drive them to tell the truth.

Step Click the Show Net Gain button to see why low-quality sellers will not lie.

Figure 3.1.8.3 shows what is on your computer screen. The price function has been superimposed on the warranty costs. The price is a step function, with a discontinuity at the warranty level of 40, because no buyer will pay $10,000 unless the car comes with the correct warranty.

We assume that all sellers seek to maximize the net gain, or profit, from the sale of their goods and services. Sellers of used cars would not look simply at the fact that they can make $10,000 by offering a warranty level of 40. This decision-making strategy completely ignores the cost of the warranty. Instead, sellers must compare the *net gain*, price minus cost of the warranty, to arrive at an optimal decision concerning the warranty level.

The table below the graph contains each type of seller's net gain from selling a car with no warranty versus selling the same car with warranty level of 40. Read the table horizontally – for each type of seller, compare the net gain without and with the warranty, and choose the higher number.

It is clear that sellers of high-quality used cars will offer the warranty level and make $7000 in profit because that beats the $5000 net gain if no warranty is chosen. Similarly, the sellers of low-quality used cars will choose to forgo the warranty and walk away with $5000 because that is superior to the $2000 net gain from choosing to lie and posting the warranty bond.

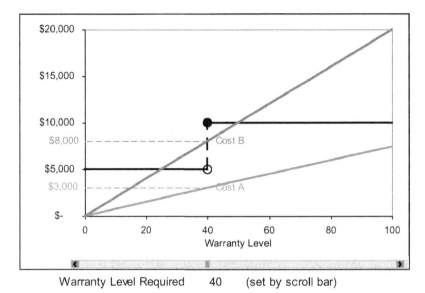

Warranty Level Required   40   (set by scroll bar)

Decision Making
Net Gain Calculation

	Warranty Offered?		
	No	Yes	Choice
A	$ 5,000	$ 7,000	Yes
B	$ 5,000	$ 2,000	No

Figure 3.1.8.3. Understanding why sellers will not lie.
Source: SignalingTheory.xls!Optimizing

This is a rather remarkable result. To restate the outcome, the sellers of low-quality used cars will voluntarily and honestly admit that their used cars are of low quality and only worth $5000. The sellers of low-quality used cars will not lie to the buyers. Is this because they suddenly were overcome by their conscience? No. They are the same fallible, less than perfectly honest people before and after the warranty scheme. Are they telling the truth because an authority figure is watching them, ready to punish liars? No. No one is watching them. The sellers of low-quality used cars can lie if they so wish. They will not lie, however, because it is not in their self-interest. They end up worse off if they lie in this situation. The warranty scheme has managed to successfully separate or sort the two qualities of cars into their respective groups. This result is called a *separating equilibrium*.

Figure 3.1.8.4 shows that the warranty acts as a screen, separating the true car qualities into two distinct groups, Xs and Ys, from which it easy to tell which cars are high quality and which are not. In essence, two markets for cars are created, one for low- and the other for high-quality cars, each with their own prices. Sellers of low-quality cars, although they are physically able to do so, will not lie and enter the high-quality car market because the price

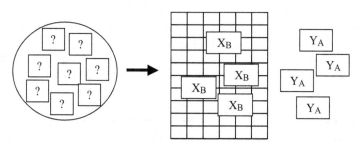

Figure 3.1.8.4. Warranty as a screen.

of admission is too high. Lying is not profit maximizing; therefore, lying will not be observed.

It is perhaps paradoxical to ponder, but no individual or organization runs this scheme. No one sets the warranty level and no one sets the price of the cars. The whole system bubbles up from the interaction of the two kinds of sellers and the buyers. Adam Smith would have called it an example of the "invisible hand" of the market; Friedrich Hayek would have described it as a "spontaneous order"; and modern day chaos theorists would speak of "self-organizing systems." It is all the same thing – individual interaction generating a quite agreeable systemwide result. To see how the equilibrating forces operate in this model, we examine how the signaling scheme can break down.

Signaling Failures and Equilibrium

One way that a signal can fail is if it is set too high.

Step Use the scroll bar to set a high signal, like 80 or so.

In this case, as shown in Figure 3.1.8.5 and your computer screen, not even the sellers of high-quality cars find it in their self-interest to accept the warranty level that brings the $10,000 price. The signal has failed to separate the two qualities of cars.

On the other hand, if the signal is set too low, sellers of B cars will find it in their self-interest to lie and claim their cars are actually high quality. They will choose the warranty level that brings the $10,000 price.

Step To see this, use the scroll bar to set a low signal, 20 or less.

Your screen should show that both sellers opt to acquire the signal. The low-quality seller will lie and claim that the car is of high quality because the net gain from lying (cell H27) is greater than the net gain from telling the truth (cell G27). Once again, this signal has failed.

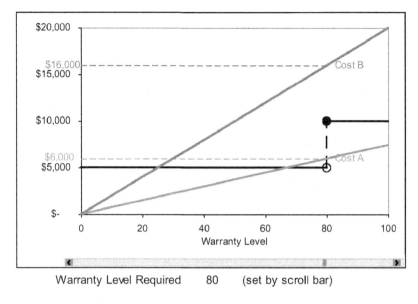

Warranty Level Required   80   (set by scroll bar)

Decision Making
Net Gain Calculation

| | Warranty Offered? | | |
	No	Yes	Choice
A	$ 5,000	$ 4,000	No
B	$ 5,000	$ (6,000)	No

Figure 3.1.8.5. Signaling failure from a warranty level set too high.
Source: SignalingTheory.xls!Optimizing

When the signal is too high, the holes in the screen are too small and no one can get through. If the signal is too low, the holes are too large and everybody passes through. In a separating equilibrium, the level of the signal is such that the two types are grouped together and easily identifiable.

It is the very fact that signals can be observed as failing that provides the key to understanding how the system can settle down to a result that effectively solves the problem without central control. If the signal is too low, self-interested sellers of high-quality cars will offer high warranty levels in order to block their lying brethren from diluting their market. If the signal is too high, no one will take it and the buyers will realize that they have lost the means by which to identify the two qualities of cars. The forces inherent in the system, self-interested behavior by the interacting agents, will conspire to generate an equilibrium signal level that effectively sorts the two qualities of cars. The process works just like supply and demand – pressure in disequilibrium pushes the signal in one direction or another until it equilibrates.

Other Applications of Signaling Theory

We have barely scratched the surface of signaling theory. There are many situations in which one party to a transaction has available information that the other party lacks and this asymmetric information puts honesty in peril.

Consider the job market (which was Spence's original example). Faced with many job applicants, all claiming to be high-quality A workers, the firm might insist on a signal, a college degree, to back the claims made by job applicants. Suppose that low-quality workers are also likely to be low-quality students, and that it is more costly for them to acquire the educational signal. As in the used car case, the successful screen will separate the two worker groups into their respective low- and high-quality categories. The signal will elicit honest responses from low-quality workers because lying requires a college degree to be believed and this is not in their best interest.

Additional applications of signaling include life insurance (in which gravely ill or sick people honestly reveal their health status because their claims must be supported by a physical exam), legal bargaining (in which plaintiffs signal the strength of their case by demanding a high pre-trial settlement), and firm entry (in which incumbent firms make reliable claims about their low costs and ability to compete by charging low pre-entry prices).

In these cases, an incentive mechanism has developed that accepts self-interest among buyers and sellers as a powerful, immutable, driving force. Instead of fighting self-interest by removing or suppressing it, the incentive mechanism uses self-interest to reach the desired end.

The Economics of Honesty

Dishonesty exacts a large cost on society. For lesser developed countries, corruption is a severe obstacle to economic growth. Getting people to be truthful is a serious, critically important goal.

The primary solutions to the problem of dishonesty have centered on utopian and authoritarian approaches. The former seeks to perfect human behavior; the latter to directly control it. A third, somewhat counterintuitive, alternative exists that relies on self-interest to yield an agreeable systemwide result.

This third alternative is marked by individuals following their self-interest. When birds fly in a V-shaped pattern, they do so not under the guidance of an authoritarian drill sergeant who tells each bird where to fly, but because they obey a simple rule that says, "If there are no birds around, fly; if a bird is in front, fly just off its wing because it is easier." Likewise, modern society is composed of millions of individual agents whose interaction establishes a systemwide pattern. Unsatisfactory results can be changed via transmuting the motivating forces of each agent, imposing decisions on each agent, or changing the incentives faced by each agent. The last option is rarely considered, but may be the most effective and best of the three.

Signaling theory says that by making honesty the best policy, we will get honesty. Sellers reveal the truth because lying leaves them worse off than telling the truth. This is the economics of honesty.

To be sure, signaling requires rules and institutional support. If the seller of low-quality used cars knows that he can renege on warranties or other contracts because the court system is nonexistent or corrupt, then signaling will be useless. There is, however, a world of difference between an authoritarian approach that relies on a central power to coerce honesty and the system that evolves out of the interaction of the buyers and sellers given appropriately supporting institutions. The decentralized system avoids the question of "Who watches the watcher?" because there is no dominant central power. And in the end, this may be its most significant advantage.

Exercises

Open Word and answer the following questions. Save the document and print it when you are done.
1. Suppose a firm is trying to determine whether an applicant is of low or high ability and it believes people with long fingernails have higher ability. Would fingernail length be an effective signal? Draw a graph to support your answer.
2. Draw a graph that shows how education as a signal could be used to separate low- and high-ability job applicants. Explain how education as a signal works.
3. Draw a graph in which education as a signal fails because the signal level is set too high. Explain why the signal fails.
4. College education as a signal clashes with human capital theory, which says that educated workers earn more because they were made more productive by their education. What does signaling theory say about the value of education? In other words, according to signaling, why are educated workers paid more?
5. Why has it been difficult to determine with data whether human capital or signaling theory is right about college education?

References

The epigraph is from page 495 of George A. Akerlof, "The Market for 'Lemons': Quality Uncertainty and the Market Mechanism," *The Quarterly Journal of Economics*, Vol. 84, No. 3 (August, 1970), pp. 488–500. This is the paper that Michael Spence described as "quite electrifying" in his Nobel acceptance lecture (available at <nobelprize.org>). The Nobel Prize was shared that year by Akerlof, Spence, and Joseph E. Stiglitz "for their analyses of markets with asymmetric information."

Akerlof's paper led to an exchange concerning the empirical validity of the claim that lemons drove out high-quality used pickup trucks. Eric W. Bond, "A Direct Test of the 'Lemons' Model: The Market for Used Pickup Trucks," *The American*

Economic Review, Vol. 72, No. 4 (September, 1982), pp. 838–840, found no evidence for the claim. Michael Pratt and George Hoffer, "Test of the Lemons Model: Comment," *The American Economic Review*, Vol. 74, No. 4 (September, 1984), pp. 798–800, conduct a "finer test" and "conclude that the market for used pickup trucks is a lemons market." In a reply, Eric W. Bond, "Test of the 'Lemons' Model: Reply," *The American Economic Review,* Vol. 74, No. 4 (September, 1984), pp. 801–804, said that "Pratt and Hoffer find used trucks to be of lower quality not because they have a 'finer' test, but because they fail to adjust for observable quality differences and include trucks that are more than 10 years old." Bond believes there is no lemons effect for used pickups because institutions have arisen to counteract the effects of asymmetric information.

The signaling model is laid out clearly in Michael Spence, "Job Market Signaling," *The Quarterly Journal of Economics*, Vol. 87, No. 3 (August, 1973), pp. 355–374. This article was based on his doctoral dissertation and published as a book titled *Market Signaling* in 1974.

George Selgin, "Gresham's Law," online at <eh.net/encyclopedia/article/selgin.gresham.law>, offers a short explanation of the history and application of this concept.

3.2

General Equilibrium

3.2.1

The Edgeworth Box

"[Irma Adelman] was an early proponent of simulation models. In addition to work with input-output and linear-programming models, she was one of the pioneers in developing computable general equilibrium (CGE) models and applying them to developing countries, especially for analysis of income distribution."

Distinguished Fellow Citation for Irma Adelman

We have become quite familiar with Figure 3.2.1.1. We have used partial equilibrium analysis to focus on a single commodity, exploring how supply and demand determine an equilibrium quantity that is the market's answer to the resource allocation question.

We have also used Figure 3.2.1.1 to set up and solve an optimization problem in which society chooses that quantity of a single commodity that maximizes consumers' plus producers' surplus.

When the market's equilibrium output equals the socially optimal quantity, the market works well. There are situations, however, when we do not get the quantity that maximizes $CS + PS$. We label these situations a market failure. An obvious example is monopoly. It produces too little output and generates a deadweight loss.

But the focus on a single commodity is limiting. In fact, the market system uses supply and demand for each good or service to answer the fundamental production and distribution questions. In other words, there are many interacting markets (one for each commodity) simultaneously in operation.

If we monopolize one commodity, we cause a misallocation of resources in the monopolized market (too little is produced) and that reverberates into the other markets. After all, the high price in the monopolized commodity will shift demand curves for substitutes and complements of that good.

General equilibrium analysis attempts to account for supply and demand in all markets. As you can imagine, it is much more difficult than partial

Production:			Which goods and services to produce with limited resources?
					How much of each kind?
Distribution:		How much does each person get of the goods and services produced?

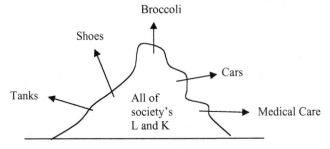

Figure 3.2.1.1. Society's resource allocation problem.

equilibrium analysis, but it is also superior because the entire resource allocation question is under consideration.

This book will focus on general equilibrium theory, but as the epigraph to this chapter explains, computable general equilibrium models are used to estimate the general equilibrium effects of tax policies, monopoly power, and other events. Economists have always been aware of the limitations of partial equilibrium analysis, but it was not until the development of modern computers that these complicated models could be solved and applied.

Before beginning our study of general equilibrium theory, two observations are in order.

1. Society can decide which goods and services are handled by the market. Society may decide that human organs or votes may not be legally bought and sold. Different market-based societies may choose different lists of commodities to be allocated by the market. We call a society market based if individual resource owners make decisions about how to allocate the inputs they manage, even if particular commodities are regulated or entire sectors of the economy (such as education or health) are not privately owned.
2. A complete general equilibrium analysis of the market system is beyond our scope. There are three parts, of which this book covers only the first one.

   • Pure exchange: Assume each consumer has endowments of already produced goods and allow trade to occur.
   • Production: Allow goods to be produced from inputs.
   • Combine pure exchange and production.

We focus solely on pure exchange and ignore the next two stages. This means we will not complete a true general equilibrium analysis of the market system. Emphasizing only the problem of pure exchange enables deep learning of the core concepts of general equilibrium, including the all-important Edgeworth Box graph.

Creating the Edgeworth Box

The canonical graph used to depict a pure exchange economy is called the Edgeworth Box. It is also commonly referred to as the Edgeworth-Bowley Box. It turns out that both names are wrong. Mark Blaug, discussing something called the "Ricardo Effect," points out an interesting thing about names:

Whether it really is in Ricardo is a nice question. The fact that the Ricardo Effect is hard to find in Ricardo exemplifies a general rule. According to R. K. Merton, 'eponymy' is the "the practice of affixing the name of the scientist to all or part of what he has found" but it is a striking fact that the outcome of eponymy is almost always to hang the right label on the wrong person. Thus, Thomas Gresham never stated Gresham's Law. Jean Baptiste Say only stated Say's Law after James Mill had stated it for him. Robert Giffen never stated Giffen's Paradox. Francis Edgeworth never drew the Edgeworth Box. Ernst Engel never drew an Engel's curve. Walras never stated Walras' Law. Irving Fisher did not invent the Ideal Index Number and actually pleaded (in vain) that it should not be named after him. Arthur Bowley did not enunciate Bowley's Law. Arthur Pigou did not state the Pigou Effect – and so on. Indeed S. M. Stigler has advanced "Stigler's Law of Eponymy: No scientific discovery is named after its original discoverer," a law which is confirmed as soon as it is stated (see *Transactions of the New York Academy of Sciences*, Series 11, 39, 1980). Nevertheless, there are also counter-examples in economics to Stigler's Law, such as Pareto-optimality and the Wicksell Effect. (Mark Blaug, *Economic Theory in Retrospect*, 5th ed., p. 523)

In case you are curious, it was Vilfredo Pareto (pronounced pa-ray-toe) who should be credited with the graph that we call the Edgeworth Box (Tarascio, 1972). Because no one has ever heard of the Pareto Box, we will continue to call it the Edgeworth Box.

The Edgeworth Box is a graph that is constructed by putting together the consumer choice problem graphs from two consumers. It ends up looking like a box; hence its name. Here's how you build an Edgeworth Box.

Figure 3.2.1.2 has Endowment Model graphs for two consumers, A and B. Consumer A has an initial endowment of 35 units of good x_1 and 10 units of good x_2. Consumer B arrives at the market with 5 units of x_1 and 30 units of x_2.

Step Open the Excel workbook EdgeworthBox.xls and read the *Intro* sheet, then go to the *A* sheet to see consumer A's optimization problem. At the given prices, the sheet shows that A will maximize utility, subject to the budget constraint, by selling 10 units of x_1 and buying $6\frac{2}{3}$ units of x_2.

Step Proceed to the *B* sheet to see consumer B's optimal solution. Given the same prices faced by consumer A, consumer B optimizes by buying 20 units of x_1 and selling $13\frac{1}{3}$ units of x_2.

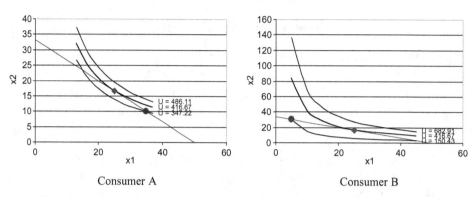

Consumer A   Consumer B

Figure 3.2.1.2. Preparing to build the Edgeworth Box.
Source: EdgeworthBox.xls!A and EdgeworthBox.xls!B

The crucial step in understanding the Edgeworth Box is the next one: Flip consumer B's graph, as shown in Figure 3.2.1.3. Sheet *B* in Edgeworth-Box.xls shows how to do this.

Step Follow the instructions in column F of sheet *B* in order to recreate Figure 3.2.1.3.

Actually flipping B's graph will help you remember that B's decisions about buying and selling are always read from the perspective of the northeast corner of the Edgeworth Box.

The last step in creating the Edgeworth Box is to join the two consumer's graphs. The result of this operation is Figure 3.2.1.4.

Step Proceed to the *EdgeworthBox* sheet. You may need to scroll down a bit to see the Edgeworth Box.

Step Click on the graph to select it, and then drag the graph to the right.

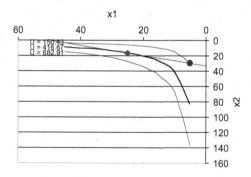

Figure 3.2.1.3. Flipping B's graph.
Source: EdgeworthBox.xls!B

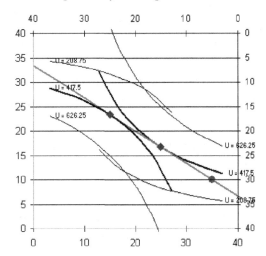

Figure 3.2.1.4. The Edgeworth Box.
Source: EdgeworthBox.xls!EdgeworthBox

It comes apart! Clearly, the Edgeworth Box is simply two separate graphs superimposed on top of each other. The top graph has no fill, so it is transparent.

Step Click the Make Box button to put the box back together. The button simply lines up the two graphs to make it easy to create the box.

Step Scroll back up to see the organization of the sheet. The two consumers' optimization problems are represented in columns A and B and columns M and N. In the middle (columns G and H), market information is displayed. Cells H16 and H17 contain the prices of the two goods. The price of good x_2, called the *numeraire*, has been set equal to 1. In the next chapter, we will see how prices respond to supply and demand.

Properties of the Edgeworth Box

1. The sides of the box give the total amounts of the two goods available.
   Total $x_1 = 40$
   Total $x_2 = 40$
2. The initial endowment is a single point that can be read from A's or B's point of view. The initial endowment is (35,10) for A and (5,30) for B.
3. Prices establish a budget constraint that is common to both consumers.
4. It is the price ratio, p_1/p_2, that matters, not the individual prices themselves. By convention, we set $p_2 = 1$, and call it the *numeraire*.
5. Net demands for x_1 and x_2 for both A and B can be read from the box. It requires careful attention because it is easy to be tricked. Remember to read B's decisions about buying and selling from the top right corner.

6. The Edgeworth Box has enough information for you to figure out how prices will change and where the equilibrium solution lies. The next chapter shows how.

Edgeworth Box Basics

The Edgeworth Box simultaneously displays the optimization problems of two consumers. A's view is the usual x–y axis configuration with the origin in the lower left corner of the graph. B's graph has been flipped so the origin is at the top right corner. Thus, x_1 rises as you move to the left on the top of the box and x_2 rises as you move down the right side of the box.

In the next chapter we will use the Edgeworth Box to see how the market equilibrates. The Edgeworth Box is used again to explain the concept of Pareto optimality and the idea of economic efficiency in a general equilibrium setting. Although it does not have the widespread recognition of supply and demand, the Edgeworth Box is the canonical graph in general equilibrium theory.

Exercises

Open Word and answer the following questions. Save the document and print it when you are done.

1. Suppose an Edgeworth Box was very tall and very skinny. What would that tell you?
2. Use Word's Drawing Tools to draw an Edgeworth Box that is the same as the *EdgeworthBox* sheet except B's utility function is $U = \min\{x_1, x_2\}$. Draw three representative indifference curves for B.
3. Click the Reset button in the *EdgeworthBox* sheet and set cB in cell M21 to 0.1. Click the Take a Picture button and paste the graph in your Word document.
4. Explain B's buy/sell decision for each good.
5. How does B's buy/sell decision make sense given that B has so little of x_1 and so much of x_2?

References

The epigraph is from "Irma Adelman: Distinguished Fellow 2003," *The American Economic Review*, Vol. 94, No. 3 (June, 2004). This book is about economic theory, but it is worth noting that advances in computers have enabled real-world, empirical applications of general equilibrium analysis. Computable general equilibrium models (CGEs) are used to find equilibrium solutions with many agents and commodities. The effects of taxes and other shocks are simulated and evaluated.

See Irma Adelman, "The Research for the Paper on the Dynamics of the Klein-Goldberger Model," *Journal of Economic and Social Measurement*, Vol. 32 (2007), pp. 29–33 to learn how Adelman and her physicist husband, Frank Adelman, used an IBM 650 mainframe computer in 1958 to produce one of her most famous articles, "The Dynamic Properties of the Klein-Goldberger Model," *Econometrica*, Vol. 27, No. 4 (October, 1959), pp. 596–625. This was the first attempt to solve an econometric model with an electronic computer. Adelman (2007) also says that the work was "I believe, a first application of Monte Carlo techniques in economics." (p. 32)

In an introduction to Adelman's description of how the model was estimated, Renfro describes the IBM 650 and how incredibly impressive it was that Adelman managed to use it to estimate the model. In addition to covering her den with pieces of paper indicating the contents of each memory register at each step in the computation and having to pay more than a month of her salary for 1 hour of computing time, Renfro (p. 24) points out that the work had to be done at night. "Throughout the entire mainframe era, those who needed to get something done quickly worked through the night. Computers in those days had multiple users; this was the time of day that provided the best turnaround, when only the most serious were awake." See Charles G. Renfro, "Introduction," *Journal of Economic and Social Measurement*, Vol. 32 (2007), pp. 23–28.

Agent-based computational economics (ACE) is related to CGE. To learn more about "growing economies from the bottom up," visit <www.econ.iastate.edu/tesfatsi/ace.htm>.

For support for the claim that it should be called the Pareto Box, see Vincent Tarascio, "A Correction on the Geneology of the So-Called Edgeworth-Bowley Diagram," *Economic Inquiry*, Vol. 10 (1972), pp. 193–197.

3.2.2

General Equilibrium Market Allocation

Without Pareto, the Theory of General Equilibrium, of which Walras was without question the real founder, would never have acquired the fame which it has now, nor indeed would it have been possible to speak of the Lausanne School.

Umberto Ricci

Partial equilibrium analysis relies on supply and demand for a particular commodity to explain how the market establishes an equilibrium output that is society's answer to the resource allocation question. The figure X traced out by supply and demand lines is perhaps the most basic and well known picture in economics.

General equilibrium analysis labors under a new graph, the Edgeworth Box, that is confusing when first encountered. However, the equilibration process in an Edgeworth Box is based on the same logic used in supply and demand analysis.

We will leverage knowledge of supply and demand to explain how the market works in a general equilibrium setting and to learn how to read the Edgeworth Box.

Tatonnement – The Equilibration Process

Intro Econ students know that shortages cause prices to rise and surpluses push prices downward. In a supply and demand graph, the price is displayed as a horizontal line that falls when it is above the intersection and rises when it is below.

In the Edgeworth Box, there are two markets simultaneously equilibrating. The prices of the two goods are displayed by a single line, which is the budget constraint faced by the two consumers. The slope of the price line, also known as the price vector, is $-p_1/p_2$.

Remember that we are considering the special case of a pure exchange economy. All products have been produced and individuals are trading from their initial endowments. Prices are determined competitively by the interaction of all buyers and sellers – every consumer takes prices as given. Unfortunately, a two-dimensional Edgeworth Box allows for only two consumers. We model price-taking behavior by supposing that there is an auctioneer who shouts out prices. Consumers take these prices as given.

Although each commodity has a price, in general equilibrium analysis, only relative prices matter. We can arbitrarily take one good and set its price to 1. This makes that good the *numeraire*.

The price line rotates around the initial endowment, *swinging to and fro*. It becomes more vertical as p_1/p_2 rises and flatter if p_1/p_2 falls. At any moment, the consumers can compute the optimal amounts of each good to buy and sell. If the amounts each wants to buy and sell are not mutually compatible, then the price line swings toward the equilibrium price vector. The word *tatonnement* (pronounced ta-ton-mon) was used by the French economist Leon Walras to describe the equilibration process. He visualized the market groping its way through an iterative process that converged to a position of rest.

You may have noticed that the terminology of general equilibrium analysis has a decidedly French language flavor to it. Walras, the father of general equilibrium theory (and described by Schumpeter as "the greatest economist ever") was French. His successor at the School of Lausanne was Vilfredo Pareto, a native Italian with a background in math and engineering, who invented the concept of Pareto optimality (and is the actual originator of the Edgeworth Box). In the second half of the 19th century, French economists were at the leading edge of general equilibrium theory and mathematical economics. This strong mathematical tradition continues today (e.g., native sons Gerard Debreu and Maurice Allais have won Nobel Prizes in Economics for their work in general equilibrium theory).

Step Open the Excel workbook EdgeworthBoxGE.xls and read the *Intro* sheet, then go to the *EdgeworthBox1* sheet. Figure 3.2.2.1 reproduces what is on your screen. We review the display, piece by piece.

The organization is similar to the EdgeworthBox.xls workbook. Consumer A's optimization problem is in columns A and B. No need to run Solver – cells B11 and B12 contain A's optimal reduced-form expression.

With a price line with slope $-2/3$, consumer A would like to sell 10 units of good 1 and buy $6\frac{2}{3}$ units of good 2. This is shown in the Edgeworth Box by focusing on A's part of the box (read from the bottom left corner). In Figure 3.2.2.1, arrows along the bottom and left sides of the box indicate what A wants to do.

Columns M and N display consumer's B optimization problem. At the initial prices, consumer B wants to buy 20 units of good 1 and sell $13\frac{1}{3}$ units of good 2. Figure 3.2.2.1 has arrows that show what consumer B wants to do.

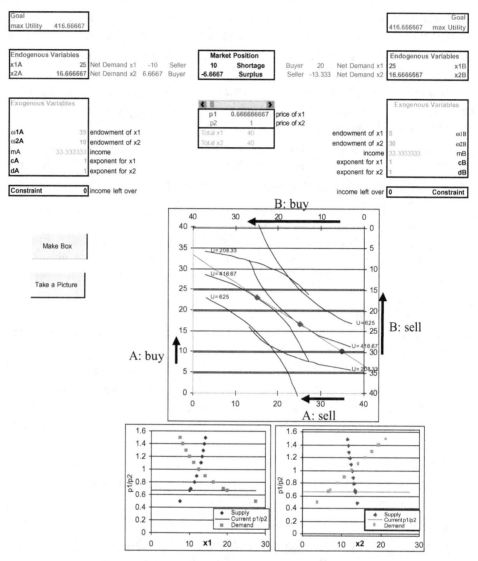

Figure 3.2.2.1. Disequilibrium in the Edgeworth Box.
Source: EdgeworthBoxGE.xls!EdgeworthBox1

Make sure you understand that the length of the arrows in Figure 3.2.2.1 indicate the amounts to be bought and sold, and the direction of the arrow indicates buying or selling. It is easy to see that A wants to sell 10 units because A's optimal solution requires that he consume 25 units of good 1 and he started with 35 units of good 1. Similarly, A wishes to buy $66\frac{2}{3}$ of good 2 to add this amount to his initial allotment of 10 units of good 2, in order to end up with $16\frac{2}{3}$ units of good 2.

B is harder to read correctly. It is easy to make a mistake. We proceed slowly.

Read B's buy and sell decisions in Figure 3.2.2.1 from the top and right axes. B wants to buy 20 units of good 1. From her initial endowment of 5 units, she wants to move *left* along the top axis, which means acquiring more x_1, until she ends up with 25 units. On the other hand, she wants to sell $13\frac{1}{3}$ units of good 2, moving *up* the right axis – which means she is reducing her desired amount of x_2.

When B moves up the budget constraint in Figure 3.2.2.1, by moving from her initial endowment point in the lower right-hand corner of the box in a northwesterly direction along the budget constraint, she is increasing (buying) x_1 and decreasing (selling) x_2. This may seem obvious, but it is easy to forget.

Of course, with the spreadsheet, you can quickly see what A and B want to do by looking at the cells in the middle of the sheet. The market position cells clearly show that there is a shortage of good 1 and surplus of good 2 at the initial price vector. This information is also conveyed in the supply and demand graphs below the Edgeworth Box. Notice that the demand and supply curves for good 2 are upside down because the y axis is the price ratio, p_1/p_2.

With a shortage of good 1 and a surplus of good 2, we know that p_1 must rise and p_2 must fall, which means the price vector must get steeper. Remember that the budget constraint in the Endowment Model rotates around the initial endowment when prices change.

Step Use the scroll bar (over cells G15 and H15) to see how price changes affect the box. Set the price ratio to 1.5.

The spreadsheet does most of the hard work for you. A's and B's optimal solutions are instantly calculated. The market position cells immediately reflect the position of markets for each good at the new prices (where good 1 is one and a half times as expensive as good 2).

The Edgeworth Box is a live graph that reflects the new price vector. It is easy to see that we have overshot the equilibrium price vector because we now have a surplus of good 1 and a shortage of good 2.

Step Practice reading the Edgeworth Box. With $p_1/p_2 = 1.5$, compute the amounts that A and B want to buy and sell. Compute the surplus and shortage of each good from the box alone. Verify (using the cells in the Market Position display) that your answers are correct.

The more you practice reading the Edgeworth Box, the more comfortable you will get.

Step Play with the price vector, adjusting the scroll bar to set different price ratios and interpreting how the consumers will respond to each price ratio by using the Edgeworth Box.

As you adjust the price ratio, the price vector swings to and fro. It always rotates around the initial endowment (which would change if and only if any of the four initial endowment parameter values change). The tatonnement process is how the market responds to shortages and surpluses by changing prices in such a way that the surpluses and shortages are reduced, until they are completely eliminated.

Equilibrium

You have seen how shortages and surpluses push the price line to and fro, swinging around the initial endowment point.

We know that equilibrium means "no tendency to change." We apply this definition of equilibrium to this particular model: when p_1/p_2 has no tendency to change, we know we have settled to the equilibrium solution. The equilibrium solution generated by the market tells us how much x_1 and x_2 each consumer will end up with if the market is used and how much each consumer wants to buy and sell of each good.

Step Use the scroll bar to find the equilibrium price vector.

The equilibrium solution in a General Equilibrium Exchange Model is an important graph that is reproduced as Figure 3.2.2.2. Your screen should look like Figure 3.2.2.2. If not, set the price ratio to 1.

As Figure 3.2.2.2 clearly shows, when the equilibrium position is reached, the optimal solution of both consumers lies on the same point. This eliminates all shortages and surpluses (as shown in the supply and demand graphs below the Edgeworth Box) so the price ratio has no tendency to change. The single point in the Edgeworth Box represents a mutually compatible solution for both consumers and is the hallmark of a general equilibrium solution. The single point is akin to the intersection of supply and demand in a partial equilibrium analysis.

The market is an allocation mechanism. It will redistribute the initial endowments of the two consumers by using prices until all mutually advantageous trades are exploited.

Notice, however, that the two consumers don't get equal amounts of the two goods. Why does A end up with more? Because A started out richer. At the equilibrium price vector, the market values A's endowment at $45 and B's at $35. General equilibrium theory does not ask why A is richer. It takes the initial endowment as given.

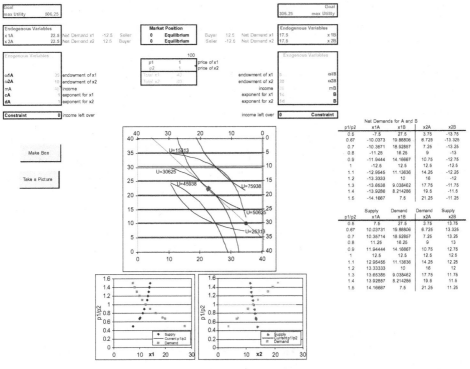

Figure 3.2.2.2. A general equilibrium solution in the Edgeworth Box.
Source: EdgeworthBoxGE.xls!EdgeworthBox1

Walras' Law

Leon Walras is the father of General Equilibrium Theory. The law that bears his name states the following: *The value of aggregate excess demand is identically zero.*

Using Walras' Law, we can deduce the following logical result: If $n - 1$ markets are in equilibrium, then the last market must be in equilibrium.

A concrete demonstration of Walras' Law is the best way to understand what it means.

Step With $p_1 = 1$ (at the equilibrium solution), change p_2 (cell H17) to 2. Find the equilibrium p_1.

You should find the equilibrium p_1 is now 2. This shows that, no matter the value of p_2, the equilibrium solution will be found when p_1/p_2 equals one.

Thus, it looks like there are two endogenous variables here, p_1 and p_2, but there is really only one endogenous variable, p_1/p_2. This is the idea behind Walras' Law.

Step Click the Reset button. Scroll right (if needed) and click the Show Walras Law button (near cell U5) to reveal calculations that demonstrate Walras' Law in action.

Step Change p_1 (via the scroll bar) and notice that no matter the price, the sum of the value of aggregate net demand is always zero. Explore the cells in the range U11:Y11 to see how the formulas are entered.

A direct implication of Walras' Law is that in a general equilibrium system with n goods, we don't really have to find n prices. If $n-1$ markets are in equilibrium, the last one automatically has to be in equilibrium.

This is why we actually have only a single endogenous variable, p_1/p_2, in the two-good case. All that matters is the relative price, not the two individual prices. With n goods, one good would be the *numeraire* (historically, gold has played that role) and all other goods would be valued in terms of the *numeraire*.

Comparative Statics with the Edgeworth Box

Having found the initial equilibrium solution, we could pursue a variety of comparative statics experiments, shocking an exogenous variable and tracking how the equilibrium solution (of various endogenous variables) responds.

We present one such experiment.

Step Click the Reset button.

Because consumers A and B have identical preferences with equal desire for the two goods, it stands to reason that the equilibrium price ratio is exactly 1.

Step Change dA (cell B22) to 0.5. What happened to the indifference curves?

They clearly shifted. A does not want to buy or sell as much as before.

Step Where is the new equilibrium solution? If you decide to use Solver to answer this question, please make the target cell H15 because that is the cell that the scroll bar is affecting. This way you will not destroy the formula in cell H16.

You should find a new equilibrium solution at $p_1/p_2 \approx 1.53$. Approximately 7.3 units of good 1 will be traded and 11.8 units of good 2 will be exchanged.

You could compute the dA elasticity of equilibrium p_1 or the dA elasticity of good 1 sold. One could do this, but it is not that exciting, so we will not.

Two Advanced Ideas

In a mathematical sense, General Equilibrium Theory is perhaps the most abstract and sophisticated area of economics. Two questions that have been studied intensively involve existence and uniqueness.

The question of the existence of an equilibrium solution was posed by Walras himself. The issue, loosely stated, is that we cannot be sure that a general equilibrium system with thousands or millions of individual goods has a place where the entire system is at rest. In fact, from an intuitive point of view, given the huge number of equations in a real-world economy, we might doubt that an equilibrium solution exists at all.

Walras and other early theorists thought that if the number of endogenous variables (unknowns) equaled the number of equations, then a solution was guaranteed. This is not so. Existence proofs in the 1950s utilized fixed-point theorems to prove rigorously the conditions under which an equilibrium solution was guaranteed to exist. Google "Brouwer fixed point" or "Kakutani fixed point" for more information on this topic.

Closely tied to existence is the problem of uniqueness. Even if an equilibrium solution is proved to exist, the worry is that there may be multiple equilibria in a general equilibrium system. Research has focused on what assumptions must be invoked in order to guarantee a single equilibrium solution.

Existence and uniqueness proofs are well beyond the scope of this book. They rely on topology and advanced mathematical concepts. This is another way of saying that our presentation of the Edgework Box and general equilibrium in a pure exchange economy is introductory and rudimentary. General Equilibrium Theory is a vast ocean and we are paddling near the shore.

Equilibrium in the Edgeworth Box

The canonical supply and demand graph is used in partial equilibrium analysis to find the equilibrium solution. General equilibrium uses the Edgeworth Box. It appears cumbersome and tedious at first, but, in fact, it is an ingenious graphical device. By representing two consumers simultaneously, while sharing a common budget constraint (given that they face identical prices), the box enables one to quickly see whether the two-good, pure exchange economy is in equilibrium. It also reveals how prices must change as the system staggers to equilibrium via the tatonnement process.

Whether a pure exchange economy is in a general equilibrium can be determined in an instant by seeing whether the optimal solutions of the two consumers are compatible – that is, if there is a single point where the two consumers want to be, given the existing price ratio.

But what about the final allocation generated by the market – what are its properties? This is an excellent question that leads to the famous Pareto optimality conditions and the First Fundamental Theorem of Welfare Economics. It is explained in the next chapter.

A final note: Although we have used numerical methods (implementing the problem in Excel) to analyze and find the general equilibrium solution, you should be aware that there are analytical approaches also. We could write down demands for goods by each consumer and impose the equilibrium condition that each market clear. This would enable solution of the equilibrium price vector with the aid of algebra (and, as soon as we left the simple world of two or three goods, linear algebra).

Exercises

Open Word and answer the following questions. Save the document and print it when you are done.

1. Use Word's Drawing Tools to draw your own Edgeworth Box. Place the initial endowment so that A has more x_2 than x_1.
2. Add a price vector to your box in the previous question that generates a shortage of x_1. Draw arrows along the bottom and top x_1 axes to show the amount of x_1 each consumer wants to buy or sell.
3. Use Word's Drawing Tools to draw a supply and demand graph for x_1. Include a horizontal line in the graph that shows the current price of x_1.
4. Add the equilibrium price vector to your Edgeworth Box graph in question 1. Explain why this price vector is the equilibrium solution.
   Hint: Add indifference curves to your graph to support your explanation.

References

The epigraph is from page 11 of Umberto Ricci, "Pareto and Pure Economics," *The Review of Economic Studies*, Vol. 1, No. 1 (October, 1933), pp. 3–21. You can learn more about Walras, Pareto, and the Lausanne School by visiting the History of Economic Thought web site at <homepage.newschool.edu/het>.

Perhaps no area of economics is as mathematically sophisticated and intense as General Equilibrium Theory. There has always been disagreement among economists regarding the use and necessity of mathematics in economics (Pareto sneered at the literary economists), but in recent years, in France, a full blown rebellion against math mushroomed. There were calls for a new, post-autistic economics, and graduate students circulated a petition that said, "We, economics students of the world, declare ourselves to be generally dissatisfied with the teaching that we receive." It highlighted, among other things, a desire to "escape from imaginary worlds" and expressed opposition to "the uncontrolled use of mathematics." You can read the entire petition online, browse the *Post-Autistic Economics Review* journal, and learn more about this movement at <www.paecon.net>.

3.2.3

Pareto Optimality

Except during short intervals of time, people are always governed by an elite. I use the word elite (It. *aristorocrazia*) in its etymological sense, meaning the strongest, the most energetic, and most capable – for good as well as evil. However, due to an important physiological law, elites do not last. Hence – the history of man is the history of the continuous replacement of certain elites: as one ascends, another declines.

Vilfredo Pareto

Our approach with general equilibrium is the same as with partial equilibrium. First we determine the equilibrium solution, then we find the optimal solution, and last we compare the equilibrium to the optimal solution.

The previous chapter used an Edgeworth Box with a price vector to find the initial equilibrium solution. We know that shortages and surpluses swing the price line to and fro until it settles down where the plans of the two consumers are mutually compatible.

In this chapter, we use the Edgeworth Box to display the optimal solution. The price line is removed because prices play no role in determining the optimal solution. Just as with partial equilibrium, we logically separate the equilibrium from the optimal solution. If the two agree, then we know we have a good result.

Finding the Optimal Solution

Step Open the Excel workbook EdgeworthBoxParetoOpt.xls and read the *Intro* sheet, then go to the *EdgeworthBox* sheet. Figure 3.2.3.1 reproduces what is on your screen.

The workbook is quite similar to the *EdgeworthBox* sheet from the previous chapter, except there is no price or market position information. We are not interested in markets right now. We are focused on determining the optimal solution.

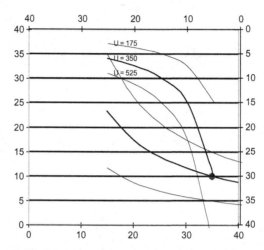

Figure 3.2.3.1. The initial endowment in an Edgeworth Box.
Source: EdgeworthBoxParetoOpt!EdgeworthBox

The OOSP, the omniscient (all-knowing), omnipotent (all-powerful) social planner, is charged with determining the optimal allocation, given the initial endowment in Figure 3.2.3.1.

With the OOSP's special powers, we can reallocate the initial endowment as we see fit. We can arbitrarily give and take from one person to the other. What should we do?

At first glance, it might seem that we would want to solve an optimization problem like this:

$$\max U_A(x_{1A}, x_{2A}) + U_B(x_{1B}, x_{2B})$$
$$\text{s.t. } x_{1A} + x_{1B} = \text{Total } x_1 \text{ and } x_{2A} + x_{2B} = \text{Total } x_2$$

In other words, we could give consumers A and B the amounts of goods 1 and 2 that maximize the sum of the individual utilities subject to the total goods available.

This strategy suffers from a serious problem: We cannot make interpersonal utility comparisons. This brings us full circle to work we did at the very beginning of this book in the Theory of Consumer Behavior. Utility is ordinal, not cardinal. Monotonic transformations (that keep rankings intact) of utility are allowed. Utility has no meaning in terms of its units.

Thus, an optimization problem that aggregates individual utilities is silly. It makes no sense to say that the utility of A is added to the utility of B to get a total utility. There are no common units with which to measure and add utility. There is, however, a way to judge and evaluate different allocations of goods to A and B.

Pareto developed logical rules that enable us to get around the limitations of utility. His basic idea was that you can compare two allocations in terms of better or worse so you can make statements about one allocation compared with another.

The Pareto Vocabulary: **Pareto Inferior/Pareto Superior, Pareto Non-comparable, and Pareto Optimal (or Efficient)**

Pareto's idea was to compare two allocations and, if possible, declare which one is better. We proceed by example. From the initial endowment point in Figure 3.2.3.1, suppose we consider the point (30,15) for A and (10,25) for B.

Step Click the (30,15) button. A red point appears at that coordinate in the box.

Is A better off at the new point compared with the initial endowment? How about B?

Although the indifference curves for A and B are not drawn through the red point, we know they exist because the indifference map is dense – there is an indifference curve through every point in the quadrant. If we draw an indifference curve for A through that point and it lies above the indifference curve that goes through the initial endowment, we know that A prefers (30,15) to the initial endowment.

The same argument can be made for B. The only trick for B is to remember that you interpret the box from the top, right corner and B's satisfaction increases as the indifference curves move farther away from the northeast corner.

Because both A and B are better off at (30,15) than the initial endowment, then that allocation is Pareto Superior to the initial endowment. We can also say that the initial endowment is Pareto Inferior to point (30,15).

Pareto Superior means that it is possible to make at least one person better off without making any one else worse off.

Consider another point that is (30,10) for A and (10, 30) for B.

Step Click the (30,10) button.

Is A better off? How about B?

Because the point (30,10) is better for B, but worse for A, then this allocation is *Pareto Non-comparable* to the initial endowment because at least one person is made worse off. You cannot compare the points by saying B's utility goes up by more than A's falls because utility is only ordinal.

Now, from the initial endowment, we can shade in *all* of the Pareto Superior points. This *lens* tells us the set of points that are improvements for at least one person (without hurting the other person).

Step Click the Show Lens button to see all of the Pareto Superior points (compared with the initial endowment).

Next, we return to the first point, (30,15). It is inside the lens so it is Pareto Superior to the initial endowment, but does it have any points that are Pareto Superior to it?

Step Click the `Hide Lens` and `(30,15)` buttons.

It should be easy to see that (30,15), like the initial endowment, has a whole set of points that are Pareto Superior to it. These points also form a lens, albeit smaller that the lens formed by the Pareto Superior points to the initial endowment, that stretch from the point (30,15) to where the two indifference curves intersect again.

Clearly, whenever indifference curves from A and B cross at a point, such as the initial endowment or (30,15), we can find Pareto Superior points in a lens from that starting point. What happens when the indifference curves are tangent?

Step Click the `Hide Lens` (if needed) and `Show B Curve` buttons.

You see an indifference curve for B that is tangent to A's highest displayed indifference curve. We will call the point of tangency between the indifference curves point PO1. This point PO1 is obviously Pareto Superior to the initial endowment.

Now, for Pareto's key idea: Does PO1 have any Pareto Superior points to it? No.

Why not? Because movement in any direction from point PO1 lowers someone's satisfaction. There is no lens from point PO1.

Thus, a *Pareto Optimal* point is one that has no Pareto Superior points to it. You cannot make someone better off without hurting someone else. Pareto Optimal points are where we want to be!

It is important to note that there are many Pareto Optimal points. In fact, wherever the indifference curves are tangent, we are at a Pareto Optimal point.

The set of all Pareto Optimal points is called the *contract curve*. A contract curve for an unknown (but well-behaved) pair of utility functions is displayed in Figure 3.2.3.2. A few indifference curves are displayed, but you should understand that every point on the contract curve is a point of tangency between two indifference curves. The sides of the box are not well labeled, but you know how to read an Edgeworth Box.

Pareto Optimal points are especially desirable because they imply that there is no way to improve the allocation without harming someone. In other words, given the limitations of ordinal utility, we can say that we have wrung out as much gain as possible. Thus, from any given initial endowment, the OOSP would want to reallocate the two goods so that the allocation is on the contract curve.

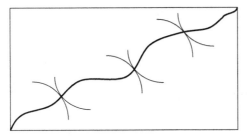

Figure 3.2.3.2. A contract curve.

One drawback of the analysis is that there are many Pareto Optimal points when starting from an arbitrary, non-Pareto Optimal point. There is no way to choose between Pareto Optimal points.

Mathematically, it should be clear that Pareto Optimal points occur only when $MRS_A = MRS_B$. When this condition holds, the two indifference curves are tangent.

Pareto Optimality with Solver

One way to find Pareto Optimal points is to solve an optimization problem. It's not the silly "sum the utilities" objective function, however.

Step From the *EdgeworthBox* sheet, open Solver. Your Solver dialog box should look like Figure 3.2.3.3.

Notice the UtilityB=Initial_UtilityB constraint. We are going to maximize A's utility without harming B. B will be indifferent between the final allocation and the initial endowment, so we are not harming B.

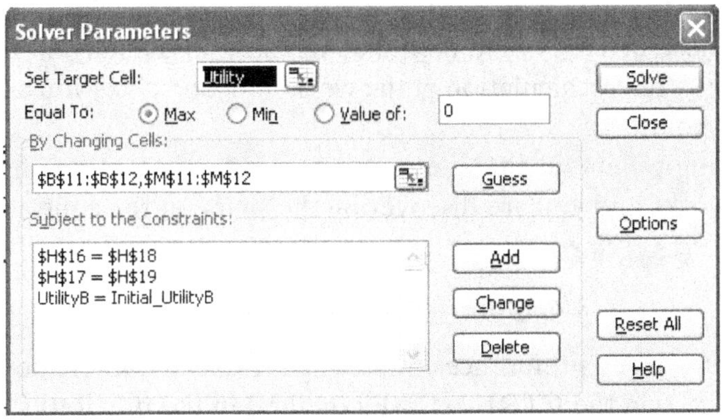

Figure 3.2.3.3. Using Solver to find a Pareto Optimal point.
Source: EdgeworthBoxParetoOpt!EdgeworthBox

Step Click Solve to find an optimal solution to this problem.

Scroll down (if needed) to see the Edgeworth Box. We are at the top most (from A's point of view) Pareto Optimal point. This point is on the contract curve.

What if we ran the same analysis, but maximized B's utility subject to maintaining A's utility constant? This is yet another Pareto Optimal point.

Most students want to make claims about points in the middle of the lens being somehow better than the two extreme points, but the Pareto analysis does not allow for such distinctions.

The Contract Curve with Excel

Step Proceed to the *ContractCurve* sheet. It is set up just like the *EdgeworthBox* sheet, except A's Initial Endowment cells (B18 and B19) have a formula, =ROUND(randomnv()*38+1,0).

This formula allows you to hit CTRL-ALT-F9 to get a new initial endowment, then use Excel's Solver to find a point on the contract curve from that initial endowment. You can use the "max A's utility keeping B's utility constant" or "max B's utility keeping A's utility constant" strategies. In the former case, you are finding the highest indifference curve of A that is tangent to B's indifference curve that goes through the initial endowment. You are doing the reverse when you maximize B's utility subject to A's indifference curve that goes through the initial endowment.

Take advantage of the live nature of this sheet.

Step Hit CTRL-ALT-F9 to move the initial endowment point around the box, then find and record a point on the contract curve. Do this several times.

To be clear, the idea is to hold down all three keys at the same time, so hold down the CTRL key first, then the ALT key, and finally hit the F9 key. This executes a full recalculation of the workbook and gives you a new initial endowment point.

By sampling points on the contract curve, you are learning how Pareto optimality works and you are discovering the shape of the contract curve.

Comparative Statics with Excel

Step Change A's preferences by setting cA to 0.5. Sample points on the contract curve (via the CTRL-ALT-F9 method in the previous step). What effect does this have on the contract curve?

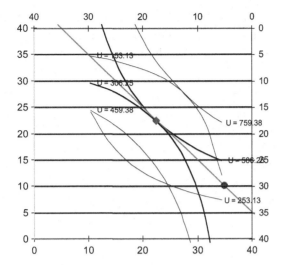

Figure 3.2.3.4. Market equilibrium.
Source: EdgeworthBoxGE.xls!EdgeworthBox

To see the answer to this question (but first try to answer it on your own), click the Show CC with cA = 0.5 button.

The First Fundamental Theorem of Welfare Economics

With the Pareto criteria in hand, we are ready to judge the market allocation. Recall that the market uses prices to establish an equilibrium solution. What can we say about the market's solution?

We can say that it is Pareto Optimal! In fact, we can say that starting from any initial endowment, a market allocation yields a Pareto Optimal solution. This is the First Fundamental Theorem of Welfare Economics.

First Fundamental Theorem:
> *If preferences are well-behaved, a properly functioning market's equilibrium solution is Pareto Optimal.*

Figure 3.2.3.4 shows the equilibrium solution from the Edgeworth-BoxGE.xls workbook. We know we have the equilibrium solution because there is a single, common tangency point. Consumer A maximizes by choosing that combination where he reaches the highest indifference curve subject to the constraint. Consumer B does the same.

Each consumer is finding a point of tangency that obeys the mathematical condition, $MRS = p_1/p_2$. From A's perspective, we have $MRS_A = p_1/p_2$. Similarly, B chooses that combination where $MRS_B = p_1/p_2$. Unbeknownst to them, they are ending up at a point where $MRS_A = MRS_B$.

In other words, by paying attention to prices and optimizing, the equilibrium generated by exchanging consumers is also generating a Pareto Optimal solution. There is an *invisible hand* aspect to this in the sense that the consumers do not know and do not care about Pareto optimality.

Geese fly in a V by drafting – wind resistance is minimized by aligning oneself at angle to the goose ahead, instead of flying directly behind or next to a fellow goose. The geese are completely unaware that they are generating a V-shaped pattern. Consumers in a market are just like geese – they are completely unaware that they are solving a much bigger optimization problem.

What can't we say about the market allocation?

We certainly can't say that it is "fair." The market will grind to a Pareto Optimal point from any initial endowment. The Pareto logic takes the initial endowment as given. What if A starts out with much more than B? The Pareto criteria have nothing to say about this.

In fact, welfare economists have worked on fairness and other ways of distinguishing between allocations, but this requires much more complicated analyses.

If there's a First Theorem, there must be a Second Theorem, right?

Second Fundamental Theorem:
> *If preferences are well behaved, a properly functioning market can reach any Pareto Optimal point if the appropriate initial endowment is provided.*

The Second Fundamental Theorem says that you can use the market to reach any Pareto Optimal allocation – that is, any point on the contract curve. All you have to do set the initial endowment appropriately, then let the market work its magic.

The last two problems in the *Q&A* sheet ask you to show that the Second Fundamental Theorem works.

That Markets Generate Pareto Optimal Solutions Is a Truly Fundamental Idea

In a way, this chapter marks the end of a long road. We began with the Theory of Consumer Behavior and learned that consumers maximize satisfaction subject to a budget constraint. An important extension of this basic model utilizes an initial endowment instead of cash income.

In a Pure Exchange Model, we combine two optimizing consumers in an Edgeworth Box. Their interaction results in an equilibrium solution.

Using the Pareto criteria, we can compare allocations and determine which ones are Pareto Optimal. These are allocations that have no Pareto Superior points. The set of all Pareto Optimal points forms the contract curve.

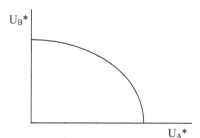

Figure 3.2.3.5. The utility possibilities frontier.

Students struggle with the term *Pareto optimality*. Its definition, i.e., that there is no way to make someone better off without hurting someone else, can become a jumble of words with little real meaning. Here is the crucial idea: Pareto optimality means no waste. The allocation at a Pareto optimal point cannot be improved upon (without harming someone). Thus, Pareto optimality means we have an unbeatable allocation.

The First Fundamental Theorem of Welfare Economics makes a powerful statement because it says that a properly functioning market yields a Pareto Optimal allocation. This is a highly desirable result.

It is also surprising, in a way, because individual consumers have no idea they are participating in solving a resource allocation problem. Each consumer is simply maximizing utility subject to a budget constraint. Like geese that fly in a V, each consumer is responding to a signal (in the consumer's case, prices).

Notice that the work here has said nothing about innovation or technological change. In fact, the analysis assumes constant technology and no new products. The analysis is completely static and based solely on the market's ability to reach a Pareto Optimal solution in terms of allocating already produced goods in a pure exchange economy.

Are all equilibria in an Edgeworth Box Pareto Optimal? Absolutely not. The next chapter shows how the market can fail.

Exercises

Open Word and answer the following questions. Save the document and print it when you are done.

1. Why do the Pareto criteria fail to provide a single point that is the best allocation?
2. What must be true about the exponents in the Cobb-Douglas utility functions for consumers A and B to generate a linear contract curve? Describe your procedure and explain your answer.
3. Use Word's Drawing Tools to draw an Edgeworth Box with well-behaved preferences and a point Z, where the $MRS_A > MRS_B$. Explain why point Z is not Pareto Optimal.
4. The contract curve (with $cA = 0.5$) can be transformed into a utility possibilities frontier, as shown in Figure 3.2.3.5. Where would point Z (from the previous question) be on this graph? Explain why.

References

The epigraph is from page 36 of Vilfredo Pareto's *The Rise and Fall of Elites: An Application of Theoretical Sociology* (originally published in Italian in 1901, translated to English in 1968 with an introductory essay by Hans L. Zetterberg, and published as a paperback in 1991 and 2000). The back jacket says, "Here in brief and incisive outline are the major ideas for which Pareto was later to become famous ... This slim volume is more readable and disciplined than most of the later elaborations, and serves well as an introduction to Pareto's political sociology ... Pareto's irony shows in his attack on elites that become humanitarian and tender-hearted rather than tough-minded."

Most economists know Pareto through his work on utility, General Equilibrium Theory, and the idea of Pareto optimality, but Pareto grew disenchanted with "pure economics" (what we would call today economic theory) and turned to sociology. His most famous sociological work is *Mind and Society* (originally published in 1916 and first translated into English in 1935), in which he explains how the circulation of elites drives history.

See Vincent J. Tarascio, *Pareto's Methodological Approach to Economics* (published in 1968) for a comparison of Pareto's views on the scope and method of economics, especially as contrasted with Alfred Marshall. Whereas Marshall saw mathematics as a language, capable of being translated so nonmathematicians could understand, Pareto believed that "mathematics makes it possible to express relations between facts which are not possible with other facilities or ordinary language" (Tarascio, p. 106, footnote omitted). Pareto saw no need to translate heavily mathematical papers for the "literary economists." Many of Pareto's ideas on optimization and equilibrium were presented in prose form by Philip H. Wicksteed, *Common Sense of Political Economy* (first published in 1910 and available online at <www.econlib.org/library/Wicksteed/wkCS0.html>).

3.2.4

General Equilibrium Monopoly

(1) Let E be an economy such that, for every i,
   (a) X_i is convex,
   (b) if x_i^1 and x_i^2 are two points of X_i and if
       t is a real number in $]0,1[$, then
       $x_i^2 \succ x_i^1$ implies $t x_i^2 + (1-t)x_i^1 \succ x_i^1$.
An equilibrium $((x_i^*), (x_j^*))$ relative to a price system p, where no x_i^* is a satiation consumption, is an optimum.

Gerard Debreu

Partial equilibrium analysis tells us that monopoly causes an inefficient allocation of resources – too little output (compared with the socially optimal level) is produced.

This chapter explores the welfare implications of monopoly in a general equilibrium setting. The procedure is the same as the one used for judging competitive markets: We determine the monopoly allocation and then test it by comparing it to the set of Pareto Optimal points (i.e., the contract curve).

Monopoly in an Edgeworth Box

Suppose we start with an initial position as described by the Edgeworth Box in Figure 3.2.4.1.

Competitive markets are modeled in an Edgeworth Box by supposing that prices are determined by the interaction of many buyers and sellers. In order to implement price-taking behavior in a two-person Edgeworth Box, we use an auctioneer who calls out prices. Each consumer determines optimal amounts to buy and sell based on the given prices. The Edgeworth Box is used to check whether the amounts that each consumer wants to buy and sell are compatible. If not, prices adjust based on the shortages and surpluses generated by the plans of each consumer.

How can we model monopoly in a pure exchange Edgeworth Box? We simply eliminate the auctioneer and give one of the consumers monopoly power.

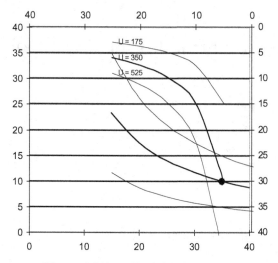

Figure 3.2.4.1. The initial position.

Suppose that A is a monopolist. What does this mean? It means that A will quote prices to B and let B decide how much to buy and sell. In other words, p_1 and p_2 become choice variables for A, to be used to A's advantage.

You can think of A as an auctioneer who first shouts out prices to see how B will respond, then picks the best prices – from A's point of view.

Step Open the Excel workbook EdgeworthBoxMonopoly.xls and read the *Intro* sheet, then go to the *PriceOfferCurveB* sheet.

Figure 3.2.4.2 (and your screen) show B's price offer curve, which tells A exactly how much x_1 and x_2 B wishes to buy given prices, p_1 and p_2.

For example, with $p_1 = 0.67$ (p_2 is the *numeraire*), B maximizes utility by selling $13\frac{1}{3}$ units of x_2 and buying almost 20 units of x_1. Figure 3.2.4.2 shows

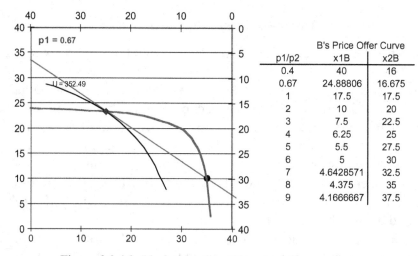

B's Price Offer Curve		
p1/p2	x1B	x2B
0.4	40	16
0.67	24.88806	16.675
1	17.5	17.5
2	10	20
3	7.5	22.5
4	6.25	25
5	5.5	27.5
6	5	30
7	4.6428571	32.5
8	4.375	35
9	4.1666667	37.5

Figure 3.2.4.2. Understanding B's price offer curve.
Source: EdgeworthBoxMonopoly.xls!PriceOfferCurveB

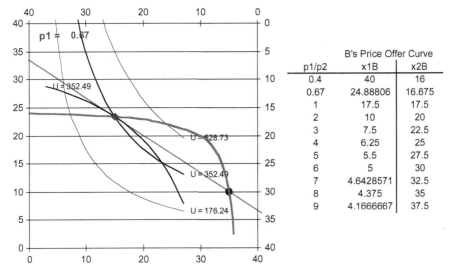

Figure 3.2.4.3. A monopolist deciding what price to charge.
Source: EdgeworthBoxMonopoly.xls!EdgeworthBox

this solution as the point at which the highest attainable indifference curve (the only one displayed) is tangent to the budget constraint.

Step Click the scroll bar above the graph to change the price of good 1. With each click, the red budget constraint line rotates about the initial endowment, and B chooses a new optimal bundle.

The locus of points that B chooses as p_1 is varied, ceteris paribus, is called the price offer curve.

Step Click the scroll bar several times. Be sure you associate the purple price offer curve with the optimal solution for B. Notice how, no matter the price, B finds the place at which the highest indifference curve is tangent to the budget constraint – and this point is on the price offer curve.

Having explained B's price offer curve, we bring A into the picture. A knows B's price offer curve and has the monopoly power to set any price (given $p_2 = 1$). Which price will A choose?

The answer is obvious: Choose p_1 that maximizes satisfaction for A. How can this problem be solved?

Step Proceed to the *EdgeworthBox* sheet. The display is the same as on the *PriceOfferCurveB* sheet, except that now we have added A's indifference curves. Figure 3.2.4.3 shows the initial position.

Does Figure 3.2.4.3 (and your screen) display a good solution for A? No, because by increasing p_1, A gets greater satisfaction.

Step Confirm that this is true by clicking on the scroll bar and keeping your eye on A's utility in cell B6. The scroll bar over cells A9:B9 can also be

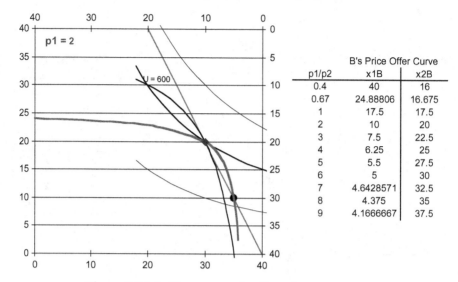

Figure 3.2.4.4. The monopoly allocation.
Source: EdgeworthBoxMonopoly.xls!EdgeworthBox

used to set p_1. It is under the heading of Endogenous Variable because A chooses the price – this is what monopoly power means.

Step Can A go crazy and charge too much? Of course. Use the scroll bar to set $p_1 = 3$. What happens?

Just like a monopoly firm in a partial equilibrium setting, A is operating under a constraint. A monopoly firm takes the demand curve as given. Consumer A takes B's offer curve as given.

Step What's the optimal p_1? Play around with the scroll bar.

You cannot beat $p_1 = 2$. This is the optimal solution. This is what A will charge B for x_1.

At this price for good 1, A gets 30 and 20 of goods 1 and 2; B gets 10 and 20. This is the monopoly allocation. It is displayed in Figure 3.2.4.4. Notice that A's indifference curve is tangent to B's offer curve. This is how a monopolist maximizes utility.

Judging Monopoly

What can we say about the monopoly allocation?

This is obvious: It is not Pareto Optimal; therefore, from society's point of view, we do not like it.

Figure 3.2.4.4 (and your screen if $p_1 = 2$) show that the monopoly allocation is at a point (from A's view it is coordinate 30,20) where the $MRS_A \neq MRS_B$ because the indifference curves intersect. This means that there are Pareto Superior points to the monopoly allocation. It also means that the monopoly allocation is not on the contract curve.

By moving northwest, into the lens created by the two indifference curves at the monopoly solution, an omniscient, omnipotent social planner could make both A and B better off.

Why doesn't A do this? Because A does not have the power of the OOSP. All A can do is set the price of good 1.

Giving A OOSP-like powers is a bad idea, but there is a turbo-charged monopoly scenario that yields a counterintuitive result. Suppose A had the ability to set different prices for good 1? In other words, A could sell the first unit at a high price and decrease the price as B purchased more units. As explained in the chapter on monopoly in a partial equilibrium setting, this is called perfect price discrimination. The *Q&A* sheet asks you to work out the welfare implications of this type of monopoly in a general equilibrium analysis. The welfare results for perfect price discrimination in partial and general equilibrium are the same.

Unlike partial equilibrium, we report no deadweight loss measure in this pure exchange, general equilibrium analysis. We simply note that the monopoly allocation is not Pareto Optimal and this is enough to doom monopoly because we know there are Pareto Superior allocations to the monopoly result.

Monopoly Is Not Pareto Optimal

We found, once again, that monopoly is inefficient. In a pure exchange Edgeworth Box, if one agent is granted monopoly power, he or she will choose a price to maximize his or her utility. Unfortunately, this does not generate a Pareto Optimal allocation. The monopolist is not interested in Pareto optimality – she simply wants to maximize her own utility.

We have shown, once again, that monopoly fails to properly allocate resources. Unlike the first time, which was based on a partial equilibrium analysis and measured inefficiency with deadweight loss (the Harberger triangle), the inefficiency of monopoly is more rigorously demonstrated via general equilibrium analysis. Recall, however, that this is simply a pure exchange economy. A true general equilibrium model would include production of goods and services and then combine production and exchange. The monopoly result stays the same; however, it still fails to yield a Pareto Optimal allocation.

Exercises

Open Word and answer the following questions. Save the document and print it when you are done.

1. Is the monopoly solution better than the initial endowment? Explain.
   Hint: Use Figure 3.2.4.4 as a reference.

2. Suppose A really liked x_1, so that cA (cell B21) was 2. How would this change A's utility maximizing price of x_1? What is the monopoly solution? Describe your procedure.
3. In an earlier chapter, we used a supply and demand (partial equilibrium) analysis to show that price ceilings in a competitive market cause an inefficient allocation of resources. Use Word's Drawing Tools to create an Edgeworth Box with a price ceiling on x_1. Explain why price ceilings are undesirable in this general equilibrium setting.

References

The epigraph is from page 94 of Gerard Debreu's *Theory of Value: An Axiomatic Analysis of Economic Equilibrium* (originally published in 1959). Debreu won the Nobel Prize in Economics in 1983 "for having incorporated new analytical methods into economic theory and for his rigorous reformulation of the theory of general equilibrium"; see (<nobelprize.org/nobel_prizes/economics/laureates/1983/press.html>).

The Nobel Prize web site explains Debreu's contribution in more detail, of course, but for the real scoop, consider this excerpt from E. Roy Weintraub's *How Economics Became a Mathematical Science* (published in 2002):

> While it was the case that most economists would have been unfamiliar at that time with the novel tools of set theory, fixed point theorems, and partial preorderings, there was something else that would have taken them by surprise: a certain take-no-prisoners attitude when it came to specifying the "economic" content of the exercise. Although there had been quantum leaps of mathematical sophistication before in the history of economics, there had never been anything like this. (Weintraub, p. 114)

Weintraub reports that he had better luck interviewing Debreu than did George Feiwel, who prefaced many of his questions with, "For the benefit of the uneducated." When Feiwel asked why existence of an equilibrium solution is so important, "Debreu shot back, 'Since I have not seen your question discussed in the terms I would like to use, I will not give you a concise answer'" (Weintraub, p. 113). In addition to providing an entire transcript of the interview, Weintraub explains how Debreu led a wave of mathematical formalism into economics in the 1950s.

In other words, the general equilibrium ideas presented in this book are a mathematical step below the more formal, axiomatic exposition of General Equilibrium Theory developed in the 1950s. Pick up Debreu's *Theory of Value* or a modern, PhD-level Micro Theory text (such as David M. Kreps, *A Course in Microeconomic Theory*, 1990) to see exactly what a formal, axiomatic exposition of general equilibrium entails.

Conclusion

But when time and the means for achieving ends are limited *and* capable of alternative application, *and* the ends are capable of being distinguished in order of importance, then behaviour necessarily assumes the form of choice. Every act which involves time and scarce means for the achievement of one end involves the relinquishment of their use for the achievement of another. It has an economic aspect… Here, then, is the unity of the subject of Economic Science, the forms assumed by human behaviour in disposing of scarce means.

Lionel Robbins

Throughout this book, Excel has been used to solve optimization problems and equilibrium models. Repeated emphasis has been placed on comparative statics and elasticity.

This concluding chapter has three parts:

1. Solver: There is a review of basic Solver skills with emphasis on the lesson that Solver is not perfect.
2. Overall view: A quick tour of the topics covered enables a clear statement of the economic way of thinking.
3. The open problem: Whereas the role of markets in a static framework is well understood, the economic growth generated over time by capitalism is not.

Solver

Consider a perfectly competitive firm with a total cost function given by $TC = 100q^{\frac{1}{2}}$. Dividing both sides by q gives us the average cost function, $ATC = \frac{100}{q^{\frac{1}{2}}}$. Taking the derivative of TC with respect q yields $MC = \frac{50}{q^{\frac{1}{2}}}$.

If this perfectly competitive firm faced a market price of \$5/unit, what is the profit-maximizing level of output?

This book has solved optimization problems via numerical and analytical methods. We will apply both methods to this problem. First, we will use Solver.

Step Open a blank Excel workbook. In cell A1, type the word *quantity*. Cell B1 will hold a number that represents the quantity. In cell A2, type the word *profits*. In cell B2, enter the formula for profit.

The price is \$5/unit and $TC = 100q^{\frac{1}{2}}$ so the formula in cell B2 is "=5*B1–100*SQRT(B1)".

Step Run Solver. The target cell is B2, the goal is obviously to maximize profits, and the changing cell is B1. There are no constraints because the firm is free to produce as much output as it wants at the given price.

Excel gives a *miserable* result. It cannot take the square root of a negative number so it gives up and announces its failure.

Step Run Solver again. Add a constraint that cell B1 be greater than or equal to zero. Click Solve.

Solver reports an optimal solution of zero. Can this be correct?
Maybe the issue is that we are starting from blank cell, which is zero. This is poor practice. We can change where Solver starts from to see if that helps.

Step Change cell B1 to 25. Cell B2 should display −375. Run Solver.

Solver appears convinced that the optimal solution is zero.
We turn to analytical methods to see if we can confirm Solver's result.

$$MR = MC \Rightarrow 5 = \frac{50}{q^{\frac{1}{2}}}$$
$$q^{\frac{1}{2}} = 10$$
$$q = 100$$

This is confusing. We now have two answers: $q = 0$ and $q = 100$. Which one is right?
The canonical graph in Figure IV.1 depicts this firm's $MR = MC$ solution and the negative profit rectangle at this quantity.

Step Enter the analytical answer in cell B1. Cell B2 should equal – 500. Run Solver.

Solver now gives a miserable result – optimal output is a huge number.
What is going here?
If you have yet to figure it out, the easiest way to understand what is happening is to draw a graph of the profit function.

Step Create a column from 0 to 500 by 10. This is the quantity. Use the profit formula to create a column for profit based on the quantity. Create a graph of the two columns.

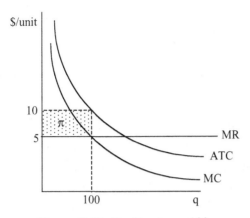

Figure IV.1. Profits at $q = 100$.

Your graph should look like Figure IV.2.

Figure IV.2 makes clear that the point where $MR = MC$ is actually a point of *minimum* profit. Although the first-order condition is met (we did find a flat spot on the profit function at $q = 100$), this solution fails the second-order condition for a maximum.

The correct answer is to produce an infinity of output. The more you produce past 100, the more profits rise. Higher output leading to greater profit continues forever so the optimal solution is infinity.

How can we explain Solver's seemingly bizarre behavior?

When Solver starts from below 100 (like zero or 25), it goes to zero (or negative output if you do not have a non-negativity constraint). When it starts from 100 or more, it goes right on the x axis and gets the right answer.

It is worth remembering that Solver's algorithm is naïve. It evaluates the function at the starting value, then moves left and right. The size of the

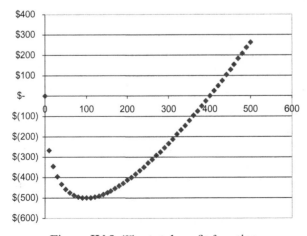

Figure IV.2. The total profit function.

move depends on the numerical values in the problem. Starting from $q = 25$, for example, Solver moves a little bit right, sees that profits fell, then decreases output. You can see Solver's steps by checking off the Show Iteration Results option after clicking the Options button in the Solver dialog box.

Figure IV.2 makes clear that a starting value below $q = 100$ means starting from the downward sloping part of the profit function. Solver keeps lowering output because profit rises (becoming less negative) until it hits zero.

Starting from an output greater than 100 will lead Solver to the correct answer because it will keep increasing output.

You might be thinking that since we are in the long run, $ATC = AVC$ and it is clear that $P < AVC$ at $MR = MC$, which means the firm should shut down. That is not bad thinking, except the rule does not work at $MR = MC$ in this case because that is not the profit-maximizing output.

This example shows that numerical methods are to be used with caution. Be careful out there.

Overall View

This book has covered modern-day, orthodox microeconomic theory at the intermediate level. The economic approach or economic way of thinking provides the framework for analyzing observed behavior. The basic idea is to set up and solve an optimization problem or equilibrium model. Next, a single variable is changed, ceteris paribus, and the new solution is compared to the initial solution. This procedure is called comparative statics. Elasticity captures the logic of comparative statics in a single number.

When the economic approach is applied to consumers, it is called the Theory of Consumer Behavior. The key comparative statics analysis is deriving the demand curve.

When the economic approach is applied to firms, it is called the Theory of the Firm. The key comparative statics analysis is deriving the supply curve. The firm is more complicated than the consumer because firms hire inputs to produce output. In fact, the firm is really a set of three interrelated optimization problems: input cost minimization, output profit maximization, and input profit maximization.

The individual demand and supply curves derived from the consumer and firm models can be added up to produce market demand and supply curves. This enables a partial equilibrium analysis of how markets solve society's resource allocation question. General equilibrium is a more rigorous and sophisticated analysis. Both can be used to show that a properly functioning market yields an optimal allocation. Both can be used to show that price ceilings, monopoly, and externalities generate inefficiency.

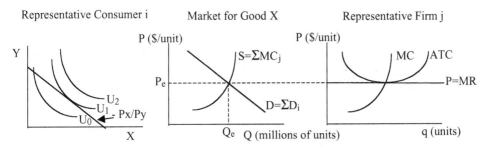

Figure IV.3. The market's resource allocation solution for one good.

Partial equilibrium enables calculation of a measure of inefficiency called deadweight loss (also known as the Harberger triangle), but this should be interpreted as an approximation because consumers' surplus requires the utility function to have special properties and the effects on other markets are ignored. Partial equilibrium analysis is commonly used in empirical work. Think of deadweight loss as a rough measure of inefficiency in the allocation of resources.

General equilibrium does not suffer from the same problems as partial equilibrium, but it is much harder to implement in the real world. In the epigraph to the chapter introducing the Edgeworth Box, mention was made of computable general equilibrium models. This shows that there is an empirical side to general equilibrium analysis, but it is a modern development – though rapidly growing.

It is reasonable to view mainstream microeconomics as a theory of the price mechanism. The market system uses prices as signals to allocate resources. Optimizing agents react to price changes and their interactions as buyers and sellers drive the system toward equilibrium. The Theories of Consumer Behavior and the Firm are stepping stones that explain how the market answers society's resource allocation question. Figure IV.3 puts the Theory of Consumer Behavior, Theory of the Firm, and partial equilibrium analysis together. These three graphs and how they fit together are worth remembering.

Another way to make sense of microeconomics is to split it into two parts – individual agents (consumers and firms) that optimize and what happens when these optimizing agents interact in a market. The former is about optimization and the latter is about equilibrium. The order that is spontaneously generated by interacting, optimizing agents is a remarkable result. Economists see supply and demand not as the simple intersection of two lines, but as a pattern that is unwittingly generated by the agents themselves – just like geese that fly in a V.

This book was designed to provide you with practice in applying the economic approach. We tackled unconstrained and constrained optimization problems, computed many different elasticities, and solved several equilibrium models at the partial and general levels.

The many applications of the economic approach demonstrate its remarkable flexibility. The Theory of Consumer Behavior, at first, seems ridiculously unrealistic – a robot consumer chooses between two goods with prices, tastes, and income given! But that is just the basic model. By changing the goods to consumption in the present and the future, it becomes an intertemporal choice model. We analyzed charitable giving, portfolio theory, and the effect of safety features in automobiles with the Theory of Consumer Behavior.

In every application, the economic way of thinking was prominent. We set up and solved an optimization problem, then changed a variable, ceteris paribus, to see how the optimal solution changed. There are countless applications of the economic approach, but they share the same framework and logic.

In fact, the economic approach is what defines economics today. Most people have a content-based definition of economics: They think that the study of interest rates, unemployment, and money is economics. But this is wrong. The proper definition of economics is the application of the economic approach to explain observed behavior. Crime, marriage, and war, if analyzed with the economic approach, fall under the heading of economics. Now, when you hear the phrase "an economic analysis of," you will know that the economic approach is about to be applied.

The Open Problem

Neither this book nor modern, mainstream economics explains the dynamic process of capitalism. A few hundred years of the market system make clear that creativity, innovation, and technological change are endogenously generated by market-based societies. No one really knows why.

Explaining the dynamism of the market system is a much different question than the static optimization and equilibrium models that explain why markets allocate resources efficiently. In the static world, there are no new products, cost-saving innovations, or new firms. The static world is stable and markets are in equilibrium.

This static model clashes violently with reality. Joseph Schumpeter's portrayal of what he called plausible (i.e., real-world) capitalism, captured in the oxymoron "creative destruction," highlights the rise and fall of firms, explosive growth, and dislocation produced by markets. For Schumpeter, the driving force is the entrepreneur, a hero whose desire to dominate the business world results in economic success for society. But Schumpeter's story (best captured in *Capitalism, Socialism and Democracy*, originally published in 1942), thrilling though it may be, is not part of mainstream economics today.

It is plainly clear that markets do generate spectacular economic growth, unparalleled by any other organizational form. Even the harshest critics of capitalism concede this point:

The bourgeoisie, during its rule of scarce one hundred years, has created more massive and more colossal productive forces than have all preceding generations together. Subjection of Nature's forces to man, machinery, application of chemistry to industry and agriculture, steam-navigation, railways, electric telegraphs, clearing of whole continents for cultivation, canalisation of rivers, whole populations conjured out of the ground – what earlier century had even a presentiment that such productive forces slumbered in the lap of social labour?

Marx and Engels, *The Communist Manifesto*

Although the productive power of markets may be obvious, we simply do not know the answer to basic questions about how markets generate growth. Beyond superficial generalities about the institutional environment, such as needing rule of law and established property rights, we have no explanation for how the interaction of multitudes of agents drives the system over time. We cannot even answer the most basic question, posed by Adam Smith, of why some countries are rich and others are poor.

If we knew how and why markets caused technological change and output per person to grow exponentially, we would know how to help those societies mired in poverty. Nobel Prize winning economist Robert Lucas puts the question well.

Is there some action a government of India could take that would lead India's economy to grow like Indonesia's or Egypt's? If so, what, exactly? If not, what is it about 'the nature of India' that makes it so? The consequences for human welfare involved in questions like these are simply staggering: Once one starts to think about them, it is hard to think about anything else. (Lucas, 1988, p. 5)

The point is this: Markets can be analyzed from static and dynamic perspectives. The former focuses on resource allocation at a single moment in time. It freezes the movie and asks how markets work in this motionless environment. We know how markets work as a resource allocation mechanism. The latter considers how markets work over time. The movie runs – spurts of rapid growth are followed by recessions, then more growth, but output per person trends upward. Will this continue? We do not know. How do institutions emerge from the interaction of optimizing agents? We do not know.

Explaining markets as a dynamic process remains the most important open problem in economics. Perhaps you can work on it.

References

The epigraph is from pages 14 and 15 of Lionel Robbins, *An Essay on the Nature and Significance of Economic Science* (originally published in 1932 and available online at <www.mises.org/books/robbinsessay2.pdf>).

We began with a famous quotation from Robbins, defining economics as "the science which studies human behavior as a relationship between given ends and scarce means which have alternative uses." This book takes this definition seriously and has stressed static optimization, but this last chapter makes clear that we have a great deal to discover and learn about dynamics and technological progress.

Karl Marx and Frederick Engels, *The Communist Manifesto* (originally published in 1848), is available in many places online, including <www.marx.org>.

Robert Lucas, "On the Mechanics of Economic Development," *Journal of Monetary Economics*, Vol. 22 (1988), pp. 3–42.

The fact that perfect competition is incompatible with increasing returns (as the Solver example with $TC = 100q^{\frac{1}{2}}$ showed) led to a heated debate in the 1920s. Economics continues to struggle to develop a model that combines the fact that average cost falls as output rises for many products with competitive markets. See David Warsh, *Knowledge and the Wealth of Nations: A Story of Economic Discovery* (New York: W. W. Norton & Company), 2006, for a review of how economics has grappled with the issue of increasing returns.

If you are interested in the trajectory of capitalism and markets, then modern economic theory will not be of much help. Try reading some of the classic works by these economists: Adam Smith, Karl Marx, John Maynard Keynes, Joseph Schumpeter, Frank Knight, Milton Friedman, and Friedrich Hayek.

For an entertaining review of capitalism and how it has been treated in economics, see Robert Heilbroner, *The Worldly Philosophers: The Lives, Times, and Ideas of the Great Economic Thinkers* (New York: Touchstone, 1999, 7th edition, originally published 1953).

Visit <www.pbs.org/wgbh/commandingheights> to see the PBS documentary *Commanding Heights: The Battle for the World Economy* (based on a book by the same name by Daniel Yergin and Joseph Stanislaw, 2002). Episode 1, *The Battle of Ideas*, tells the story of the intellectual currents around the world during the 20th century, highlighting Keynes and Hayek. You will also meet players from the Austrian and Chicago schools of economics.

Index

Printed in the United States
By Bookmasters